ADDICTIONS
&
SPIRITUAL
TRANSFORMATION

MAKING TWELVE-STEP RECOVERY MORE EFFECTIVE

Richard W. Clark

Richard W. Clark

Addictions & Spiritual Transformation
Third Edition, January 2007
The author's website: www.richardwclark.com

Note for Librarians: A cataloguing record for this book is available from Library and Archives Canada at www.collectionscanada.ca/amicus/index-e.html
ISBN 1-4120-8398-2

Printed in Victoria, BC, Canada. Printed on paper with minimum 30% recycled fibre.
Trafford's print shop runs on "green energy" from solar, wind and other environmentally-friendly power sources.

Offices in Canada, USA, Ireland and UK

Book sales for North America and international:
Trafford Publishing, 6E–2333 Government St.,
Victoria, BC V8T 4P4 CANADA
phone 250 383 6864 (toll-free 1 888 232 4444)
fax 250 383 6804; email to orders@trafford.com
Book sales in Europe:
Trafford Publishing (UK) Limited, 9 Park End Street, 2nd Floor
Oxford, UK OX1 1HH UNITED KINGDOM
phone 44 (0)1865 722 113 (local rate 0845 230 9601)
facsimile 44 (0)1865 722 868; info.uk@trafford.com
Order online at:
trafford.com/06-0153

10   9   8   7

For Michael George Perry
1951-2003

Welcome to this book...

It was conceived, and my decision to write it was made, in April of 1986. After eleven years of research, in the fall of 1997, I finally put pen to paper and started the first draft. What followed was several more years of research and seven years of writing. Finally, after five rewrites, and four earlier editions, in this pleasant summer of 2006, the book is now complete. I do hope you find value in it.

Richard Clark
Vancouver, Canada
June, 2007

Permission

The author is greatly indebted to Alcoholics Anonymous World Services, Inc., for their generous permission to quote at length from their published material. The material quoted and excerpted from *Alcoholics Anonymous, Twelve Steps and Twelve Traditions*, and other published material they hold copyright on is used with permission of Alcoholics Anonymous World Services, Inc. Permission to use this material does not mean or imply that AA has reviewed or approved the contents of this work, nor does it mean or imply that AA agrees with the views expressed herein. Alcoholics Anonymous is a program of recovery from alcoholism only; use of their material in connection with programs and activities which are patterned after AA, but which address other problems, or in any other non-AA context, does not imply otherwise.

Formerly published under the title:
Addictions and Getting Recovered
The Myths and Realities of Twelve-Step Programs
(ISBN 1-4120-3131-1)

Copyright

Photographs & Cover Design

The rear-cover photograph was taken by Sylvain Lefebvre. Cover design and graphics: Flash Lewis, <www.atrdesign.com>.

A Note About The Index

Due to the limitations of space and to avoid duplication of the Table of Contents, the index is not exhaustive. It is only to assist in following a few of the topics and themes that thread throughout the book. Index page numbers may refer to the main text or a footnote.

"God is. That is the primordial fact. It is in order that we may discover this fact for ourselves, by direct experience, that we exist."

Aldous Huxley
Huxley and God, Essays
Edited by Jacqueline Hazard Bridgeman
Harper San Francisco, 1992, p. 17.

"The philosophers of all ages have taught that the visible universe was but a fractional part of the whole, and that by analogy the physical body of man is in reality the least important part of his composite constitution. Most of the medical systems of today almost entirely ignore the superphysical man... Paracelsus [1493-1541], noting the same proclivity on the part of physicians during his day, aptly remarked: 'There is a great difference between the power that removes the invisible causes of disease, and which is Magic, and that which causes merely external effects [to] disappear, and which is Physic, Sorcery, and Quackery.' (Translated by Franz Hartmann.)

"Disease is unnatural... . Permanent health cannot be regained until harmony is restored. The outstanding virtue of Hermetic medicine was its recognition of spiritual and psychophysical derangements as being largely responsible for the condition which is called physical disease."

Manly P. Hall
The Secret Teachings of All Ages
Tarcher/Penguin Books, 2003, p. 354.
[Originally published by The Philosophical Research Society, 1928.]

"The world is not a 'prison house,' but a kind of spiritual kindergarten where millions of bewildered infants are trying to spell 'God' with the wrong blocks."

Edwin Arlington Robinson
Edwin Arlington Robinson, Selected Poems
Penguin Classics, 1997, p. xx.

"It is... our decided conviction, that to become a genuine spiritual entity... [a person] must first create [themselves] anew, so to speak — i.e. thoroughly eliminate from [their] mind and spirit, not only the dominating influence of selfishness and other impurity, but also the infection of superstition and prejudice."

Helene P. Blavatsky
Isis Unveiled
Theosophical University Press, 1988 edition.
[Originally published 1877, emphasis on 'create', H.P. Blavatsky]

Acknowledgements

If it weren't for Michael Perry this book would most likely never have been completed. His friendship, support, and editing expertise over the five years it took to complete the first four drafts were crucial in my finally getting twenty years of work between the covers of this book. I would also like to thank Carmen Wittmeier, editor to the first edition. Her interest in the material, her general observations, and her editorial expertise were a significant contribution to the overall tone of the book.

Richard Hansen's interest and contributions to the 1996 lectures, and Tammy Ford's effort in transcribing the recordings, were pivotal in encouraging me to persevere. Ron Jordens and Ryan Angel's comments and feedback were most helpful in eliminating my oversights. Sylvain Lefebvre and Melody Winter's encouragement and support are greatly appreciated.

As for therapists and associates, a special note of thanks goes to Rowan Scott, Danny Novak, Holly Jones, Joel Brass, Leonard Shaw, Lynne Zettl, and Ed Josephs. I remember, with affection and great respect, two monks, one Christian and one Buddhist. Their generosity of spirit, their profound sense of spiritual peace, and their insights that at times bordered on the mystical, have guided me in my own pilgrimage in ways that are beyond words.

Respect & Dignity

Readers may encounter ideas they disagree with. The intent in writing this book is neither to insult people, nor to persuade them to reject what they believe or cherish. I simply want to put words to the reality that I see around me, and to offer alternatives to people who are foundering, confused, or dissatisfied in their pilgrimage out of addictions. The world is quite large enough for different beliefs, and yet small enough that acceptance and respect are necessary for us to live in harmony.

In alternating between nouns (addicts, alcoholics) and pronouns (you, we), my descriptions of the process that relates to addictions and spiritual pilgrimages are for convenience and grammatical style. Some people who read this won't be addicts and the pronouns aren't intended to be accusatory, nor are they intended to include readers where they wish not to be. In anecdotes and examples, the names chosen are generic and do not represent any particular person.

A Note About Quotations and Citations

I refer to other authors and books, and to social leaders, actors, artists, therapists—to people who are successful or famous in various fields of endeavor. By quoting them, or referring to their ideas, I do not mean to imply that they agree with or endorse the views I offer in this book; and, I may not necessarily agree with everything they say. Regardless of this, I wish to express my gratitude to all of them for provoking and challenging and teaching me. For whatever my own contribution to Life may be, I am aware that I stand on the shoulders of giants. The observations I make throughout this book are entirely my own.

Richard Clark

Table of Contents

4. Step Four: How "I" Have Become Me   160

5. Steps Five, Six, and Seven: What I Do With Me   207

6. Steps Eight and Nine & The Promises: Social Re-Entry   244

Prologue: The Manner of Presentation

Addictions and spiritual transformation are multi-dimensional, interrelated, and layered. To say they are complex is a magnificent understatement. Imagine an intricate, three-dimensional spider's web where every point of intersection of web is somehow directly connected to every other point of intersection: nothing is linear; everything is connected to everything else. The dynamics of addictions and of getting recovered exist like a massive spider's web of symptoms and issues that are all connected, and it all happens at once. You get sick everywhere and throughout your entire personality all at the same time, and you become spiritual everywhere and throughout your entire personality all at the same time. This is why getting recovered is so painstakingly slow. Being addicted, like being spiritual, is a state of existence.

Everything in this book, from discussing the many and varied issues that create a firm basis for understanding and exiting addictions, to embracing personal transformation, to becoming Spiritual, is important in the overall task at hand. And, it is complex. However, because of this complexity—the extreme subtlety of the material and the multi-dimensional topics, you may believe some topic of discussion in this book is out of sequence or better suited elsewhere. At times the segue from one item to the next may seem disjointed or random.

Outside of the specific steps, any one topic could be presented in several different places in the overall sequence of the information in the book. The flow of information may seem disjointed to you, but quite natural to someone else. And, while some people think I don't spend enough time explaining one particular point, others think I'm belaboring the same point and impatient I move on.

This happens because the information we each absorb is filtered through our perceptions and values (our ego[1]). Each person who reads this book will have a different perception of it than anyone else who reads it. In addition to personal filtering, the subtle disjointedness you may experience is partly due to the limitations of a book—in fact, the limitations of education. Education requires that information be presented in some linear fashion, which isn't how addictions happen and certainly isn't how spiritual transformation happens. Nothing about this process is linear, but we can only write or talk about it that way.

I have been asked whether this book is for therapists or for ordinary people getting recovered. First there's this: Counsellors and therapists are ordinary people. Second: There have appeared two closely related and pervasive myths; not even myths exactly, but a malignant ambiance in the attitudes about addicts and alcoholics. These are that addicts don't really want to get recovered, and they're incapable of comprehending complicated things. Granted, there are exceptions, but for the most part, addicts are capable and do want to get recovered. However, this requires a determined and focused effort, over a long time, in a very specific direction. *"The*

---

[1] Ego is discussed at Appendix IV.

unfolding of [person's] *spiritual nature is as much an exact science as astronomy* [or] *medicine."* [2]

Understanding the progressive, ubiquitous, and destructive nature of addictions, and how psychology can assist but only spirituality can resolve them, is incredibly complicated. This requires discussion of subtle detail, the use of words that may be unfamiliar to some readers, and hard work. Therefore, this is not an "easy" read. Of those who read the first edition, close to 140 people were kind enough to offer thoughtful comments. Of that group, eleven were therapists, three were doctors, several never completed high school, and about 80% were in twelve-step programs. Understanding the content was well within the grasp of these "ordinary" people. What they had in common was patience and determination.

To understand this book, some people will need a dictionary near to hand and will have to ponder carefully the information in its considered detail. Both recovering and helping others to recover from addictions is incredibly complex. If you aren't willing to work enough to understand this book, you're probably not willing to work as hard as is required to get recovered, or to effectively help addicts to get recovered. Comprehension has to be earned. Nothing is free.

This book presents ideas and perspectives that will generally contradict (a) much of what is presently, commonly thought to be "addictions" treatment, and (b) most of what is routinely said and done in modern twelve-step groups. Misconceptions about twelve-step programs and addictions are reflected in the media, treatment modalities, and in the carnival-like atmosphere of many twelve-step meetings.

Respect cannot be offered to people, nor can this subject be held in the regard it deserves, when people and addictions are treated in a superficial or trite manner. Your rewards will be commensurate with your efforts. When someone desires to transform themselves, and they undertake to resolve their addictions, throughout that process, they gradually become more graceful in assimilating deeper awareness. The further along they are towards achieving spiritual integrity, the more they can appreciate spiritual nuance. It's very complicated.

You have the difficult task of trying to assimilate extremely complicated information that is multi-dimensional, interrelated, and layered—and it all happens at once: the three-dimensional spider's web. Many of you are trying to do this with an ego that will resist much of what's in this book. By reading this slowly and thoughtfully, you will eventually sense how it all fits together.

Be kind and patient with yourself. Be gently determined. From wherever you are right now, at this immediate point in your own transformation, you are a newcomer to the rest of your life.

---

[2] *Secret Teachings of All Ages,* Manly P. Hall, Tarcher/Penguin Books, 2003, p. 120. Procrastination and working grudgingly, which are characteristics of an alcoholic/addict (*Twelve Steps and Twelve Traditions,* p. 49), should not be preemptively interpreted as disinterest. These can be overcome, which is a specific part of the process of getting recovered. *Twelve Steps and Twelve Traditions,* and *Alcoholics Anonymous,* and this book, are an explanation of that process.

1

Begin at the Beginning

*"We owe a definite homage to the reality around us, and we are obliged,
at certain times, to say what things are and to give them their right names
and to lay open our thought about them to the men we live with."*

Thomas Merton[3]

Twelve-step programs have been proven to be the most (and some might say the only) effective method for addiction recovery. However, in addition to the long, difficult process of comprehending and completing the twelve steps, there are the addict's ego defenses, their suspicious and defiant attitude, puzzling program clichés, confusing jargon, various myths and inaccurate information, and (very often) preexisting therapeutic issues. Interventions that support abstinence or the normalizing of addictive behavior (such as in work or sex addictions) often fail because of this profoundly complex constellation of symptoms and issues. What adds to the addict's struggle is the often-heard, fear-based, blaming statement: "Well, addicts who relapse don't really want recovery. They don't try hard enough."

Since about 1984, there has been a huge surge of awareness in North America about twelve-step groups, and a dramatic increase in the number of professionals and institutions catering to the specialized needs of people with addictions. These changes still can not adequately address the needs of the population explosion around addiction and recovery. The resulting chaos and problems aren't entirely due to the identification of greater numbers of people with an addiction. It is much broader and more complex than that.

With the advent of an insightful family-systems theory of shame, many therapists have unknowingly acted in concert with the machinations of addictions. They created a decided tendency to shift the responsibility for addictions and getting recovered off the shoulders of the addict and onto community and family.

Additionally, with the restructuring of psychiatric hospitals, the reductions in funding for the treatment of mental disorders and support programs, and the discharge of many people from these programs, there came another set of problems for twelve-step groups. Through publicity, easy availability, and promises of support and healing, came a wave of new people. With their open-armed welcoming of any and

---

[3] *A Thomas Merton Reader,* Rev. Ed., edited by Thomas P. McDonnell, Image Books, 1974, p. 121.

all who were (or might possibly be) afflicted with an addiction, and their self-diagnosing rule of membership, twelve-step groups received an influx of people who were formerly being cared for in professionally structured programs and facilities.

With the increase of professionals (many with minimal training, with addictions themselves, or serious unhealed wounds) catering to addicts; with the plethora of healing and treatment centers; with the huge influx of new people, some of whom were only marginally appropriate to the mandate of twelve-step programs; with too much publicity and false promises about twelve-step programs being a panacea (they decidedly aren't); and with insightful psychological theories, there came a disastrous blurring of the boundaries between therapy and twelve-step work. This drastically obscured the spiritual vision presented in the original twelve-step literature. The efficacy and spiritual integrity of twelve-step programs (especially AA and NA[4]) could not withstand this tidal wave of change. A critical mass was reached and in the mid 1980s, cultural awareness simply exploded. It became trendy to be in AA or NA, or for that matter, any other twelve-step program (except the ones for sex addictions).

Two results are a subtle, treacherous trend within "self-help" groups and within society at large to marginalize and demean proper therapy, and a dangerous myth that twelve-step groups are a modern therapeutic panacea. In concert with these, many therapists and people within twelve-step groups misunderstand addictions, or see twelve-step groups and treatment centers at odds with a traditional therapeutic mandate. For the most part, neither the therapist nor the twelve-step participant clearly understands how to effectively enroll the other discipline as an ally in the healing journey, and neither are clear on the crucial importance of maintaining the independence of each process. The result of this misunderstanding has been to naively force each process together or to belligerently keep them apart. People are lost in this confusion and too often the consequences are relapse or death.

The Origin Of This Book

In 1986 I was working in a treatment center. On Fridays, a very informal group of clients would convene in my office and we would ruminate about the vagaries of life. One time a delegation requested that I sort out some confusion about depression. So, I gathered several reference texts and some old course notes and, over the next couple of hours, delivered an impromptu lecture. Their interest astonished me. A week later, I was approached by another delegation of clients who wanted another presentation on something else.

I was, at that time, subtly intimidated by the request for more impromptu lectures. I was anxious about setting a precedent whereby clients could closely examine me. I could possibly, thereby, be held accountable by them for my own lack of therapeutic integrity. Much later I realized how I had adopted the belief that client lethargy, perceived lack of ability, or disobedience were the sole problems responsible for high recidivism. I began to see how deeply the clients were foundering in ignorance, myths, contradictions, and the dislocation of ethics within the bureaucratic and coercive care being offered to them (both in their treatment *and* in their twelve-step groups). I admitted all this to them, and with noticeable anticipation, the lectures became a regular event.

When those clients finally got it—that there was understandable, learnable information beyond trite clichés—many became proactive in their own healing. At their insistence, it developed into a regular Friday lecture: for me to offer information and for them to listen, puzzle over dilemmas, relax, laugh, debate, take notes, and ask questions in an informal setting. They decided the general topics; I'd do the research and lecture. As they acquired knowledge, they evinced a new interest in self-care and developed the courage to advocate on their own behalf. They began to discard that which was never real and to reorganize and embrace that which was.

Those people had been written off as only suitable for therapeutic babysitting. Those men and women, who were referred to as dead-end, low-bottom junkies and drunks, hadn't until then asked for reference books or videos. They began banding together in support of each other and questioning what they didn't understand. Many started using the center's reference library, which had been largely dormant.

Within a few months the other counsellors and management felt threatened by the clients' new assertiveness and, in true wounded-healer fashion, became defensive and blamed me. Some professionals see demands for information from clients perceived as psychologically blind, no-account failures to be intimidating, confrontational, or representative of defiance—especially professionals and caregivers who carry their insecurities and prejudices well concealed.

Those clients offered me the opportunity to uncover and examine my own subtle prejudices about addicted people, which prejudices were also being held against me by myself. I realized the significant need for caregivers and sponsors to be more than just "aware" of the vicious machinations of addiction, and to have thoroughly resolved their own well-concealed arrogance and prejudice, and to be insightful and sensitively attuned to the unique and complicated needs of those who seek their help. Do not be deceived about the malignant and inexorable power of untreated addictions. There are two rules here. The first rule is that people die from addictions; the second rule is that you can't change the first rule.

I am forever indebted to that first group of clients who trusted that they could push hard against the edge of their treatment (meaning me). I am grateful to the thousands of people who have attended my presentations, and to the many hundreds of clients who have shared their lives with me. After fourteen years of lecturing and research, and six years of writing, there is this book. Ultimately, my responsibility is to demand of myself what I can only encourage in others, and to live by my convictions regardless of the respect or antagonism this generates.

Therapy and Twelve-Step Work

Many addictions-treatment service providers and many people in twelve-step programs offer ineffective services, and within twelve-step groups, "carrying the message" is offering a service. For any number of reasons, noted throughout this book, including the ease with which a Misalliance of Commitment is established

---

[4] AA and NA refer respectively to the groups Alcoholics Anonymous and Narcotics Anonymous.

(which is discussed in Chapter 6), these people fail to maintain a proper segregation between the mutually exclusive requirements of well-managed, long-term, formal therapy, and a twelve-step spiritual pilgrimage.

The Sphere of Human Health

In the sphere of "the human condition", there are three general treatment modalities for addressing issues of ill-health. These are:

Medical Model (including psychiatry)	Psychological Model	Spiritual Model
Generally organic mental disorders, illness, and trauma, treated with medication, surgery, massage, diet, or chiropractic.	Generally mental/emotional dislocations that are addressed with variations of talk, art, or dynamic therapy and adjustments of perception.	Addictions treatment.

Certainly there is a great overlap, especially between the medical and psychological modalities, which is ever more apparent with recent breakthrough treatment strategies like Self Regulation Therapy® and Emotional Freedom Technique.[5] There are also people with dual- or multi-diagnosis concerns where one of the issues is addiction and the others belong in the other modalities. The issues do interweave themselves.

It's crucial to understand that in relation to derivative medical issues that stem from addictions, and where there are multiple-diagnosis concerns, there is a need to incorporate medical or psychological treatment of those "outside" issues. The addiction itself, however, is treated and resolved with spirituality.[6]

Spirituality treats addictions. That is the foundation of the *original* twelve-step program, and is what is outlined in its reference texts. Separating out the addiction from all other health concerns and treating it independently (spiritually) is certainly delicate, but it is essential because an addiction, in its ubiquitous origin and unique manifestation, stands segregated from all other types of health concerns.

It's essential to understand and enroll the complimentary importance of psychology and/or medicine in the treatment of the derivative issues, but to also maintain the segregation of spiritual twelve-step work when addressing addictions. This becomes incredibly delicate when a person is attempting to resolve any abstinence not-available addiction.

Abstinence-Available & Abstinence Not-Available Addictions

There are many ways of categorizing addictions. For the purpose of this book, and to more clearly understand addictions, they are divided into two main

---

[5] See Appendix III.
[6] This book is almost entirely concerned with the effective treatment of addictions. There is some reference to their origin and their cause, but only to the extent of helping addicts get recovered.

categories. Which addiction you are addressing (which category it belongs to) will significantly affect the early stages of your healing work.

Abstinence Available	Abstinence Not-Available
These are addictions to alcohol, tobacco, drugs, and gambling. The spiritual pilgrim can clearly establish complete abstinence; hence, an abstinence available addiction.[7] *This category commands virtually all government attention, policing, research, and press coverage. Yet, these are the least common of the addictions. Sex, work, pornography, relationships, television, computers, and violence addictions are* <u>much</u> *more prevalent and just as destructive to the human condition.*	These are addictions to sex, work, relationships, anger, food, violence, adrenaline, etc., where complete abstinence is not available. Addicts desiring recovery must *first* establish an ethical and credible standard of "bottom line" behavior at and during Step One before other twelve-step work begins. This means they establish and maintain a standard of behavior which, if it were not met, would be considered a relapse. The difficulty is the standard is subjectively interpretive. Abstinence, here, has to be negotiated with and between personal perceptions, instinctual influence, and sometimes pre-existing psychological issues, all of which causes all manner of confusion. It easily lends itself to irresponsibility, repeated failures, and constant relapse.

There are various theories that addictive acting out is self-medication, self-regulation, a reaction to unresolved trauma or abuse, an expression of rebellion, from genetic flaw, or a result of unfulfilled developmental dependency needs and despair. There is research and psychological evidence to lay some claim to all of these; however, none are, independently or collectively, sufficient to encompass a consistent theory of origin. What is common is a profound spiritual dislocation in all addicts, and self-annihilation that sits at the core of all acting out.

Addictions are the self-destructive outcome of deep spiritual dislocation. Access to a spirituality that resolves addictions is what the original twelve-step process established. And, access to that spirituality is completely dependent upon the ability to abstain. This is crucial: The fundamental prerequisite to all bona fide spiritual endeavor is to be not acting out in any addiction.

Achieving this prerequisite, although difficult, is rather straightforward with abstinence available addictions. With abstinence not-available addictions, however, any chaos around establishing bottom-line behavior—any failure to maintain a spiritually credible standard of abstinence, renders all twelve-step work ineffective. There is no end of abuse and confusion about this in the twelve-step and counselling communities. With abstinence not-available addictions, cautious and well-conducted cross-over work[8] is essential to establishing and maintaining an ethical, non-addicted

---

[7] Here I refer to gambling as wagers and various games of chance. Yes, it's a "gamble" to cross the street, but the generic risks of life are not what we're discussing here.

[8] Cross-over work, meaning a combination of therapy and spiritual twelve-step work done coincidental to each other, is necessary for abstinence not-available addictions (some of which were noted in the chart above). This is to establish ethical, non-addicted bottom-line behavior. Cross-over work is also necessary when newcomers respond to invasive "Step One Guides" that are discussed in Chapter 2; and it's always required when addressing a religious or sex addiction. There is also a reference to cross-over work in Chapter 3 regarding Step Two and the fifth type of spiritual newcomer. (cont'd: Fn. next page...)

standard of bottom-line behavior. Without this, any medical, therapeutic, or twelve-step work is only temporary crisis management.

Two crucial requirements early in the process of addictions treatment are reducing the self-annihilating quality of behavior, and eliminating all self-serving, shallow definitions of bottom-line behavior. Once ethical, bottom-line behavior is established *and maintained*, and there appears to be some element of spiritual curiosity, the twelve steps are only then undertaken and applied to the addict's life, exactly as they are laid out in the original twelve-step literature.

With the abstinence not-available addictions like sex, relationships, adrenaline, work, righteousness, food, and religion, any kind of heavy-handed approach to establishing bottom-line behavior, or any generic "group" approach, invariably entrenches the following vicious relapse-cycle in the addict[9]:

(1) **Desire** (to heal): "I want to get recovered. I want to change my life. I'm really going to do it this time. I'm dying. I'm serious."

(2) **Action**: "I am going to quit acting out, stop attending addictive social events, leave abusive relationships (or whatever), and establish abstinence." This is tremendously difficult because abstinence is intimately personal. Too often, in a twelve-step or therapeutic environment, addicts meet up with generic, impersonal abstinence strategies that can't work. Abstinence fails. This entrenches more...

(3) **Guilt** and a deep sense of personal inadequacy. The abstinence strategy that was generic and political (imposed by peer- or therapeutic pressure) is rendered meaningless. The subsequent self-doubt, fear, and shame generates...

(4) An **aversion** to self, to treatment, to twelve-step spirituality. This causes the addict to...

(5) **Retreat** from recovery, from therapy and "their issues", and from spirituality. The viciousness of addiction, and a faint hope of recovery, however, soon leads to another...

With abstinence not-available addictions, which are directly related to instinctual drives, establishing an ethical/spiritual level of meaningful abstinence requires a unique and personalized approach with each individual. A metaphor that I use is that I must discover the addictions fingerprint for each client and then we create a completely new strategy around that.

Cross-over work is very delicate and time-consuming, and should only be undertaken with an insightful therapist who: a) is very well versed in spirituality, addictions, and the intricate requirements of twelve-step programs, b) has a well-established relationship with you (longer than several months of regular weekly appointments), c) is patient and generous of spirit; and, d) is someone you intend to continue working with. In cross-over work the focus is always to end up with spiritual integrity more than psychological health, which priority is mandated by the addiction. This work facilitates access to the truths of psychology, but eventually these become subservient to the principles of spirituality, which are outlined at Appendix II. This process is *very* delicate. The consequences of mismanaged cross-over work are far more onerous than they may seem. The possible rewards are often not worth the risk of undertaking the work where the four criteria are not reasonably well met.

[9] This cycle is discussed from a different perspective in relation to traditions in Appendix I.

Because people must contend with food, sex, work, relationships, and spirituality, and cannot eliminate them as someone can eliminate alcohol, drugs, gambling, or tobacco, establishing abstinence (bottom-line behavior) is one very delicate task of well-conducted cross-over work. Once this is established, which may take upwards of one year of regular therapy, treating any abstinence not-available addiction is a matter of twelve-step work, with ongoing supportive therapy.

The Ubiquitous Nature of Codependence

It is important to realize that the nature of addictions, as I discuss throughout the book, will not allow only one addiction to be present. An addiction is "a state of existence" and not limited to participation in any single acting-out ritual or substance. Poly-addictions are a given.

All addicts will have, at the minimum, a relationship addiction[10] that sits near the core of their acting out, and then at least two other associated addictions at the same time. It is therefore important, if you are addressing a substance addiction like alcohol, drugs, or tobacco, to understand that if you intend to get recovered and be truly spiritual, you will eventually have to address the underlying, associated relationship addiction.

In short, *all* addicts, while getting recovered, will have to address at least one abstinence not-available addiction—relationships—wherein they will have to understand, establish, and adhere to bottom-line behavior.

I am very aware of people's ability, through their ego, to convince themselves that there is nothing wrong within themselves, and that solutions to problems they face belong with someone else: externalizing responsibility.[11] This is often just as true for people offering help as for those seeking it. Caregivers, whether sponsor or professional, are ineffective when they consistently interpret multiple client/newcomer "failures" or repetitive conflict in the treatment dyad, as independent of themselves, the caregivers.

People trying to get recovered will unknowingly rely on misinformation from wounded service providers, where those service providers, especially sponsors, unknowingly live in a misalliance of commitment (discussed in Chapter 6). Newcomers often hope for or participate in the illusion of an expedient or easy process, while enmeshed in a subtle conspiracy theory that someone else is to blame for their addiction and misery. No one is to blame, and there is no expedient process.

Therapy and twelve-step programs complement each other, but have to be combined with extremely careful consideration and forethought. Integrating psy-

---

[10] Codependence is usually a generic catch-all label for all manner of relationship dysfunction. You'll have more clarity and success in addressing "codependence" if you understand it's very likely relationship addiction. In my view, relationship addiction is the more accurate name for codependence. All alcoholics... all addicts, regardless of the style of acting-out behavior, live with relationship addiction (which is abstinence not-available).

[11] Externalizing responsibility (blaming someone else—the mindset of accusation) is a crucial aspect of addictions and is discussed throughout this book.

chology, the five principles of Spirituality[12], the medical model of addiction, twelve-step programs, and formal therapy, into a personalized, effective *spiritual* pilgrimage out of any addiction is profoundly complicated.

Many books have been written about twelve-step programs and their wonderful healing powers. The mass of published literature that misrepresents or recasts the original twelve-step spiritual process onto various and sundry problems is overwhelming. There are literally hundreds of different twelve-step programs (and adaptations and variations and mutations of programs) that try to address everything from drinking too much soda pop to being a child survivor of war. I don't question the need for help, but I do question the insecure and greedy misapplication of the original twelve steps.

This book is designed for people who want or need to eliminate confusion, and get recovered from addictions, within the framework of a twelve-step program (which is a process *into* Spirituality). It's for twelve-step pilgrims who would like clarity regarding the spiritual intent of the twelve steps and the role of appropriate therapy. I have been told that this material is valuable in helping professionals and interested outsiders gain insight into the workings and intent of the twelve steps and addictions in general. It offers detailed explanations of the nature and symptoms of addictions, the twelve steps, the spiritual philosophy that underlies those steps, and the subtle dynamics being recovered. It also explains how to effectively incorporate medical, psychological, and therapeutic assistance into a twelve-step journey.

This is not a quick-read book. It's a very detailed examination of the journey "from addicted to recovered" within the spiritual framework outlined in the original twelve-step program. There is a specific view to exit all addictions via Spirituality, with encouragement to compliment and enhance personal recovery with well-conducted formal therapy and wise spiritual counsel.

Someone once asked me to sum all of this up. I replied that clamoring for simplicity is one manifestation of addiction that is significant in creating the mess we are in. Demanding expedience is fatal to Spirituality. However, for better or worse, and subject to change, this is my answer:

You are a sexual being, in a physical body, trying to be a spiritual entity, in a human context, within a limited but unknown segment of eternity. Even without dysfunction and abuse, or addictions and a selfishly oriented ego, it's incredibly complicated.

As an addicted person getting recovered, somehow realize within yourself that simply learning and doing will not guarantee your becoming Spiritual. Knowledge and action are not the solution—in its broadest sense, God is. Be patient. Labor with devotion for many years. Live intimately with trusted loved ones. Respect the earth and all living things. Have an intimate long relationship with a mentor or therapist. And, in all of this, hold

---

[12] These are outlined in Appendix II. Spirituality (with a capital 'S') refers to that type of spirituality that is ethical, has integrity, and is deeply sincere—spirituality that stands the test of very close scrutiny—the type that we "ought" to aspire to.

personal responsibility, truth, respect, humility, kindness, charity, and non-violence as the highest values. Labor with devotion and patience only to this end: through the maintenance steps be forever obedient to the five spiritual principles.

You will eventually cross some ubiquitous line and then sense, but only in hindsight, and only by embracing your ever-present frailties, that you are recovered. Some might then call you wise, many will resent you, and you will smile gently because, for you, it will be sufficient to quietly repose in the safety of knowing that the mysterious machinations of Providence are beautiful.

The Ordinary Alcoholic: Fact or Fiction?

When people stumble into a twelve-step group and begin to address their most obvious addiction, they suffer from terminal uniqueness. "You're not alone," is the resounding and repeated refrain. It's meant to be reassuring and, to a large extent, it is. As newcomers, they may not be unique within the group of people getting re-covered, but they are alone and isolated from their relationship with God, from themselves, and from others. Isolation from all things is the nature of addictions.

How often have you dimly or secretly sensed how profoundly alone you are in the whole mess called "Your Life"? Within the camaraderie of groups there's iso-lation, too big to handle, and too frightening for the socializing glad-handers to acknowledge. I recall a wonderful story called *The Loneliness of the Long Distance Runner.*[13] Our lives are a lonely, long distance run, which is in many aspects an es-sential and healthy component of a spiritual life. Fears, myths, and a fanatic devotion to superficial social interaction repress the truth of spiritual loneliness. A significant part of unhealthy loneliness and fear is inculcated by people explaining (often in a patronizing way) that we don't *have* to be lonely: smile more and try harder; it was our own fault that we misunderstood; or we were wrongly focused, so when we felt lonely we were at fault for feeling that way.

When I discovered and carefully examined the contradictions I was being fed, sorted out the dilemmas, and puzzled through the paradoxes, I was able to see that very often other people's claim that they weren't lonely was a sham. [In a truly spiritual life, there are no dilemmas or paradoxes.]

Being gregarious, telling ribald or racist stories, precipitating practical jokes, bragging about acting out, talking loud, getting laid a lot, belligerent celibacy, gossiping, teasing, staying in the adrenaline of a chaotic life, constantly regenerating the Life of a Victim—all of these behaviors merely keep the loneliness at bay. It's difficult to confront the socially imposed, long-believed-in myth that isolation and loneliness are curable. They aren't: they are modifiable.

True Spiritual pilgrims eventually understand and accept the essential isola-tion and loneliness inherent in a Spiritual life, which is remarkably different than the relationship-addicted loneliness that people "in recovery" experience most of the

---

[13] Allan Sillitoe, *The Loneliness of the Long Distance Runner,* Plume/Penguin Books, 1992.

time. Spiritual loneliness in a life of devotion to a higher power always carries fulfillment and love within it.

It is also difficult to accept and enjoy that life is randomly benign. Calamity isn't ever directed at anyone personally. This component of life has been identified for thousands of years (by many wiser than me) and cannot be dismissed without the presence of some self-serving agenda. Struggling to see what signs "God" may reveal in the mundane trivia of life, or to understand the spiritual message in random calamities, are ego-driven exercises in vanity that trivialize both the human spirit and God. All circumstances are opportunities to love God, which takes life beyond all temporal coincidence.

In my own struggle to fit in, I had to go through several transitions. Yes, I belonged to a group and I did fit in, but secretly I believed I really didn't. I participated and shared until it hurt, and took everybody's advice so I would be liked—and stayed lonely. After years of confusion, and using intellect and arrogance to conceal the fear and doubt, I cut back on my social participation in my support group and began to study the original twelve-step texts, meaning *Alcoholics Anonymous*[14] and *Twelve Steps and Twelve Traditions*.[15] I was determined to find out what was so powerful about the original twelve steps when they were done exactly as suggested. I sensed there were strong and familiar aspects of the perennial spiritual philosophies, but they were hardly visible beneath the social hype and psychobabble.

I think it was M. Scott Peck who said that as future generations look back on the 20th century, it won't be nuclear fission they remark on; it will be Alcoholics Anonymous and what happened to the world because of it. What is it that makes Mr. Peck's statement true? For better or worse, with all my inadequacies, that's what I set out to discover. What I eventually learned, among other things, was that I was an ordinary person, with or without my addictions resolved, and I could openly participate in the spiritual pilgrimage of the human race. I wanted to *be* ordinary, but most twelve-step people wouldn't let me.

Principles Before Personalities (maybe)

In the world of twelve-step programs, thousands of times each day people ask one another: "How long have you been sober?" or "How long have you been clean?" The only answer is "one day", but there's a hierarchy within the meetings that denies this—the status that's associated with celebrating dry dates and abstinence anniversaries. Key fobs, medallions, marbles, poker chips, parties, cards, and cakes have become more important than spirituality.

Someone will always put you on notice where you fit in the ubiquitous pecking order. A measure of amazement or a tone of awe can be heard in the gossip about the local twelve-step legends. In some meetings special chairs are actually reserved for "sobriety dinosaurs", which is usually nothing more than catering to

---

[14] *Alcoholics Anonymous,* refers to the book published by Alcoholics Anonymous World Services, Inc., third edition, seventh printing, 1980. Alcoholics Anonymous in Roman script refers to the groups.
[15] *Twelve Steps and Twelve Traditions*, published by The AA Grapevine, Inc. and Alcoholics Anonymous World Services, Inc., 1983.

their irascible petulance. Most introductory social conversations will include, besides names, information on drug of choice, alcohol of preference, home group (especially if it has any historical status or local legend attached to it), and the infamous sober or clean date. There's often information on who the respective sponsors are (especially if the sponsor is a local "character") or how many people each person is sponsoring — all to establish the pecking order: personalities before principles.

Then there are "The Hunters" — those men and women in twelve-step or self-help groups who peruse and cruise for relationships, people to sponsor, sex, marriage partners, jobs, transportation (anywhere), loans, housing, food, someone to look after them, or someone to look after. These hunters (whose opening conversations exaggerate or minimize status, depending on what they are hunting for) will work either end of the status game to gain advantage.[16] Any of this defeats any hope of being spiritual. I've often commented that in just about any twelve-step group it's easier to find a wife, a husband, or a good deal on a used car than it is people with dependable, sound, spiritual qualities. It's sad. Really.

Another status tactic is creating a spectacular, flamboyant story, and telling it *repeatedly*. Tales of violent adventures, extreme suffering-and-degradation, sexual imbroglios, graphic descriptions of insanity and reprehensible behavior, are all gambits that actually defeat the purpose of sharing. This doesn't promote belonging, it subverts it, creates isolation, and clearly establishes another pecking order. Sensationalism defeats spirituality and creates distance, not intimacy.

Everyone who hears these stories is affected in some unhealthy way. Those who are of a spiritual nature might notice a poignant sadness at the emptiness of it all and the harm it causes. Those who resist flamboyance or have more gentle sensibilities are often offended, and some become decidedly uncomfortable about their own non-dramatic story. Others shame themselves: "I didn't have it *that* hard; I should have quit sooner," or they criticize themselves and demean their own feelings: "I didn't have it that bad. What have I got to talk about?" Others confabulate or lie to match the notoriety by aggrandizement, and others say nothing and withhold a simple heartfelt story to avoid looking as if they are whining complainers.

There are many honest, emotionally moving *ordinary* stories of pain in addiction that are, by implication, demeaned by the purveyors of excess. Grand stories of debauchery, conquest, violence, abuse, racism, sexism, trainloads of alcohol, degradation to the Nth degree, and escapades of crime, when recast as humor and presented as entertainment, are seriously damaging. Flamboyance defeats spirituality and entrenches cliques and isolation. When you hear it, don't laugh. The tellers are expressing deep insecurity and shame. They need compassion, not applause.

There's another type of subtle, petulant uniqueness that often runs unchallenged. Yes, newcomers belong and are "understood" by those in the group, but they are too often manipulated into believing the quiet rumor that nobody "out there" un

---

[16] The "humble" end of the status game is: "I'm not special, and we are all equal and clean only one day," as the old-timer hits on yet another newcomer for something (usually sex). The arrogant end of the status game is: "Yes, I've been sober much longer than you, so I'm offering my experience and wisdom to help you along, you poor thing."

derstands. "Insiders" are special, and people outside twelve-step groups didn't care, don't understand, don't want to care, wouldn't help if they could, or can't help. Addicts petulantly lick their collective wounds, and thereby create the Evil Blue Meanies[17], labeling various outsiders as stupid, mean, selfish, cruel, and inept.

Many addicts proudly wear the badge of "The Heroic Minority of Recovering Addicts". This attitude is easily reframed into, "I'm a good person for doing this and you're not because you're not doing it," yet another isolation tactic. With self-congratulatory undertones, it ends with bragging about being dedicated to spirituality and helping others. This is arrogance, which is camouflaged by false humility and rhetoric about carrying the message.

All of these are variations on a theme: Personalities Before Principles. In this pervasive oppression, any chance of sincere spirituality is lost. Groups and members cling to the illusion of moral superiority: they're actively seeking "God" and everyone else really needs to do this. This justifies hiding in recovery groups, and avoiding step work, spirituality, and the community at large. It successfully maintains a destructive isolation, which is a core issue of all addictions.

The pecking orders of moral superiority and entitlement are rigidly enforced. There is always someone nearby who will compete using their own more ribald or spectacular story; or spiel off slanderous details of the unsympathetic, uncaring "Normies" that reside outside of the twelve-step membership; or subtly put you on notice that abstinence seniority harbors wisdom and carries political privilege. The fact of the matter is that generally, Principles Before Personalities is held in low regard.[18]

What dovetails with this, is a sometimes well-concealed arrogance about helping others. In the process of becoming recovered, newcomers are unknowingly duped by people in the program who pretend to "know" but don't (people who spout recovery rhetoric); or people who hope they know but conceal that insecurity (dishonest about their lack of faith and experience); or by still others who know they don't know what they're talking about, but claim they do and just don't care (cruel indifference). The more I learned about all of this, the more I appreciated the fascinatingly unique symptoms of the disease of addictions.

Prior to becoming recovered, addicts often decide something is untrue because they don't like it. At other times they refuse to admit the truth of something to avoid embarrassment, such as when they learn that something they've believed in is false. They're insecure and manipulate others to agree with them so they, themselves, feel secure. When I first recognized these traits about myself, I expected to encounter similar behavior from people who, like me, were in the initial stages of their recovery. I didn't expect it from those who had been around for a while, and I was shocked out of my naiveté by old-timers who claimed to be on a spiritual path but weren't.

---

[17] The "Evil Blue Meanies" is a phrase taken from the AA pamphlet *A Member's Eye View of Alcoholics Anonymous,* Alcoholics Anonymous World Services Inc., 1970.
[18] *"This odd trait of mind and emotion..."* and *"This subtle and elusive kind of self-righteousness...,"* *Twelve Steps and Twelve Traditions*, p. 94.

Egos are resourceful and tenacious in clinging to old ideas — a non-spiritual exercise in being right. Other people's attempts to avoid their own insecure loneliness by telling me to get involved, to get social, to smile more, to take responsibility for not trying hard enough, used to arouse my own suspicions of myself. It now arouses gentle curiosity about them.

As I began to understand and experience what could happen through the process of meticulously following the original twelve-step path, and saw the beauty inherent in the universal concepts of Spirituality (which are contained within the original twelve-step writing as much as they are in the perennial philosophies), I knew there was profoundly more available to me than membership and isolation in a terminally unique subculture. My own dissatisfaction with the changing priorities in twelve-step groups, and a rising philosophical conflict, set me on a journey.

When I would discuss some aspect of the original twelve steps that took me out of this addicted, political/spiritual isolationism, and into the greater spiritual community, I would almost always be dismissed, ignored, or argued with. Rarely would anyone listen with any real interest. I assumed that I was being arrogant in how I presented what I believed were profound truths. Later I realized that those who criticized me were envious or insecure, and they circumvented their feelings by making me wrong — just as they did with people outside twelve-step programs.

There is something timeless and profound about the original twelve-step path. Most people, although they have the instructions, miss it almost completely. There is a perennial philosophy at work here, but to me, very sadly, people get abstinent, get popular, get employed, get socially alive, and remain spiritually dead.

By questioning not so much what I was doing but what I was told to do, and by entering therapy[19], and by studying the literature, and by learning to trust my own intuition (which I had been too afraid to speak openly about to others), I identified myths and misconceptions that were being touted as "program". As I studied the perennial philosophies of spirituality, I found similar themes in the original twelve steps. I noticed, beginning immediately in Step One, respect for the body-temple, veracity, and responsibility[20], three of the five spiritual principles. I struggled to become voluntarily obedient to the principles embodied in the twelve steps, and saw the themes of other Spiritual disciplines. I realized in the secret dark corner of my heart that I had a place in the world's pilgrimage. I was deeply relieved.

There's a synergy to the world, stronger and more beautiful than the sum of its parts. Twelve-step people are a part of that synergy — they add to it — but where do they fit? If twelve-step people buy into the historical, cultural perspective of addictions, there's shame and isolation — they lose. If they buy into the twelve-step myth that they're unique and that "outsiders" can't help them, they're arrogant and iso-

---

[19] I was fortunate to meet and work with Dr. Rowan Scott who, at that time, although not strongly informed about twelve-step groups, worked in helping us both to examine and understand the exclusive and inclusive aspects of his expertise (therapy) and my "expertise" (the twelve steps). That work was invaluable. Thank you, Rowan.

[20] Most people in twelve-step programs avoid obedience and responsibility like the plague, and yet these personal commitments to ourselves form the essence of integrity. Without these two qualities there is no access to spirituality. See Appendix II.

lated—they lose.[21] If twelve-step people participate in the social hypocrisy rampant in groups, they may be popular but won't become spiritual—they lose. Any of these take them out of that universal synergy.

My work and presentations, and this book, are my explanation, in real terms that people can understand, of how to escape these destructive and isolating traps. It's okay that I had addictions. The world is mine, too. I contribute to the beauty and strength of the universe. My struggle for spiritual integrity is no different than the struggles of billions of other people over thousands of years.

With increasing frequency over the years, people asked for transcripts of this material, for reference handouts, for permission to record my presentations. There have been hundreds of demands for a book. I was at first flattered and embarrassed. When questioned about what stopped me from writing this book, I made excuses about being very busy or that I was fine-tuning the material. I would patronize or stall, silently wrapping myself in the convenient myth that people like "me" didn't know how to handle success (arrogantly presuming my book would be successful). It wasn't that I couldn't handle success (or failure). I was afraid of being held accountable. I would rationalize that there was no need to write this—if I could figure it out, others could too; they just didn't want to. So…

Why Bother?

There have been books upon books written about counselling and addictions. It would appear there is too much *writing* about it and not enough *doing* about it, and yet here's another book. Why bother?

Over the years, as I became more aware of my life's journey and became more aware as a therapist (the journeys are the same), I've repeatedly encountered a series of problems that manifest in different ways, but can usually be reduced to:

- poor client/newcomer individuation with counselors, sponsors, and communities too invested in the success or failure of the newcomer's process;
- difficulty in transposing theoretical concepts into cognizant therapeutic interventions and definable spiritual behaviors, which if reduced, would make the process of exiting addictions into spirituality a more tangible reality;
- people unnecessarily complicating, or irresponsibly simplifying, the requirements of the steps of the original twelve-step program. The consequences are more deeply entrenched confusion, failure, and self-perceived repetitive inadequacy, which altogether reflect the hopeless confusion and failure in untreated addictions;

---

[21] There is no such thing as an "outsider". We all have a membership in the Everybody's A People Club, whether your ego likes it or not. Gracefully accepting this is spirituality in action.

- various myths, illusions, delusions, social success equations, and acquisitions of tenuous sobriety, that are promoted in groups and by sponsors and professionals as "spirituality"; and,
- a debilitating shift of responsibility for an addiction and the consequences of an addiction (derivative damage, if you will) away from the addict onto community, family, or life circumstances.

It never fails that some of the pain that needs to be resolved in people who struggle in twelve-step groups isn't related to (historical) emotional or physical trauma *per se*. It's also related to the confusion and sense of failure that arises from the corruption in caregivers. Contradictory information is presented, and emotional abuse is perpetrated, by self-styled, self-help gurus, unspiritual sponsors, and poorly trained or still-wounded professionals. This is compounded by the client/newcomer's complete inability to confront the subtle contradictions and abuse from people who hold themselves out as caring and capable. It exacerbates and entrenches the newcomer/client's shame at believing they're inadequate. This engenders a pervasive fear of relapse, reinforces mistrust, and perpetuates a self-defeating confusion.

Caregivers, sponsors in self-help groups, counselors, and spiritual advisors — anyone in addictions-treatment — are charged with the paramount responsibility to do no harm. It appears that too many of them haven't done enough work on themselves to enable them to help addicts without abuse and interference.[22]

People with addictions (especially relationship addiction, and all addicts are inherently relationship addicts) have pervasive fear, mistrust, shame, and pain to some serious degree. These are noticeably worsened by the attempted short-cuts to spirituality embodied in the myths and psychobabble that permeate many twelve-step groups and consulting rooms. Many people who are caregivers, and twelve-step spiritual pilgrims beyond the stage of newcomer, perpetuate these myths. They evince pervading fears of relapse, recidivist acting-out, obsessive hyper-vigilance, a noticeable lack of spiritual self-discipline, dishonesty, phasic addiction substitutions to a consistent and unsettling degree, and demand newcomers comply with self-indulgent and arbitrary rules.[23]

For over twenty years I have focused my studies, healing, and spiritual inquiry not so much on the assumption that I didn't get it right or that I didn't try hard enough, which is what I was told often enough, but on the distinct possibility that I may have been misled. I discovered that I had been offered myths as truths, and had often allowed myself to be manipulated into someone else's spiritual insecurities.

---

[22] Regarding addictions treatment: Certainly there is significant pain from addictions, and everyone carries varying degrees of unresolved developmental/family trauma. In the last twenty years these are very often exacerbated by the confusion, conflict, contradictions, and hypocrisy that is more and more prevalent within the healing community in general, and within twelve-step groups in particular.

[23] I suspect that this is *some*times related to an undiagnosed and subtle anxiety disorder or learning disability. For an insightful and important view of learning disabilities and the influence that family of origin, addictions, and stress have, see *Scattered Minds,* by Gabor Mate, Alfred A. Knopf (Canada), 1999.

I soon became too impressed by the confidence, clarity, and spiritual truths that I read in *Alcoholics Anonymous* and *Twelve Steps and Twelve Traditions* to believe that the petulance, bitterness, and spiritual shallowness I witnessed in meetings was the best that I could hope for. Being "accepted" by others because I allowed them to manipulate me into agreeing with them was no longer acceptable. Within twelve-step groups, the amount of peer pressure that's exerted through gossip and covert ostracism to ensure cooperation, all the while denied by loud rhetoric about love and tolerance, is staggering.

I know that me and my book will be soundly disapproved of by some people. They may accuse me of telling tales out of school, interpret my observations as harshly judgmental, or express disbelief and angry disagreement. I had to develop the courage to contend with the patronizing dismissal (by people with more education), the condescension (by people with more sober time), the overt rejection (by people who are fanatical about some other belief system), and the disrespect from insecure people who need to punish me for breaking their rules.

Years ago, in anticipating these responses, I was afraid to share my ideas and beliefs through a book. I delayed responding to the needs of those people who asked for help, by way of my writing this, and who asked for it out of a genuine interest and desire to learn more and change.

I wrote this book to put a name to what is happening, and to provide clarity through detailed information about the spiritual intricacies of the original twelve steps. This book is neither an improvement nor a short-cut. It explains what monumental work is involved, and offers spiritually-oriented alternatives that challenge the pop-psychology that permeates twelve-step meetings. I encourage a shift to hold spiritual principles as the highest value. I am living up to my commitment to hundreds of people who asked for this book so they could carry these ideas with them. And, finally, I wrote this book to continue to live within the five spiritual principles.

Many times I resisted writing this, and at times I decided not to write it and hid the manuscript away from view. As much as I sometimes tried to ignore it, I couldn't. It seemed that writing this book was the job that I had been given to do.

2

Step One, and Many Other Things

In order to apprehend what someone is up against in getting recovered, it is necessary to examine many topics that are directly and indirectly associated with addictions and spiritual transformation (getting recovered). This requires that I explore various topics that are apparently unrelated to Step One. They aren't. Before someone can wisely re-educate (which I discuss in detail later) and discipline themselves into being recovered, they must first unravel the misinformation and dislocation that pervades twelve-step groups and treatment programs.

Walled Up Consciousness

Expending the energy to beat yourself into an all-encompassing addictive mess takes a sustained effort over a long period of time. Being a successful addict of any kind is very hard work. In telling about a different type of chaos and pain, Matthew Arnold wrote a poem called *Dover Beach*. The last stanza of that poem is:

> *"Nor certitude, nor peace, nor help for pain;*
> *And we are here as on a darkling plain*
> *Swept with confused alarms of struggle and flight,*
> *Where ignorant armies clash by night."* [1]

I am of the opinion that this about best describes the confusion people face when they set out on a journey to get recovered from addictions.

Life is dark. You don't know where to turn. Nothing is certain. Everything hurts. Certainly you're confused. You hear opinions about therapy and twelve-step programs and God and the medical model of addictions and abstinence and spirituality and self-help books and sharing and your ego and your inner child, and it just doesn't seem to stop. You hear opinions about Narcotics Anonymous and Emotions Anonymous and Smokers Anonymous and Alcoholics Anonymous and Overeaters Anonymous and Cocaine Anonymous and Debtors Anonymous and Gamblers Anonymous, and many others.[2] They're all publishing their own reference/text books and it just doesn't seem to stop. There's Sex Addicts Anonymous (SAA) and Sexaholics Anonymous (SA) and Sex and Love Addicts Anonymous (SLAA). If it's a

---

[1] *The Poems of Matthew Arnold*, Matthew Arnold, Oxford University Press, 1961, p. 212.
[2] These names, and others similar to them, refer to the names of twelve-step groups and organizations.

sex-addiction, which twelve-step group should you belong to? Alternatively, is your problem a relationship addiction (which hides under the label "codependence"), and should you also attend CODA or ACOA or Alanon or Naranon?

At the core of it all, there's this thing called *Spirituality*. What about you and your spirituality? Do you have to deal with the low or the high "perspective" of being an Anglican, or is that Episcopalian if you're in the U.S.? Are you the Catholic version of being a Christian, and is that Orthodox or Roman? Don't forget Presbyterian, Alliance, Gospel, Unity, Baptist, the all-faith churches, Unitarians, Jehovah's Witnesses, and the United Church (only in Canada). What *exactly* is Christianity, really? What about Buddhism? Being Sikh? Being Jewish? Being Muslim? Being Wiccan? Shamanism? Hinduism? Jainism? Baha'I? Of course there's God (which is more specific than a Higher Power), and The Goddess, Tao, Allah, Mother Earth, the Atman-Brahmin, YHWH, and many hundreds of other names to choose from.

Is that spirituality with a capital "S" or a small "s"? Is it spirituality that is apophatic or kataphatic?[3] What about meditation — is it transcendental, mystical, or the kind described at Step Eleven? What *exactly* is Step Eleven meditation? Is the Step Seven prayer petitionary, as opposed to contemplative? Which style of prayer should you be doing? Does it matter? Are you praying in the style of whichever tradition that you may or may not be temporarily attached to? Maybe you're angry at praying in the tradition you were raised in, or feeling guilty for not praying before you go to bed. Do you have to?

All of this is dark, confusing, and threatening to people in twelve-step programs; it can't not be. It's so threatening and overwhelming that most veterans of twelve-step groups barely scratch the surface of spirituality. People aspire to only the absolute minimum so they can appear "devoted" while they, themselves, remain lost, confused, and preoccupied with fornication and shiny things. This is dangerous, for they are the sponsors and role-models of spiritual commitment.

The point lost in all of this is that the original twelve-step literature is very specific The point is to get recovered and to be sincerely spiritual, eventually living a life that reflects the will of a higher power, and carrying out the will of God in every area of life, *and* to do this willingly (joyfully). Sadly, this appears to be less and less of what is actually going on.

In spite of the blatant spiritual dislocation within twelve-step programs, I believe what keeps addicts coming back is a glimmer of realization that there's something for them in twelve-step programs, and whatever that may be, they can get it nowhere else. In its broadest sense, a psychic shock happens, and crossing the threshold into "recovery" becomes possible. Regardless of how nebulous, vague, or distant, they sense it and search for it. But, because they can't see what they're look-

---

[3] Kataphatic approaches place a high value on the content and images of spiritual experiences; Apophatic approaches place a high value on the consciousness aspect and argue that content and images are a hindrance. Most popular religions including Hinduism and Buddhism are kataphatic. Zen and many of the truly mystic disciplines are apophatic. For an insightful and detailed exploration of spirituality and psychology read *Will & Spirit, A Contemplative Psychology*, by Gerald G. May, Harper & Row Publishers, 1982.

ing for, and don't know how to look, and because there are so few people to turn to for sound twelve-step spiritual guidance, they flail away at spirituality and end up with a tentative resolution and mediocre recovery.

There used to be a rumor in the late nineteen-thirties, and thankfully it's been proven true (even though today that truth is often misapplied, and in many circumstances rendered ineffective), that *Alcoholics Anonymous* described a method to get recovered from alcoholism. By the early nineteen-forties, AA[4] was only a few years old, and the method it presented for alcoholics to become spiritual was still largely an experiment and not well trusted. Over the next thirty-five years, the original twelve steps and the "self help" groups[5] that embody them, were proven effective and reliable. Now, seventy years later, that history, which borders on legend, is one attraction to those who follow.

Regarding counsellors at treatment centers, therapists that offer specialized services, and sponsors: many attempt to take the proven process of the original twelve steps and re-work it into a brand of psychological healing. Unless these people are exceptionally clear on both what the mandate of a twelve-step program is (spirituality), and what the mandate of therapy is (which varies considerably), and are at the same time generally healed themselves (and at the very minimum absent of all addictions), any program they devise that combines these processes will backfire. The people seeking help from them will be damaged more than they already are.

Despair from repeated, failed efforts to combine and negotiate therapy and twelve-step programs is far too common. Addicts are being sold a bill of goods that suggests there's a combined, expedient process. There's no expedient process. And, unless the counsellor (or sponsor) is well informed, themselves reasonably healed, and spiritually insightful and adept, the newcomer/client gets lost.

To be recovered from addictions—to become Spiritual via the original twelve steps—is long, hard, delicate, painstaking, and (up to Step Seven) painful. Each addict is so unique in their requirements for healing that any heavy-handed, generic intervention is doomed. The individual's special needs are primary. Certainly, recovery-communities and support networks are elemental to success; but equally important, there must be a significant focus on individual uniqueness in spiritual endeavor. Considering that we are playing with lives here, no less than surgeons do in operating theaters, delicate touch, prudence, and consideration of the individual are paramount in addictions treatment.

I believe that many service providers, and most people in twelve-step programs, deliver ineffective services. They don't understand the mutually exclusive

---

[4] AA: The coveted acronym that represents Alcoholics Anonymous (the groups). *Alcoholics Anonymous,* in italic script, refers to the book, cited at an earlier footnote.
[5] Twelve-step programs are not self-help. "Self-help" *groups* don't exist. If you belong to a group that helps and supports you, it's not self-help in its truest sense. There are times when the phrase "self-help" is used by someone to brag about vigorous independence from everyone (which is a dysfunctional symptom of addiction). More often, self-help is used to mean that lay people are doing something without the aid of a professional; and there's often a prideful and belligerent exclusion of "professionals" when touting their healing endeavors. There is no such thing as self-help. All our successes, in every endeavor, are interdependent to some noticeable degree.

dynamics of therapy and the original twelve steps. What works in one discipline is often detrimental if applied in the other. They complement each other like salt and pepper but cannot be substituted for each other.

When the lecture series that led to this book was in its early stages, I was astonished (and still am today), that the majority of addictions-affected people "in recovery" could articulate nothing substantive about the phenomenon that was killing them—beyond being glib about drinking or drugging. I drew a parallel with the Dark Ages when people would die of disease and know nothing about it except superstition and myth.[6] Considering how epidemic addictions are, people still know very little about them; about spirituality; or about the difference between the therapy and the twelve-step programs people are expected to facilitate or participate in.

Knowledge dispels ignorance and supports awareness, but knowledge isn't awareness and it *never* substitutes for healing. Clients will often acquire knowledge and then quit therapy, presuming they're healed. Many "sober" addicts become counselors and abusively use their jobs and education as "proof" of their health and wisdom. Practicing addicts "counsel" addicts, which is very often destructive, and at best marginally effective, and everyone is left in dislocation and myth. Many professionals who live with secret or visible, socially-approved addictions offer treatment that is harmful to those they claim to help. In all these circumstances, the abuse is concealed under rhetoric, clichés, education, socially-approved addictions, and socially-approved dysfunction like greed, aggression, and irresponsibility.

The poignant aspect is through unexamined stereotyping, addicts are too often seen as incapable of change or morally weak, and knowledge is withheld. No one informs them, which tends to abet denial (a symptom of the disease), and that works to preclude awareness. This guarantees more damage and no substantive change.

Taken together, this book and its companion volume *Facets of Personal Transformation,*[7] are intended to take you from active addiction, through the original twelve steps and the related issues surrounding addictions, to being recovered (spiritual). At the end, you should be informed enough to differentiate clearly between a therapy and a twelve-step issue, and to maintain some integrity, and therefore achieve some notable success, in getting recovered. Altogether, this should eliminate recovery-confusion so you'll know where you're [supposed to be] going.

As a client, my own first serious course of therapy began around 1982. I'd be talking to my sponsor about something and he'd ask: "Have you got your therapist's card?" I'd answer, "Yes." He'd say: "Phone him, I don't know anything about that." At other times I'd be sitting in my therapist's office and going on about my alcoholism. He'd push the phone towards me and say, "Phone your sponsor." I'd ask: "What do you mean, phone my sponsor? You're the psychiatrist." And he'd say, "Yeah, but I'm not an alcoholic. Phone your sponsor."

---

[6] The damage and destruction from addictions leaves me with no doubt we are facing an addictions-plague of epidemic proportions. Alcohol and drugs are only a very minor part of the problem.
[7] *Facets of Personal Transformation* is scheduled for publication in 2007. See p. 445.

My therapist and my sponsor and I, with some stumbling about, became clear on each of our roles. Of course, it ended up that my role was to do all the work of healing myself, which, if the truth be known, annoyed me to no end. Those were days of sometimes petulant struggle—me trying to get those two men to indulge my perception of my own inadequacy. I wasn't inadequate to the tasks and they didn't indulge me. This was my first (very strange) experience of being in non-codependent relationships, which meant there was no relationship addiction. I began to see both the profound and the subtle distinctions between therapy and spirituality.

Addicts cling desperately to excuses for acting out and have an endless supply of reasons for blaming others. Their *un*usually *un*healthy egos are brilliant at externalizing responsibility.[8] Coercive mentor-ship, counselors and sponsors being invested in the personal or spiritual lives of others, and mountebanks who use abstinence seniority or education as a masquerade for wisdom or authority, are all irresponsibility in disguise. Irresponsible behavior manifests itself in countless ways.

Irresponsibility is secretly hoping/praying that love will go right, food will taste good, bills will get paid, or that someone will arrive with a panacea for all your ailments. Irresponsibility is waiting for a benevolent hero to hold your hand and tell you it's okay to do whatever you want; or searching for someone who has a magic formula or secret mantra to make spiritual healing easy. Irresponsibility is complaining about anything, especially that Life hurts, your pain won't go away, people won't stop being mean to you, that it's someone else's fault, or that Life isn't fair. These, and ten-thousand variations of them, are all irresponsible. With irresponsibility, secret, subtle, or otherwise, there can never be spiritual peace or true commitment to anything, intimate love will be absent, contentment will be tenuous, fulfilling sex will be unavailable, Life will at best be mediocre, and God will never be trustworthy. For irresponsible people, the implacable grandeur of life will be forever elusive.[9]

If, after some period of abstinence, people claim to be puzzled about suddenly ending up drunk; or plead they really couldn't help it that they committed adultery, lied, stole, seduced yet another newcomer; or are angry they had to declare bankruptcy because they mysteriously ended up in huge debt; or are particularly belligerent about honesty or spirituality, they are irresponsible. Their claims to have "suddenly" ended up in trouble, and the justifications for their irresponsibility, are not usually challenged in meetings. This is twelve-step political deal-making at its best. Irresponsibility is spiritual cancer.

Myths and Misinformation

Before I get into the details about doing an actual Step One, which is: *"We admitted we were powerless over alcohol—that our lives had become unmanage-*

---

[8] When addicts become curious about the freedom that's inherent in complete responsibility (which curiosity should begin to dimly appear at Step Four, and be marginally clear by Step Seven), they take responsibility and stop blaming others or finding fault elsewhere. Equally important, at the same time they cease feeling non-contractual guilt—they only feel as guilty as they've agreed to.

[9] *"For if there is a sin against life, it consists perhaps not so much in despairing of life as in hoping for another life and in eluding the implacable grandeur of this life."* Albert Camus, *The Myth of Sisyphus And Other Essays*, Vintage Books/Random House, 1991, p. 153.

able,"[10] I want to talk about a few myths and "rules" that are often touted as being part of healthy recovery. These horrendously complicate, delay, or entirely prevent your getting recovered, which is complicated enough already.

The Two-Part Step One

One myth exists in the way that some people represent Step One. They claim, usually as an excuse for relapse, or yet another defense of their irresponsible or insensitive behavior, that they have only done the first half or the second half of the step. This explanation is usually given in a tone of self-castigation (which often rings hollow), and now that they are back for the 7th or 23rd time, they are determined to focus on whichever half of Step One they had been ignoring. This excuse is flawed: There are not two halves to Step One.

Remind yourself, and it is so obvious that we don't think about it, that one reason we can impart knowledge through writing is the rules of grammar. If you took any book and removed the punctuation and the capital letters, the book would make no sense. If you substituted commas for periods, or semicolons for dashes, the writing would take on a different meaning. Editors insist on correct grammar, especially in books of instruction. Grammar is what organizes words so people can transmit ideas in some manner close to what they intend. Those who wrote *Alcoholics Anonymous* were schooled in traditional English and grammar and they were intelligent. It would be reasonable to assume they wrote the words they intended to write and used the grammar they intended to use.

In Step One, the short line between *alcohol* and *that* is a dash. A dash is a specific piece of punctuation—an abrupt interruption which advises the reader that what follows the dash is an appositive phrase or summary. Whatever phrase or clause follows a dash, within the same sentence, is an explanation or summary of what preceded the dash. So, *"—that our lives had become unmanageable"* is an explanation or a definition of the phrase *"We admitted that we were powerless over alcohol—"*. They are the same idea, represented by different words, so we can understand the point that the author intended. The phrases immediately before and after the dash do *not* offer ideas independent of each other.

And, additionally, note that there is no writing regarding Step One in *Twelve Steps and Twelve Traditions* or *Alcoholics Anonymous* that reads "and now for part two." Nowhere does it read: "Now, for the second half of Step One." There are serious risks in creating the illusion that Step One is in two separate parts. These are subtle and the consequences are vicious. When people view Step One as being in two parts, they create serious complications that allow them to dramatize the simple idea presented in the step. One result, among others, is that they are provided another excuse for irresponsibility

Step One is in the past tense. One purpose of this is to begin, and then to expand awareness during abstinence, of the consequences and repercussions of your acting out. Regarding the original Step One, unmanageability is directly attached to

---

[10] *Alcoholics Anonymous*, p. 59, and *Twelve Steps and Twelve Traditions*, p. 21.

acting out. They are symbiotic. Should you change the dash to an "and" or a semicolon, or when you reject the correct grammatical use of a dash, you thereby create two parts to Step One. You now have an opportunity to redefine an unmanageable life as independent of the context of your former acting-out behavior. This separates the drinking/acting out from the unmanageability. This is subtle and dangerous.

When this happens, acting out stays "in the past", but unmanageability, now erroneously independent from acting out, can be examined by itself. This allows "unmanageability" to be used in present, or to be projected into the future, as an excuse for irresponsibility. Unmanageability can thereby become an independent, preeminent issue: "It wasn't *really* the drinking [acting out], it was the unmanageability, so maybe if/when I get my life manageable I will be fine."

As soon as you isolate acting out from "unmanageable"; once unmanageability stands independent unto itself, there's an escape route to avoid responsibility in sobriety. With Step One in two parts, when in sobriety, unmanageability becomes an easily-available excuse for irresponsible behavior rather than a defining quality of active addiction. Irresponsibility that's justified (concealed) by calling it "unmanageability" can not be addressed properly because it has become camouflaged as legitimate. Many people tout their irresponsible behavior in abstinence as unmanageability, when, in fact, it's a complicated justification for deliberately spiteful, mean, irresponsible, or petulant behavior.

Drama & Pain

Addicts love drama: having crises, hardship, pain, love, angst, joy, and successes all larger than life. An ego controlled by addiction is especially relentless in finding ways to create and justify drama. Related to this is the self-serving arrogance associated with rewriting, editing, or rearranging the original program, which often serves as an escape clause into drama.

Drama is created attendant to some authentic pain or insecurity, and is often evinced as a distorted sense of entitlement, harsh judgments, or comparisons: "I didn't try hard enough." "They didn't try hard enough." "My penis isn't big enough." "I'm not pretty enough." "My breasts are too small (or too big)." "I'm too tall (or too short)." "I can't run fast enough." "I'm too heavy." "I'm too horny, too often." "I've got bad teeth." "It's not fair..." "My car isn't fast/shiny/new enough." "I'm poor (or rich)." "...*and nobody understands the anguish I endure!*"

Creating drama is a way to add to, and intensify, already existing pain and shame. Once the drama is created and goes unchallenged, there are now two "types" or sources of pain within the addict. There's the (first) insecurity/pain that originally motivated the drama, which is now buried underneath the (second) pain arising from the drama itself. The despair and futility arising from the drama is no less "painful" than the pain, insecurity, or shame that originally motivated it. All of the pain is experienced as real but arises from two different sources—trauma and drama.

There's a long-term crippling effect of trying to address pain, that is generated by self-created or imposed drama, with the usual therapeutic pain-relief strategies like compassion, empathy, validation, applied problem solving, or assertive re-framing. In this context, with poorly trained, naïve, or still-wounded thera-pists, or with self-styled self-help gurus, or still-wounded sponsors (abetted by spiritually unfocused groups), the drama will be validated as externally authentic.[11] The vicious complication is that this entrenches and reinforces the drama as real.

The usual therapeutic strategies for relieving emotional pain are only effec-tive provided the pain they are addressing is not based on drama. Resolving emotional pain where the origin of pain is rooted in drama (i.e. "dramatic" pain) re-quires a very different healing strategy. To relieve pain caused by drama you must eliminate the drama, then that pain goes away. However, there's the horrendously complicated and delicate task of sorting out which pain is rooted in drama and which isn't. [Drama-reduction is directly related to taking complete personal responsibility, the explanation of which is part of the theme of this book.]

Besides exaggerating for dramatic effect, there is excessive minimizing for dramatic effect. In the midst of real calamity you hear: "Ah, it's *nothing*! My house burned down after the fire-insurance expired, someone stole my car, my partner left me, I lost my last pair of glasses so I can't read the instructions for my heart medica-tion; and yes, I also lost my job, my wallet, and my dog died, and I can't afford bus fare to the Food Bank, but really, I'm fine." This ego-style creates drama by making legitimate hardship inconsequential.

I do not imply that all pain is always dramatic. Pain and hardship are legiti-mate. However, the suffering arising from the drama; the plaintive wail, "Nothing's My Fault;" the justifications of the relationship-addicted martyr; the magnificent struggle of the twelve-step hero, are drama. And, of course, the bigger the drama, the harder it is to resolve the pain, and to get started on organizing your life around ab-stinence and the five spiritual principles.[12] A client, after months of struggle, finally admitted, with a shy smile, that he was responsible for organizing his own happiness, which included a responsibility to eliminate his ego-created drama.

Drama and irresponsibility are always directly or indirectly associated with a belief that Step One is in two parts. Greater complications and more drama are al-ways the consequence.

Another issue that arises from dividing Step One into two halves is you get to marginalize the consequences of drinking or acting out. The speech goes like this: "Well, yes, I couldn't control my drinking [the first half], and of course my life was unmanageable [the second half], but my life is still unmanageable, so I guess unman-ageability doesn't have very much to do with drinking. It wasn't the drinking that was the problem, it was the unmanageable life. If I learn how to manage my life, I guess I'll be able to drink." This rationalization is *carte blanche* permission to re-lapse. In any of this, character defects are never resolved, abstinence is never stable, and there's constant compensation to stay ahead of the fear. The compensation tactic is to create [more] drama.

---

[11] Pain and shame from shock, emotional, or developmental trauma (see Appendix III) is authentic. Pain arising from drama is experienced as real; however, its origin is only "real" in relation to the self-generated or imposed drama, not to the original pain-causing circumstances.
[12] See Appendix II.

When you extend yourself into a Spiritual lifestyle, which is done by willing obedience to the requirements of the steps, it is for the most part to eventually become benignly indifferent to the transient circumstances you experience—not to transcend them, but to lovingly ignore them in favor of the five spiritual principles. When you create drama, you are avoiding the reality of your own ordinariness. When drama is perceived as reality, and you attempt to be spiritual without *first* eliminating the drama, the resulting "spirituality" becomes an extension of the drama and is either obsessive and rigid,[13] or maudlin and sentimental.[14] Your faith and relationship to the divine are then rooted in drama (delusion), and of no substantive value.

———

After any reasonable period of abstinence in a twelve-step group, what precedes any "relapse" is some combination of petulance, blaming, anger, and dishonesty. These are related to Isolation Thinking that is discussed in Chapter 11. These covertly guarantee the probability of relapse; but the reasons you present for relapse are most often misrepresentations and cover-ups that are rooted in drama.

You wanted to teach someone a lesson (vindictiveness); you wanted to rub some misdemeanor in someone's face (righteous pride); you're not going to be told what to do (defiance); or you resent spirituality (arrogance/insecurity; can't show off). These are expressions of fear and insecurity which are witnessed as character defects. To admit this doesn't promote sympathetic responses from other drama junkies. However, a plaintive cry that you're trying really, *really* hard, and you didn't get the other half of Step One, is good for garnering sympathy. It's awkward to admit that the step is relatively simple, and embarrassing to admit you relapsed into your primary addiction because you were pouting and behaving irresponsibly.

Is It Really Relapse?

When seen from a more responsible point of view, most relapses aren't "relapses" because the person concerned didn't exit their addictions. The common experience called relapse should be more accurately described as the resumption of an obvious addiction, in association with ongoing subtle addictions.

Consider people who are addicted to tobacco, relationships, and alcohol. This is a common combination of addictions. They quit drinking and join AA but continue acting out in their socially acceptable, less destructive (sic) addictions to tobacco and relationships. After some period of not drinking, called sobriety, which may be years, all the while still acting out in the other two addictions, they start drinking again. They then attend their twelve-step meeting and confess their "relapse." Yes, technically, they relapsed into alcoholism, but they didn't relapse into addiction: they never got out of it.

---

[13] Religious devotion that arises out of drama, or that is compensation for insecurity and character defects, usually manifests as obsessive, rigid, or arrogant. Intrusive proselytizing, fundamentalists, "born-agains", and fanatic "twelve-steppers" are evidence of this.

[14] Beware of the thwarted sentimentalist. Their viciousness when crossed is only exceeded by their phony benevolence and deeply camouflaged insecurities.

For the most part, people who claim to have relapsed, haven't. They've only resumed some blatant addiction they'd discontinued, that garners more attention than the subtle ones they've continued to practice that don't garner attention. Should people exit all their addictions, they are so spiritually aligned that they don't relapse at all. Use the word relapse carefully.

The Manageable Truth About Unmanageability

In the original literature, the concept of unmanageability is used in relation to active addiction.

You meet a person, you date, sincerely love them, and desire fidelity in the relationship. You get married. A year later you wake up in bed with somebody else and you're getting divorced; yet, when you got married, your love and commitment were sincere. Maybe it's your child's birthday and certainly you love your children. You make a commitment about the birthday, but because you have a couple of drinks on the afternoon of the party, you cause a huge scene and the party's a disaster. Or, you really enjoy your career, but you blow it by getting stoned and missing work just before that one big project is finished. Remember that at the moment you made the commitment, you were sincere.

How many times have you had a sincere intention and were later irresponsible because of your acting out? The unmanageability that's attendant to your active addiction makes it appear that you weren't sincere or serious about your marriage, your children, or your job. Not showing up for a commitment doesn't necessarily mean you were insincere when you made it. When you are actively in your addiction you are irresponsible. An unmanageable life, in this context, is a symptom of, and intended to be a part of, the truth of what active addiction does to a person. By people who are abstinent, it's intended to be read in the past tense, and it offers clarity on what active addiction encompasses.

Step One is in the past tense. That our lives *had become* unmanageable is a reference to the historical chaos attendant to alcoholic drinking or other acting out. Knowing that a dash means what it means, it follows *"—that our lives had become unmanageable"* means you *were* powerless over alcohol [acting out]. If your life "in sobriety" is still unpredictable and unmanageable, similar to what it was when you were in your obvious addiction, then you're acting out in another addiction, although not the one from which you've been abstinent.

In sobriety, because you don't like your life, because your life is hard, because you don't get your own way, does not mean your life is unmanageable. Notice the number of times "unmanageable" is misused in twelve-step conversation to complain about the state of affairs in someone's life of abstinence. What I'm getting at here is, while you become recovered, your ego will want to define a life you don't like as "unmanageable", and blame your addiction, rather than viewing yourself as petulant and slothful.[15] Blaming is fatal to spiritual integrity.

In early abstinence, you probably begin to show up for your appointments on time. Although you don't like visiting the probation officer or the banker or the doctor, you show up on time, which you rarely did when drinking or using. You show up for work on time although you don't like your job or your boss. Maybe you don't like living in a recovery house and your life circumstances are unpleasant: you're broke, you have to take the bus because you don't have a car, you've got to stand in line to use the bathroom, the food is too salty, everything's overcooked, and your roommate snores, but you still show up for meals and appointments. You don't like that you've got to get a minimum-wage job and start paying rent.

These typical "unpleasant" life situations are your excuses to label your life as unmanageable. But, none of these circumstances mean your life is unmanageable; they just mean your life is difficult and you don't like it.[16] Unpleasant circumstances are *not* a symptom of the disease, they are the result of it. Symptoms are not external, they're internal. The symptom of addiction is in the irresponsible, cynical, or petulant way you blame Life and people, and misuse the term *unmanageable*. External unpleasantness is the result of the disease, not the motivator of it.

Addicted egos cling to an entrenched belief that addicts are somehow, supposed to be exempt from the routine pains and irritations of life. Addicts complain that life isn't fair for them, and by that imply it should be more unfair for others.[17] Lives in early sobriety aren't unmanageable: they are hard work, often unpleasant, and for a long while, painful.

When you're getting recovered and label a difficult life as unmanageable, you are possibly using "unmanageable" in the wrong context. Unmanageable is symbiotic with acting out; it's not intended to legitimize whining and complaining, after all, it is a self imposed crisis. And, regardless of any of this: At first glance, it would appear that unpleasantness is a condition attendant to Life, addicts included. The magic of the a truly spiritual life is that all unpleasantness becomes optional.

Step One "Guides"

There are many instruction sheets that are circulated in the recovery community that are referred to as Step One Guides. I've collected quite a few over the years and they have several things in common. I will choose to assume they were all written by well-intentioned people, but who have missed the point, and made getting recovered that much more complicated than it needs to be.

Many tell you to write and talk about your parents—describe what kind of people they were emotionally, mentally, spiritually, and physically. In contrast, *Alcoholics Anonymous* suggests that you examine your own drinking behavior. I

---

[15] Your ego defines your life in the way it filters and interprets the relationship between the Matrix of Your Soul and the Corporeal Universe; see Appendix IV. And, in Chapter 8, I discuss The Two Step Dance which is this dynamic in action.

[16] Remember that most of the work in the world is done by tired people who don't feel very good.

[17] Life is neither fair nor unfair, it is benignly indifferent to everything. There is no meaning to Life, except what meaning we each assign to it.

cannot find, in either AA text, any direct or indirect suggestion requiring you understand the emotional or mental attitudes of your parents. What kind of family you had is not mentioned as a factor contributing to the difficulty of becoming spiritual.[18]

In a Step One guide from a recovery house, whose stated mandate is to address addictions in a twelve-step model, respondents are asked to analyze their family of origin. Many counselors can't do this; why demand it from a confused newcomer? It implies some "family-of-origin" responsibility for the addiction. Not only does this misrepresent Step One, it lays the groundwork for a Victim Mentality and exacerbates anxiety and futility within the newcomer. This is blatantly contrary to the idea presented in the AA literature, that alcoholism/addiction (with all its unsavory ramifications) is a self-imposed crisis.[19]

Similarly: Another treatment center asks, "How did your parents [in other questions, siblings and grandparents] express their love and affection toward each other?" Yes, some dysfunction arises out of the inability to express love, or from never having received unconditional positive regard.[20] And yes, relationship patterns are passed on through generations, and sometimes fail to meet developmental dependency needs. These guides imply, however, that these troubled relationships explain the addiction, which makes it easy for the addict to externalize responsibility for the life damaging consequences. The client/newcomer reasons, with an ego-smile of absolution: "It's not me, it's my parents and grandparents. My siblings didn't properly express their love; that's why I'm an addict. What a relief! I thought for a moment that it was *my* fault." Addicts go to great lengths to avoid responsibility, and far too many treatment centers and professionals are complicit in this.

In many Step One "guides", newcomers with minimal insight are asked to puzzle out complicated psychological paradigms. By implication, they are being told that an addiction and the self-annihilation related to it, are somehow the responsibility of some classification of caregiver. [As a complicated aside, the counselor who uses this type of guide goes to great lengths to avoid responsibility, too.] Caregivers may have evinced unsavory behavior, but they did not cause the addiction.

I have another Step One guide that presents this: "We accepted that we were powerless over the *effects* of our addictions, that our lives had become unmanageable;" [emphasis added]. The original Step One is for you to clarify the obvious relationship between unmanageability and powerlessness during and attendant to drinking [acting out], so you can admit the truth of that. This particular guide requires acceptance of significantly more than unmanageability and powerlessness:

---

[18] Being aware of the neglect or abuse you experienced may contribute to an understanding of why you are ashamed, neurotic, or racist, etc. Developing that awareness, however, is not the purpose of twelve-step work. Becoming spiritual is the purpose of twelve-step work. Psychological health is noticeably different from spiritual integrity. Crossover work, which I described earlier (footnote, p. 17) may be necessary to establish abstinence, but crossover work is not necessarily focused on historical family dynamics.

[19] *Alcoholics Anonymous*, p. 53.

[20] Unconditional Positive Regard is one aspect of Client Centered Therapy, developed by Carl R. Rogers, *The Carl Rogers Reader,* Edited by Howard Kirschenbaum and Valerie Land Henderson, Houghton Mifflin Co., 1989, p. 225.

Being powerless over the *effects* of an addiction (the derivative consequences, such as poverty and ill health) is significantly different from being powerless over the behavior of acting out. This change expands the scope of responsibility and acceptance to include circumstances that the addict had or has no control over. It creates a sense of hyper-responsibility, and a need to control the consequences (environment). This type of hyper-responsibility is a facet of relationship addiction.

Acceptance of anything more than the basic relationship between acting out, unmanageability, and powerlessness, is quite impossible to a newcomer at Step One. In *Alcoholics Anonymous,* Step One is to establish a clear and definite relationship between unmanageability and acting out, which is the initial major inroad to the truths of powerlessness and irresponsibility, *and* which is the only effective precondition for Step Two. This guide, and many other psychologically reworked Step Ones, dangerously obfuscates the relationship between acting out and powerlessness, which subsequently, seriously undermines the efficacy of Step Two.

The author of this particular "guide" rewrote the step to psychologically spoon-feed clients, and thereby imposed an expanded, personal interpretation of Step One. This counsellor is emotionally invested in the success of clients, which indicates abusive expectations on the counsellor's part, and subtly legitimizes relationship addiction. In the subtle nuance of the underlying issues here, the writer of this guide is an untreated relationship addict.

Another guide states a goal of Step One is to achieve humility, and defines humility as "a clear reckoning of who we really are". In the original literature, humility is only vaguely implied in Step One by the required admission of truth—*silently* inferred by the unstated spiritual axiom of humility-via-honesty. However, spiritual humility is *not* identified as a specific goal of Step One, and it is certainly much more complex than "a clear reckoning of who we really are". This guide has taken the complicated concept of humility, offered a very inefficient definition of it, and pushed it visibly into the middle of Step One where it doesn't belong.

Step One has a reference to being humbled by the admission of personal powerlessness, and humbled by the truth of the newcomer's devastating weakness. "Being humbled", in this context, refers to the introduction of reality and the loss of delusion in a newcomer's life; not humility vis-à-vis a spiritual principle.

People who have been abstinent for years struggle with humility. Priests, ministers, yogis, monks—the experts, never mind the laity—see humility as a life-long quest fraught with pitfalls. Psychologically and spiritually defiant newcomers. detoxing from years of insane thoughts and self-annihilation, are not to be given the impossible and unnecessary burden of understanding humility at Step One.

Other guides have Step One as: "We admitted we were powerless over alcohol; that our lives were unmanageable." Or: "We admitted we were powerless over alcohol and that our lives were unmanageable." These changes: (i) the dash to a semicolon, (ii) the dash to an "and"; and, (iii) changing "had become" to "were", alter the very nature of the step. Unmanageability is here presented as independent of the addiction, and creates unnecessary complications and opportunities to justify irresponsible behavior. These guides go on to say specifically in relation to Step One: "Furthermore, here in this treatment center, which uses the twelve steps, the only real source of unconditional love is God as you understand Him."

There are serious problems in these guides. (1) Step One is in two separate parts, which creates the problems discussed earlier. (2) Spirituality is presented as an *active* part of Step One; it isn't. (3) The author has interjected their own spiritual values into Step One: they declared love as the gift of a divine being, which denies freedom of choice in spiritual matters. (4) By changing "had become" to "were," the guide edits the original scope of Step One, which is supposed to allow an awareness of the progressive nature of untreated addiction and not its singular end result.

Another document is called a Step One Assessment, which is quite different than a guide, and is comprised of 49 questions and instructions regarding Step One. Here are seven of them:

- Briefly describe your memories of your father in your early childhood years.
- Have you or your partner ever had an abortion, miscarriages, or given any children up for adoption?
- Briefly describe any significant sad or happy events that you remember in your childhood.
- Briefly describe your home life as you remember it in the first ten years of your life.
- What parent are you most like?
- Have you ever been physically, sexually or emotionally abused as a child or as a teenager? By whom? How has this affected you?
- Have you ever had or desired sex with animals? How has this affected your life?

Of the 49 questions, 24 are related to substance abuse and 25 are therapeutically intrusive, related to various and sundry psychological issues. There is no theme or structure to the 25 intrusive questions, six of which are of a prurient sexual nature, and all 25 are overall, a random inquisition, fishing for something dramatic.

In a twelve-step meeting or an addictions treatment center, the Step One issue is the unmanageability from your acting out, not that you were abused or your parents didn't like each other. This information *may* be important as far as being in therapy goes, but within the context of early abstinence, these questions are inappropriate. Acting out must be kept generally separate from family of origin influence so that abstinence is entirely a function of personal responsibility and commitment.

There are two long term, devastating implications in these various corruptions of Step One. The first is the clear implication that if you ended up in formal treatment for addictions there must be horrible abuse or major trauma, otherwise, you wouldn't be in treatment. The second is that trauma (real or imagined) is the primary cause of your addiction. It decidedly isn't.

Far too many addicts and caregivers fail to appreciate that the degree of self-harm through addictions is rarely proportional to the trauma experienced in childhood, and that having an addiction doesn't mean there are egregious childhood "issues". Misunderstanding this leads to the dangerous, erroneous supposition that by resolving the trauma, you resolve the addiction. It also sets up a psychological witch hunt: The addict gets to hunt for someone to blame. These styles of "Step One" make abstinence more difficult than it is, and irresponsibility more difficult to address.

Some twelve-step/support groups encourage discussions about how caregivers and early family relationships didn't meet childhood needs, and how this historical deficiency is now compensated for by the love or acceptance in the addict's twelve-step group. This is a nice thing to say, but it is, more often than not, political and probably not true. Subtle peer pressure that limits participation to whatever is within the group's comfort zone, the rampant and abusive gossip, the often overt and always covert rules for acceptance, aren't demonstrations of love. Being told you are loved unconditionally when you really aren't is very damaging and often a re-creation of the hypocrisy in many families. Whether or not you were (or are) loved has nothing to do with the requirements of Step One.

These are only a few examples of how the seemingly innocuous altering of Step One can cause harm, and identifies a destructive combination of therapy and twelve-step work. From one perspective, these so-called Step One "guides" represent an effort to make abstinence easier to attain. At a deeper level, this is indicative of the various counsellors' confusion or insecurity, that is being acted out in a form of relationship addiction, which is concealed by altruistic rhetoric.

Now, combine this with a second perspective: These guides were all written by staff at treatment centers. When viewed as treatment centers needing to generate or maintain funding by creating a psychological version of step one (because "becoming spiritual" won't get government money), these rewritten steps are motivated by commercial enterprise. (This is explored in Appendix I at Self Supporting.)

Doing "good" things like rewriting the steps to make them easier for the suffering newcomer is very often a mercenary endeavor so a treatment center can generate and maintain funding. It may appear benevolent, but upon close examination, it is very likely not as efficient, honorable, or wise as is claimed. Every newcomer has to pay the full admission price for spiritual integrity. Nothing is free, and getting recovered is expensive.

The original Step One offers that the resolution of addiction and unmanageability begins with abstinence, and taking full responsibility for that abstinence, and admitting the truth of powerlessness. The majority of treatment centers' Step One guides imply that the resolution of addictive crisis and unmanageability is in insight psychology. Insight into developmental trauma and shame will make you psychologically less confused, but that won't make you spiritual, and you will invariably end up being only a more insightful drunk.

The majority of clients that I have worked with in the last fifteen years are drowning in pop-psychology. Their command of therapeutic jargon would rival many therapist's; and invariably, the more they have experienced relapse and recidivist indoctrination in programs and treatment centers, the worse off they are. When they relapse for the 8th or 23rd time, yet another doctor/therapist/sponsor sends them to yet another program/therapy group, or even the same program, with the admonition to "try harder". The clients are trying "harder" otherwise they wouldn't be back in a professional's office or a twelve-step group. The client, or someone else, then pays ten or twenty or thirty thousand dollars and the Recovery Opera in One Act starts over again. Everyone waits for the repeat ending, which happens 95% of the time. The professional's keep their jobs and the addicts die. [It's hard to describe this without sounding cynical. I'm not cynical: that's just what's happening.]

Where there are unresolved addictions in caregivers; where prurient interests are camouflaged as psychological investigation; where a belief exists that addiction treatment is an issue of morality or social responsibility; when caregivers push expedience or avoid spirituality for financial considerations; or when people seek to heal themselves by sponsoring or counselling others, there is abuse to the client/newcomer. All of this is a part of the significant mess that most caregivers, treatment centers, and twelve-step programs are in.

Sentimental commiserating isn't appropriate in getting recovered, and neither is being socially good. Substitutes for hard work, attempts to replace inner self-discipline with external obedience, expecting sympathy to resolve suffering, blaming others, creating scapegoats, suppressing spirituality, denying freedom of choice in spiritual matters, and suggesting quick-fix solutions to tremendously complicated problems, are all manifestations of relationship addiction, which used to be called codependence. In wounded caregivers—be they parents, therapists, counselors, priests, ministers, friends, spouses, or sponsors—it foments disaster.

Guides that use intrusive psychological questions are inappropriate vis-à-vis the intent of the original twelve-step program. Moreover, when the client's responses are not addressed by an experienced, non-relationship-addicted therapist, who understands the intrusive nature of the questions and the intricate multi-dimensional relationships of the issues—a therapist who can actually do something appropriate and can negotiate effectively between psychology and spirituality—then these self-styled guides always make things worse. *Always.*

This wise counsel from M.C. Richards should be never far from the awareness of caregivers: *"Do not be deluded that knowledge of the path can be substituted for putting one foot in front of the other."*[21] Writing down histories of childhood abuse, reading about spirituality, scanning self-help books, taking courses, knowing things, being a counselor, or sitting around at meetings sharing (which is usually either gossiping, bragging, or complaining) will accomplish nothing spiritually.

---

[21] Mary Caroline Richards has written at least two books that I know of: *Centering*, Wesleyan University Press, 1969, and *Towards Wholeness*, Wesleyan University Press, 1980.

Client selection for treatment is often addictions-generic. The fact that you're addicted, claim to desire abstinence, are facing calamity, and can get the fee, means you meet the admission criteria. Given this, and that all early recovery is about poly-addictions[22] (personality structures that harbor addictions are horrendously complicated), an effective Step One must simply be a recognition of the powerlessness or unmanageability, with a single view to establishing a successful continuation of abstinence. Anything else misrepresents the actual requirements of the step and the spiritual dynamic of the original program. That's why the chapter on Step One in *Twelve Steps and Twelve Traditions* is so short: recognize the direct relationship between unmanageability/insanity and drinking/acting out, get and stay abstinent, and wait until the fog clears. In doing anything beyond this, within the boundaries of something called a Step One, the caregiver will create additional problems, which must eventually be resolved by the client, not the caregiver.

Twelve-step members, sponsors, and recovery-house staff aren't usually trained to handle the trauma associated with abuse and unmet developmental dependency needs, which do contribute to the viciousness of an addiction but are not responsible for it. And even if these people are trained, they shouldn't necessarily be facilitating that work in early recovery.

Addicts who are healing from developmental- or shock-trauma, need abstinence and a safe crucible for therapy. And: The twelve-step group that supports abstinence and encourages a spiritual pilgrimage must also offer a safe crucible. The mandates are quite different. These must not be confused with each other. Only very cautiously should these be combined, and more often than not, they shouldn't be. Investing Step One with psychologically intrusive material is risky, and for the most part self-defeating, because the original twelve steps are not for psychological health: they're for developing and maintaining spiritual integrity.

———

Addicts may well be the most dysfunctional, quasi-successful group of complicated people on the planet—the sickest of the functioning sick. It's interesting to me that we don't spend more time impressing upon people the life or death nature of this reality.

Take a look around any meeting room. There's anywhere from a dozen to several hundred people, most knowing nothing substantive about what it is that's killing them. Probably well over half are clean and sober less than two years, more than 70% of them will probably not maintain their abstinence, and someone in that room will very likely be dead from their addiction in the next year. Who will it be? Untreated addicts and early newcomers are living on borrowed time. Don't have any illusions about the dangers of addictions.

Every time an addict in recovery tells a lie, they're collecting relapse points. Those who smoke, use pornography, are Victims, work addicts, whatever... they'll never understand spirituality in its deeper beauty: they're practicing addicts. Every time they avoid responsibility, their abstinence is that much more tenuous. There's a

---

[22] No addict lives with only one addiction. At the outset of all healing journeys, they all have *at least* two

serious price to pay for disobedience to, or deliberate avoidance of, the instructions outlined in the original twelve-step literature. Nothing is free.[23]

If you're an addict, and desirous of the spiritual integrity that is available via twelve-step work, then I want to impress upon you that your journey is a life-or-death matter. Remember, the first rule is that people die from addictions, and the second rule is that you can't change the first rule.

If you go to a meeting to try to find a girlfriend or a boyfriend, you're in trouble. If you go to a meeting to try to find a job, you're in trouble. If you go to a meeting to find somebody to lend you twenty dollars or take you to the dance, you're in trouble. If you go to a meeting to get and stay sober and thereby enable you to find a higher power, you'll be fine. If God and Spirituality scare you, well… that's tough; I mean that gently: that is tough. God might scare you; addictions will kill you. Do you want to be scared or do you want to be dead?

Take as much time as you need to make this palatable, but understand, in no uncertain terms, right from the start, that spirituality and a higher power are at the core of twelve-step work. The purpose of participating in a twelve-step program is to (one day at a time) maintain abstinence, get rid of character defects, participate sincerely in a Spiritual way of life, and devote yourself to the will of a Higher Power. It's to be of service to God, not to serve yourself a good life. Accordingly, by far the most important step is Step Two, and the most difficult step is Step Six. Over the course of this book, you will read why these statements about Steps Two and Six are true. Yes, social and financial stability often result from abstinence, but these are not the intended goals, nor are they the real rewards.

Rights, Freedoms, and Values

The following exposition isn't directly related to the topics at hand. There isn't a smooth segue into it; but it is crucial and related to everything. In the realm of human relations, to achieve true intimacy and fulfillment, you need, probably more than anything else, to claim and offer your rights and freedoms.[24] You should have been offered them when you were an infant; before you knew you had them; before you even knew you were a person.

As adults, in relationships with everyone, and especially in any healing journey, too often your rights are vaguely implied out of muddy notions of dignity and self-esteem. Here are your rights in intimate, personal relationships:

- You have the right to say "No" without fear of malicious or punitive consequence. If you decline or limit what you do or say, there should be no other-imposed harmful consequence.
- You have the right to expect confidentiality; what you say or do will be kept appropriately or respectfully private. Gossip is always a betrayal of trust. Confidentiality isn't limited to the legislated

---

and usually three addictions operating.

[23] My favorite proverb is Spanish: "Take what you want," God said, "and pay for it."

[24] This will be expanded upon in *Facets of Personal Transformation*.

privacy of privileged information, and it doesn't automatically mean keeping secrets. Confidentiality cannot masquerade as a device to perpetuate abuse, or to conceal reprehensible behavior. To offer confidentiality is to offer respect.

- You have the right to your dignity and respect: you will not knowingly be shamed or humiliated, maligned, or misrepresented.

- You have the right to question or challenge anything that happens in relation to yourself or to those under your legitimate care. You have the right to ensure that you understand what's going on in relation to you.

Children live with authority figures that wield tremendous power. Hopefully their caregivers are loving and benevolent, since personal rights are only available to a child if they are generously offered by the authority figures who control the child's life. The time to learn to say "No" and to set boundaries is when you're three, not when you're 37 sitting in a treatment center.

As an adult, whether or not you have your rights and freedoms in relationships is a function of how you allow yourself to be treated (primarily by yourself).[25] Without them you can only act at being a grown-up.[26]

There were many insightful, pioneering books that were less than specific on definitions of codependence, and many early theories were long and somewhat inconsistent. As we discovered years ago, when trying to understand the many facets of addictions, codependence was a phenomenon that was not easily defined. However, it became clear that if you were an addict, you were codependent.[27] All codependence is some variation or combination of relationship addiction, sex addiction, or romance addiction.[28] If you are in Alanon, Naranon, ACOA, CODA, or some other similar twelve-step group, you're a relationship addict.

What's the connection to your rights? Briefly, and this is oversimplified: having limited or no access to your rights and freedoms; allowing someone to have emotional privilege over yourself; or demanding emotional privilege over others, indicates a relationship addiction.[29]

Attendant to your rights, you have this primary responsibility: *You are responsible to ensure that you offer these rights to others*; to offer them gracefully, as a matter of course. The fact that someone doesn't know their own rights or freedoms doesn't mean you have license to withhold them.

These rights are embodied in spiritual principles. Invariably, the people I've discussed "rights" with have been unclear on what they might expect in spiritual,

---

[25] See Appendix IV.

[26] Many adults only mimic what they've seen other adults do, and so they "act like grown-ups", whatever that means. They don't really have a clue about what "being" themselves entails, and can only make it up as they go along, which most often ends up with them in awkward and unfulfilling circumstances.

[27] See: *Co-Dependence, Healing the Human Condition,* Charles L. Whitfield, M.D., Health Communications, Inc., 1991; and *Bradshaw on: The Family,* John Bradshaw, Health Communications Inc., 1988.

[28] *Escape From Intimacy,* Anne Wilson Schaef, Harper Collins, 1990.

[29] I will explore this in greater detail in *Facets of Personal Transformation*.

personal relationships. No one I've ever spoken to, including professionals, has spoken of them in a manner that touched on all four. A surprising number of people concerned with emotional health are genuinely puzzled and mumble some dismissive comment like, "Don't know, never thought of it." Usually any discussion of rights and freedoms is vague and borders on legislated culpability. Work at having these rights perceptible, defined, and visible in your life. Insist on them for yourself and offer them to others.

Out of your rights, which under ideal developmental conditions would have been offered to you freely and graciously by your caretakers, before you were old enough to know you had caretakers, you would have automatically evinced your freedoms. If you're given your rights, acquiring your freedoms is automatic. The first five freedoms are from *Making Contact,* by Virginia Satir.[30] The sixth is my addition to the list.

(i)   *The freedom to see and hear what is here instead of what should be, was, or will be.*

(ii)   *The freedom to say what one feels and thinks, instead of what one should.*

(iii) *The freedom to feel what one feels, instead of what one ought.*

(iv) *The freedom to ask for what one wants, instead of always waiting for permission.*

(v)   *The freedom to take risks on one's own behalf, instead of choosing to be only "secure" and not rocking the boat.*

(vi) The freedom to desire and create for one's own benefit, instead of catering to the wishes or demands of others.

This is tremendously important: After a person lives with their rights for an extended period, they will naturally accrue their freedoms. The sequence is important: rights first, freedoms second. Then, out of being free, you'll figure out how you are to "be" not what you are supposed to "do". And, after you've lived with your freedoms, out of these comes a gracious expression of your values. Being the person you are, as opposed to the person you are expected to be, is the way your declare your values: Rights –>Freedoms –>Who "I" am –>Values.

These rights and freedoms are sometimes not available in politics and commerce. People knowingly surrender them in favor of some perceived gain. In political or contractual situations, or when facing danger and overt power, or with your employer, it may be wise to not demand your rights and freedoms. Wisdom and values will govern your behavior. Notwithstanding that, if you don't routinely have these in your life, especially in your intimate or sexual relationships, with your family and friends, you're in trouble. Those who deny you your rights are also in trouble, but more importantly, you are for allowing it.

---

[30] *Making Contact*, Virginia Satir, Celestial Arts (Press), Berkley, CA, 1976.

The only way we realize our potential is by living with our rights and free-doms, regardless of the cost. You may have to forego relationships with family, friends, or spouses, but unless you are willing to insist on your rights and freedoms for yourself, you will remain unfulfilled. Try this: post your rights, freedoms, and your one responsibility somewhere prominent in your home and read them *out loud* every third day for a year. Examine your relationships with *every*one and notice if you insist on them for yourself. Who offers you these and who doesn't? Do you offer them freely to others? Estimate the cost of living without them.

What you value is evinced in how you are as a person. Should you have been raised in optimum circumstances, where rights were offered as a matter of course, and freedoms were available for you to claim, you would develop and adopt values that were determined by you. Again, this should have been done as you grew up, not when you're 43 and sitting in therapy. All practicing addicts, and too many abstinent ones, don't know what adopting values is, or how to go about doing that.[31]

When you live gracefully with your rights, are responsible, claim your free-doms, and adhere to your own values, all the while respecting these in others, you will experience a spiritual sense of "being". (It's very complicated.) And, of course, being in *any* addiction makes all of this is unavailable to you.

Addictions Prohibit Spirituality

Many addicts in recovery presume of themselves that they're spiritual, or "kind of" spiritual, or spiritually on track, or at least making an effort to be spiritual. All this usually means is they are making an attempt at the secular notion of being morally good. Many also believe that they're "spiritual" because they make a spo-radic effort at praying, or belong to step-group of one kind or another. Other people attend church services and so label themselves spiritual.

However, if they're participating in any addiction: adrenaline, aggression, aggressive-sports viewing, alcohol, anger, drugs, food, gambling, compulsive mas-turbation, moral self-righteousness, pornography, relationships, religion, sex, shop-ping, sports, tobacco, twelve-step meetings, violence, work, workshops, to name a few—*any* addiction—they can't be spiritual. How can people be spiritual when they are actively negligent to their own welfare, are being willfully irresponsible, or are degrading and harming themselves and others? How can people be spiritual when they take pleasure from watching people beat up, injure, and dominate other people (which some people call sports)?[32] The conditions that must exist within anyone to enable any addiction, preclude absolutely the person being sincerely spiritual and living with their rights and freedoms.

---

[31] Discovering and abandoning old values and adopting new ones is a profound exercise unto itself, and is the point of this book. It is discussed more specifically in Chapter 5 and at Appendix I.

[32] What follows is one specifically Christian view of violence that has a universal application. Dr. Martin Luther King, Jr. said: *"I am expert in recognition of a simple, eloquent truth. That truth is that it is sinful for any of God's children to brutalize any of God's other children…"* As reported in *Martin Luther King, Jr.,* by Marshall Frady, a Lipper®/Viking Book, 2002 Viking/Penguin, p. 188.

Be aware that, even though abstinent from their primary addiction, people who curse and swear with vehemence and rudeness, who participate in violence through sports, who are sexually irresponsible, who are racist or sexist, and who *also* claim they're spiritual, aren't. They may believe in a higher power and probably do; however, their spirituality is an illusion and lacks integrity.

An addiction is a disease of Impression Management and delusion.[33] It embodies self-annihilation, deceit, arrogance, selfishness, and blame. These conditions of personality are mandated by the addiction itself. To be spiritual there must be a willing posture of deep respect for self and others, veracity, humility, charity without contract, and responsibility and obedience. *Being in any addiction and being Spiritual are mutually exclusive.*

Being despairing, isolated, not participating in Life in a meaningful way, enduring loneliness, and self-annihilation are conditions of addictions, regardless of how gregarious, healthy, or spiritual you *act*. After you've quit all addictive acting out, you start to find out what's really going on inside you, and what being spiritual really is. If you desire to be sincerely spiritual, you have to stop all of your addictions, be responsible, and abandon your devotion to the accumulation of shiny things and influence. Being an active addict and being Spiritual are mutually exclusive.

The technological tendency to ignore matters of the spirit is demonstrated in the medical/scientific determination to categorize addiction as a medical concern. Certainly there are derivative medical or psychological consequences of addictions (detoxification, physical damage, shame, etc.) that require expert medical or psychological attention. Addressing the derivative consequences is crucial, and certainly it's important to do skilled cross-over work for the abstinence not-available addictions. But, doctors and therapists can't heal addictions because the actual addiction *itself* isn't a "medical" illness. Only ongoing spiritual integrity resolves it.

Addictions encompass such a wide range of manifestations, that they defy any consistent scientific classification. The only perspective that, so far, *is* consistent and effective is that addictions are a manifestation of spiritual corruption, and can appear "everywhere". (Notice, too, that "God" also defies any scientific or cultural classification. God fits everywhere.)

Elementary Truths For Addicts

The Forward to the Second Edition and The Doctor's Opinion[34] report these anecdotal statistics: *"Of alcoholics who came to A.A. and really tried, 50% got sober at once and remained that way; 25% sobered up after some relapses, and among the remainder, those who stayed on with A.A. showed improvement."*[35] They're telling you that if you really try, you've got three to one odds of making it. [As a teenager, I was told several times that the odds of me living to 30 were very slim. When I joined a support group fifteen years later, I was told in no uncertain terms that if I tried

---

[33] Impression Management: investing energy into making oneself appear as one isn't—a devious self-advertising campaign designed to conceal aspects of personality that would meet with disapproval. This is a significant manipulation strategy that addicts use, and it will be referred to many times.

[34] *Alcoholics Anonymous*, pp. xiii and xxiii respectively.

[35] Ibid., p. xx.

hard, and did *exactly* what is outlined in *Alcoholics Anonymous,* I had a 75% percent chance of making it. Those were the best odds anyone ever gave me, for anything.]

Of course, that success is dependent upon making a real effort. Obedience (the "**O**" word), and responsibility (the "**R**" word), are often a curse to addicts, but nothing is free. If you are obedient to the instructions, and responsible for your self-imposed crisis, according to the AA textbooks, you have a 75% chance of becoming recovered.

The two AA reference texts are the source material for all twelve-step programs in the world. Everything effective regarding addictions and spirituality is contained in those two books. They are more dependable than sponsors, meetings, and conventions (but not as entertaining). I'm not cautious about applying the original twelve steps to any addiction; I'm only cautious about rewriting the material. Rewrites always obscure the spiritual integrity of the original material, which is intended to be a program of spiritual instruction, not psychological help. Regarding all addictions, once abstinence is established, I suggest that people getting recovered read *Alcoholics Anonymous* and *Twelve Steps and Twelve Traditions,* pencil in their addiction in place of "alcohol", and change nothing else. More than anything else, that will guarantee spiritual results. *Go to the source.*

Alcoholics Anonymous and *Twelve Steps and Twelve Traditions* are textbooks, and offer instruction like other textbooks do.[36] What is notably different about them, and crucial to understand, is in all other areas of study you seek knowledge which is outside of your spiritual nature. This includes studying psychology and religion, which are respectively the scientific study of your personality, and the sociological study of cultural rituals. All knowledge-seeking is a [secular] pilgrimage external to your deeper spiritual nature, and you will thusly not find The Great Reality which lies deep within you.[37]

Alcoholics Anonymous and *Twelve Steps and Twelve Traditions* are for spiritual transformation; nothing else. The purpose of studying the AA texts is not to understand them *per se,* and not to acquire external knowledge. You study the AA texts to study yourself, and thereby understand how and why you are not accessing your deeper spiritual nature. They advise how to transform yourself so you can become spiritual—entirely an *internal* process. Excluding the AA texts, all the twelve-step instruction books that I've examined are recast in such a way as to include some psychology, which dilutes the spiritual intent and renders them less effective.

If you believe that participating in a twelve-step group is a journey to psychological health and social contentment, you will study the original literature as an external process. The steps will be used as a set of social improvement tools to get ahead in the temporal world, and you will use willpower to manage your defects. You will then view yourself as the agent of change (which, paradoxically, is partly what got you into trouble in the first place). Studying the original literature to acquire

---

[36] *Alcoholics Anonymous*, p. xi.
[37] Modern psychology, which is the "technology" of spirituality, is doomed to spiritual inefficiency.

knowledge results in the illusion of recovery. The result will be a spiritual disaster. I discuss this in the next section: 811 Facts About "Rigorous Honesty.

 Alcoholics Anonymous tells you: *"…that's what this book is about. Its main object is to enable you to find a Power greater than yourself which will solve your problem."*[38] In the same book, a few pages earlier, it asks, not rhetorically but specifically: *"But where and how were we to find this Power?"* The answer is *"We found the Great Reality deep down within us. In the last analysis it is only there that* [God] *may be found."*[39] Always, *always*, look inside yourself. Anywhere outside defeats the process. Finding a good sponsor, a good meeting, or memorizing page numbers and passages, will not solve your problem. It therefore follows that anyone who gets involved in a study of *Alcoholics Anonymous* or *Twelve Steps and Twelve Traditions* should be studying themselves, not the book.

 The vast majority of people I've encountered act like becoming spiritual is a scavenger hunt: being under pressure, with a time deadline, to discover unique things in strange places: some type of vague competition hoping to win something. People get a book and they hunt for God in knowledge. They search for a higher power outside themselves in meetings, service work, religious buildings, statues, authority figures, esoteric rituals, and education. A scavenger hunt to find God never works.

 Insightful adherents to the original twelve-step program, as rare as they are, understand that social success is not what you're [supposed to be] hunting for. In studying the AA textbooks you're not studying the literature: you're studying yourself (an internal pilgrimage). Sit still. Use the steps. Look inside. Wander through the dark and hostile areas of your own personality. Examine how you defeat access to your own spiritual nature. Here is an example: The Search for Rigorous Honesty.[40]

811 Facts About "Rigorous Honesty"

 As a rule of conduct, rigorous honesty is so straightforward that it defies definition. However, you can study the AA literature to learn why it was important to those who wrote the books and memorize how many times rigorous honesty is mentioned. You can study dishonesty as a symptomatic aspect of addiction. You can research religious and psychological literature to learn how religious and secular authorities discovered honesty was important. You can hunt for references to "withholding the truth to spare others". In a couple of years, with all this studying, you would sound like a twelve-step guru, and impress everyone with your 811 facts about rigorous honesty. But, even after all that, *you* are no closer to being rigorously honest yourself. You may have become an expert on the theoretical development and spiritual implications of honesty, but you remain dishonest. You would have the power of knowledge, and could make potent speeches about rigorous honesty, but still be an inveterate liar; no closer to being honest or spiritual yourself.

---

[38] *Alcoholics Anonymous*, p. 45.
[39] Ibid., p. 55.

For the most part, the AA texts (excluding the personal stories) are revealed truths. That's why it's never necessary to rewrite them. After all, what's confusing about "rigorous honesty" or "a self-imposed crisis"? The required understanding is self-evident. The material doesn't need "understanding", and bragging to anyone who'll listen that you're struggling to understand it is a diversion from the responsibility of doing it.

I think of how many thousands of times I've heard addicts complain they are not fulfilled within their Life—and it's obvious they aren't following the instructions. The only reason for participating in discussions about the AA textbooks would be to figure out what you are doing that's contrary to the instructions. Don't investigate the instructions; investigate your disobedience to the instructions. Getting recovered is simply an exercise in obedience, (the "**O**" word again). A book-study is to understand yourself vis-à-vis why you're not willingly doing what you are told. Study the literature to understand why *you* are disobedient to the identified principles and your life will take on a completely different texture.

In Step One, you begin to generate some commitment to obedience to the instructions. That small kernel of responsibility allows a belief at Step Two that will eventually transform your life into a sincerely Spiritual one. It's about committing to the instructions in *Alcoholics Anonymous,* exactly as they're outlined—your apprenticeship to Spirituality. When listening to the opinions of others about addiction and recovery, regardless of their length of abstinence, education, or reputation, listen to determine how closely their opinions follow *Alcoholics Anonymous* or *Twelve Steps and Twelve Traditions*. If their opinions are not detailed within those books, be cautious about adopting their opinions. Your only real safety is in trusting people who willingly follow those instructions in a humble manner.

When you adopt personal, anecdotal interpretations of spirituality and the steps, you are playing with your life: suicide gambling with a fatal illness. The consequences are devastating. Remember Matthew Arnold's poem:

> *"Nor certitude, nor peace, nor help for pain;*
> *And we are here as on a darkling plain*
> *Swept with confused alarms of struggle and flight,*
> *Where ignorant armies clash by night."*

For addicts and alcoholics who are exhausted by the insanity and self annihilation of their illness; tired of the conflict, turmoil, shame, and anger; drained by the struggle to avoid the fear, they are to frequently remind themselves of the sentence on page 45 of *Alcoholics Anonymous*: *"Well, that's exactly what this book is about. Its main object is to enable you find a Power greater than yourself which will solve your problem."*[41] The importance of obedience to the original twelve-step in

---

[40] Here are a few references to rigorous honesty: *Alcoholics Anonymous*, pp. 58, 64, 67, 70, and *Twelve Steps and Twelve Traditions*, pp. 59, 60, 72. There are many others.
[41] Emphasis added. Notice it doesn't say "which will solve your parent's problem, which they passed on to you." Your addiction is always your spiritual problem, no one else's.

structions cannot be overstated. They are designed specifically to resolve whatever it is within you that forces your extreme distance from spirituality and God. Your addiction is not evidence of how hard your life was, or how badly you were mistreated: it is evidence of your separation from the spiritual realms of life.[42] The steps are intended to mentor you from the addictive, darkling plains of self-annihilation to spiritual health, not social success. Granted, some social success and stability accrue from doing the steps, but these are not what is intended, and are of no account in the matter at hand.

I offer an analogy that might show that this general theory of spiritual regeneration isn't new. In doing this, I'm not advocating for Christian hegemony. St Benedict (c. 480–547 CE) was the next major Christian spiritual influence after Saint Augustine, and is considered to be the founder of western monasticism. He established The Order of Benedictine Monks and wrote *The Rule of Benedict*, affectionately referred to as The Rule.[43] It is a short and profound manual that instructs how to transform the dislocation of daily life into a serene life via Christian beliefs—ethically practicing "a life in Christ". The Rule is about spiritual faith, love of God, charity, humility, and responsibility, not social accomplishment and popularity. It concerns itself with developing a devotion to God and maintaining a sense of spiritual community. Granted, this is over-simplified, but these are the themes.

In *Alcoholics Anonymous*, the theory is very similar: healing of the inner life of the alcoholic, then developing a devotion to a higher power (of your own understanding). As evidence of the success of this, three major principles would operate: (i) a life of abstinence and rigorous honesty, (ii) a sincere humility and love of a higher power; and (iii) service to a higher power by demonstrating spiritual principles in all activities, and carrying the message of spiritual transformation out of addiction to those people who are interested. The original twelve steps are a very general parallel to The Rule of Saint Benedict. [This is only to make a point about the perennial and recurring nature of spiritual transformation presented within the twelve steps. There are equally appropriate non-Christian spiritual alternatives. The steps also have ethical themes and responsibilities that are similar in aspect to The Four Nobel Truths of Buddhism.]

Spiritual principles contained within the *Alcoholics Anonymous* program were not invented by the cofounders. The path of *Alcoholics Anonymous* is stylistically unique for a specific spiritual dislocation—effective and inspired, but the themes are not original, which is good.[44] Spiritual regeneration, the manner and path to spiritual integrity through inner-cleansing, truth, responsibility, and humility, is at least 3000 years old. The AA cofounders did, however, tailor it to the specific needs

---

[42] Being spiritual does not mean you will have an easy life. At times, in spiritual realms, life is very difficult. The difference is in the underlying serenity with which you approach the "problems" of Life, and having a benign indifference to the outcome.

[43] Many books have been written about *The Rule*. Two of my favorites are Esther de Waal's *Seeking God, The Way of St Benedict*, The Liturgical Press, 1984; and Joan Chittister's *The Rule of Benedict - Insights for the Ages*, Crossroad Publishing, 1992.

[44] Profound spiritual truths appear when they are needed to address specific issues at some particular time when humans become involved in grand-scale self-annihilation particular to their eras: The Ten Com-

of people with alcoholism (addictions). If you put into your life what *Alcoholics Anonymous* has to offer, you are adopting universal spiritual principles.[45]

Your Pilgrimage Begins

How are you going to save your life beginning with Step One? What does it actually require? Clichés and shallow metaphors are as dangerous as drinking. Someone said that violence is the repartee of the illiterate. I offer that rhetoric is the repartee of the insecure, and clichés are the haven of the confused. By masking your insecurity and confusion with rhetoric and clichés you make Impression Management your lifestyle. Sincerity then becomes political, and successes are illusions. When [if] you ever get through this by demanding rigorous honesty only of yourself, you'll be able to relax and not take it too seriously; after all, it's only Life.

In presentations I often ask: "When you plan a journey of any kind, what do you need to know? You're planning a trip, so what information must you have?" The usual replies are about where you're going, the type of transportation, the route, when you'll travel, knowing the cost, the dates of travel, obtaining special clothing or equipment, and who's going. There is an essential piece of information, however, that is very rarely offered as one of the answers. You need to know very specifically where you are leaving from. The travel agent who books your holiday will need to know your point of departure. If you are going to the Caribbean, your point of departure must be more specific than western Canada. If you want to get to someplace where you're not, you've got to leave the place where you're at. I know it may sound silly, but it's symbolically important.

Then I'll ask: "On your pilgrimage out of addictions, what's your point of departure?" I usually get replies like insanity, drinking, drugging, chaos, alcoholism, or the disease. These are all partially correct but, from a spiritual point of view, the answer that everything depends upon is that you're leaving from *powerlessness.* Admitting and then beginning your pilgrimage from powerlessness precedes everything. In the AA steps this is the very first thing you read: *"We admitted we were powerless... ."* Addicts begin their journey from *powerlessness,* vis-à-vis addictions, to get to spiritual peace.[46]

In the all-protecting safety of sincere Spirituality you find great strength, which allows you to serenely cope with life on life's terms—the courage to govern yourself by the five spiritual principles. Step One is to figure out where you are leav-

---

mandments, *The Four Nobel Truths, The Sermon on The Mount, The Koran, The Rule of Benedict,* The Protestant Reformation, The Twelve Steps, Zen, are examples of this. There are others.

[45] See Appendix II.

[46] All relationships with a higher power, regardless of the cultural/ethnic structure that surrounds them, must originate from powerlessness. One principle that humility is based on is abandoning influence—being *voluntarily* absent of power. This applies as much to ecclesiastical/religious power and authority as it does to temporal/secular power. Having any kind of power detracts from humility. Faith is what counteracts the ego-insecurity attendant to powerlessness. "It's easier for a camel to get through the eye of a needle than it is for a rich person to get into heaven." Or, "How can I be saved?" "Give away all of your possessions and follow me." (Jesus of Nazareth) The subtext is: abandon power, political clout, authority,

ing from. Abstinence, and the remaining steps, allow you to actually leave.[47] That introduces another simple notion that is crucial.

Now you know you are leaving powerlessness you must ask: Where am I going? There are many speeches about going to The Promises, into community, back to work, to a happy life, to a healthy relationship, to success. In the work that lies ahead of you, these are non-issues. Understand that you are going very deeply *inside yourself,* to embrace your frailties in the *inner* presence of a higher power of your own understanding. A twelve-step pilgrimage, any true spiritual pilgrimage, is always a journey *In,* finding The Source, which is known *a priori,* and boundless, and called by many names.

The original twelve steps are not concerned with whether or not you make lots of money or find that happy love affair. They are not concerned with whether or not you make president of the company or get a new car. The original program *is* concerned with taking you from self-destructive powerlessness (evidenced by your addiction) to a place deep inside yourself to God (as you understand God)—the source of courage and power.

Once Upon A Time

Consider that in all of the fairy tales we tell children, the poor person never goes to the rich person to find spiritual peace. It's always the king or queen going to the poor hermit to learn of inner peace. There are powerful metaphors in this traditional motif that are reflected in the original twelve steps.

The direction of these "fairy tale" pilgrimages is always away from commerce and wealth (the pilgrim leaves the city and the castle), and towards poverty (to a humble cottage and a poor person). Spiritual pilgrimages are always away from crowds and groups (leaving parties and courtly celebrations), and involve traveling alone, over unused, faint paths, without a map, deeply into a dark forest (through the pilgrims' unknown insecurities and frailties, deep into the darkness of their own personality), towards a single wise person (to solitude and God).

As evidence of this, Siddhartha Gautama, Yeshua, Benedict of Nursia, Gio. Francesco Bernardone, and many others, abandoned comfort, wealth, or power to pursue spirituality.[48] Regarding spirituality, all of this implies that inner turmoil and non-fulfillment are always associated with unnecessary wealth or political/social power.[49] This is an unalterable truth about lifestyle and spirituality.

The original twelve-step program doesn't care about your job, but it is big on responsibility. It doesn't care whether you've got a lover, but has a clear position

weapons, possessions, wealth. Why? This forces an opening for humility, and only in humility can spiritual association with God be realized. There are similar secular themes in Buddhism's "middle way".

[47] This is not a play on words, it is true. Addictions are a self-destructive compensation for (or a reaction to) spiritual dislocation and powerlessness. You are not leaving your addictions, you are leaving powerlessness.

[48] Respectively, these people are The Buddha, Jesus of Nazareth, St. Benedict, and St. Francis of Assisi.

[49] Benevolence and wisdom are never justifications for the accumulation of power. This is my alteration of Alan Watts' general observation about our culture: *"...we feel justified in using dangerous powers when we can establish that there is a relatively low probability of disaster."* From *This Is It,* Alan Watts, Vintage Books, 1973, p. 152.

on rigorous honesty, both in and out of sexual relationship. The original program is only concerned with teaching you how to create and live a life of spiritual integrity (embodied in the maintenance steps).

You start the journey by admitting you were powerless (over alcohol and acting out)—that your life had become unmanageable. Step One is for you to admit your powerlessness when you acted out, and then by inference from that historical experience, to believe that if you act out again unmanageability will reappear. Out of the general particulars of your past, you can reasonably anticipate the consequences of repeating old behaviors.[50]

Seeing and admitting your powerlessness through Step One is a fundamental precondition to Step Two. Being able to understand Step Two is completely dependent on seeing God/Spirituality as the source of power that the pilgrim doesn't have (which they learned at Step One). When Step One is diverted away from powerlessness towards family of origin and insight psychology, the fundamental nature of powerlessness remains vague and unrealized. This makes Step Two impossible to accomplish, which renders the remaining steps meaningless: they are all structured to access a higher *power*, not to enhance insight psychology.

Powerless, Helpless, Hopeless

I have been asked: Would powerless be the same as helpless or hopeless? No, but to understand this, it's important to reflect carefully on what I am about to say. There are two perspectives to consider: spiritual and psychological.

Generally, *psychology* advises that feeling helpless or hopeless are issues of perception: evaluating temporary circumstances through an ego that creates the illusion that there are no options, hence, helpless or hopeless. From a *spiritual* perspective, the AA reference texts, and the observations of various spiritual masters, describe helpless or hopeless as directly or indirectly related to lack of faith or neglect of spiritual commitment. And so, psychologically *or* spiritually, the feelings of helplessness or hopelessness are optional. To change them requires responsibility, commitment, self-discipline, wise counsel, abstinence, and hard work. You may feel hopeless, or believe you are helpless in the face of your addiction or difficult life circumstances, but these feelings are optional. In abstinence, as powerful as the sense of helplessness or hopelessness may be (psychologically or spiritually), it is the result of faulty perceptions, irresponsibility, or spiritual sloth.

Being powerless regarding an addiction is another matter altogether. Powerless, by definition, means lack of ability, or being without sufficient force or resources to accomplish something. Time and again, over the last seventy years, in millions of situations, for millions of people, we have learned that the unaided individual human will (or aided only by psychology, or the willpower of another person) is entirely insufficient to resolve an addiction. Without sincerely participating in spirituality, there is *in*sufficient "power" available for the afflicted person to recover. This establishes the direct relationship between powerlessness (meaning *in*capable of accomplishing recovery), and the requirement for spirituality (being the source of power that enables transformation). Powerlessness is a fact in relation to active addiction, and *Alcoholics Anonymous* offers a process (the steps) to acquire the necessary "power" (spirituality).

Out of the repetitive emotional disasters in acting out comes a sense of despair and a false, but very powerful belief that hopelessness and helplessness are facts. They're not. These are issues of perception. But, the fact of powerlessness (re: addictions) can be overcome with devoted spiritual work. You will eliminate your addictions and live serenely in the maintenance steps. Voluntarily following the spiritual principles won't give you power over Life, that you can never have. (If we had it, we'd get bored.) What you can achieve, however, is a noticeable measure of influence and appreciable serenity as you participate gracefully in the circumstances that Providence presents.

This was put to me once: If someone were to swallow rat poison, they'd be powerless over the fact that rat poison is going to kill them. They thought similarly about powerlessness over alcohol: as an alcoholic, if they drank alcohol it would kill them. It may seem to make sense at first glance.

In these scenarios, rat poison and alcohol are spoken of as the agent of destruction; they aren't—the addiction is. Spiritual integrity requires that addicts not blame alcohol, drugs, rat poison or anything else, even caregivers, regardless of how they treated them. *Alcoholics Anonymous* advises this is a *self*-imposed crisis (p. 53). Active addiction is active self-annihilation. Acting out doesn't kill you: you kill yourself.

When addicts are exposed to the alternative of not drinking or acting out (which is a surprising option to many of them), they may start to accumulate hope. The first year of any abstinence is breathe in, don't drink, breathe out, don't drink. So the new person asks: "Yeah, but what do I *really* have to do?" Well, you breathe in, and you don't act out, you breathe out, and you don't act out. That's all you do. "But how long do I do that?" they ask. Until you don't know you're doing it. You breathe in, you go to a meeting, you breathe out, and you don't act out. You breathe in, you go to a meeting, you breathe out, and you don't act out. Try praying.

If you want to get married, get married and don't drink. If you want to get a divorce, get a divorce and don't drink. If you want to move, move and don't act out. If you want to change jobs, do that, and don't act out. If you need to quit your job, quit, and don't act out. If you want to go to a movie or not go to a movie, then do that, and don't act out. Go to a meeting. *Breathe in, don't drink, breathe out, don't drink, one minute at a time*. Regarding your "program", that's all you do for the first year. And, say your prayers.

Out of the success of not acting out is created a legitimate sense of hope (that was always available but not appreciated). The initial year or two of "breathe in, don't drink, breathe out, don't drink, and pray", coincidental to the sense of suc-

---

[50] The saying: "Insanity is repeating old behavior and expecting different results," is a reflection of this.

cess and joy, creates a very powerful two-choice dilemma (which expression itself is redundant, but the phrase lends authority to the situation). It's either…

- act out and remain insane/powerless and die; or,
- maintain abstinence and face the unknown, fearful require- ments of abstinence and honesty. [Abstinence and honesty are terrifying enough to keep some addicts acting out.]

This dilemma is associated with Step One but does subtly recur throughout the first nine steps. Its resolution (and it must be resolved to avoid tenuous absti- nence) is brought about by coming to believe the following two sentences:

- The pain, fear, and self-annihilation in acting out is permanent and always slowly escalates for as long as you act out.
- The fear of abstinence and honesty (which are always painful and difficult at the outset) may appear to be excruciating and insurmountable but, with perseverance, are always temporary. (Temporary may mean many months, but they *are* temporary.)

———

What do you do when you are seeking help from someone—a doctor or therapist, for example—who doesn't support the twelve-step philosophy? If you are convinced that twelve-step philosophy is intrinsic to your survival, then discuss that with them. Advocate *respectfully* for your beliefs. Professionals are often insightful and caring people. Consider what they offer, for they are well trained and may have much to contribute. Decide *for yourself* your course of action. The harder part fol- lows: Live responsibly with the consequences of *your* decision. Do not externalize responsibility: Don't blame them. You must account only for yourself.

My Group is the Drug

For people in twelve-step programs, there are, at times, healthy, spiritually- related reasons for staying away from certain meetings. Terry Kellogg wrote, a num- ber of years ago, that the most common solution to an addiction was another addiction.[51] I see this as the motivation for many people who attend meetings— they're addicted to the hype, chaos, sex, and gossip. Being addicted to meetings has the appearance of respectability, and carries a built-in defense for abusive behav- ior—you're "in recovery" and your neglect of responsibility or selfish disregard for others is at least for a "healthy cause". The most common, instant defense to pro- gram/workshop addiction is this: "Well it's better than being addicted to cocaine or alcohol." Maybe so, but it's not that simple.

---

[51] *Broken Toys Broken Dreams*, Terry Kellogg, BRAT Publishing, Revised 1990, p. 72; and, see the dis- cussion of EFT and SRT at Appendix III, for related information.

Participating in an addiction is inherently self-destructive and damaging to your family and your community. It may be perceived as "less" damage, but it's damage nonetheless, and you cannot be spiritual while practicing any addiction.

An addiction, according to The World Health Organization, is *"a pathological relationship with any mood-altering experience that has life-damaging consequences."*[52] I've seen, hundreds of times in my personal and professional life, the damage that arises from an addiction to recovery groups—irresponsible parenting, perpetual welfare, belligerent arrogance, shaming, divorces, irresponsible expressions of sexuality, racism, sexism, and more, all justified as "healing".

If you believe the original twelve steps are a route to anything other than spirituality, there is an ever-present danger you will substitute your program for your drug of choice. Your meetings become the mood-altering experience. The inner turmoil and never-ending despair of unfulfilled recovery creates shame just as any other acting out does. This is often apparent in those who attend multiple twelve-step groups. If you're a person who is perpetually in recovery and cannot fathom eventually being recovered, you are possibly in an addictive cycle with your program(s) being the mood-altering experience.[53]

The One-Addiction Myth

A person who requires eye glasses to function may have prescription sport-goggles, reading glasses, and all-purpose glasses. The permanent, constant nature of the eye condition requires they use eye glasses all the time.

Like bad eye sight, addiction is an unrelenting condition. Spiritual dislocation is a state of existence, and addiction is the automatic compensation for this. It affects *every* aspect of someone's life, *all* day, *every* day. An addict isn't an addict only when they're acting out; they are an addict all the time, and must constantly compensate for their spiritual dislocation. At the same time, addicts cannot "act out" in their *primary* addiction all day every day. They may be drunk every evening, or at the track every afternoon, or masturbate five times a day, or go on eating binges every other day, but the primary addiction is not sustained *all* the time; however, the spiritual dislocation is an all day, every day condition. An addict requires secondary and tertiary addictions to compensate for the always-present spiritual dislocation, for those periods when they are not in their most visible addiction. This dynamic is what underlies Mr. Kellogg's statement about substitute addictions. (Fn. pg. 74)

Aside from the primary addiction, there will be at least two other addictions operating, one of which will be a relationship addiction, and then, additionally, substances, sex, work, religion, pornography, gambling, television, tobacco, adrenaline, anger, or variations and combinations of these, or others. An *un*spiritual addict *must* participate in some addiction every waking moment because that is the only way to continuously compensate for global, constant spiritual dislocation. If you're abstinent from your most obvious addiction, you've a second full-fledged addiction going, and a third one hovering in the background. Poly-addictions are a given.

---

[52] *Bradshaw on: The Family*, John Bradshaw, Health Communications Inc., 1988, p 89.
[53] This will be discussed in *Facets of Personal Transformation*.

The Doctor's Opinion

For its time, The Doctor's Opinion[54] was one of the more profound pieces of writing on addictions. It is essentially a letter of reference. The cofounders of AA wanted to give credibility to their newly written book and their fledgling program. They invited a knowledgeable and respected doctor to write an introduction, so people would treat the book more seriously than seeing it as a couple of drunks singing the praises of being religious teetotalers. Dr. Silkworth wrote that he'd specialized for many years in the treatment of alcoholism; he had seen the cofounders' plan work, and saw the possibility of rapid growth. Dr. Silkworth pointed out that the twelve-step plan was often a successful intervention[55] in working with alcoholics of a kind that he had formerly considered hopeless.

Historically, to 1935, the interventions for addictions (primarily alcoholism) had all been spiritually belligerent and caustic in their view of alcoholics, and very limited in terms of success. The important diagnostic issue Dr. Silkworth made clear is the body of an alcoholic is as abnormal as their mind.[56] He, and the AA cofounders, knew that to get recovered there had to be a strategy to address the behavior of alcohol consumption, and there had to be some sort of mental/spiritual treatment. Beginning with Dr. Silkworth (and Dr.'s Jung and Tiebout) and the cofounders of AA, there was evidence that a dual approach (physical and spiritual) was elemental to successful treatment. These two categories each have two sub-categories.

Physical Recovery

(1) This is from the behavior of drinking or acting out. Out of desperation, addicts, with frequent guidance from fellow pilgrims, consciously and deliberately decide to focus their willpower on behavior modification: Don't go to the bar, go to a meeting instead. Stop drinking and start reading *Alcoholics Anonymous* or start making phone calls. By the exercise of willpower, they force their bodies to go to places where people don't act out rather than places where people do; and,

(2) There must be recovery (or stabilization) from the physical damage that results from acting out, including detoxing. Addictions are not medical diseases in a purist sense, but medical care is essential to address any physical damage that is derivative of acting out. Addicts should consider consulting a physician and follow instructions in this regard.

Spiritual Recovery

(3) There is an entrenched, defiant, sub-conscious mindset that perpetuates long-term, self-destructive behavior. An active, practicing alcoholic, a tobacco

---

[54] The Doctor's Opinion, *Alcoholics Anonymous*, p. xxiii.
[55] Intervention means a behavior or action of some sort intended to stop or change a process. Penicillin given to cure an infection is a pharmacological intervention. If someone is drinking incessantly, then treatment centers, therapies of many types, Alcoholics Anonymous, or *Alcoholics Anonymous* would be intervention strategies intended to stop (or sometimes only modify) the drinking.
[56] *Alcoholics Anonymous*, p. xxiv.

smoker or other drug user—*any* addict—is on a long-term run of self-annihilation.[57] This arises partly out of a vicious ongoing process of isolation. Addicts isolate from others in an unhealthy way, and isolate from themselves. Subsequently, whatever self-perceptions practicing addicts have, will be inaccurate.

Out of being alienated from themselves arises their inability to rely on themselves. This guarantees the never-ending painful misadventures of an addict's life. The dynamic of self-abandonment and isolation enables the abuse "of self" which then shows up as self-annihilation/self-destruction. Because they can't rely on themselves, or be responsible to themselves, addicts do far more damage to themselves than anyone else. Getting recovered requires that addicts commit themselves to the work of self-discovery; and,

(4) Addicts *"have lost their reliance on things human."*[58] This profound observation identifies an unalterable truth: Addicts can no longer rely on human willpower, intellect, or psychology, for healing. Most importantly, since they themselves are human, *they cannot rely on themselves to ensure their recovery or use "themselves" as a reference for wise choices.* It's crucial to understand this unalterable dynamic of alienation that sits at the core of lost reliance on things human.

Items 3 and 4 are (partly) what mandates spirituality as the only effective addictions "treatment"; and: The fourth subcategory, the inability to rely on things human, is one of the two most unique aspects to this disease.[59]

Social scientists, doctors, and psychologists can analyze addicts regarding abuse, neglect, shame, loss, natural- or human-made calamity, unmet developmental dependency needs, vitamin deficiency, or diet (make up your own list). They can categorize addicts, prioritize the issues, and write books about addicts until the world runs out of ink. Addicts can cooperate in therapies, be obedient to psychology, read self-help books, find love, be generous, accumulate money, and demonstrate social skills until the cow jumps over the moon, but regarding their addictions: never will they be able to deeply and sincerely rely on things human.

Dr. Silkworth's observations identified and clarified the basis for all successful intervention strategies for addictions. Dr. Silkworth refers to the required (spiritual) psychic change and the poor success rate of other approaches[60], and to do any less than address all four areas leaves the treatment unbalanced and ineffective. Resolving addictions must go beyond the realm of science. Only a deeply sincere relationship with a higher power can compensate for the self-annihilating alienation from "things human" and precipitate the necessary psychic change. *"Well, that's exactly what this book is about. Its main object is to enable you to find a Power greater than yourself which will solve your problem."*[61]

---

[57] A smoker once said to me, in a serious, reflective tone: "I am committing suicide by cigarette."
[58] *Alcoholics Anonymous*, p. xxvi.
[59] The other unique aspect is it's the only disease that has a built in ego-script that tells addicts that nothing is their fault, it's everyone else's; or that they're not sick, everyone else is.
[60] *Alcoholics Anonymous*, p. xxvii. This clinical observation was also made by Dr. Harry Tiebout and Dr. Carl Jung, both of whom I refer to later.
[61] Ibid., p. 45.

Symptoms

The words in bold print in the next few pages identify attributes that all addicts manifest, which, for the sake of this examination, might be called symptoms. These are all consistent with the phenomenon of addictions, and when all addictions are resolved, they largely disappear.

Acting out is engaging in any behavior that is detrimental to yourself or others in any manner—**life-damaging consequences**. There are endless variations of minimizing or explaining away life-damaging consequences so addicts can maintain the illusion that they aren't addicts. One brief example is: "I'm not an addict. I know I'm unpredictable and I black out when I drink, but it's only two or three times a year." (Infrequency is the *ex*clusionary excuse.) Because you infrequently participate in destructive behavior; because the life-damage is subtle, socially acceptable, or it appears no one is hurt, does not exclude you from having an addiction.

Some life-damaging consequences, that are often not viewed as addictions-related, are contained in the failure to achieve common, universal social goals like graduating from high school, holding a job for longer than a year, staying out of jail, paying taxes, or buying a car. Not to achieve any one of these is not necessarily of itself a symptom of addiction. But, if not achieving the usual social accomplishments is the ambience of your life, there's a good chance you're addicted. Other life-damaging consequences and destructive patterns of addictions *might* be:

- divorce (one or many, it doesn't matter),
- contracting HIV/AIDS and other sexually transmitted diseases,
- some pattern of medical treatment regarding injuries from lifestyle,
- admission to psychiatric wards, asylums, and treatment centers,
- unemployment, marginal or erratic employment, being fired,
- abandoning children and significant others,
- sexual anorexia or promiscuity; using pornography; neurotic or belligerent celibacy; adultery, infidelity, erratic or moody sexual lifestyle; "hunting" relationships and sex through dating clubs, personal ads, internet chat rooms, twelve-step meetings,
- erratic, inconsistent, repetitively unfulfilling friendships and sexual relationships,
- some eating patterns and food-relationships,
- inability to make and maintain commitments—regardless of whether it's in one or many areas of your life,
- violence, ongoing threats of violence, repetitive arguing and fighting, participating in violence in sports (vicariously as a spectator or as a participant), excessive competition,
- gossiping and bingeing on righteousness (self- or other-oriented righteousness, often apparent in rigid religious beliefs),
- being noticeably angry much of the time, rage binges, road rage,

- having your private life noticeably different from your public life (maintaining significant secrets about private attitudes and behavior); Impression Management (see Fn. P. 50),
- being frequently in trouble with landlords, creditors, relatives,
- living on the edge of poverty, recurring debt, financial instability,
- getting drunk or stoned, having black-outs, smoking,
- any drinking or drug use and driving,
- gambling, crime,
- shopping, buying, excessive working hours,
- compulsive exercise, preoccupation with body image, some cosmetic surgeries,
- isolation via reading, television, videos, computers, internet.

To experience any one or two of these isn't necessarily indicative that you are an addict. If, however, you experience a few of these to any noticeable recurring degree, you are likely an untreated addict, or destructively compensating for some other serious problem.

Many people in twelve-step programs are abstinent from their obvious acting out and still experience many of these destructive behaviors. Maintaining abstinence from only the obvious mood-altering experience looks good, and often gives them a marvelous defense to avoid addressing the more socially acceptable or secret addictions: "Hey, I quit drinking, so get off my case about the smoking." "Quit complaining about six hours of TV every day; at least I'm not in the bar." "So what if I rent a porn video once in a while; at least I'm not doing drugs anymore." Poly-addictions are a given.

Another possible indicator of addiction is **neurosis**[62], although it isn't usually talked about as a part of an addiction. Neurosis is a mental/emotional disorder, characterized by strong inner conflict, that does not have an organic cause. The routine symptoms of neurosis are insecurity, anxiety, irrational fears, or depression, but not to the degree that a person would be generally incapacitated. A neurosis leaves your inner life out of balance in an exaggerated way, although your outer life may appear reasonably normal.

If someone casually observes that the color of your shirt doesn't quite match your jacket, then later you tear the shirt up and agonize for hours over the comment; or should you worry for an hour, trying on a dozen outfits to look perfect for a casual lunch with friends, and these are ongoing, secretly typical behaviors, you would be neurotic. No one would see the unreasonable, anxious behavior in response to these everyday situations. The anxiety and inner conflict must be significantly *dis*proportionate to the extant conditions, but a person can still function in community. It's often a limited participation because of the secret conflict and turmoil, and there's often little joy or pleasure in life, despite outward appearances.

---

[62] Carl Jung said that neurosis was a way to avoid legitimate suffering. At another time, when asked if he believed in God, Jung said very calmly, "I don't believe. I know." As reported by Gerald May, *Will and Spirit*, Harper & Row, 1982, p. 135.

Addicts, when they are acting out or in the early stages of recovery, and many people in twelve-step programs with extensive abstinence, are neurotic to some noticeable degree (noticeable in therapy, not always noticeable in ordinary life). Some neuroses are resolved in the normal course of getting recovered and going through proper twelve-step work, but the more serious ones aren't.

Denial, another requirement of addiction, is an unconscious, automatic ego defense mechanism (one of several), that is characterized by an inability to recall and acknowledge painful realities, thoughts, or feelings. Denial is an unconscious, automatic mind-survival technique of "not remembering". All addicts have denial to some degree. [To Alcoholics and Addicts: Congratulate each other that you're in denial: it helped you survive your self-imposed crisis so you could enter recovery.]

Repression is very common amongst addicts and is different from denial in that it begins with a more conscious effort. It's not automatic. When reality is repeatedly painful, the memories and emotions that stem from the conflict are consciously thrust aside (willful forgetting). Over years of repetitive willful forgetting, the incident is repressed out of memory.

Regarding Denial and Repression: Suppose your life is completely falling apart. Within a short while, your siblings are killed in a train wreck, your house burns down, you get laid off from work, the dog has fleas and bites the neighbor and now you're being sued. Your one-and-only best friend moves away, your partner leaves you, you get a speeding ticket on the way to the doctor's office, and you're told you have cancer. The pain of it all is too big to handle, so you'd naturally (and appropriately) develop these ego defenses which would allow you to cope.

If calamities befall someone in otherwise optimum circumstances (i.e. over time and not closely impacting one upon the other) this person could experience the pain in a supportive environment, in increments that their psyche could stand. If there was no supportive environment and the trauma was continuous (like when addicts continuously act out and regenerate crisis and trauma), the denial and repression become "permanent". This sets up a cyclic re-experiencing of crisis and is the source of an astonishing number of physical ailments.[63]

For people who have suffered repeated trauma (especially self-inflicted), ego defenses allow them to survive. Developing Denial and Repression, and to some extent, being neurotic, are ways addicts compensate and survive. It is how they avoid legitimate pain because at the time they experienced it, with circumstances as they were, they were unable to cope any other way. These conditions are entrenched, and prevent addicts from being proportionately aware of the realities and pain in the circumstances of their life. That's the way people with addictions live.

Try to not use words like denial, repression, neuroses, abandonment issues, inner child, or dissociation, unless you're well informed and know exactly what you're talking about. Even then, don't use them too often. Because you have skimmed through a few self-help books, or have a Psych-101 course, or are other wise an opinionated new-age workshop/therapy junkie, does *not* mean you are well-

---

[63] Self Regulation Therapy® and/or Emotional Freedom Technique both address body-energy dislocation that is associated with physical and psychological trauma. (Appendix III)

informed. In fact, with this type of self-serving limited information, you are probably dangerous.

Misuse of complicated psychological words hurts people. Using them is often loaded with bias and prejudice—power-mongering and a mean-spirited analysis of someone else's character. I use them here to assist you in comprehension, not to call people names. Millions of people, for thousands of years, have been spiritual without these scientific words that dissect and analyze another's character. Unless you know what you're doing, and there is a specific reason for doing so, and you are truly compassionate, don't use them.

Addicts often base their values and beliefs on **assumptions.** They assume (1) various "things" about other peoples' character, which beliefs are rooted in ignorance or supposition; and, (2) that most people believe, or if they don't they should believe, as they, themselves, do. Assumptions are created out of fear, ignorance, naiveté, or out of the insecurity that underlies cynicism and arrogance. Assumptions keep people trapped in destructive, limiting thought patterns. This leaves prejudices and stereotypes unchallenged. As Herbert Spenser said, contempt prior to investigation keeps us trapped in ignorance.[64]

Shame[65] is arguably the most powerful emotion and the greatest block to human development. Other emotions are certainly influential, but none carry the power to contaminate personal awareness or defeat personal accomplishment to the degree that shame does. It is the emotion that separates us from ourselves: internal isolation. Shame mandates that we be "human doings" rather than human beings.[66]

The destructive influence of shame sometimes (but not always) begins in early childhood; and, in an addict's life, shame is always created, reinforced, expanded, and entrenched further by acting out and by societal values and mores in relation to addictions. Shame is also, and certainly, a significant factor that helps to keep addicts in a cycle of acting out. It is, however, easy for people to erroneously believe that shame is the cause of addiction, and to therefore hunt for some (possibly nonexistent) severe circumstance in childhood and then blame caregivers.

Some addicts are shamed in childhood significantly less than others, and yet are *not* shamed to the degree that would correlate to the vicious addictions they have. Not all (and sometimes very little) of an addict's shame came from their family of origin-caregivers, and it is irresponsible and abusive to insist otherwise.

Addicts are psychologically **isolated** from themselves (by denial, shame, and repression) and have no dependable sense of self.[67] They are often socially isolated through shame or excessive, **disproportionate fear**. Addicts who present themselves as gregarious are still isolated, regardless of their claims to the contrary.

---

[64] *Alcoholics Anonymous*, p. 570.
[65] Shame, fear, and guilt will be discussed at some length in *Facets of Personal Transformation*.
[66] The phrase "human doing" carries an edge of satire from over-use. Nonetheless, it is still very appropriate here.
[67] "No dependable sense of self" is explained in more detail in Chapter 11: Thought, Form, Fascination, Fall.

Being an addict requires that you lie and deceive as a matter of course. **Dishonesty** (and its emotional-cousin **withholding**) is a tactic to garner power or manipulate for selfish advantage. Addicts lie because their addiction requires it, not because they are bad. You cannot be a practicing addict (in *any* addiction) and be honest. An "unrecovered" addict's dishonesty or deceit or withholding may be calculated, spontaneous, deliberate, or unconscious, but it is not optional.

Selfishness is also intrinsic to addiction. Selfishness is the manipulation of people and circumstances, or the disregard for the rights and dignity of others, to avoid exposure of your own shame, frailties, fears, and mistakes. Selfishness is any behavior that avoids personal responsibility or accountability and unjustly (irresponsibly) externalizes responsibility onto someone or something else. Selfishness is avoiding exposing your limitations, defects, errors, or resentments at the expense of others—making them guilty, bad, wrong, or responsible for your own faults and misdemeanors. Selfishness is one facet of being irresponsible.

Irresponsibility permeates *all* aspects of an addict's life. Here's a short alphabetical list of behaviors that harbor irresponsibility: accusing, admonishing, arguing, attacking, avoiding, blaming, censuring, cheating, condemning, deceiving, defending, defying, demeaning, embellishing, evading, exaggerating, finding fault, gossiping, hiding, invading, lying, minimizing, moralizing, petulance, rebuking, reprimanding, undermining, whining and withholding.

Addicts are masters at irresponsibility. One of the greatest challenges they face is becoming completely responsible for everything in their character, and for the historical, ongoing, or developing circumstances of their addiction and their life.

Cynicism, among other things, embodies a belief that the cynic is superior to whatever they are cynical about. It's often rooted in assumptions about the shortcomings, failings, or hypocrisy of others, and implies the cynic's self-held conviction about their own superior character attributes and/or superior insight and wisdom. The more cynical someone holds themselves, the more they demean others, and the more they are isolated and out of touch with their emotions. This leaves the cynic living with illusion, delusion, and loneliness.

Arrogance is the demonstration (or secret existence) of a belief in some personally held superior quality. One common understanding of arrogance is that it is the opposite of humility. With arrogance, there is isolation.

Within a recovery program, there are three obvious paradigms of arrogance, and these are very often silent: (1) Believing that because you are the smartest or most perceptive or most experienced person around you don't need help. (2) Believing you are (or someone else is) the sickest or the most depraved person around, so nobody can help. (3) Believing you (or someone else) is the most worthless or useless person in the room, and nobody should then waste time giving help. These are arrogant.

The more cynical or arrogant you are, the more distant you are from your feelings, and the more you are isolated from yourself and others. Cynicism and arrogance are emotion-avoidance tactics. If you are openly or silently arrogant or cynical, you cannot be spiritual, and you're isolated, afraid and lonely, even if you aren't aware of it.

And finally, these symptoms of addiction, regardless of how obvious or subtle, will be **chronic** and **entrenched**. They will be so pervasive that the addict will be unaware of their all-encompassing nature.

Blindness To The Disease

In The Manner of Presentation, I described the three-dimensional spiders web of symptoms and issues. Addictions are incredibly complicated. I wrote this: *"You get sick everywhere and throughout your entire personality all at the same time."* Addictions affect *everything* about an addict's life: how they brush their teeth, how they make love, how they drive, how they eat, what art and music they like, how they think, how they work, how they celebrate holidays, how they earn a living, how they sleep, how they dress, how they comb their hair... literally *everything* is affected by an addiction.

Other diseases (except possibly some rare mental illnesses) don't have the all-encompassing effect on a person that addiction does. When someone gets some disease *other* than addictions, it affects aspects of their life but not *every* aspect of it. With other illnesses, they're noticeable because the illness is experienced in a specific area—the person can "notice and feel" some particular disruption. Illnesses affect certain aspects of a person's life, but not their selection of clothes, the type of food they eat, the type of music they like, or the type of person they choose to love. Other illnesses have defined boundaries of influence. An addiction exists globally; it's a state of existence. [Being spiritual is also a state of existence.]

This all-pervading quality, and the *un*usually inexorable trickle-effect of addictions, makes them invisible to the people who have them. Out of this blindness comes the famous first line of defense when an addict is confronted: "What? There's nothing wrong with me. What are you talking about? I'm fine."

Altogether, addicts manifest acting out and life-damaging consequences, neurosis, denial, disproportionate fear, repression, isolation (from self and others), assumptions, shame, dishonesty, withholding, selfishness, irresponsibility, arrogance, and cynicism—all chronic and entrenched, and they are largely blind to them.[68] Some of these symptoms are not usually talked about in terms of addictions, and I'm sure that some will disagree that I call them symptoms. However, these attributes manifest consistently in addicts and alcoholics, and they are significantly reduced or eliminated when they stop *all* acting out and become sincerely obedient to spiritual principles. [Note: These are the external symptoms of the disease, they are not the disease itself. The disease of addictions isn't resolved by making the symptoms go away, but by healing the spiritual dislocation that allows these symptoms to exist.]

It's no wonder, then, that <u>The Doctor's Opinion</u> identifies restlessness, irritability, and discontent as hallmarks of an addict.[69] *Restlessness* is an absence of

---

[68] This blindness remains forever subtly present, unless there is a sincere devotion to the spiritual principles that inform the maintenance steps. The all-pervading self-blindness is what mandates constant self-examination and wise, ongoing spiritual counsel, throughout the addict's life. It takes *years* for self-examination to become accurate and dependable.

[69] *Alcoholics Anonymous*, p. xxiv.

quiet or repose; not being able to relax or be still; being worried, anxious, or uneasy. *Irritability* is being easily irked or annoyed, and sensitive to stimulus. *Discontentment* is being unhappy with circumstances and desiring change—a dissatisfied and impatient longing for different circumstances. These are traits of the addict, and they arise from the symptoms. People cannot continuously use a mood-altering experience, over an extended period of time, without entrenching restlessness, irritability, and discontentment in their personality.

Honest Misrepresentation

A man once said to me, with very dramatic intensity: "I was *literally destroyed* as a child going through foster homes. Did abuse, denial of my rights, and trauma create my addiction before I started drinking as a teenager? I've been clean and sober a while and a lot of times I'm back to acting like a child. I believe the damage caused my addiction. Did it?"

No. Childhood abuse can appear to set the stage for addiction, and it does make addictions more complicated, but addictions aren't a guaranteed result of abuse. To believe they are isn't scientifically accurate, and it isn't spiritually responsible. Some addicts with vicious addictions had a childhood relatively free of abuse, and others with heinous childhood abuse didn't become addicts, or if an addiction did develop, it might be comparatively "mild".[70]

When addicts begin recovery, they go through a *long* phase of being anxious, angry, afraid, very confused, and insecure about life. These emotions are often evident in their sexuality. Coincidental to this, sexual acting out can be an addiction and not necessarily symptomatic of overt abuse. All of this is too easily explained away as the result of childhood neglect or abuse. Certainly some addicts were sexually or otherwise overtly abused, but many were not. A general assumption that serious abuse must have happened—otherwise the person wouldn't be an addict—is erroneous. This misperception sometimes leads to confabulation in sobriety. It fosters exaggeration, witch hunts, blame, and drama, and creates serious complications in an already very complex dynamic.

Clients and newcomers seek approval and are afraid of rejection. Many will alter their story to fit the pet theories of those who help them. Caregivers who don't understand the dynamics of the horrendous damage that addicts do to themselves, irrespective of childhood, and who endorse more recent, culturally popular theories about addictions, too quickly label fear, confusion, irresponsible sexual behavior, or vague memory, as evidence of childhood abuse. This eliminates the aspect of self-imposed crisis, and makes caregivers, or some calamity, responsible for (i) the addict's addiction; and (ii) their recovery experience of pain, confusion, and insecurity.

Now, back to the man's statement: "I was *literally destroyed*... ." The dramatic inflection he used, more than its content, will help to begin to sort out the dynamics of what's afoot here. Much was implied by the passion and conviction he had in believing he was *literally destroyed*; but is that accurate? Through his own

---

[70] I use the word mild only to make a point about some theories on the origin of addictions, not to pass judgement on the authenticity of someone's life experience. I go into this in more detail elsewhere.

perception-filtering mechanism, it is honest, but it misrepresents the circumstances. If he was *"literally destroyed"* would he be alive? Would he be sober in a twelve-step group, or at the lecture? Using that phrase with the pretentious, passionate conviction he did has a self-serving advantage related to drama, and various other factors like culturally imposed guilt and shame. So… what does he *do* about it?

First, I would invite him to examine what the ego-payoffs[71] are for being so theatrical and intense in his descriptions of his childhood. I do not intend to demean his (or anyone else's) pain; however, there are times when legitimate pain is exaggerated or minimized to accomplish some subtle, unhealthy, self-serving agenda.

In this, and in similar scenarios, there are three areas to examine that are connected, but, at the same time subtly independent of each other. One: How and to what extent were they abused as children and (from that) developed an unhealthy personality? Two: Later, as adult-addicts drinking and acting out self-destructively, they caused additional, *serious* damage to themselves: To what extent? Three: What complications arose, and what self-serving advantages were accrued by them (consciously or unconsciously) altering their perceptions of their experiences?[72]

For addicts who are getting recovered, the first thing to address is always abstinence, and then understanding it's a self-imposed crisis: what they did to damage themselves by acting out.[73] These are always first. If they are not reasonably willing to accept responsibility for their addiction, and all the crises and damage done to themselves and to others from it, *and* for getting recovered, then that irresponsibility must be addressed before anything else. Without accepting full responsibility, any therapy or twelve-step work simply entrenches the unspiritual ego-posture of addicts being victims. Taking personal responsibility must be reasonably well-established and present *before* addicts can successfully negotiate the deeper areas of healing. Yes, perpetrators of abuse should rightly be held responsible for that abuse; however, addicts should rightly be held responsible for their addiction and the consequences of that.

The nature of active addiction requires that perceptions of personal history be altered. This is commonly seen in externalizing responsibility. When people begin their recovery, it is essential they begin to shift from avoiding to taking responsibility. With addicts, any premature attempt to heal pre-addiction trauma, especially healing which is encouraged by naive caregivers, creates all manner of horrendous complications. At the very minimum, these caregivers will reinforce the victim mentality that's attendant to addictions, and abet addicts in finding someone (other than themselves), to hold responsible for their life and how it turned out. [From another

---

[71] All behavior is purposeful. For a discussion about ego, see Appendix IV.

[72] Perceptions of childhood trauma may be changed in many ways for many reasons. Three more obvious ones are minimizing it and thereby rescuing the abusers, exaggerating it and thereby persecuting them, or exaggerating it and thereby attributing accountability for outrageous or egregious behavior to a cause other than the addicts themselves. Regarding the unconscious nature of this memory manipulation, there is a parallel theme in Thought-Form-Fascination-Fall (Chapter 11). This is not to undermine the sincere representation of trauma. This is to understand more clearly how the mind of an addict works.

[73] *Alcoholics Anonymous*, p. 53.

complicated perspective, this is self-serving for the caregivers.] Extricating the alcoholic/addict from a blaming mentality is an extremely difficult thing to do.[74]

The harm from childhood trauma, and the self-inflicted damage from addictions, exacerbate each other. Over years of acting out, as the life damaging consequences become more destructive, an addict creates subtle tactics for justifying the self-destruction. By tweaking memories, they find ways to explain their blatantly self-destructive behavior, which, at the minimum, includes (1) creating enemies where none exist, (2) minimizing their own culpability; and, (3) exaggerating, or at times minimizing, the influence of the damage done to them by others. Addicts experience so much damage specific to their acting out, that if encouraged at all, they will confabulate or modify their memory of historical circumstances to make their addiction more palatable to themselves and "justifiable" in the eyes of society.[75]

One of the more subtle and debilitating demonstrations of relationship addiction (codependence) occurs when sponsors, mentors, or professionals (doctors, counselors, therapists, social workers, priests, ministers, etc.) cooperate in this. Without addicts *painstakingly* and *patiently* separating the actual from the perceived traumatic circumstances, and without eventually accepting addiction as a self-imposed crisis, the degree of responsibility they accept for the state of affairs in their life will always be insufficient and self-serving. Their mythologizing, minimizing, exaggerating, or blaming remains unexamined. The results of this, for everyone concerned (caregivers, communities, professionals, families, loved-ones, and the addicts themselves) are disastrous over the long term.

About half of the people I work with spend a large part of the first two years of their therapy overcoming the confusion and pain from mismanaged and ineffective "help" at the hands of poorly-trained or still-wounded caregivers who don't understand addictions, and who confuse spiritual fitness with social success. And, easily 75% of the clients I work with, who are attending twelve-step meetings, spend well over a year sorting out the confusion and misdirection they experience in meetings. The misunderstanding and chaos about therapy, spirituality, addictions, twelve-step programs, and responsibility is horrendous.[76]

The Ripple Effect of Irresponsibility

Consider this scenario: As a child, Jack was abused by a priest. It's now thirty years later. The offender is old, retired, and moved away (maybe dead). The church's congregation has changed: there's a new priest; the committee of elders has changed. If the abuser is alive, Jack charges him with abuse and sues him for damages. And, whether or not the offender is alive, Jack sues the church (meaning the registered nonprofit organization, the bishop, etc.) Eventually, Jack "wins" a settlement. Now the new congregation, the new church, the new priest, the new bishop, or some insurance company (whoever), has to come up with the cash. Going to church

---

[74] I refer to this again in Chapter 4. Also see *Twelve Steps and Twelve Traditions*, p. 47.

[75] Recall I wrote earlier about the propensity of some addicts to significantly dramatize their addiction in the way they "share" at meetings. This theme applies here.

[76] There's a well-considered perspective of responsibility in Nathaniel Branden's book, *Taking Responsibility*, Simon & Schuster, 1996.

costs more, everyone who uses that insurance company has their rates go up slightly, and the church's insurance premiums double. Yet the new priest, the new congregation, the insurance company, are innocent. They didn't abuse Jack, but they are made to pay for the crime of someone else.

Jack is demanding reparation from, and making innocent people pay, for something they didn't do. Yes, Jack was completely innocent when he was abused. Historically, the priest, as a child, was also innocent when he was abused. And this now-gone/retired/dead priest, who abused Jack, made Jack pay for something that was done to himself [the priest] long before Jack was born.[77] Moreover, as Jack struggles in the irresponsible activity of suing innocent people, abetted by an addicted system of civil law that enables revenge, Jack will harm the people that are close to him. Jack is perpetuating the cycle of abuse by making innocent people pay.

Holding people accountable for their own behavior is always appropriate. In all sincerity, every effort should be made to hold offenders accountable. When, for whatever reason, perpetrators escape accountability, that is hard to accept; but making innocent bystanders pay for someone else's crime is much worse.

Children are completely innocent of whatever abuse was done to them. As a child, if you were abused, you are *not* responsible for it. However, it appears that from a spiritual point of view, as an adult, only you are responsible to clean up the mess. Waiting for someone else to clean up the mess of *your* life, while you as an adult stay bitterly "sick", demand reparation from innocent people, and hunt up scapegoats, continues to harm everyone... especially yourself.

Indirectly harming innocent people like employers, children, friends, and spouses, because someone was mean to you when you were a child, is mean and irresponsible on your part. Put another way: You cannot externalize the responsibility for cleaning up your life onto innocent people without seriously harming people who are innocent of responsibility for the trauma that was done to you.

Most people in twelve-step programs and in our culture generally, wander aimlessly inside themselves, isolated and lonely, acting out in socially approved addictions. They often pounce like jackals on the weakness of others, seek scapegoats, and are ambivalent about their careers and relationships. Their ethics are situational and opportunistic, and they wonder what life is about—subtly demanding purpose and meaning from the outside, and punishing innocent bystanders when they don't get their own way. Because they live this way people become disposable. [When Jack sues the innocent church people they become disposable.]

"Some of us have tried to hold on to our old ideas and the result was nil until we let go absolutely."[78] This observation has far-reaching consequences for the spiritual pilgrim as it relates to spiritual integrity and accountability.[79]

---

[77] All people who were sexually abused do not themselves become abusers. All people who are abusers were themselves abused.

[78] *Alcoholics Anonymous,* p. 58.

[79] Norman Allan MacEachern, MA, DD, was a Presbyterian minister. In a speech he wrote and delivered to the graduating class at Presbyterian College (Montreal), he told them that they should be wary of ministers who do not make the laity uncomfortable. A minister's job, according to him, was to challenge and confront various forms of spiritual inactivity, to encourage the hard work of being spiritual, and for ministers to push themselves and their congregations out of their comfort zones—to call everyone to a higher

Old Ideas and The Disease

Within both addicts and our culture, one of the old ideas to be confronted is the belief that this is not a disease.[80] Recall the symptoms I listed: acting out and life-damaging consequences, neurosis, denial, repression, isolation from self and others, disproportionate fear, assumptions, shame, dishonesty (including withholding), selfishness, irresponsibility, arrogance, and cynicism—all chronic and entrenched.

There have been many debates on whether an addiction is a disease. There are incredibly complex spiritual and psychological issues in play, and lives are at stake. What needs to be said, in defense of the use of the term, is that any addiction isn't a matter of simple defiance or disobedience. Paranoia isn't a disease in the classic virus-like medical-model of interpreting life's problems; but neither is it a matter of willpower or intellectual weakness.

Addicts and alcoholics go through definable phases of being powerless to their mood-altering behavior. It is long known they are as puzzled about their self-annihilation and flagrant irresponsibility as anyone. Doctors, therapists, treatment centers, and twelve-step programs are all rather busy with addicts wanting, but unable, to achieve recovery. [This book is encouraging a return to a formerly more successful, and now largely ignored, avenue to successful treatment.]

Calling alcoholics weak-willed, bad, or defiant, in relation to the condition, says more about the naiveté or prejudice of the person saying it than the addict or the addiction. Because science isn't clear on the *exact* nature/cause of the disease (and may never be) doesn't mean that addicts are to be called names. They, and their treatment, are entitled to be treated with respect and dignity.

———

As an alcoholic/addict, in one conversation you may declare you have a disease. In other conversations, you condemn yourself for doing something you believe you shouldn't have: "I shouldn't have got that divorce," or "I was really stupid to tell that lie." These self-condemnations are contrary to the declaration that your addiction is a disease. If you think that you *should* have done something differently than you did (shouldn't have lied, shouldn't have divorced… , or whatever), that implies you believe you had choices regarding your symptoms.

Having a fever is a symptom of pneumonia. After you've recovered from pneumonia it would be foolish to declare: "Oh, that was stupid of me to get that fever; I shouldn't have done that." It's acceptable to have a fever with pneumonia—it's a part of the pneumonia package. Addiction is a disease. Symptoms are not optional.

---

way of living. (This is my precis of what I consider to be an insightful and detailed address.) That is my purpose here. I don't hold myself out to be a minister, but my intent is to invite you to challenge yourself. Dr. MacEachern's address was entitled "The Common Factor in All Great Preaching", from *The Pilgrim Heart*, Thorn Press, Toronto, 1948.

[80] Medical science is very clear about the treatment of the derivative damage and side effects of alcoholism and addiction. The actual addiction, itself, is not resolved by the elimination of the symptoms or the resolution of its consequences.

An addict who harbors harsh self-criticisms of their own addictions-related symptomatic behavior, or of other addicts displaying symptomatic behavior like lying, cannot also hold a simultaneous belief in addictions being a disease. This contradiction arises from deeply ingrained confusion about the nature of addictions, cultural misunderstandings, cooperation with externally imposed guilt, and poorly defined ego boundaries.

Demanding that you (or someone else) should have done or not done something that is contrary to the symptoms of the disease implies that you think there were choices where no choice existed. You declare you have a disease and then criticize yourself for having the symptoms. This denies the truth that symptoms aren't optional. To claim that you believe an addiction is a disease, and then to ridicule yourself or another for having the symptoms, means you don't understand or accept the nature of the illness that is killing you (or them).

My describing destructive or "irresponsible" behavior as symptomatic (meaning unavoidable) does *not* offer an excuse to avoid accountability for it. Addicts must be held accountable, especially by and for themselves. *Alcoholics Anonymous* advises that this is a self-imposed crisis—addicts are responsible, but they're not to be blamed or called names, especially by themselves.

The Selfish "Program"

Being selfish is manipulating people and circumstances to avoid exposure of your shame, insecurities, fears, and mistakes. You avoid exposure of your humanness or meanness by unjustly (deceitfully) shifting responsibility away from you and onto someone or something else.

"This is a selfish program," is a frequently-heard statement which dangerously misrepresents the spiritual intent of the original twelve-step process. The original twelve-step literature isn't selfish, and the other twelve-step program outlines that I've reviewed are not intended to be selfish. Regardless of their efficacy, each of them, in their own way, suggests a path which stands in opposition to addictions. Yet there is ample evidence of neglect and irresponsibility under the guise of attending meetings. If the programs aren't selfish, how do they become selfish?

What has been verified time and again in my work is that the most common "solution" to an addiction is a substitute addiction.[81] A twelve-step group can easily become a substitute acting-out ritual. Put another way: Recovering addicts become (more) selfish when their twelve-step program becomes a substitute addiction, in which case their program would be inappropriately interpreted as requiring selfish behavior. There are many ways addicts can be selfish under the guise of becoming recovered. Addicts' selfish behavior is especially destructive when it's camouflaged as a spiritual endeavor. Here's a true story…

A woman owned a company, was an alcoholic, and a work addict. Her ritual was to get up early and go to work, start drinking at lunch, and work and drink all afternoon. She'd come home in the evening and drink and work, or sometimes stay

---

[81] Recall the earlier discussion about poly-addictions. And, see Terry Kellogg's book, *Broken Toys Broken Dreams*, BRAT Publishing, Revised 1990, p. 72.

out and drink and work with employees. Day in, day out, often seven days a week, for years: get up, work and drink, go to bed. She had a spouse and children. Finally her spouse had enough, got some help, and advocated for change. She eventually entered AA. After getting sober her general ritual was to get up early and go to work, meet program-people for breakfast or lunch, and work, and talk with program people whenever possible, all day. She would come home and work, and talk on the phone to program people all evening. Often she'd work late and go to twelve-step meetings. Finally (again) after a few years of this, her spouse had had enough, got some help, and advocated for change. They divorced.

In this case, and many others like it, the meetings and groups become a substitute addiction, and participation in recovery becomes the justification for irresponsibility: "Honey, I can't watch the kids, I've got to go to my meeting," (1,713 nights in a row). Or: "I'd love to spend time at home but I'm sponsoring twenty-seven people. I have to meet them and I have to carry the message or I'll relapse. I think I'm free two weeks from next Thursday between 4:30 and 6:00 PM."

As soon as the partner talks about neglect, absence of commitment, or avoiding responsibility, the response is an ominous defense of the substitute addiction. "Listen, I know I've been gone seven nights a week and every Saturday morning for four-and-a-half years, but that's better than drinking, isn't it? At least we didn't get a divorce, right? *Right*? I know I'm never home, but I'm getting help and that's what *you* wanted, right? So would you rather have me drunk?" This is justifying a substitute addiction.

Being busy in recovery is fine, and a significant commitment is necessary at the outset. However, the intent of going to meetings is to become spiritual and to eventually create a spiritual life without addictions; to get back into community and healthy relationships. It's actually a self-less program. However, when the program becomes a substitute addiction, it is used selfishly to avoid responsibility.

People stay on social assistance for years getting someone else to pay for their "recovery". Victims lick their wounds, whining about how hard Life is; how they were so horribly abused by their father, mother, wife, husband, ex-wife, ex-husband, grandparents, children, bank managers, the police, politicians, lawyers, the school system. The list is endless. This is irresponsible, and others in society who get up and go to work every day have to pay. There are no free rides. Social pampering and rescuing people out of personal responsibility is fatal to getting recovered, for both those who are rescued and for those who rescue them.

If you break your leg, it's a ludicrous proposition to accuse you of being selfish when you go to the hospital. You broke your leg and going to the hospital is generally considered intelligent. And yet going to the hospital is an inconvenience. You'll miss work and need special help from your partner or family. Friends might miss a meal or cancel an engagement to help you. Breaking your leg is an inconvenience to other people in your life. But you go to the doctor, get over it, resume your life such as it was, and the inconvenience to others stops.

You were selfish when you were acting out. That's a symptom of the disease. Once you decide to get recovered, you need help. If you have to inconvenience people to get beyond early recovery, you're not being selfish: you're being intelligent. A twelve-step program or treatment center, *properly* used, is like an "addictions hospital". Inconveniencing people is necessary; however, remember to only inconvenience others only as much as is necessary for proper self-care to get recovered. As soon as the program becomes a justification for irresponsibility, it's become a substitute addiction. This is often the case when participation in twelve-step programs is motivated by a desire to be healthy rather than spiritual. Granted, some are sicker than others, but years and years of excessive participation in twelve-step meetings isn't evidence of spiritual fitness.

People sometimes see me for an addictions-assessment. Since the symptoms of this disease go far beyond "acting out", I don't [really] want to find out *exactly* how much they drank or drugged. Yes, I am interested, but that isn't my primary focus. I want to also assess how much they lie; how isolated they are, even though they claim to be gregarious and have friends; how they try to manipulate people (including me); how they misrepresent themselves and others. I want to assess their fear, loneliness, desperation, and the subtle ways they self-annihilate. I will notice their assumptions and arrogance and cynicism. For a professional to assess for addiction on only the evidence of acting-out behaviors, in any but the most blatant cases, is insufficient.

Step One isn't concerned with whether or not your grandmother loved you, your parents were mean, you were forced to take music lessons, you went to a strict school, or went to school at all. Step One is interested in how you drank or acted out (not how much, but how), and the unmanageability that was generated in your life. Using a broad definition of trouble: how you got *yourself* in trouble. [At Step Four, regarding 'trouble', you will be advised that *"We thought 'conditions' drove us to drink..."*[82] Addicts think this, but conditions really don't.]

In getting recovered, beginning at Step One, addicts begin to accept ever-more responsibility regarding the truth of their self-imposed crisis. But, they have a perspective of Life that resists this by creating excuses for acting out: their parents, their brother, their boss, their wife, their husband, the government, the schools, the policeman, the judge, bad TV reception, road traffic, and on and on.

Addictions are an issue of corrupt spirituality, which is yours alone to deal with. You're not in control of what is done to you, but you are responsible for cleaning up after it. Out of uncompromising, personal responsibility comes the beauty inherent in spiritual devotion and humility. Spirituality is only truly available in the deeply self-responsible life.

How many times have you heard that plaintive cry of the suffering addict: "It's not fair! I don't deserve this!" That life is supposed to be fair is one illusion that addicts live with.[83] It often shows up like this: "I'm going to be nice (meaning fair)

[82] *Twelve Steps and Twelve Traditions*, p. 47.
[83] When this illusion goes unchallenged, it ends in all manner of abuse and irresponsibility. One is in situations like "Jack" (from a few pages ago) suing the innocent church people. Jack believes the world wasn't fair to him, and so he doesn't have to be fair either. People justify gossip, crime, meanness, betrayal, lying, harsh judgments, etc., thusly: Life wasn't fair to me (past tense), so I don't have to be nice or fair to you (present and future tense). This is spiritually corrupt and dooms you to an unfulfilled life.

so other people will be nice to me". Unlike TV shows and commercials, life isn't neatly solved in thirty minutes of rudeness, sarcasm, and sympathy which, sadly, passes for entertainment. The number of people who find violence and disrespect entertaining is evidence of the poignantly sad state of affairs in modern culture. Life is not a television show. We're dealing with a terribly dislocated culture, globally addicted lifestyles, and gross personal and cultural irresponsibility.

In my small corner of the world, as a therapist, lecturer, writer, and musician, I'm known somewhat by reputation. Many people also know that I'm a member of a program. When it's appropriate, and when I am asked, I am a twelve-step apologist.[84] But what if my character defects and my ordinariness are publicly visible? Won't this reflect badly on the program? Only to people who are already looking for excuses to blame others and be self-righteous.

Cynics, manipulators, and arrogant, dishonest, envious people already have 173 excuses for blaming everything. I've been maligned, gossiped about, and irresponsibly blamed many times. My own ordinary defects will only add a little fuel to their already blazing fire. I'm human, so therefore I'll make mistakes (it goes with the package of being human). My life isn't a reflection of any program: it's a reflection of my humanness.

Whether or not I do lectures, play in a band, write or don't write a book; and whether it's ten or ten-million people who know anything about me, there will be mean-spirited criticism. The fact some people are entrenched in vicious self-justification, and are unable or too insecure to examine themselves instead of me, guarantees they will disparage my character regardless of what I do. What they don't realize is it also guarantees they will continue to live an impoverished life. My own observation is that if we eliminated gossip from twelve-step meetings, the vast majority of conversations would screech to a halt. Mean-spirited back-biting leaves too little time for stringing pearls for the delight of heaven.[85]

To Whom It May Concern

Tragedy was originally a term for fictitious/literary drama. It has become a word that alleges the "true nature" of some circumstance of life. As much as it may appear that Tragedy is rampant in modern life: tragic car accidents, tragic illnesses, tragic crimes, that's an illusion. Life isn't more (or less) "tragic" now than at any other point in history. In part, what has happened, is modern culture has inserted technology in between People and Life—and created the fantasy that Life should be free of misadventure. Technology fosters irresponsibility and the illusion that there should be fewer bad things happening. But technology can neither reduce the frequency of death (it happens once to everyone), nor can it improve the odds of

---

[84] An apologist is someone who defends something. There'll be much discussion later about "I'm sorry," and "I apologize."

[85] This poetic phrase came from *Blues ain't nothing but a good soul feeling bad,* Sheldon Kopp, Fireside/Parkside Books, Simon & Schuster, 1992, the entry for January 19. This is the most useful and thought-provoking daily-reflection book I have found.

avoiding random calamity. However, Victims and Romantic Sentimentalists transform random circumstance into a tragic, personal event.

Tragedy and calamity aren't personal. They're always addressed "To Whom It May Concern" and you happened to be standing there when the bus crashed around the corner. Life is randomly indifferent to everyone and the only meaning it has is the one *you* give to it. Your childhood difficulties weren't targeted at you in particular. Understand that any other child born in your approximate space in the universe, plus or minus a few months, as the result of an act of intercourse between the same two adults, would have more-than-likely ended up with some variation of what you had. Tragedy and calamity are not addressed to you personally.

Some people got slammed pretty hard with addictions, but that isn't about them *personally*. Neither is gray hair. Yet, in the dynamics of your addicted personality, with a victim mentality, your ego generates an illusion about life not being fair, and you soon "believe" that Life is out to get you personally. Life isn't anybody's fault. Chance exists, and misadventure happens. Everyone has a randomly equal opportunity to escape disaster. Pain is required and suffering is optional. Believing otherwise is one of the greatest blocks to spirituality and serenity there is.

Life isn't fair, *but also it isn't unfair*. It just is. If you heal enough to not take it personally, then you don't have to personalize random calamity by blaming whomever you assume was your oppressor. You need to heal from the pain, but beyond that, there isn't anyone to blame.

The International Association of Petulant Victims (The I.A.P.V.) was going to have a convention, but they couldn't get any one to take charge so they cancelled it. The complaining was horrendous. Eventually they had to disband because everyone wanted someone else to make a decision. Watch out for members of The International Association of Petulant Victims in twelve-step meetings: they are everywhere and always on the lookout for someone (else) to blame. Most addicts cling tenaciously to their I.A.P.V. membership, but there's no spirituality there. The more you believe you are a valiantly struggling oppressed victim, the less you are recovered.[86] (Members of the I.A.P.V. live with a mindset of accusation.)

It's only by adopting a doctrine of obedience to spiritual principles, and complete responsibility for your life, that an addict can have access to freedom and spirituality. When addicts are completely responsible, regardless of whatever situation they are in, it frees them up to respond however they choose. If, however, they see the problems in their life as someone else's fault, then the person they're blaming is in charge of their life because the addict/victim can only wait (and complain) until the other person does something.

Imagine this: A courier, dressed in elegant, formal evening attire, knocks at your door and delivers a large parchment envelope decorated with flourishes and

---

[86] There's common sense required here. I'm not referring to bona fide hostages of crime and terrorism, or to children who are abused. Yes, the perpetrators have to be held accountable; but once children become adults, and once hostages are freed, responsibility for healing becomes theirs alone. It's the law of spiritual healing. Right or wrong, good or bad, that's the way it is.

cherubim. Trumpeters sound a grand chorus to herald the arrival of your beautiful, expensive invitation. With surprise and anticipation, you break open the fancy wax seal. Slowly you pull out a very expensive, gold-embossed card.

> *Dear You:*
>
> *You are cordially invited to attend the celebration of Your Life. It will begin tomorrow at 6:00 P.M., at wherever you are tomorrow at 6:00 P.M. Please dress in layers and bring an umbrella because it might or might not rain (on anyone). You are advised to pack a lunch, and do what you want to enjoy yourself, because Life lasts a long time. If, however, you've started celebrating Your Life without receiving this invitation, you're having a good time already and life won't last long enough.*
>
> *We would like you to know, that we know, that you're sorry for the delay in our getting this invitation to you, but there are so many people who wait for us to invite them to celebrate life that we're rather behind schedule.*
>
> *Be advised: You only have this one life to live, and if you won't live your life for yourself, you'll end up living your life for someone else.*
>
> *Sincerely,*
> *An Unnamed Deity,*
> *Asst. to the Co-chair of The Invitation-To-Life and Spiritual Oversight Committee.*
> *- RSVP not required –*
> *(Dictated/not read; per AUD/mgp)*

No one gets this invitation. Your own invitation to live was actually the ritual of your creation. "You" are in this Life by way of *You*, and no one else. Nothing will ever arrive in the mail inviting you to be happy or to make something of yourself. You'll not be getting permission from anyone to do anything with your life. You'll not be getting a certificate of exemption from calamity. Your birth was your invitation to get the life *you* want. Maybe your caregivers didn't tell you that, but that's the fact. No one will ever give you permission; you just jump into Life and elbow out your own space. Joseph Campbell, the expert on mythology, once said that Life was like a big free-for-all: It isn't a private fight; anyone can join in.[87]

I was giving a lecture once and I expressed a contrary opinion—not rude or mean, just contrary and uncommon. A man became *very* indignant, rose to his feet, and said loudly in front of 200 people: "How dare you say that! What gives you the right to say that?" I answered, "Me." He stalked out of the lecture hall in high dudgeon, deeply believing that I had no right to espouse a value that, by *his* standards, offended his sensibilities, unless I was given permission to have my opinion by some outside authority that he approved of, like a priest or the prime minister.

He did not understand that I am the highest authority there is for my life; as is he, for his. I don't need an invitation, nor do I need permission, to be Me. I was born and my inherent birthright is to be Me. Granted, my responsibility is to clean up

---

[87] *Joseph Campbell & The Power of Myth, with Bill Moyers*, PBS TV, Apostrophe S. Productions, Inc., Public Affairs Television, Inc., 1988.

the messes in my life (regardless of who created them) but only so that I can get on with the job of being Me, because, after all, being me is my job. And while being Me, I must take care to not infringe on the rights of others to be Them.

If you happen to be standing on the spot marked "X" exactly where the plane crashes, you will never get a telegram or an email that reads:

Dear You:
We decided it's your turn. Good luck with the plane.
Sincerely,
The Calamity Gods,
Ad-hoc Crisis-Distribution
Sub-Committee, #55
(12 for; 1 against; 2 abstentions. Carried by majority.)

Calamity is random; therefore, since no one is really to blame, the responsibility for your life remains with you. Becoming who you want yourself to be is only available as the result of your choosing to live with loyalty to the code of complete personal responsibility. You cannot be what you want to be if someone else is responsible for the circumstances in your life. Be completely responsible (for yourself) and obedient (to the five spiritual principles) if you wish to be recovered and fulfilled; if you are not both, then you are neither.[88]

Your attitudes and biases, which are simply the events of your life filtered through your ego; and your commitment to (or rejection of) personal responsibility, are the magnets that attract or disarm the calamity in your life. That's why trouble gravitates towards you, and this is especially true in personal relationships.[89] I remember this anecdote from a book I enjoyed: A woman was complaining about the men in her life. "There's no nice guys left, They're all irresponsible, poor prospects for long-term, fulfilling relationships, and just generally jerks." Her therapist observed that it appeared that there were some nice, dependable men available, but the woman gave only the poor prospects her phone number.[90]

It isn't that *all* men or *all* women are poor prospects for fulfilling partnerships. It's about people behaving in ways that repeatedly invite only the irresponsible (angry, dishonest, addicted...) types of people into their life. This behavior is always rooted in irresponsibility, a disrespectful self-concept, and fear. It's a matter of long-term therapy and hard work to learn how they set this up themselves, and how they stop it, without blaming their neighbors, their parents, some ex-spouse, or the dog that lives down the lane. (It is very complicated.)

In the mind of a practicing alcoholic/addict, "looking after oneself" means getting away with things and not getting caught. Should addicts enter recovery and

---

[88] Being abused is a valid reason for a sad and painful childhood. It's a poor excuse for an unfulfilled life. Also see: *Blues ain't nothing but a good soul feeling bad.* Sheldon Kopp, Simon & Schuster, 1992, the entries for Jan. 12 and July 15.
[89] I will discuss this in *Facets of Personal Transformation.*
[90] *A Return To Love*, Marianne Williamson, HarperCollins, 1992.

continue to believe this, they neglect their true needs and all of their energy goes into maintaining the "game" of hiding and misleading—Impression Management.

Emotional self-care requires always gently offering and advocating for truth, responsibility, and respect.[91] There's a certain hypocrisy about insisting that others treat you with respect when you keep putting yourself in disrespectful situations, or secretly think disrespectful and abusive things about yourself or others.

What makes you continuously invite dishonest, disrespectful people into your life? The key is to unravel and challenge your own abuse and neglect of yourself and to develop inner integrity. Accomplishing this isn't done by controlling others so they treat you with respect; it's done by being aware and negotiating yourself out of your own internal, self-abusive, self-neglecting ego-scripts. It's gently "moving on" when people don't care enough about themselves, or others, to respect your commitment to spiritual values. Responsibility *always* begins and ends with you.

Once in a while we are innocent and happen to be standing on the corner exactly where the plane crashes, but the large majority of times, people attract the calamity in their lives into their lives. In this culture, being responsible is a lonely prospect. Think carefully about this truth: It is a sign of spiritual health that you consistently and gracefully choose loneliness over conflict and chaos.[92]

Focus your effort on not abusing yourself in your own mind. Don't associate with dangerous, disrespectful, abusive people. If you do, you're putting yourself in emotionally or physically dangerous situations. Decide that anger won't be a part of your own day-to-day life.[93] You will sometimes feel angry, which is only being the human that you are, but your decision will require that you take complete responsibility for it. [Recognize that the consequences of anger are far-reaching.]

Decide that people who are irresponsible about anger will not be personally close to you. Period. No exceptions. Decide that people who are irresponsible, violent, or dishonest (aggressive sports fans, racists, sexists; people who blame, gossip, or lie and cheat) will not be in your intimate/personal life. They can do those things anywhere other people will let them, but you won't subject yourself to this. Period. No exceptions. Quietly rearrange the circumstances in your life to exclude them and that behavior. Make no demands on them.

The more you are *completely* responsible for your feelings and your life—regardless of the circumstance—the less time you will spend in "negative" emotions.[94] You will experience more and greater joy, and the more graceful your self-care will become. Invariably this is true, but members of the International Association of Petulant Victims don't believe me.

---

[91] Some people, under the guise of "working their program", use honesty as an excuse for meanness and belligerence.

[92] Over the course of several gigs a few years ago, a fellow musician and I discussed lifestyles. I offered that I didn't drink or smoke, was a vegetarian, and didn't participate in sports, racist or sexist jokes, etc., *and* that I made a noticeable effort to be spiritual. With a wry smile, he admitted he had a similar lifestyle and commented: "No wonder we're single, we've priced ourselves out of the market." In this culture working towards spiritual integrity has a significant price tag attached to it. What are you willing to pay?

[93] Firmly deciding to live without anger, and being willing to pay the price for that, regardless of the cost, *before the fact,* is one fundamental prerequisite to a serene life.

I was once asked: "What happens if it's your roommate who's angry and throws things or kicks holes in the wall?" The person who asked this was obviously upset by their roommate's anger. I asked how long it had been going on and was told that the behavior had been continuous for over a year. I offered them this:

"What is it inside *you* that believes you must subject yourself to that angry behavior? You put yourself in that situation. Many people, and right now you, claim to desire a peaceful life. You make splendid speeches that you're sick of conflict, rage, anger, and meanness. You've probably talked with your roommate about this, maybe given meaningless ultimatums, complained to friends, and solicited sympathy. Yet you're still living with this person. You're *choosing* to live in conflict and fear, and complaining about it to anyone who'll listen. You're making your roommate responsible for the lack of safety in your life, which is irresponsible on your part. You must make your life safe: no one else can. In spite of your pretty spiritual speeches that you desire peace in your life, you really don't because you are allowing anger and abuse to enter it. You (your ego) obviously needs the conflict, which justifies your complaining, and makes you appear innocent and superior. You avoid the fear, criticism, and loneliness that comes with being responsible.

"Think about this: 'It's not acceptable behavior.' Do I mean your roommate's behavior of irresponsible anger is not acceptable, or *your* behavior of passively sitting in the rage and abuse and complaining about it is not acceptable?

"I mean both. But right now, more importantly, I mean it is not acceptable that you voluntarily and willingly subject yourself to aggression, and then do nothing but complain about it. When you [eventually] learn how to properly self-care, and quietly insist on respect from others—even at the cost of being lonely, socially unpopular, poor, criticized for being too demanding, or rejected by your peers because they think you are a snob—then you will immediately leave this roommate and begin to stop attracting calamity and misadventure into your life."

How many times have you secretly thought: "Here I go again with another crazy relationship." So you change meetings, change jobs, and pick new partners with a different body type, different hobbies, different education, and, "Oh my goodness, the same personality. Here I go again!" How do you keep attracting these crazy relationships, one after the other; the same arguments, again and again? It's because you are unaware of, and unwilling to challenge, the subtle *self*-abusing nature of your personality. You are *un*willing to work hard, to face loneliness and pain, to take responsibility, so your ego chooses conflict because in being a victim and being in disharmony and failure, there's always someone (else) to blame.[95]

It's always very rewarding for clients when, after *long* periods of therapy and struggle, they finally announce that life is peaceful, and I ask, "What happened?" Their answer is always some variation of: "I met an angry (dishonest, rude, mean) person and they asked me out and I said no. I may be alone, and now I have to do

---

[94] From one perspective: There is no such thing as positive or negative emotion.
[95] I will discuss this at some length in *Facets of Personal Transformation*.

everything by myself, but I'm happy." There it is—all taken care of by sensing when to say no and firmly saying it. Become responsible to the spiritual principle of self-care, and obedient to your declared value of inner peace, in spite of solitude, poverty, or being labeled unpopular, unforgiving, arrogant, or a snob.

Oversimplification Never Works

One of the horrendous problems that we have with many self-help/twelve-step groups and counsellors, is that healing from addictions (becoming spiritual), is oversimplified.[96] How many people have read a self-help book and actually done any sincere, noticeable, long-term self-helping? This is exceptionally rare. They read two chapters, skim the rest, and their good intentions fade away. Many people do, however, skim a book and then play junior-therapist by pushing it onto others whom they think it would really help.

One of the disservices people do to themselves is to go through a long history of reading self-help books without the wherewithal to do anything but read them. People spend thousands of dollars hunting for expedient solutions. The journey of exiting all addictions and becoming Spiritual is the most complicated process that I have ever read about, studied, or participated in. For the most part, in the first decade of spiritual transformation, egos don't self-modify, they self-justify. There's nothing more complicated than trying to restructure your ego and become Spiritual— not eliminate or reduce your ego, but to actually restructure it.[97]

Alcoholics Anonymous is not a self-help book, and neither is this one. You're on a journey with other people, are encouraged to be with like-minded individuals, and you're encouraged to assist others. There's nothing "self-help" about it. To be successful, you have to be spiritually motivated, but that's not self-help, either. The thing about personal transformation is you can't do it alone. It is spiritually untenable for an addict to insist that self-help is the solution.

People with "socially approved" addictions like relationships, work, religion, twelve-step groups, exercise, and self-help books, participate in community in a superficial and addicted way. The *Alcoholics Anonymous*' instructions are intended to develop spiritual integrity and to reintegrate addicts and alcoholics in community, but in a spiritual way. Sadly enough, in recent years, twelve-step groups have lost that focus.

There's so much talk about treatment centers, and so many self-help books being pushed on everyone (as substitutes for hard work and devotion), that God and Spirituality are hardly visible.[98] For the most part, twelve-step programs have be-

---

[96] For an accurate and considered approach to the complicated nature of codependence, read Dr. Charles Whitfield's book *Codependence, Healing the Human Condition*, Health Communications, Inc., 1991; and Anne Wilson Schaef's book, *Escape From Intimacy*, Harper Collins, 1990.

[97] Any therapy or spiritual discipline that attempts to reduce or eliminate your ego may sound good but is generally ineffective. Becoming humble is not an exercise in ego reduction. Humility is *not* an absence of ego. In fact, only someone with a strong definition of self—with strong ego boundaries—can be sincerely humble or spiritual. This is expanded upon in Chapter 9 and Appendix IV.

[98] The larger the group of people, the less probable is the presence of God. In very large groups, the conscious presence of God almost vanishes. *Huxley and God, Essays,* by Aldous Huxley, edited by Jacqueline Hazard Bridgeman, Harper Collins, 1992, p. 123.

come social clubs, with entrenched pecking orders, that focus on dances, anniversary parties, and cake. Any excuse is given for a party—one-day chips, thirty-day chips, sixty days, ninety days, this birthday, that anniversary, Christmas, golf parties, summer parties, barbecues, camping parties, ball games, and bowling. Any excuse is given for a party—just as it was in their addictions. Now they're showing off, unspiritual, and sober, which isn't emotionally much different from showing off, unspiritual, and drunk. From my reading and personal experience, the original twelve-step community was devoted to two things and little else mattered: to support each other in sobriety, and to work at becoming spiritual.

———

Talk about family of origin from an unregenerate addict invariably includes some subtle blaming of someone else for the suffering in their life. I have often attended abstinence-related support groups where people talk at length about family of origin and childhood trauma, and don't mention addictions, a higher power, or abstinence at all. They speak of themselves as Victims of Life and their story is The Grand Journey of Suffering. These people are angry, lost, and in desperate need of spiritual sponsorship and well-conducted therapy.

Family histories and detailed recollections of childhood trauma are sometimes, but not always, valuable in a well-conducted therapeutic process. These have very little value in authentic, spiritual twelve-step work. When the original literature advises alcoholics to talk in a general way about *"what we used to be like, what happened, and what we are like now,"*[99] they are referring to:

> a) *"what we used to be like"* (not what anyone else was like, and not what *it* was like): i.e. during the period of using, drinking, and acting out; the insanity, unmanageability, and early abstinence,
> b) *"what happened"*: the circumstances that caused a shift out of addictions and to desire a better life: the transition from acting out to abstinence, and the various recovery experiences that pushed them deeper into spirituality; and,
> c) *"what we are like now"* (not what anyone else is like, and not what *it* is like): i.e. your relationship with a higher power, any inner transformation struggles, and your successes or failures at responding spiritually to the circumstances of life.

For a twelve-step spiritual pilgrim to belabor, to mention, or to describe at all, the sins and misdemeanors of *any*one, including family of origin, isn't forgiving, charitable, kind, responsible, or spiritual. *Alcoholics Anonymous* advises and teaches you to live humbly in a community of like-minded souls, who are [hopefully] only interested in three things: maintaining abstinence, developing a relationship through the steps with a higher power, and carrying this specific message to interested others.

---

[99] *Alcoholics Anonymous*, p. 58.

I am aware of a debate between a newcomer and someone who'd been around for many years. The old-timer would ask: "Did you say your prayers?"

"No," the newcomer would answer.

The old-timer would smile gently and say, "Well, you're probably going to get drunk, and you'll stay miserable."

"Well, I don't want to get drunk," countered the newcomer.

"Then say your prayers," was the old-timer's considered reply.

Days later, the old-timer would ask: "Did you say your prayers?"

"No, not really."

"Well, you're probably going to get drunk."

"I don't want to get drunk," the newcomer would say.

The old-timer would say, "Well, then, say your prayers."

And again, the newcomer would say, "But I don't want to say my prayers."

The old-timer said, "If you don't work at saying your prayers, you're probably going to get drunk. Regardless of this, you're taking an awful chance, and you'll stay miserable, too."

The newcomer finally said: "You keep telling me I've got to say my prayers or I'm going to get drunk or be miserable. I don't want to pray, and I don't want to be miserable *or* get drunk. Aren't there any other options?"

The old-timer's answer was: "If you're an alcoholic, no, there aren't." He wasn't invested in the success or failure of the newcomer's life. He was only interested in honestly carrying the spiritual message in a gentle way, and then leaving the choice to the newcomer.

To become sane and rid yourself of addictions—living in serenity—leaves you with one very limited option: get spiritual. Unregenerate egos cherish the promises of easier, other "solutions" that [are supposed to] happen between the covers of books like "Finding God Without Emotional Sweat," or "Vitamins, Pets, and Personal Grooming: The Undiscovered Solution to Addictions," or "Heal Your Life Between TV Commercials." As far as I know, these aren't books, and if these are books, they're misleading. These titles are as alluring as they are empty and dangerous. There are no easy or quick solutions.

Becoming spiritual, at the outset of your transformation, is the most challenging work you will ever undertake. Provoke and challenge yourself, not others, into thinking differently, and hopefully you will abandon some of your old ideas and [then] be closer to a spiritual life.

Pity, Self-Pity, and Suffering

People are very often told, when feeling sad or hurt, that they are feeling sorry for themselves—it's just self-pity. They're instructed to get over it, or to smarten up and get off the pity pot. These instructions are evidence of disrespect and intolerance, and nothing more than a belligerent demand they must change.

Anyone in any twelve-step program has "unresolved issues" (whatever that means). It's not a perfect world, and quite probably *every*one has unresolved pain and sadness from the past, but not everyone is an addict. Unmet needs and trauma are not the reasons for your addiction, but they are a complicating factor.

Once addicts have remained abstinent for any noticeable period beyond a few months, they often feel quite sad (or lonely and hurt) at the tremendous losses and damage they inflicted on themselves in their addictions. Years and years of buried sadness and hurt are now available to be felt. Mixed in with this will be all the unaddressed historical issues. This sadness isn't self-pity.

In my experience, very few people, including many counselors, know how to wisely ask where it hurts, and know how to help sort out "pain". Is it pain from childhood? Is it minimized or exaggerated? Is it pain (and shame) from acting out? What acting-out pain is exacerbated by cross-over pain from childhood? Is it pain and sadness from the realization of opportunities lost in self-destructive behavior? What acting-out pain is fused by shame to historical issues? How clear can the experience of pain be after years of self-destruction and foggy, overlapping memories? When and how do you offer empathy? How do you facilitate resolution, without co-dependence, rescuing, or entrenching a victim ego posture? How do you sort out reality from illusion, and authentic from imagined? If there is drama, where is it, and how much is there? This is incredibly complicated.

All of this can be largely resolved—enough to sincerely enjoy Life—but there are different resolution strategies, and it takes a *long* time. Empathy doesn't resolve pain. Empathy is only part of the stage for healing, but it isn't healing. Very often, empathy and sympathy make matters worse. Accusations of being in self-pity, true or not, also make everything worse. Yes, many of us do feel sorry for ourselves part of the time, and, at times, manipulate the world to get sympathy, but self-pity isn't a given when someone is sad and lonely.

All self-pity and suffering is based on some underlying legitimate pain and sadness. Sorting out what is legitimate sadness, and what is drama and self-pity, is difficult, even for many therapists. How do you sort this out? Carefully. Consider well-conducted, *long*-term professional help. Your insecure "friends" will discourage this. Forge ahead on your own initiative. Examine how you see yourself as a victim and your belief that life isn't fair. Remain abstinent. Go very slow.

You probably often feel hurt and sad, but lack the insight and ability to articulate that clearly. This inability alone can make it sound like you are living in self-pity. Because self-styled do-gooders, and home-made "wanna-be" counselors in twelve-step programs don't know what to do with their own feelings, and your own sadness provokes something in them they must avoid, they'll tell you: "Smarten up—you're just feeling sorry for yourself."

Too many people compensate for their own discomfort and inadequacy by making someone else's sadness a bad thing. Also, some sponsors or professionals may dismiss as unnecessary, the subtle dynamics and required detailed work that I describe here. These people are actually blaming others, and making others responsible for circumstances that they, themselves, are uncomfortable with (which conceals a self-serving agenda on their part, rooted in fear and shame).

Pity is that feeling of sympathy, combined with sorrow or sadness, which is aroused by the misfortune or dire straits of another, and always contains some element of a belief that the person who is pitied can't help themselves. There's an implication that the suffering person doesn't know any better (ignorance), and/or can't escape whatever the "tragedy" is. Pity includes a cynical or patronizing attitude on the part of the beholder: the person being pitied just can't or will never get it right. Feeling pity (sorry) for someone, and telling them, often occasions a very strong reaction: "Don't you *dare* pity me." This is because of these patronizing and demeaning implications inherent in the transaction of expressing pity.

When people hurt, it's natural to try to make the pain go away. The two most common and ineffective tactics are to control or blame others, and to repeatedly talk about the pain and solicit empathy or sympathy.

An aspect of futility develops when legitimate pain is demeaned, and no relief is found over the long term. If you can't find support and empathy in response to your pain, two things happen: (i) You will develop a mindset that you're helpless, and it's hopeless; and, (ii) You will offer support and sympathy to yourself. This turns into the dynamic that is often referred to as self-pity, which evolves from ineffective efforts to resolve continuous pain.

Self-pity contains the same elements as feeling pity for someone else, but these are turned inward by you upon yourself. Self-pity originates out of authentic, original pain; develops from long-term unsuccessful attempts to heal; and is coupled with your own, erroneous view of yourself as being helpless and hopeless. Self-pity rescues yourself out of responsibility; carries an element of aggrandizing the underlying, legitimate pain; and subscribes to the belief that you are a tragic victim. [Regardless of whatever participation others may have had in your pain, it is still your responsibility to resolve self-pity without blaming others for your plight.]

Here's the key to understanding the contribution of self-pity to suffering, and how to make them both optional. Suffering is a combination of three things: (i) feeling some "legitimate" pain, fear, loss, loneliness, hurt, or distress; (ii) aggrandizing that by perceiving yourself as a victim: it's tragic; and, (iii) having an attendant perception that you are helpless and the situation is hopeless. If you're *suffering*, then attendant to the legitimate pain you are trapped in self-pity: your own sense of hopelessness that the object of pity (yourself), is incapable and helpless; having the belief and the sense that you are doomed. [These are all issues of perception.]

Here's the viciousness: Because a person trapped in self-pity believes they cannot change, they won't; and because they believe it's hopeless, they will unknowingly try to sabotage their own therapy (and are often successful).

Perceiving yourself as a victim automatically makes someone else responsible for the "healing journey" in your life. If "They" are responsible then you can't do anything about it, only they can. With a victim mentality suffering is guaranteed: "It's not *my* fault. *They* aren't doing anything to help me, and so I am helpless." That is suffering. Do you want to stop suffering? Stop blaming people for the state your life is in. Take responsibility for yourself and the suffering will immediately stop. You will be left to deal with the underlying original pain, but without suffering.

Denial and Newcomers

Denial: Within the psychobabble of twelve-step groups there is noticeable confusion between being in denial, and the defiance or belligerence that is routinely present in unspiritual addicts. Denial, the ego-defense mechanism that allows you to not remember, is not the same as belligerence or denying something.

Imagine this: You walk into the kitchen and someone is chewing something and swallowing. You see brown crumbs on their lips, brown crumbs on the counter, a cookie jar with the lid removed, and a few brown cookies in the jar. You ask this person if they are eating cookies. They mumble "No," as they swallow and shake their head vigorously. This person isn't "in denial"; they are denying. To berate them that they are in denial is inaccurate and ineffective.

Refusing to admit the obvious is not being in denial; it is denying something obvious. Being belligerent or stubborn is not necessarily representative of psychological denial. And, in the face of demeaning criticism, like being berated for being full of self-pity or in denial, people become belligerent and stubborn, and distrust becomes more deeply entrenched.

Accusing an addict, in recovery or otherwise, of being in denial is like accusing someone of having a nose. If addicts weren't in psychological denial (and they've all got some), they'd be dead or clinically insane from the overwhelming pain. The psychological state of denial is only relieved by being in a very safe environment of acceptance, and with gentle and competent therapeutic technique. It's important to be in denial *and* to come out of it gradually. Accusations of denial, akin to berating others or attacking their character, are harmful.

Newcomers: With consecutive days of abstinence, and continuous efforts to "follow the suggestions", you're a newcomer in any twelve-step program for at least five years. It doesn't matter how hard you work, how well you do the steps, how diligently you study the book, how devoted you are in prayer, or how much service work you do. The five-year rule is due to the subtle, painstaking work that must go into reorganizing how you think and how you perceive the world. Reeducating yourself regarding the incredibly complex issues (the three-dimensional spider's web), is always a long, trickle-effect transformation. Here's the catch: if you don't pursue spirituality, you'll always think and act like a newcomer, regardless of how long you've been abstinent.

Having an addiction is a state of existence. If it were purely an issue of intellect you could take a course and resolve it. However, since you're challenging deeply rooted and immaculately justified, self-defeating perceptions; *and* eliminating subtle and entrenched patterns of self-annihilation; *and* doing so in the context of overcoming spiritual dislocation in a spiritual pilgrimage (in an unspiritual culture), it takes years to cast off the cloak of "newcomer". You cannot race into recovered, so learn to enjoy the ride. You're a newcomer for at least five years.

Heliotropism & Impatient Step Work

Heliotropism is when a plant turns naturally to face sunlight. It does this without the ability to think. Within each step is the potential to access what I refer to as Spiritual Heliotropism—tan effortless turning of yourself towards Spirituality. If you're painstaking and thorough in the assigned tasks, patiently complete them in order, and seek wise spiritual counsel, you will unconsciously and gracefully sense when it's time to move to the next task. There's a natural, spiritual heliotropism in the original steps, which requires no decision from you; one that will shift your gaze to draw you deeper into yourself and closer to God.

Whenever you're struggling, delaying, fearful, or impatient with any specific step, you've missed the point. Go back at least two steps and reexamine your work. Impatience or "forced decisions", are evidence of insecurity and a misalliance of commitment (explained in Chapter 6). Being badgered by impatient sponsors or counselors, or harassed by your own insensitive ego, as in: "Hurry up, you've been around nine months and you've not finished Step One," or, "You've been here six months and you haven't done Step Three," creates problems. Anxiety, pressure (from *any* source), or impatience, always demonstrates insecurity and intolerance in the person doing the demanding; this embodies nothing Spiritual.

When you absorb the *intrinsic* nature of the step you're on, the way it's spiritually designed (not psychologically or socially designed), it will inherently draw you onward without pressure or fear, like a flower turning to face the sun. One day you will think, without planning it: "I wonder what the next step has in store for me?"—a simple and peaceful, willing desire to move on to the next step to accomplish what's required. It's very subtle, which is the nature of Spirituality. You can't smell the roses if you run through the garden. In your pilgrimage *you are your only enemy*. Spirituality is a patient, friendly discipline of devotion.

You may be concerned that you've forced yourself impatiently through the steps a few times and wonder if there's any sense in going back to Step One and starting over. Yes, there is. If you're struggling with any individual step; if you've completed any of them in a forced, impatient manner; or if you've repeated the steps a few times, and are somehow still anxious about not getting it right, you've missed the point. If you believe you have to repeat the steps over and over, or you think that you have to do any of them every year or two, you've missed the point.

What do I mean by "completing" the steps? For this to work in the manner I'm describing, you must be willing to abandon *all* your addictions and work towards Spirituality. Study *Alcoholics Anonymous* and *Twelve Steps and Twelve Traditions.* When I refer to *Alcoholics Anonymous,* I mean up to page 192 and the appendix entitled <u>Spiritual Experience</u>. The rest is personal stories. Don't take the personal stories as "the program", they're just personal points of view which you hear at meetings all the time. The two AA pamphlets I would encourage you to study are *A Member's Eye View of Alcoholics Anonymous* and *The Jack Alexander Article.*

By studying, I mean reading *each sentence* carefully, with a dictionary close by, and paper and pen for the copious notes and cross references you will make. For each sentence and paragraph, ask yourself:

- What do these words mean? (use the dictionary)
- What does the meaning imply?
- Does this relate to another part of the book? (cross-reference)
- How does this apply to me and Spirituality?
- What am I doing to avoid being obedient to this instruction?
- What must I do to incorporate these guidelines into my life?

Begin at the beginning, and *gently* incorporate the specific instructions into your personal life so that you can become Spiritual, not so you can become socially successful or mold yourself to someone else's view of the world.

The Inappropriate One-Year Rules

Two instructions that newcomers are often admonished with, that are so controlling and destructive, and are becoming so common, merit special attention. **The first inappropriate instruction** is that newcomers are told that staying out of sexual relationships for the first year is a good "recovery" thing to do.

The focus of abstinence-available programs[100] is to get clean and sober and maintain it, then through the steps, work diligently towards being Spiritual. That's the end of it. For the abstinence not-available addictions, the first priority is to establish a spiritually credible standard of bottom-line behavior. Adhere to it. Then, through the steps, work diligently towards being Spiritual. That's the end of it.

There are places in the original twelve-step literature where it tells you that anyone's sexual life, newcomer or otherwise, and their intimate relationships, are nobody's business. It advises: *"...where 'boy meets girl on A.A. campus,' and love follows, that difficulties may develop. The prospective partners need to be solid AA's... ."*[101] For people in twelve-step programs, this is a guideline, not a prohibition.

If you're interested in getting married, or by implication, dating, because that's what usually happens before marriage (although I know of several marriages, old-timers' included, that didn't noticeably include dating), the AA literature advises caution. It doesn't say not to. In the discussions on Step Four and sexuality, there is this: *"Here we find human opinions running to extremes—absurd extremes, per-*

---

[100] Remember the two categories of addictions. One is abstinence-available addictions (alcohol, drugs, tobacco, gambling), meaning those addictions that allow *complete* abstinence. The other is abstinence not-available addictions (sex, work, relationships, food, etc.), where complete abstinence is never available and you must establish an acceptable standard of "abstinence", which is interpretive and not legislated. This second category can severely limit the effectiveness of twelve-step programs because access to spirituality in the original twelve steps is designed around the ability to abstain. Which category you and your addiction fit into will significantly affect your healing work. There is no end of abuse and confusion about this in the twelve-step community.

[101] *Twelve Steps and Twelve Traditions*, p. 119.

haps,"[102] closely followed by: *"We want to stay out of this controversy. We do not want to be the arbiter of anyone's sex conduct."*[103]

There are a few advisories throughout the original literature that when carrying the message, you need to strictly adhere to your expertise—drinking or drugs or other acting out, becoming abstinent, and developing a relationship with a higher power. Have no opinions on anything else, including dating or sex. The arrogance in imposing this one-year-newcomer's no-sex rule is astonishing. In some circumstances, it may happen that someone (newcomer or otherwise), decides to be sexually abstinent on their own, and on their own behalf. That's well and good, but it's no one else's business what they do with their private life.[104]

One exception for having a sex guideline *might* be in well-conducted therapy where a therapist might make suggestions for sexual behavior. Hopefully the therapist is well-trained and thoroughly aware of the personality dynamics of the client(s). The therapeutic agenda must be very clear, and the client(s) willing. Even with all that, it's advised only after thoughtful and considered discussion.

Regarding newcomers: What's to be done with newcomers who are in long-term partnerships? If they are not supposed to be in a sexual relationship for the first year, do they have to separate? And, how many times have you heard from someone who has been sober for years: "I never should have got into that crazy relationship." Many people with longer sobriety frequently get in and out of crazy relationships. Harmony in any relationship has little to do with length of sobriety.

The idea of anyone in a twelve-step program instructing anyone else not to be in a relationship/have sex for a year is an opinion running to extremes, and irresponsibly meddling in the lives of others. This is self-righteous interference. Twelve-step people are [supposed to be] experts on abstinence and spirituality, not sexuality and dating. It's completely outside of the twelve-step mandate.

If you're interested in a newcomer's sex life, then date one; otherwise it's none of your business. In twelve-step programs, in fact anywhere: mind your own business about other people's sexuality unless you are involved in sex with them. Even then, accept your partner's sexuality as it is presented to you: enjoy it or leave. Don't try to control them. Don't gossip. Don't moralize.

If addicts and alcoholics make "poor" relationship decisions after years of abstinence, why have the one-year rule? There's the usual patronizing, sentimental reply that new people might relapse if they have sex because they're so helpless and confused (the poor things), and the sponsor has the new person's best interests at heart. The sponsor who insists on a no-sex rule has an inappropriate investment in the life of the new person. It's intrusive and abusive moralizing. The newcomer, who doesn't know the original literature, can only assume they are being advised ethically. They aren't. This rule takes advantage of the uninformed newcomer and imposes a morality that isn't freely chosen.

---

[102] *Alcoholics Anonymous*, p. 68.
[103] Ibid., p. 69.
[104] This refers to sex between consenting adults, not violence or crime.

What is it about relationships or sex that so threatens sponsors, and who really benefits from the no-sex rule? The exact reasons are particular to each situation, but here are a few general themes:

- Sexual relationships always introduce some chaos and drama into Life. When you get into a sexual relationship there may be lies, secrets, and power struggles, whether you are sober ten months or ten years. There is heartbreak and celebration, which makes life more complicated, which can also make sponsoring more difficult. The sponsor thinks: "I'm sponsoring them and they're in *another* relationship... more phone calls about heartache and conflict." For a sponsor who may be codependent, irritable, celibate, insecure, lazy, unhappy in their own relationship, or jealous, the one-year rule makes life more peaceful — for the sponsor.
- I know of situations where sponsors developed a desire for a relationship with the person they were sponsoring. They were adamant that "their" newcomer stay out of relationships because they secretly wanted a relationship with them for themselves.
- Independent of the previous point, are sponsors jealous because the newcomer is having sex and they're not? I've encountered noticeable envy in many of the advocates of the "no relationship" rule. If the sponsor isn't getting laid, nobody is. Being a petulant spoilsport isn't limited to newcomers.
- There are claims that, with this rule, there will be less chance of the newcomer's relapse into primary addiction. That's only biased opinion, and a minor point of passing comment. This is no different than saying that maybe they shouldn't drive, too. Road rage and traffic jams may prompt the newcomer to drink. Since people spend more time fighting traffic than having sex, maybe newcomers should take the bus for a year. When any twelve-step person, regardless of their sobriety, is in a relationship and relapses into their obvious addiction, someone blames the relationship, and that's *not* where responsibility lies.

The Example: Two people in a twelve-step program are dating. They quite like each other; maybe they love each other. They're relaxing one evening. One says: "I'm going to take a hot bubble bath," and goes into the bathroom. Both people are feeling romantic and aroused. A few minutes later the other person walks down the hall and stands in the doorway of the bathroom. The first person has just finished getting undressed, gets in the tub, snuggles back into the bubbles, and says hopefully: "Would you like to scrub my back?" As the other partner is getting undressed, they notice it's 7:00 o'clock, and their home groups starts at 7:30.

I've heard a thousand variations of this story a thousand times. Now ask: What priorities were brought into the relationship? It has nothing to do with whether or not they're in a relationship, or have sex, or don't have sex. How easily will either of them place their relationship commitment ahead of their spiritual commitment?

Imposing "no-sex rules" doesn't resolve the problem of not having spirituality as the priority, which has nothing to do with any external circumstance like relationships, employment, or road traffic. After attaining a few weeks of abstinence, any relapse more often identifies a problem of priorities more than anything else.

Here's a true story: A man in his early thirties was in AA and was just over a year sober. He was single, healthy, had a well-paying job, was living in a high-rise apartment building with a rooftop pool, and drove a new car. He knew his way around the city and enjoyed restaurants, clubs, and dancing. Surprise, surprise... he had a girlfriend. One weekend they had dinner out, went to a concert, then an after hours club. Later, they swam in the rooftop pool, watched the sun come up, had a light breakfast, and went to bed. Two hours later the phone rang.

"Hello?" the man answered in a sleepy voice.

It was his friendly sponsor. "Hello... I'll pick you up in a half an hour."

The man said, "I'm going to pass on the meeting. I was up all night... had this date... " Of course, he briefly told his sponsor the story, expecting his sponsor to understand. His sponsor *did* understand.

"Listen," his sponsor said, "if you don't maintain your priorities, you place your sobriety at risk. Your home group's in forty-five minutes. Do I pick you up?"

They went to the meeting. His sponsor made no negative comments about the relationship or staying up all night—it was none of his (the sponsor's) business. In fact, the sponsor was curious what the band was like (they were both musicians). The sponsor's only *brief* comment was that it seemed that the newcomer almost got his priorities backwards.

When sponsors invade the private lives of those they sponsor, or struggle for dominance in the relationship, the esteem and credibility of the sponsor and the sponsor's "program" is dependent on the success of those they sponsor. Any newcomer should be told plainly that whether or not they have sex is no one's business but their own. Sex makes for a more interesting life, but their program allows them to have a life, so: establish your priorities.

A sponsor should be spiritually stable enough (meaning they should have a strongly defined, spiritually focused agenda) to maintain the relationship based only on abstinence, the steps, and God, but that would mean tremendous work on the sponsor's part. It's far easier to make up rules for newcomers so the sponsor's own insecurities and jealousies aren't prodded awake.

Sponsors shouldn't recast their role from spiritual role-model to relationship consultant. No one is in charge of anyone else's sobriety or sexuality or life. We are each in charge of our own. What matters is the spiritual attitude and priorities that are brought into any relationship, including the sponsor-relationship. Remember that who anyone has sex with, and how often, is not your business (unless it's you). In therapy, maybe it's the therapist's business, but this is sponsorship, not therapy. If you're a counsellor who is also a sponsor, the people you sponsor are *not* your clients. If you treat them as clients and dispense psychological advice, you're in worse trouble than they are.

As a sponsor, there may be a circumstance where you decide to comment on your own relationship and sex life, details *not* included, but only to gently explain how that relates to the five spiritual principles. Role-model devotion to the quest for Spirituality, instill a respect for the priorities, and mind your own business.

Some people in relationship-focused twelve-step programs like Sex and Love Addicts Anonymous, SAA, etc., ACOA or CODA, may question this. What if they're relationship or sex addicts? In all fairness, it isn't any different. Help them create and maintain a definition of bottom-line behavior, and then role-model spiritual principles. Apart from that, be friendly and mind your own business.[105]

A woman with a few years of sobriety was told by her sponsor: "Go ahead, get in a relationship. It won't work and you'll bring yourself lots of grief. So, go ahead, waste your time and break your own heart. Just don't drink." This attitude is arrogant and presumptuous. The sponsor was claiming to be so wise and all-seeing, and was so confident of her "authority and insight", that she believed she could patronizingly dismiss another woman's life. The sponsor didn't know how it would turn out, and made a mean-spirited assumption that any attempt to create a romantic relationship was doomed, implying that the woman she sponsored was a fool. (What does this judgment and harsh criticism say about the sponsor?)

Who really knows if any relationship will or won't work? From another point of view, relationships *always* work. Even if you argue a lot and break up, the relationship provided opportunities for love, kindness, and awareness; it gave opportunities to learn about amends, and opportunities for insight. Just because it didn't last, or because it causes pain, doesn't mean it didn't work. Every circumstance embodies the potential for learning, transformation, and love, if you approach it from the right perspective, breakups included.[106]

If someone makes a sincere effort to be abstinent, and to live by the spiritual principles contained within the steps (meaning they're following instructions), that's all a sponsor need be concerned with. Even if they aren't making a sincere effort, their private life is *still* no one else's business. As a sponsor, offer gentle comments on the overall spiritual nature of their life—their prayer and meditation, rigorous honesty, program-commitments, etc., and have no opinion on whether or not they should be in any relationship. If you, as a sponsor, disagree with their relationship or sexual lifestyle, then quietly excuse yourself from their life. Don't gossip.

Until Step Seven, no amount of cajoling or rule-making will change the fact that addicts learn the hard way. [And, until such time as they appreciate Step Seven, they will always learn the hard way.] Struggling to boss newcomers or clients around

---

[105] Notice, in that sentence, it was to help them create and maintain *a definition* of bottom-line behavior. Whether they adhere to it or not is their responsibility, not the sponsor's.
[106] The actor and author Peter Coyote once said in an interview: "Consistently reach for the most enlightened possibilities in any given situation."

by making rules and demands, with the codependent and shallow justification of helping them (which is only your own relationship addiction) is abusive meddling.[107]

Everything depends on the attitudes and priorities you bring into a relationship, and those you leave it with. And don't forget the early-recovery success stories about love (which never get any press). And don't forget that many people in programs with years of abstinence are still all screwed-up about relationships.

While in treatment centers, there's usually a "no sex" rule, especially sexual relationships with other clients. It's often an automatic discharge offense. There are reasons that range from insurance liability and possible civil suits, to keeping chaos out of the treatment environment as much as possible and keeping clients focused on their therapy. (Notice I did not say focused on their spirituality.)

Residential treatment is usually intense, short-term, and addresses psychology, not spirituality. Preventing distractions like romance and sex helps keep attention focused and reduces chaos for short-term therapy. By entering therapy in a treatment center, the client would, beforehand, knowingly agree to the guidelines of the treatment program. Therapy, and the professionals who offer it, maintain a very different mandate than any spiritual pilgrimage. This is only right.

Outside of a treatment center's rules, or in voluntary cooperation with the obvious wise counsel of a well-trained, bona fide therapist, be very cautious of anyone (friend, sponsor, counsellor, self-appointed guru), who tries to impose sexual-conduct/abstinence rules. If someone you are associated with is conducting their life in a manner that offends your sensibilities, then you should *gently* excuse yourself from their life. Don't gossip, and especially don't try to control them. Role-model spirituality and mind your own business.[108]

The second inappropriate instruction to newcomers is: Don't make any big decisions for the first year. This might be wonderful if the machinations of Life would cooperate with the rule, but Life has a tendency to do whatever it wants, regardless of the puny rules people make up to suit their convenience or cater to their insecurities. Granted, stability is important, but people must respond to the vicissitudes of Life. Choices are forced upon us. There is a major element of foolishness present when people try to live by a rule of making no big decisions because there is no way that they can trust that Life will cooperate.

People who are newly abstinent and insecure about many things are easily influenced into greater insecurity. Trying to avoid big decisions, when they have no control over what circumstances may befall them, generates anxiety. Even if nothing happens, and no big decisions have to be made, the anxiety of hoping that nothing big happens, so as to avoid the possibility of making a big decision, makes abstinence more difficult than it needs to be. There is the additional concern of being

---

[107] *"If he is not interested in your solution... you may have to drop him until he changes his mind,"* and *"We find it a waste of time to keep chasing a man who cannot or will not work with you."* Alcoholics Anonymous, pp. 95 and 96 respectively.

[108] This is not about sexual abuse, pedophilia, or other conduct that may be illegal. I intend that these observations be about adults in the normal course of their life.

forced to make a big decision and possibly incurring the disapproval of their sponsor. Besides that, isn't it more appropriate to instill confidence that with faith in a higher power, and commitment to abstinence, you can negotiate through anything?

Assuming that making no big decisions for a year is a rule that you agree to, and some major choice is then thrust upon you by life's circumstances, you will face indecision when responding to the choices that you have to make. In other words, in addition to Life forcing you to make a big decision, you now have to contend with whatever guilt accrues from breaking the "no big decisions" rule.

Life forces choices on people. When you are required to make decisions in response to the vicissitudes of life, the decision is immediately more difficult when you think you aren't supposed to make decisions. You will want to avoid the decision (thereby being irresponsible), because of an arbitrary rule that's impossible to uphold. Addicts spend much of their addicted life avoiding responsibility. It's hard enough making big decisions without some intrusive, arbitrary rule that complicates an already difficult situation. And, besides that, forcing yourself to avoid important decisions to please someone else may cheat you out of fulfilling opportunities in your own life; and *again* besides that: Who decides what decisions are big? Usually the sponsor (or counsellor), but how qualified are they to decide on your life?

Two "big" decisions, if they can be called that, are staying abstinent and finding a higher power. Abstinence and pursuing spirituality are what enable addicts and alcoholics to make big decisions and wiser choices—about everything. Deciding to be abstinent and spiritual, and to overthrow an entire lifestyle, are huge decisions in themselves and they're made in the first year.

If the role-models and more senior members of twelve-step programs work at being spiritual and responsible in their own lives, rather than meddling in the lives of others, we'd all be the better off for it.

The Relationship Between Abuse and Addictions

To make this easier to investigate and comprehend, I will offer two spectra. One is for family dysfunction, where the right end will represent a Mild/Subtle variety, and the left end will represent Severe/Blatant dysfunction. The second spectra will be for addictions where the right end represents Mild/Subtle evidence of addictions, and the left end, Severe/Blatant. This is not intended to minimize or aggrandize anything or insult anyone. It's to make a general observation about families and addictions.

1: Spectrum of Family Dysfunction

Severe / Blatant	Mild / Subtle
overt sexual abuse	no sexual abuse
repetitive or severe violence	minimal or no violence
cruel, shaming atmosphere	somewhat accepting
isolation, poverty, hunger	social life, no deprivation
crime	generally law-abiding
no support or caregiver attention	some support and attention

2: *Spectrum of Addictions*

Severe / Blatant	*Mild / Subtle*
crime, unemployment	*generally law-abiding*
sexual promiscuity	*minimal or no sexual acting out*
no family, homeless	*have family and/or home life*
chronic diseases	*"generally" healthy, employed*
destitute, poverty	*have lifestyle/disposable income*
significant instability	*reasonably stable*
chronic, visible acting out	*less obvious, subtle acting out*

Putting these two side by side would leave you with a diagram similar to this:

1: *Family Dysfunction*

Severe / Blatant	*Mild / Subtle*

Severe / Blatant	*Mild / Subtle*

2: *Addictions*

Consider each spectrum separately and estimate the overall, general state of your life in terms of (1) your childhood and then (2) your addiction. Mark where your life fits on each spectrum, and then join the dots. Find several other people who are getting recovered and ask them where they would place themselves on each spectrum. Join the dots for their choices. After several people have chosen for themselves, you will end up with a crisscrossing web of lines.

Family Dysfunction

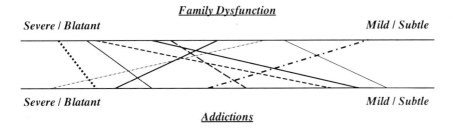

People with mildly dysfunctional families ended up on the severe end of the addictions spectrum, and others with severe family dysfunction ended up with "milder" addictions (or possibly none at all). You will find that being severe on one spectrum does not guarantee that you will be severe on the other.

Within a family, siblings that were exposed to similar parenting may not develop similar personality issues. The appearance or virulence of an addiction cannot be reliably predicted in relation to family issues. Yes, on a balance of possibilities, being from the severe end of "family" may tend to put you on the severe end of "addictions", but that is not to be depended upon. Do *not* buy into the myth that because you had a horrible childhood, you must be a severe addict; or that because you had a pretty decent family, you are less entitled to be an addict or to have a virulent addiction.

Multiple Variables and One Phenomenon

Genetics is the base out of which you were created. As a child, your family crucible molds your personality further.[109] These set the stage for your own perceptions of whatever happens in your life. Your personality (ego) is created in the crucible of genetics, physiology, infancy, temperament, childhood, and multiple cultural variables, and is then profoundly altered by addictions (one phenomenon). As an unspiritual addict in sobriety, you will continue to choose some particular world view that is always a subtle variation of the view your genetics, your family, and your addiction gave you.

Children have caretakers and adults who provide for them: efficient, loving, or otherwise. No origin-story is perfect, but some are better than others. You can go into any book store and find dozens of books on "inner child", addictions, spirituality, healing, and meditating, each with varying degrees of credibility. You'd be very hard-pressed to find one book on ego that is for the layperson and relatively easy to understand. In short: Your personality is your ego in action.[110]

Egos are amazing things. They can make you completely responsible for everything that's gone wrong in your life and, a moment later, blame someone else for exactly the same things. Outside of the phenomenon of addictions, the real problem is that your ego is brilliant at externalizing responsibility onto everything except itself. To many, this seems an almost mystifying paradox, but it is understandable. You can reorganize your ego to take the heat off of yourself, but more importantly, off of whomever else you happen to be blaming.

Siblings sometimes have remarkably different views of their parents and often develop remarkably different "issues". And, sometimes people from rather dislocated families develop very few "issues". Family and personal history is what it is: factual, and subject to personal interpretation, and always has (often) unpredictable consequences.

Your own personal world view, your physiology, your personality, and various other factors like culture, educational experiences, and random calamity, will altogether decide where you end up on the addictions spectrum, but these do not put you on the spectrum. Being an alcoholic or an addict of any description does not depend on whether you were beaten, abused, neglected, or abandoned. There is, or has been, dysfunction in everybody's life. Your acting-out rituals are too easily classified (read: dismissed) as a metaphor for various and unresolved dynamics of rebellion and abuse. Realize that many people with addictions were raised in pretty decent families. There may have been subtle emotional repression, irresponsibility, codependence, deceit, depression, unhealthy religious affiliation, manipulation, or

---

[109] This will be discussed in *Facets of Personal Transformation*. I refer you again to Gabor Mate's book *Scattered Minds*, cited at p.27.
[110] See Appendix IV.

covert power struggles. Whatever degree of family corruption existed, it often shows up in the children, but not all of them, and not always. And certainly, it's only the "flagrant abuse and horrible addictions" that get press coverage.

With all of the exceptions to the "dysfunctional family therefore I'm an addict" theory, none of the factors noted in the previous paragraph will explain why any particular individual ends up with an addiction. The factors may only influence where a person fits on the spectrum of addictions. It *is* possible to achieve some understanding of the relationship between all these factors, but only in long-term, in-depth therapy, with a therapist who authentically understands addictions, therapy, *and* spirituality, and is themselves either recovered or not addicted, and meets the other criteria for cross-over work that I described earlier.

Regardless of the countless variables in genetics, family systems, and cultural mores, addictions will sometimes appear where we predict they will, and sometimes they appear unexpectedly. The reverse is often true as well. Furthermore, addictions are often virulent when we expect they shouldn't be, and not virulent when they're supposed to be, and again, vice versa. There is a decided phenomenon-factor (which I examine later) in the appearance of an addiction.

Family dynamics, personality, and lifestyle are not reliable predictors of an addiction, nor of its possible virulence. Some people get addictions and some don't. It's unpredictable as to whether addicts can find spirituality and recover, and many transplant themselves into a socially approved addiction and stumble through their lives lost and confused, never really knowing "why". And regardless of the apparent cause, it's always the individual's responsibility to take charge of their life. Regarding addicts, there are no victims in this self-imposed crisis.[111]

Time and again it has been shown that when you attempt to categorize an addiction from some specific sociological or psychological perspective, the result is an externalized hunt for scapegoats, and after all is said and done, the addict will maintain a Victim's perspective of Life. If you're an addict, the oftentimes confusing relationship between you and your choice of mood-altering experiences can be unraveled enough to be reasonably understood. The dynamics of that relationship, and those choices, operate within a complex paradigm, and are a metaphor for a corrupt relationship pattern within yourself, related to your spiritual nature.

The only thing that appears to be consistent among addicts is some long-standing, deep-seated, spiritual corruption. This is why religion, new-age workshop-awareness groups (and the like), and twelve-step participation, are very appealing acting-out rituals. They provide a socially approved avenue to self-righteous behavior (sanctioned arrogance), and the illusion of health.

Craving

Dr. Silkworth observes that craving may be the manifestation of an allergy,[112] and that a medical perspective of "allergy" may account for the unique

---

[111] *"Hurt once, shame on you! Hurt twice, shame on me!"* from *Blues ain't nothing but a good soul feeling bad.* Sheldon Kopp, Fireside/Parkside Recovery Book, Simon & Schuster, 1992, entry for December 12.
[112] Alcoholics Anonymous, p. xxviii.

relationship between some people and the consequences of their ingesting alcohol. I'm cautious about using the word allergy; however, if you're a substance abuser, you will experience physical craving while you are using and during early abstinence. You'll also mentally obsess about your acting-out behavior, which generates a variation of craving. Resisting this is crucial. EFT can be significantly beneficial in eliminating cravings. (See Appendix II)

There are times when the "craving" isn't a craving in the classic sense of having an intense physiological desire for a substance. It may be that you're experiencing emotional pain, or dealing with unpleasant circumstances in your life, and you know from your history you could avoid this by consuming a substance or acting out. You become obsessed with making the pain go away, or making the circumstances disappear, which, after a time, will feel like a craving. This obsessing isn't necessarily a physiological craving.

Epinephrine addicts, whom we casually call adrenaline junkies, are addicted no less than other addicts. Epinephrine is the hormone secreted by the adrenal glands (near your kidneys), which is produced in response to fear or stress. It stimulates bodily changes: increased heart rate, blood pressure, and blood glucose concentration, among others. Withdrawal from a diet high in epinephrine is responsible for the craving sensation in people with excitement, anger, danger, or aggression addictions.

Relationship and sex addicts who cruise through bars or twelve-step meetings, gamblers, high-risk financial investors (sanctioned gambling), criminals, high-risk sports participants, people who binge on rage are, among other things, generating high levels of epinephrine. Usually they live with an addicted relationship to it.

Exercise addicts get three rushes. The first is from the ego-created vision of being more "desirable" (slim, muscular, curvaceous)—watch them watch them*selves* in a mirror. The second rush is from the adrenaline produced during the exercise. The third is from the binge of self-talk (either self-righteous or self-castigating), after the exercise, about the perceived success or failure of their effort. People can talk or think themselves into an adrenaline rush. Here, as with anger and religion, nothing is quite so satisfying, and so quick to conceal shame and insecurity, as a good binge of self-righteousness.

Intermittent reinforcement is another significant factor in adrenaline production—the bigger the bet, the greater the odds, the bigger the risk, the more unpredictable or sudden the surprise... the greater the rush. For illegal behaviors, the risk of getting caught is powerfully addicting. Consuming gratuitous violence and sex through films and literature (touted as art/action/drama) generates the rush, too. It's not participation in art: it's addiction. [There is valid purpose in some representations of violence or sex in art, and certainly it is in the eye of the beholder. I am *not* touting censorship. I am advocating for enlightened common sense.]

Competition creates an adrenaline rush. I recall a football advertisement that declared that fans had the opportunity to "watch a war" from the safety of their living room. "Sports fans" participate vicariously in abuse by their endorsement of dominance, violence, cruelty, and injury. From boxing, football, rugby, basketball, and hockey, through to sports car racing, tennis, golf, and the Olympics, there is the deliberate infliction of emotional or physical pain on oneself and on one's opponent.

The issue here is competition that's rooted in a dominance model of relationship; an aggressive win-lose mind-set, not physical health.

The determination to win is grasping for the opportunity to feel good (gloat) at someone else's expense. There's excitement, the possibility of grand failure, and the potential for huge success. Winning is the empty bolstering of self-worth arising from the illusion of superiority. Fans, from occasional observers through to fanatics — the degree of participation doesn't matter — are compensating for some lack in themselves by endorsing violence. [The fact that it's men who are usually injured and considered "disposable" for the sake of entertainment is entirely another matter. As women are disposable when they are unattractive or old, men are disposable when they are poor or weak. The consequences for all are horrendous.]

It's interesting how this is justified. I was told by someone that hockey, in between the fights, shaming, insults, violence, aggression, arguing, injuries, and abuse, had grace and beauty in it. The physical grace and skill somehow made the violence acceptable. This rationale requires that violence be called "competition". When I asked what he did for leisure, outside of his family chores, he replied that he watched sports as often as he could.

It's well known that in the second half of the world war c. 1939-45 (the first half was 1914-18), came many advances in technology, communications, transportation, medicine, surgery, and prosthetics. These advances don't justify the deaths of over fifty million people. Physical fitness and grace don't justify violence. In a truly spiritual life, violence is never acceptable. How is it, then, that violence and brutal competition masquerade as entertainment? Through insecurity, addictions and shame.

Notice that promoting and developing competitive skill is training people to perceive weakness in others so they can take advantage for themselves (quite un-spiritual). That's the nature of competition — taking advantage of weakness or inability. This creates the temporary illusion of superiority. On the other hand, promoting collaboration, which excludes competition, is promoting skills that perceive strengths and compatibility in others — an advantage for all.

———

All of the foregoing information regarding myths, inappropriate rules, mis-information, violence, and misapplication of the twelve-step process, may not appear to have too much to do with Step One. However, it is essential to create an aware-ness of exactly what unnecessarily complicates or prohibits your entry into a spiritual lifestyle. Have no doubt that if you don't get spiritually on track in the first two steps, there are disastrous consequences throughout the journey.

Some Important Reminders

Part of the purpose of Step One is to show you that you're leaving a state of powerlessness in order to begin your spiritual pilgrimage. The focus is to generate an insightful self-awareness about the content and context of your life when you were acting out. At the end of this chapter, the exercises I suggest regarding Step One are designed to expose the insanity (in both content and context), and the consequences, of your self-imposed crisis.[113] That's not always obvious with subtle or culturally approved addictions like relationships, work, sex, anger, and religion. It *is* obvious with the culturally disapproved of addictions like crime, illegal drugs, tobacco, and gross alcohol consumption. Aldous Huxley wrote:

> *"In most civilized communities public opinion condemns debauchery and drug addiction as being ethically wrong. And to moral disapproval is added fiscal discouragement and legal repression. Alcohol is heavily taxed, the sale of narcotics is everywhere prohibited, and certain sexual practices are treated as crimes."* [114]

The twelve-step journey must begin with you thoroughly understanding the intrinsic unmanageability attendant to your acting out. Step One is to identify your personal powerlessness so you know exactly where you're starting from. Approached with the right perspective, it instills appropriate hope that if you become obedient to "the steps" (and forego your defiance), and work *very hard*, you will change. At Step One you will come to believe in the impossibility of becoming sane while you are in any addiction. It is simple and straightforward: *"We admitted we were powerless over alcohol—that our lives had become unmanageable."*[115]

Step One is not in two parts. It requires no information about family history or childhood, and only calls you to account for your addictions. Should someone expect you to provide details of your childhood and family as part of Step One, quietly inquire about the reasons for that. It isn't what's prescribed in the original twelve-step literature; however, question them respectfully because with professionals who are experienced and properly trained, it can be of benefit, and it might well be in your best interest to provide it. Discussing family history with twelve-step "gurus", lay counsellors, or in any twelve-step discussion group is always ill-advised.

Admit & Accept

There is a remarkable difference between admit and accept. They are not interchangeable. Beware of people who tell you that in Step One, you're supposed to admit anything other than the fact that you're powerless over alcohol (or any other acting out)—that your life is unmanageable.

In *Twelve Steps and Twelve Traditions*, the authors described acceptance of the devastating weakness (p. 21), and admission of personal powerlessness. At Step One, if there was more than that required, they would have written something other

---

[113] Over and above the Step One concerns I have written about thus far, there is this: A crucial error in the first nine steps is in examining only the content and not the context of Life that is created by the addict. Realizing the dynamics of context (how they enabled calamity before calamity ever happened, i.e. you orchestrated the divorce before you ever got married)... has more impact than rehashing the mundane content of an addict's life. It's in examining context, in the first nine steps, that addicts come to appreciate accountability and responsibility. This is especially true regarding relationships. The regeneration steps address the context of Life, the maintenance steps address the content.

[114] *Huxley and God, Essays,* by Aldous Huxley. Edited by Jacqueline Hazard Bridgeman, HarperSanFrancisco, p. 122.

[115] *Alcoholics Anonymous*, p. 59, and *Twelve Steps and Twelve Traditions*, p. 21.

than what they did. Because of the raw nature of a newcomer's defects, and the glaring symptoms of addiction, and delusion that conceals painful reality, acceptance of anything else isn't possible until the addict has gone beyond Step Six. Newcomers are only capable of becoming aware enough to admit and accept the reality of their helplessness and devastating weakness. Here's why…

The ability of anyone to "accept" something requires certain attributes of character in the person trying to be accepting. These are a willingness to be responsible, understanding that Life is neither fair nor unfair, authentic self-insight, the ability to be kind, and a noticeable presence of an egalitarian mindset. True acceptance of anything is only possible when these attributes of character are sincerely present; they're inherent in the nature of acceptance.

Newcomers are oppressed by their defects, especially irresponsibility and anger, and they live with delusion.[116] It's outside of a newcomer's ability to accept anything but the blatant, obvious truths of powerlessness and unmanageability. (Acceptance is discussed in the sections <u>Forgiveness</u>, and <u>Covenants</u>, Chapter 6.)

Here's another perspective of this: Because of the nature of addictions, addicts require spiritual assistance to address any character defect. However, spirituality can't begin to become "detectable" until Step Two, and can only become somewhat apparent beyond Step Five. When still at Step One, there isn't enough spiritual awareness or faith to have any positive impact on character defects. The very nature of acceptance requires graciousness and serenity, and an absence of belligerence. Acceptance is impossible for a newcomer to achieve for anything beyond Step One because spiritual integrity is absent, and there is too much interference from their defects of character.

A newcomer is only capable of admitting the fatal nature of the disease—an obvious truth, which is all that's required. For a sponsor or therapist to demand or expect from a new person, acceptance of anything beyond this, is a set-up for failure. When anyone tries to accomplish too much recovery too fast there is this devastating consequence: there automatically develops a sense of inadequacy in relation to completing the steps. This subtle and never articulated sense of inability to "do" Step One, because of a caregiver's unreasonable expectations, becomes the attitude that undermines all future step work.

At Step One it's okay to be angry that you're an addict or that your life is in a mess. It's acceptable to somewhat grudgingly complete Step One. Admit it cleanly, be angry if you have to be. Admit the obvious truth of powerlessness. You'll eventually be able to accept more than this, but not for quite a while.

---

[116] Many twelve-step participants who are beyond "newcomer status" are irresponsible in not more diligently eliminating their anger. Some anger, in a very few shocking situations, may be unavoidable (we are human), but even then, a spiritual person must be willing to be completely responsible for their anger and its consequences, which will be subtle and far-reaching, *and* they must ensure that it doesn't last longer than a few moments. For addicts, anger is always representative of a character defect. Beware the long list of justifications for anger, including being "helpless". Any justification for anger is a justification for abuse and will skew spiritual truths to selfish advantage. This is discussed from another perspective in The Two Step Dance (in Chapter 8).

Spirituality is Attractive

And so you may be wondering, with all the problems there are today in twelve-step groups, how is it that anyone stays abstinent at all? The sad, short answer is, most people stay clean or sober on belligerence and defiance as they act out in some socially acceptable addiction. The original twelve-step program, beyond Step One, isn't about being sober: it's about how spiritual you're willing to become. In meetings, notice the predominance of bragging about escapades, struggles about sobriety, and the absence of sincere discussion about obedience, humility, or God. You cannot be angry, dishonest, and spiritual; but you can be angry, dishonest and sober. Compared to being Spiritual, staying sober is quite easy.

Saint Augustine wrote that spirituality is not efficient.[117] It's awkward, elusive, demanding, and sometimes frightening. At times it seems contradictory. For addicts in particular, it is all of these things—and it's also very attractive.

Spirituality is opposite to anything an addict has ever experienced. The peace, confidence, harmony, composure, and serenity that are dimly perceived as available are a powerful magnet. When newcomers see spiritual principles in others—even only corrupt and faint shadows of them—they are drawn in. But for me, sadly, the metaphor is of moths crashing into bright lights at night: newcomers are drawn in and slam up against hypocrisy, myths, misrepresentations, social success equations, psychobabble, and politics. They crash into relapse and despair because of most people's shallow investment into carrying the message of Spirituality. Newcomers celebrate abstinence, but are dazed and confused about what to do next, and it's not their fault that they aren't getting it.[118]

Re-Education

Here are some words and phrases picked at random from *Twelve Steps and Twelve Traditions*: personal powerlessness, complete defeat, no self-sufficiency, bankruptcy, absolute humiliation, utter defeat, devastating weakness, and fatal progression. These describe the state of life that's attendant to acting out. By studying Step One carefully, a newcomer would develop their self-awareness, and reasonably understand and admit how those eight aspects of powerlessness governed their life, when they were in their addiction.

This is important: In Step One, *Twelve Steps and Twelve Traditions* makes no reference to love or the absence of love, or violence or the absence of violence,

---

[117] *The Confessions*, St Augustine.

[118] What are they not getting? Step Two will become the cornerstone of your life. It is therefore the most important step beyond abstinence. Up to Step Five, you are not transformed, you are made aware. Steps One to Five are insight- and awareness-oriented. This process (albeit embarrassing) is safe since self-insight and awareness are logical and can be influenced by self-will. In Steps One through Five you are simply discovering things about yourself that are already there. You deepen your awareness of yourself and gain self-knowledge. Step Six is the cornerstone of your transformation, and is therefore the most difficult. At Step Six, and thereafter, you are no longer just made aware, you are required to actually transform. All transformation is spiritually influenced, and therefore frightening because it's unpredictable. Surrendering to transformation (beginning at Step Six), leaves you entirely in a position of unknowing at the hands of Providence (a higher power). Steps Two (the most important) and Six (the most difficult) are deftly avoided because they demand so much.

between your parents. *Alcoholics Anonymous* asks you nothing about sibling rivalries and nothing about the sexuality of anyone in your family of origin. The original literature is entirely concerned with, and specifically focused on, your addictive behavior, and what that self-imposed crisis created in your life. Staying abstinent, and maintaining that focus, gives you a chance to get recovered (spiritual). Your Step One is *your* re-education, not your family's and not your friends'.

There's something interesting about education and re-education. One thing happens in education. Two things happen in *re*-education. In education, you are in a process of adding new information to your mind—putting new facts into your brain. It is simply acquiring knowledge and learning new things. In re-education, you are doing two things: adding new information and unlearning old information. You cannot be re-educated without giving up old ideas or modifying old beliefs. Becoming spiritual is always re-education, and often called a letting-go process—letting go of your judgments, letting go of your old ideas, letting go of your prejudices, letting go of your old beliefs: in short, unlearning, and at the same time that you unlearn old information you take in new information.

Many people who have achieved long-term abstinence haven't really changed. They've only learned things which supported their pet theories, and haven't *un*learned much. They cling to old beliefs, like racism or religious elitism, even in the face of overwhelming evidence that refutes their old beliefs. The added dimension of unlearning old beliefs is complicated, and takes spiritual courage. Notice a sentence in *Alcoholics Anonymous* where one of the cofounders admitted his tendency to do what was convenient, and to disregard what wasn't (p. 11).

In simple terms, the re-education process is to maintain abstinence, read and *study* the appropriate literature, and challenge your old ways and beliefs. This is the posture of spiritually committed people. How many times, in twelve-step meetings, have you seen people act exactly as they did in the bar: party hard, be dishonest, gossip, curse and swear, argue, force their opinions on others, tell racist or sexist jokes, show off, be irresponsible, be aggressive, hunt for sex, and treat people as if they are disposable? Many new people are told to not go to the bar anymore. Consider telling yourself not to bring "bar" behavior into meetings. There is a specific reference to *un*learning in *Alcoholics Anonymous*: "*Some of us have tried to hold on to our old ideas and the result was nil until we let go absolutely.*"[119]

The process of Step One gets you involved in a community that is supposed to allow you to spiritually re-educate yourself.

Recurring Chaos: Content and Context

Unmanageable, *recurring* conflict is on the list of life-damaging consequences noted earlier. You can identify this unmanageability where you haven't achieved the reasonable, common goals of your culture: i.e. graduating high school or holding a job longer than a year by the time you're thirty are reasonable, common achievements; as are: being stable enough to get your name in the phone book, living at the same address for a year, being in a relationship for more than a few months, or saving a few thousand dollars before you're in your forties. These are "content". Never managing to accomplish these usual life goals often indicates addictions.

The themes that support any lifestyle—the paradigm of beliefs and perceptions that underlie the content—is the context. *Content* would be multiple relationships, adultery, recurring conflict, divorces; and *context* would be subconsciously defining Life as hard, People as unfair/mean, and Self not worthy of peace or love. Achieving *authentic* spiritual serenity begins with context adjustment (which begins at Step Two and is the purpose of the first nine steps), not reorganization of content (like changing spouses, jobs, or meetings).

In Recovery vs. Being Recovered

When contemplating being "in recovery" vis-à-vis "being recovered"[120], learn these equations:

- Active addiction equals increasing, permanent pain.
- Always "being in recovery" equals repetitive pain without relief.
- Becoming recovered equals very intense pain and fear at the outset, but gradually leads to true serenity.

What newcomers need to hear, what you need to convince yourself of, is that becoming recovered may be frightening or extremely painful, but the pain eventually subsides. It requires being meticulous in the completion of the first nine steps and a gradually increasing obedience to the five spiritual principles embodied in the maintenance steps. This entails a significant demand for self-discipline and a determination to confront only yourself.[121] Getting recovered may hurt more intensely at the outset, but the pain eventually goes away if you painstakingly follow the instructions.[122] With willing obedience to the original twelve steps, you will eliminate the in-recovery cycle of self-harm (entrenched inadequacy), which is much more damaging than the vicissitudes of life.[123]

---

[119] Alcoholics Anonymous, p. 58.

[120] Being recovered is discussed in detail in Chapter 7.

[121] In 1927, the American blues singer Bessie Smith (1895 - 1937) was performing for her fans in a large tent in the southern U.S. She was warned of the approach of several Ku Klux Klansmen and advised to flee. Ms. Smith left the tent but rather than flee, confronted them with threats and shaking her fist at them. The KKK people fled and she finished her concert. In becoming Spiritual, you must marshal the courage and determination to shake your fist at your own addiction. Don't shake your fist at your parents addiction or family history of addiction—only at your own. If you are truly committed to emancipation from the slavery of your addictions that's your job and your responsibility. [The anecdote about Ms. Smith is part of a larger commentary from Episode Three of the PBS film series *Jazz*, directed by Ken Burns and narrated by Keith David.]

[122] Staying "in recovery" doesn't seem to hurt because the historical experience of repetitive pain of inadequacy and failure is familiar. A new experience of pain from responsibility and commitment is more frightening, but only because it's unfamiliar.

[123] One of the reasons there is so much dislocation and mismanagement in completing the steps is people "read ahead". Reading ahead and trying to understand some step before you are there, or getting caught up in anticipating doing it before you are actually there and ready to do it, is self-defeating. The spiritual...

In Step One everything "should" begin to shift. Some addicts are emotional and others are intellectual; some are loners and others are gregarious—all are lonely. As newcomers maintain their abstinence, they will (hopefully) gently shift the focus of their personality from isolation to union, from superficiality to sincerity, from gregarious behavior to an appreciation of solitude, from emotion to intellect, and for these foregoing examples: vice versa; and in all events, from irresponsibility to responsibility. Step One is the beginning of all these things.

Multi-programming

People often see me to sort out twelve-step recovery confusion. One person was attending four different twelve-step groups (AA, NA, CODA, & SLAA), had three sponsors (AA, NA, and SLAA), saw them each once a week, saw a psychiatrist (bimonthly), a therapist (monthly), and sought counsel from a medical doctor every so often for some phantom ailment. This person's collection of self-help books numbered over one-hundred volumes, and each one was only partly read and discarded. They attended church sporadically, and occasionally sought confession and counsel with that religious official. They wanted to add me to this list of chaos, thinking that I could help them stay focused on church so they could become more spiritual. We eventually sorted it out, but it took over a year.

This type of chaos is very common, and is an unstructured, addictive cycle that uses "helpers & groups" as the mood-altering experience. This is frantic, reactionary recovery and is very self-destructive. People must exit the damaging pattern of addicted, erratic, fear-driven, frantic healing and stabilize into a coordinated effort. A scattered, multi-program approach is never successful, and entrenches an even deeper sense of shame and failure through repetitive inadequacy.[124]

How many different twelve-step programs you should attend is an individual decision. Remember that there are abstinence available and abstinence not-available addictions. For the first category, decide what your primary substance of addiction is and check out the major substance-abuse twelve-step programs. They're different and will each expect that you speak primarily about the substance that that particular program focuses on. Respect that request. Decide which one appeals to you, and participate with a view to be spiritual.

As far as actually doing the steps goes, it should be no surprise that my view is that you should use the original material (*Alcoholics Anonymous* and *Twelve Steps and Twelve Traditions*). That will give you the best chance of creating a Spiritual lifestyle. It's always wiser to go to the source material; but that's only my view. This is your quest, so embrace spirituality and not your addictions.

If you are addicted to alcohol, drugs (including prescription drugs), tobacco, or gambling—the abstinence-available addictions, you will also be a relationship addict (abstinence not available). Or if you believe that you have abstinence not-available addictions like sex, work, religion, etc., again, you will also be a relation-

---

discipline that's required for any step is only achievable and non-threatening when you have thoroughly completed all the steps that precede it.

[124] This addictive cycle will be explained in ore detail in *Facets of Personal Transformation.*

ship addict. These are more complicated addictions and formal therapy is a wise option to consider. You must decide what ethical abstinence is. It may be beneficial to attend a twelve-step program for what seems to be the most destructive addiction, always maintaining abstinence. Reflect carefully on where you will focus your energy. Don't squander or scatter your efforts. If you're locked into twelve-step/workshop/therapy/church chaos, that *in itself* is an addicted pattern. With proper balance and focus, no one ever needs to attend more than two twelve-step programs.

All addicts inherently embody corrupt and broken relationships with people. What sometimes offends people in Alanon, CODA, ACOA, and other similar programs, is that they are, in fact, addicts, working on an addiction to people: Their drug of choice is the mood-altering experience of being in a relationship with an addict. Here's a way of looking at it that may make it simpler to understand. The metaphor may sound a little outrageous, but bear with me.

You go to a doctor and report a horrible pain in your left thumb. The doctor thinks it's a very rare disease—the mysterious Left-thumb Luxation, but isn't sure. The doctor advises that there's a unique blue pill which is the *only* pill capable of curing the painful Left-thumb Luxation. The blue pill has no side effects and cures nothing else. The doctor isn't really positive that you have this rare disease, but since this blue pill is only effective for Left-thumb Luxation, and there are no side effects, it's worth taking. And if you take the pill and your thumb gets better, then you'll know what disease you had. You take the pill and your left thumb gets better.

We know that twelve-step programs are successful in treating addictions. It is the only thing they can treat. They resolve nothing else. The blue pill for addictions is a twelve-step program. If you go to Alanon or CODA (twelve-step programs, which can only treat an addiction), and get better by doing the steps, you've proven you're an addict.[125]

We're dealing with a life-threatening disease. Remember the two rules about addictions: The first rule is that people die from addictions; the second rule is that you can't change the first rule. If you don't understand these rules, your addiction may kill you, and it will seriously harm you and people who care about you.

Years ago, I was working at a treatment center and received a call from a police constable who thought I might be able to identify a body. I went to the local morgue. The body had on only a pair of torn, ragged, dirty jeans. He had no money, no identification, no socks, no underwear, no shirt, no shoes, no jewelry. When they found him in the stairwell of a sleazy hotel, he had a syringe stuck in one arm and a "graduation medallion" from the treatment center clenched in his fist. Four weeks earlier, the man had completed the treatment center's program, smiling and happy like everyone else.

---

[125] Enabling behavior, which is commonly discussed in these programs, is indicative of relationship addiction. Any person who enables an addict is also an addict. The general themes of these programs is to disengage from the person with the addiction—not rescuing and not taking responsibility for their problems. This is actually the struggle of establishing bottom-line behavior in an abstinence not-available addiction.

Step One

Doing a Step One is that process of taking the general information about addictions, described in Step One, and personalizing it, so it has intimate meaning for *you* and you alone. Step One is actually coming to believe what is written is true for you, without exception. That can only be done by personalizing it. The personalized version of Step One might be: My unmanageable-uncontrollable acting-out — how the symptoms of the disease showed up in me and my life.

Learn exactly how addictions showed up in you (*not* how they showed up in your family). Step One teaches you how your addiction made your life unmanageable—what you did to yourself to make your life more difficult (*not* what was done to you by others). The disease has to be personalized in a way that is specific to you so that you can own it. After all, it is a *self*-imposed crisis.

Remember to challenge these misperceptions and myths: (1) It's a selfish program; (2) Don't make any big decisions for the first year; (3) Being criticized and badgered eliminates denial; (4) Step One is in two parts; (5) Staying out of sexual relationships for the first year is an important recovery thing to do; (6) You're just feeling sorry for yourself; it's self-pity—get over it.

Work at understanding these truths, and take your time while doing it:

- Don't confuse an unmanageable life with a life you don't like. Not being happy, or not getting your own way are not evidence of an unmanageable life. Once you achieve regular abstinence and some measure of support (secular and spiritual), your life becomes generally manageable. It may be painful, and you may not like it, but it is manageable. If your life is still unmanageable, there's another blatant addiction to abstain from.
- It's a disease of isolation—from others and from yourself, because of the shame, fear, and pain you carry within yourself.
- Step One only requires "admitting". Demanding that newcomers accept anything beyond Step One is a set-up to undermine confidence and will further entrench a sense of inadequacy.
- *"We admitted we were powerless... "*[126] is in the past tense and it means exactly that. Once you achieve regular abstinence, and some measure of spiritual support in the process of getting recovered, you are no longer powerless. Do not justify petulance, sloth, or irresponsibility underneath claims of being powerless.
- In a twelve-step group, people who are desirous of being spiritual, and who rigorously work towards that by being obedient to the approved literature, are the safest to seek help from.
- Notice, and remind yourself: *"We of Alcoholics Anonymous, are more than one hundred men and women who have recovered..."*[127]. It's about getting recovered, not perpetual recovery.

---

[126] *Alcoholics Anonymous*, p. 59, and Twelve Steps and Twelve Traditions, p. 21.
[127] *Alcoholics Anonymous,* p. xiii; see also pp. 17, 20, 29.

- Active addiction equals permanent pain. Being forever in recovery equals repetitive pain. Getting recovered equals temporary pain.
- Getting recovered from any addiction is unconditionally dependent upon complete abstinence *or* rigidly adhering to bottom-line behavior that's representative of health (no compromises). Be abstinent.

What You Actually Do

In Step One, many things are accomplished at the same time. Start with this: Get a copy of *Twelve Steps and Twelve Traditions* and go to the beginning of <u>Step One</u>. It's the shortest of all the step chapters, which might at least indicate it's the most straightforward. On lined paper, write out in long-hand, verbatim, the entire Step One chapter from *Twelve Steps and Twelve Traditions*. Leave at least three blank lines between each of your own hand-written lines.

Now, closely following the theme and meaning of the original text, write out your own version of Step One (in a different color of ink) in your words. Carefully follow the meaning in the original text. Put another way: personalize the original Step One by writing your own experience, so that your words are different but the story is identical. What you are doing is "translating" the English used by the author(s) into English used by you.

In the example that follows, the bold italic text quotes the first lines of Step One from *Twelve Steps and Twelve Traditions* (p. 21). The plain italic text underneath uses different words someone might use to personalize Step One into their own words and story so it follows the same theme, but has a specific personal meaning.

<u>The Book:</u> ***"Who cares to admit complete defeat? Practically no one, of course. Every natural instinct cries out against the idea...***
<u>Your Words:</u> *"Who wants to say truthfully they're beaten and licked? Not me! Everything I ever believed in, every thought and idea, was to fight...*
<u>The Book:</u> ***of personal powerlessness. It is truly awful to admit that, glass in hand, we have warped our minds... "***
<u>Your Words:</u> *against being whipped and losing. I hated the truth when I admitted that with liquor and sex, I screwed up my entire life and my mind..."*

When you read both stories, they will compare in theme, but the second one will be your personal version of the original chapter. When you're done, you'll have your story and words, in sync with the theme of the original. This written Step One will embody *both* the theme of addictions in your life, and the theme of Step One in the original AA literature (context). Read and discuss your Step One story with a few trusted people in your group, individually or a few at a time. Invite them to ask you questions about it. Add information to your version that deepens your awareness of *your* disease. As you personalize Step One (without showing off), you will experience insights and the nuances of your self-imposed crisis.

Here are two more exercises that will keep you in line with what the original program requires. Again, these are about the context of your life.

- Here are five general areas of your life: i) Personal, ii) Family, iii) Work-Education, iv) Community, v) Leisure/Recreation. Identify and write out five (try for ten) examples for each area to show how you structured your life to make drinking/using drugs/acting out, easier.[128]
- List 30 people you associated with during your acting out and then, in relation to each person, identify at least five (try for ten) lies you told, and secrets you kept, about your acting out.

When you're done, you will have identified at least 25 ways you organized your life to make acting out easier, and over 150 lies and secrets so you could act out with impunity. You can also work at accomplishing these:

- Maintain your abstinence. Absolutely.
- Demand only of yourself ever-increasing honesty in *all* circumstances with *all* people.
- Don't gossip. *Ever.* Stop telling "stories" about other people.
- Begin the letting-go process: Stop doing it your way and start doing what *Alcoholics Anonymous* suggests. Work hard at doing what you're told to do in the original literature. It's obedience to, and compliance with, the instructions that gets you recovered.
- Be thorough and painstaking and patient in all aspects of your step work. Your life depends on it.
- Take complete responsibility for your addiction; it's yours and no one else's.
- Don't blame anyone for anything about your addiction. *Ever.*

The authors of *Alcoholics Anonymous* offered the world a program that is universal beyond any secular or religious boundary. It incorporates no classes or hierarchy within its membership. Gender and orientation are non-issues. All ages, religions, colors, cultures, and creeds are welcome. It challenges hypocrisy, misunderstandings, and harsh judgments about addicts and addictions and spirituality that have permeated human affairs for all time. It does all of this unobtrusively and gracefully. "The Program" minds its own business.

With your determined cooperation, it's powerful enough to break through your addictions and offer you an opportunity that's available to few, and that still fewer take meaningful advantage of. Your dues were paid, and your initiation was completed, prior to joining. Once you join you can't be denied membership. Of their own accord, without advertising or proselytizing, twelve-step programs have become international and are thriving and expanding. Alcoholics and addicts each have the opportunity to leave behind what is possibly the most puzzling, devastating, and in-

---

[128] Here's an example for Work-Education to show "structuring your Life": You may hate your job as Area Manager, but turn down a promotion because all the business travel makes it easy to have affairs.

sidious illness known to humans, and it offers us all an equal chance to be Spiritual. Remember...

You are a sexual being, in a physical body, trying to be a spiritual entity, in a human context, within a limited but unknown segment of eternity. Even without dysfunction and abuse, or addictions and a selfishly oriented ego, it's incredibly complicated.

As an addicted person getting recovered, somehow realize within yourself that simply learning and doing will not guarantee your becoming Spiritual. Knowledge and action are not the solution—in its broadest sense, God is. Be patient. Labor with devotion for many years. Live intimately with trusted loved ones. Respect the earth and all living things. Have an intimate long relationship with a mentor or therapist. And, in all of this, hold personal responsibility, truth, respect, humility, kindness, charity, and non-violence as the highest values. Labor with devotion and patience only to this end: through the maintenance steps be forever obedient to the five spiritual principles.

You will eventually cross some ubiquitous line and then sense, but only in hindsight, and only by embracing your ever-present frailties, that you are recovered. Some might then call you wise, many will resent you, and you will smile gently because, for you, it will be sufficient to quietly repose in the safety of knowing that the mysterious machinations of Providence are beautiful.

In a Zen way, remember your addiction fondly. You have been led to an opportunity that's so rarely available to addicts or alcoholics—the opportunity to influence your destiny, which was absolutely unavailable until the exact moment you forced yourself to study... Step Two.

3

Steps Two and Three: The Specific Direction

I have been asked if becoming a good person, without actually being spiritual, is sufficient to recover from addictions. Is aspiring to being Spiritual essential to being recovered?[1] In my view the answer is yes, but the explanation is complex.

First: There are people who are psychologically healthy, moral, who live a principled life, and who are atheists or agnostics. There's a notable distinction between atheist and agnostic, but regardless of that, there are non-spiritual people who are ethically principled. Excluding addictions issues and the claims of religious zealots, it is possible to be a good person and deny or be disinterested in God—a morally committed atheist.

Second: In a general way, a morally-committed non-spiritual person would demonstrate attributes similar to these: (1) respectful self-care, (2) veracity, (3) secular humility[2]; and, (4) some manner of sincere concern for community/humanity. These four, acting in concert, might be called a morally-based system of inner-personal ethics. I'm going to repeat this another way; it's important.

Should a person not believe in God, and live with (1) respect and consideration in their general attitude towards health and life, (2) honesty at all levels of interaction with others (meaning no manipulation or deceit), (3) universal equality as a governing principle; and, (4) considerate or responsible participation in community, then they would generally qualify as a non-spiritual "good" person. [Note that these are also some, but not all, of the attributes that a recovered addict/alcoholic or a spiritual person would have.[3]]

And, finally, before I leave you with a firm "yes" to the question: Is being Spiritual essential to being recovered?, there is this to consider...

The Phenomenon

A phenomenon is an occurrence or an observable event that arises and is perceptible by the senses, which is unusual, significant, and unaccountable regarding its origin, vis-à-vis scientific insight. In philosophy, a phenomenon is something that

---

[1] Recall the distinction between spiritual and Spiritual described in a footnote, pg. 20.
[2] Secular humility is the recognition of our human limitations and the honoring of the inherent value of all people—being sincerely egalitarian, and offering and receiving support in the celebrations and calamities of life. (See the first requirement of Humility at Appendix II.)
[3] A religion that has Spiritual integrity would have to embody and advocate for these virtues. I will expand on this in *Facets of Personal Transformation* in the chapters on religion and spirituality.

appears real to the mind, regardless of whether its underlying existence can be proved, or its nature understood.

Addictions don't automatically show up in everyone who was abused, neglected, exposed to family tyranny, or forced to contend with calamity. Some people with serious abuse issues don't develop addictions, and, conversely, some with fairly decent upbringings do. Addictions manifest in ways that can't be reliably co-related to trauma or environment. Childhood issues, shame, depression, etc., are not the root cause, and if they're not the cause, their resolution will not embody the solution. As regards addictions, there is a phenomenon component to their manifestation.

Research has offered various hypotheses about genetics that are interesting, but these are always inconclusive and insufficient. The vagaries in the appearance of an addiction; the varying degrees of its virulence; its duration and phasic nature; the myriad manifestations, substances, and behaviors; and, the inconsistent pattern of its onset, indicate it is unusual, significant, and unaccountable regarding its origin, vis-à-vis scientific insight (therefore a phenomenon).

Addictions have become the province of medicine. Yes, there are consequences that must be treated by doctors and therapists, but the resolution of the addiction itself isn't in the sphere of medicine, and it certainly isn't an issue of will-power or insight-psychology. Considering the ever-increasing problems with sex, greed and violence, and a parallel increase of alienation in modern culture, *and* the corresponding drastic rise in people manifesting addictions, the last twenty years of intense psychological and medical attention to addictions have done little, if anything, to curb this trend (and in the case of twelve-step programs it's decidedly made things worse). An addiction is entirely independent of medicine or psychology, and purely and entirely a phenomenon of corrupt spirituality (which is only my reframing of what's in the original twelve-step literature).

As millions can attest: An addict may be given wise and generous secular help, but it will be insufficient for recovery to prevail. Depending on science or psychology to get recovered is temporary at best. When you consider the tenacious, self-annihilating, all-pervading nature of addictions; their often mysterious appearance; the ubiquitous influence of the myriad symptoms; and the paltry influence of "will-power" or "medicine/psychology" in their resolution, then living by spiritual principles and maintaining an authentic relationship with God (of your understanding) is the only paradigm that addresses all facets of addictions, facilitates a non-harmful response to all the vicissitudes of Life, and does so without contradiction. Addictions are a phenomenon related to unexplainable, deep spiritual corruption.[4] This is crucial so it bears repeating in another way.

The strategy to resolve addiction must be so universal that it is the antithesis to *all* of these: the ubiquitous nature, the lack of predictability, the phenomenon component, all the symptoms discussed earlier, the self-annihilation, the defiance to socio-cultural influence, and the *in*ability of the addict to rely on things human. And, it must also be effective in such a way that cooperates with and allows harmony in

---

[4] In the sphere of addictions, in the process of actually getting rid of them, try as some of us might, it is difficult to deny the machinations of Providence.

all secular/worldly circumstances, and enhances Life in all its aspects (because addiction affects *all* of Life's aspects).

This requires significantly more than the limited capabilities of science and psychology, thus: psychology and medicine or being good, are insufficient to resolve an addiction. Only authentic spiritual endeavor confronts and resolves everything that an addiction entails. So, the answer to the question is yes: sincere spirituality is crucial to getting recovered. [Yes, there are many addicts who are clean and sober, but being sober only indicates sobriety, not recovery or spirituality.]

Surviving Calamity

Many people, including addicts, wonder if surviving egregious trauma or calamity is evidence of a spiritual awakening, and they often interpret this as divine preference. According to Appendix II of *Alcoholics Anonymous*, surviving danger and escaping death are not a spiritual experience, only a personality change is.

How you perceive the historical events of your life, before, during, or after any event, is a function of your ego. The theory of "divine preference" (meaning Providence has some special purpose for you, and you were kept alive to fulfill that purpose), is a very risky belief for an addict, and is fatal to humility and getting recovered. A traumatic event may be a catalyst for personal change, but simply surviving calamity is not evidence of anything but surviving calamity.

In my own life I've been in many violent and life-threatening situations. Considering my history of illness, injury, and violence, had I lived prior to 1900, I would have been long ago dead, well before reaching thirty, simply because medicine was not sophisticated enough to save me. And so it is for millions of others. Does this mean that those who survive grievous injury are divinely chosen, or simply born after 1900? Notice that as medicine becomes more sophisticated, more people survive serious illness and injury. That doesn't mean that "God" favors people in this century more than in centuries past.

If I allow my spiritual insecurity to recast the role of efficient ambulance drivers, competent doctors, and modern medicine as Divine Preference, my ego views me as having special spiritual status. If I believe that I escape trauma or death because God is doing something especially on my behalf, it's easy to believe this is because God has some special purpose for me: I am "specially chosen" over anyone who has an ordinary story, or who doesn't survive calamity.

When I respect that calamity is random (which in itself is scary enough), and that I was born in the era of "modern" medicine, I force myself to eliminate the arrogance inherent in believing I'm especially chosen. Addicts getting recovered cannot afford to participate in any belief that offers them special status with God. They may have sobriety, but they don't have Divine Privilege.

Recall that two of the symptoms of addiction are arrogance and isolation. As much as addicts may humbly claim otherwise, as soon as they believe they have divine preference, they justify a subtle arrogance. There's also isolation in believing they're closer to God than anyone who lacks a hair-raising survival story. It certainly implies a divine preference over those who don't survive, and that the "chosen" addict has privileged spiritual status—slippery ground for any mere mortal.

These beliefs are enmeshed with the arrogance of self-aggrandizement and the need to isolate from shame, which arise out of a severely skewed concept of "self". Any time any addict sets themselves up for that degree of uniqueness, they end up in serious social and spiritual trouble.

To make it a bit confusing, there's a different perspective to this I sometimes ponder. In any twelve-step program it's [supposed to be] a given that no one is more special than anyone else. This policy of equal ordinariness, although not often followed, must extend itself into the community-at-large. No one is more entitled than anyone else. No one is closer to a higher power than anyone else. It follows that because someone survives egregious trauma, they are not entitled to more respect or consideration than someone who hasn't. However, I sometimes do meditate against this conundrum: What is it about twelve-step pilgrims *collectively* that allows them the opportunity to pursue Spirituality and influence their destiny, when many millions of addicts don't? I do not know what Providence may intend regarding the entire twelve-step pilgrimage as a whole, *and* at the same time, I don't believe anything spiritually special accrues to the individual.

As an aside, as we are told through legend, the prophets God has apparently directly influenced—Jesus, Mohammed, Moses, and the other chosen few, had a very hard time with that privilege. The spiritual responsibilities that accrue to people to whom God has apparently spoken certainly appear to be more than a recovered addict can handle. Addicts can hardly handle being honest, so how can they handle being especially chosen by God? Avoid believing that you are especially chosen by, or spiritually closer to, God. Be watchful for arrogance and a need to feel special at the expense of others, and especially a need to believe that your path to God, or your own perception of God, is somehow more special than other's.

Misadventure and bounty are really quite random. All of us are no more or less safe from calamity than anyone else. This fact is very hard to appreciate, and insecure people will generate all manner of divine theory and superstition to avoid the truth of our vulnerability and helplessness. We live by geological consent. Being spiritual is a continuing exercise in humility. As much as anyone may fall short of the goal to achieve humility in both its manifestations, it is wise to adopt beliefs that keep you away from the doctrine of Privilege with the Almighty.

A Standard of Conduct

For myself: I will not allow myself to participate in any relationship, or subscribe to any belief, that is morally squalid or ethically questionable in order to gain the tenuous security of being popular or socially successful. I will not be in a relationship that embodies deliberately unspiritual behavior. I'm not willing to abandon the pursuit of Spirituality (my commitment to the five spiritual principles as they appear within the maintenance steps[5]) for a confined and suffocating "membership" in socially popular organizations and rituals. I routinely and respectfully discuss insensitive behavior directed at me, and when I'm made aware of my own, I make an effort to challenge myself. [I am not too sensitive or too honest, as I have often been accused; actually, I am not sensitive enough.]

As best I can, I make spiritual principles the basis of my relationships, and if there isn't a desire from the other person to reciprocate, I quietly move on. This very often generates insecurity in many people, and rather than examine themselves, they usually attack me. (Remember Bessie Smith and ask: "At whom must I shake my fist?" In all inner- *and* inter-personal conflict, the answer is *yourself.*)

Being Recovered

People often tell me that when they speak about being recovered at twelve-step meetings it generates insecurity in others—so much so, in fact, that at times they have been openly warned by many against trying to achieve it. This is one example of how insecure people groom newcomers so the newcomers will not challenge the insecurities of older members.

My deliberately chosen beliefs about getting recovered—and I am recovered—arise from my commitment to Spirituality as it is presented in the original literature, not from some arrogant idea I've cooked up on my own. This endears me to a few, offends many, and frequently makes me unpopular. If you examine this material closely, and begin to subscribe to the ideas that I am telling you about (which, for the most part, derive from the original twelve-step literature), you will become recovered. If you painstakingly follow the instructions in *Alcoholics Anonymous* and *Twelve Steps and Twelve Traditions*, you can't not become recovered.

"*We... are more than one hundred men and women who have recovered from a seemingly hopeless state of mind and body. To show other alcoholics pre-cisely how we have recovered is the main purpose of this book.*"[6] This statement was made in 1938 to a world that was disbelieving and suspicious about any treatment for alcoholism. At that time, it must have seemed outrageous. Considering all the debates, the psychobabble, and the ineffective treatment programs that exist today, this is still a very courageous statement, let alone in 1938 when it was first made.

In the AA literature, being recovered is specifically referred to or implied in several places. That being the case, why would anyone argue with it or caution someone against it? My answer is they are trying to conceal their own lack of faith and commitment, and to camouflage their own irresponsibility. I recall once I was remarking on something from the AA text, and someone was disagreeing with me rather intensely. I offered I was only trying to point out the instructions in the literature, and that their disagreement with me was akin to killing the messenger.

---

[5] This also includes my adherence to the rights and freedoms which I discussed in Chapter 2.

[6] *Alcoholics Anonymous*, p. xiii, emphasis theirs.

If you are participating in a twelve-step program, do exactly as you are told according to the instructions in the books *Alcoholics Anonymous* and *Twelve Steps and Twelve Traditions*. Don't add suggestions that simplify the requirements or be swayed by myth or opinion. Don't modify any requirements. When you're in turmoil, examine yourself for disobedience to the instructions, and *never* blame anyone for any feeling you have or circumstance in your life. Study and be obedient to the instructions in the AA reference texts so you can [eventually] enjoy the serenity of a spiritual life (called being recovered).

Talking in meetings about being recovered often generates insecurity in others. Nevertheless, "recovered" is in the literature and it *is* possible. In conversations, I tend to keep quiet about this, trying not to generate controversy. However, when I'm asked, and it's appropriate, I state my beliefs. I adhere to my values in the face of criticism, for if I don't, they are of no value; but I also try to not flaunt them. In Chapter 7, I discuss being recovered in detail, and argue that if you painstakingly follow instructions you can't help but be recovered when you get to the maintenance steps, or stay recovered if you painstakingly follow those instructions.

Relapse and Obedience

In order to add depth to the discussion of the dilemmas (which is next), I will first offer this bit of information about abstinence and "relapse". In the beginning, anyone who attends a twelve-step group has at least two addictions operating, and probably three. Newcomers usually only address the most destructive, obvious addiction. For example: a person smokes tobacco, is a relationship and sex addict, and has alcoholism. They attend AA, addressing the obvious alcohol addiction and become sober, and talk like that's all there is to it. They are still practicing addicts: tobacco and addicted to relationships and sex, and there's a very destructive atmosphere to their life, which they ignore and gloss over. Assume things "don't go well" and they start drinking again. The discussion is then about them "relapsing", but since they never got out of the other addictions, they aren't relapsing.[7] They're simply expanding the range of their ongoing addictive behavior. Relapse—in the usual twelve-step meaning—misrepresents the actual dynamic of what was happening during the previous period of "abstinence".

Addictions are a self-annihilating compensation for severe spiritual dislocation. New abstinence creates an horrendous inner imbalance, which is very obvious and temporarily extremely painful. Without: (a) an *internal* resource, i.e. "God", as understood by the individual, to provide the courage to persist in recovery and confront the dislocation; and (b) an all-encompassing, non-belligerent paradigm that addresses all the dynamics of addiction (a spiritual lifestyle within the maintenance steps/five spiritual principles), it's impossible to transform oneself out of addictions.

While abstinent from any blatant addiction, other ongoing addictions like relationships, sex, anger, or work, may not be enough to compensate for this new

---

[7] Once addicts are recovered (meaning *completely* free of addictions), they don't relapse because they are reasonably spiritually fit, which is the only way you can be free of addictions and safe from relapse.

abstinence-induced dislocation. When support from caregivers is wrongly focused, and spiritual effort is inadequate, what happens is a socially approved addiction and gossip/self-righteousness reestablishes some manner of ersatz inner harmony. Relapse into the blatant addiction means the associated addictions were not sufficient to compensate for the newly exposed and unaddressed spiritual dislocation. Only concerted spiritual effort will compensate for this in a healthy way. Without spiritual effort, and properly focused secular support, relapsing is inevitable.[8]

Considering how technology and cultural arrogance (fear) have so drastically changed the human condition, it's extremely difficult to establish and maintain an authentic spiritual lifestyle. Technological, modern culture is actually designed and structured to encourage greed, irresponsibility, a quick-fix mentality, and the classification of people as disposable. This perverse and vicious cultural ambiance makes it astonishingly easy for groups and sponsors to quote psychology, send people to treatment, lecture rather than role-model, and evade the all-encompassing demands of spiritual integrity. Not only must twelve-step pilgrims stand against their addictions; to be truly spiritual, they invariably have to stand against their culture. It takes tremendous courage and perseverance to actually be obedient to the instructions and to spiritual principles.

Don't delude yourself into believing that non-compliance with the original program is wise or viable. Clinging to self-reliance, and disobedience to the spiritual mandate, allows only insecure, conditional abstinence. This entails grave risk and always leaves you potentially at the mercy of any twelve-step guru/charlatan who presents a good story. Without spirituality, there's always the possibility of relapse, and abstinence depends on nothing "too big" happening to you. Since you are forever unaware of what circumstances life may present, your abstinence is conditional.

The Three Dilemmas

The essence of a dilemma is experiencing pain or anxiety when being forced to choose between alternatives with equal consequences. Being forced to choose between equally wonderful alternatives is a dilemma, just a much as alternatives that are perceived as equally painful. If you don't understand the following recovery dilemmas, and how to address them, you will always be in danger of relapsing or remaining in a conflicted spiritual condition.

Once an addict initiates the process of going from active addiction through to being recovered, they must resolve a few major dilemmas along the way. If any of these are not resolved in favor of a deepening of spirituality, regardless of the social cost, the addict immediately intensifies their confusion and will either regress from spirituality and remain in turmoil, or relapse. Living in painful dilemmas is the sad lot of those people who refuse to pursue spiritual integrity.

Active addiction means generating permanent increasing pain. Abstinence and honesty will also generate intense pain. The non-resolution of this dilemma is often evident in the short-term relapses: in for a year, out for a year; in for a month,

---

[8] Properly focused secular support would be that which is addictions-insightful, spiritually oriented, absent of expectations, non-relationship addicted, non-belligerent, and consistently dependable.

out for a month. People are creatures of ego-habit. If you are not told clearly, by people whom you sense have spiritual integrity, that the pain from abstinence and honesty is temporary, you will continue in some "relapse pattern" of addiction. Exiting this pattern is done by reorganizing your Life of abstinence from social to spiritual (new context), and learning that when you follow the instructions of getting recovered, the pain is always temporary. It may last a few years, but it is temporary.

People resolve dilemmas by challenging assumptions and acquiring new information. Newcomers trapped in dilemmas must be gently offered information on the consequence of inaction: increasing frustration/confusion that leads to substitute addictions or a renewal of their prominent addiction. When offered honest, credible information, and properly focused support, addicts most often choose to exit their dilemma towards Spirituality (the 75% success rate mentioned earlier).

In Step One, you face the painful dilemma of living with an addiction, which is terrifying at the best of times, or living with abstinence and rudimentary honesty, which also is terrifying. Talk to anyone who has been in AA anywhere between twenty minutes and six months, and you will hear (maybe not articulated clearly) that this is probably one of the more painful choices they have had to face.

Dilemma One in the Early Stages of Step One

either (a): continued acting out, addictions, drinking, drugs, death; continuing irresponsibility and insanity etc. ...	or (b): continued and increasing commitment to abstinence and honesty, and "going through" the pain.

The resolution strategy is three-fold: to acquire additional information, to self-challenge, and to unlearn old beliefs about helpless/hopeless (issues of perception) and powerless (the absence of a higher power). Choosing to resolve the first dilemma and forge ahead will soon present a second dilemma. This is created by the requirements of Step Two: *"Came to believe that a power greater than ourselves could restore us to sanity."*[9]

Dilemma Two Near the End of Step One and Step Two

either (a): stay sober, insane, angry, lonely, in danger of "relapse" into the primary addiction...	or (b): continue abstinence, incorporate increased honesty, and develop beliefs about a higher power and spirituality.

The added dimension of spirituality increases the degree of anxiety, the depth of self-examination, and the level of commitment. The resolution strategy is to acquire additional information, to self-challenge, and to re-educate yourself about God and spirituality, which is the essence of Step Two. This will soon present...

The In-Recovery or Recovered Dilemma

Contemplate carefully what follows. In the third dilemma (below), people who choose to be always in recovery have chosen to live at 3(a) and they avoid the hard work of spiritual commitment.

---

[9] *Alcoholics Anonymous*, p. 59, and *Twelve steps and Twelve Traditions*, p. 25.

Dilemma Three Near the End of Step Two and at Step Three

either (a): stay abstinent and be "in recovery"—live with repetitive inadequacy; recycle the steps; re-experience recurring doubt, and failure; sentence yourself to perpetual, repetitive labor…	or (b): commit to becoming recovered; increase spiritual faith: be *completely* responsible, and be *obedient* to Spiritual principles.

I have repeatedly witnessed an innate and almost unconscious awareness in addicts in recovery that they cannot manage recovery without spiritual assistance. They may not admit it, but they are aware of it. They also faintly know of their grossly irresponsible behavior *and* that they are somehow responsible for the chaos in their lives. Getting recovered entails bringing these faintly perceived truths to the forefront, which is an anathema to the unregenerate addict. It is so threatening that the majority of addicts in recovery address only their obvious addiction by belligerent abstinence, and remain noticeably irresponsible, choosing to live at 3(a) rather than 3(b), in Dilemma Three. (A parallel to 3[a] is The Myth of Sisyphus.)

These dilemmas force huge choices on addicts. Choosing the "a" side of the dilemmas above always results in personal stagnation, or regression into relapse. The pain of insanity and addictions will remain, and the struggle to become spiritual through the steps will seem insurmountable. The result is being perpetually "in recovery" and adopting a life built on clichés and rhetoric.

Recycling through the steps generates the following, insidious cycle of addictive behavior: You will repeatedly re-experience acting out through rhetoric and fantasy (or relapse) at Step One; revisit insecurity and distrust at Step Two; re-experience the fear of spiritual commitment at Step Three; justify insecurity and irresponsibility at Step Four; re-experience guilt and shame at Step Five; declare willingness at Step Six when in fact you're not, and be dishonest and participate in hypocrisy and politics; this fosters shallow faith and Impression Management rather than humility at Step Seven, which leads to another exercise of guilt and blaming at Step Eight, and guilt and apology at Step Nine. The Promises remain unavailable.[10] Serenity (inherent in the maintenance steps), and the potential to be Spiritual, aren't available to the perpetually in-recovery addict. Facing this cycle repeatedly, for as long as you are sober, is the consequence of being always in recovery.

Repeating the steps in the way just outlined is thematically similar to the cycle of addiction. Being forever "in recovery" is simply another example of repetitive inadequacy and failure, two of the hallmarks of an addict who is acting out. It's the posture of someone who is secretly or subconsciously unwilling to resolve their spiritual belligerence. (This means changing only content, not context.)

Living in the unappealing cycle I described two paragraphs above unconsciously generates and entrenches the belief that you never get anywhere. It guarantees you'll never experience the beatitudes of spirituality or acquire enduring faith in a higher power. Living like this is painful, but the always-in recovery addict becomes quickly inured to it because it is very similar to the dynamic of being in addiction; and without strong spiritual grounding, addicts choose the familiar pain.

---

[10] The Promises are in *Alcoholics Anonymous*, pp. 83-84, and discussed here in Chapter 6, p. 298.

The Perpetual Excuse

Irresponsibility and willfulness are ever-present in people who are always "in recovery". For every incident of insult or abuse; for every situation that shows a character defect, they always have a defense: "I'm in recovery—I'm working on it." Commitment becomes a euphemism for convenience. Being "spiritual" is rooted in Impression Management and depends on the prevailing social climate. As soon as the five spiritual principles (which are universally embodied in the maintenance steps) require the addict to be socially unpopular, make a significant effort, or jeopardize some coveted belief or prejudice, they will abandon spirituality and blame their disease, blame someone else, personalize some random calamity and pout, or hide behind dogma. Do not underestimate the insidious and ubiquitous nature of self-destructive irresponsibility in the unregenerate addict.

Being recovered does not include being cured. Because you become *"...recovered from a seemingly hopeless state of mind and body"*[11] doesn't give you license to drink or act out. You are recovered, but your recovery/spirituality depends absolutely on continued abstinence. The insane thinking, the craving, the dishonesty, the need for acting out, the manipulation are gone in that they won't exist within you anymore. But... only your sincere and continued obedience to abstinence and the maintenance steps will keep you that way.

If being recovered means having spiritual serenity in the maintenance steps, which sounds desirable, why do so many in-recovery addicts avoid it? Avoidance comes from the addict's innate knowing what being recovered implies: a global respect for self and others; an active seeking of humility; unconditional gentle honesty; willing prayer and meditation; unqualified responsibility; and very hard work. They're afraid Life won't work out in their favor if they're truly spiritual.

If you choose to view the program from the position of getting recovered—and this always depends upon obedience to the AA texts, not the personal stories—you will do Steps One to Nine once, slowly and painstakingly, and then incorporate Steps Ten, Eleven, and Twelve regularly, consistently, and sincerely in all ways, in all circumstances, with all people, regardless of the cost to yourself, and regardless of the effort required. Being responsible, in addition to the obvious spiritual connotations, would mean that:

- your anger and rage, depression, moodiness, unhappiness, frustration, selfishness, greed, petulance, dishonesty, and arrogance about anything are completely *your* responsibility;
- your being unemployed or under-employed or poor, is always *your* problem;

---

[11] *Alcoholics Anonymous*, p. xiii.

- all conflict with everyone; all your addictions both past and present; and all your failed relationships and romances, are completely *your* responsibility;[12]
- as an adult, if you see yourself as being abused or taken advantage of in any way, it is always completely *your* problem; and,
- there would be three cornerstones to your life: (i) prayer and meditation; (ii) obedience to the five spiritual principles (which are embodied in the maintenance steps); and, (iii) always holding a willingness to let go of old ideas.[13]

Subscribing to these requirements gives you a limitless potential to experience joy, and to continuously transform and enhance your secular and spiritual life. If, as an addict, you choose to become recovered, you must abide by these. The vast majority of addicts will do anything to avoid diligent spiritual work.[14] There are few truly Spiritually disciplined people. It is very difficult to convince newcomers at Step Two that, although terrifying at the outset, and certainly emotionally demanding, making these commitments eventually becomes a pleasure.

Pain-Induced Willingness

I have often been asked about the value of, or necessity for, pain-induced willingness as the motivator for personal change. Is it healthy?

Addicts initially enter into a twelve-step program because of pain. They are (or feel like they are) dying, falling completely apart, or going insane. There's very often an unstated belief that others should make the addict's pain go away by that other person changing some behavior and, other than pain relief, the addict's life won't need to change much. Addicts generally arrive in twelve-step programs as pain-filled, self-destructive neurotics (or worse), and hope that without any concerted effort on their part, they will end up pain-free. Attending a twelve-step group and being always "in recovery" (i.e. sober with shallow spirituality) is often evidence that the addict has only learned how to be a more effective neurotic.

Personally, I didn't attend my first support group because I wanted the glories of spirituality. I attended because *at that time* I thought that my wife was crazy, my boss was a jerk, and nobody liked me. I had constant nightmares, would frequently break out in cold sweats, was twenty pounds underweight, and hardly ate. I was in huge debt, owned nothing, drank every day, believed the world was generally

---

[12] This doesn't mean the other person is innocent. It means that regardless of how blameless or partially responsible you think you are, you cannot allow your ego to "investigate" the other person's share of the conflict, or to point out what they did wrong, regardless of how obvious it is. You are completely responsible because you participated. If there is one rule about relationships that is absolutely true, it's this: Each person in any committed or long-term relationship has the same capacity or incapacity, or the same ability or inability, to bring love and commitment or conflict and tension, to the relationship. Neither person is healthier or unhealthier than the other person — even though it may appear otherwise.

[13] *Alcoholics Anonymous,* How It Works, p. 58.

[14] The reason there are so few saints is that it is such hard work. *Huxley and God, The Essays,* Aldous Huxley, edited by Jacqueline Hazard Bridgeman, HarperSanFrancisco, 1992.

evil and notoriously unsympathetic to my plight, and if someone else didn't do something, I was going to die; hence pain-induced willingness.

Pain-induced willingness is "good" as the motivator of your initial participation; however, "no pain no gain", the usual cliché, is only applicable to the spiritual newcomer.[15] At a specific time later in your spiritual growth, at a point that I'll identify clearly later on, pain-induced willingness is completely unnecessary. In fact, pain-induced willingness as the motivator for change eventually becomes evidence of spiritual neglect.

It is easier to be a sober social success living insincerely than it is to be Spiritual. Bill Wilson wrote that he discarded those parts of spirituality he found less than convenient.[16] How far away you are from spirituality, or the less diligent you are about constant self-examination and spiritual responsibility, is exactly how far away you are from being recovered and how close you are to relapse.

Exiting the in-recovery cycle, described earlier, is done by thoroughly re-addressing Step Two, and changing your perception of the program. When you re-design your life as instructed—painstakingly towards spirituality, a higher power, and spiritual principles—the pain and fear of responsibility, truth, etc., regardless of its intensity, is always temporary. When you don't follow the instructions, the result is lack of faith, permanent pain and stagnation, dishonesty (which is fatal to Spirituality), and shallow manipulative behavior. These consequences are not optional—the disease dictates this.

———

My assertion that you only do Steps One to Nine once (and thereafter remain in the maintenance steps) does not imply that you must do those steps perfectly. Doing them by following the specific instructions in great detail[17], to the best of your ability, is entirely sufficient. Repeating the steps in a shallow manner demonstrates repetitive disbelief (no faith), repetitive inadequacy (I'm not smart/good enough to do them only once), and repetitive failure (I'll get them right next time). When you recycle the steps, you diminish their impact, remain subtly petulant, and have little faith. Faith is the key, but it has two aspects:

---

[15] If someone stays sober/abstinent, but with minimal spiritual effort, then "no pain no gain" will forever be the theme of personal change—an unappealing prospect at best. However, once a person goes beyond being a *spiritual* newcomer (which is very different than a program newcomer), change happens without pain. Change will actually embody the sense of joy—regardless of what the change is.

A *twelve-step* program newcomer is just that—a newcomer—for at least five years. A *spiritual* newcomer (a beginner at spiritual devotion and transformation) remains a spiritual newcomer until such time as they are *well* practiced at Step Eleven, and have at least ten years of *sincerely and continuously* living in the all maintenance steps, and have regularly sought and followed wise, bona fide spiritual guidance. It is no mean feat to go beyond the level of spiritual novice, but it is certainly worth it.

[16] *Alcoholics Anonymous*, p. 11.

[17] Four references to thoroughness from *Alcoholics Anonymous* are: "*thoroughly followed our path*," p. 58; "*if we have been thorough*," p. 70; "*painstaking*," p. 83; and "*carefully followed directions*," p. 85. There are many others.

- faith in the program and its instructions, that they are accurate, sufficient, and need not be adjusted, *and* that the results promised are not
an illusion and are attainable; and,
- faith in the unseen influence and benevolence of a higher power, and
the related belief that you will be supported both in abstinence and in
the vicissitudes and random calamities of life.

These faiths develop simultaneously and your certitude of them is directly related to
your hard work. Most people don't get that being sober is not evidence of a spiritual
life; being sober only means that you're sober.

Now that you've read this far, you may see the possibility of getting recovered, but be somewhat overwhelmed and intimidated. Approach each step—
approach getting recovered—*"with willingness, patience, and labor."*[18] You must
undermine your anxiety, and ignore social peer pressure which will demand you be
only as spiritual as the group can tolerate. When you approach the steps in this manner, there is an intrinsic sense of when you are done any one step and ready for the
next one. (We're back to spiritual heliotropism.) However, this is not revealed until
you complete the step in the manner demanded by its spiritual content.

Please Stop Jumping Around

Chapters in a book are in a certain sequence for a reason. Knowledge must
be presented so that it builds on itself; otherwise, it's chaos. Nobody can do differen-
tial equations before they understand addition. A novel has a structure. The author
had some dramatic intent in mind. You don't generally read Chapter 11 for ten minutes, read the end of Chapter 5, read Chapter 2, and then check out the first page.
You read from beginning to end, which allows the novel to deliver its dramatic impact. In school, how often were you told not to read ahead in the textbook?

Spiritual transformation happens in a ubiquitous but subtly rigid, structured
manner. I refer to this in Chapter 4, in the section There Are Laws Here. People cannot change the steps with impunity.

I offered this once to someone who was struggling with the steps. Buy
Twelve Steps and Twelve Traditions and separate it into twelve "packages" so that
each package is the writing on each individual step. Put all these packages in a
drawer someplace, and then start with Chapter 1 (Step One). Study it all by itself, for
many weeks. Look up words in a dictionary. Be thorough in completing the Step
One exercises I suggested. Understand them. Do not go chasing off into any other
step. This prevents intellectual and spiritual chaos. More importantly: (1) it stops you
from looking for an easier, softer way by jumping ahead; and, (2) it prevents your
avoiding an awkward/difficult step (like Step Two) by plunging into the drama of
Step Four. Command the philosophy and truth of each step in a focused and deliberate manner.[19]

---

[18] *Alcoholics Anonymous*, p. 163.
[19] It is worthy to note here, the different purposes of the two AA reference texts. At their essence, *Alcoholics Anonymous* is "what to do" and *Twelve Steps and Twelve Traditions* is "why to do it". The later steps,

The problems you encounter within each step are resolvable from within the step itself, with the help of what insights you've acquired, and self-discipline you've established, in the steps previous to it. Stay where you are until you are finished. Then, when you sense spiritual heliotropism (which takes a long time), read the next chapter, which would be the next step, and work at that one.

Once you have completed a step in this manner, there should be no reason to repeat it or refer back. The philosophy, the problems and their resolution, and the spiritual tasks are integrated as a part of you. (Once you command calculus, you won't periodically review addition just to make sure addition works.)

There are not enough people in twelve-step programs who see this as a spiritual apprenticeship, which is what it is. In any apprenticeship, you can't do fourth year work in the first six months. Apprentices are not allowed to attempt tasks beyond their training. We need more of this in twelve-step programs. This is an apprenticeship—you are attending Spirituality School and you should not attempt tasks that are beyond your training and faith.

Twelve-step pilgrims always increase their confusion and spiritual dislocation when they encounter a problem in any one step and hope to find the solution by leaping ahead in ascending sequence to steps they have not completed. This manifestation of fear and impatience is fatal to abiding spiritual faith. It inculcates shallow understanding, spiritual and intellectual sloth, and impatience, into an already insecure lifestyle. (The fact that they jump around means they are insecure and didn't do the steps as required.)

You also demonstrate insecurity when you jump backwards for solutions that you are supposed to have already incorporated into your spiritual lifestyle. The fact that you're jumping backwards indicates you didn't *really* get it. "Jumping around" problem solving, which avoids diligence, patience, and labor within the step that the problem manifests out of, is debilitating in the extreme.

There is No Group Experience

The original literature is written using plural pronouns, which is simply a grammatical structure for describing what each member of a group did individually. The pronouns do not imply that people sat in a group and did the steps together. It is a grammatical representation of individual journeys.

The instructions, as outlined in the first 192 pages of *Alcoholics Anonymous,*[20] and all of *Twelve Steps and Twelve Traditions,* are a spiritually revealed truth that enables addicts to become Spiritual and get recovered from addictions. The purpose for attending a study group of the literature is not to understand the literature; it is to identify the specific instructions, and then to figure out which fears prevent you

---

and especially the maintenance steps, are significantly more spiritually complex. If you don't understand the "whys" of the early steps—their spiritual intent—or haven't done that work, should you read ahead you will undermine your confidence and faith and confuse yourself.

[20] In my view, the text *Alcoholics Anonymous* is essentially limited to the first 192 pages, this being the Introduction through to page 164 and the first personal story (being Dr. Bob's) which ends at page 192, plus pp. 563-569. The other material is personal stories and anecdotal information that has little to do with the task at hand (spiritual transformation).

from doing exactly what you are told, exactly as you are told to do it. Book study groups are dangerous if you're simply accumulating knowledge, debating the wisdom of the step, or forcing yourself (or someone else) to attempt a step before you (or they) are ready.

Addiction is an inner spiritual dislocation and has similar emotional themes for everyone. As a social, external structure, it shows up differently. My own story is rather flamboyant. I ran around a lot, got in fights, and drove places at a hundred miles an hour. I drank hard, played fast, and lived with danger. Other people's addictions showed up differently. They drank less (or more), got in less (or more) trouble—but felt just as horrible about the whole thing. They viewed their addiction just as seriously life-threatening as I did mine, regardless of the fact that, at the social level, we were remarkably different.

The steps are highly personal. Doing them individually is important. Doing the steps *as a group experience* is ill-advised. The purpose of Step One is to figure out how your addiction showed up in you. It is a personal statement. That's why, when you share your experience, strength, and hope, it's important that you share a minimum of social content and personalize your self-annihilation at an emotional level. When you disclose your story quietly, at an emotional level, you can potentially reach everybody. When you aggrandize and show off, you reach no one.

What You Do and Where You Go

If you wake up in the morning and you've got a terrible, persistent stomach-ache, somebody will probably tell you to go to a doctor. If you fall down and break your leg, you'll go to a hospital. When you have an illness, there are places for you to go. That's part of the social structure in our culture.

You realize you have addictions. Many members of a twelve-step group will tell you where to go: Step One, where you learn and believe that you are sick and not crazy, and that abstinence is essential. People will then suggest solutions: go to meetings, go get a sponsor, go do service work, go read the literature. It all seems to make sense, *except...* those are what you *do*, but it's not where you *go*.

Step Two does not read, "Came to believe that having a good sponsor could restore us to sanity," or "...that doing service work could restore us to sanity." These may keep you sober, and it is what you do, but you are to go to God, as you understand God. *Where you go is to God; what you do is the steps*, which teach you how to gracefully abide by spiritual principles. Only that restores you to sanity. If you confuse "what you do" with "where you go" the results are disastrous—for you and for everyone else in your life.

Every time anyone recasts the original AA instructions, they dilute the spiritual integrity of the original message. The various myths that you are led to believe, and the deification of psychology (which is only an inadequate technology of spirituality), imply that something other than Spirituality will restore you to sanity: going to meetings, sponsorship, service work, literature, therapy. They won't. The greatest source of program chaos and misalliance arises at Step Two. If you don't get Step Two, you don't get anything except maybe abstinence/sobriety based on will-

Two, you don't get anything except maybe abstinence/sobriety based on willpower, and a social life rooted in peer pressure, politics, and Impression Management.

I have never yet met anyone who was working towards *sincere* Spirituality who relapsed. I have seen many people get drunk because they didn't go to meetings or they went to too many meetings, or they were sponsoring too many people, or they didn't have a sponsor, or they lied, or they... well, there are thousands of "reasons" for relapse. Over the long term, if you want "guaranteed" abstinence and peace of mind, become sincerely Spiritual. Dependence upon a higher power is the only solution, and believing this is the essence of Step Two. Addicts either become sincerely Spiritual or they stay sick to some noticeable degree.

This ultimatum, dictated by the phenomenon of addiction, can be threatening. Some alcoholics [addicts] will do anything to avoid getting spiritual—even relapse and die. They'll get three sponsors; they'll sponsor seventeen people; they'll go to 16 meetings a week; they'll donate until it hurts; they'll have seven good reasons for one "harmless" lie; they'll answer the phones five nights a week until four in the morning (and not complain or brag about it very much). They will do almost anything to stay sober and *appear* spiritual rather than *be* spiritual.

Disease, Clarity, Health

Self-awareness about their own addiction is not readily available to an addict. Except possibly for some mental illnesses, addiction is the only disease that has an entrenched "self-blindness" that specifically tells the addict they're not sick. This is related to the fact that an addiction is a state of existence rather than an isolated condition of health. This mind-set (self-blindness) is often suddenly fractured by a transformative moment. That moment, a type of unitive experience of insight, informs addicts that something is terribly wrong with *them* and there is [possibly] another option, both of which they were previously unaware. The trenchant and entrenched phenomenon of self-blindness is cracked enough so that clarity (sometimes later perceived as a divine intervention) pierces the addicted condition.

This sudden clarity has very decided spiritual tones to it, and is never people-induced. People can arrange secular circumstances so that the fracturing of self-blindness may happen, which is the purpose of twelve-step work—to set the stage for the second event in the chart below—but its appearance is never guaranteed. It might look like this:

First	Second	Third
The presence of an Addiction: blindness to the conditions of self-annihilation, deceit, arrogance, greed, defects, selfishness, irresponsibility, disobedience, and defiance.	An opportunity comes out of a spontaneous, insightful moment that fractures "self-blindness" and allows some insight that something is terribly wrong. A new option becomes available that heretofore didn't exist. This is sometimes referred to as a divine moment.	With diligent step-work, the awareness of sickness transforms itself into a commitment to spiritual health, i.e. devotion to spiritual principles.

Consider: (1) Providence provides the initial transformative moment; (2) the varied and inconsistent etiology, virulence, and duration of addictions; (3) the historically demonstrated success that the tenets of spirituality have in eliminating addictions; and, (4) the generally conflicted and erratically unsuccessful attempts of medicine/psychology to resolve addictions. These should altogether provide enough convincing evidence that addictions are an issue of spirituality, not science.

Alcoholics Anonymous advises that it is deep within us that the Great Reality is found.[21] This philosophy, in one form or another, has been around for about three thousand years. If your physical body and mind are corrupted, in this case by addictions, you cannot get deep within yourself to find that Great Reality.

By definition, the attributes you need to be Spiritual are the exact opposite of the symptoms that comprise active addiction. To be Spiritual in the fullest sense of the word, you have to properly care for the thing that encapsulates your soul, which is your body, and live by spiritual principles. This commitment must be in *all* of your affairs: sexuality, parenting, leisure, relationships, education, recreation, employment, career; with people you love, like, and don't like; with people you have authority over; with people who are being mean, insensitive or dishonest—literally everywhere with everyone.

Sponsors, abstinence, sponsoring, speaking at conventions, studying the texts, service work, attending meetings, sharing—these are only what you do (the avenues to the solution); they are not the solution. The solution is a relationship with a higher power. Believing this truth is what underlies Step Two.

Beliefs, Experiences, and Awakenings

This following section may seem like semantics, or it may read like a shallow effort to appear erudite. It is neither. Having clarity in the nuance of spiritual issues is crucial for the development of an abiding faith, and for the acquisition of sincere humility. I cannot overstate the importance of thoroughness in Step Two.

You may wonder about the difference between a spiritual experience, a religious experience, and a spiritual awakening. According to the literature, there isn't any difference; but, there are certainly misunderstandings about them. There are misunderstandings about the relationship between the [often] alternating sequence of having a spiritual belief and having a spiritual experience. And, you might have a religious experience without believing in anything spiritual; and you can believe in spiritual things without having a spiritual experience. Many people think they've got to find God first and then accumulate faith—it doesn't often work this way. Having a spiritual awakening without believing in a higher power is very often how spiritual transformation begins. A spiritual experience or a spiritual awakening is what usually happens before you believe in a higher power, not after.

The reason for writing the appendix Spiritual Experience[22] was that many readers got a false impression from the first edition of *Alcoholics Anonymous*. From one perspective, that appendix is an amend for being less than clear when the book

---

[21] *Alcoholics Anonymous,* p. 55.
[22] Ibid., p. 569.

was first published. The first paragraph asserts a spiritual experience, or awakening, or religious experience, *"shows that the personality change sufficient to bring about recovery from alcoholism has manifested itself among us in many different forms."* This information is intended to make the spiritual journey easier in two ways.

The first has to do with language. In all specialized fields of endeavor, there is a lexicon of words that have special meanings because of the nature of the subject. Medicine, philosophy, mathematics, computing—all have their own unique jargon. Spiritual endeavor is no exception. However, *Alcoholics Anonymous* advises that you use everyday language when discussing spiritual matters so there is less possibility of misunderstandings.[23] Using uncommon words, where the definition more clearly articulates a point, isn't creating jargon.

As regards to getting recovered, a phrase was needed to describe this unique process: the changes that occur as an alcoholic/addict endeavors to become spiritual. This positive change is healing (but not exactly), and it increases awareness (but it's more than that), and there is a personality change (but it's much deeper than psychology). The phrases "spiritual experience", "spiritual awakening", and "religious experience" are used interchangeably and refer to a personality change sufficient to bring about recovery. This takes the twelve-step pilgrim away from complicated definitions and esoteric meanings, which lightens the burden of transformation.

The second way the appendix Spiritual Experience lightens your burden is by lowering your expectations. Many people become trapped in the expectation that they'll witness some extraordinary phenomenon, which will become the basis for having faith in a higher power (which would require less hard work on their own part). Some people wonder why they've been around a program for a while, and haven't seen burning bushes or divine visions attendant to their prayers. Is God overlooking them? Are they not doing this right?

Spiritual Experience advises that many alcoholics concluded from the first printing of the book that *"in order to recover* [notice: it's not to be in recovery] *they must acquire an immediate and overwhelming God-consciousness... "*. If they sit around long enough (they secretly hope) a divine flash of transformation will eventually occur, and they won't have to do any real work. Addicts simply generate drama while they wait for an easier, softer way. After months or years of waiting, with no divine revelations, many spiritual complications are created. If addicts proclaim they've prayed and nothing happens, they can become insecure. This can generate so much anxiety they'll withdraw from their support group. Insecurity requires they create delusions or illusions about themselves and spiritual uniqueness, which requires a supporting drama (which they'll relentlessly reinvent).

Defect-laden personalities inject all manner of self-serving meanings into coincidence. Some people perceive uncommon circumstances as validation that God exists. They interpret dreams and coincidence in some context of divine message. I've known people to claim God spoke to them because there was a powerful gust of wind at a particular moment of prayer. Others entreat a higher power to provide

---

[23] *Alcoholics Anonymous*, p. 93. It is important to recognize that "everyday language" isn't restricted to one-syllable words, and that spiritual language is absent of cursing and swearing.

parking spots so they won't be late for appointments, and still others characterize the Atman-Brahmin as a trickster, a social secretary, or an omniscient Santa Claus. Curious coincidence, anxiety-induced visions, and dreams do not prove God is paying particular attention to someone, nor do they prove the existence of God. To believe that they are, is proof that our minds are powerful in creating distractions from humility and hard work.

Most people completely overlook (or ignore) the subtle personality change that is a valid manifestation of a spiritual experience. For example: In the middle of an argument with your partner you suddenly realize you are wrong, so you spontaneously and humbly make an amend. That is a spiritual awakening that arises from deep within you, but it doesn't look like one because you only feel regret and take responsibility for hurting someone you love. You're just making an amend. If your sponsor understands spirituality, and you told them what happened, they might comment on the lovely spiritual experience: a moment of personality change that was sufficient to bring about recovery from addiction. That type of behavior is a spiritual awakening and the world is a safer place for it. However, it didn't occur with a celestial-trumpet fanfare.

Realize these small personality changes are satisfying the definition given in Spiritual Experience. Don't look for "Omnipotent Manifestations of the Great Spirit", or "The God-Inspired Selection of Parking Spots". As far as I am told, God has *apparently* had direct contact with only a very few people. It's a pretty short list. I don't think that run-of-the-mill alcoholics are on it, windstorms notwithstanding. Celebrate the fact that spiritual awakenings require very hard work, which enables you to treasure the experiences, and develop a stronger faith in God. Humble, honest effort is the order of the day, *every* day.

Most people will have slow, gradual spiritual awakenings—the educational variety. If you look for burning bushes, you will become disillusioned and disappointed. You may wonder: "What's the point? I'm going to meetings and nothing's happened. Why am I hanging around?"

A spiritual experience (or awakening or religious experience) appears in different ways. Any of you who are participating in a twelve-step program, and who are willing to be more honest today than you were a few months ago, have had a spiritual experience. You're probably noticing, in the same period, that you may be slightly more interested in kindness. The fact that you can't pinpoint exactly when, or exactly what happened to motivate you to be more kind or honest (and certainly no person "caused" these changes), indicates the change is of a spiritual nature. This in no way undermines its authenticity. Suspicious egos have a tendency to cast about frantically looking for some secular reason, when in fact, it's spiritually oriented.

It's interesting that there is little or no talk about having a religious experience. I wonder how popular you'd be at your next twelve-step meeting if you spoke eloquently and passionately about a *religious* experience? Many people in twelve-step groups are vehemently opposed to religion. It's also interesting that these are most often the people who misrepresent the philosophy of the twelve steps, and thereby create social prejudice against twelve-step groups (just as other fanatics have misrepresented the invisible beauty of their religions and so helped to create prejudice and opposition to religion).

What Makes An Addict Honest?

Trying to understand these personality changes as a function of psychology, rather than viewing them as religious experiences, as described in the appendix of *Alcoholics Anonymous,* obfuscates the evidence you need to develop spiritual faith for the yet larger trials ahead. If you attribute an increase in honesty to your own willpower, your ego takes the credit. If you attribute it to your sponsor, your therapist, your therapy, your ego takes the credit for picking that sponsor: What a good person I am; see how hard I'm working?

In addictions, you had countless opportunities to be honest, even when there was no risk to being honest. Still, you weren't. If you believe your own willpower gets you honest, you may well be honest, but no farther ahead since one defect (arrogance about yourself) is as bad as the other defect (being dishonest). For the addict getting recovered, any sincere increase in honesty, however slight, is a spiritual experience. When you define these changes as the mysterious derivative of praying and spiritual commitment, developing faith is inevitable.

In a twelve-step program, there's no sanctioned punishment for being dishonest. People continue to be dishonest in many areas and there appears to be no overt consequences (except spiritual corruption). Really, then, why get honest? There are three reasons. **First**: Honesty requires less energy than deceit, so you'll have more energy and pleasure in life. **Second**: Honesty always feels better than dishonesty over the long term—looking at yourself in the mirror is easier. **Third**: The more honest you are, the farther away you are from relapse.

Self-challenging vigilance is always the order of the day. Here are two declarations to consider, and in order to become recovered, they are not negotiable.

Declaration I:
(approximately the first five years of spiritual/step work)

If I drink, use drugs, act out, or lie, in any circumstance of my life, my destiny is in the hands of those around me.

Declaration II:
(after five years)

If I manipulate anyone to disadvantage or participate directly or indirectly in anything morally squalid; if I am overt or covert in disregarding any of the five spiritual principles; if I blame anyone for any condition in my life, then my spiritual condition is tenuous and my destiny is in the hands of those around me.[24]

---

[24] These declarations are related to the two types of relapse that are discussed in Chapter 11.

These declarations are hard to live up to; they're all-encompassing. I wrote them that way. I am in charge of so little in the universe. Life's benign indifference to *me* motivates me to keep as much influence over my own life as I can, without controlling or imposing on others. The only position that consistently allows this is to live up to these declarations. Being Spiritual is a very difficult thing to achieve. That's why few people seriously attempt it, and why its rewards are so sincerely and wholly blissful.

Steps One to Nine allow you to accomplish everything you need to become recovered and then to embrace Declaration II. Many people "in recovery" are only as honest as they need to be to get by. They are still liars (but not very often), and on any occasion when someone points that out, they become defensive and present some self-serving interpretation of rigorous honesty. For them, honesty is a matter of convenience and lying is a solution to awkward circumstances. At the minimum, the error is in equating sobriety and spirituality — they mistakenly believe that [somehow] long-term abstinence indicates some degree of spiritual integrity.

The spiritual authority and beauty of the original twelve-step program, as revealed in the first 192 pages and Appendix II of *Alcoholics Anonymous,* and in *Twelve Steps and Twelve Traditions*, is two-fold. Firstly, it never contradicts itself. There are very few "guide" books on spirituality which don't somehow contradict themselves.[25] Secondly, it is its own training ground. If taken as presented, it's a completely self-contained program for achieving regular, deep, and sincere association with a higher power, without attacking any other religious doctrine.

The original twelve-step instructions are so humbly confident about what they offer, that they don't allow for any troubling circumstance to be too difficult for them to resolve. They deny any spiritual problem as too sophisticated to be beyond the scope of what *Alcoholics Anonymous* and *Twelve Steps and Twelve Traditions* have to offer. There are no philosophical or spiritual contradictions within them (excluding the personal stories, for after all, they are only personal stories). These books are probably the most profound writings on spirituality and the human condition written in the last 1500 years — since *The Rule of Benedict* (c. 520 CE). For people with addictions, the precision and clarity of the AA texts' spiritual intent, that path's proven effectiveness, cannot be overstated.

————

In the first few years of becoming recovered, you will have spiritual experiences without really believing there's a higher power. For example: You may subscribe to any number of reasons by which you explain any increase in your honesty — your willingness, your determination, you're working your program, or because you believe it's worth it. These reasons will appear valid at the time, so your increase in honesty, which brings about recovery from addiction, won't be inter-

---

[25] Very often, the authors of spiritual guide books, or the defenders of formal religious doctrine, will allow a contradiction in their doctrine, or the doctrine will embody some glaring injustice in its program of salvation. They will then explain this away by blaming God, some long-dead prophet, the mysterious machinations of Providence, or their own inability to explain Divine Prerogative (which is blaming God). *There are no contradictions, paradoxes, or injustices in a sincerely spiritual life.*

preted as a spiritual awakening but as an ego exercise of willpower. And, during that spiritual experience, you may not believe in God.

At the early stages of getting recovered (or if you're forever in recovery), you will tend to credit yourself for these personality changes and conveniently forget the historical fact that while acting out, or in unspiritual sobriety, good intentions, determination, and willpower never changed anything.

When getting recovered, any consistent increase in *sincere* spiritual effort will bring about a spiritual experience, regardless of where *you* place the credit. Personality changes like honesty or being more responsible for your abuses and misdemeanors, will creep into your personality. You'll be in the middle of these various spiritual experiences/awakenings that bring about recovery *before* you have a strong faith in a higher power (of your own understanding). It's very common to have a spiritual awakening prior to having strong faith.

Don't confuse spiritual experiences with spiritual beliefs. You do not have to believe in a higher power to begin this journey. All you have to do is follow the instructions in the original texts.[26] It can also work the other way: people may have spiritual beliefs without spiritual experiences: i.e. There are people who believe in a higher power of some description who are also mean, dishonest, or selfish, and who don't have spiritual experiences. There are still others who believe fervently that their system of spiritual belief is superior to all others, and who are silently or openly racist or mean on behalf of "their" God: spiritual elitism. [Insecurity motivates these types of beliefs, and abuse always results from representing any spiritual doctrine as superlative. The spiritual path presented in *Alcoholics Anonymous* is the most effective for addicts seeking recovery, but it isn't "the best" for everyone.]

In this book, I'm explaining that the original twelve steps, as a route out of active addiction and into spirituality, guarantees the best results. They are quite "perfect" the way they are written, and require no modification or amendment. They do, however, require hard work and commitment. Be cautious of people who present guidelines and advice that promise an easier, softer, quicker way. The spiritual masters throughout history have consistently told us the way to a higher power and a sincerely spiritual lifestyle is the most difficult personal journey there is. The original steps are very particular in their demand for commitment and detail; you are well advised to do this exactly as instructed if you intend to become recovered.

For addictions, experience has proven that the original twelve steps work. Other addiction/recovery programs may or may not work; however, in order to find out if they do or not, you may have to pay with your life. Is it worth the risk?[27]

---

[26] If you're being advised to do anything regarding your "recovery" by apparently well-intentioned friends or sponsors, ask them where their advice to you is found in the approved literature. If it isn't in *Alcoholics Anonymous* or *Twelve Steps and Twelve Traditions* (and watch they don't take something out of context to win a useless argument), be cautious about following it. The advice will be more for their benefit than yours. If you do as the literature instructs, you will start to have religious experiences, regardless of whether you believe in a higher power of your own understanding.

[27] People without addictions can attempt a spiritual lifestyle and, for any number of reasons, decide to abandon their quest. For them, there are no dire consequences. For addicts who abandon the spiritual path, the consequences are disastrous.

The point of this book is to offer some clarity on the original instructions, along with an awareness of how therapy and psychology might assist, and what the risks are for disobedience to spiritual principles. Be cautious when the AA textbooks are used as general guides. Be cautious about following the advice of people who did any of the steps "their own way". You are putting your life in the hands of people who think they are wiser than *Alcoholics Anonymous* or *Twelve Steps and Twelve Traditions*. I don't know of too many people who are that wise.

At this point, I assume you understand that when you drank or acted out (past tense) you were powerless over alcohol or acting out, meaning inherently that your life *was* unmanageable. You believe there aren't two halves to Step One. You've carefully examined your life and have figured out how you structured it to facilitate drinking or acting out. You're convinced that continuing abstinence is crucial. Once you establish abstinence and are convinced of these truths, and admit that you are powerless, you are ready for Step Two—not before.

Step Two

In Step Two, you first come up against the phrase *"Came to believe... ."*[28] At face value, and do take it at face value, it means that, over a period of time, you judged something as accurate and truthful. Because of what it is you must come to believe, accomplishing Step Two is time-consuming. I am never surprised or concerned when people take six months, or a year (or longer), to complete Step Two. What you have to accomplish is subtle and there's a lot to it. What you came to believe must be clear. You must also be confident; otherwise, everything you attempt thereafter is undermined by ambivalence, and *ambivalence is spiritual cancer*.

Everything in your recovery and in your life that transpires after Step One is dependent upon how you addressed Step Two. After abstinence, Step Two is by far the most important step.[29] The ease of everything you do is predicated on your relationship to a higher power. Step Two is where you begin that relationship. It's the foundation for how you reorganize your values and perceptions. The basis for your spiritual journey, which, according to Step Three is your life, begins here. Spirituality must take an ubiquitous and pivotal position in your life. As an addict getting recovered, *how* you come to believe that spirituality is the solution, and *what* you believe about that, will affect every decision you make for the rest of your life.

Believing encompasses a very specific attitude. People believe 2 + 2 = 4. It isn't negotiable. If you believe something, you don't "kind of" believe it. When you believe a thing, you accept it as true and allow that it's not open to debate. You either believe something or you don't. You assume an intellectual position of conviction and confidence: no substitutions, vagaries, or equivocations. Notice one of the AA co-founder's declarations on page 11 of *Alcoholics Anonymous*—how he once ac-

---

[28] *Alcoholics Anonymous,* p. 59, and *Twelve Steps and Twelve Traditions*, p. 25.

[29] Regardless of any topic under discussion, always understand that everything is dependent upon complete abstinence from acting out behavior. Clean, sober, abstinent, adhering to bottom-line behavior—it doesn't matter what you call it, everything Spiritual depends on abstinence from all acting out behavior.

cepted moral teachings he liked and disregarded those that were inconvenient. A sincere belief requires that something be true, even when it may be inconvenient.[30]

Beliefs of "convenience" are treacherous, and the exact thing to avoid in Step Two. Should you believe as you are advised, you will soon reorganize all of your old ideas, change previously cherished behaviors, and voluntarily impose *on yourself* new values and attitudes. Should you believe, with conviction, what the original literature counsels (and of what use is believing something if there is no conviction behind the belief?), and if you adhere to the five principles of spirituality with quiet determination, I can assure you that you will be viewed as suspicious and face disapproval from many people; even within your twelve-step group. But, your life will become your own and change in wonderful ways you cannot imagine.

What "Came To Believe" Encompasses

There is significant work involved prior to believing *"that a Power greater than ourselves could restore us to sanity."*[31] You must select the idea of god that you believe in: Spiritual Essence, a Universal Consciousness, a higher power, the Great Reality, Allah, YHWH, Atman-Brahmin, Jesus: there are hundreds of names and points of view for this conception. You *start* to get clarity on your point of view concerning the name and concept of God. This is very personal.

What isn't personal is what this higher power will help addicts accomplish. Picking a personal conception of God is important, but each individual higher power does the same thing for each addict getting recovered: it restores them to sanity. The following four processes will all be happening during Step Two:

- deciding upon which concept of God is right for them to start their pilgrimage;
- working to eliminate their spiritual belligerence (which I discuss later in Spiritual Dislocations);
- slowly understanding the "theory" and content of Step Two; and,
- coming to believe (being convinced) that How It Works is true, and that a higher power will restore them to sanity.

No Substitutions

It is especially important to not substitute anything in place of the phrase, *"a Power greater than ourselves."* Step Two does *not* read: Came to believe that going to lots of meetings could restore us to sanity. It also does not read that getting a job, or being a circuit speaker, or getting someone to love us, or sponsoring lots of people, or attending lots of twelve-step social occasions, or studying the books, or doing service work could restore us to sanity. More particularly, it does not say that

---

[30] At the beginning, for probably the first ten or so years, becoming spiritual will be the most inconvenient thing you'll ever do; but take heart: after ten years of diligent application and hard work, spiritual transformation does become graceful.

[31] *Alcoholics Anonymous,* p. 59, and *Twelve Steps and Twelve Traditions,* p. 25.

doing the steps could restore you to sanity. Substitute nothing for the phrase, *"a Power greater than ourselves."*

Yes, the AA textbooks advise you to: be at meetings, be at a time and place where other people can share their problems, be charitable, carry the message, pay your own way, be honest. These, and many other instructions, are to facilitate your becoming Spiritual. These are not the solution; they are the avenues to the solution. The substitutions I listed (above) may allow you sobriety, but you will remain not-spiritual, and therefore at risk. Being always "in recovery" is proof that substitutions have been made, and getting recovered does not allow for substitutions.

The reason addicts are "supposed to" keep the meetings going is so that people can learn about Spirituality. They're not supposed to keep the meetings going so they have something to do on Friday night, or so they have someplace to go when they're bored and want a laugh (which is often at someone else's expense). Everything you do in twelve-step groups is "supposed" to facilitate and promote your relationship with a higher power of your own understanding. The glad-handing, socializing, and psychological success equations that substitute for a relationship with a higher power are each as dangerous as they are epidemic.

If you don't believe that getting recovered depends upon your relationship with a higher power, and sincerely act upon this, then you believe that recovery rests on some combination of willpower, therapy, getting in touch with feelings, social success, fulfilling sex, meetings, and sponsors. Of course, if all you want is sobriety, then these may well be sufficient: You'll be in the social loop, and popular, but living on the edge of insanity and relapse. Relying on anything other than a higher power to resolve your addictions is relapse-gambling with your life as the stakes.[32]

What newcomers use for their higher power in the initial stages of participation is very often a survival/grasping-at-straws reaction to the fear of acting out and failure. That's fine. There is much encouragement to use the group, your pet, or anything else that is neutral or has psychological safety. Believe in what you have to at the beginning. If this rudimentary concept persists beyond the newcomer phase, however, it is risky for several reasons.

Over an extended period of time, if you use the group as a higher power, you are allowing yourself to be dependent on something that is loosely organized and subject to the ego-pressure of charismatic members. Groups and meetings are untenable as a "higher power" because the traditions and steps are not scrupulously adhered to. If you use the group as your higher power, you limit your ability to participate in the community at large. A higher power that is defined secularly, and that does not extend beyond some arbitrary intellectual concept, is thereby limited in scope and will not allow you to participate beyond that narrow limit—the intellect.

---

[32] In recent years, "getting in touch with your feelings" has become possibly the most popular (and most ineffective) strategy to resolve addictions. Addictions are not an issue of emotions. If you are resolving an abstinence-available addiction, then belligerence, social networking, and entrenching yourself in thirty meetings a week may be enough to keep you clean and sober. This is because of the hard line you can draw between abstinence and acting out. For any abstinence not-available addiction (like anger, sex, or relationships), sobriety based on meetings, sober-networking, and willpower, will not allow sobriety for any length of time because a hard line cannot be drawn between abstinence and those addictions that generate directly out of instinctual needs.

Using "a group" will eventually restrict you to the limited knowledge and prejudices manifested within the group itself. Using anything finite, be it a cat, the memory of your nice grandmother, or nature, as your higher power, also places limits on your spiritual resources. I cannot find any respected treatise or major writing on God or Spirituality, including the original AA texts, that suggests you pray to your dog, the sunset, or any group. The spiritual masters teach this would be idolatry and defeat any sincere spiritual endeavor. From a "Western" perspective, yes, I grant that God may talk through people (which is usually a trite euphemism for something pithy), but God is not people or the groups they form. *Twelve Steps and Twelve Traditions* discusses different attitudes of spiritual newcomers and what you have to do to go beyond this narrow and limiting spiritual perspective.

Step Two advises that a power greater than yourself *could* restore you to sanity, which implies that this restoration is dependent on something. It depends on your continued abstinence, appropriate prayer and meditation, and your continued devotion to sound spiritual endeavor. This is what is implied by the word could. *Restoration to sanity and sincere spiritual endeavor are intrinsically interdependent.*

Just because you don't cheat or lie, and do go to meetings, have a sponsor, and answer your phone late at night, doesn't mean that you are going to stay sober; nor does it mean you are spiritual. In fact, people go to meetings, sponsor others, go to the round-ups, and still relapse. What happened? What happened is that they didn't come to believe that sound spiritual principles and devotion to a higher power (which can only arise out of "believing" at Step Two) is the solution.

Restore

Notice this: *"When dealing with such a person, you had better use everyday language to describe spiritual principles."*[33] Restore means to bring back, or return something to an original, former condition or position. These are straightforward definitions found in any dictionary, which have far-reaching implications for the addict getting recovered.

Creating a unique jargon to discuss addictions and spirituality defeats the intent, which is to reach everyone. Pious or insecure people try to compensate for their perceived "inadequacy" when describing the indescribable, such as God, by creating obtuse or abstract words and meanings: jargon. This doesn't mean people shouldn't use uncommon "big" words, nor does it mean that we have to use one-syllable words. It means jargon and slang words with unique meanings are to be avoided. These create cliques and allow clique members to exclude others and avoid truths. Getting recovered is somewhat complicated; it is arduous; it is not beyond ordinary language, and neither is God. The AA textbooks use ordinary definitions to present the ideas and describe the process.[34]

At one point in time, you were okay. Then you became not-okay (by virtue of an addiction). With proper application, you are going to become okay again. Re-

[33] *Alcoholics Anonymous,* p. 93.
[34] With the massive presence of television, videos, movies, computers, etc., we are becoming more and more linguistically lazy. Buy a dictionary. Nothing is free.

store means exactly what it means. It doesn't say create—it says restore, and yet you will hear both old-timers and newcomers say: "I've been broken and defective from the moment I was born." What arrogance and drama is in that claim?

Some addicts expend a lot of energy trying to prove they were the meanest, wildest person in town, which in a very few cases and in very small towns, might have been true. There is drama and insecurity in their claim to have been sick *all* of their life—addicts from the moment they were conceived. It's pretty hard to top that story. If they can convince you that they were sick from the moment they were born, and by age three were killing and pillaging the countryside (or at least swearing and stealing cars), they have status and notoriety. They are now more special by virtue of being the sickest person in the meeting.[35]

Balance what follows with common sense. Fetal-alcohol or -drug syndrome are serious medical concerns. There are other seriously damaging congenital conditions. I'm not talking about these, nor am I denying there may be valid genetic links that influence a predisposition to addictions. I am referring to drama and exaggeration. Evading the implication of *restore* contains a justification for status and irresponsibility. Granted, for some of you, you can't remember when you weren't "crazy" so you may have to act on faith regarding *restore*; so, act on faith. The next time you're around an infant, notice it's not a psychologically debilitated, dysfunctional, mean-spirited, deceitful, corrupt alcoholic. It's an infant—an innocent, beautiful child, and so were you. Respect that about yourself.

When you are deciding to *"thoroughly follow our path"*[36] then *restore* implies at some time in the past you were not insane. You can't go beyond Step Two if you believe you were "created" insane. What degree of self-abuse or grandiosity pushes you to that degree of self-rejection? What ego pay-off is there for convincing anyone, especially convincing yourself, that you were an addict from conception? Is it to put responsibility on your family? Is it to avoid the pain of being ordinary? Is it to justify or excuse your gross irresponsibility as an adult? Is it to maintain special status and impress people? Is it to frighten people away? All claims to uniqueness defeat spirituality, create isolation (especially from yourself), and maintain your own unheeded loneliness.

Blank Spots

Addicts often feel a need to explain away, justify, or compensate for, a memory blank-spot—especially big ones. They do this by deliberate dishonesty, or by assumption and confabulation[37], which aren't necessarily dishonest.

---

[35] While acting out, such people go to unusual lengths to be extravagant or outrageous—deliberately generating calamity to command attention. They do the same thing "in recovery"—command attention by flamboyance and drama.

[36] Part of the opening sentence of How It Works, *Alcoholics Anonymous*, p. 58.

[37] Memory blank-spots themselves are caused for different reasons, possibly for as mundane a reason as extended, repetitious boredom; or alcohol/drug use and acting out; or as important a reason as the concealment of historical trauma. From one point of view: Confabulation is a compensatory defense against insecurity or shame and fear, where memory blank-spots are filled in, or unsatisfactory memories are replaced, with some more acceptable fantasy that, over time, becomes a "truth". Cont'd...

Addicts sometimes have very few memories of their early life, and all addicts have memory blank-spots from their childhood and during times of acting out. With a propensity to blame, and a tendency to label themselves as bad, and often enabled by poorly informed therapists and helpers, they easily assume that memory lapses mean they were doing something horrible, or something horrible was being done to them. Couple this with an insecure need to be seen as unique, and a need to explain away their destructive behavior, they will try to fill in these memory lapses in a way that compensates without responsibility and keeps fear and shame at a distance by blaming.

If addicts repeat to themselves, for years, that having a memory lapse means something horrible happened, that memory lapse will eventually become something horrible—as much from any legitimate trauma or abuse that *may* have occurred, as from the self-inculcated idea of "very horrible". Addicts can convince themselves of just about anything.[38] The truth here is addicts will need therapy to resolve the self-harm that results from living with self-inculcated, imagined, horrible memories, just as much as they would for real trauma that did exist.

If you look at a blank piece of paper, it's exactly that—blank. There isn't pornography on it, there isn't an abstract painting on it, there isn't a poem written on it; it's just blank. Many people (themselves wounded) assign intrusive therapeutic labels and make risky assumptions about memory blank-spots, with only two pieces of evidence: one, that someone is complaining they can't remember; and two, that they're an addict. Some of you will have memory blank spots because of serious abuse (given or received), and others because life was repetitive and mundane. Not having memories is not in and of itself evidence of trauma or abuse. Be very careful about making assumptions about memory blank spots and trauma; it is exceptionally dangerous without accurate, qualified, thorough, cautious, "un-biased", in-depth clinical support in addictions-related symptom recognition and diagnosis.

Twelve-step programs are not treatment modalities for psychological problems, *per se*. They do not address childhood-onset psychiatric disorders (or any other psychiatric disorder for that matter). They only address spiritual dislocation, which is Addiction. Inasmuch as it is true that you will, throughout your spiritual life, challenge all of your old ideas, it's nonetheless tremendously important to accept this as true: *"To believe that the alcoholic who approaches A.A. is an unprincipled, un-*

Confabulation is sometimes ego-deliberate, in that a fantasy scenario is created and replaces reality, where the historical reality is unacceptable to a later specific ego agenda like needing to justify behavior. Over the course of years, the memory manipulation is subsequently suppressed, and the created memory is held to be true since the ego-generated manipulation is forgotten. This does *not* imply that all memory is false or is confabulation. It's very complicated. It can only be resolved in well-managed, *long-term* therapy, and if there is any organic damage it may never be resolved. Competent therapeutic counsel is essential if this seems to be of concern for the recovering addict.

[38] Prisoners in wartime are brainwashed. They are kept tired, hungry, in pain, cold, confused, disoriented, lonely, and frightened, and are repeatedly told some story. Addicts treat themselves like prisoners of war, and they repeatedly tell themselves stories.

taught barbarian, suddenly transformed by the previously unavailable spiritual illu-mination of the Twelve Steps, is, to me, utter foolishness."[39]

Addicts are ordinary people and innocent when they were infants and children. Through a process of spiritual dislocation, they manifested an addiction. The good parts became hidden through their addictions and yes, sometimes through abuse inflicted by others. Addicts are now charged with the responsibility of resolving their addictions by slow, painstaking spiritual transformation.

The essence of Step Two is that over some period of time, you become convinced that a higher power could restore you to sanity. Substituting meetings or the steps, or anything else for a higher power, or skimping on the requirement of *being convinced,* will corrupt the outcome and prohibit you from realizing the freedom and beauty of being recovered (and all it implies). In getting recovered, your soul isn't recreated; spirituality is restored.

It's impossible to realize spiritual integrity (meaning much more than "sober and happy") without firmly entrenching these two fundamental pre-conditions: abstinence (from Step One) and belief (from Step Two). Lacking these will show up as reversion into primary addictions, the intensification of subtle addictions, a failure to exit all addictions, a shallow commitment to honesty and responsibility (you'll be honest and responsible providing it's not too inconvenient), recycled step completion, or as a reorganization of or an attempt to camouflage your character defects (Impression Management). Not *being convinced* results in your having shallow faith in the program (regardless of how loudly you proclaim otherwise), being suspicious and fearful of those who are sincere and honest, and never achieving an abiding sense of safety in intimate relationships.

People in this painful quandary often work hard, but they work hard in the wrong direction.[40] Twelve-step spiritual misalignment always starts in Step Two.

Spiritual Dislocations

There are five types of spiritual problems, more aptly called dislocations, that newcomers face at Step Two. At the minimum, this means that although the newcomer desires transformation and has a belief that spirituality is good, something is subtly wrong and persists in interfering with their pilgrimage. The spiritual novice (the newcomer) has to appreciate the nuances of these dislocations to resolve them so they can stay on track spiritually.[41]

The first type of spiritual problem is defiance—the person who won't believe. This defiance can be well concealed underneath many apparently well-justified, stalling tactics like studying religions and checking out alternatives. Be

---

[39] From the pamphlet A Member's Eye View of Alcoholics Anonymous, Alcoholics Anonymous World Services, Inc., 1970.

[40] Many people work hard at completing the steps. I mean that in all sincerity. They are diligent and painstaking; however, sincerely working hard in the wrong way is just as ineffective as making a half-hearted effort in the right way.

[41] One of the more applicable and lucid explanations of dislocation is found in *The World's Religions,* Huston Smith, Harper Collins, 1991, p. 101.

aware of the consequences of continued defiance to spiritual principles—relapse, continuing humiliation, self-destruction, anger, chaos, and possibly death. Review the top of page 26 in *Twelve Steps and Twelve Traditions,* where you will find paragraphs which describe what the spiritually belligerent person has to do.

If you fit into this category, *Twelve Steps and Twelve Traditions* advises the hoop you have to jump through is bigger than you think. You don't have to believe everything all at once. Take your time. With continued effort, you only need a little honesty, open-mindedness, and willingness. A spiritual experience has already happened and your belligerence will lessen.

There are two important side issues to this first type of spiritual problem that need to be examined in detail—HOW and WPL.

HOW — Honesty, Open-mindedness, Willingness

These three attributes, hereafter referred to as HOW, allow addicts to work on the specific problem of spiritual belligerence at Step Two. Step Two is a perception and faith step, as are Steps Six and Seven. The other steps (One, Three, Four, Five, Eight, and Nine) are "action" steps. [The maintenance steps are in a separate category altogether and are exempt from this discussion.]

When addicts or alcoholics take the problem-solving paradigm of HOW out of Step Two (a perception and faith step), and apply it to any of the action-oriented steps, they usually fall into a destructive trap. In doing this, they take HOW out of context, and end up unknowingly using it as a justification for sloth. (See Fn. p. 261)

Addicts must abandon their victim ego-posture that the messy state of affairs in their life isn't their fault, and must begin to take personal responsibility. If a victim mentality goes unchallenged, addicts will whine and commiserate with other Victims while they wait for someone or some*thing* else to "take charge" of their transformation. Not addressing this victim posture allows them to be misapply HOW and it camouflages inactivity (sloth).

When HOW is applied out of context to any problem within an action step, *and* the person also has a victim mentality, they won't "act" within the action step. They'll wait—again, for someone else to take charge or some*thing* to happen. They will make passionate speeches about HOW, but their victim-attitude keeps them inactive. Other than the fact they'll make speeches about HOW, nothing will happen. Here are two examples:

Example One: I knew a person who had been planning on doing a Step Four (an action step) since their second year of abstinence, and had been "planning" it for about eight years. For all the years that I knew this person, they had been proclaiming: "I'm Honest, Open-minded, and Willing to do my Step Four. I really am. I'm serious." And, they were serious, and they sat there. Years later, this individual was still making sincere speeches about Step Four and honesty, open-mindedness, and willingness. They had taken HOW out of Step Two (perception and faith) and applied it to Step Four (action), therefore, out of context.

Example Two: People who are controlled by an addiction like sex or rage will claim, over the course of years of sobriety, to be honest, open-minded and willing to address their defects or other addictions, but will never actually do anything about them. They have unknowingly taken the problem-solving attribute of HOW out of a perception and faith step, and (inappropriately) applied them to a problem that requires action. They've taken HOW out of context. The speech about HOW *sounds* good, but carries no weight.

The misapplication of HOW results from not relying on a higher power for the courage to transform. Relying on a higher power is essential to effect any change, and praying, for the addict, is *always* the first step in problem solving and transformation. Passionate speeches about HOW are usually evidence of taking honesty, open-mindedness, and willingness out of context (meaning out of a perception and faith step), and using speeches about commitment as a way to conceal their fear and spiritual inactivity It is irresponsibility and fear cleverly hidden underneath political speeches about devotion and effort.

If you apply honesty, open-mindedness, and willingness *by themselves* to problems other than those regarding perception and faith, you apply the theory out of context. You will actually create more problems than you are trying to solve. HOW is designed for spiritual defiance at Step Two (or similar issues within Steps Six and Seven). For all other problems, you may be honest, open-minded, and willing, and that *is* all well and good, yet these are entirely insufficient without two additional attributes: patience and labor, which must be added to the application of HOW, to make the resolution of other problems effective.

WPL — Willingness, Patience, and Labor [42]

Be aware that the underlying essential requirements for *all* spiritual endeavor (including HOW) are identified in this sentence: *"To duplicate, with such backing, what we* [the AA pioneers] *have accomplished is only a matter of willingness, patience and labor."* [43] So being honest, open-minded, and willing is, by itself, always insufficient. Without labor (meaning action and effort) and patience, all claims to spiritual devotion through honesty, open-mindedness, and willingness are rhetoric (and a subtle version of Impression Management). [44]

"Faith without works is dead." [45] "Works" is labor and consists of the following: Pray and Meditate, regularly. Shut off the TV, go to a stationery store, and buy pads of paper, pencils, and a dictionary. At home, study the AA textbooks. Search for meanings; look for themes; cross-reference the information; examine your own defiance, doubt, and evasiveness. *Study* the texts with an intent to discover how you may be more obedient to spirituality as a life-discipline. If you struggle with

---

[42] Patience and labor, as presented in *Alcoholics Anonymous,* are two aspects of Right Effort, which is one tenet of The Eight-Fold Noble Path of Buddhism. How you focus your energy (willpower) is one theme of Right Effort and something that all spiritual pilgrims must examine, regardless of the religious path they choose. For an insightful view that has a universal twelve-step application, see *The World's Religions,* by Huston Smith, p. 108. On the large scale, *Alcoholics Anonymous* is the "what to do" and *Twelve Steps and Twelve Traditions* is the "why to do it" of Right Effort for twelve-step participants.

[43] *Alcoholics Anonymous,* p. 163.

[44] Impression Management is defined in a footnote in <u>Addictions Prohibit Spirituality</u>, Chapter 2.

[45] This is one of the observations from *Alcoholics Anonymous* (p. 88) that has an unqualified universal application in all spiritual endeavor.

dictionaries and "book studying", then spend a lot of time talking sincerely about this with someone who can and does study the original material.

"Work(s)" may mean taking a course on the history of religions, or making effort to persevere in the face of others' disapproval when you quietly distance yourself from their unspiritual behavior. It may mean meeting regularly with a therapist or a spiritual advisor, and working extra to pay for that yourself. Labor always means challenging only yourself to achieve greater levels of responsibility in every area of your life, and not challenging others. "Work" at minding your own business, which calls for a lot of silence on your part. Serenity often resides in silence. Serenity and silence aren't destroyed by talking, they're destroyed by the desire to be heard or the need to conceal insecurity. Work towards never showing off at a meeting, and *never* impose your will on others—even if you "know" you're right, or are a group's founder, an old-timer in sobriety, or in a responsible service position.

Meetings are not supposed to be social gatherings *per se,* they should be safe and pleasant places where people can search for truth and establish integrity by carrying the message of a spiritual awakening. Keep this in context—I am not saying that you can't or aren't supposed to enjoy yourself, but "fellowship" is not the first priority of meeting attendance. Fellowship is fourth on the list behind learning about spirituality for yourself, helping others to establish a spiritual life, and providing a place where people can bring their addictions problems. Twelve-step meetings [are supposed to] contribute to people's restoration to sanity (not to their sex life), and are for establishing and maintaining a commitment to God *as you understand God.*

If you're belligerent and argumentative about spirituality, review page 26 of *Twelve Steps and Twelve Traditions.* Do what is suggested, for a long time.

The second type of spiritual problem encountered at Step Two is that of the person who does believe in God, a higher power, etc., but has no faith. One way this shows up is believing you have been too bad. God has a book of celestial coupons and you're only allowed nine major transgressions (or eleven, or some vague number you can't pinpoint). Every time you did a big one, God tore out a coupon, and by the time you were old enough to vote you used up all your celestial coupons. Now you couldn't get into heaven for love nor money. These spiritual newcomers believe in God, but have no faith that God will act on their behalf.

Confusing God with Santa Claus, i.e. I have been bad and will get no presents, results in weak faith. People believe in God and pray for optimal parking spots, nice weather, and deliverance from illness and trying circumstances. When God doesn't give them what they want, they may continue to believe in God, but their faith becomes tenuous. Or, not having their "morally good" prayer requests answered leads to self-condemnation: If I was good enough, God would have answered my prayers. God didn't, so I mustn't be good enough or trying hard enough.

In reference to this person, page 28 of *Twelve Steps and Twelve Traditions* discusses the roadblocks of indifference, fancied self-sufficiency, prejudice, and defiance. There's often an arrogance about their "sinning ways" [sic]. These are the usual attitudes of people who believe but have no faith. The book talks about these attitudes prohibiting a well-grounded approach to spirituality, and what to do to resolve them. If you are not willing to read and follow these instructions, you will be-lieve, but live with a weak faith. Your abstinence will therefore be tenuous.

The third type of spiritual problem is found in the intellectually self-sufficient person: "You can't prove God exists. I can't accept this spirituality stuff." This results from arrogance and cynicism, often rooted in the theory that the presence of selfish or cruel behavior is proof of the non-existence of God: God does not exist because there are mean, nasty people in the world. This logic about God has elements of racism in it.

As soon as everyone's perfect (read: wonderful and kind), this person will believe, i.e. some truth about God. If you live with this type of spiritual dislocation, the instructions on pages 29 and 30 of *Twelve Steps and Twelve Traditions* tell you what the route is for you to begin challenging your old beliefs.

The fourth type of person that has difficulty coming to believe in God is the one who is devout and religiously perfect: self-righteous. *Twelve Steps and Twelve Traditions* advises that this person is so arrogant that they have come to suspect that God doesn't believe in them. This person's view of themselves and of faith is usually related to wallowing in self-aggrandizement and emotionalism: "I'm praying perfectly. I'm devout. I'm spiritually pure. The fault is that God doesn't see this. God doesn't recognize my righteousness and my unwavering fabulous devotion. It's God's fault, not mine."

There's often an analytical-elitist approach towards religious communities (superlative comparisons and belaboring the faults of other paths). The melodrama of immaculate faith and superb devotion (quantity rather than quality) is the barrier. The transformation guidelines for this problem are on page 31 and 32 of *Twelve Steps and Twelve Traditions*.

There is a fifth type of spiritual problem that isn't discussed in the AA texts. When these books were written, this specific spiritual problem wasn't commonly identified. It is today, and is worthy of special attention. There are those addicts and alcoholics who want to, but are terrified of, abandoning an entrenched and painful system of religion: cults and extremely orthodox religious systems.[46]

This is usually present when people leave a rigid point of view that was imposed on them. Or, being psychologically damaged, they join and are indoctrinated into a tyrannical belief system (cults, etc.) and then, for whatever reason, choose to leave. Often, God, or the cult leader, is represented as omnipotent and vengeful. While they know what they believe is unfulfilling and unhealthy, they cannot, through fear of retribution, let their old beliefs go for something new and fulfilling. This is, essentially, a struggle to change the indoctrination that happens in a closed-loop, bigoted, elitist "religious" structure. Besides cults, this indoctrination can be

---

[46] This discussion is for people who wish to voluntarily change the views they have been indoctrinated with—they recognize the importance of that fact on their own, and decide to voluntarily adopt different religious values. Conducting formal interventions to rescue people who are trapped in cults and who will resist leaving them is another matter entirely. In this latter case, find competent professional help.

present in any religion where there are rigidly extreme orthodox beliefs.[47] Getting out of this is a complex process.

If you are frightened about abandoning beliefs that you were indoctrinated with, wish to heal from the abuse you endured in a fundamentalist religion, or wish to get recovered from a religious addiction (which is far more common than can be safely discussed here), there are some things you can do. This (as with sex and relationship addictions) requires going beyond a twelve-step program.

- Go "counsellor shopping" for a therapist who is gentle, sincerely open-minded, and patient. Make an appointment with a few therapists and ask them questions about their style, training, and religious beliefs. *You interview them as much as they interview you.* If the therapist is defensive about being interviewed, what does that tell you? Bring a tape recorder and record the session, and then listen to it later.
- The therapist should be well-versed in addictions, especially abstinence not-available addictions, and religions (or cults if that is applicable). Their having a reasonable working knowledge of Buddhism or Unitarianism (or some other ethics-based, middle-way philosophy) can facilitate a safe avenue to begin exploring non-dogmatic alternatives.
- If other addictions are a concern, maintain your abstinence.
- Take a Contemporary Religions or History of Religions course at a non-religious university. Read books by authors like Karen Armstrong, Huston Smith, and Joseph Campbell. Avoid books that promote a one-option or superlative point of view.

Then *slowly*, over a *long*, gentle course of therapy, and if applicable participating in your twelve-step group, you will acquire accurate knowledge about alternatives. The fear, shame, and guilt will gently abate and, *by your own initiative*, you will acquire the ability to choose a safe spiritual path. There will some traumatic dysregulation that will need to be addressed. (See Appendix III)

It is important to make choices that are not a reaction to the tyranny you are escaping from.[48] Choosing without reacting is crucial in order to create your own spiritual value system, which will eventually allow you to emotionally exit an oppressive system with dignity and confidence.[49]

---

[47] Keep this in context. I'm referring to religious extremism, not well-intentioned, respectful personal conviction.

[48] In this situation, a reactionary choice isn't limited to choosing another oppressive religious system. It can also be to enter abusive/oppressive relationships with lovers, employers, sponsors, and friends.

[49] Spirituality is needed to resolve any addiction, but at the same time, the fusion of "spirituality" to cults, extremely fundamentalist religious structures, and religious addictions, creates very unique problems which are coupled with issues related to personality and trauma. Leaving a tyrannical religious structure and at the same time exploring addictions and spirituality is a very delicate, very slow, process. This is incredibly complicated.

While you are learning about other religious traditions, you may experience a desire to pray. This will probably be frightening. At those times of fear and image-confusion in your prayers, adopt a "neutral" stance. Try this: Assume a comfortable position—at a minimum, have your eyes closed or almost closed, and sit quietly. Arrange it so you're comfortably warm. In your mind, picture or imagine a limitless, empty panorama of blue-black nothing-ness. Clear your mind of images and concentrate on a space of blue-black nothingness. If some traditional or threatening image appears, then quietly refocus your attention and concentrate on some other section of the limitless blue-black emptiness. In your mind, don't "fight" the intrusive image, just quietly ignore it and look beyond or away from it. Focus on another area of the limitless, empty panorama of blue-black nothingness, and then simply talk to *It*. Several brief attempts of only fifteen to twenty seconds throughout the day will generate better results than one or two long attempts.

In all of this, if you persevere, you will be rewarded with a new religious or spiritual world view that is a comfortable extension of you, rather than some subtle aspect of the tyranny you're escaping. Be patient. Remember page 569: Spiritual experiences are personality changes. Trust your personality changes, and you will learn that a higher power is working inside of you in spite of the fear and oppression you experienced in the past.[50]

Healthy Spirituality transcends all alienation. How you transcend alienation is delicate. However, with perseverance and wise counsel, it is inevitable. When newcomers are unsure of how to focus their attention, they often just give up too soon.[51] If you are presently too scared to strongly challenge your old views, go slowly, seek out some authentic support, and trust Step Two in *Twelve Steps and Twelve Traditions*. Desire only a personality change that will bring about recovery, not an experience of divine revelation. Spirituality will grow in you like a flower; maybe a flower that takes years to bloom, but it will grow.

When people are ready to attempt meditation as it is described in Step Eleven, and they seek my counsel, I sometimes suggest that they spend a few months meditating in the style of Step Eleven, but on the content of Step Two.[52] When I work with people who want to escape religious oppression into a healthy form of spirituality, I draw heavily on the material contained in Step Two.[53]

As an addict it is crucial that you come to believe that acquiring Spirituality is the solution. If you repeat the steps over and over you've missed this, and will be

---

[50] George Santayana wrote: *"My atheism is true piety towards the universe and denies only gods fash-ioned by men in their own image, to be servants of their human interests."* Having a similar perspective is said of William Blake by Thomas Merton in *A Thomas Merton Reader,* Edited by Thomas P. McDonnell, Doubleday, 1996, beginning at, *"How incapable I was of understanding... ,"* p. 228.

[51] The reason there are so few truly spiritual people is because it is such hard work. *Huxley and God, The Essays,* cited at earlier footnotes.

[52] This is not to re-do Step Two. It is to expand their awareness about their own on-going, subtle variations of spiritual resistance.

[53] Re: Religious addiction, etc.... A few pages ago I briefly described praying to a space of blue-black nothingness, and I also state that I draw heavily on the content of Step Two. There is much more that has to go into resolving extreme spiritual dislocation.

living a life that is governed by subtly "tolerable" or not-very-noticeable levels of dishonesty, insincerity, manipulation, meanness, gossip, and irresponsibility.

According to *Twelve Steps and Twelve Traditions,* there are four types of spiritual newcomers. I have added a fifth. There are specific ways of getting past spiritual dislocation. Each technique is a little different. They work if you spend time carefully figuring out which type of spiritual newcomer you are and then eliminate your dislocation according to the instructions. You may overlap between two types, or go through phases of having variations of all of them. Be aware of the resolution-strategies and then realign yourself as suggested.

Notice: *"There was a feeling of awe and wonder, but it was fleeting and soon lost."*[54] *Alcoholics Anonymous* reports, in its own way, that we each have some experience of mystery and awe in appreciating a higher power. Because it is covered up with all manner of dislocation, it is fleeting and soon lost.

Many people are frightened of pursuing spirituality—(a) it's so at-odds with technology, (b) we're afraid if we're truly spiritual things won't work out in our favor; and, (c) and as soon as we find a way to achieve it that's minimally sufficient, we tend to take a dogmatic stance and give it limits. Then, if we can convince someone else to do it our way (proselytize) we feel reassured for three reasons: (i) because this is perceived as saving a soul, and "we" take credit, (ii) because we're no longer "alone" in our quest; and, (iii) we have (before the fact) prevented another person from going beyond the place we're at in spiritual awareness—if they did, we'd feel guilt or embarrassment at recognizing our own lack of commitment. Very often, when we experience a sincere breakthrough into a true awareness of something divine—a unitive experience—it is so ego-threatening that we abandon it for the suffocating reality of socially-approved rituals: living by consensus.

In *Facets of Personal Transformation,* I will discuss a unitive experience, which is that fleeting and rare sense of profound union with the universe. Absolute unity (actually: atonement [at-one moment]) is present and the person, as an individual, ceases to exist. In a few moments it's gone. A unitive experience, which is so threatening to our egos and our sense of individuality, is one of the rewards we seek in living a spiritual lifestyle. The mystics know it well.[55]

When spirituality becomes meaningful for you, you may find yourself uplifted, relieved, and eager to share that. You may feel impatient and annoyed that others don't get it or they don't marvel at your revelation. Be patient and accepting of yourself and others. It is important not to impose your ideas, values, or spiritual experiences on others. Encourage only yourself to labor diligently according to the instructions.

The instructions in Step Two in the original twelve-step program are to help you access a higher power. They're not guidelines on how you can convince others to live as you do. Never offer advice unless it's invited, and even then, be very cautious. Your opinions on relationships, careers, love affairs, parenting, recreation,

---

[54] *Alcoholics Anonymous*, p. 46.
[55] Gerald May explains a unitive experience, in *Will and Spirit*, HarperCollins, 1987, Chapter 3.

lifestyles, diet, sexuality, exercise, prayer, God, and religion are all a result of how you look at the world. Any advice is *your* solution to their predicament, not theirs. When you encounter people who have different values and lifestyle and, if your association with them leaves you judgmental, angry, disapproving, unable to be free and safe, then quietly shift your priorities. Examine yourself for religious or moral arrogance, *never* gossip, mind your own business, and quietly move on in your own life. Right association is essential.[56]

What is How It Works?

The two-and-one-half page summary, colloquially referred to in AA as How It Works,[57] extends from the beginning of Chapter 5: *"Rarely have we seen a person fail... ,"* through to *"...God could and would if He were sought."*[58] This is read at the start of many meetings. Besides the fact that it begins Chapter 5 in *Alcoholics Anonymous*, what is it? What's the point of it being *exactly* there? Why are only those two-and-one-half pages read at the start of many (most?) AA meetings? The author(s) didn't write these specific words and then stick them where they did because it seemed a nice thing with which to start a chapter.

When you have finished Step Four or Eight, you know you are done because you put a period after the last word on the last page. That period signals completion. But Step Two is one of the perception-and-faith steps. How do you know when you have finished Step Two?

In meetings and discussions there is a slurring of the boundary between Steps Two and Three. Do people sort-of-come-to-believe and say the prayer; or do they check out Step Two for a while before someone arbitrarily tells them to get on with Step Three? How do they *know* when they're finished Step Two? What event signals that it's time to move from Two to Three? There is a very clear indicator of when that is, but first you have to know what How It Works is (the two-and-one-half pages, not the chapter).

How It Works describes a successful journey from active addiction through to being recovered in a spiritual lifestyle. These two-and-one-half pages contain probably the most succinct version of the whole process: the shortest complete description of becoming spiritual. *"Well, that's exactly what this book is about. Its main object is to enable you to find a Power greater than yourself which will solve your problem."*[59] All the writing in *Alcoholics Anonymous* and the step chapters of

---

[56] In addition to abstinence (for addicts); for anyone endeavoring to transform into a spiritual lifestyle, Right Association is the single most important ongoing requirement. This is implied in *Alcoholics Anonymous* regarding carrying the message: *"...don't waste time trying to persuade him,"* p. 90; and *"We find it a waste of time to keep chasing... ,"* p. 96. Both of these statements imply addicts are to associate with others who "want what we have"—a spiritual solution, which is referred to several times in the chapter Working With Others. For more on Right Association, I refer you to Huston Smith's book *The World's Religions*, pp. 104, 105.

[57] "How It Works" is the title of Chapter 5 of *Alcoholics Anonymous*, beginning on p. 58. And colloquially, How It Works also refers to the passage from the beginning of p. 58 through to the middle of p. 60, ending with *"...if He were sought."* How It Works contains, in those two and one-half pages, the essence of the entire transformation process outlined in *Alcoholics Anonymous*.

[58] Ibid., pp. 58-60

[59] Ibid., p. 45.

Twelve Steps and Twelve Traditions are explanations that expand on what is written in How It Works (the two-and-one-half pages).

This is immediately followed by a paragraph that begins, *"Being convinced, we were at Step Three."*[60] In the book, *"Being convinced"* is followed by a comma and *"we were at Step Three"* is stressed by italics. That grammar means that the phrase *"Being convinced"* refers back to the preceding information in How It Works, and to the three pertinent ideas (noted as [a], [b], [c]) that immediately precede it.

Read How It Works through to *"Being convinced,"* and at that point stop and ask yourself: "Being convinced of what? What am I to have convinced myself of?" The answer is: You are to be convinced that How It Works (the two-and-one-half pages) and the three pertinent ideas [(a), (b), and (c)] are true. You must understand the absolute truth of the preceding two-and-one-half pages; that what they describe applies to *you*, personally. To make this point more clear, I'm going to insert some words into the middle of the sentence "Being convinced, *we were at step three."* Try it this way: *"Being convinced,* [that How It Works and the three pertinent ideas are true and apply completely to me—that Spirituality is the solution— then I was...] *at Step Three."*

When people aren't willing to put serious effort into understanding the nuances and subtle meanings of the words—exactly as they are written; when they instead rely on the loose interpretations of others, and substitute anything for "a power greater than ourselves", they cheat themselves out of a meaningful, spiritually rewarding life. They won't get recovered. You must hunt for the instructions within the instructions and be obedient to them. (This is "working the program".) The degree of your willingness to do this is directly related to how convinced you are that How It Works is true.[61]

When you "do" Step Three without being convinced, all of your subsequent effort will be less than effective, repetitious, and therefore it will foment futility. All recovery work will be more difficult than it needs to be.[62] Being pushed into Step Three prematurely, by yourself or anyone else, is fatal to getting recovered. Once you are *thoroughly* convinced of the absolute truth of How It Works, you'll have significantly less difficulty in addressing any of the steps following Step Two, and you'll exit the always-in-recovery cycle.

Completing Step Two is that process, over considerable time, of overcoming your defiance and doubt enough to develop a conviction that the program, exactly as it's described in How It Works, is true *for you*. Or: When you contemplate How It Works, and are deeply comforted by those two-and-one-half pages— convinced they contain *all* the answers regarding getting recovered that you will

---

[60] *Alcoholics Anonymous*, p. 60, emphasis theirs. This emphasis is very important. It has grammatical as much as spiritual meaning.

[61] Twelve-step pilgrims are unable to minimize spirituality in any way, with impunity. They are only human and cannot stand with only other humans against addiction.

[62] *"Difficulty at the beginning works supreme success. / Furthering through perseverance. / Nothing should be undertaken / It furthers one to appoint helpers."* Cary F. Baynes, Translator. *The I Ching or Book of Changes*, Princeton University Press, 1950, p. 16; as reported by Sheldon B. Kopp in *If You Meet The Buddha On The Road Kill Him*, Bantam Books, 1985, p. 3.

need, you've completed Step Two. Or: When you have a deep and abiding inner be-lief that access to Spirituality, specifically as outlined in <u>How It Works</u>, is true and exactly what *you* need to do—that is completing Step Two.

<u>How It Works</u> is the substance of Step Two, but why is it read at the begin-ning of most AA meetings? Step Two is what unites *everyone* in AA, *every*where in the world. Step Two is [supposed to be] the common starting point; the foundation of everyone's recovery; the guide for *everyone's* conduct. Reading <u>How It Works</u> sym-bolizes in words the path everyone follows, and reminds all members that: *"...Step Two [<u>How It Works</u>] is the rallying point for all of us. Whether agnostic, atheist, or former believer, we can stand together on this step."*[63] Members are to be reminded of their singular purpose and universal unity every time <u>How It Works</u> is read.

Leading Into Step Three

"Being convinced, <u>we were at Step Three</u>."[64] And Step Three is: *"Made a decision to turn our will and our lives over to the care of God <u>as we understood Him</u>."*[65] What exactly does Step Three imply?

The speeches often go like this: "I want to turn my will over, but I don't know what that really means or when I've done it." "I get in this struggle with God about who's in charge." "This is making me crazy—turn it over, take it back, turn it over, take it back." The confusion and struggle around Step Three is unnecessary when you understand it in relation to the philosophy of the program, and especially in relation to Step Two. First, here's a story:

In November 1989, I was living in Edmonton. Outside there was a foot of snow on the ground, and I decided I was fed up with winter. I also decided I would move to Vancouver (you don't have to shovel rain). My partner agreed. I went back to school to enhance my qualifications to make it easier to find employment. Every Sunday morning, for ten months, I drove to an Edmonton newsstand and bought a Vancouver newspaper. I checked the apartment and employment ads, and I sent out dozens of resumes. The next November I got a job.

Moving to another city is not a simple thing. Literally, there was a ton of books, never mind bookshelves, guitars, CDs, stereo equipment, and other less im-portant things like furniture and dishes. We hired a mover and started saying good-bye to friends. We quit our jobs, packed our property, and left. On December 24, 1990, we arrived in Vancouver.

From the time I decided to move, until I actually arrived in Vancouver, thir-teen months had passed. The *decision* to move to Vancouver didn't mean I was there. There were months of work and preparation prior to the decision becoming a reality. You may have decided what you are going to do next Saturday. That doesn't mean that you're doing it—it's not yet next Saturday. Because you *made a decision* to turn your will and life over to the care of God, as you understand God, doesn't

[63] *Twelve Steps and Twelve Traditions*, pp. 34, 35.
[64] *Alcoholics Anonymous,* p. 60, emphasis theirs.
[65] Ibid., p. 59, and *Twelve Steps and Twelve Traditions*, p. 34, emphasis theirs.

mean that you can "turn it over", and it doesn't mean that you are "turning it over". It only means you have decided to do that.

Back to the story of my move: Yes, I decided to move, but that decision meant nothing without action. For five years prior to that, every November I would decide to move away from the snow, as my Edmonton friends could attest to. It was always good for a laugh at first snowfall—me deciding to move to Vancouver (again). However, my decision in November 1989 was different. How did others know it was different? I followed the decision up with the action required, regardless of the difficulty or inconvenience.

A decision by itself is only a passive "thinking action". It's meaningless without behaviors that arise out of a commitment to whatever the decision is. There is deciding. Then there is acting (on the decision), which eventually results in the original decision in your mind becoming a reality in time and space.

Let's assume, only for the sake of this discussion, that someone reading this book is a counsellor and has decided to change their counselling style because of things they've read here. They've thought about it, read this book a few times, and have firmly committed themselves to changing their style of work. After their decision, they must do whatever behavior is required to make their decision real. At the minimum, they would have to study this book more closely, possibly go back to school, and maybe go to therapy themselves. They would study the books I cite in the footnotes. They may even decide to track me down and work with me for a while (whatever it takes, right?). They would have to actually do these things or their decision by itself is meaningless.

Consider that even after having done all of those things, in order to actually change, they'd also eventually have to *act* in the new ways they would have learned. They would behave differently. In order for the decision to become absolutely real, they must *do* the things that demonstrate the commitment to what they have not only decided, but learned. Any decision has no value if you don't work to accomplish it, and then actually *do* it.

All of this applies to Step Three: *"Made a decision to turn our will and our lives over to the care of God <u>as we understood Him</u>."*[66] Assume, right now, in this moment, you are completely and absolutely convinced that <u>How It Works</u> is true, and you *decide* to turn your will and life over to the care of God as you understand God.[67] That precise moment often contains a subtle and crucial misperception in the expectations that many addicts have regarding Step Three.

Spiritual newcomers cannot turn their will and life over, and "leave it over". They haven't learned how or acquired the skills yet. Simply making a decision does not spontaneously create the ability to be spiritual. Commitment, self-discipline,

---

[66] *Alcoholics Anonymous,* p. 59, and *Twelve Steps and Twelve Traditions,* p. 34, emphasis theirs.
[67] An interesting aside is that I don't hear people talk about how hard Step Two was, and I hear many people talking about how hard Step Three *is*. Yet, in the actual requirements of the steps, Step Two is the hard one: coming to trust the program, coming to believe that God is the solution, coming to trust with no reservations that being Spiritual and a higher power will restore you to sanity. This is the hard part, and once you have ample faith, making the decision is relatively easy. Most addicts in recovery slide past Step Two because it really calls them to task.

willingness, labor, and training do that. Because you decide that you want to be a doctor, a therapist, more spiritual, a musician, or anything else doesn't mean you are that something: You've only decided, and not taken the steps or completed the training. It is no different here. Once you've made the decision to "turn it over" the remaining steps are the apprenticeship that teaches you how to "leave it turned over".

At Step Three you are still struggling with fear, character defects, irresponsibility, guilt, shame, etc. With proper research at Step Two, before you make the decision, you will trust that <u>How It Works</u>, and the steps, are the itinerary for learning "how" to turn it over. At Step Three you can neither turn your life over nor be sincerely spiritual; you don't know how. You're an untrained beginner at being spiritual. If you make the decision at Step Three, and at the same time think you can do it (and berate yourself when you don't), it will entrench a vicious sense of spiritual inadequacy. You hear people in meetings all the time: "I made a decision to turn my will over and I took it back, and I turned it over and I took it back." The frustration, confusion, and the often growing despair, is obvious.

When you have completed your training i.e. the steps, and are eventually comfortable with Step Eleven, you will only *then* be somewhat trained in the basics of spirituality. You won't be good at it, still largely a novice, but you will have some training (via the first nine steps). You will then also notice some regular, but limited, success at "leaving your will turned over", but only because, and if, you've been obedient to *all* the instructions. Step Three is making a decision to live a spiritual lifestyle. Long after that decision is made—after living in the maintenance steps with spiritual integrity—you will realize the reality of that decision, not before.

Turning Over My Life, Too?

Addicts complain and lament about turning or not turning their will over to the care of God. The discussions that revolve around the intellectual struggles of "willpower" seem never-ending. Challenging your more easily identifiable behavior is avoided by constantly debating the abstract notion of willpower. I have never heard addicts debate turning or not turning their "life" over to the care of God.

How often do alcoholics and addicts who claim to be "in recovery" participate in unspiritual behavior, i.e. adultery, aggression, blaming, cheating, harsh criticism, defiance to the principles, dishonesty, gossip, greed, insensitive jokes, cruel judgments, manipulation, pornography, prejudice, racism, rudeness, irresponsible sex, sexism, slander, violence, etc.? Addicts turning their *Life* over requires a very dedicated commitment to the opposite of the behaviors I just listed.

Turning your will over and taking it back (whatever that might mean) is a dissembling intellectual debate. It easily sounds sincere, but demands nothing of the addict but a good speech, and addicts are great at speeches. Addicts are significantly less accountable when they concentrate on theories and words like "willpower". Acting and behaving as if they were *living* God's will is entirely another matter.

Turning your *will* over is a specific reference to your thoughts and emotional energy. In turning your *will* over, you work at focusing your mental energy on ideas of honesty rather than deceit or manipulation; on having kind thoughts, not angry, mean thoughts; on ideas of sharing and equality, not on manipulating privileges for yourself. Focus your willpower (intellectual energy) on challenging yourself, not others; on not showing off, not being demanding, not gossiping, not arguing, not being petty. Deliberately focus your thoughts and energy—your will— on taking responsibility and not blaming. This requires constant vigilance. Altogether, these might be the exercises of turning *your* will (or mental energy) towards the will of God, as you understand God. For the first few years it is exhausting.

Turning your *life* over to the care of God means acting and behaving in a manner that demonstrates respect for the body-temple, veracity, humility, charity, and responsibility—obedience to spiritual principles. It means: Promote peace in *all* the relationships in your life; *always* behave graciously; and offer courtesy, respect, and consideration towards all others (especially towards people you're mad at or that are mad at you). These living behaviors demand incomparably more effort than the usually spurious, spiritual debates about the ego-construct of willpower and who's got how much focused in what direction.

When was the last time you discussed someone else's character defects and justified this cruel gossip by not telling who they were? This is feeling intellectually or spiritually smug because you can smear their character and conceal their identity, justifying it by explaining you were trying to help, trying to share your struggles, or "working your program". Remember the last time you were in the company of others who were racist or sexist in their "humor". Did you participate or did you quietly excuse yourself and not socialize with them any more? How have you tacitly justified your own meanness, disrespect, dishonesty, or irresponsibility? When was the last time you told an anecdote at someone else's expense and people laughed at the other person's expense, and you were the entertainer? What about driving badly? What about knowing you're guilty and still fighting over parking and speeding tickets? Being rude to store clerks? Littering? Ignoring the common-courtesy rules about owning pets? All of this is how you respect the people in your community. These are the questions to ask about a spiritual *life*.

An authentic Step Three decision requires a huge commitment to Spiritual behavior: turning your Life over, too. This would require an ongoing diligent effort to stop all unspiritual conduct—gossiping, lying, violence, manipulating, bossing others around, cheating, arguing, being slothful, breaking rules, raging, irresponsibly depending upon others, complaining you're sick when you're not, blaming, showing off, etc. And it would include praying often, regularly, and sincerely.

A Spiritual *Life* is: put money in the meters; stop giving people "the finger"; stop at yellow lights; don't complain the sale price expired yesterday; pick up after your dog; if the sign says don't (whatever)… then don't; put your shopping cart back where you're supposed to; pay your parking tickets; don't litter; return the items you borrow; buy the pet license; don't talk during the movie; don't be impatient in the checkout line at the store. *In addition to the obvious praying and meditating, a spiritual person extends courtesy and respect into their community and never excuses their own mean or irresponsible behavior.*

Turning your life over also means you complete the Step Three prayer, which is the first behavior that demonstrates the sincerity of your decision, and then complete the rest of the steps, as instructed, in a deliberate and thorough manner. The fact it may be inconvenient and require you drastically change your lifestyle doesn't matter—your decision was voluntary. Once you've *decided* to turn your will and life over, if the decision has any credibility, unspiritual behavior must stop.

The investigation leading to your Step Three decision (called Step Two) and the actions that follow it, are what determine whether you'll remain in recovery, or become recovered. The first nine steps are your Spiritual apprenticeship: how you learn to live doing God's will. Keeping spiritual principles visible in your life, approaching the work with anticipation and interest, and being honest in all of your relationships, are what prove that your decision was sincere. In order for the decision to be genuine, the follow-up action must be thorough, regardless of the "cost" to yourself. It is never a matter of convenience.

Your willingness to do exactly as you are told will prove how sincere your decision was.[68] Your decision to live Spiritually can only be trusted by others if you consistently behave spiritually, regardless of how difficult that is. Your conduct proves your desire to live up to the commitment you made. You must consistently recommit yourself to spiritual behavior, which allows you to become what you've decided you want.

I was once asked: "In Step Three, aren't we asked to become powerful instruments of God's love on earth?" Because of the interpretive license in the way this person reframed Step Three, my answer was, "No." I point this out here, partly because of its bearing on Step Three, but also because it shows how easily recovering addicts reinterpret the original program to the detriment of spiritual principles. There are three main observations on that person's question.

One: "God", as an entity (which is limiting in itself and therefore not effective, but more about that later), doesn't "ask" anyone in a twelve-step program to do anything. Addicts are in pain (acting out), they discover (unitive moment), they choose abstinence, they volunteer for spirituality. In the vernacular, I would put it that God asks for nothing, and waits for the pilgrim to volunteer. *It's all voluntary.* What do you demand of yourself on behalf of God, as you understand God? There's a difference between being asked to do something, and voluntarily understanding the value of something and being quietly devoted to it, without being asked.[69] We volunteer to be examples of the life that is available when we live spiritually.

The concept of responsibility is very subtle. Think about these two statements: (a) I'm on this spiritual-devotion trip because God asked me to; or, (b) I'm on this spiritual-devotion trip because I see it's inherently good for me and I want to. When you consider the motivation and responsibility in either statement, you'll notice significant differences. Regardless of how close you believed you were to your

---

[68] This is subtle and very important: Willing obedience to the instructions is the solution; being grudgingly obedient solves nothing.

[69] "Surprise" your higher power with a generous gift: devote yourself to spirituality. *You* are the gift.

own insanity or death, at the moment you made that decision, it was voluntary, so there's never any reason to complain.

Two: Being "an instrument" has a tone of intrusiveness. The question was asked with a quality that implied people getting recovered are on a mission to do God's work. Well, a very tentative *maybe,* but only with this firm qualifier: the "mission" is to only work on themselves, and to *never* proselytize.

Three: Describing this twelve-step pilgrimage as some aspect of God's "love" imposes a specific and highly personal view of God on those you would help. Pushing the view that "God is love" onto others is against the crucial freedom-guaranteeing injunction: "as you understand God".

Step Two (Revisited)

If you don't develop a very firm belief that a higher power is the only thing that can restore you to sanity, then your recovery will be politically motivated. Too many people in twelve-step programs don't understand that Step Two is the hard one and Step Three is the easier one. They skip lightly over Step Two on their way to the sober dance, wrongly believing that service work, committees, round-ups, sharing, and doing the steps, will restore them to sanity.[70]

Certainly these people will be honest—most of the time. They'll knock around in the program, stay sober and get a job—that'll be good enough. So what if they gossip or win a useless argument once in a while. They won't lie to their sponsor or to the important people in their life… very often. This political focus to step work is one reason why people carry a nagging sense that the steps are always unfinished. The Promises remain elusive, and being recovered will never be available.

Getting recovered arises out of a consistent devotion to learning about the five spiritual principles as they are embodied in the regeneration steps (Steps One to Nine). If you don't acquire belief and begin commitment to a higher power in Step Two, the decision at Step Three is meaningless as far as getting recovered goes. Spend a year on Step Two, then a week on Step Three, and you'll be fine.

If you're struggling with Step Three, tired of repeating the steps, or unsure of your higher power or the program, go back to Step Two and stay there for a *long* time. If you're convinced that you are an addict and you can't act out, yet you keep on relapsing, you missed the crucial spiritual import of Step Two. If you're generally discontented or angry with recovery; if your abstinence is tenuous; if you're subtly confused about where you are in your program; if it vaguely doesn't make sense; if spirituality is confusing or frightening; if the twelve-step process is burdensome or repetitious, go back to Step Two and stay there for a *long* time.

Anyone who sincerely understands Step Two has no serious difficulty after that. Resolve your spiritual belligerence as suggested, and *then* do Step Three. Include both your will and life, and know that intellectual debates about willpower are actually evidence of willfulness. This is hard work—in Step Two you are refocusing

---

[70] Without Spirituality as the essential foundation of everything you do, not even doing the steps will restore you to sanity. Doing the steps without sincere Spirituality is an exercise in Impression Management.

your entire existence. If you're properly oriented in Spirituality, you'll see things you've never seen before. Your transformation has implacable grandeur, and is solely to the credit of God and not to the credit of anything else. The only motivation for praying is because God is worthy of being prayed to.

Step Three

The first paragraph of Step Three in *Twelve Steps and Twelve Traditions* begins*: "Practicing Step Three is like the opening of a door, which to all appearances is closed and locked."*[71]

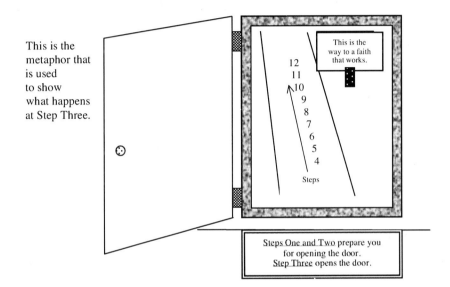

It goes on to say that willingness opens a door, and through the door you will see a path leading to a faith that works. The metaphor also advises that through the door you will see a sign: *"This is the way to a faith that works."*[72] It means that beyond Step Two the steps are the route to an ever-deepening faith. Whatever depth of conviction you achieve in Step Two will be deepened into a faith that works (for the larger spiritual trials that lay ahead).

How willing you are to do this isn't a matter of magic or luck; it's a matter of prayer and hard work. The harder you work at laying the foundation at Step Two, the more willing you will be. It's this simple: Everyone is willing to invest where they are guaranteed to gain. If there is no doubt about the outcome, people are willing to work for something they want. So, if there's poor research before the decision, there's less willingness when it's time to make the decision. With significant effort at Step Two you will come to believe that Spirituality is a guaranteed success. You'll then have no doubt and that makes the decision easy: You know, from your own effort, the results are guaranteed. It all depends on *your* hard work.

---

[71] *Twelve Steps and Twelve Traditions*, p. 34.
[72] Ibid.

The Step Three Prayer

"God, I offer myself to Thee—"[73] Here is the offering of yourself (will *and* life) to your higher power. If you decide to do this, it means completing the steps, following the instructions, and forcing yourself to learn how to think, live, and behave according to spiritual principles. And of course it's in all endeavors from planting your garden and doing laundry to… well, everywhere.

"—to build with me and do with me as Thou wilt." Remember, a dash indicates that what follows the dash explains what's before it. When you offer yourself it must be motivated by a desire and willingness to become what "God" wants, and in God's way; not what your peer group, insecurities, or culture wants.

The steps are the actual process of building: the process of restoration. You allow God to re-build you by you doing the steps yourself. Too many people speak as though they are waiting for God to actually do something in their life. God "building" you is only a metaphor. God mysteriously supports you as *you* do all the work.

"Relieve me of the bondage of self, that I may better do Thy will." This is a supplication to God that your selfishness (which is nothing more than irresponsibility via the usual character defects) be removed so you can better do God's will, not so you can have a leisurely, peaceful life.

"Take away my difficulties, that victory over them may bear witness to those I would help of Thy Power, Thy Love, and Thy Way of life." The intent of asking God to remove your difficulties is only so other people can see that living a Spiritual life is good. Your difficulties are not removed so that you have a good life, but so that others will be attracted to a similar way of life. This hard work is in service to your higher power, not in service to yourself.

"May I do Thy will always." This implies a voluntary desire that regardless of how difficult it may be, this will be a permanent way of life, without exception.

This is a deeply unselfish prayer and excludes praying for righteous "charities", like your friend recovering from an illness, your children finding happiness, your sister finding true love, or your picnic not being called off on account of rain. Because something is perceived as morally good or charitable (for instance, that some person doesn't die from cancer or get hurt on their canoe trip) it doesn't follow Spiritually that you should pray for that. All petitionary prayer for "good" things is, to some degree, self-serving.[74]

And, almost finally, regarding Step Three, consider: *"We found it very desirable to take this spiritual step with an understanding person… ."*[75] In Step Three, which is one of the six action steps, there must be a demonstration of your sincere commitment to a higher power. In doing your Step Three prayer with someone, you're making a public declaration of your sincerity. The books offer that the decision and prayer is vital, but has little lasting effect unless:

---

[73] *Alcoholics Anonymous,* p. 63.
[74] Ibid. p. 87, and *Twelve Steps and Twelve Traditions,* pp. 102, 103.
[75] *Alcoholics Anonymous,* p. 63.

- it is preceded by an exceptionally thorough reorganization of your spiritual views in Step Two; and,
- it is followed by vigorous effort,[76] which is Step Four, and then the remaining steps.

In this book, in this chapter, about 85% of the material is about Step Two, and about 15% is about Step Three. As I said earlier: Spend a year on Step Two, then a week on Step Three, and you'll be fine. Really, that's all there is to it.

---

[76] *Alcoholics Anonymous*, pp. 63-64, and *Twelve Steps and Twelve Traditions*, p. 42.

4

Step Four: How "I" Have Become Me

"Ride your horse along the edge of the sword.
Hide yourself in the middle of the flames.
Blossoms of the fruit tree will bloom in the fire.
The sun rises in the evening."[1]

This poem describes a life of individual self-determination. Some people might interpret it in relation to things external; others may see in it the dynamic of being yourself and challenging your own demons. Challenging your own demons is at the core of all spiritual work; challenging anyone else's demons is a significant aspect of relationship addiction.

Ride your horse along the edge of the sword. Develop a sense of yourself underneath imposed social attitudes and rituals. Step out from under the mantle of Victim, ignore peer pressure, and put yourself on the edge of your own personality. If you manage to do this without imposing on others, you will appreciate your own freedom. Take risks that are appropriate to accomplish your aspirations, all the while reining in your ego's need to control or criticize others. This accomplishment involves achieving independence, claiming individuation, and taking responsibility.[2]

Hide yourself in the middle of the flames. To remain in tune with a *spiritual* pilgrimage, the place of struggle is within your own inner dislocation and contradictions, rather than in external controversy. You are the flame. Hide in the middle of who you are. Don't abandon yourself or "come out" from who you are. The more arduous struggle is deep within yourself.

Blossoms of the fruit tree will bloom in the fire. As you wrestle with your dislocation, and develop your own spiritual personality, you will be able to more quietly say, "I am truly *Me* in my relationship with the universe." This accomplishment that you sense, as you pursue who you are without imposing on others, is

---

[1] This is from the I Ching. I cannot verify the specific translation, but I'm quite sure it's from *The I Ching or Book of Changes* by Cary F. Baynes, trans., Princeton University Press, 1950, (my copy of which has gone missing).
[2] There are social risks for being assertive and strongly self-motivated. As a general rule, although there are variations, the range of human conduct is on the spectrum of passive to assertive to aggressive. Each one of these types of personality has a certain view of the other two types. Decidedly aggressive people often think that passive people are wimps and hold them in disdain, and view assertive people as "being okay". Passive people are often insecure around, or envious of, assertive people and quite afraid of aggressive people (who, according to them, are mean, pushy, and demanding). Assertive people often view passive people as simply "okay" and aggressive people as only an annoyance, but no real threat (because they, themselves, are assertive).

magnificent (blossoms blooming). You appreciate the fragrance of the universe in the midst of your struggle with yourself.

The sun rises in the evening. You won't know the joy or beauty (sun rising) of any of this until after you've accomplished it (in the evening). Your life is a symphony being conducted by you. There are a hundred and twelve instruments being played, all at the same time, with different tempos, volumes, and tones. *Your* symphony is composed of your career and relationships and recreation and leisure and sexuality and values and likes and dislikes and preferences and calamities and successes. You are the symphony; you are the conductor.

Because a note was missed in the 152nd bar doesn't mean it's a bad symphony. It means that there was one note missed in two hours of music. No one knows it's a beautiful symphony until the last note is played. Even then, whether or not the symphony is good or bad is only an opinion. Play your own symphony as if there's no audience.[3] That's the only way you'll know about *you*. You won't know it was a glorious life until the last note is played.[4] You won't know the value of riding your horse along the edge of the sword, or hiding yourself in the middle of the flames, until your life is well along its course. That's the beauty of it.

When I'm old I'll not likely be saying to someone: "Remember that time I played it safe?" And I wouldn't want to remember very many times when I had a chance to be me and didn't take it. The purpose of your life is to be you. That's all. I suppose that's one purpose of this book—to show you how, by deliberately (or properly) using the original twelve steps, you discover yourself in healthy Spirituality, and reap the rewards of your own personality. It's far too easy to abandon yourself within the dysfunctional community of twelve-step programs or culture, just as you abandoned yourself to illness or within in your addictions. Abandoning yourself is much easier than being spiritual and living honorably with your own values.

I was aware of the import of this as I was writing this book, and contemplating how different readers (be they victims, or passive, or assertive, or independent, or aggressive, etc.) might react to what I write. I would occasionally resist being political when I found myself hedging my words when writing something that went strongly against popular opinion. At other times, I was too assertive and needed to recast a sentence into a softer tone. I live most often with respectful disregard for the opinions of others about *my* life. I also work at having no opinions about theirs. For as much as you agree or disagree with what I write, I certainly wouldn't have written it if I had not agreed with the message of the poem.

Here's an interesting perspective and subtle application of the poem: You may casually remark that you are a member of a group or a member of a program. "I belong to AA," or, "I am a member of SAA." That may be true; however, it's more

---

[3] Moments before going on stage in front of several thousand people at a jazz festival in Europe, Miles Davis was reported to have said to a nervous member of his quintet: "There's no need to be nervous, it's just practice."

[4] Musicians, other live performers, and teachers often experience a decided shift partway through a presentation and notice that the last half of a set of songs or presentation was an improvement over the first half. It's always possible to feel the mood and improve as the performance progresses. You can always improve the quality of your own life as it progresses; it's not over yet.

intimate, and it subtly changes your perceptions of responsibility, if you say that you are not "a member" of a group, but that you *are* the group.

I'm told in some Aboriginal languages, when people talk about themselves they can't say, "I'm *from* such-and-such community." The literal translation is: "I *am* the community." The syntax and nuance of the language is that they *are* their community. [I describe this from a spiritual perspective on p. 323.]

This is an awkward view for people to accept because it puts greater accountability on them for how they act, knowing they actually *are* what they are members of.[5] You are what you do. Your behavior is purposeful and is always an advertisement for the integrity of your spirituality. You are your group, and to present yourself otherwise easily fosters superficial or artificial associations.[6]

When your ego has you believe that you are "from" AA, or NA, or the PTA, "from" implies that there's a separation between you and the group. Should the group be unsavory you can distance yourself "from" them; likewise, the group can distance itself from you and your unsavory behavior. You (or they) get to opt out of responsibility. Your ego has it set up that AA, or NA, or your church, or union, or friends, are all somehow no reflection of you i.e. I am me; the group is them. As much as this perspective may be appealing, it is spiritually untenable. You *are* your behavior and your associations.

How many times have you heard some variation of "I did a mean (or a dishonest) thing, but that's not *really* who I am." Nonsense. Behavior is purposeful. You are what you do. Twelve-step groups are the animated reflection of the people who comprise them. When people are absent, the group doesn't exist. As the members behave, so *is* the group; as you behave, so you are.

By the time you get to Step Four, which is the first of the two major preparations for a public declaration of your spiritual devotion, you've ridden along this "sword" long enough to understand that one purpose of the program is to assume ever-increasing responsibility for yourself and the state of affairs in your life. It demands that you be completely accountable. You are your associations. Your twelve-step group, your religion, your profession—these don't live in a book or some building; they live in you. You are the way you behave and think, and it's not spiritually tenable to ignore the unalterable fact that you're *It*.[7]

---

[5] This is readily apparent in the way the traditions of AA are presented, which are so easily disregarded in favor of politics.

[6] *"There's no use for artificial discipline, / For, move as I will, I manifest the ancient Tao."* Hsiang-yen, as quoted in *This Is It*, Alan Watts, Vintage Books, 1973, p. 88.

[7] Notice that fifteen years ago, and before that, twelve-step groups were mentioned in movies and books with a tone of respect. Today they are more the brunt of sarcasm and racy humor. The members of twelve-step groups, by not taking themselves more seriously, contribute significantly to this cheapening of recovery and spirituality. Nothing is free.

As an important aside: Therapists, ministers, sponsors, priests, yogis, counselors, etc., are only capable of bringing someone to whatever level they, themselves, are at. If the helper is neurotic, honest, fearful, serene, mean, carries subtle addictions—whatever—the best that can be hoped for is the people they help will be as (dys)functional or (non)spiritual as the helpers are. For the newcomer/client that *may* be an improvement, but it says little for the integrity of the helper when they refuse to address the dislocation in themselves. Whatever the helper "is" the best the client/newcomer can hope for.

You, as an individual, are the focus of the first seven steps; these are yours, personally. Everybody else gets the last five; they are for others. [Ultimately, all of the steps are done on behalf of your higher power.] At Step Four there's a *much* greater demand for you to be accountable, both to yourself and to your higher power. It isn't about having a good time or a good life; it's about being spiritually accountable. You're learning self-discipline, accountability, and commitment in order to become a person who demonstrates a sincere and unassuming spirituality. This is far more onerous than being socially successful.

Disciple, Discipline, Obedience

A disciple is an adherent to a movement or a philosophy. Being disciplined is being consistent in living up to commitments, values, or rules: regularly holding yourself to specific standards of behavior. The roots are from Latin—*discipulus* (a pupil) and *discere* (to learn). Only discipline allows you to accomplish anything, and only being a disciple of the original twelve-step philosophy allows you to become recovered. Being spiritual requires discipline and determination.

At face value, it sounds logical and straightforward, but the number of ways an addict's ego can slip justified irresponsibility into a spiritual pilgrimage is amazing. You're up against a disease that will kill you if you let it, and a culture that pays lip-service to integrity. Becoming spiritual is an uphill battle to say the least (but the effort required eases noticeably beyond Step Seven). Spiritual freedom, among other things, is freedom from the annihilating bondage of addictions, and an exercise in self-discipline and obedience. It's no mean feat if you accomplish it.

Near the beginning of getting recovered, obedience is perceived and felt as a confining thing. In some ways, compared to the erratic, flamboyant behaviors in active addiction, it is. However, near the end of your spiritual pilgrimage, obedience isn't a confining thing at all. When you're living in the maintenance steps, obedience is actually the only guarantee of freedom you have.

Obedience to the principles identified in the original literature (not to opinions about the literature) makes you a disciple of the program's spiritual intent. Obedience is what creates safety. It's interesting that proselytizing is discouraged in the two most effective transformation processes in the world's history, Buddhism and the original twelve-step program.[8] If you're obedient to the principles, your success is guaranteed. You don't have to figure out Step Four: you have to do it. But that, of course, requires self-discipline, which addicts often lack in spiritual pursuits.

The instructions in *Alcoholics Anonymous* and *Twelve Steps and Twelve Traditions* are written in a somewhat confusing style. [Usually anything that chal-

---

[8] Buddhism wasn't always the overt, stylized rituals and ornate temples that we see today. It was originally, via the wisdom of Siddhartha, without icons, statues, or formal places of worship. There was no proselytizing. The intent of Buddhism was to acquire contemplative peace by taking complete personal responsibility for the entire state of your own life, without recourse to anything external. Through the adoption of new values by personal insight, via The Eight-Fold Noble Path, it demonstrated an *inner*-personal system of ethical conduct that allowed complete respect, in thought and action, for *all* other living things. The Four Noble Truths and The Eight-Fold Noble Path provide a method to detach from the dislocation of life. Original Buddhism was not a religion in our modern view of religion, and is probably closer to authentic self-help than anything else.

lenges the dislocated and self-serving perceptions of an unregenerate ego, is labeled as confusing, and heard with skepticism.] The AA reference texts are hard to read as books of psychological instruction because that's not their intent. What with the long metaphors, which sometimes seem incomplete, the symbolism, and the apparently poorly defined structure, they make little sense psychologically. However, when you study them as spiritual reference texts they make complete sense, even in their incompleteness.[9] *Alcoholics Anonymous* and *Twelve Steps and Twelve Traditions* make you work for the insights. Nothing is free, especially spiritual peace.

As much as you may hope otherwise, *this* book won't make your work easier. This book may make the path a little smoother, but only because you'll realize the "bumpiness" was your old way of addressing the steps, which really means your old way of addressing your life. Your own insights, wherever they lie within you, won't be easier to find because insights aren't universal; they are particular to you. Understanding of *your* path cannot be found while walking on someone else's. What I offer here may help to keep you "on track", or prevent you from wandering off into unfruitful endeavor, but your own transformation won't be any easier.

I have no slick tricks, short-cuts, or rules that will ease your burden. Without doing *all* the work yourself, you cannot openly demonstrate the commitment you made at Step Three, and you cheat yourself out of the opportunity to develop faith, which is the sensed, subtle reward of diligent effort. Faith isn't free for the asking. When you're working hard, and insight finally clicks, there's an indescribable, comforting little jolt of true peace and relief. But you've got to sit in meditation, in prayer, in quiet discussion, by yourself and with a spiritually trustworthy mentor, with the books and a dictionary, *one sentence at a time*, for long contemplative hours, weeks, months, and then years, to get successively deeper insights.[10]

Properly focused, disciplined effort is what creates humility and spiritual confidence. Filling in the blanks of someone else's Step Four-quiz creates a prison: you become some version of whomever wrote it. The authors are creating followers. It's often patronizing, and certainly indicative of a facet of relationship addiction on the part of whomever writes them, and fear and unhealthy compliance (again, relationship addiction) on the part of whomever completes them.

I cautiously add: There are exceptions. When you're involved in formal treatment, there are added psychological agendas and limitations of time. This structured approach to early intervention requires some generic forms, accelerated crossover work, and forced disclosure. Outside of these time-limited professional settings: For addicts in the course of spiritual transformation, avoid generic guides and remain with personal exploration through the original literature.

---

[9] All of the insightful treatises on spiritual transformation, i.e. paths to "divine peace", like *The Bhagavad-Gita, The Upanishads,* several of the Buddhist sutras, *The Rule of Benedict, The Kabalah, The Sermon On The Mount, The Koran, and* the AA reference texts (there are others) are found lacking or contradictory when they are examined in a scientific or psychological manner. That's because the writings are most often poetry and complicated symbolic metaphors, but are read as scientific, literal prose.

[10] "Take what you want," said God, "and pay for it." A Spanish proverb quoted from *Taking Responsibility,* by Nathaniel Branden, Simon & Schuster, 1996.

Think about this: someone writes a one-hundred question Step One guide. You don't have to read the approved literature—just fill in the blanks on some photocopied handout. It's symbolic of your filling out a job application: You're applying for the job of being just like whoever wrote the guide. Doing the much harder work of being an unassuming, quiet disciple of the original material, and absorbing its revealed wisdom *directly* into your own life, is where real faith and insights come from. This will guarantee you never become an extension of someone else. (Being an extension of someone else is one aspect of the addictions issues that got you here in the first place.) Yes, it's much easier to go to a bookstore or some treatment center and buy a step guide and follow someone else's path. This easier, softer way cheats you out of the exercise of self-discipline, which is essential for spiritual integrity. Ask: Do I want to become them or do I want to become me?

The metaphor of a butterfly leaving a cocoon applies here. Yes, it's a time-worn metaphor, but it's very true in spirituality. If you force open the cocoon and help the butterfly, it dies because its wings don't become strong enough through the exercise of breaking out to fly. It needs the struggle. *You need the struggle.* You can buy step guides and search for gimmicks that promise success with less investment of energy and emotion. That's a fool's game. To achieve the intimate relationships or the serenity you declare you want, but complain you don't have, there is no easy solution and no easier path. Your propensity to pander to your own, or another person's, sloth and irresponsibility is killing you, as well as them.

Faith and Tradition

There are essentially three ways that people acquire faith:

The first way people acquire faith is to assume the faith of the authority figures in their life (which begins in childhood). Here, traditions and beliefs are imposed, and sometimes the indoctrination of the young person is absolute and all-encompassing. "Outside" knowledge, other perspectives, and personal/alternative experience are rigorously excluded. When people live with imposed traditions, their safety and peace of mind is dependent on obedience to that which was imposed.[11] As the child becomes older, their faith (or trust) in the imposed tradition becomes intellectually and emotionally "easy". There's little risk because there's no personal responsibility: "I have faith because I was told this is true."

This paradigm fosters faith with little enduring strength. When the authority figure dies, the underling's faith is undermined. Or, should the minion encounter a stronger authority with great charisma and a different experience, or should some startlingly new truth arise that's at variance with what they've been taught, their faith is shaken. Faith that hinges on indoctrination and obedience often becomes unten-

---

[11] There's a very fine line here that I am mindful of: Some imposition of values and religious tradition is by tyrants and is blatantly abusive; imposed so that the tyrants can remain secure with various illusions about truth and validation. There is also the imposition of values and tradition by parents who are sincerely doing well by their children: kind and judicious parenting. In the areas of religion and sexuality, in my experience, there is far too much of the former being disguised as the latter. As regards to sponsorship within twelve-step programs, sponsorship should never involve the imposition of values or assume the dynamics of parenting.

able. With this scenario, indoctrinated people often grow into adulthood imposing a similar tyranny on themselves, and on those they can control.

A stringent imposition of tradition indicates deep insecurity and the need to control others. It does not foster healthy psychological or spiritual development within the people on whom the tradition is imposed. "Faith" is protected by dogma and defensiveness. In order to avoid acknowledging doubt, the defense becomes more inflexible. Whenever there is self-doubt and insecurity, it can only be repressed by an ever-increasing adherence to dogma. This type of faith is not dependent on sincere spiritual investigation and informed commitment but on dogma, and the success of political indoctrination.

The second way to acquire faith is to overtly reject *all* imposed tradition through general rebellion, and create your own traditions through your singular experience, and end with faith only in yourself, and trusting no one.

I'm not talking about rebellion as violent insurrection and revolt, although it sometimes ends up that way. Rebellion here means exaggerated rejection and defiance to anything inherited. [The proper transition from early developmental dependence to a non-addicted, adult independence, with a clear and stable identity of self (which, sadly enough, is quite rare), is thwarted by a need for rebellion.] This person struggles to create beliefs and acquire faith out of a combination of their own defiance, experience, and the belaboring of the flaws in the system or in the person they've rejected. The result is: Faith only in *me*.

Rebellion that rejects a tradition isn't necessarily a revolt against tradition *per se*, although it's usually described that way. It's often a revolt against the authority figures and the manner in which the tradition was imposed—retaliation for the disrespectful and aggressive imposition of tradition by tyrants. Out of this, which is often undisciplined or chaotic, people develop an angry, independent belief system, largely based on rejection of authority. As with the tyrants they reject, their beliefs and "faith" are often vociferously defended. This is a weak basis for faith. It doesn't have any historical experience to support it when intellect and defiance fail, when personal perceptions are limited, or when life circumstances change drastically.

The third way to acquire faith is by balancing the wisdom of tradition and the convictions that arise from individual investigation and experience. When you incorporate a clear declaration of "self" with a considered inclusion of established tradition, you create unshakeable faith. Over the long term, you would then be able to conduct yourself with discipline and determination (which is, situationally, an appropriate spiritual response). You participate in life and influence your destiny in such a way that spiritual principles, tradition, and personality, form the basis of faith. This type of faith allows you to get recovered.

Within the twelve steps, and especially Step Two, there is a significant respect for your personality. Your pilgrimage is noticeably molded by who you are as an individual. This is crucial in developing a strong faith in your own conception of a higher power. Your faith must reflect who you are because your faith is what will allow you to address the trials that lay ahead—not because the trials are so arduous, but because they are particular to you and the nuance of your addiction.

Personality is Important

In religions that are of notable influence, there's an overbearing suppression of personality. This is fatal to an appreciation of God because any suppression of personality requires an abandoning of "self". The suppression of anyone's inner self must always end with them seeking external validation. That external validation is then centered around the religious dogma. "God" and "self" are now removed from the equation and replaced by dogma and politics.[12]

This creates a need to depend more on the religious organization or religious dogma, than on "my inner-self" and my relationship with whatever deity the organization represents. This foments spiritual/emotional disaster. When people deny or suppress themselves on behalf of external dogma (an overbearing religious structure), and since it is deep within us The Great Reality is found, then people cannot access "God" because they cannot access themselves. Suppression of personality and impersonal religious structures are fatal to sincere spirituality.

Outside of the consideration of "addict", the original twelve-step literature has four factors that make it significantly more effective than many other spiritual pilgrimages which require faith. These are:

- a clear and authoritative influence of tradition, that is not suffocating, which arises from the specific experience of the early twelve-step members (as detailed in the AA reference texts). The traditions address the flaws found in the historical experience of earlier, similar organizations. They are particular to the needs of addictions recovery, and *not* the needs of the organization;
- an egalitarian philosophy and the exclusion of politics;
- a crucial inclusion of personal experience and personality through the work of completing the steps, with the clear proviso that personality is important but gently subservient to principles; and,
- an underlying and stabilizing presence of the strengths and themes of the perennial philosophies (within the five spiritual principles). These, altogether, represent the wisdom of the mystics and the *invisible* beauty of all spiritual disciplines, which are present in the maintenance steps.

These four factors are inextricably connected and balanced. The way they weave themselves together creates the necessary "unshakable" foundation for faith, upon which your transformation is built. Whenever the original material is rewritten or transposed for psychological health, the relationship between them is altered, and the result is spiritually less effective. Addictions are then not resolved. Altogether, this makes four things available to twelve-step pilgrims that weren't available before. These are:

---

[12] Spiritual disciplines that embrace and pursue an authentic experience of mysticism, beyond dogma and culturally popular meditation practices, are generally exempt from this observation.

- a previously inaccessible self-insight, primarily regarding their addiction, irresponsible behavior, and personal belligerence that blocks access to spirituality;
- with discipline and obedience, an eventual recovery from addictions;
- the acquisition of unshakable faith; and,
- the *primary* and established life condition of being in sincere relationship with a higher power.

Recovered alcoholics/addicts remain within the safety of revealed truth (the perennial philosophies); they address the specifics of their addiction (the etiology of the disease and its anamnesis related to them) and become recovered[13]; *and* they incorporate their own personality into their spiritual pilgrimage. This is done without insulting any authority figure (because there are none; or there aren't supposed to be any), and without infringing on anyone else's right to do the same. Through obedience, adherents foster individuation within an effective spiritual philosophy.

As far as I'm aware, this unique combination exists nowhere else. Certainly none of the cultural religions have it, for they were formed out of the folk myths and social-cultural needs particular to the eras they were born in. [As opposed to the original twelve-step program which, although presented in Christian terminology, was formed in response to a spiritual, *universal* cultural problem: death by alcoholism.] Twelve-step spiritual philosophy integrates its principles within any personal relationship with any higher power.

Cultural religious dogma fosters an overpowering, vigorous molding of personality, rather than taking the wiser position of fostering a relationship between personality and deity, which would make formal religious structure secondary to the primary need of a personal relationship with God. Also Note: None of the psychological disciplines are capable of allowing for Spirituality as the ultimate goal of healing. Modern personality technologies (meaning therapies) are not universal enough in their focus to address the varied needs of addiction, dislocation, trauma, culture and spirituality, which are profoundly unique and complex.[14]

---

[13] Being recovered doesn't imply clinical psychological health. It does imply an absence of addictions and a lifestyle that demonstrates sound spiritual principles.

[14] Dislocation and trauma aren't the same thing. Trauma (meaning a wound), in its varied presentations, is anything from being battered or assaulted, to being yelled at or ignored. There is developmental trauma (emotional wounds from childhood) and shock trauma (pain from incidents, illness, and events), which have both common and unique requirements for resolution. And, the circumstance that initiated the trauma, the incident itself, generates different reactions and symptoms depending on any number of variables. I had once audio recorded group counselling while someone was weeping deeply because of the trauma of having been sexually abused. In another segment someone else wept because a parent wouldn't pick them up after a social engagement (which was in the recognition of emotional neglect). When I later played the tape for a class of counsellors in training, they couldn't identify which person was more deeply wounded; the weeping was equally intense.

Dislocation is that ubiquitous sense that, regardless of your efforts and presentation, the machinations of life are capricious and indifferent, and nothing seems to fit or make sense. Life is confusing, random, and hard: bad people win; good people die young; other people work hard and finish last. There's joy and sadness, pleasure and pain, bounty and poverty, it's all capricious... and suffering is optional. There is a *huge* misunderstanding about "suffering" in relation to the First Noble Truth of Buddhism. The First Noble Truth has been translated as "life is suffering," which translation was more for a Protestant political

Alcoholics Anonymous presents the only method of spiritual transformation I'm aware of that encourages an individuation of self, combined with a wise and insistent invitation to be obedient to tradition and principle, that's strongly respectful of the perennial philosophies[15], *and* where politics and authority are seen as dangerous. This is remarkably different than the offerings of any available cultural religion.

Your perceptions of the world and your existence (Life filtered through your ego) are amazingly unique. This requires that you create and establish a subtly unique and very personal spiritual ambience in your relationship with each of the five spiritual principles. The principles are universal (context); their manifestation within you is unique (content). What's personal is how you inculcate yourself within them. That is the purpose of the steps and it requires a delicate, patient touch.

––––––

In the first decade of the original twelve-step program, the mean age of members was significantly older than today. Being significantly older, and it being in the 1930s and '40s, the members would have grown up with different traditions in their personal lives, and would have been quite differently established in relationships, religion, friendships, and careers. Also, the groups were smaller. I was told in the early 1980s, by the then very-old old-timers, that there was no focus on family of origin, and significantly more introspective discussion about the application and misapplication of "self" to Spirituality. It follows that the steps were approached and interpreted differently.

In the last twenty-five years, with all the drastic cultural changes, a huge increase in the number of members, with their mean age being considerably younger, and the overwhelming deluge of self-help psychology, the groups have focused themselves on psychological health, intimate relationships, careers, and extended social circles. That doesn't mean that career advantages and romance didn't happen in groups sixty years ago, and it doesn't mean that the newer people are to blame. It means that demographics, culture, and psychological technology have drastically changed the spiritual efficacy of twelve-step groups.[16]

As I've described elsewhere, as regards spirituality, twelve-step groups are foundering badly. This is the result of the members' refusal to maintain a spiritual interpretation and perception of the original instructions and traditions, now supplanted by "attractive", but ineffective psychological/social solutions. These are

––––––

agenda than philosophical accuracy. It isn't that life is suffering, *per se*; it's that life is dislocated. Without strong spiritual grounding and non-attachment (meaning non-codependence), everyone suffers the struggle of trying to make sense out of Life. Whether you continue to suffer is a personal choice. There is some related discussion of this in the chapter Buddhism in Huston Smith's book, *The World's Religions*, HarperSanFrancisco, 1991.

[15] In the last fifteen years, many religious organizations have implemented various "modernizations" like jazz music at worship services, or folk music sing-alongs at mass, or renting their sacred space out to artistic endeavor. This has included having congregation members undertake administrative and service positions called "Personal Ministries" which may suit their individual interest or temperament. This is for the survival of a rigid religious structure responding to drastic cultural change and greatly reduced membership. It may appear that services are being "personalized" but only to the degree of that religious doctrine remains unchallenged. These modernizations are not for the incorporation of a wise relationship between personality and deity.

[16] Where two or three are gathered together on behalf of God, spiritual grace may well be present. As the size of the crowd increases, the presence of God decreases. *Huxley and God, Essays,* cited at an earlier footnote, p. 123.

manifestations of the cultural malaise embodied in righteousness, greed, disposability, and illusions about psychology—a poor technology of spirituality. Within the sphere of addictions recovery, nobody is guilty and everyone is responsible.

All of this prohibits the development of adequate faith which must combine insight from personal experience with adherence to tradition. Addictions recovery is dependent upon commitment and obedience to a "higher authority", not to psychological astuteness. For the purposes of this discussion, the higher authority is both spiritual principles and the AA reference text books. Without this focus there is no spiritual faith, and without spiritual faith, you cannot get recovered.

I cannot overstate the importance of gently applying your personal life experience to the original steps and traditions, with this ever-present caveat: principles before personalities. In this way, when you get to the maintenance steps, your faith is strong, your inner vision is clear, and spiritual principles are quiet demonstrations of behavior rather than entertaining rhetoric and political maneuvering.[17]

Spiritual ineffectiveness results from the neglect of these principles and loss of your individuality in favor of a political agenda (religious, psychological, or social). Because of cultural changes, this is happening in all twelve-step groups; however, in all of them, except AA, the fragmentation is assisted by the rewriting of the original literature. Regardless of the secular reasons that might have instigated the rewriting, and although well-intended, rewriting subtly refocuses the intent away from spiritual integrity and towards psychological health.

Technology, politics, and psychology, acting in concert with addictive irresponsibility, have increased this fragmentation. I've noticed for years, and I make the observation sadly, that in a twelve-step group it's easier to find a new wife or husband, or a good deal on a used car, than it is a wise spiritual sponsor. The spiritual mandate of twelve-step programs is vanishing, and in spite of their being more popular, available, and visible, they are less effective, which is reflected in the individuals that comprise the group.

All of this is repairable, but certainly not easy. Rigorously apply yourself to the original literature and ignore popular opinion. Vigorously stress individual study and strong personal devotion to the original steps and traditions, as they embody spiritual principles. Your spiritual life, and often your physical life, depend on it.

The steps, in their application, aren't group activities. They are not spiritually effective when done as collective experience. Yes, they are written, "we did this" and "we did that", but that's a function of grammar, not an instruction for a group of people to do a step collectively. For example: *"Made a searching and fearless moral inventory of ourselves"*[18] is simply a grammatical way of representing what each person did individually.

In order to provide a different sense of the steps, I'm going to offer a shift in perception so you might see more clearly how the specifics of the steps apply to you

---

[17] When I suggest you personalize the five spiritual principles by the judicious influence of personality and life experience, I do not imply that personality should prevail.

[18] *Alcoholics Anonymous*, p. 59, *Twelve Steps and Twelve Traditions*, p. 42.

individually. For the purpose of clarity, and not to make your work easier, I'm going to "personalize" the first four steps by taking them out of their collective representation, and put them into a singular, personal perspective. I am not suggesting that you should rewrite the steps; I am trying to offer insight on how they apply to *you*.

Step 1: My life had become unmanageable—I admitted I was powerless over ___(acting out)___. I'm sick not crazy.

Step 2: I learned and now believe that only a higher power could restore me to sanity. (Where I get help.)

Step 3: I decided, above all else, I was going to behave and think spiritually—I decided to live a life of spiritual integrity. (How I get that help.)

Step 4: My self-imposed crisis started at an instinctual level. I wrote out, in detail, what was specifically wrong in my instincts, fears, and sexual behavior. (How I got myself into trouble.)

Some Relevant Side Issues

The nature of addictions presents dilemmas and apparent paradoxes These exist because of an unspiritual mindset. However, once you learn enough truth about yourself, and apply that to the five spiritual principles embodied in the maintenance steps, these cease to exist. When dilemmas arise, all that is required is to study "yourself" and uncover your belligerence, dishonesty, or irresponsibility.

The original twelve-step program is a revealed truth and needs no explanation. Upon close examination, its integrity becomes self-evident. The questions and complexity are generated by the addiction, so the resolution of dilemmas and problems lie within the addict and not the original program. Search the original literature, identify what instruction you are not following, and then follow it. Go deeper within yourself. And, at the same time, don't read ahead looking for answers to problems; you'll only frighten and confuse yourself.

Alcoholics Anonymous and *Twelve Steps and Twelve Traditions,* are two books on spiritual transformation that don't contradict themselves. This is one strength that allows this process to have such success in resolving addictions.

Addicts often believe they are uniquely sick, and very complicated, and harbor secret beliefs they will need much more that just "the program". They're trapped in extreme terminal uniqueness, and can't believe that two "simple" books like *Alcoholics Anonymous* and *Twelve Steps and Twelve Traditions* have all the answers to their addictions problems.[19] Lack of faith forces them to rush off in all directions, looking for something that keeps them terminally unique, all the while hoping they'll find an expedient, painless solution and beat the odds.

---

[19] Another extreme form of terminal uniqueness is that addicts assume they are smart enough for their own good: "I'm creatively insightful and need little or no help at all." Their addictions and arrogance keep them unaware of how much harm they are causing themselves and others.

At the outset, completing the original twelve steps is neither expedient nor painless. As time passes, transformation gets much simpler, and eventually becomes graceful.

———

With continuous abstinence, you're a newcomer for five years. It doesn't matter if you have a Ph.D., if you're a bus driver, or a priest, or are coming off welfare—you're a newcomer for five years. It's the mandate of the disease and not an insult to your ability or devotion. If you're patient and diligent, demand much of yourself, expect little from others, regularly pray and meditate, and are willing to self-examine more than blame, you will find all of the answers within yourself. However, the answers are only available in conjunction with a rigorous application of yourself to the regeneration steps (Steps One to Nine).

Steps Ten, Eleven, and Twelve are the maintenance steps. It stands to reason if you were forever "in recovery", you wouldn't need maintenance steps because you wouldn't have acquired anything that required maintenance. When you painstakingly appreciate and accomplish, in detail, what's required in each of the first nine steps, you can't *not* become spiritual.[20]

Nine Steps, Three Columns

Each of the steps has a complex spiritual purpose. They aren't sequenced haphazardly. In their aspect, composition, structure, and nuance, they each address specific facets of addiction, spiritual belligerence, and transformation in a non-interchangeable, non-exchangeable, ascending order.[21] They lead directly to the maintenance steps and a higher power. There are non-negotiable spiritual reasons for them being *exactly* as they are. Yes, there is some derivative psychological healing, but that is not their substantive intent. When they are rewritten for other "issues", to make healing "easier", or altered for personal convenience, the new versions become less- or in-effective for resolving addictions. They cannot be altered with impunity.

Here's an awareness and integration exercise that will take some time, but is worth the effort. At the beginning of your work on a step, at the top of a sheet of paper, write out the step and draw three columns underneath. In the first column, list the symptoms of the disease (from Chapter 2), and in the third column, list the five spiritual principles. In the middle column, note some aspect of the step that would counteract a symptom and, at the same time, would incorporate a spiritual principle.

---

[20] I have been asked whether getting recovered is available to a newcomer who is spirituality very defiant. Yes. All addicts are defiant to some degree. For however anonymously Providence moved on their behalf, people who are successful in reducing their defiance enough to achieve abstinence have all they need to begin. In the realm of addictions, there is no situation too corrupt or sophisticated that the original twelve steps cannot address spiritually, *providing* the mendicant maintains abstinence and slowly embraces willingness, patience, and labor. Continuous abstinence is evidence of some willingness. Within the original twelve-step literature, the process of becoming willing is gradual. The intricacies of each successive step reduce defiance and draw you closer to the Atman-Brahmin. A spiritual life is available when you begin with abstinence and persevere at Step Two. It's what the steps are designed to do. It's inevitable.
[21] *"The unfolding of* [person's] *spiritual nature is as much an exact science as astronomy* [or] *medicine."* *The Secret Teachings of All Ages,* Reader's Edition, Manly P. Hall, Tarcher/Penguin Books, 2003, p. 120.

Learn how each step reduces and eliminates the symptoms *and at the same time* engenders spirituality. Here's what the Step One sheet might look like:

1) *"We admitted we were powerless over alcohol—*
that our lives had become unmanageable."

SYMPTOMS	WHICH SYMPTOMS ARE COUNTERACTED AND WHICH SPIRITUAL PRINCIPLES ARE INCORPORATED	FIVE PRINCIPLES
excessive fear assumptions shame dishonesty selfishness irresponsibility arrogance and cynicism being isolated acting out arrogance selfishness/greed	Stops major self harm and annihilation. Incorporates some veracity. Begins to reduce irresponsibility and increase responsibility and obedience. Reduces and addresses isolation and begins self-care. Stops acting out and begins the practice of obedience.	(1) Respect for the body-temple; respectful self-care (2) Veracity (3) Humility (4) Charity (5) Responsibility and obedience

This exercise will facilitate insight into the intent of each step and the reasons for meticulously following the instructions. If you do this exercise, keep your work. I'll be referring you back to this later.

How you approach the maintenance steps is different than approaching the regeneration steps.[22] The first nine steps are applied *to* your life; the maintenance steps *are* your life (a parallel theme to what I wrote earlier: you are not a member of a group; you are the group). Steps Ten, Eleven, and Twelve become a part of your persona, rather than exercises to be performed. But you won't appreciate the importance of this distinction unless you study the original textbooks regularly, for years; regularly pray and meditate as instructed; frequently seek well-defined, wise spiritual counsel; and constantly examine your motives and level of honesty.

As I've said: Changes in demographics, new social and psychological perspectives, scrutiny of the process by professionals (who may have unresolved prejudices, are not spiritual themselves, or are twelve-step participants at various levels of spiritual integrity), informed consumers, and media-hype about famous people being in-program, are reflected in the changes in twelve-step groups. Members are now largely focused on anything but Spirituality. The twelve steps are

---

[22] You complete the first nine steps, and they "take" you someplace. The maintenance steps have a completely different function. The maintenance steps are never "completed". You never *leave* the maintenance steps, but you leave each of the other steps up to nine. This isn't semantics; it's the tenor of *being* spiritual as opposed to *becoming* spiritual. Applying yourself to the maintenance steps is remarkably different than applying yourself to the others.

subsequently less effective, and are losing credibility. They weren't designed for anything but exiting abstinence-available addictions and becoming Spiritual.[23]

I suppose you could weld large wings onto a car and try to make an airplane, but it wouldn't be an efficient airplane and it wouldn't be an effective car. This doesn't mean the car itself was poorly designed or that airplanes aren't efficient. It means they aren't being utilized as originally designed. This new contraption may fly a little bit, but the car-plane will garner a reputation as being ineffective. So it is with psychology that's injected into the original (spiritually intended) twelve steps.

As soon as twelve-step programs were restructured or rewritten as mandates for agencies, formulas for creative success, avenues to psychological health, or routes to relationship happiness (and some have tried to rewrite them to include all of these), they became ineffective. They were designed for something much more profound and beautiful than mere social efficiency.[24]

If you, as a member of a twelve-step group, or as a professional enrolling the aid of these groups, wish to have them as effective and powerful as they were originally, then use them only for what they were designed: the transformation out of addictions and into Spirituality. They aren't a panacea for any illness that is similar to an addiction. They aren't a substitute solution for people who can't afford, or refuse to pay for, therapy.

You've Got A Broken Ankle

One day while out walking, you trip and fall stepping off a curb. Of course, if you're an addict, you immediately look to see who pushed you. You may secretly know that you tripped, but for any number of reasons, you look for someone to blame. You're disoriented from pain and aren't exactly sure how it happened. Finally, you ask someone for help. They help you sit on the curb and gently point out that you tripped—no one pushed you—and you apparently have a broken ankle. They tell you out of kindness that they have done similar things themselves. You finally realize that you do have a badly broken ankle and that no one pushed you.

The person who is helping you now advises that you could resolve this problem by going to a hospital. They quietly explain that was what worked for them. Certainly, you don't *have* to go to a hospital. You could limp off to a bar, or go home, or go to the S.P.C.A., and not go to the hospital. You can go wherever you want; but they kindly point out that the most effective thing to do would be to go to a hospital. You admit that a hospital makes sense, and you decide to go there.

How *exactly* do you get to the hospital? You can crawl, ride a bicycle, be carried, call a taxi, or call an ambulance. After some discussion you agree to call an ambulance. It would be the fastest and safest way to get to the hospital. You would

---

[23] For abstinence-not-available addictions, like work, sex, or relationships, the twelve steps do work, provided there is a sensitive and determined effort to understand and maintain bottom-line behavior and abstinence. The need for delicately interweaving psychology and spirituality for these addictions makes this incredibly complicated.

[24] Addictions are vicious. Achieving relationship bliss or financial security are completely insufficient for the task of eliminating your addictions.

be supported en route by people who knew what they were doing, and you would have a guaranteed result: efficiently getting to where you needed to go.

You've Got An Addiction

You're destitute and defeated from your addiction, and "wake up" in a meeting. You think you were "pushed" into your insanity and, in the midst of your pain and disorientation, Step One is learning you weren't pushed at all. You're going to [hopefully] be helped to learn that you hurt yourself. You eventually believe that you have an addiction, and that you're sick from your self-imposed crisis. No one is to blame. (You tripped and broke your ankle, all by yourself.)

After you admit you're an addict, the process of getting yourself pointed in the right direction begins. From guidance, reading, and studying *yourself*, you understand and believe that a higher power could restore you to sanity — spirituality is the solution. You can't resolve anything yet, only now you know where to go. This signals the end of Step Two. Next is you decide to live spiritually: Step Three.

You accomplish this by following the most efficient method for addicts: the steps.[25] You can try to get better by being social, popular, professionally successful, generous, happily married, kind, or physically fit. Over the long term, however, these don't work. Obedience to the steps is the most efficient way for getting where you need to go; and hopefully you will be supported along the way by someone who knows what they're doing. (The parallel was going to the hospital by ambulance.) You get to a higher power via the steps.

Years ago I spent a week with an old friend from college. We had long conversations about twelve-step programs and he was happy because I wasn't destroying myself any more. Regarding the steps, he said: "Well, those don't seem too hard." He commented that he'd been doing similar things throughout his life. I said to him something like: "Don't you see how hard these steps are?" He thought for a moment and said, "Well, no I don't." Later he added: "I'm glad this program is as important to you as it isn't to me." We laughed. He understood the precepts as a matter of his everyday life: they weren't hard for him — he wasn't an alcoholic.

Being a successful addict requires that you live your life opposite to the steps. The more you're reluctant to do the steps, the harder they are for you, the more this indicates you have an addiction. If you are confused over whether or not you are an addict, try the steps. If they're difficult, you probably are.

Throughout this I would encourage you to remember: *"When we became alcoholics* [addicts] *crushed by a self-imposed crisis we could not postpone or evade… ."*[26] Your addiction is a disease. Even though it may appear otherwise, no one is to blame. The original literature is clear that your crises are self-imposed. It's

---

[25] I imagine that people with*out* addictions may pursue spirituality in any number of ways: they don't need these steps. However, for the addict, *getting recovered* and *being spiritual* are identical. To achieve this requires significant devotion to the exact instructions in the original twelve steps. The existence of an addiction prohibits other options.

[26] *Alcoholics Anonymous*, p. 53.

important to heal from the effects of any abuse and violence—for these things there is therapy—but you're not an addict because of them. Drop the word "blame" from your vocabulary.[27]

Alcoholics Anonymous offers this: "*...we believe that early in our drinking careers most of us could have stopped drinking;*"[28] and, "*...we feel we had gone on drinking many years beyond the point where we could quit on our willpower.*"[29] Should you complete Step Four (and Step Eight when you get there) exactly as it's outlined, you will, among other things, begin to sense when your acting-out went out of control and you crossed that unknown-before-hand invisible line into addictions. And if you do your Step Four exactly the way it's outlined, you will learn how you motivated your self-imposed crisis.

The original twelve-step program is amazingly rich with potential, but you've got to work for it. Nothing is free. At the prospect of spiritual (or the related psychological) work, unfortunately, most addicts stay lazy.[30]

————

I've been asked many times if there's a difference between a drug addict and an alcoholic. Some say there is, I imagine so they can lay claim to some spiritually-defeating uniqueness. Underneath the preferred mood-altering experience there really isn't any difference. Your addiction of preference is a ritual of self-annihilation, and it often changed with circumstances. Compensation strategies, your particular generation, social pressures, and subculture indoctrination will influence your choice of mood-altering behavior. And, of course, the medical requirements of detoxing will vary from substance to substance. The consequences of your acting out—the damage done and amends required—may vary somewhat. These are external differences. Underneath it all, after detoxing and moving beyond Step One, there's very little difference (which is the import of How It Works—the rallying point I discussed earlier).

Four Big Topics

Spiritual Integrity and Psychological Health are remarkably different and both of these disciplines are quite fascinating because of their intimate application to Life. They are particularly fascinating and especially important to alcoholics and addicts. Psychological Health carries the hope of personal competence and integration, and Spiritual Integrity carries promise of salvation and deliverance. There aren't enough warnings, however, that these two disciplines and the routes to achieving them, are not interchangeable.

In relation to this, twelve-step people precipitate all manner of never-ending discussions and debates about the (apparently) critical nature of these Four Big Topics: (i) addiction of preference, (ii) acting-out behaviors and self-damage, (iii)

---

[27] *Twelve Steps and Twelve Traditions*, p. 47.
[28] *Alcoholics Anonymous*, p. 32.
[29] Ibid., p. 34.
[30] "*...at the prospect of work... we procrastinate or at best work grudgingly and under half steam.*" *Twelve Steps and Twelve Traditions*, p. 49.

detoxing or withdrawal; and (iv) the struggles of abstinence or sobriety. It's important to understand that any of these four topics can be discussed from either a psychological *or* a spiritual point of view. Because Psychological Health and Spiritual Integrity are so remarkably different, it follows that discussions about any of them would have remarkably different tones to the conversation, depending on which discipline—spirituality or psychology—the discussion pertained to.

The Four Big Topics are, appropriately enough, important to a newcomer. However, to anyone beyond the status of newcomer, debates about these are usually by people who desire to be viewed as erudite addictions gurus (which is spiritually inappropriate). Egos, pushed by character defects, create contentious debates, apologies, comparisons, and analyses of these four topics.

Do not lose sight of this important fact: In any *spiritual* pilgrimage, the farther along you are in the steps (i.e. the more spiritual you are), the less important these four subjects are. But, from a *psychological* perspective, because of the nature of psychology, your addiction of preference, acting-out and harm caused, detoxing, and abstinence struggles, must always be important, and carry a noticeable priority over spirituality. Here's why:

In a Spiritual pilgrimage, the relationship between "importance of self" and "a higher power" increasingly changes thusly: a decrease of "self importance" in favor of an enhanced and soulful awareness of God. "Me and my struggles" i.e. the Four Big Topics, become increasingly *less* important. "God" is viewed and applauded as the primary agent of change. By comparison, in psychology, "self" and will power are the primary agent of change. A psychological recovery process is always steeped in willpower, self-awareness, and self-determination (all secular attributes of character). In psychology, the grand "I" takes the credit. Regardless of length of abstinence, a psychological bias to the twelve steps requires that "me and my struggles" (the four big topics) always be held in high regard.

Within the realms of Spirituality, the four topics of addiction of preference, acting-out and harm caused, detoxing, and abstinence struggles are only a very minor part of what needs to be addressed. When people with years of abstinence still wallow in these debates, they have missed the spiritual point of the exercise. Those who sincerely pursue spiritual integrity speak less and less of any of them.

Two Views of "Potential"

When the first few groups of AA started, the initial members were described as very desperate cases. They faced imminent insanity or death. Because of that, and because of the limited understanding of the disease, the original members' definition of an alcoholic was largely a simple association test. They knew what they, themselves, were like—extremely desperate—and so, if you were like them, then you were an alcoholic. Over time, despite that narrow definition, people who weren't so desperate were self-diagnosing themselves as alcoholics. The original members, formerly desperate but now sober, referred to these newer, *apparently* not-so-desperate members as "potential" alcoholics. This only meant that, in the opinion of those formerly desperate original members, the new people had a ways to go before they were as desperate as the original members were. Since membership is always self-diagnosing, the original, colloquial definition of extreme desperation used by the program founders had to change.

Another view of "potential" is in the process of addiction. Usually people start out with sporadic levels of substance use, which, over time, becomes more intense or frequent. Eventually, this becomes categorized as "addicted". Early in their acting out, there may have been a time when these people were "potentially" addicts; a time when, had they been more informed, they might have been able to alter their behavior and not evince an addiction. (Recall Blindness To The Disease, p. 68)

Many people say something like: "Oh, I used to drink a lot, but it was getting out of hand, so I quit," or "I did a lot of drugs when I was a kid, and I was getting into trouble, so I stopped." These people perceived, in time to make the choice, that they had a choice, and made it. The original literature comments that should alcoholics have been able to recognize that "choice point" before they were entombed by the disease, they might still have been able to avoid addiction. That may be true. As pleasing as that insight is to your ego, in a fashion similar to what I mentioned earlier about the four big topics important to newcomers, it's only an intellectual observation that, over the long term, has no spiritual import.

Should you do Step Four by painstakingly following the original instructions, you will have an opportunity to determine, in hindsight, approximately when you might have been a potential alcoholic (or addict). In the first few years of recovery, this awareness is important because when you see, in hindsight, that you may have had a choice and for whatever reason didn't make it, it helps you adopt a more sincere posture of responsibility. Step Four takes a lot of particular effort (as I will soon outline), without which people never attain the level of responsibility that's needed to become recovered. People memorize clichés, impress others with how soon or fast they did their steps, create racy, self-condemning autobiographies, and end up knowing very little about what's offered in the miracle of spiritual choice.

Resentments

There are three parts to Step Four, the first of which is specifically about instincts gone awry and exceeding their function.[31] Listing resentments is only important as an exercise to lead you to understand why you imposed your gone-awry instincts on others; to learn what caused you to demand too much control, protection, or affection.[32] How do you get from "resentment is the number one offender" (a frequently misapplied quote[33]) to instincts gone awry?

---

[31] *"Yet these instincts... ," Twelve Steps and Twelve Traditions*, p. 42.
[32] Ibid., p. 44.
[33] Addicts or alcoholics getting recovered frequently attach themselves to one or two appealing sentences or phrases out of a chapter, and then reduce their interest in, and give less attention to, the other information. One example is the preponderance of discussion about resentments. Resentment permeates an addict's existence, which makes anger and resentments the most commonly visible, but not necessarily the worst, "shortcoming". Similarly, parking offences may be the most common illegal activity, but they are not the most serious one. As an addict getting recovered, resist clinging to tidbits of recovery jargon. Study each particular point, but not to the exclusion of anything else.

What precipitates making unreasonable demands upon, and generating revulsion in, the people who love and care about you? Understanding the mechanics underneath resentments is far more important than categorizing or itemizing them. Resentments are only a minor part of Step Four, and yet discussions belabor them to the exclusion of all else. What this means is popular discussion about Step Four is, for the most part, empty rhetoric because of this exaggerated bias.

"Creation gave us instincts for a purpose."[34]—self-preservation, food, shelter, reproduction (sex), and a social instinct. What's written in the literature is that virtually every emotional problem for the addict can be traced to an instinct exceeding its function. These misdirected instincts are liabilities and cause great trouble, but there is no suggestion that they cause our addictions. Be mindful of this important distinction: Your addiction manifests at a behavioral/psychological level, but it exists at a spiritual level.[35]

Ultimately, Step Four is not about being bad or about your resentments at all. Many Step Fours are a wrongly focused list that tries to prove that their authors were the sickest person in town—they did 768 very horrible things, 532 medium horrible things, and lied to 1,943 people. By page twenty-nine of this style of inventory, they're depressed or smugly proud. Some become resentful of the program, God, and Step Four because this style of inventory resolves nothing, and adds no insight. Step Four is not a litany of what a disgusting miscreant you were. When the founders wrote that addicts were to understand the *nature* of their wrongs, nature refers to the instinctual conflict beneath the resentment.

Throughout this exercise, what will become obvious is, it's impossible to be resentful or angry without having some associated fear. Yes, you've got to start with the resentments to get to where you're supposed to end up, but resentments are only the starting point, and of minor consideration in the larger scheme of things.

"We want to find exactly how, when, and where our natural desires have warped us."[36] This means instinctually, not geographically.

> How: by your blaming and frustrated efforts to control others; *not* How: by others doing something to you.
> When: when you were irresponsible and when you saw yourself as an insecure victim; *not* When: they wouldn't do what you wanted.
> Where: in one of your instincts; *not* Where: in Toronto or in the bedroom.

The original twelve-step literature talks about being warped by our natural desires, and what harm this caused others and ourselves.[37] Step Four's focus of examining your behavior and no one else's is one requirement of spirituality. *"We wish*

---

[34] *Twelve Steps and Twelve Traditions*, p. 42.
[35] As you read this, remember that psychological issues from your childhood didn't cause your addiction. Some *un*definable spiritual corruption did. That's why psychology can not resolve your addictions. Bear in mind, as you trudge through all the detail of Step Four, that its *primary* purpose is to draw you closer to God, not to resolve developmental dependency issues or enhance your human relationships.
[36] *Twelve Steps and Twelve Traditions*, p. 43.
[37] Ibid., p. 43.

to look squarely at the unhappiness this has caused others and ourselves."[38] You will not be looking at what you did or what others did to you, but your instincts, fears, and selfishness.

Notice: *"...by discovering what our emotional deformities are."* It doesn't read that you're to discover what your resentments are. It's easy to figure out who you're mad at; you've probably been telling that to anyone who'll listen to you for years. But knowing your emotional deformities is another matter entirely. The requirements of spirituality demand a deeper investigation of responsibility and truth than any superficial discussion of resentments can ever allow.

In addition to abstinence, Steps One (action) and Two (insight) are "thought and awareness processes". They are by and large an initial, fundamental rearranging of your inner emotional and intellectual relationship with yourself. They reorganize your perceptions, deepen your awareness, and facilitate a commitment to spiritual values. (Context.) This is the set up that enables a proper effort at Step Four.

———

Here's an analogy to make another point: You bring your car to a garage for repairs. Suppose you just say: "My car's broken, please fix it," and leave. That won't be enough. The mechanic will expect some description of what's wrong. Doesn't it start? Is it the exhaust system? The point being that it probably isn't necessary to fix the door handles, the seat belts, or any of a thousand other things. You don't have to fix the entire car.

The purpose of Step Four is to figure out what's wrong in relation to your instincts. You only have to fix your emotional deformities. Yes, that may be a lot, but you don't have to fix everything about your entire personality.[39] Even with knowing that, in Step Four you don't fix it: you simply identify it. You are not, and I repeat, you are *not* to go marching through your personality attacking everything about yourself. There are very specific, limited things you're supposed to do; it's a clearly defined path that you have to walk.

In *Facets of Personal Transformation,* I will explore the dynamic of a "real you" that is disowned, denied, and kept hidden.[40] The point of a spiritual pilgrimage is to experience yourself at levels more profound than shame resolution. Underneath this is a poignant loneliness. People go through life compensating for spiritual dislocation by being overbearing, cynical, angry, dependent, promiscuous, celibate, drunk, stoned, bitter, shy, over-achieving, helpless, arrogant, and so on. These self-administered compensations are traceable to psychology and resolving them at that level is, in my view, certainly satisfactory—for non-addicts.

---

[38] *Twelve Steps and Twelve Traditions,* p. 43.
[39] *"To believe that the alcoholic who approaches AA is an unprincipled, untaught barbarian, suddenly transformed by the previously unavailable spiritual illumination of the Twelve Steps, is, to me, utter foolishness."* From the AA pamphlet *A Member's Eye View of Alcoholics Anonymous,* cited earlier. Should you decide to vigorously pursue spirituality and humility, you may certainly end up changing "everything" about your personality over the course of your life. However, that's not the point of Step Four.
[40] This is described in John Bradshaw's book *Healing The Shame That Binds You,* Health Communications Inc., 1988. For an important, related view of our critical nature oppressing ourselves, read *Embracing Your Inner Critic,* Hal Stone & Sidra Stone HarperSanFrancisco, 1993.

For addicts (and for others, too) who pursue spiritual integrity, there are levels of integration that people can attain which are much deeper than effective psychological/social-consumerism. Yes achieving this is socially, financially, and emotionally expensive. It's worth it. There's more serenity and joy than can be imagined or described, if people pursue sincere spiritual integrity.

Step Four identifies resentments as one entrance point to your deeper nature. As with the entrance to a mine: There may be only one entrance to the mine, but there will be miles of tunnels underground. Resentments are one of the entrance points to the underground tunnels of your nature. (Regarding Step Four, the other two entrances are fears and sexual selfishness.)

In order to hide their fears and insecurities, or to conceal that they know absolutely nothing about "why" they are so self-destructive, alcoholics and addicts have an array of tactics to keep everyone, including themselves, out of their own underground tunnels. Alcoholics try to convince everyone, especially themselves, that they aren't hiding, when in fact they are hiding, and regardless of how they explain it away, can't understand their own destructive behavior at all.

If you're an unregenerate addict, regardless of whether it's your sex partner, your boss, a relative, or a friend, as soon as they speak or behave in some way that puts you where you have to look at the real you, you'll blame, get angry, leave, get sick—do anything to keep yourself and others from knowing about your shame, loneliness, and pain. It's a terrible emotional push-pull because people are drawn, by instinct, into relationships and we desire intimacy, but addicts are terrified of this and sabotage their own best intentions.

The belief and conviction developed at Step Two, and a determined decision at Step Three, are crucial prerequisites for addicts to successfully self-examine at Step Four. They can only discover what needs to be changed by going inside, and that's *exactly* what they don't want to do. Without properly aligning themselves at Steps Two and Three, addicts doing Step Four can only list their resentments and examine other people. Until addicts get deeply inside themselves, all of their relationships, especially with God, will be power struggles for control, and end up mediocre at best.

People embark on inner child work (which is an oversimplified, largely misused metaphor for a complex therapeutic strategy) and address their shame issues.[41] That work takes a long time, and then they'll eventually become aware of how lonely they are. Many people are amazed at the depth of loneliness that exists

---

[41] Regarding the resolution of shame, I've heard all manner of psychobabble, like "transforming my shame into guilt and resolving the guilt because I stop disesteeming myself," and "distancing myself from shame through positive thinking and service work," and "my shame left because I did the steps and my higher power only wants good things for me." These are not resolution strategies, but appear so, only because of the tightly bound and limited lifestyles, and the intellectual defensiveness and strong character armor that accompanies them. To make the speech look like it's true, there's a tremendous investment in rigidly controlling their environment, and shame is only held at bay and not resolved at all. Resolving inculcated shame is a delicate process, and at its deeper levels, always requires a balanced relationship between unconditional positive regard in talk therapy, an enhanced self-regard through understanding the dynamic of the interpersonal transfer of shame, placing and taking responsibility, and some dynamic of physiological healing like SRT or EFT. (See Appendix III).

within them. That's when they appreciate a new aspect of becoming recovered, and only then is a wise perspective of Spirituality available to them. Resolve the shame, embrace the loneliness, and learn to rely on things spiritual. It's always a sign of spiritual integrity and emotional health when addicts, or anyone for that matter, voluntarily and quietly chooses loneliness over conflict.

Shame is one of the more painful things people experience, but for spiritual pilgrims, once the shame is largely resolved, they touch that deep sense of how alone they really are. This awareness isn't available to people of little faith, which is why so very few people appreciate that on the *other* side of this loneliness is where the profound relationship with a higher power lies.

I've worked with addicts who are diligent and arrive at the cusp between insight and authentic transformation. They stand on the brink of addressing their loneliness and isolation from God and then quit therapy. They know some things, and sound insightful, but choose Impression Management rather than Spirituality—looking good and playing politics; taking the larger share of control and attention for themselves, while they convince you they're not—selfishness at its best.

Finger-Pointing By Numbers

Step Four is the exercise that takes alcoholics and addicts inside themselves and away from the historical game of externalizing responsibility (blaming and condemning). Addicts are brilliantly schooled in the fine art of Finger-Pointing, which is vicious at the best of times. Practice Finger-Pointing by first making your selections at 1(A) or 1(B) and entering this selection at line 7. Then, go back to #1 and read through the exercise, making your preferred selections at 2 through 6.

1 (A) **My life is...**
( ) hard   ( ) unfulfilled
( ) empty   ( ) lonely
( ) painful ( ) chaotic
( ) intolerable

1 (B) **I am feeling...**
( ) hurt   ( ) annoyed
( ) angry   ( ) lonely
( ) sad   ( ) depressed
( ) empty   ( ) miserable

(2) because... ( ) you ( ) he ( ) she ( ) everyone
( ) they ( ) it ( ) no one

(3)... ( ) didn't ( ) couldn't
( ) won't ( ) can't
( ) should have
( ) shouldn't have

(4) _____.
(insert description of their bad behavior)

(5) And besides, don't you know that...
( ) no one   ( ) he doesn't
( ) she doesn't   ( ) they don't
( ) you don't   ( ) it doesn't

(6) ( ) really appreciate me.
( ) care enough about me.

( ) like me.
( ) really love me.
( ) ever help me.
( ) support me.
( ) understand me.

(7) And so it's *your / his / her / their fault* that
(A) My life is _____, or
(B) I am feeling _____.
[insert selection from 1(A) or 1(B)]

Step Four is the first of two major exercises you must complete in order to gently negotiate yourself past this vicious mindset.[42]

Conditions Didn't Do Anything

There is crucial information in the paragraph that begins: *"We thought 'conditions' drove us to drink… "*.[43] As the frequency and intensity of your resentments increased it meant that you were trying harder to correct conditions. You were trying to get people to give you what you wanted; trying to get people to let you get away with things; or demanding people live their lives on your terms. This will become self-evident if you complete the Step Four List chronologically.

In *Alcoholics Anonymous,* the point made is that anger is invariably reduced to some perspective of alcoholics/addicts not getting their own way: As "we" tried to manipulate others to do what we wanted, *"and found that we couldn't to our entire satisfaction, our drinking* [acting out] *went out of hand and we became alcoholics."*[44] Your drinking, drug abuse, violence, shopping, sexual behavior, rage, religious righteousness, gambling, work, physical exercise, etc., went out of control when you tried to manipulate the world to suit yourself and the world wouldn't cooperate.

Your boss didn't understand you, your spouse was mean, the kids were too loud, you were underpaid and overworked, or overpaid and under worked, or they preempted your favorite TV show. You believed conditions and circumstances caused your acting out. Things and people drove you to it.[45] This world view is directly related to the way your instincts are filtered through your ego. Your ego is the operating agent between the external world and your inner soul-nature and instincts.[46] *"It never occurred to us that we needed to change ourselves."*[47]

How many times have you heard something like this: Two people are arguing. Kim says to Jan: "Every time we disagree, you start throwing things and

---

[42] There is always some element of righteousness or envy in gossip. One of the most important reasons to stop gossiping is that it forces you to look at yourself more than you look at others.
[43] *Twelve Steps and Twelve Traditions*, p. 47.
[44] Ibid., p. 47.
[45] This attitude of blaming is outrageously obvious in most people in our culture. "You made me mad," "I'm upset because you… ," "I'm unhappy because they… ," and so on. This is all irresponsible.
[46] See Appendix IV.
[47] *Twelve Steps and Twelve Traditions*, p. 47.

screaming and shouting." Jan, who screams and shouts and throws things, immediately becomes super-reasonable and makes a speech: "Well, look Kim, I *tried* saying please. I *tried* being nice. I *tried* negotiating. I *tried* asking. I *tried* talking about this. Nothing works! The only time you listen is when I yell and throw things." This really means Jan believes that Kim is "listening" when Kim does what Jan wants. This is classic behavior in addicted relationships.

Jan's speech: "I *tried* saying please. I *tried* being nice. I *tried*... ," is an itemized list of the control tactics Jan uses to try and manipulate obedience or compliance from Kim. When Kim says "No," Jan's insecurity interprets "No" as not listening or being argumentative, when, in fact, Kim may be listening, and simply disagreeing. When nothing else works, Jan becomes dangerous.

Alternately: Passive-aggressive "helplessness" is also punishing whomever isn't giving the alcoholic/addict what they want. This is another version of trying to *"correct conditions* to *our entire satisfaction."*

Resentments are a character defect and only one small facet of your personality. They indicate where you're supposed to start looking for the problem, but they aren't the problem.

Listen for people who avoid responsibility by staying focused on resentments. They won't talk about sex addiction as they buy a pornographic magazine or a beefcake pin-up calendar, or watch a stripper at a stag(ette). Listen to the hue and cry: Step Four! Resentments! They won't talk about tobacco, that they're irresponsible and committing suicide—those resentments, aren't they something? They won't talk about greed and cheating on their income tax—everyone cheats, right? My, my, those resentments are powerful things. And, of course, they gossip and spread rumors, which is evidence of righteousness and envy and very harmful to others, but that's minor compared to resentments: resentments can kill you. They avoid their racism, sexism, offensive humor, and crude language because resentments; well... those resentments are something, aren't they? Certainly the lies they tell are only *small* ones, and their boss or children or friends or partner won't find out—they'll worry about lying later; right now they have to focus on resentments. This is a massive campaign to look good while being irresponsible.

At Step Four, you painstakingly look at the patterns of conflicts and irresponsibility in relation to your acting out. If you are fortunate and determined enough to be in well conducted therapy, you will more easily see that your ego, often referred to as "the addict in me", not only tried to control conditions, but actually orchestrated the difficult circumstances in the first place so you had something to complain about.

Whatever conditions addicts believe drove them to drink, act out sexually, binge, rage, gamble, steal, spend... whatever, were actually arranged by them in the first place. They blame external conditions for their problems, and try to change these conditions by arguing, fighting, punishing others, harming themselves, spending, quitting, lying. leaving relationships, moving, playing dumb, drinking, getting stoned, being sexually irresponsible, gossiping, etc. There are no external reasons for addictions or alcoholism. It's never been Life. It's spiritual dislocation, which is demonstrated in how they, themselves, orchestrated the circumstances in their life in such a way that their self-annihilation appeared to be someone else's fault.

People come to see me for various addictions-related problems. We talk for a *long* time and eventually, finally, everything gets sorted out. They realize that, after all that work, the world hasn't changed very much. They have become much less focused on controlling external events. What has changed is their perception of themselves and their relationship with a higher power. They've become internally responsible and willing to live by spiritual principles.

In *Facets of Personal Transformation*, there will be a detailed discussion of how your ego is created, and establishes and maintains relationships and perceptions (here, covered briefly in Appendix IV). You recreate patterns of relationships and maintain themes of chaos and conflict. There's nothing haphazard about it. It isn't conditions. It's you. Your life and your world are your perceptions of circumstances selectively filtered through your ego.

Addicts live inside a massive campaign that externalizes responsibility. *"But in AA we slowly learned that something had to be done about our vengeful resentments, self pity, and unwarranted pride."*[48] The AA literature refers to alcoholics [addicts] being victimized by their own erratic emotions. I can *not* overstate the importance of this absolutely crucial observation: *"We had to drop the word 'blame' from our speech and thought."*[49] As far as spirituality and getting recovered go, there is never a justification for complaining about anything. No exceptions.

The Buried Treasure

Recall the children's stories about pirates. Black Bart and Evil Erma, the nasty pirates, have hidden their treasure. There's a map of a deserted coastline on The Dark Continent, and on the map is a trail of little dots. The dots go along the river, through the jungle (with snakes!), past Pointy Peak, over the dangerous rapids, around Lost Lagoon, past the crocodiles, under the waterfall, thirteen paces into the cave, against the east wall, under the big rock, and "X" marks the spot! Of course it's a big rock and Black Bart and Evil Erma have to work hard, and dig deeply, and fight off other pirates, to get their treasure.

Resentment is one "X" on your map that marks one emotional spot showing you where you want to dig into yourself. You also want to look "under" the big rocks of jealousy, envy, pride, sloth, greed, and the rest of your character defects. You have to fight off justifications, blaming, and excuses for not digging. Character de-

---

[48] *Twelve Steps and Twelve Traditions*, p. 48.

[49] Ibid., p. 49. This all-encompassing requirement eliminates *all* complaining about *every*thing: family of origin, lovers, ex- or present spouses, the government, children, friends, employers, co-workers, the program, newcomers, in-laws, out laws, relationships, the weather, the police, sponsors, sponsors who act like the police, authors of books, politicians, television, money, movie stars, and any other "thing" that an alcoholic or addict is disappointed, frustrated, scared, sad, unhappy, angry, envious, lonely, upset, confused, or displeased about. What addicts complain about and blame for the state of affairs in their life that they, themselves, have orchestrated, is literally endless. All blame must be eliminated from your speech and thought. No exceptions. If people in twelve-step programs stopped blaming, complaining, and gossiping, most of their conversations would screech to a halt.

fects are emotional clues that, with hard work, lead you to the treasures of insight, faith, compassion, and serenity.

Listing resentments is to start looking at patterns, but *not* patterns of resentments. Establishing the pattern of resentments is easy: Addicts resent anything that prevents them from doing or getting exactly what they want, when they want it, or losing anything they want to keep. That's the pattern, but that's not the problem.

Examining the underlying instinctual insecurities, which also operate in patterns, is the task. Should you identify only your patterns of resentment, without addressing the underlying instinctual motivators of all your defects, you will precipitate another self-defeating pattern (like repeating Step Four every year for the rest of your life). You will also further entrench the already established posture of being victimized and blaming others, and insisting that life isn't fair.

———

Earlier I mentioned that emotions commonly classified as "negative", especially anger, are always experienced attendant to some experience of fear.[50] This is clearly pointed out regarding pride: *"For pride, leading to self-justification, and always spurred by conscious or unconscious fears, is the basic breeder of most human difficulties, the chief block to true progress."*[51]

It's sad how many people in twelve-step programs stay spiritually corrupt and fear-driven. They constantly, selectively interpret the written material in a self-serving manner to avoid challenging their secret or subtle addictions and character defects—especially arrogance and prejudice. There are any number of justifications that cause someone to alter the original twelve-step program. Each justification is evidence of unchallenged spiritual sloth. Every time anyone justifies disobedience to spiritual principles, they demonstrate fear, and defeat the true intent of the steps.

This relates to the concept of the seven deadly sins. "Sin" was used in times long past as an archery term that meant "to miss the mark". I suppose, in the struggle to be perfect, when character defects control your personality,[52] people often miss the mark, and are therefore "sinners". If you want an interesting exercise, put a sign on your fridge noting the seven sins (pride, greed, lust, anger, gluttony, envy, sloth) and beside each one write a day of the week. Do some research on the meaning of each sin. Give them a liberal definition. Reflect on them individually, daily. It'll make for interesting dinner conversation with friends. Start talking about important things.

Of the list of sins, notice that anger (resentment) is only one of seven. People who talk about their defects primarily in terms of anger are missing the point. That would be an unbalanced representation of both themselves and the task at Step Four. I encourage you to take a careful look at what you're being told by people who've modified or ignored the instructions in the original twelve-step literature.

---

[50] There are no "negative" emotions, but there are no positive ones either. To label some emotions as more desirable than others is another ego gambit to establish grounds for complaint and struggle.
[51] *Twelve Steps and Twelve Traditions*, pp. 48, 49.
[52] Ibid., p. 48.

There is a clear and succinct description of the entrenchment-process of fear and character defects. It begins: *"All these failings generate fear... ."*[53] I've set this up graphically, and at point #2, added an alphabetical list of tactics (read: "defects") which represent controlling behavior. The cycle is:

(1)
Fear and insecurity are hidden by pride, greed, lust, anger, gluttony, envy, and sloth. This causes an...

(4)
generates *greater* fear and insecurity and that leads to more...

(3)
the struggle to control others (at 2) is met with resistance, which generates more conflict and failings[54] which...

(2)
attempt to control conditions, circumstances, and people by: acting out, arguing, blaming, bullying, clinging, complaining, defying, demanding, drinking/drug use, exaggerating, flirting, forgetting, gossiping, helplessness, hiding, caustic honesty, mean or racist humor, ignoring, feigning illness, intimidating, joking, leaving, lying, being miserly, neglecting, over-achieving, patronizing, procrastinating, quitting, refusing, sarcasm, selfishness, sex, shaming, shirking, shouting, sickness, silence, spending, stinginess, teasing, threatening, underachieving, violence, withholding... all done with speeches of self-justification[55]; and then...

Here's another exercise: Set a timer for five minutes and repeatedly read through the cycle for the five minutes. Think about the behaviors listed at position #2. Reflect on some conflict where you tried to control someone or punish them by acting in a way that is listed. Do this exercise once every three days for three months. Drive the point home, within yourself, that this cycle *is* the state of affairs in an unspiritual addict's life.

"...with genuine alarm at the prospect of work, we stay lazy" and *"...work grudgingly and under half steam."*[56] People "work their program", but too often that means their energy goes into recasting and selectively interpreting the steps and traditions. From another point of view, they really are working hard at their own program, but not working *the* program as it's laid out. Editing and recasting the AA literature is evidence of character defects controlling your effort, and a lack of effective investigation at Step Two.

Everyone is insecure about some things, and addicts are very insecure about many things. If you're an addict (practicing, in early recovery, or one who has manipulated or ignored the instructions), there are these two givens: you have a noticeably unspiritual mindset, and *all* of your relationships are dysfunctional be-

---

[53] *Twelve Steps and Twelve Traditions*, p. 49.
[54] *"...the more we fought and tried to have our own way, the worse matters got." Alcoholics Anonymous,* p. 66.
[55] This list represents *"self manifested in various ways* [that] *had defeated us."* Ibid., p. 64.
[56] *Twelve Steps and Twelve Traditions* p. 49.

cause of your character defects. Demands on others, like on your boss for a raise, your partner for more (or less) sex, your parents for more love, your children for more obedience, your friends for more phone calls, people you sponsor for more gratitude, or your committee for more recognition, are all fear-based and unspiritual. Any effort to control others will generate tension and fear.

Fear is an emotion that people experience as a result of chemicals naturally generated within their bodies when they are in a situation that is perceived as dangerous or unsafe. "Dangerous" could be because of someone chasing them with a knife, or because someone else may discover their insecurities or mistakes. Fear is the emotion that causes you to want to flee, freeze, or fight (in addict's terms: leave, go silent and sulk, or argue).

The perception of danger, regardless of the type, occasions the experience of fear, and in addicts, fear motivates all character defects.[57] Fear in people with generally balanced or non-addicted personalities, or in recovered alcoholic/addicts, is significantly less than fear in unregenerate addicts. Step Four is the process of beginning to make your fears, which show up as character defects, optional.

In order to do this, you have to do exactly what is suggested in the original twelve steps, and possibly go into long-term, well-conducted therapy. Shortcuts always defeat spiritual fulfillment. Consider that doing what you are told is the real shortcut: work very hard for several years and experience authentic spiritual peace, *or* stay in untreated addictions, hold onto your old ideas, and work painfully and repetitively through the steps for the rest of your life.

———

Immediately after the Step Three prayer, it reads: *"Next we launched out on a course of vigorous action* [a general reference to Steps Four to Nine], *the first step of which is a personal housecleaning* [a specific reference to Step Four]…".[58]

The Step Three decision requires vigorous follow-up action for it to be meaningful. I suggest this means doing it the detailed way, and not to fill-in-the-blanks of someone else's interpretation. Choosing the detailed way would be a demonstration of your sincerity regarding the decision you made in Step Three. Nowhere does it recommend that you take a shortcut and do someone else's interpretation of Step Four. Neither does it advise (or ever imply) that while doing Step Four, you are to worry about Step Five. Be mindful of your ego's determination to subvert the ever-deepening commitment to spiritual integrity.

With all character defects there is an associated fear. Resentment may head the list because it is the most common, but pride is apparently the more dangerous because it heads the procession.[59] It heads the list because it is diametrically opposed to humility. Fear is the universal common denominator in all character defects and underlies all the harm done to others. However, be mindful that *"Instincts on ram-*

---

[57] At the moment you feel afraid, the fear is authentic. Whether or not the extant circumstances might "objectively" be considered dangerous is a matter for well-conducted therapy, and sincere meditation and prayer.

[58] *Alcoholics Anonymous*, p. 63.

[59] *"Pride, leading to self-justification… spurred by conscious or unconscious fears, is the basic breeder of most human difficulties, the chief block to true progress." Twelve Steps and Twelve Traditions*, p. 48.

page balk at investigation. The minute we make a serious attempt to probe them, we are liable to suffer severe reactions."[60]

Depressed or Self Righteous

These two types of general temperament are described as having unique needs in addressing Step Four. *"If temperamentally we are on the depressive side, we are apt to be swamped with guilt and self loathing."*[61] Within this melancholic group are people who tend to blame themselves for everything, or view any situation as hopeless. *"Comforting the melancholy..."*[62] refers to this group that, secretly or not, often feels so badly, all they see about themselves are character defects. From their point of view, there's no need to self-examine because of the foregone conclusion that everything's their own fault, and they'd probably fail at the task anyway.

The next paragraph describes the second type: *"If, however, our natural disposition is inclined to self-righteousness or grandiosity... ."* And, the next following paragraph offers another perspective of this same self-righteousness: *"...another wonderful excuse...* [to avoid Step Four because] *our present anxieties and troubles are caused by the behavior of other people."* [Blaming] The members of this group are generally blind to their liabilities, and think they need no inventory, or at best, have a very short list of defects.

The nature of self-righteousness and blame requires a belief in personal superiority and/or innocence. Whether they admit it or not, self-righteous types cling desperately to their (always exaggerated) good qualities, and avoid any sincere examination or admission of the ubiquitous nature of their own defects. From their point of view, there's no need for detailed self-examination—everything wrong is, for the most part, someone else's fault.

The metaphor used at Step Four is "a business inventory", one object of which is *"to disclose damaged or unsalable goods, to get rid of them promptly and without regret."*[63] If you interpret this from a psychological perspective, it's then easy to view the metaphor as incomplete or unbalanced, and to recast the instructions and reasonably justify the addition of an inventory of character assets—even though "assets" are noticeably *not* mentioned at this point. So, psychologically, the metaphor of a business inventory is easily seen as incomplete; but the book isn't intended to have a psychological perspective. The step is to be done to facilitate being closer to God, as you understand God, not for psychological balance, and so when the inventory metaphor is contemplated from a *spiritual* perspective, nothing needs to be added. A Spiritual life isn't concerned with fairness or psychological balance.

Listing assets won't bring them (or you) closer to God, it will further entrench irresponsibility and gloss over any defects related to arrogance. A list of character assets has no spiritually authentic reason here.[64] Generally, people who

---

[60] *Twelve Steps and Twelve Traditions*, p. 44.
[61] Ibid. This, and the uncited quotations following it, are from p. 45.
[62] Ibid., p. 46.
[63] *Alcoholics Anonymous*, p. 64.
[64] Step Eleven does refer to addicts being mindful of their successes (but some restrictions apply). The reasons for assets being included at Step Eleven are notably different than at Step Four.

advocate listing assets in Step Four, without regard for the qualifier of temperament, are in the grandiose or righteous category. That's why they insist on including them. Challenging their own arrogance by *not* listing their good qualities is the related exercise in humility and that brings them closer to God.

Should you be generally melancholy and depressive, a list of your assets would be advisable; but here too, listing assets won't bring you closer to God. It does, however, create some relief of the ongoing despair of being temperamentally depressed. The assets list offers a balance in self-perception for the melancholy types. That balance allows for energy and interest to examine their defects, and *that* brings them closer to God.

So, the two general types are "melancholy" (everything is my fault), or "self-righteous" (everything is someone else's fault). Each temperament is offered different counsel, to get out of their inaccurate perceptions, at which point they can then address Step Four with the thoroughness required. Notice which type usually applies to you, and study the strategy the book describes to overcome your inability to be thorough in completing Step Four. The business inventory metaphor is from a spiritual perspective and needs nothing added to it.

Recall that in Step Two, honesty, open-mindedness, and willingness were for a specific type of spiritual newcomer; and that HOW, used outside of Step Two, contains a built-in opportunity to procrastinate. The same theme of using something out of context, and the subsequent danger of misapplying it, applies to the list of assets. For those who tend to be grandiose or self-righteous, including assets in Step Four is taking an instruction out of context. That won't foster responsible self-examination and insight; it will prevent it.

Some addicts are phasic—they'll switch between self-righteous and depressive for long periods, and others will be in so much chaos they'll be in either mode at any given moment. If you are in this category of alternating/erratic focus between melancholy and self-righteous, it will help to go back to Step Two. Reflect on your attitude towards spirituality, and again disarm your spiritual misgivings. Enhance your faith, which may take months. Be patient.[65] Over time, with thoughtful self-examination at Step Two, you will notice more stability in your spiritual devotion. Then, when a new spiritual heliotropism brings you back to Step Four, you will be less erratic and have more success in attending to the tasks at hand.

A Change In Focus

In all the years you acted out, as a general rule, you talked about how good (or innocent) you were and complained about everybody else—with an exception made for whomever your present company was. At the same time, you managed to mention your good qualities, proclaim the other person's guilt, or remind whomever would listen that you were certainly a Victim in the whole mess of Your Life. You

---

[65] Addicts act in very complex and individually unique patterns—their addictions fingerprint. Because of this, being patient with yourself is imperative. Impatience never allows for contemplation, which is essential to unravel the subtle ways you cheat on your commitment to spirituality and a higher power. Spirituality suffers at the hands of impatience, however slight.

were too short, or too tall; you were not rich, or so rich people only loved you for your money; you had too much hair, or it was too straight, or too wavy, or the wrong color; or you had mean parents. You complained you had big feet, were born into a minority group (or into a majority group and complained about the backlash against you for that), or you complained that someone else was complaining about something that they really shouldn't be complaining about. It was always something.

Sadly, that sounds a lot like twelve-step programs today—the gossip, the blaming, and complaining about everything imaginable are not only vicious, but decidedly unspiritual. In Step Four this focus is changed. You cannot properly complete Step Four, and remain a Victim at the same time. You must write specifically about your instincts and your responsibility, and what eventually will need to be fixed in you (by you).

Earlier I mentioned the metaphor of a business inventory. *"We did exactly the same thing with our lives. We took stock honestly. First, we searched out the flaws in our make-up which caused our failure. Being convinced that self, manifested in various ways, was what had defeated us, we considered its common manifestations."*[66] *"Flaws in our make-up"* implies much more than resentments. It's described in the next sentence as *"self, manifested in various ways"*—selfishness: having your ego put you first in a way that's dishonest, self-serving, or harmful to others. This wears many masks,[67] but the common manifestations are generally classified as seven deadly sins.[68] Each character defect is a demonstration of selfishness: behaviors and beliefs that are motivated by fear and instincts gone awry. Your instincts gone awry became your character defects.

Step Four is done after you have become abstinent, and it necessarily requires that the list be about instincts and fears when you were acting out. It would also include defects that interfere with your relationship with a higher power in that period from when you became abstinent up to the point where you complete Step Four. [An important shift in perspective here is: Character defects are commonly thought of as causing yourself or other people problems. More importantly, they are what separate you from a sincere relationship with your higher power.]

Notice that there are no grounds for the exclusion of any resentment. The AA textbooks do not suggest that because you may have been resentful at someone, but aren't now, you have a reason to exclude it. There are no exclusions. Often people in twelve-step programs will stop being mad when those whom they perceive have hurt them make an amend. Or, if the addict is the person hurt, and never receives an amend, they may magnanimously announce that they have let the resentment go. Of course, they mention to several people how so-and-so hurt them (gossiping), and that they've let go of their resentment (bragging).

Part one of your Step Four is to examine your instincts gone awry, that exist underneath resentments and character defects (past or present). Because you believe

---

[66] *Alcoholics Anonymous*, p. 64.
[67] For a definition of harmful, refer to *Twelve Steps and Twelve Traditions*, p. 80.
[68] Ibid., p. 48.

you're "over" a resentment is not a reason to exclude it from the list. There is still a wealth of self-awareness available from that. Avoiding insight by shirking thoroughness is expensive.

The author(s) used ordinary words to describe spiritual principles,[69] and so the words should be taken at face value. A resentment is defined as being *"angry, sore, burned up,"* and having a grudge (*"grudge list"*).[70] Resentment is given a broad definition. Don't create a self-serving definition of resentment that allows you to avoid work and responsibility. I've heard many confusing and narrow definitions of resentment; here's four of them:

- Resentments are feelings like anger that last a long time. If they don't last a long time, then they're not resentments (followed by the debate over what "a long time" means).
- Resentments are angry-type feelings that are "bigger" than angry feelings.
- Resentments are emotions that are more than being mad and recur over the same things; and,
- Resentments are the "more important" angry feelings.

This esoteric babble is rooted in insecurity and fear, and represents shallow spiritual commitment. It's modifying the original program to avoid self-examination and hard work because the more exotic the definition, the shorter the list. The book advises that generally, a resentment, whether present or past, is feeling angry, sore, burned up, or having a grudge. That's going to make for a *long* list. (There's great spiritual opportunity in thoroughness.)

You have the instructions for Step Four, but at what point in your life do you start? This work is in relation to your addiction, not childhood trauma. It would seem obvious, then, that you would start your list at about the time you started to drink or act out.

One of the more "endearing" traits addicts have is they're notoriously brilliant at selective remembering. One significant reason for doing what I'm going to suggest, which may seem like tedious nonsense (but is compliant with the instructions) is: It counteracts selective remembering. [Only you can call yourself to task on your spiritual journey, so enjoy your Step Four-stroll down memory lane and have fun with this. Be willing, patient, and thorough.] It will pay off. To begin:

Let's assume you were born in 1960, your primary addiction is alcohol, and you started drinking when you were thirteen. At the top of the first page write "13/1973"; on the next, "14/1974"; on the next, "15/1975"; and so on, until you are as old as you presently are. Allow yourself at least one page per year. Maintaining chronological order offers advantages and insights that aren't available otherwise.

---

[69] *Alcoholics Anonymous,* p. 93.
[70] Ibid., pp. 64, 65.

Next: Write a list of everything and everyone in your life, from each particular year of your life, on the page that represents that year. What I mean is, you would write a list on the page "13/1973" of *everyone* you can remember from that year, even if you liked them and weren't mad. Put them on the list. [I'm not changing the instructions in the original literature, I'm showing you how to be painstaking and thorough; which means honest. We'll get to your resentments soon enough.]

So, at the top of the page noted "13/1973," write the names of *everyone* you can remember who was in your life at that time: friends, enemies, teachers, family members, relatives, neighbors, classmates, bosses, coworkers, cops, lawyers, pets (yours or other people's)—literally *every* person. If you can't remember their names, write "the girl with the blue dress" or "the boy with the green shoes". Write down literally *everyone* you can remember, whether you were mad at them or not, when you were thirteen.

Include places and institutions that were a part of your life in that year such as cities, neighborhoods, houses, apartments, camps, cottages, hospitals, social clubs, restaurants, vehicles, jobs, churches, schools (reform or otherwise), government agencies, courthouses, the police, and the legal profession. And finally, include principles—the ideas, traditions, and rules that influenced your life, like honesty, Christmas, capital punishment, immigration policies, income tax, traffic laws, being polite, bus schedules, insurance, religion, birthdays, fidelity, monogamy, divorce, adoption, probation, parole, seat belt and helmet laws, curfews, child-support payments, alimony, smoking by-laws, school grading policies, homework, the age of majority, and voting.

Do this list in detail for each year (on each page) of your life. For each successive age, add new items that weren't listed previously. When you've finished one age, go to the next age. The same person or item will recur at different ages. There's no need to duplicate entries unless there's some notable change in circumstance, such as someone who was in your life when you were seventeen and disappeared for years, then showed up again when you were thirty-one; or you may have been angry with child-support payments as a teenager because one parent wasn't paying them, and then again at thirty-eight because as an adult you had to pay them. Principles and people will affect us differently at different ages.

This part of the exercise is about creating a complete autobiographical list. You might write two-hundred names for one year and only twenty-seven for the next year. Don't omit anyone, any place, any "thing", any principle. If you can't remember names, write a brief description to identify who they are. Don't be concerned with not remembering everything; just painstakingly note whatever you do remember. *Be very thorough* and for now, don't be concerned with resentments. It's important to take your time. Be patient. This is a voluntary labor of love, which is true spiritual devotion.

Avoid pressure, impatience, and competition (with some imaginary standard of performance, or with what someone else has told you about their work). You will trigger memories and have to go back and add names. Challenge your selective remembering. From one (p)age to another, if there's some special change in circumstance, enter a name on the list again. *Thoroughness and great detail is imperative.* At this stage this is a simple exercise of making a *long* autobiographical list.

If you think I'm suggesting tedious nonsense, challenge yourself on those spiritually limiting thoughts. This does not have to be painful. If you're angry for having feelings—sadness, love, loneliness, sexual feelings—they go on the resentment list too. So does being mad at me for suggesting this.

Continue in this manner up to the present, ending with the people, places, and principles of your twelve-step program. When you've finished your autobiographical list, you may have well over a thousand entries. Now what? Consider writing the list out neater, keeping it in general chronological order, and leaving three empty lines between each entry. You will then have a neat, very *long* list of your whole life. Make a copy and keep it in a safe place; you'll need it later.

Now, from the beginning, go slowly through the list, reflecting on each entry, and cross off those entries that you weren't (or aren't) mad at or resentful towards, or that you didn't (don't) have a grudge against. If you once had, or still have, any resentment or grudge at all, old or new, big or little, past or present, don't cross them off. Be rigorously honest. If you do this sincerely, it can be very emotionally rewarding to see how many entries you crossed off. Your resentments and character defects were selective. Later, when you realize how and why you resented some and not others, you will put that insight to good spiritual use. Remind yourself this is about honoring your decision at Step Three.

You may have resented someone, but since the incident, believe you have forgiven them. Often this means you haven't really forgiven them, but the grudge is dim because of time past. The former resentment is often easily triggered awake, and therefore more sincere spiritual work is required. Regardless of this, if you had a resentment and now don't, the person or principle remains on your list. There are no exclusions for "former" resentments.

If you follow the process I've outlined, you will notice that for the early phase of your acting out, you probably crossed off more than you left on. Then later, as your addiction worsened, you probably left on more entries and had more resentments and grudges. Later still, in abstinence, you started crossing off more names than you left on.

The frequency of resentments (of defects) is a reflection of your struggle to control situations and people. You will notice when your addiction went out of hand, not by the amount you drank—which is relatively unimportant—but by insight into your personality. *Your addiction isn't in your acting out, it's in your flawed spiritual character.* Step Four requires you change your perceptions of Life *from* a preoccupation with what you did—hurt yourself, proclaim your innocence, blame others, take their inventory, and justify, *to* a reflection of who you are—your insecurities, and instincts gone awry. (This relates to the information in the earlier section, "Conditions Didn't Do Anything".)

This is where addicts must realign their fundamental operating principles from blame and dishonesty to responsibility and truth. This transition is done exactly here, and it's the genesis of the awareness of an addict's self-imposed crisis. This is not a weekend exercise. Do *not* do your grudge list during the advertisements in a movie. Your commitment to spirituality is [ideally] to work patiently and diligently for as long as it takes. Any impatience or pressure to hurry, or any lack of thoroughness, is fatal to the process.

————

Many addicts ask about including resentments about having an addiction. Yes, these could go on the list, but there are some important cautions. After having the flu, you may be regretful that you missed a party because of your illness—having an illness can be inconvenient—but you don't necessarily *resent* yourself for being sick. It's reasonable that you briefly regret the fact that you missed a party, but that doesn't mean feeling guilty and resentful. (If you do, find a therapist.)

It's crucial that addicts get it that they have an illness of spiritual origin. The symptoms of the disease are very often what they resent—they were dishonest, angry, afraid, or made "bad" decisions. Symptoms aren't optional, so why should addicts be resentful of themselves when these symptoms are part of the disease? Here's where the importance of getting Step One "right" becomes more obvious.

The pressure of socially imposed guilt is significantly reduced once addicts understand it's an issue of disease, not morality. Dishonesty, or any other symptom, wasn't a conscious, intellectual choice. When addicts take this to heart, no guilt or resentment will accrue from symptomatic behavior. Once people getting recovered sincerely understand that they had a disease; that it wasn't their "fault" (nor was it anyone else's), they feel sad and have regrets, but the guilt disappears and they don't resent themselves. If you feel noticeably resentful or guilty about your addiction, you very likely misperceive the nature of "illness".

So, regarding Step Four, should you resent yourself, list these specific resentments separately and reflect on them carefully. Review the list of symptoms in Chapter 2 in this book, read Step One in *Twelve Steps and Twelve Traditions*, and read More About Alcoholism in *Alcoholics Anonymous*. Reflect on the spiritual nature of the disease. Realize that the behaviors that you resent are more than likely derivative of the symptoms, and not something that you "chose" to do.[71]

Another tactic that must be considered is evasiveness by exaggerating or minimizing your defects, resentments, and progress. If you convince yourself that you used to kill people and pillage the countryside, and now only beat someone up every few months, it makes for a remarkable improvement-story: "I'm so much better than I used to be, so I don't really need to look at myself *that* thoroughly."

Watch you don't exaggerate in glorious detail how much you've improved, or minimize to triviality your defects and fears. You may impress yourself, but these tactics are used as justifications for shallow self-examination and sporadic abusive behavior. When reflecting on your list, watch for embellishment or minimizing. Rigorous honesty is also a euphemism for accuracy.

———————————

[71] Certainly there are times when addicts or alcoholics deliberately/consciously lied, and they must always hold themselves accountable; but underneath this, the addiction requires dishonesty, no differently than pneumonia requires a fever.

Let's assume that your complete list has 1,987 entries. After crossing off all the people, places, and principles where you had no resentments, anger, or grudges, you are left with 456 entries. If you are overwhelmed by this apparently huge number, remind yourself it's just information about how resentful you were. Notice how many you have crossed off. But, if on the other hand, you've crossed off 1,976 and end up with only 11 entries remaining on your list, there's something amiss. In this case, find a wise, spiritual mentor. Reflect more carefully on your emotional past, and you'll (probably) need some professional help as you work through this.

You will end up with an accurate list of resentments and grudges. If it's cluttered, you're probably going to balk at this, but, keeping them in approximate chronological order, write a neater grudge list with four or five empty lines between each entry. This becomes column one, as shown in *Alcoholics Anonymous*.[72] Now, examine each entry carefully, and for each one, ask yourself why you were mad: What did they do that you resented? Itemize and note what you believed the external cause of your grudge was. This will become column two of your list. Don't use ditto marks. Be honest, brief, and thorough.

And finally, *Alcoholics Anonymous* refers to five instincts: self-esteem, personal security, ambitions, personal relations, and sex relations.[73] Think about these instincts and reflect on them in relation to your anger and character defects in general. Your fears and insecurities relating to these instincts, and how those fears interfered with their natural expression, is the root cause of resentments and grudges.[74] Your task is to identify your fears and insecurities, in relation to these instincts, *for every entry on the list*. This information becomes the third column. Be very specific about how your instincts were threatened. Every entry gets the same devoted attention. If you're not willing to work in the detail *Alcoholics Anonymous* suggests, evidently you didn't really come to believe (in Step Two), or you didn't understand the nature of your commitment (in Step Three).

Here, for the first time in this process, you begin to intimately understand how *you* created the crises in your life. You started with whom and what you were mad at, then noted what was "done" to you, and ended by paying detailed attention to how *your* instincts had gone awry through *your* fears and insecurities. Character defects are only the "entrance points" that allow you to delve deep inside your personality. Resentments themselves play a pretty minor part in all of it.

Invest a lot of time in this; be diligent and at the same time be patient. Don't be obsessed and fanatical. Do a half-an-hour a day, or an hour every other day, until it's finished; take breaks and continue to live your life while you do this.

In all times of punishing others, trying to get your own way, or arguing—which are the behaviors of coveting resentments and defects, the victor only appears to win. Needing to win; being pleased that someone else has beat another person; or

---

[72] *Alcoholics Anonymous*, p. 65.
[73] Remember, the authors were spiritual, not scientific, in their use of the word instinct. Don't quibble about this. This is a process in getting recovered, not a lecture on genetics or biology.
[74] *Alcoholics Anonymous*, p. 65.

being pleased that someone you don't like has lost, must all be abandoned. Triumph is always short-lived and empty because the need to dominate is always motivated by fear and insecurity.[75] Winning doesn't make the insecurity go away, it only camouflages it. This is a truth about a Spiritual life, but eliminating the underlying insecurity is only available if the work is done as outlined. Struggling to control anyone is a fool's game, regardless of its disguise.[76]

This part of your Step Four points out your irresponsibility, which is related to your instincts gone awry. When contemplated spiritually, you expose your insecurity underneath your efforts to dominate and blame.[77] Any other model of a Step Four won't dovetail with the intended, long-term spiritual result. Remember: *"We went back through our lives. Nothing counted but thoroughness and honesty."*[78]

There Are Laws Here

The laws of physics and the mechanics of material determine how things are made. If people want planes to fly, or water to freeze, there are rules. The laws of nature determine these processes, which are not negotiable. "Nature" isn't concerned with convenience. The properties of material, the truths about mathematics, and the laws of physics and chemistry are unyielding. People obey these laws, or planes don't fly and water doesn't freeze. If we want any mechanical endeavor to be successful, we must figure out the rules of nature (physics), and follow them.

Regarding spiritual regeneration, this is admirably stated by Manly P. Hall: *"The unfolding of* [a person's] *spiritual nature is as much an exact science as astronomy, medicine or jurisprudence. To accomplish this end religions were primarily established; and out of religion have come science, philosophy, and logic as methods whereby this divine purpose might be realized."*[79]

All spiritual transformation, whether it begins from within an unfulfilling, psychological outlook on Life, or within the dislocated/self-annihilating position of addictions, has a required sequence of tasks, and a *non-*modifiable process and structure. The entire process of regenerating yourself into a more spiritual person is resolutely mandated by the inherent requirements of Spirituality. There are laws here. If I were to personify spirituality and nature, I would say, "Nature" doesn't care that making planes fly is complicated and expensive. People, if they want planes to fly and want to travel quickly, have to follow the rules and pay the price. Likewise: "Spirituality" doesn't care that regeneration is arduous and time consuming. If peo-

---

[75] Proselytizing is the intellectual contest of trying to convert someone into another value system or doctrine. It's insecurity and arrogance, etc., disguised under the illusion of religious or moral superiority.

[76] Keep this in context. I'm referring to adults in the spiritual and judicious course of their lives.

[77] Winning, dominating others, arguing, all have damaging consequences. A spiritual being considers actions and their consequences far beyond the immediate result. There are Primary, Secondary, and Tertiary consequences to be considered. A person [an addict] does something: (1) What are the consequences to themselves? (Primary); (2) What are the directly related consequences to people close to them? (Secondary); and, (3) What are the consequences to the community, their careers, to the world/the environment? (Tertiary). The Doctrine of Competition (or of selfish self-interest) continues to exist when people consider the consequences only at the primary level, which by definition, is selfish.

[78] *Alcoholics Anonymous,* p. 65.

[79] *The Secret Teachings of All Ages,* Manly P. Hall, Tarcher/Penguin, 2003, p. 120. Also: See the quote from *Isis Unveiled,* H.P. Blavatsky, cited at p. 5.

ple want to experience the bliss of a truly spiritual life, or if addicts want to save their life, they must pay the price of following exactly these guidelines.

How to be obedient to the laws of spiritual transformation—how to effect that change—is brilliantly presented and explained in *Alcoholics Anonymous* and *Twelve Steps and Twelve Traditions*. That process can not be altered in its content or sequence without dire consequences.

Two-At-A-Time Programming

People getting recovered often use expressions like: "When I was doing Steps Two and Three," or "I'm worried about Steps Eight and Nine." This pairing usually happens with "two and three", "four and five", "six and seven", and "eight and nine". When any of the first nine steps are perceived as yoked together—seeing any two steps as somehow joined in execution—problems are created. These pairings are pervasive, and based on the perception that these steps are somehow more connected to each other, than as say, three is to six, or five is to eight.

There is a crucial relationship between the innate paradigm for spiritual transformation and the order of the first nine steps. In this paradigm, any step is just as intrinsically connected to any of the other eight steps, as it is to one that appears adjacent to it. There are no preferential pairings, and creating these pairings causes serious problems. Steps One to Nine should not be viewed in pairs or done out of sequence (they are independent of each other). If they are paired up, or done out of sequence, you'll be doing work that's at odds with the paradigm of spiritual transformation. For the addict getting recovered, the results are disastrous.

No one can effectively appreciate the nuances, or negotiate through the requirements, or absorb the spiritual tone of any step while carrying the intellectual or emotional burden of anticipating any other step. Each regeneration step can only be accomplished and absorbed within you, as it is spiritually intended, when it's addressed individually and independent of *all* the others. Getting recovered is not possible if, during any one step, you puzzle over the intricacies of any future step, or have failed to acquire the faith, insight, and spiritual grounding that accrues from doing the previous step(s) painstakingly and independently.

It's spiritually untenable to anticipate, plan for, discuss, review, analyze, attempt, puzzle over, meditate on, or contemplate any of the first nine steps in pairs or "together". [Steps Ten, Eleven, and Twelve are remarkably different—they're steps of spiritual maintenance, and therefore inseparable from each other; done simultaneously, but more about that later.]

———

So, the first part of Step Four was about the relationship between resentments (character defects) and fears in relation to your instincts gone awry. There's a paragraph that contains the segue into the second part of your Step Four. It begins: *"Notice that the word fear... ."*[80] This paragraph takes your new-found awareness of

---

[80] *Alcoholics Anonymous*, p. 67.

the fear and insecurity inherent in resentments, and expands your focus to identify *all* your fears. Fears must be thoroughly reviewed by *"putting them on paper, even though we had no resentment in connection with them."*[81] On a new sheet start listing all of your fears, whether or not you had a resentment in connection with them. Begin at the time or shortly before you started acting out.

Are <u>or were</u> you afraid of being poor? Are <u>or were</u> you afraid of Spiders? Are or were you afraid of… Self-awareness? Responsibility? Honesty? Kindness? Fire? Flying? Dying (suddenly *or* slowly)? Being old? Being alone? Eating different food? Beautiful women? Handsome men? Anger? Assertive people? Rich people? God? Sex? Intimacy? Commitment? Teachers? Snakes? Drowning? Dancing? Doctors? The police? Make a list of *all* your fears. Include a brief reference to the instinctual fears you listed in column three of the previous exercise.

If you're too embarrassed to admit them all, or annoyed at the thoroughness required, you've missed the point that this is a labor of devotion. Go back to Step Two and review your commitment to spirituality, and then reconsider your decision at Step Three. The solution is in spiritual obedience.

Be cautious about probing into fears from infancy and childhood without professional support. For these, and possibly for all of your fears, you should seek out an experienced counsellor who is wisely empathetic to your participation in a twelve-step program. If you've gotten over some of your fears, include them anyway. Old fears are worthy of examination and can often offer substantial insight.

And now for more patience and self-discipline, from *Alcoholics Anonymous*: *"We asked ourselves why we had them. Wasn't it because self-reliance failed us?"*[82] Contemplate this, then write something down beside each fear.

Notice that in this section of the AA text, which applies to fears and Step Four, there is no guarantee or implied expectation that by this process, all your fears will go away. They *may* be reduced, or they *may* go away, but escaping your fears is not the specific goal—there are two more important goals. The first is to be completely honest about your entire inner experience. There is relief in microscopic truth-telling.[83] The second is to gracefully and gratefully depend on a higher power; to enroll prayer and meditation as ways to embrace your fears and still have a fulfilling life. This exercise has a spiritual, not psychological, focus.

Getting recovered is a huge undertaking, and carefully reflecting on your fears is an essential, on-going spiritual discipline. Be patient with yourself.

Nine Sex Questions

The third and final part of Step Four is *"…about sex. Many of us needed an overhauling there. But above all, we tried to be sensible… ."*[84] It says that with opinions running to extremes, *"We want to stay out of this controversy,"*[85] that: *"We do*

---

[81] *Alcoholics Anonymous*, p. 68.
[82] Ibid.
[83] *Conscious Loving,* Gay Hendricks, Ph.D., & Kathlyn Hendricks, Ph.D., Bantam Books, 1992, p. 111.
[84] *Alcoholics Anonymous,* p. 68.
[85] Ibid., p. 69.

not want to be the arbiter of anyone's sex conduct."[86] In essence, twelve-step participants are told to mind their own business about other people's sex lives. You are to closely examine your own sexual behavior and not the behavior of others.

Make a complete list of *all* the people you have had sex relations with. You can refer back to the extensive autobiographical list you kept a copy of. Your sex partners' names will be there. If you've ever masturbated, put yourself on your sex-list.[87] Some people will have a long list and others will have a short list.

There are two general categories of sexual relationships. These are:

- those people you knew: wives, husbands, longer-term partners, boyfriends, and girlfriends. You may have only been with them for a short while, but you knew them. List these individually; and,
- the group of nameless strangers you "woke up" with. You don't know the one-night stands and mystery partners. Make an honest estimate of how many mystery partners there were and write at the bottom of your list: Mystery Partners – 142, or 6, or whatever number you come up with.

Don't take the easy way out by lumping as many as you can from the first group into the second group. Don't underestimate the number of Mystery Partners to conceal shame, or overestimate the number to impress anyone (especially yourself). If any particular Mystery Partner stands out as startlingly different from the others in the mystery group, place that one on the list of ones you know. The fact that this person stands out, for whatever reason, affords them special consideration.

Some addicts will be ashamed they have only a very few names, and some will be ashamed they have hundreds. Nothing counts but thoroughness and honesty. Leave at least six or seven empty lines between each name on your list.

What I'm about to suggest is in line with thoroughness, responsibility, and spiritual principles. There are two types of "sex partner" that are frequently overlooked. (1) There are alcoholics and addicts who've lived with obsessive fantasies about others. They've invested significant emotional and sexual energy in fantasizing about someone: a movie star, a neighbor's spouse, one of their co-workers. Or, (2) they may have come dangerously close to having sex with someone where the result would have been particularly disastrous: *almost* having sex with a relative, with a

---

[86] *Alcoholics Anonymous*, p. 69. This peremptorily eliminates any rules about newcomers in relationships. Note the item on p. 111 of *Twelve Steps and Twelve Traditions* about giving advice that addicts aren't competent to give.

[87] If, as an addict, you acted out with animals, children, or were involved in incest, pornography, prostitution, or adultery, these must be included in your Step Four. This is essential so you can complete later spiritual tasks within yourself, within the steps, and as a recovered person helping others. I know this may seem tremendously difficult, possibly beyond your comprehension; however, you are capable of doing this if you approach the instructions with patience, *professional support*, faith, abstinence, and a relationship with a higher power. When approaching Step Five be mindful of the qualifying guideline (p. 74 *Alcoholics Anonymous*) *"Perhaps our doctor or psychologist..."* and review the paragraph on page 79 of *Alcoholics Anonymous* that begins, *"Although these reparations take innumerable forms...."* If you have to hire a therapist, do that. Take responsible action; don't evade.

boss, or with the spouse of a close friend. It would be wise to include these sex-relationships for two reasons: (i) there is much to be learned from these demonstrations of sexual insecurity; and, (ii) it will help to prevent a recurrence of this.

When your list of names is complete, begin reviewing your sexual conduct. *"Where had we been selfish, dishonest, or inconsiderate? Whom had we hurt? Did we unjustifiably arouse jealousy, suspicion, or bitterness? Where were we at fault, what should we have done instead? We got this all down on paper and looked at it."*[88] This requires that you ask, and answer, nine questions about every sexual relationship you were in—for every person in the Ones You Know section (which would include the obsessive fantasies and dangerous close-calls), and one general answer for the group of Mystery Partners. Here are the questions again:

1. Where was I selfish?
2. Where was I dishonest?
3. Where was I inconsiderate?
4. Whom did I hurt?
5. Did I unjustifiably arouse jealousy?

6. Did I unjustifiably arouse suspicion?
7. Did I unjustifiably arouse bitterness?
8. Where was I at fault?
9. What should I have done instead?

It is crucial that you answer these questions about every sexual relationship in your life, in relation to your addiction. If you've been selfish, dishonest, or inconsiderate; or aroused jealousy, suspicion, or bitterness, in a sexual relationship, somebody has been hurt. Carefully examine each one, write a brief answer, and don't use ditto marks. [If sexual abuse or rape is a part of your history, or if you struggle with your sexual preference/orientation, then your sponsor, meetings, and the steps, are *not* the venues to resolve this. Seek competent, professional help.]

Consider that the people you harmed through sexual irresponsibility may not have been just the people you had sex with. You may have emotionally harmed the children of your sex partner (or your own children), friends, co-workers, or relatives. Did your sexual acting out harm a business or a group?[89] This is an exercise in awareness about harm you have caused. It's fine to be brief, but be thorough.

For this final part of Step Four, you may want to list yourself as someone you hurt by irresponsible sexuality—contracting a disease, ending up in jail, being divorced. Should this be the case, at the end, note the harm your sexual behavior did to you. This isn't to itemize your resentments and fears about sex (which should be already noted in the first two parts of this step). Listing the consequences to yourself of your sexual irresponsibility, which is the result of your character defects controlling your sexuality, and then deciding what you might have done instead, contributes to creating values regarding a spiritual expression of sexuality.[90]

---

[88] *Alcoholics Anonymous*, p. 69.

[89] In this book, in the section A Change In Focus there is a footnote about Primary, Secondary, and Tertiary consequences. The ripple effect of irresponsible sex is considerable.

[90] Because of "modern" culture's notions of sexuality (repression, orientation, gender stereotyping, etc.), and the powerful dogma of sexually repressive and righteous religions, some readers may believe that there's no such thing as spiritually based sexual expression. Others may believe that spiritually based sex must be boring, or occur only in the missionary position, or exclude homosexuality—or any number of other repressions and prohibitions. This is definitely not the case regarding Step Four in the original twelve steps, and not the case regarding sexuality in general. Spirituality only requires responsibility and

Without including everyone and answering the first eight questions, you cannot intelligently and thoroughly answer question nine. The answer to #9 is where you start to create new values about sexuality (governed by the five spiritual principles that are embodied in the maintenance steps).

This is a huge undertaking, much of it repetitious, and for some, embarrassing. However, notice in the way outlined here, which is an explanation of the original twelve steps, it becomes a moral inventory (not a list of bad things), and is fear-less (done largely without fear). Nothing counts but thoroughness and honesty. Take your time, get it all down on paper, and keep a record of what you should have done instead, because: *"In this way we tried to shape a sane and sound ideal for our future sex life. We subjected each relation to this test—was it selfish or not?"*[91]

Morality

You're creating new values and incorporating spiritual principles into your future sexual conduct. Neither of the AA texts subscribe to any religiously oriented moral position. They do, however, subscribe to spiritual principles that are to become foremost in *all* areas of your life.

We each have different desires and preferences for how we express our sexuality. Some people like oral sex, and some don't. Some people prefer missionary position sex; others don't. Some people like to have sex only in the bedroom and others enjoy different places; some like tickling and giggling; some don't. When you answer the first eight questions, you identify the problems that arose in the way you conducted yourself sexually (not necessarily in your sexuality, but in your conduct). Question nine identifies what you should have done instead. This creates your own standards for a spiritually based sexual relationship.[92]

For example: Jane really likes and enjoys tease-and-tickle sex, and is sexually assertive. In her Step Four, she identified the many misunderstandings and conflicts about this from her past. She learned, by detailed self-examination, how to incorporate spiritual principles in her conduct to avoid conflict. John sees himself and his personal taste as not "adventurous". This is equally wonderful and acceptable. He learned this from his Step Four and knows how to conduct himself to avoid sexual conflict with partners who have different tastes and values. Two other people,

---

adherence to spiritual principles as ongoing parts of your sexual expression. There's an important commentary on sex and religion in John Shelby Spong's book *Rescuing the Bible from Fundamentalism,* HarperCollins, 1992, beginning at page 1.

[91] *Alcoholics Anonymous,* p. 69.

[92] Too often, problems in sexual conduct are incorrectly coupled to problems in sexuality. The elemental, instinctual nature of sexuality, which is similar to the elemental nature of spirituality, requires that it (and spirituality) embody a quality of attracting problems into them, which are unrelated and don't belong there. This often renders Step Four (or therapy) ineffective when problems with sexual conduct (anger, shame, competition, greed, betrayal), aren't effectively disengaged from issues of sexuality (orientation chaos, incest, fetishes). And: In as much as Step Four is about conduct, ethics, and spirituality, there is the related and horrendously complicated phenomenon of sex addiction. Sex addiction immediately shreds into an almost Gordian Knot, the already complex issues of conduct, sexuality, culture, and spirituality. After establishing abstinence, it takes a minimum of two years of on-going regular cross-over work in therapy, with *continued* abstinence, to extricate a recovering sex addict from the self-annihilating mess of sex addiction into a comfortable awareness of respectful, self-defining choice.

Jack and Betty, have learned similar things in their own Step Fours. If these four people meet at a party, they can, with devotion to spiritual principles and what they've discovered in their Step Fours, and regardless of their orientation, pair off (or not) in a respectful way and avoid sexual conflict.

Within the original twelve steps, there is no imposition of opinion about "acceptable" sexual values.[93] Each person develops their own standards of sexual expression. There are no guidelines regarding heterosexual or homosexual sex, length of sobriety, frequency, body oil, chocolate syrup, celibacy, masturbation, lights on or off, or kitchen table or not. There *are* guidelines about the commitment to abstinence, and the adoption and adherence to spiritual principles in the expression of your sexuality, but only so you are responsible, and you stop hurting yourself and others. Step Four is brilliant in the way it achieves this for each individual. There's no imposition of "morality". From page 69 of *Alcoholics Anonymous*: *"We do not want to be the arbiter of anyone's sex conduct."*[94]

If you and your present (or any future) partner don't have similar sexual values, don't fight about this. Just say thank you very much, but no thank you. Mind your own business, *don't* gossip, *don't* criticize, and quietly move on in your own life. You may be annoyed you didn't have sex, but that's of no consequence; being angry and mean is.

Spiritual principles, and your sane and sound sexual ideal (meaning what you should have done instead), will now arbitrate your sexual expression before the fact, not after the fact. You will end up with a clear view of your sexuality within the larger context of spiritual principles. This affords a better chance of spiritual harmony as you express the deepest part of your physical existence: your sexuality. Without answering all the questions for each person on your Step Four sex-list, including the ones you swore you'd never tell about, you won't be able to figure out how to avoid conflict and harming others in the future.

One thing that many alcoholics and addicts believe, especially overt relationship and sex addicts, is that as soon as they're physically attracted to someone (aroused), they've *got* to do something about it. Know that because you are physically attracted to someone, or just horny, doesn't mean you have to do anything about it. A physical attraction may be only a signal to consider investigating the other person's personality as far as being a potential partner goes (meaning dating). The vast majority of "horny attractions" are notoriously unsuitable for healthy intimacy because of different values, expectations, and life circumstances. One of the interesting things about addicts in general is that they will date someone, break up, and afterwards wonder why they dated the person at all—they didn't even like them. This is one indicator of sex or relationship addiction.

---

[93] Bear in mind this is about consenting adults in the normal course of their life. None of this implies the approval, tacit or otherwise, of abusive, incestuous, or violent behavior.

[94] If people conduct their lives in a way that you disapprove of; if you notice you are envious, insulted, or offended by their sexual behavior (or their lifestyle in general), do not try to control them. Mind your own business, *don't* gossip or criticize, and quietly move on in your own life. If your disagreements and judgments are mean or persistent, that indicates something amiss in you.

If you're in a long-term committed sexual relationship, and find yourself almost (or actually) acting upon a physical attraction for someone other than your partner, that indicates problems that are probably outside the scope of Step Four. Committing adultery and then leaving your old partner to marry or take up residence with the person you committed adultery with, never legitimizes the adultery. And, being the sexual partner of an adulterer is equally irresponsible. Should you believe you must act on sexual impulses, or that you are always turned on/horny, or that flirting and romance with others while you're in a committed relationship is harmless, or that adultery is largely inevitable for you, it would be wise to undertake therapy.

———

You don't often hear people at twelve-step meetings talking about making their list of fears: it's too embarrassing and not as dramatic as resentments. You also don't hear anybody talking about sex in the manner required by Step Four. If they were *that* spiritual about their sexuality, the chances of getting laid would be greatly reduced. A clear understanding of your sexual selfishness, and demanding only of yourself that you express sexuality within the context of the five spiritual principles, is crucial for attaining a self-defined and sincere lifestyle.

There are these statements in *Alcoholics Anonymous*: *"When we were finished we considered* [the list] *carefully." "We turned back to the list... ," "Referring to our list again... we resolutely looked... ," "We reviewed our fears... ,"* and *"We reviewed our own conduct... ."*[95] The number of times that reviewing your work is suggested makes it obvious this is to be a patient and reflective endeavor. There's a wealth of important self-awareness to be gleaned here. Don't burden yourself with impatience or pressure from *any* source; work steadily and slowly. Don't create anxiety with visions of Step Five.[96]

From *Alcoholics Anonymous*: *"In meditation, we ask God what we should do about each specific matter. The right answer will come, if we want it." "We avoid hysterical thinking or advice."* And further on: *"We earnestly pray for the right ideal, for guidance in each questionable situation... and for the strength to do the right thing."*[97] These three general injunctions apply specifically to sex. Interestingly enough, and sadly, it seems that most addicts aren't willing to pray before they have sex or go on a date. It's very often the furthest thing from their mind. It shouldn't be.

---

[95] *Alcoholics Anonymous,* pp. 65, 66, 67, 68, 69, respectively.
[96] Here again, there may be conflict with the time restrictions of treatment centers. The mandate of a treatment center requires restrictions on time, and there are deadlines. I see these institutions as valuable. They do (a) help addicts stabilize, somewhat, in their new lifestyle, (b) initiate a formal course of treatment and education that may create the opportunity for permanent change; and, (c) expose the addict to the first few steps at an entry/training level. This is important. It is also important to bear in mind that most of these programs are psychologically oriented, and a few have a decided Christian focus. For the addict getting recovered, all of this is only an initial and *very brief* exposure to the real spiritual transformation work that lies ahead. The time restrictions of treatment centers require that the initial work be incomplete. My counsel has always been: Once formal treatment is finished, time limitations regarding the steps are gone. Maintain abstinence *at all costs*, and then begin again at Step One (if necessary), or begin at Step Two, and complete the steps as thoroughly as the original twelve-step program requires.
[97] *Alcoholics Anonymous,* pp. 69, 70, respectively.

Now you know what they meant by: *"If we have been thorough about our personal inventory, we have written down a lot."* [98] That paragraph outlines what you are beginning to learn and understand. You can now begin to comprehend the futility and corruption, and the terrible destructiveness of your old lifestyle. At this point you are very much a spiritual novice, and only a beginner at self-examination, but at least you're (finally) finished Step Four. Seal all of it in an envelope and give yourself a present; you've worked hard.

No One is Disgusting

If you notice, the original literature *never* instructs you to write how many disgusting things you did, or how horrible you were. Step Four, and in fact, no part of any of these steps, is about your being disgusting or being bad. These cultural perceptions of addictive behavior have only a detrimental contribution to make to getting recovered. Step Four has everything to do with instincts gone awry, fears, and sexual selfishness, which are all reasonably routine and not spectacular. This is entirely about how you got yourself into trouble and your self-imposed crisis. [As an aside: If you are not required to write down how horrible, bad, disgusting, or mean you were, then there must be no requirement to talk or brag about these perceptions of your behavior at meetings.[99]]

This all may seem boring and tedious, which usually means you are annoyed and impatient. Step Four is a labor of spiritual devotion, not an exercise of psychological integration. What is it that makes you bored and impatient? Give yourself a few months for Step Four. You've got nothing to do but be sober for the rest of your life anyway, so you might as well do yourself a favor and take your time.

Redoing a Step Four every year or two, forever, is indicative of being insecure, and always associated with weak faith and substitutes for spirituality. To get out of this cycle, go back to Step Two and unravel the nature of your spiritual defiance. Understand the spiritual intent of getting recovered. There is no psychological intent here. *Believe* that How It Works is true and is personally applicable to you. *Decide* that spiritual endeavor will be the superceding aim of your life. In *Alcoholics Anonymous* and *Twelve Steps and Twelve Traditions* you read again and again that faith did for you what you could not do for yourself.

Sex, God, and Death

Some people subscribe to the belief that there are only three subjects worthy of serious discussion: Sex, God, and Death. People passionately pursue or neurotically avoid sex throughout their lives. People talk, write, and make movies about

---

[98] *Alcoholics Anonymous*, p. 70.

[99] In Step Four, overall, you have written fifteen "columns" of information about yourself: (1) resentments, (2) what the other person did, (3) instincts gone awry, (4) fears, (5) handling fears differently, (6) sex partners, (7) to (14) answering the first eight questions about sexual selfishness, and (15) what you should have done instead. Notice that you have devoted only one column of fifteen to resentments (less than 7% of your work), yet it appears that resentments occupy 95% of the conversations about Step Four. This exemplifies the quirk of addicts to focus on the theatrical aspect of their life (resentments), to the virtual exclusion of all else.

relationships, sex, and intimacy *ad nauseam*. Regarding God and Spirituality: People covet beliefs, kill each other, and debate endlessly all manner of notions and theories. The emotional and physical violence that people inflict on each other and on the earth, justifying this brutality on behalf of "God", is as insane as it is horrific, and *every*one in the world lives with the shame of this. Then there's Death—how near, how far, how sudden, with or without agony, deliberate or accidental, and what (if anything) follows it? There's the self-vilification often experienced when people perceive their death is near and believe their life has been meaningless or wasted. Sex, God, and Death—that's all folks.

I see within the complex simplicity of the original twelve steps, recovered alcoholics and addicts might experience peace and spiritual grace at a very deep level in the expression of their sexuality. They can experience an abiding faith in their relationship with God—in facing any circumstance of Life; and they can live with a benign indifference to the appearance of death. This is all available to those twelve-step pilgrims who are willing to work for it, and yet, so few are willing to work.

———

I have been asked many times: "How often do you do a Step Four?"

In addition to my prayers, I make a point to read or study some specific aspect of the original literature and/or spirituality, every day. About every two years I take a few days to enjoy carefully rereading *Alcoholics Anonymous* (to page 192), and all of *Twelve Steps and Twelve Traditions*. This reading is to reflect on any new insights or nuances, as I contemplate my own humanness and the amazing grace and harmony of the maintenance steps, where I attempt to live daily. This is a gentle review—I don't repeat any of the first nine steps. In doing this, it has so far never failed to allow me to again experience a deep appreciation for the single most profound blessing I have ever received—the ability to choose spirituality and God over addictions and death.

Throughout any given day, I notice how I do (or don't) live in the maintenance steps, and in the five spiritual principles. When I fall away from these, I don't castigate myself or rush back to the beginning and start over. I sharpen the focus of my energy into being completely responsible, making amends where necessary, and quietly minding my own business. Then, such as it is, I get on with the business of my own life. I thoroughly studied Step Four, and painstakingly followed the instructions once—that's enough.

5

Steps Five, Six, and Seven: What I Do With Me

A Few Reminders

Thus far, some of what you are reading may well provoke anger or discomfort. This is certainly true when I offer this information through lectures. Keep in mind that challenging yourself, not others, is at the core of all spiritual work, and in the early stages of the process, being upset is the admission price you pay for transformation.

One of the many things you have to accomplish in healing and being Spiritual, is to be always cognizant of your rights and, while retaining them for yourself, offer them to others.[1] I've tried to offer them to you in the way I have written this book, and I ask that you offer them to me as you read it. (Respect & Dignity, p. 6)

I suggested, near the end of the previous chapter, that when people conduct themselves in a way that offends your sensibilities, or in a way that you "disapprove" of, then mind your own business, don't gossip or criticize, and quietly move on in your own life.

Regardless of the degree of joy or horror, your task as a spiritual pilgrim is to continuously reach for the most enlightened possibilities in any given situation.[2]

Regardless of any topic under discussion, addicts becoming spiritual are locked into this unalterable fact: Abstinence and sobriety are essential and never negotiable. Everything spiritual created in the recovering addict's life is dependent on complete abstinence from addictions. If you're acting out in any way, in any addiction, you cannot be sincerely spiritual.

In becoming recovered, addicts do not become cured. They cannot return to any acting out behavior without disastrous consequence. In being recovered, they are only being spiritual as outlined in the five spiritual principles[3], which are themselves, embodied in the maintenance steps.

Remind yourself that being sincerely spiritual does not necessarily imply the achievement of "mental health," or vice versa. In fact, being sincerely Spiritual in a modern culture of technology, would have many people doubting your sanity.

When you're confused, slow down. (Go slow anyway.) The relationship between these issues is very subtle and complex. Challenge and question only yourself about your spiritual defiance, impatience, lack of veracity, or reluctance to be obedi-

---

[1] Rights, Freedoms, and Values were discussed in Chapter 2.
[2] This view of behavior and life's circumstances was a comment made by the actor Peter Coyote during a television interview.
[3] See Appendix II.

ent to the principles. Notice your reluctance to challenge either your character defects or old, coveted beliefs.

Reread the Manner of Presentation.[4]

Addiction shows up in each of us differently. In some, it shows up as heroin and crime; in others, it's cocaine and prostitution; in others, it's wine and divorces; and in still others, it may be chronic poverty and beer, tobacco and pornography, cocaine and violence, shopping and sex, or marijuana and... the list is long. Addictions always show up in at least two blatant ways and one subtle way, and at least one of those three will be a relationship addiction. The purpose of your doing Step One is to figure this out. Identify *your* symptoms, which will be slightly different from the symptoms of others.

The process of exiting your addictions into healthy (and complete) abstinence, completing the steps, and then creating, thinking, and living a sincere expression of responsible spirituality, is a monumental undertaking. Sharing the stories and circumstances about your transformation rather than your acting out, without bragging or complaining about the content of your addiction, in the context of becoming spiritual, is carrying the message. This creates insight and unity in yourself, and is significant in getting you out of isolation, and helps you to learn that you are spiritually sick and not crazy.

The program teaches you to live your life spiritually, meaning without addictions, and without the desire for affluence and social accomplishment. The purpose of recovery is *not* to get you beautiful, handsome, laid, happy, married, or rich; it's to allow you to become spiritually sound. There's a difference between having a happy life (which underneath all the rhetoric usually means getting your own way), and a joyful life. The original steps, and obedience to them, are intended to replace your addictions with spiritual attributes and spiritual grace—nothing else.

Abstinence and spirituality are always good. When your ego perceives life as troubling, it isn't; it's your perceptions. Should you be annoyed, frustrated, angry, or bitter for longer than a few seconds when there's a minor inconvenience, or for a couple of minutes in bigger calamities, you're in precarious spiritual condition. [Notice I referred to angry and not to feeling sad, afraid, or lonely, which *may* or may not indicate other spiritually limiting value structures.]

Attend meetings with a spiritual agenda. If you're taking penicillin for an infection, you create stress and guaranteed disappointment if you expect the penicillin to also correct poor eyesight. Penicillin has a very specific task and has its limitations. So it is with the twelve steps. If you expect happiness, hot sex, social success, acceptance, employment, absence of calamity, or love, in addition to Spirituality; or attempt to impose psychological agendas on the steps, you'll be perpetually disappointed. Eventually you'll become disillusioned. This is a tough one because our culture confuses social altruism (whether corrupt or not) with spirituality.[5] This is disastrous for addicts.

---

[4] The Manner of Presentation is at page 11.
[5] *"He who would do good to another must do it in minute particulars: General Good is the plea of the scoundrel, hypocrite, and flatterer."* William Blake, from *Complete Writings,* ed. by Geoffrey Keynes, 1957.

Service work and twelve-step work are not, by themselves, evidence of being spiritual; neither is serving food to the homeless or volunteering at a crisis center. Most often, and sadly enough, these are evidence of being not-spiritual. Social responsibility is important, generosity is nice, happiness is pleasant, and financial success comforts your ego, but these should not be interpreted as evidence of success at spirituality. These never substitute for the difficult inner searching for some brief glimpse of your spiritual nature (and it may take years of committed devotion to get one brief glimpse).

Countless addicts in recovery do all of the approved "twelve-step" things: attending meetings, working on service committees, chairing meetings, driving newcomers around, and getting a sponsor. To their amazement, they still relapse, or they're secretly afraid and lonely. Others recite a litany of social responsibility, declare offerings of friendship, and perform countless acts of service work; they are well-liked and approved of (by the other social do-gooders), yet they often appear insecure, scattered, angry and petty, and forever on the edge of chaos. There' often an edge of belligerence or arrogance to their life.

Altruism and service work are not evidence of spirituality.[6] People are very loyal to the secular belief that being morally good, kind, and generous are sufficient to qualify as spiritual. Logic has it (and being spiritual has little to do with logic) that we are good or should feel good because we do good things; hence, we are therefore "spiritual". People then hope for the ancillary benefits of an amazing love relationship and a sizeable investment portfolio. Not so. The original twelve steps are designed to create a value system that stands in opposition to both addiction and culture.[7]

These steps are not to enable popularity or affluence, or to prohibit calamity. A person struggling out of addictions and into spirituality must wade through an imbroglio of shallowness and greed, and go beyond cultural values. Addicts getting recovered have often unknowingly made our incredibly *un*spiritual cultural value system their higher power: get abstinent (but only from the disapproved-of addictions), get a job, get money, get sex, get successful: be good, be loved, be influential, be happy. The truth is that Spirituality is not concerned with any of these accomplishments, and, in fact, places some limits on many of them.

An addict getting recovered has to undermine and replace the modern values of disposable consumerism and greed. The myths around power, beauty, and affluence "should" be replaced with adherence to the five principles as they are embodied in the maintenance steps. Modern culture and spirituality are diametrically opposed, which makes Step Two (the cornerstone on which all spirituality rests) more difficult than in times past. Taking a year, or longer, to solidify a new belief system at Step Two isn't unreasonable. Reorganizing your personality from "ad-

---

[6] *Peace of Mind*, by Joshua Loth Liebman, Simon & Schuster, 1946. The chapter Love Thyself Properly presents an explanation of how being spiritually based and spiritually ethical within yourself, is fundamental to healthy charity.

[7] With the changes in technology and culture, and the demands made on any individual in a technologically advanced society, to be socially successful, affluent, powerful, intellectually astute, precocious, famous, slim, or muscular, it is often necessary to generate an obsessive or addictive lifestyle to achieve success. Being sincerely spiritual leaves you at odds with addiction *and* culture.

dicted and culturally obedient" to "recovered with spiritual integrity" is the most difficult thing you will do, and that's exactly what's required of you.

When recovering addicts finally understand this, they take the pressure off of themselves, and everything about the twelve steps comes into focus. What's to be done isn't confusing at all. The first nine steps, which are a regeneration of your personality, are the process out of addiction and into a value system and lifestyle that is contained within the three maintenance steps.

I am long convinced that the original Buddhist teachings, meaning The Four Noble Truths and the dislocation attached to desire, anger, and delusion, and what is offered in *Alcoholics Anonymous,* are the only paths of pilgrimage that embody an unrelenting focus on being egalitarian and personally responsible. They have an attractive aura, and appeal to many because of their (valid) promises of inner peace. However, and most often, when acolytes are presented with the actual depth of work and self-discipline required for either discipline, they recast the philosophy into a self-serving political or social context, pollute the teachings with personal interpretations, and manipulate the tenets to some personal advantage—pretty speeches, with delusion and without substance.[8]

Petulance and greed are subtle, deeply rooted, and more a way of life than addicts or alcoholics realize.[9] Very often, declarations of love, commitment, and spirituality are tainted by convenience (albeit well hidden, immaculately justified, and easily deniable). Cultural perceptions about success and what constitutes "spirituality" are at odds with the offerings of the original program.

Getting recovered requires addicts to actually dismantle the blaming and selfishness they are permeated with. At Step Four, the struggle to replace these with honesty and responsibility begins in earnest. That's one reason the original program's instructions suggest you meditate carefully on your completed Step Four *before* moving on to Step Five.

Changing Values

From my own perspective, my life is always good, and when it isn't, that's only my perception. Yet, according to my 1975 beliefs—that pursuing wealth or power was good and Life was monumentally unfair towards me—my life today is a complete failure: I'm not wealthy and I have no power over anything (except my

---

[8] The spiritual issues around honesty and sincerity are beautifully described in Part Two, Section Seven: Sincerity, *A Thomas Merton Reader,* Thomas Merton, edited by Thomas P. McDonnell, Image Books, Doubleday, 1996. The entire section is applicable here, but the immediate reference begins *"But the fact that men spend so much...,"* p. 121.

[9] From birth we are imbued by disposable consumerism, including the reprehensible attitudes that people are disposable, power is good, and that everything "wrong" must be fixed quickly or it isn't worth saving—the self-denigrating, vicious, quick-fix mentality. Alice Miller, in her book *The Untouched Key,* Anchor Books, Doubleday, pp. 10-11, points out the earlier a child learns something, the more entrenched it becomes. If this be positive, the more consistent the successes; if it be negative, and the harder it will be to unlearn. This is discussed in another of her books: *For Your Own Good: Hidden Cruelty in Child-Rearing and the Roots of Violence,* Farrar, Straus & Giroux, 1985.

attitude and my adherence to my values, which are today noticeably different). So therefore, I have "failed" at Life according to my 1975 values.

The values that I embrace today are vastly different from the ones I had in 1975. They are also different from the ones I had in the early 1980s (early abstinence). And my present-day values are different from the ones that, in early abstinence, I imagined I wanted (or would have) when I envisioned reaching the point I am at today. My life today is more in line with the tenets of spirituality—I'm very ordinary—but, my life forever unfolds in remarkable ways that I never could have imagined. That is the beauty of a spiritually oriented life.

Yes, I have the disease of addictions, from which I have recovered, and I'm sometimes a little scared or depressed or insecure (I'm human). However, I respond differently to these, and to the vicissitudes of Life, because I am able to perceive everything differently.[10] When I ponder this change in myself carefully, it's beyond anything I'd ever imagined or could imagine.

Authentic spiritual self-discipline will keep you confused—as soon as you get to where you thought you wanted to get to, you realize it's only approximately what you thought you wanted. You are there, but not exactly, so you refocus onto some newly envisioned spiritual posture, and off you go again. True "spirituality" only allows you to get closer, and when you're closer it's never exactly what you imagined or desired that you wanted or needed. Yes, you get recovered, but that's only to enable you to enhance your own spirituality and deepen your commitment to a higher power.

―――――

In Chinese, the symbol for "crisis" is made up of two characters; one, "danger," and the other, "opportunity". Out of the spiritual crisis of your addiction, in Step Four, you learned about the danger of blaming others and expecting them to clean up your mess. This created the opportunity to view your life as a self-imposed crisis. Recall in Step Four the tasks were very specific and you couldn't write whatever you wanted. In a convoluted way, you forced yourself to appreciate, in a responsible manner, this idea: *"To believe that the alcoholic who approaches AA is an unprincipled, untaught barbarian, suddenly transformed by the previously unavailable spiritual illumination of the twelve steps is, to me, utter foolishness."*[11]

Aside from how Step Four undermines culturally imposed guilt and offers spiritual opportunity, it is also important to deflate the addicts' untrue, pervading view that they're completely corrupt. The steps are a finely tuned, *very specific* procedure that allows for a clean delineation between (1) what is wrong, (2) what isn't wrong, and (3) what you think is wrong (which, until you are well into being recovered, is usually incorrect). The distinctions are crucial and, with rigorous honesty, will come into sharper focus throughout the remaining steps.

What I explained earlier regarding Step One "guides" applies here: Be cautious around a Step Four guide that includes invasive questions about pre-addiction,

―――――

[10] Changing perceptions is working with your ego—Appendix IV. Changing perceptions is also presented as a fundamental tenet of *A Course In Miracles,* The Foundation For Inner Peace, 1985/92.
[11] *A Member's Eye View of Alcoholics Anonymous* © AA World Services Inc., p.16.

childhood, and early family-of-origin issues. These can't (and don't) clearly separate what is wrong, from what isn't wrong, from what the author of the guide thinks is wrong, from what you think is wrong. In truth, these aren't Step Fours: they're psychological questionnaires.[12]

Your Step Four is an exercise that identifies what needs fixing in relation to your addiction and your personality so there is less interference in your relationship with God (of your own understanding). What's obvious, but not talked about, is that when you arrive at Step Five, telling someone what needs fixing isn't fixing it.

The Disease and Guilt

From a cultural point of view, for most diseases, most people offer and receive compassion and are allowed some consideration for being sick. The following story is true: A patron at a movie theater had a serious epileptic seizure. An ambulance was called, the movie was interrupted by the disturbance for a few minutes, and the person was taken to the hospital. With some courtesy, the theater manager offered free movie passes to this person and their partner so they could view the film at another time. All ended well.

The following story is fiction: Imagine another couple who are alcoholic/addicts and relationship-addicted. They go to a movie. Shortly after the film begins, they argue loudly and accuse each other of various relationship misdemeanors and betrayals that are addictions related. The manager stops the film because of the disturbance. The police are called (not an ambulance). There are no free passes back to the movie, and minimal courtesy. The addicts go to jail.

Both situations involved minor inconvenience to the other patrons, yet one situation is acceptable and the other isn't. One person is sick; the other people are bad. Epilepsy and addictions are treatable illnesses. Generally, if you have an addiction, there is very little cultural empathy. Notice your own instant response, and imagine the general response of people, to these two statements:

"I found out Lee's got cancer and will probably die from it."

"I found out Lee's a drug addict and will probably die from it."

We (*you*) live in a culture where addictions are not seen as a real disease, which is because they are the disease of our culture.[13] As an addict getting recovered, like it or not, you carry that attitude within you. Deny it if you must, but it's there, and this paradigm manifests itself as subtle self-criticism, self-condemnation, and self-rejection. In the medical model of disease, there's no reason for you to feel guilty about being sick, so you needn't necessarily feel guilty for having an addiction — but you do.

---

[12] Intrusive or insight psychology has much value, but not necessarily in relation to Step Four. And, oftentimes, cross-over work is necessary and wise because of the globalization of addictions and the possible influence of pre-existing psychological concerns. This is delicate, and should only be undertaken with a therapist who meets the four criteria that I described in a footnote in Chapter 1. The consequences of mismanaged cross-over work, and wrongly established abstinence, are far more onerous than they may seem. Where the four criteria are not reasonably met, whatever harm arises from poorly conducted counselling will eventually have to be cleaned up... by the client.

[13] This will be explained more in *Facets of Personal Transformation*. For an important, and presently undervalued perspective see *Peaceful Measures*, Bruce K. Alexander, University of Toronto Press, 1990.

Often, out of your Step Four comes an awareness of an overwhelming sense of culturally induced guilt that you continue to own. In spite of all the new-age rhetoric to the contrary, having an addiction still amounts to having done a bad thing. The original twelve-step program allows addicts to regain their integrity and dignity while believing that an addiction is a sickness—but only when they take responsibility for it.[14]

Most addicts and alcoholics probably feel guilty about things they did when they were acting out—not sad or ashamed, but guilty. Reflect carefully on what I am about to say: personally, after a few years of reflection on this[15], I feel guilty about nothing I did while in my addiction. I didn't have any choice: The disease dictated the behavior and it was *not* a matter of willpower. This does not excuse me from responsibility. I have felt sad, afraid, hurt, etc. (all resolved), and I am responsible, but I don't feel guilty.

Guilt is about breaking rules. Notwithstanding the influence of fear and shame, if a person feels guilty, they believe they broke a rule.[16] The "rules" of addiction—the mandated behaviors, are the symptoms: acting out and life-damaging consequences, neurosis, denial, disproportionate fear, repression, isolation (from self and others), assumptions, shame, dishonesty, withholding, selfishness, irresponsibility, arrogance, and cynicism; all chronic and entrenched, and addicts are largely blind to them. The disease demands these, even though our culture (you probably included) believes you had a choice. There was no choice; hence there's no psychologically "authentic" reason to feel guilty.[17]

Freedom from the guilt associated with addiction is only available when you contemplate your discoveries for a long time, through the specifics of the steps, the nature of disease, the symptoms, and spiritual principles. There's a great benefit to the freedom and relief from guilt when you accept that your addiction is a disease, but there is a price to pay for this. Once you realize freedom from guilt, you take on

---

[14] Guilt and its cultural imposition, in relation to the disease of addiction, is to be [eventually] eliminated. Guilt is to not to be confused with regret or sadness, nor is this in any way an avenue to avoid responsibility. In fact, subscribing to this view, and achieving a guilt-free perspective of yourself and your addiction, actually increases your responsibility. See: *Twelve Steps and Twelve Traditions*, p. 62.

[15] Insight can only come through reflection or meditation. It cannot come through only belief. You cannot, as a willful act, make yourself realize an insight. Insights can only arise through contemplating and pondering truths; through your mind being open and receptive to teaching. Blind belief is not advised, but neither is belligerence or arguing. The mind should be willing to be receptive through pondering and quietly meditating. *The Four Noble Truths,* Venerable Ajhan Sumedho, Amaravati (Buddhist Center) Publications, Hertfordshire, England, 1992, p. 39. Also: *"When there's something you don't understand, you have to go humbly to it. You don't go to school and sit down and say 'I know what you are going to teach me.' You sit there and you learn. You open your mind. You absorb. But you have to be quiet, you have to be still."* John Coltrane, jazz musician.

[16] I discuss this from a related perspective in Appendix I, and will examine it at length in *Facets of Personal Transformation*.

[17] The entitlement to "no guilt" only stands with integrity for that period while you are in your addiction, and in your abstinence up to that transformative moment when you realized you have a choice. Once you can choose, guilt will accrue if you choose wrongly because now there *is* a choice, and guilt is about breaking "rules" and knowingly choosing "wrongly". Should you willfully break some law, you must be responsible. However, should some former behavior like lying be symptomatic of your addiction, then the presence of "guilt" for that is optional. Ponder this carefully: You are still and always responsible to cooperate with the sanctions of your community *and* to take yourself to task for harm caused, but feeling guilt for symptomatic behavior is optional.

the mantle of complete personal responsibility, and that obligates you to do something more than whatever is just good enough. Nothing is free.

Other themes that begin to be more clearly understood at this point are the notion of willpower and spiritual self-determination. It follows, but I've not heard it discussed as such, that since an addiction is a self-imposed crisis[18], there must be a self-imposed solution, not an other-imposed solution. An other-imposed solution would be addicts expecting to get better when someone other than themselves accepts (some) responsibility for the addiction.

In other words: Addicts' wrongfully-focused "willpower" got them into their predicaments. When they refocus their willpower from blame and self-annihilation to responsibility and spirituality, spirituality becomes an issue of self-determination. Providence may have moved to put them *in* a twelve-step program, but they must act to stay in it. Colloquially: Providence may have presented an addict with the opportunity to change (at and during Step One), and no one knows why. Hopefully the addict will then assess the opportunity and come to believe in the plan that's outlined at Step Two. Finally, the addict decides to choose spirituality and "God" at Step Three, which makes them spiritually self-determined. There is nothing accidental about a fulfilling relationship with God—it's entirely deliberate.

The insidious cultural view of addictions is that addicts are "bad" because they somehow choose to do what they do, and could expediently change if they made up their minds to try harder.[19] Therefore, the major reprehensible insult that addicts and alcoholics must atone for is being willfully bad (deliberately irresponsible), and destroying themselves to be mean or spiteful. The *cultural* position we are saddled with is that addicts are simply irresponsible, and if they somehow just smartened up and tried harder... well, you know how it goes.

Every addict I've ever spoken with or counseled, to any noticeable degree, has always experienced sadness about the fact that their lives have been devastated. Without exception, they regret the pain they've caused and deeply desire it were otherwise. This is sincere and painful but seldom admitted because they're rarely believed. In the midst of acting out, they don't feel that way, but addictive acting out isn't representative of the morality of the addict—it's the reality of the disease.

Step Five

When you complete Step Five it will deepen the shift in inner perception that addicts aren't bad, and will reduce culturally imposed guilt. Step Five further expands the awareness that you aren't alone in your wretchedness. These new perspectives (that weren't available before) are dependent upon your obedience to the

---

[18] *Alcoholics Anonymous*, p. 53.

[19] Do not be lured into the cultural deifying of expediency (the quick-fix) and disposable consumerism, where people are disposable objects. That is the underlying truth of "quick fix", "harm reduction", and "substance-use management" programs: The best solution (spirituality) isn't expedient, and therefore addicts become disposable. Many care-givers and addicts view themselves (and other addicts) as not worthy of a considerable and determined investment of time, effort, or money.

original program.[20] The person who shares your Step Five with you, who is willing to hear you with unconditional positive (spiritual) regard[21], is in a position to lighten your burden of loneliness and isolation—one theme of Step Five.

At meetings, you tell your story in a general way, and probably throw in some exciting, exaggerated, or embarrassing details. In the ears of trusted friends or a sponsor, you allude to more shameful details, which in itself is often attention-getting. The original Step Four works to prevent exaggeration and flamboyance by demanding accurate detail about very specific parts of your personality.

Step Five is the first time that you are required, by a mandate of the steps, to tell completely accurate truths about yourself, to be specific about your *instinctual* excesses, to not blame anyone, to not condemn yourself, and to trust you will not be shamed or judged. If you're inaccurate or insincere; if you attempt to bypass Step Five with a generally painless admission that you were sometimes a bad actor[22], or imbue it with exaggerated (or minimized) descriptions of your behavior—all of which is only "sober" acting out—you will not initiate the process of guilt-reduction, and will live, to some extent, distrusting of the steps.

Bearing all of this in mind, notice: *"get rid of that terrible sense of isolation"*[23] and *"emerging from isolation"*[24]. If your Step Five is primarily a list of bad things, the isolation and loneliness will remain. Beginning to end your isolation from yourself and from God is dependent upon pushing through all types Impression Management, and being accurate and specific in a quiet, sincere way.

Addicts, too often immediately after the writing of Step Four, make an appointment for their Step Five. I've often discussed this with them and ask if they have admitted it [their Step Four] to God or to themselves? They're usually puzzled and mumble something vague about God watching over their shoulder as they wrote Step Four. I point out that the sequence of instructions in the step is: admitted to God, then to themselves, and (finally) to another human being.

Review the first sentence of <u>How It Works</u>: *"Rarely have we seen a person fail who has thoroughly followed our path."* Then immediately read Step Five: *"Admitted to God, to ourselves, and to another human being the exact nature of our wrongs."*[25] Accordingly then, by specific instruction, it is not sufficient to tell only another person.

Each step is a spiritually self-contained unit. This means that whatever work transpired prior to Step Five has no influence over the detail or effort you put into Step Five. The fact that you wrote Step Four doesn't diminish the attention you must pay to the instructions in Step Five, which is to be read independently of the work in

[20] Meaning *Alcoholics Anonymous* (minus the personal stories) and *Twelve Steps and Twelve Traditions*. I also recommend the AA pamphlet, *A Member's Eye View of Alcoholics Anonymous*.
[21] "Unconditional positive regard" is a phrase used to describe one significant aspect of the therapist's attitude in client-centered therapy, developed by Carl Rogers. *The Carl Rogers Reader*, edited by Howard Kirschenbaum and Valerie Land Henderson, Houghton Mifflin Company, 1989, p. 225.
[22] *Twelve Steps and Twelve Traditions*, p. 55.
[23] Ibid., p. 57.
[24] Ibid., p. 62.
[25] *Alcoholics Anonymous*, pp. 58 and 59, respectively.

the previous steps. Before any admitting can take place, however, it is important to remind yourself what exactly you are to admit. Notice these:

- *"The objective look at ourselves we achieved in Step Four..."*[26]
- *"We have written an inventory and we are prepared for a long talk."*[27]

Step Four is the list of the exact nature of your fears, etc., so this means in Step Five you only admit exactly what's in your Step Four. Just as there were limits on what you wrote, there are equally specific limits on what you are to admit, and there are also equally specific limits on whom you can admit all this to.

In taking the instructions at face value, and using everyday language to describe spiritual principles, addicts would first admit the exact nature of their wrongs "to God". Consider sitting in a meditative mood in prayer and offer your entire Step Four, item by item, to your higher power. This prayer is a specific task of Step Five, not to replace any daily prayer routine. In this prayerful reflection get more honest, with a view to relying more on your higher power for courage in these matters. As you pray reflectively through the exact nature of your insecurities, fears, and sexual selfishness, notice where you may have glossed over a few minor details — just "tiny" omissions — so you wouldn't look too bad. This is the second time (of three), in the first nine steps, where you commend yourself directly to your higher power.

The next phrase is: *"...admitted to yourself..."*. Consider actually making eye-contact with yourself in a mirror, and at the same time, ask these questions of yourself about each Step Four entry: "Was I *completely* accurate and thorough in my self-examination about this?" And: "Have I avoided any responsibility by *secretly* blaming others for this trouble?" Determine if you have admitted the *entire* truth about your insecurity, fear, and sexual selfishness.[28] As you ask yourself these while looking *at* yourself, pay especial attention to any hint of blaming. You may notice little glitches of guilt if you've been evasive. Amend your Step Four where you have to. You, and those important to you, will pay dearly for any inattention to detail here.

These two reviews may seem excessive. After all, you've spent weeks writing Step Four, you've read it, you've reviewed it, you've reflected on it. Isn't that enough? Again, notice the exact wording of Step Five. When I have occasion to discuss these two requirements with others, they often become defensive, and I'm often dismissed outright, and accused of being too picky and too thorough. Your defensiveness regarding your own disobedience to the instructions is evidence of fear, which makes for a shallow commitment.

As you begin to develop new values molded around a spiritually oriented conscience, and understand the importance of truth and commitment, these first two

---

[26] *Twelve Steps and Twelve Traditions*, p. 58.
[27] *Alcoholics Anonymous*, p. 75.
[28] Recovering addicts often speak of being unable to make eye-contact with themselves in a mirror. Thinking about doing this may provoke anxiety, or some criticism of my being too particular about detail. What might that indicate about you?

admissions of Step Five are neither difficult nor foolish. Only you know when you're lying and withholding. Only you are responsible to force yourself to stop weaseling out of responsibility. This is a labor of love, and a deep and moving experience.

One fact about honesty is: As long as you deceive yourself, to *any* degree, you will deceive others. The moment you achieve the willingness to be completely honest within yourself and see this as a Spiritual virtue, you will not perpetuate deceit outside of yourself. Honesty is an inside job. Only you can look into your soul. Only you can see the edge of the abyss beyond which faith carries you to God. The final arbiter of your spiritual conduct is you.

When you do the steps and meditations as instructed you occasionally, and then increasingly, get a glimpse of *You*; the you that's connected to a higher power in a deep experience of unitive truth. Only this can cause a permanent, unpremeditated correction in your previously addictions-twisted structure of values.

"I am personally convinced that the basic search of every human being, from the cradle to the grave, is to find at least one other human being before whom [they] can stand completely naked, stripped of all pretense or defense, and trust that person not to hurt [them], because that other person has stripped [themselves] naked, too. This lifelong search can begin to end with the first AA encounter."[29] Among the many important things that are contained in this quote, two points stand out in relation to Step Five. The first is that truth and trust are essential to the search. The second is that the search only begins to end — it doesn't end.

You must develop accuracy in all aspects of self-knowledge so that you are capable of standing stripped of pretense or defense in front of yourself first.[30] Without this vulnerability you can never be loved for who you are, and will always be loved for your pretensions. The exercise of doing Step Five in the manner prescribed is the only way that you begin any in-depth, accurate self-disclosure. The task here is not to expose historical data — it's to initiate accurate self-disclosure and eliminate the subtle self-deception that you practice. This self-disclosure will help to keep you spiritual, honest, and soulful in times of turmoil and temptation.

Tom Waits sings in one of his songs: *"How do the angels get to sleep when the devil leaves the porch light on?"*[31] It's a wonderful metaphor for the addict's struggle to be Spiritual while noticing temptations. What beliefs prevent you from accepting that *you* are in charge of leaving your own porch light on? You're responsible for your temptations and how you respond to them. Your view of yourself and the world creates your temptations. Accurate self-awareness and responsibility are essential keys to turning your porch light off. More importantly, to keep temptation turned off, you must develop insight about how tenaciously you cling to your ability to deceive, to avoid, and to conveniently misrepresent yourself.

---

[29] From the AA pamphlet *A Member's Eye View of Alcoholics Anonymous*.

[30] At a concert, jazz musician Bill Evans was asked where he was going with his music. The question was framed in a musical context. He answered, *"In."* He answered in a soulful context. *Inside* is where all truly creative and spiritual journeys go; never "out", always in.

[31] From *Heartattack and Vine,* written by Tom Waits; the album: *Heartattack and Vine*, Fifth Floor Music Inc., ASCAP, 1980.

You finished writing your Step Four a while ago. You have now meditated through it three times: once as a part of Step Four—reflecting on the source of your insecurities and searching for responsibility; and twice more as parts of Step Five: once with God in prayer, and once by making eye contact with yourself, all the while making necessary amendments to further entrench honesty, accuracy, and responsibility. You are now ready to tell someone else; but who do you tell?

Making The Selection: The Four Conditions

If, in the past, you have done a Step Five and suspect that it didn't work as well as described, yes, it may be because you were not thorough enough in completing the earlier steps, or were lax in preparation at Step Four. However, you may also have been negligent in choosing a confidant who didn't meet the four conditions.[32]

As with so many other things, this is subtle. Within the human relationship you create in Step Five, it's safe to presume that one of you is (apparently) the wiser of the two. The person hearing it is supposed to be farther along in their own pilgrimage than the person offering it, and should therefore know more about what's supposed to transpire. Certainly the accuracy of the content is the complete responsibility of the person sharing. However, the greater share of responsibility for spiritual effectiveness is on the person hearing the disclosure. That effectiveness is related to the four conditions noted in *Alcoholics Anonymous*, and are entirely the province of whomever hears it.

If you belong *"...to a religious denomination which requires confession* [you] *must, and of course, will want to go to the properly appointed authority whose duty it is to receive it."*[33] However, those who cannot, or would rather not, do this can look for someone else—a psychologist, doctor, therapist, religious professional, or understanding mentor. And, whomever you choose to tell *"must understand, yet be unaffected."*[34] Certainly you should trust them to some degree, but considering you may know this person only by reputation or recommendation, how does it come about that they can be trusted?

First: Make yourself thoroughly aware of these requisite four conditions that the person you choose must satisfy. Firs̲t̲: this person must be able to keep a confidence. You have to rely on their ability to be absolutely silent regarding you and your disclosure. Secon̲d̲: the person you choose must fully understand what you are doing. *Alcoholics Anonymous* doesn't advise that they only "partially understand" or "have a general idea". Your confidant must fully understand, which implies a lot. Thir̲d̲: this person must approve of what you are doing. Since (and because) you are being obedient to the instructions, you will not add, change, or take away anything. Your confidant should likewise change nothing. So, it's not enough for this person to fully understand; they must also approve. Fourt̲h̲: they must not try to change your

---

[32] *Alcoholics Anonymous*, pp. 74-75.
[33] Ibid., p. 74.
[34] Ibid. If the person you choose is socially or personally involved in your life: a friend, co-worker, twelve-step comrade, coffee companion, sports partner, spouse... they will be affected. Also, if the person you choose admits they sometimes share at meetings they hear Step Fives—even if they guarantee your anonymity—they have been affected. Hence, none of these people should be chosen.

plan. According to Steps Two and Three, your plan should be to simply follow the instructions.[35] Attempts to change your plan are usually very subtle and indicate they do not approve of what you are doing.

Second: Do not rest on the recommendations of others. Get a few names and conduct pre-Step Five interviews. Your first meeting with them is to discuss their view of Step Five, and to enable you to satisfy *yourself* that this individual meets the four conditions. Do not bring your Step Four to this pre-Step Five interview. Bring *Alcoholics Anonymous* and *Twelve Steps and Twelve Traditions* with a few things highlighted that you want to talk about.

Ask about confidentiality—do they keep a record? How would they address confidentiality if someone asked them about you? What is their understanding of twelve-step programs? Do they ever talk about or mention to others that they hear Step Fives? Do they understand what a Step Five is? What do you think you are to accomplish? Will they read the applicable paragraphs from the reference texts to ensure there's no misunderstanding? Do they approve of what you're doing? Will they try to change your plan by adding anything? How do they end a Step Five? Do they expect you will say a prayer or do Steps Six and Seven with them?

These questions ensure there'll be no surprises later on when you are into your Step Five disclosure. This pre-Step Five interview is not an attack on their character, it's you being self-responsible. What if they are annoyed, argue, or are defensive about your thoroughness? What does that tell you about them? Be prepared to discuss anything they don't understand, and make clear your intent to follow the instructions in the approved literature.

In a spiritual sense, all of these precautions should be redundant since both you and your confidant "should" desire to enter into this wanting to follow the instructions. Your plans should be the same. However, the only guarantee of your success in getting recovered is your own thoroughness in following instructions. You invest effort into ensuring that the person you choose meets the four conditions. You need the practice in spiritual assertiveness and self-care.

Be wary of the person who agrees, but kindly suggests some small amendment. They may say they understand, and proclaim Step Five is quite wonderful, but if they suggest some change, they're suggesting you follow "their" program, not *the* program. Here are common suggestions made by people who don't fully understand or accept what is required in Step Five:

- "You don't really need to refer to your Step Four since you know it all anyway. It's all about your fears, so you can just refer to it from memory. Put it away, and we'll just talk."
- "Listen, your fears, and all that sex-stuff, it's all pretty similar, so you can just lump them together. There's no need for repetition. Hit the highlights and we'll save some time."

---

[35] Philosophical analysis of the tenets of *Alcoholics Anonymous* or *Twelve Steps and Twelve Traditions*, and esoteric discussions about any facet of the five spiritual principles, may be interesting and important, but are always only an adjunct to doing what the literature tells you.

- "If everything goes well, we can do Steps Six and Seven right after. You'll get all three steps out of the way."
- "I've heard a lot of Step Fives, and it seems to help people if they come around to my step group. I get to help you out if it gets rough, and you get to expand your spiritual resources."
- "We'll spend a bit of time talking about your childhood troubles. That often helps. We'll set some time aside for that—but of course only if you want to."
- "When we're done we can say a prayer together."

What any of these suggestions really indicate is the person doesn't fully understand or approve of Step Five, as it is written. Are you willing to put your life in the care of someone who thinks they are wiser than *Alcoholics Anonymous* or *Twelve Steps and Twelve Traditions*?

If you suspect they can't be trusted to follow the guidelines, or you aren't sure of their integrity, or something in their demeanor doesn't meet the conditions, there are two spiritual options. You might respectfully discuss your concerns with them. If they are in the least bit defensive or autocratic, then they are not respectful of your concerns. Will you do your Step Five with someone who doesn't respect you? The other alternative is to respectfully say thank you, but no thank you, and quietly move on, without gossiping or complaining. Interview someone else.

Should you push ahead and do your Step Five without clearing up your concerns, then, during your Step Five, you'll cut corners and evade. When you're not rigorously honest, you're dishonest. Dishonesty and ignoring any "danger signs" are symptoms of your addiction. By ignoring your concerns and going ahead with this person, you're being disrespectful of yourself, and willfully choosing to withhold and isolate. You will end up participating in addictive behavior during your Step Five. Addictions are insidious—follow the instructions.

———

Many people grew up with the illusion that somehow, someday, a savior would come along and make their lives safe and happy. Not so. And, even if you can lure someone into looking after you, it will eventually backfire. If you don't stick up for yourself, no one else will. Whether they're in a twelve-step program or not, go through this ritual of caring for yourself. Take responsibility for your life by taking responsibility for your pilgrimage.

Remember the two rules: Rule #1 is people die from addictions and Rule #2 is you can't change Rule #1. I offer this next point gently so keep it in context: Make your mentor or confidant earn the right to hear your Step Five. You are playing with your life here—they aren't playing with theirs. Make every effort to ensure your Step Five will not go awry. At Step Five you are allowing someone to significantly influence your spiritual pilgrimage. Think about this: If it doesn't work, you will soon feel empty and unfulfilled. You might get drunk, act out, or otherwise relapse. The person who heard your Step Five might then say in all sincerity: "Gee, that's too bad," but they haven't relapsed—you have.

Should you be asked to hear someone's Step Four, and they don't suggest a pre-Step Five interview, then you, as the more experienced twelve-step person, should ask for one. You must verify that the newer person is on track spiritually. In the event they aren't, refocus the interaction, and with gentle consideration, start an education process on what a Step Five is. Supposedly you're the more responsible spiritual person, so you must turn the event into a sponsorship process of carrying the message. Have your own AA reference texts handy and initiate a discussion on what's required. This is never about what anyone did wrong, it is only about how it might be made more effective. Reach for the most spiritually enlightened possibility.

For those who hold themselves out to be capable and willing to act as mentors, hearing someone's Step Five requires significant insight about the steps and long-term *spiritual* sobriety. What is required is subtle. By changing the guidelines, through arrogance and insecurity, people presume of themselves they are wiser than the original literature, or want to show off playing therapist and twelve-step guru. They may enter into it well-intentioned, but good intentions aren't good enough when dealing with things as vicious as addictions and as subtle as spirituality.

If you're invited to hear someone's Step Five, you're being offered a very special gift. It's an honor to be thusly respected. Veracity, humility, and obedience to the principles and instructions are crucial. To have the opportunity to contribute to the healing of the world; to help resolve addictions in another's life so they may carry on to find spiritual peace, carries a profound responsibility.

———

It would appear from the literature that the only time Step Five can legitimately be postponed is when you cannot find someone suitable.[36] This implies you have searched, done pre-Step Five interviews, and not found anyone. Keep looking.

In Step Four, you admitted certain defects, ascertained what the trouble is (fear), and identified weak items (issues around spiritual faith) in your personal inventory.[37] You have not inventoried your sins or catalogued your exploits and debauchery. Once you feel generally content about what you've accomplished thus far, including your pre-Step Five interview, only then do you make the appointment for your Step Five. If you make the appointment before you've completed *all* the preliminary work in a thorough and patient manner, there'll be pressure to "get it done". Impatience and deadlines are fatal to contemplative thoroughness.

Some questions about Step Five are: What if I relapse? What if they relapse? What if they can't handle what I have to tell them? What if they gossip? What if I see them at a meeting later on? What if I trigger their stuff? What if they start to cry? What if I start to cry? Do they have to be in a twelve-step program?

My replies are fairly standard: *"Rightly and naturally, we think well before we choose the person or persons... ."*[38] Notice *"or persons,"* implying you may decide to share your Step Four with more than one person. For example, you may

[36] *Alcoholics Anonymous,* p. 74.
[37] Ibid., p. 72.
[38] Ibid., p. 74.

discuss your instinctual insecurities and fears with one person, and your sexual self-ishness with someone else.[39] This may be wise or it may be evasive. Carefully examine your motives with a spiritual advisor or sponsor.

Be cautious about choosing self-styled, self-proclaimed program gurus, or anyone who has splintered their pilgrimage with outside step guides or treatment center outlines. This might indicate they have a poor understanding of, and weak faith in, the original program. If you can, notice the ambiance of their program, the subtleties of their spiritual attitudes, and how willing they are to follow the instructions. Don't automatically choose people by their reputation. Look towards those people who have an emotionally peaceful demeanor. No, they don't have to be in "the program"; they only must satisfy the four conditions.

As you enter your Step Five meeting, if you have followed the directions carefully, the result will be a peaceful confidence and closeness to your higher power. Talk about your Step Four in a sincere and straightforward manner. You're on a life-or-death errand. Your purpose is to illuminate every dark cranny of your personality, which is thoroughly outlined in your writing. As you go along, thoroughness and honesty may jog your memory and provoke greater detail. During your Step Five, you may remember subtle things that aren't in your notes. Include these.

Spiritual comfort and inner serenity, which are perceived in thought-logic as the nearness of your higher power, cannot arise from a grandiose disclosure of sins. They flow from a humble sharing of your instinctual conflict, a quiet examination of your fears, and taking responsibility for your sexual selfishness. Out of these actions, providing they are done with spiritual integrity, will come some noticeable relief from loneliness and isolation. You'll now begin to appreciate a sense of belonging — that you have a right to your relationship with your higher power and are entitled to earn a spiritual, peaceful life.

The Two Big Ones

When you join a twelve-step program, and in order to get recovered, the two general problems that must be resolved are the obsession to drink or act out, and the insane thinking. Notice at Step Five: *"The feeling that the drink problem has disappeared will often come strongly."*[40] Accordingly then, you've resolved one of these two general problems. During your Step Five, or shortly after it, you may well be aware that you are *in* a spiritual experience.[41]

The pamphlet *A Member's Eye View of Alcoholics Anonymous* offers information about "terminal uniqueness". Step Five contributes to eliminating this spiritually fatal self-perception which then permits the experience of an increased

---

[39] Should you decide you must disclose behavior that carries legal sanction, it need only be told to the professional authorities (including possibly a therapist and/or lawyer), that are qualified/responsible to receive this information. It is wise to tell a *bona fide* spiritual mentor for trustworthy spiritual counsel, and a therapist, but this decision is yours alone to make. It is never for general conversation in meetings.
[40] *Alcoholics Anonymous*, p. 75.
[41] Ibid., *"We… are delighted* [and] *begin to feel the nearness of our Creator.* [We] *have a spiritual experience."* Being able to appreciate being *in* a spiritual awakening as it happens rather than recalling the experience after the fact, indicates much progress in being spiritually sensitive. The main advantage to this difference is that in the former circumstance there is a more consistent sense of gratitude and serenity.

sense of being ordinary. Never malign your ordinariness—it's the substance of saints. Being sincerely ordinary allows you to experience spiritual sensibility.[42]

In your life you've experienced trauma, had difficult decisions thrust upon you, and endured Life, but so have billions of others. You are an ordinary alcoholic or addict; an ordinary person with the ordinary wants and needs and desires of everyone on the planet. You belong *to* the world and *in* the world, no more and no less than anyone else. You are ordinary *and* you have now finished Step Five.

Honesty

Step Five is overtly concerned with rigorous honesty. One of the hardest things addicts have to do in their lives (but certainly less arduous as devotion to spirituality increases) is to understand that dishonesty or withholding are *never* the answer. It doesn't matter what you've got to tell, or to whom you've got to tell it. Withholding information about gifts or because of a legal obligation are, of course, accepted social standards of behavior. Outside of these, and excluding the one *rare* exception identified in Step Nine, rigorous honesty is always the answer.[43]

Taken together, veracity and not withholding comprise one of the only two types of behavior that prohibit guilt; the other is responsibility. Veracity and responsibility (or their opposites) are the masters of your conscience. When you're indecisive about whether to be honest, you're entangled in anticipating the consequences of honesty based on your perceptions of hardship, discomfort, or loss of personal advantage. These consequences may be accurate or exaggerated; but regardless of this, the fact that honesty may be tough on *you* is of no consequence, since your dishonesty (or some other character defect) is what got you into feeling awkward in the first place. Honesty may create discomfort; dishonesty may create death.

In order to maintain a soulful union with God or another person, or to appreciate any abiding spiritual peace, you must strive for veracity. This is fundamental to all spiritual transformation (but so are the other four spiritual principles). Honesty may well be more painful for the short term, but the pain of deceit lasts as long as the deceit does. If a lie is permanent, the guilt and pain are permanent. *Only honesty makes your world less painful. Only responsibility makes your world safer.*

The Honesty Police

If you believe someone is being dishonest, is it your place to say something? Each circumstance is different. If their dishonesty affects you directly, then yes; if not, you have a decision to make. It's not your job to be running around challenging or reporting everyone you perceive as being dishonest. It may be important to say something, but... it may be more important to quietly excuse yourself from someone's life, and move on, saying nothing.

---

[42] There's an interesting aspect to the notion of "sensible" in relation to being spiritual. Once you're on the other side of the chaos of addictions, and well into being recovered, all of the significant travail, inner struggle, pain, and social calamity, amount, in the final analysis, to very little. Being spiritual, even with the years of monumental effort you put into it, is simply the sensible thing to do.
[43] I go into this in greater detail regarding amends in the next chapter.

Be advised: The way you say something is as important as what you say. Attacking people through "morally superior honesty" is always ineffective. It is your job to create a safe environment for your life, and a respectful environment for others around you, not to save the world or to save lost souls. Being kind, not attempting to impose your morality, being responsible for how you put yourself in some awkward position, not being angry, not demanding behavior change from others, are inherent to spiritual problem solving.

If someone emotionally close to you is dishonest in some way, the focus isn't on that person's dishonesty. What are you doing in an intimate relationship with a dishonest person? It is wise to feel *un*safe when you are with people who are willing to lie, commit crimes, be mean, or defend their racism or sexism. Be wary of people who will condone irresponsibility. If they're willing to condone or do those things, it's a fool's delusion to believe you are forever exempt—eventually it will be your turn because their honesty (and integrity) is only a matter of convenience to circumstance. Regardless of how sincerely they promise otherwise, it will eventually be your turn (if it isn't already). Examine the insecurity within you that motivates you to continue to be around people like this.

If you know, or remotely suspect, that some person you associate with is untrustworthy, and subsequently they lie or cheat you, it's entirely your fault: You were victimized because you ignored the evidence. When you get left, burnt, ripped off, ignored, or cheated, you have nothing to complain about since you volunteered to be there. If you are concerned about their unethical/unspiritual behavior, what are you doing there?

You must decide how much energy you will invest into reorganizing your life and personality around spiritual principles. Integrity, and its emotional cousin Serenity, are more expensive than most people are willing to pay. You may share your concerns with whatever scoundrels, meanies, liars, cheats, drama junkies, and ne'er-do-wells you associate with, as an explanation for your distancing yourself from them. You may even decide to report illegal or dishonest behavior to whichever civil authorities would respond to that information. These are decisions *you* have to wrestle with. Don't gossip. You are in some awkward situation because of your own questionable integrity. You alone, are responsible for your discomfort.

———

As an addict getting recovered you were granted, by whatever grace that Providence allows, some window of opportunity to see that your addictions were optional, but only with very hard work and huge commitment. You may well become recovered and achieve the promises, but with the unalterable requirement that you pay for them. Uncompromising commitment to the five spiritual principles as they appear in the steps, and continuing to demand more personal integrity from yourself with ever fewer demands on Life and others, is the price.

The stated fact is that a higher power could restore you to sanity, and here that means acquiring the courage to act in a way that honors the five spiritual principles. Your decision at Step Three requires that you forever acknowledge: *"Well, that's exactly what [Alcoholics Anonymous] is about. Its main object is to enable you to find a Power greater than yourself which will solve your problem."*[44]

Being recovered requires the maintenance steps govern all of your affairs — voluntarily and willingly continue to rededicate yourself to a spiritual way of life. You might not keep your job, you may have to move or divorce, you will lose all superficial relationships, but you'll achieve spiritual integrity — serenity and a relationship with a higher power. You cannot dilute your commitment to the tasks of the original maintenance steps, or avoid any principle of spirituality without the immediate consequence of losing whatever spiritual harmony you've earned.

After Step Five, and *before* Step Six, you are in this position: *"Step Four was, after all, only a look..."* and *"...it didn't necessarily mean that we had yet acquired much actual humility." "Though now recognized, our defects were still there. Something had to be done about them." "[We] could not wish or will them away by ourselves."*[45]

The Review

There's a significant piece of work that's done before you move to Step Six. It's outlined in the paragraph that begins *"Returning home we find..."*, which sits immediately before the instructions for Step Six.[46] It advises you to go home, be quiet for a while, and review your work thus far (the first five steps), to determine if you have omitted anything. This necessitates reviewing (yet again) your Step Four and the interaction and content of Step Five. In this review you are to be mindful of your gratitude and express this to your higher power. Your willingness to carefully review everything is evidence of your commitment.

The metaphor offered is that you are building an arch through which you shall walk, *"a free [person] at last."*[47]

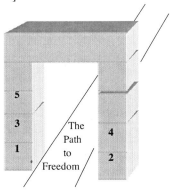

---

[44] *Alcoholics Anonymous,* p. 45. Note this is present tense. At any given moment Providence distributes another set of problems to "whomever", from broken shoelaces to bankruptcy and illness. Since problems appear relentlessly, *Alcoholics Anonymous* continuously takes the recovered addict back to "a higher power" that will solve those problems.

[45] All from *Twelve Steps and Twelve Traditions,* p. 58.

[46] *Alcoholics Anonymous,* p. 75.

[47] Ibid.

You are being told to examine how you have built your arch thus far. There are nine steps in the completed arch; you've now finished the first five. The obvious implication of "free" is you will eventually be recovered. So, *"...be quiet for an hour, carefully reviewing..."* those proposals.[48] The book asks is your work solid so far? Are these first stones [steps] properly in place? Was there skimping on the cement in the foundation? Should you find something you were lax on or overlooked, call your spiritual advisor or sponsor, possibly speak again with your step-five person, and repair it.

The implication is: If your work is not thorough, the arch will collapse, meaning you will not become recovered; you will not become free; you will not properly access the maintenance steps. If it does collapse, you'll have to rebuild the arch (re-do the steps) over and over—I suppose until you get it right.

This review is similar to school where you review your work before any big test. It's important to notice this is the only place in the original twelve-step literature where you are advised to review all of your spiritual work before proceeding further. This pre-Step Six review precedes the toughest "test" you'll face in the process of getting recovered. Something big is about to be asked of you.

"If we can answer to our satisfaction, we then look at Step Six."[49]

Step Six

The first sentence of Step Six is: *"This is the Step that separates the men from the boys."*[50] I am not enamored of the metaphor itself—it's shaming to men and boys, and insulting to women; but be that as it may, Step Six is the *only* step that opens with such an implied warning. No other step requires an entire program review prior to attempting it. This speaks to the import of Step Six.

The underlying philosophy, and the tasks you are required to complete at this point, are harder to assimilate and accomplish than what's required at any of the other steps. I don't assert this only through personal opinion (although that is my experience), but through the writing in the original twelve-step program, and through the truths regarding the opposing paradigms of addictions and spirituality.

In brief it is this: At Step Six you become *willing* to permanently and completely change the fundamental operating system of your personality. [At Step Two you came to believe that this difficult job could be done.] Step Six is your becoming willing to do it. This sets up two serious, subconscious fears: who will you become, and how can you survive (or succeed) in the new alien system you are to adopt?

The paragraph that begins, *"When men and women pour so much... ,"*[51] likens the vicious self-destruction that addicts are bent upon—alcohol, drugs, smoking, gambling, sex addictions, whatever—to suicide. Notice the opening sentence of the paragraph following: *"But most of our other difficulties don't fall under such a category at all."*[52] Most of an addict's difficulties are in the ordinary sphere of everyday

---

[48] *Alcoholics Anonymous*, p. 75.
[49] Ibid., p. 76.
[50] *Twelve Steps and Twelve Traditions*, p. 63.
[51] Ibid., p. 64.
[52] Ibid.

life: flat tires, forgotten appointments, money mismanagement, hurt feelings in romance, etc., yet so many addicts live as if they are martyred victims, heroes in the grand and magnificent struggle, noble characters standing against the treachery of addictions, or self-help psychology gurus with wisdom to dispense.

It's interesting that the most difficult step has only one short paragraph of instruction in *Alcoholics Anonymous*. Granted, it's a straightforward outline of the work you are to do, but its simplicity belies the monumental inner-personal realignment and reorganization that's required. Step Six permeates every facet of your life. It's interesting that Steps Two, Six and Seven are the steps that very few twelve-step people give any insightful discourse on. This mass-avoidance is a reflection of the spiritual depth and power of these steps.

Willingness

"We have emphasized willingness as being indispensable."[53] Willing, from various dictionaries, is defined as consenting without begrudging; pleasantly inclined; eager to go along; cheerfully consenting. A willing worker completes a task with cheerful readiness. Being "willing" means to go along agreeably; to cheerfully or eagerly consent to a commitment; to be pleasantly inclined to do something; or to have a pleasant, friendly attitude—without feeling irked, begrudging, or annoyed. All of this is *willing*.

Willingness is used frequently in relation to getting recovered. *Alcoholics Anonymous* is written for alcoholics [addicts]: stubborn, isolated, defensive, dishonest, depressed, suspicious, selfish, insecure, and especially begrudging. For them to become willing, especially willing to change the fundamental way they participate in life, in the fullest sense of Life, is a monumental undertaking,

Addicts are brilliantly schooled in adding, "Yes, but... " to anything they're doing, and still be able to convince themselves they are willing. It looks like this: "I'm willing to be spiritual, except that sometimes... ," "Of course I'm willing to be honest in all areas of my life, but... ," "I'm willing to be completely responsible, except that... ," "I'm willing to stop pirating software or music, but after... ," "Certainly I'm willing to make amends, as long as it's not... ," "Yes, I'm willing to go to therapy, but... ," "Sure, I'm willing to drive you home, but I hope... ," Adding any exception (openly or silently) to your claim of willingness means you're not.

Similar ideas about passion and caring, that are important to life and transformation, and which also closely parallel what we're about here, were wonderfully illustrated by the actor Nicole Kidman. She was talking about her perspectives of, and great respect for, the late film director Stanley Kubrick. Here are Nicole Kidman's observations of Stanley Kubrick:

> *"His* [Stanley Kubrick's] *understanding of humans was that we are very bittersweet, but he admired... passion, commitment, and loyalty... .*
> *The whole process of the film* [Eyes Wide Shut] *was a discovery. It was never about the result. It was never about... 'Well, we have a week to*

shoot this thing so quick, quick, quick, we have to do it; let's see, we may not fully explore it, but we'll get something good.'

  Stanley wanted to explore every avenue and then make his decisions based on that. Stanley was not restricted by time. He refused to be, and that is a great luxury. Do you want to know what's gold with filmmaking? Time is gold. Not having to walk away from a scene before you feel like you've really perfected it.

  The other thing Stanley hated doing was ever explaining himself... 'So what's the film about, Stanley?' He'd look down, look away, and not answer. And the same thing applied to a scene: 'So what do you really want this scene to be?' He would never answer that.

  Part of Stanley's legacy on my life is that... well, you believe in something. You passionately believe in something, so devote yourself to it— completely, utterly, and don't apologize for doing it."

Nicole Kidman[54]

Other people in the documentary referred to Stanley Kubrick's view that either you care or you don't. You can't really "partly care", either you do or you don't. In your own bitter-sweet existence, people are not disposable. Care about what you do or don't do it. Be passionate.[55] Don't apologize for passion. I'm sure other people share similar views, but none I've found have been stated quite as articulately as Ms. Kidman's. I invite you to ponder rather carefully what she said. It is entirely applicable to how we do, or don't, live our lives, and is particularly applicable to any struggle to move through the steps, get recovered, and become spiritual.

You are asked to become willing to let God remove all your defects of character: *"...any person capable of enough willingness and honesty to try repeatedly Step Six on all* [their] *faults—without any reservations whatever—has indeed come a long way spiritually... ."*[56]

Here are examples: Are you looking forward to, pleased and agreeable, cheerfully compliant, or graciously consenting, to be gently honest *all* the time, in *all* situations, with *all* people, regardless of the consequences to yourself? Are you willing to be honest all the time, no matter to whom you're speaking? Are you willing to be charitable and kind, all the time, regardless of what the other person has done, or is doing, to you? I imagine some people may wonder: "Can't I be willing and complain a little bit sometimes?" No. Either you are or you aren't. When that clergyman wrote, *"This is the step the separates the men from the boys,"* he meant that this step is spiritually the most difficult because of the requirement of willingness.

---

[53] *Alcoholics Anonymous*, p. 76.
[54] This is taken from *Stanley Kubrick, A Life In Pictures,* Warner Bros. Pictures, Time Warner Ent., Co., 2001. In the film, Ms. Kidman's comments were offered in shorter excerpts to fit with the style of that documentary. They are reprinted here as one commentary to fit with the requirements of this book.
[55] As an aside that is indirectly related: *"Of all forms of caution, caution in love is perhaps most fatal to true happiness."* Bertrand Russell, from *The Blues ain't nothing but a good soul feeling bad*, Sheldon Kopp, Fireside Books, Simon & Schuster, 1992, entry for Sep. 17.
[56] *Twelve Steps and Twelve Traditions*, p. 63, emphasis theirs.

Survival Skills

All families have some degree of dysfunction—dishonesty, greed, avarice, sloth, manipulation, aggression, "codependence", oppression, sexual problems, envy, shame, etc. These dysfunctions are very often subtle or covert. They require each of us to develop a "compensation strategy" for whatever the dislocated power alliances are (or were) in your environment. You adapted as required and survived.

Depending on any number or variables, and on the power alliances in your family, and to varying degrees, you survived by being overtly sexual or sexually repressed; hiding your emotions or overtly displaying them; being invisible or showing off; being direct or subversive; being overachieving or underachieving. Perhaps you were deceitful, greedy, a comedian, prone to rages, bad, disobedient, obsessive, political, manipulative, brave, slim, or overweight. Perhaps you took the role of caretaker in your family, or were prone to self-harm. You may have engaged in dozens of other strategies and combinations of strategies, all "unhealthy" [sic] to some degree, and became good at whichever of these you chose. These are often ordinary, compensating survival skills, often very subtle, and done as a matter of course.

In our culture's clamoring for convenience, hunting for scapegoats, obsession with shiny things, and our separation from our souls, human ordinariness has become a defect. The genesis of the animal called "human" now has no room for error. However, character defects are inevitable, as are compensation strategies (both, functions of our ordinariness), and they exacerbate the spiritual condition called addiction. Having character defects or a dysfunctional family—now overly used and trite phrases—doesn't make you an addict. Those sometimes quite ordinary defects, in your addiction, evolved into destructive survival skills... which are exactly what you must be willing to abandon.

Regardless of the degree of dysfunction, families are so psychologically rooted in their misalliances, that any maladaptive survival strategies are experienced as absolutely normal. Children sometimes experience a psychic jolt—a sudden, blunt shock of realization that their family isn't like others. There can be a host of "awareness problems" that result from this rupture of perceived normalcy. Be that as it may, this only aggravates an addiction that may develop later, but it doesn't cause it.

Addicts develop new self-annihilation strategies and further entrench any old ones from childhood. Addictions create new personality problems which become fused to the old ones, making the old ones worse. Should these pre-addiction, often quite routine compensatory behaviors from childhood (after all, some addicts did come from pretty decent families) be altered by the phenomenon of addictions, it is easy to perceive that your "childhood" caused your addiction. It didn't.

Step Six requires that you be willing to quit using the very behaviors that allowed you to be a successful addict. Spirituality, and "the program", are requiring that you *willingly* quit doing the things that made you brilliantly successful at destroying yourself. Consider that addicts approach this step with only a few months or one or two years of sobriety, and come from years or decades of self-annihilation. It is monumentally difficult, even with good role-modeling and strong faith, to become completely willing to abandon your addictions-based survival skills.

Psychologically violent behaviors like shaming, teasing, verbal abuse, arguing, moral superiority, pity, intrusive questions, and threats have no place in a spiritual lifestyle. These are the behaviors of addiction. Tough, hard-line, angry, insensitive "recovery" is about dominating, shaming, and humiliating people into obedience—doing what the sponsor (or, in many cases, the counsellor, the church, the recovery house) wants, so "they" can look good and brag they saved somebody. This is entirely inappropriate and has no place in any *spiritual* recovery program.

This is why your mentor, sponsor, therapist, or doctor (whomever you seek counsel from) should be someone who is *well*-conversant with, or obedient to, the principles of an ethical, non-violent life.[57] Anyone who covets any underlying anger, prejudice, or contempt will have no persuasive power to attract another person into a spiritual, non-addicted lifestyle.[58] Gentle self-discipline, and sincere commitment to the maintenance steps (spiritual principles), and a sincerely ethical life, is the order of the day, *every* day. Seeing this in others is a prime ingredient and an essential motivator towards willingness at Step Six.

You have to take into your heart the truth that becoming the exact opposite of every character defect, of every symptom of the disease, is where you *willingly* go. You cheerfully volunteer for it. Eventually you would pursue this with pleasant anticipation. Read this carefully: Step Six requires that you become *willing* to be respectful, honest, humble, generous of spirit, and considerate and responsible in *all* situations, in *all* circumstances, and with *all* people, regardless of the consequences to yourself and regardless of how people behave towards you.[59]

If you don't have an abiding conviction (established at Step Two) that spirituality is the key, it is impossible to do Step Six. At Step Six, which is the third of the three major demands for a complete realignment of your perceptions, you are required to prove that your decision at Step Three was sincere.

*"Are we now ready to let God remove from us all the things which we have admitted are objectionabl*e?"[60] This reference to Step Four and Five refers to your insecurities, fears, and sexual selfishness. The defect-removal process must, and can only, begin with willingness. If Step Four or Five is in any way a catalogue of acting out behaviors, rather than a disclosure of instincts gone awry, fears, sexual selfishness, then you're in trouble. Here's why:

The intent of Step Six is to establish a willingness to remove your defects. You can remove defects, but you can't "remove" historical events. You don't "have" old behaviors; they're gone. You cannot be successful when praying for the willing-

---

[57] Addictions are violent. They involve self-annihilation, psychological abuse, shame, disrespect, deceit, etc. These, directly or indirectly, have no place in any spiritual endeavor.
[58] My belief, and this comment, is my adaptation of this: *"You have no morally persuasive power when you possess any underlying contempt,"* said by Dr. Martin Luther King, Jr., which is found in *Martin Luther King, Jr.*, by Marshall Frady, a Lipper®/Viking Book, 2002.
[59] Keep this in context. These may be somewhat modified in emergent situations of violence or danger; however, even then, do not abandon spiritual principles.
[60] *Alcoholics Anonymous*, p. 76.

ness to remove something that you don't have. Past *behaviors* are not removable. Character defects, on the other hand, are removable; they aren't gone; they're still present. If a Step Four or Five identifies a list of "bad behavior" there's nothing you can do at Step Six because spiritual willingness can't resolve past behaviors. However, what is still present and objectionable are the instincts gone awry, fears, and sexual selfishness. You have the ability to remove or modify these. Completing Step Six is impossible if Steps Four or Five are about behavior.

"We have emphasized willingness as being indispensable."[61] Ponder carefully what that sentence implies because your own getting recovered depends on it. With minimal faith in a higher power, you have no resource for the courage it takes to be willing. "If we still cling to something we cannot let go, we ask God to help us be willing."[62] Become willing to abandon your addictions-related survival skills (defects) and adopt a spiritual way of life.

The Objective

Twelve Steps and Twelve Traditions advises you to work towards an objective defined by God, not defined by you (meaning defined by your defects and insecurities).[63] I suppose each of us has a certain level where some arbitrary degree of honesty is good enough: "I've got a good life now. I'm honest (enough)." Having a strong attachment to a peer group means your life is only as spiritual as the group's, which is an objective defined by the group and not by God: honest enough to get by, but not honest enough to risk social discomfort.

Whatever degree of spirituality you have attained has allowed you to achieve a certain comfortable lifestyle, and you often judge that level as "good enough". You're tired of the hard work; you'll just relax and maybe not be as vigilant. Overcoming your own complacency to deepen your spirituality, which flies in the face of everything cultural, is what "separates the men from the boys."[64]

I wonder what "God" might think of receiving a prayer like this:

Dear God:
I've been trying this spirituality/getting recovered thing for a while. My friends think I'm too demanding of myself about honesty. They're uncomfortable. And all this humility stuff. Well... this spiritual work is really hard. Like, it's really hard! So I'm going to take a break. Besides... well... my sponsor's life is okay. I know they sometimes tell little lies and complain and gossip, but they've got a job and a nicer car than me. God, I don't want to have to make all new

---

[61] *Alcoholics Anonymous*, p.76.
[62] Ibid.
[63] "...between striving for a self-determined objective and for the perfect objective which is of God." *Twelve Steps and Twelve Traditions*, p. 68, and "Reminding ourselves that we have decided to go to any lengths to find a spiritual experience...," *Alcoholics Anonymous*, p. 79.
[64] Remember the proverb: 'Take what you want,' said God, 'and pay for it.' The long transition from deceit and manipulation to rigorous honesty is always awkward. Making this transition is both wise *and* difficult, but once you reasonably achieve it, it's a pleasure to maintain.

friends just because I'm honest. Jeez! I mean, finding people who are really trying to live by spiritual principles might take forever and... well, anyway, I don't want to be working at Spirituality all that hard all the time. Life's pretty good now. I'm going to take some time off.

Sincerely,
Me

P.S.: God, can I please keep my abstinence and maybe a little serenity while I'm ignoring you? Thanks.

There is never a vacation from the maintenance steps and the principles they embody. And, if the truth be known, eventually the five spiritual principles become the vacation that you've always wanted but were too cheap to pay for.

The majority of twelve-step pilgrims are just honest enough to get by, and often grumble about how hard it is, which is because they're just trying to get by (like trying to swim without getting too wet). To constantly be responsible, to struggle for deeper levels of willingness, and to adopt completely the spiritual principles in the maintenance steps is to aspire to a standard set by God. It eventually becomes graceful, but in the meantime, remind yourself that you voluntarily chose a spiritual lifestyle. When you are noticeably willing to live, *all of the time*, by a Spiritually-defined objective, and are reasonably consistently determined to get back on track when you find that you're not, you are done with Step Six.

Read the single paragraph in *Alcoholics Anonymous* about Step Six. Meditate on how simple and complete it is. It may take several months to understand its all-encompassing nature and to become truly willing. Thoroughness is how you demonstrate your commitment to live a Spiritual life. Step Six is acquiring a willing devotion to abandon all of your "addict survival skills"—actually *being* a spiritual pilgrim. Are you completely willing to change completely?

I get variations of two general reactions from people who have a stubborn mindset prior to reading or hearing this. They often strongly disagree, and become angry or defensive (they've been jarred out of their comfort zones). Or if they're foundering or confused, they experience a sense of relief that it does make sense and there is hope. In either situation, there is anxiety (fear) at all of the work involved.

Old Ideas

As I mentioned earlier, I was once offering a seminar on "Christianity and Spirituality" at a treatment center. A man got up in the middle of the lecture, pointed at me, and proclaimed loudly: "How dare you say that!" He went up to his room, packed his bags, and quit treatment. He decided two things: I was wrong and he was offended. When you think you're right, you can't learn anything, and even if you are "right", there's disadvantages to being arrogant about it.

"Some of us have tried to hold on to our old ideas and the result was nil until we let go absolutely."[65] It's easy to understand that this sentence refers to old ideas from drinking and acting out. That's only part of it. In their first year of abstinence, people getting recovered have to let go of old ideas from when they were acting out; in their second year, they must abandon some old ideas from their first year; and in their fifth year, they must let go of old ideas from the third or fourth years of getting recovered. An old idea is an old idea—ideas from an hour ago and thirty years ago qualify as old ideas. If you're not willing to let go of old ideas, you're in serious spiritual trouble.[66] It isn't that old ideas are automatically wrong because they're old: It's your willingness or unwillingness to self-examine and change that's at issue.

The more you have invested in an old idea—the more passionately you believe in it, the more you brag about it, the longer you have cherished it, the more difficult it will be to challenge it. Your being willing to let go of old ideas, old "truths", old perspectives, old behaviors, is related to humility (i.e. being spiritually teachable), an attitude you are to maintain for the rest of your life. Forcing yourself to shift out of your ego's willful blindness[67] and into willingness is always a significant ingredient in re-education.

When do you let go of an old idea, an old value, an old behavior? When you realize it operates contrary to any part of any of the five spiritual principles within the maintenance steps. When an insight illuminates some very subtle corrupt motive, or when a more recently felt experience has a more sincere spiritual perspective, then the old idea goes.

Become convinced that spirituality is essential (Step Two); commit yourself to achieving this in your own life (Step Three); be responsible and view yourself properly (Step Four); be transparent and honest about yourself (Step Five); desire to be willing (Step Six). And that brings us to...

Prerequisites and Observations Regarding Step Seven

Very soon now, two things will be possible that weren't before. You will be capable of acceptance, and you will not require pain to be the motivator of change.

Step Six is so subtle and overwhelming that it seldom gets the attention that it deserves. Achieving willingness, as difficult as that may be, is a fundamental quality of character that must be present for humility to exist. *"Since [Step Seven] so specifically concerns itself with humility, we should pause here to consider what humility is and what the practice of it can mean to us."*[68]

---

[65] *Alcoholics Anonymous*, p. 58.
[66] "Willingness" will now become a mindset that is essential to all transformation work.
[67] Willful Blindness is a principle of jurisprudence. A stranger on the street offers you an obviously new, expensive sports car for $500.00. You buy it and are later charged with some crime related to possession of stolen property. At trial you claim you didn't know it was stolen. You willfully chose to be blind to the obvious, hence "willful blindness", and you may well be found guilty of a crime. In a similar manner, forcing yourself to be blind to obvious unspiritual/abusive behavior (your own or someone else's) is a transparent, irresponsible ego-tactic of addicts. See again the quote of Thomas Merton at the beginning of Chapter 1.
[68] *Twelve Steps and Twelve Traditions*, p. 70.

Humility

Humility is not the intellectually passive adoption of a philosophical concept. You cannot think yourself into a relationship with a deity. Humility is misunderstood; it's tricky. Humility, as with the other four spiritual principles, goes against every trait of any addiction. Spiritual endeavor requires that you adopt both aspects of humility (see Appendix II) so that [eventually] Grace can operate more freely within you. Humility is the primary underlying theme that operates in concert with all spiritual attributes, without exception.

Humility is active. It's an actual physical set of behaviors, accompanied by a contemplative, willing mindset, where you surrender gracefully to, and put yourself in the position of, rendering service to a higher power. That may manifest as service to people but that, by itself, is only being socially charitable. Humility is rooted in service to, and love of, a God of your understanding—an outgrowth of the spiritual principles that form the context for an egalitarian mindset.

I have heard people subtly complain after a twelve-step call, or after working with someone, about the ingratitude they encountered. How many "spiritual" people secretly expect gratitude? Do you quietly revel in the subtle praise and glances of respect from others? How many nod in a *self*-satisfied way about the compliments they receive? What's it really like in the shadows of your heart when no one says: "Thanks for your effort."? Being spiritual requires that all of your effort be in the humble service of a higher power, not in the service of your ego's notions of *quid pro quo* and reward, which is what largely underlies most petitionary prayer.

A story: Once upon a time, a monk (or a sponsor or a therapist) had an acolyte (substitute a newcomer or a client) who was absolutely devoted to her. The monk thought her spiritual student dull-witted and inept, but was pleased she had such a devoted follower. One day the monk heard rumors that her acolyte had walked on water. The monk questioned the young acolyte, who immediately prostrated himself and humbly said, "Yes, Master, they told me that I did that, but I was in walking meditation at the time, contemplating my reverence for you, Master, chanting your name in meditative bliss when this happened. I was unaware of it." The monk marveled at this. In an effort to demonstrate her own spiritual prowess, she walked into the river chanting, "Me, Me, Me," and sank.

When living in dislocation, humility is often viewed as dangerous. Many people, especially addicts, perceive that being humble is boring, or that when they are humble, they're weak and they run the risk of being humiliated.[69] These are two of the more subtle dynamics of spiritual misinformation that have to be challenged. These perceptions automatically set up a very subtle resistance to humility, and then spirituality becomes that much more distant. The further along you are in the steps, the more responsible you must become. The more responsible you must become, the more you need humility. You've got to sincerely want to be the acolyte and not the monk.

---

[69] The truth is that when you are sincerely, spiritually humble, you cannot be humiliated.

Here's another perspective. You think "pick up the pen," so you pick up the pen. Or you intuit that a smile is appropriate and so you smile a pleasant, friendly smile. You never notice the process of doing either of these, and have no real comprehension of how these incredibly complicated things happen—brain cells, synapses, nerves, muscles, memory, coordination. Millions of tiny energy impulses all "did something", and you picked up the pen, or you smiled. It was unconscious and graceful. Humility has to act that way. Work hard at not noticing your humility. However, at the outset of your transformation, there is a necessary and concerted intellectual effort required to *be* humble. You have to force yourself into it. Initially, it isn't graceful or voluntary at all. When you talk about how humble you are trying to be, or force yourself to be humble, you aren't. It's forced, but it still has to start with you acting "as if".

All spiritual transformation begins with your acting as if you are what you cannot yet be. Force yourself to do it. Diligently belabor the action within yourself, and embrace your incompetence as natural. The desire to become humble is sufficient to begin. Humility grows out of an unassuming devotion to achieving the spiritual principles in the maintenance steps. Force yourself to surrender gracefully, and be silent about that. When you do this, without want of reward, without knowing it is happening, you are in a humble moment.[70]

I've tried not to offer any specific definition of what humility is. The definitions are legion. Two things they all have in common are that the definitions are quickly reduced to clichés, and they are always incomplete (words themselves are inadequate). Additionally, any concerted, energetic effort to define humility fails because of the underlying and camouflaged arrogance of trying to write the "perfect" definition of humility (or likewise, of God).

Humility is also present in authentic love. Or, from another view, neither love nor humility can exist without some noticeable presence of the other. Where, within this thing we call our mind, did some abstract concept like Humility come from? Where *exactly* does Love reside? These two are inextricably linked, and are impossible to define. Love and humility appear to be the two human attributes that are innately present at birth and never need to be taught.[71] They cannot be taught and exist somewhere underneath our physical existence.

The potential to be spiritual exists within everyone. It exists underneath the biological and secular trappings of personality and culture. Becoming spiritual requires unlearning old ideas, clearing away defects, abandoning pride, and having faith that your insecurities are meaningless. Humility will be present as you endeavor to know God inside yourself. All of the spiritual principles exist inherently within us. The three maintenance steps are the rituals that demonstrate those pre-existing five principles. Willingly surrendering to this truth is the task at hand.

---

[70] *The World's Religions*, by Huston Smith, HarperSanFrancisco, 1991, The Way to God through Work, is an articulate explanation of "work" through karma yoga, as one path to God. Any work in service to God, and without a personal investment in the outcome, is an aspect of humility.
[71] People never need to be taught how to love. *The Blues ain't nothing but a good soul feeling bad,* Sheldon Kopp, Fireside Books, Simon & Schuster, 1992, entry for March 11.

The Gift is the Opportunity

In studying the writings of the spiritual masters, and from my own ordinary experience, it seems the gifts people receive, which appear to arrive from divine sources, are of this specific nature: If they are to be appreciated, they cannot be withheld from general distribution. What you must give away; what you have to share freely or lose, are: understanding, charity of spirit, serenity, compassion, love, and joy. Once you have these blessings, which are the after-effects of a spiritual lifestyle, they are available to anyone who comes into contact with you, by virtue of the fact that you have them. When these spiritual gifts are husbanded or withheld, they wither and disappear; they are destroyed by selfishness. With some irony, you keep them for yourself through giving them away—generosity is how they are retained. The spiritual attributes of respect, charity of spirit, serenity, compassion, love, and joy are always retained by egalitarian distribution.

Conversely: People who accumulate or receive secular "gifts" like property, money, influence, and temporal power must withhold them from others in order to keep them for themselves. Withholding them—selfishness—is how these are retained.

Now consider the circumstance of sobriety or abstinence. Many addicts, prior to their first experience with twelve-step programs, don't understand that sobriety is an option. Suddenly they are presented with the awareness that they do have a choice, and are then given the opportunity to chose. This is often described in terms of "gifts from Providence", and are variously referred to as a spiritual experience or awakening, or a religious experience. Doctors Jung, Silkworth, and Tiebout refer to this as a psychic shift. And so, it would appear that sobriety extends out of the opportunity to choose, and that awareness-opportunity is provided by Providence. There is no actual "labor" involved when an alcoholic or addict is suddenly presented with that first uninvited *opportunity* to become spiritual.

Spiritual transformation isn't free, the opportunity is. Transformation is earned by working hard to take advantage of the opportunity to choose. In the vernacular: "God's" gift to you is the opportunity to choose sobriety. Then, you work hard in a very specific way (the original steps) to take advantage of that opportunity. Spiritual virtues subsequently appreciate in you, and your gift to "God" is to embody those virtues in such a way that Spirituality becomes attractive to others. You do the work; God, as you understand God, gets the credit.

––––––

If you want to be a great therapist, you have to study great therapists and (to some degree) act as they acted. Students of painting and music study the great painters and musicians. Study Yeshua of Nazareth, the Buddha, Lao Tzu, Gandhi, Da Mo, Mohammed, whomever—work to understand what they understood, all the while embracing your resistance and incompetence as natural. You're always a newcomer to the rest of your life.

Force yourself inside the steps and principles; force them inside you. This effort is the spiritual use of willpower and the effective use of a strong ego. If you want to have humility as a graceful part of your life, study the people who live humble, spiritually courageous lives. You don't need to do this on a mountain top in the wilderness. You need to do this *exactly* where you're standing at any given moment of any given day. Here is when it starts and now is where it's found.

The Monumental Shift

Humility, partly because of the cultural disparagement of Spirituality, and the deifying of greed and power, is routinely discouraged as a desirable attribute. Initially, entering a twelve-step program is always motivated by fear, shame, humiliation—the consequences of your addiction. At Step One you are forced into your first rudimentary exposure to "humility" which, at this stage, closely resembles humiliation only because you are beaten into it. Nobody comes to humility easily, not even the saints. The process I am about to describe is crucial to spiritual success, and takes you directly into one of the most important value shifts in getting recovered.

At the outset, you were beaten into humility by acting out, which is only the external tip of the problem. The acquisition of humility is initially evidenced by a subtle and constantly increasing inner motivation to do the steps while you are in fact doing them. However, if you haven't followed the instructions thus far, you cannot lay the foundation required for the monumental shift that I am about to describe.

The initial motivation to become abstinent is from shame and fear of insanity, death or punishment. At Step Two you believe that spirituality is the solution. The motivation changes slightly from "all fear" to include some small portion of a desire for spirituality. Through Steps Three to Five, fear as the motivator is further reduced, with a correlated increase in a desire to be spiritual. At Step Six, where the task is to acquire willingness to lose your defects, you're now (or "should be") primarily motivated by a desire for spirituality. You're now beginning to believe that spirituality is inherently good for its own sake, which is remarkably different from the Step Two perception that spirituality is good because it's going to save your life. Your view of spirituality is changing from something imposed by fear and shame to something desired. This shift is *the* essential prerequisite to Step Seven.

Should you have done *these* original steps meticulously, there's an underlying fundamental shift happening in your world-view—humility and honesty are becoming intrinsically good unto themselves, and are willingly pursued personal attributes. Loyalty and allegiance to the principles are increasingly inner imperatives. By Step Seven, the work has thus far set up the maintenance steps (even though you aren't there yet) to become cherished, internalized foundations of non-negotiable conduct. If this isn't becoming more obvious to you, then something important has been missed *en route* to this point.

If you believe you've done the steps but are always "in recovery", if you're sometimes political rather than honest, if you avoid awkward truths for your own sake, if you talk about someone rather than to them, if you're interested in being honest, generous, kind, etc., because it's what's expected, you've missed the shift from begrudging spirituality to willing spirituality. Your motivation for recovery is still rooted in addictions-based fear and shame. In these situations, go back to Step Two and reexamine your commitment to spirituality.

It's impossible to be spiritual and at the same time harm yourself or others. It's impossible to be spiritual if you are irresponsible.[72] It's impossible to be humble if you disrespect yourself or others by abuse, neglect, withholding, or lying. Humility and truth are an integral part of self-respect.

Begrudging participation and shallow commitments are the breeding ground for dilemmas and confusion. When spiritual principles are understood and adhered to, dilemmas and confusion evaporate. *"We saw that we needn't always be bludgeoned and beaten into humility. It could come quite as much from our voluntarily reaching for it as it could from unremitting suffering. A great turning point in our lives came when we sought for humility as something we really wanted, rather than something we must have."* [73]

As soon as you experience in your heart that humility, both spiritual and secular, is desirable for you, that moment is a sunrise to the rest of your life. You stay committed to responsibility and truth, and integrity is consistently available. You'll no longer be motivated by pain and shame. While you're forcing yourself to be humble, fear of being humiliated will disappear. There won't be any confusion about how to conduct yourself. And, there's this fine point about "voluntary" participation: arriving as a newcomer, and through the first six steps, your participation is motivated by crisis, fear, and pain. Yes, you voluntarily participate, but you volunteered only to get rid of pain and chaos. That's how everyone starts. However, when these steps are done meticulously, and spiritual heliotropism carries you through Step Seven, your voluntary participation becomes motivated by the attractiveness of humility, i.e. *"...we needn't always be bludgeoned and beaten into humility."*

Being an addict, and the tasks that facilitate transformation in the first six steps, require the cliché "no pain, no gain" to be true. In the continuing absence of willingness in spiritual commitment, "no pain, no gain" is the prerequisite to everything you accomplish. However, when you really "get" Step Seven, the struggle for growth is over—growth *without* pain—and when you desire humility as a good thing, veracity is automatic and painless. These are permanent benefits of changing your perspective of humility, and it's here that living without suffering becomes possible. If you claim to be beyond Step Seven, and are still generally motivated by pain and turmoil, or if there's recurring conflict and struggle in your life, your spirituality is political; you've missed the point.

---

[72] What follows will be explained in detail in *Facets of Personal Transformation* (see p. 445). I have described people in therapy who get to the cusp between knowledge and insight and then quit. If you are in therapy and it seems to have worked for you for some period of time, laborious or expensive as it may be, don't quit when you get the urge to take a break. The stronger the urge, the more important it is that you stay. You will dredge up several rationalizations that justify quitting: The therapist didn't.... . My friends say... . Keeping the appointments is hard because... . Work through your resistance. If the therapeutic alliance has worked up to that point, and the therapist has been generally effective, then persevere. *Don't quit.* It's exactly at that point that something important is happening for you and insight is on your horizon. Don't quit; in fact, ask for extra sessions—challenge yourself, not the therapy or the therapist.
[73] *Twelve Steps and Twelve Traditions*, p. 75, emphasis added.

"The chief activator of our defects has been self-centered fear—primarily fear that we would lose something we already possessed or would fail to get something we demanded."[74] You have character defects because you're scared. Do you want to know why you lie; what motivates betrayal; why you manipulate people? You're scared. Why are you greedy? Why are you slothful? Why are you mean? Why are you spiteful? You're afraid. You are angry because you're afraid. The chief activator of your defects has been self-centered fear.

When you find yourself in the middle of a character defect, ignore the defect itself and examine yourself for fear. The skill of identifying your fears and instincts gone awry was developed at Step Four. Getting honest and avoiding theatrics about your fears and sexual selfishness was practiced in Step Five. Because of this training, bypassing the actual character defect to expose the underlying fear should be a fairly straightforward task of self-reflection, and should occur without the need to blame anyone. If it isn't, you've missed something along the way.

Step Seven

"I hope you like the wedding gift I bought
you. It's a broken toaster oven."

The instructions regarding Step Seven are contained entirely within one paragraph. And, of course, they presume you've done what you were told to do to up to this point. The Step Seven prayer is profound and rather straightforward.

> *"When ready, we say something like this: My Creator, I am now willing that you should have all of me, good and bad. I pray that you now remove from me every single defect of character which stands in the way of my usefulness to you and my fellows. Grant me strength, as I go out from here, to do your bidding. Amen."*[75]

"When ready… " means when you have done *all* the prerequisite work, and have achieved the (reasonably consistent) willingness described in Step Six, regarding each of your character defects. That's when you'll be ready.

"My Creator, I am now willing that you should have all of me, good and bad," has a subtle catch to it. Addicts live with shame, and deep inside believe they are flawed and unworthy. The first sentence is the offering of yourself as a gift to your higher power, but nobody likes to give or receive defective gifts. Did you ever go into a store to buy a gift and say: "I'd like to buy my partner a watch. Have you got one that's scratched and doesn't work right?" There's a social stigma attached to offering broken gifts: "I hope you like the wedding gift I bought you. It's a broken toaster oven."

People usually give gifts that are pristine and shiny and work right. In Step Seven, you are giving yourself to God. *You* are the gift. If you believe there's some-

---

[74] *Twelve Steps and Twelve Traditions*, p. 76.
[75] *Alcoholics Anonymous*, p. 76.

thing broken in the gift, there is a reluctance in the offering.[76] You've been ashamed of yourself for so long, so how could *anyone* want you? Part of your step work has been to eliminate self-condemnation, which began back at the "I'm not crazy. I have a disease," realization at Step One. If you haven't unequivocally resolved the "I'm bad - I'm sick" debate, you can't offer yourself sincerely at Step Seven. If this be the case, then the shift to desiring humility won't happen. You'll remain stuck in the "no pain, no gain" mindset (which clearly doesn't exist in a spiritual life).

At Step Two you learned that social success was *not* the order of the day. At Step Seven, you're not offering only your energy or social accomplishments, but also your love and spiritual devotion. Your devotion to Spirituality is the actual gift of "yourself" to your higher power.[77] Your willing commitment to spiritual principles is the gift and what allows the offering of flawed gifts to God. Without sincere willingness, the Step Seven prayer is only Impression Management.

"I pray that you now remove from me every single defect of character which stands in the way of my usefulness to you and my fellows." The prayer is basically petitionary, but not for personal advantage. The purpose of your gift of "you" to God is service to God and to others. It does not read: Please remove my character defects so that I have a serene personal life. The prayer contains no aspect of selfishness and nothing about personal success or popularity. Your defects are to be removed because they limit your usefulness to God.

Ask of God that your character defects be removed *only* so that others can see that praying is good. Ask of God that regardless of whatever life circumstances befall you, you remain steadfast in your commitment to God, so that others will see (by observing you) that God is worthy of being prayed to. When next you say your prayers, plead to remain anonymous and in the background of *all* your good deeds, so that God will get more credit than you do. Pray because God is worthy of being prayed to.

Petitionary prayer almost invariably reduces itself to the petitioner trying to control the agenda of life, based on some comparative or superlative analysis of moral values: trying to advise God that the world should be run according to their plan; trying to impose their will on whomever or whatever it is they are praying about; trying to avoid loss, inconvenience, pain, responsibility, or calamity. Most often, petitionary prayer has little to do with God, and is motivated by the selfish agenda of whomever's praying. Outside of praying only for things that are to the advantage of a universal deity, petitionary prayer is the attempt to impose some personal agenda on Life, on God, on others. (Which agenda is what addicts begin to eliminate at Step Three.)

---

[76] Outside of spirituality, in the dynamics of love and relationship, one perspective of a long-term sincere commitment to another person is the notion of giving yourself to them: the metaphor of gift-giving in love—I offer myself to thee. If you believe (especially subconsciously) you're broken and defective, you'll withhold on your commitment in the relationship; or you'll give yourself to someone who will agree with you that you are flawed, and they'll treat you disrespectfully.

[77] This theme is expanded upon in the section on prayer in Chapter 9.

The steps are intended to reduce the dominating presence of character defects and insecurities, and eliminate addicts' never-ending struggle to get their own way. Confusing God with Santa Claus, under the guise of altruism or moral or religious righteousness, is a potent error in prayer. There's an identifiable arrogance—an obvious flaw of hubris, in trying to dictate the terms of Life and advising God on how things should be run. From various religious points of view, the more ethically suspect this is, because "God" is supposed to know much better than we how to run the universe. What arrogance is there in suggesting how God run things?

Selfishness, camouflaged under altruism, righteous proselytizing, and charity, is the refuge of a fearful person who patronizingly believes they know what is good for everybody—even God. Altruism or charity that isn't rooted in reasonably sincere, non-controlling, egalitarian values; that doesn't emanate from someone who is, precedent to the charitable act, spiritually humble and self-responsible, is to some degree, corrupt. Altruism that conceals moral superiority, or presenting a selfish agenda as the will of God, is the rationale for imposing your will on others, and is corrupt in the extreme.[78]

The prayer ends: *"Grant me strength, as I go out from here, to do your bidding."* Notice it doesn't say: "Grant me the strength... to find a lover (or) get the promotion." In twelve-step programs there are many pointless debates on people's confusion about God's will. The debates are an intellectual stalling tactic while searching for an easier, softer way, i.e. trying to discover some gambit to justify fear and selfishness while claiming spiritual commitment. Claiming to be confused about God's will justifies any delay in making a meaningful commitment. This willful blindness enables continued unspiritual behavior, and avoids the unaddressed dishonesty and irresponsibility underneath the debates.[79]

The twelve steps allow you to become Spiritual and to maintain that. Page 15 in *Alcoholics Anonymous* advises that your job is to work and sacrifice yourself for others; page 19, your job is to have respect for others' opinions; page 77, your real purpose is to be of maximum service to others and to God; and on page 128, that giving rather than getting is the principle of your existence. These are what God's "will" is—from the literature.[80] People who are confused about God's will haven't done the requisite work to clearly understand the focus and spiritual nature of the original twelve steps. If they had done the work, there would be no confusion.

---

[78] Some may argue that when charity is offered with corrupt motives, it's still to be endorsed because it fills an immediate need, and the immediate need is seen as a greater good than the need to withhold the charity until spiritual integrity is established. It isn't that simple when you expose the consistently unexamined secondary consequences of corrupt charity: shame, dishonesty, rescuing, arrogance, implied obligation and debt, pity; and the tertiary consequence of perpetuating the social cycle of shame on both the part of the giver and the receiver. As a spiritual endeavor, charity is oftentimes risky business.

[79] For an in-depth explanation of responsibility, see *Taking Responsibility* by Nathaniel Branden, cited at an earlier footnote. Gerald May's book *Will and Spirit* has important observations about God's "will".

[80] And, of course, remember your self-assigned task is to make real your decision at Step Three—to turn your will and life over to the care of God, as you understand God. It isn't "My will for God," it's "God's will for me." There's a remarkable difference.

The Principles Aren't the Steps

There is much talk about whether people are or aren't following the principles, and what those principles are. I've referred many times to the spiritual principles inherent in the regeneration steps and embodied in the maintenance steps.

A spiritual principle is a universal truth against which we evaluate our behavior and attitude. Huston Smith writes, near the end of *The World's Religions,* that the three universal principles of the wisdom traditions are veracity, humility, and charity. Because of the inherent qualities of addictions, and how I understand the perennial philosophies regarding spiritual wisdom, I have added two more—respect for the body-temple and responsibility/obedience. These are what would be aspired to in the acquisition and demonstration of spiritual integrity. (See Appendix II.)

The steps themselves are not principles. Each step is an instruction for a task you are to complete. Principles, which would apply to all of the steps, are the foundation upon which the steps are built, and the guidelines for how you do them. For example, veracity is a principle—an essential theme upon which all the steps are constructed—which also guides the nature of your behavior while doing the steps.

Earlier, I discussed that there is an external difference in types of addictive behavior and detoxification, but underneath the behavior, addicts are generally the same.[81] The symptoms of addiction, listed in Chapter 2, are present to varying degrees in all addicts. The self-destructive acting out behaviors are different, but the symptoms are the same. I also pointed out that the first nine steps are individual tasks to be completed, and the three maintenance steps aren't ever completed—they're ongoing and interrelated. You *do* the first nine; you *are* the last three. The principles of spirituality are within each individual step, but the content of the step (the addictions fingerprint) will vary from one addict to another. The principles won't vary, which is what makes them principles.

One of the more profound things about the twelve steps is related to Huston Smith's observation about the three universal spiritual principles from the wisdom traditions: veracity, humility, and charity. The maintenance steps, by spiritual design, are virtually perfect representations of those three principles: Step Ten — Veracity; Step Eleven — Humility; Step Twelve — Charity.

In any twelve-step program, the first fundamental spiritual requirement, crucial to your ability to carry the message and eventually be recovered, is to heal yourself first. This is why the first seven steps belong to you. These have little or nothing to do with anybody or anything else. You get the first seven steps; everyone else and God get the last five.

Because of the nature of the disease of addictions, your only guarantee of "success" is to negotiate yourself through the original twelve-step steps, exactly as they're written. Each step, up to nine, eliminates various facets of the disease and

---

[81] This does not contradict the truth that the therapeutic and spiritual strategy in establishing abstinence must be very particular to each addict (identifying and responding to a person's addictions fingerprint). Each addict harbors a unique interaction of personality and addiction.

incorporates aspects of the maintenance steps and the five spiritual principles. Recall that earlier, I explained that each step, up to Step Nine, counteracts some combination of the symptoms and incorporates spiritual principles. Earlier, I suggested a three-column exercise for each step. Review that exercise now: it will help with your willingness (or lack of it).

Step Six is the third major turning point after you achieve abstinence. Overall, it's crucial that you change your worldview, and Step Six (willingness) creates the foundation for that fundamental change. The generosity and sincerity in your Step Seven prayer is only a reflection of your personal devotion and determination to focus your willpower towards willing humility.

The President and The Janitor

Once upon a time, there was an exceptionally huge, multi-national corporation that employed 675,000 people. This *mega*-corporation had investments and controlling shares in 561 smaller companies. The corporation had huge offices and warehouses in 42 countries around the world, and had gross production and sales in the tens of billions of dollars. Overall, this massive, global business conglomerate directly or indirectly governed the livelihood of over three million people, and the economy of small countries. (This company was *really* big.) The CEO/President worked out of the very largest office, on the highest floor, at the very top of the tallest business tower, at the very center of the biggest city in the world.

There was a janitor who had one lunchroom to clean in a small subsidiary company, away around on the opposite side of the world. This janitor couldn't balance a check book, and would often grumble about other workers being untidy. The janitor certainly knew nothing about running the big international mega-corporation. One day, however, the janitor sent a note to The President on the other side of the world. The janitor politely insisted that a company policy be changed—a policy that the janitor didn't know too much about, but didn't like. The janitor implied in the note that The President didn't know how to run the corporation, and things would be improved if The President did what the janitor wanted.

In personifying God, which is what I have done here, a risky venture at the best of times, "God" somehow operates the universe and I keep my life clean. I have come to enjoy sending notes to The President (by way of prayer), reporting that my lunchroom is clean and I'm grateful I have a job.

Getting Step Seven done properly demands tremendous faith and devotion. It's no place for the faint of heart.

6

Steps Eight, Nine & The Promises: Social Re-entry

The paragraph immediately after the Step Seven prayer begins, *"Now we need more action, without which we find that 'Faith without works is dead.'"*[1] Two obviously important points in this sentence are that without effort your faith is rendered meaningless, and that you are urged directly into the next step.

I wrote earlier about the profound psychological shifts within Steps Two, Six and Seven. It's these paradigm shifts, embodied in these steps, that make them the most avoided. There's yet another major shift within Step Eight, which is again about taking more responsibility, and begins a new focus to your pilgrimage—away from you and towards others.

People in twelve-step programs talk about Steps One, Three, Four, and Twelve the most. These are the easiest about which addicts can declare their "struggles"; the easiest to be dramatic about; the easiest to "act like" they've done them without having really modified anything deep inside themselves. These are the steps that fall most easily into the category of Impression Management.[2] It's rare that you'll hear anyone say anything at all substantive or insightful about Steps Two, Six, Seven, or Eight.

Step Eight is specifically about identifying the harm you've done to others, not about the harm you've done to yourself. Regardless of how deeply ensconced you are in your twelve-step subculture, you are here taken back from whence you came—the community at large.

Lingering Obsessions

In its essence, *Alcoholics Anonymous* advises that you will eventually accomplish two main things. The first is relief from the obsession to drink [act out] and the second is the elimination of insane thinking. Every addict getting recovered has these two fundamental issues to address. The successful elimination of these over the long term, indicates you're recovered.

It's written that by the time you get to Step Five, you will often have the feeling that the drink problem has been removed (if that hasn't already happened). So, if you follow instructions and are continuously abstinent, the first of the two major problems is more than likely gone by the time you get to Step Five. If an addict is still noticeably preoccupied with drinking and acting out, or has disturbing and lin-

---

[1] *Alcoholics Anonymous*, p. 76.
[2] I suspect that if the effort expended on Impression Management (any self-advertising campaign) was diverted to spiritual endeavor there'd be saints all over the place.

gering obsessions *after* Step Five, this is more than likely because of the presence of one, or a combination of, the following four circumstances.

One: Lingering obsessions, often attached to anger, may be the result of an unidentified and/or undisclosed major error in step-work. Anger almost always arises from a victim mentality, and is often directed at someone who is being blamed for the addiction or for other problems. Anger will allow obsessions and preoccupation about acting out to persist. This will occur regardless of whether or not the blamed person is taking some responsibility (which is always ill advised) for the addict's addiction. Global anger directed at Life has the same result. Regarding step work, at the minimum this means the error was impatience, a lack of thoroughness, and improper focus at Step Four. Lingering obsessions can result from irresponsibility and anger. Resolving irresponsibility and stopping blaming can't be accomplished without a painstaking and patient re-addressing of Steps One, Two, and Four.

Two: Preoccupation with acting out may also be a result of unresolved guilt and self-condemnation about the insecurities, fears, and sexual selfishness that were identified in Step Four. This sometimes occurs because of misunderstandings and unresolved conflict regarding the "I'm Sick vs. I'm Bad" debate, and the resulting confusion or ambivalence about "disease" and moral choice.

This can persist because of the negative influence of a significant authority figure that the addict is associating with; or, they've not sufficiently reduced the historical, cultural/family imposition of guilt, which is demonstrated in a deeply entrenched, and subtly concealed, self-shaming/self-castigating mindset. Disengaging from the relationship with the abusive authority figure, and/or defeating the self-destructive messages about moral turpitude, are the resolution strategy.

[These two previous situations are related to a Misalliance of Commitment, which I discuss in some detail later in this chapter.]

Three: A third reason for a lingering obsession is that the addict is still acting out in another unaddressed or not-acknowledged addiction. Acting out in secondary or secret addictions (tobacco, work, food, pornography, violence, sex, gambling, relationships, *especially* relationships, etc.) *always* destabilizes the primary abstinence. If you're preoccupied with acting out and you believe you've carefully followed the instructions, maintain your abstinence and examine yourself for other addictions that you're ignoring. For other addictions, which are often abstinence not-available[3], go back to Step One and establish abstinence in these additional addictions.

Four: Lingering obsessions are (on occasion) indicative of an undiagnosed mental health concern, of untreated trauma disorders, or indicative of some pre-addiction problem that is unaddressed The desire to act out, in these situations, *may* be an indication of the need to medicate or stabilize the mental health issues, or ad-

---

[3] Abstinence not-available addictions are discussed in Chapter 1.

dress the trauma-induced dysregulation. (See Appendix III.) Maintain your abstinence and seek some well-qualified medical or therapeutic help.

Resolving lingering obsessions and preoccupation with acting out is incredibly complex. From the addict themselves, it requires a willingness to be responsible and abstinent. It will also require a well-grounded, authentic spiritual mentor; and, very probably a well-trained and insightful therapist or counsellor.

The second of the two main problems, the insane thinking, is beginning to be addressed, and is probably greatly reduced. It should be largely resolved by the end of Step Nine. If the insane thinking is still noticeably present, the reasons will be related to the four situations I just described, and resolved similarly.

When the obsession and insane thinking are gone, your addiction becomes a non-issue. In the next chapter I discuss, from various perspectives, the philosophy and state of being recovered *"from a seemingly hopeless state of mind and body."*[4] It doesn't matter how you define the disease, with Right Effort and Right Concentration[5], the original twelve-step program enables you to become recovered.

Why Don't I Belong Here?

Many addicts and alcoholics wander without direction all their life, looking for some place to belong. Maybe, at some time in their past, they did feel they belonged in a social group like a family or a club, but lost it because of their addiction, and now carry a sense of aimless wandering.

If you are presently in a twelve-step program, there was probably some point early in your participation when you sat in a meeting and "figured out" that you were sitting in *your* chair. You felt as if you finally belonged, and some of that aimless wandering disappeared. Be that as it may, it is often short-lived, and there are any number of factors that contribute to losing it.

Whatever motivates you to attend a meeting, the attitude that you carry at the meeting, and what you encounter when you're there, will all affect your sense of belonging—just "attending" isn't enough. There are two considerations. **The first** one is your personal agenda for attending the meeting. Is it to: (1) seek God and get recovered? (2) socialize because you're lonely? (3) find a sex partner? (4) find a job? (5) tell jokes? (6) look for the person who owes you money? (7) __insert your own__. **The second** one is the group's agenda—the group's conscience that's embodied in the meeting ambiance. Is "the group" to (1) be spiritual and get recovered? (2) arrange social events? (3) create a dating club? (4) provide a venue to network for jobs? (5) organize an amateur entertainment club? (7) __insert other reason__.

Of course everyone would like everyone else to believe that they, or their group, are both in the "# 1" category, but this is rarely the case. It's rare that people, and so subsequently the groups they form, are spiritually motivated. Regardless of what the real motivation actually is, should your personal agenda not match with the group's agenda, you will neither belong, nor feel safe.

---

[4] *Alcoholics Anonymous*, p. xiii.
[5] These are two self-imposed disciplines from The Eight-Fold Noble Path of Buddhism.

This dynamic is equally applicable when you're completing any of the steps. People often describe a sense of dissatisfaction with step work. Yes, they follow the instructions, but it just doesn't seem to work. What's the reason for your step-work? Is it because: (1) you wish to be spiritual, (2) your sponsor told you to, (3) you're confused and don't know what else to do, so you'll try the steps, (4) you want to get these steps over with, (5) they're cheaper than therapy, (6) because that's where the step group is, (7) because your counsellor said... ? Usually people claim it's #1, but again this is rarely the case. If you approach each step as an extension of what you came to believe at Step Two, that seeking a higher power is the solution, the steps then make sense. Your purpose for doing them is consistent with the reason for the step's existence, and you'll feel like you belong "in" the steps. If your reason is anything other than #1, you're at odds with the original intent of the step.

In theory, meetings are to carry the message of a spiritual awakening, to enable people to recommit themselves to spiritual principles, to show other people how to access a higher power so they can recover from their addictions and attain peace of mind. Spirituality is the path out of addictions. Considering the major realignment of priorities within twelve-step meetings, the more determined you are to be truly spiritual, the fewer are the places where you will sense you belong.

At Step Eight, when the harm you caused is identified out of a spiritual agenda, there's often a peaceful loneliness, and a sense of quiet pride without any need to exonerate yourself. This arises from the loss of chaos, some reflective sadness, and the subtle separation from people who are not of a truly spiritual intent, which is often described as a sense of poignancy.[6]

So, in Step Six you got over the significant hurdle of clinging to your survival skills (character defects) and in Step Seven you saw humility as a virtue of the highest order. These changes allow you to "gain without pain", and you can now actually examine the harms you caused in a non-selfish way. *In theory*, you now possess the resources to do the work of caring generously for the welfare of others (called making amends) regardless of what they may have done to you, and with little attention paid to the advantage for yourself.

The Return

As you became more destructive in addictions, you withdrew more and more from your community, family, and friends. You then joined a twelve-step group and became a member of an organization that was, by definition, quite separate from the community at large. Initially, the process from Steps One to Seven indirectly reinforced this new isolation in an "underground" community, where the focus of the first seven steps was entirely on you.

At Step One you discovered that your addictions showed up in at least three ways: two obvious and one subtle, and one of these was a relationship addiction.

---

[6] This is partly representative of the quiet sensibility present in truly spiritual people who, although they conduct affairs in the secular community, oftentimes sense they don't belong. It's a poignant and simple consequence of being Spiritual. It's rare.

You understood that unmanageability and acting out were synonymous, and the reality of this was self-annihilation. You learned you were sick and continued abstinence was crucial for any continued success, *and* you did all of this without going outside the confines of your meetings. You might have also found a counsellor to help you with that early work and still never went outside of your twelve-step community.

At Step Two, through your experience and investigation of Steps One and Two, you came to believe that a higher power (of your own understanding) could restore you to sanity. You became involved in a social life within your fellowship. Step Three was also about you: *your* decision and *your* higher power. Once you decided to turn your will and life over to the care of God, and did the prayer with someone else (probably within the program), you were ready for Step Four. As you figured out who you were, and not what you did, you probably decided which twelve-step member you would do Step Five with.

You likely completed your Step Five with someone in "the program", and felt safe in that world. Step Six was certainly the most difficult of them all—you became completely willing, without reservation, to leave behind your survival skills. But, notwithstanding that, it too, was done inside your twelve-step world, and was about you. At Step Seven you adopted a spiritual view of humility, and you made a sincere offering of yourself to your higher power.

Thus far, up to and including Step Seven, everything has been about you, and you never had to go outside your group. You develop friendships in your twelve-step program, expand your social skills, find employment, find sex partners, find a real-estate agent, buy a car, complete the steps to Seven, and learn to dance, all within the social club of twelve-step meetings. You never have to do anything but think about yourself, *and* you can exist completely inside "the fellowship".

From the drastic isolation of addictions, you recreate yourself inside a closely-knit, small, self-protective, quasi-underground community. Now, combine this isolated social sub-structure with these personality attributes: suspicion, fear, insecurity, anger, envy, cynicism, and defensiveness. These two sets of attributes become spiritually defeating when combined with a decided tendency to blame others for any self-generated crises. Altogether, this allows addicts to create the "Evil Blue Meanies"[7]: people outside of a twelve-step program. A nasty variation of this is calling people "Normies"—people who haven't faced the grand calamities, suffering, chaos, or hard times that addicts in recovery have faced. The addict's resulting elitist, self-serving theory that "Normies don't get it" is always unspiritual. To become spiritual, addicts must force themselves to abandon these self-limiting perceptions.

Altogether, this creates a spiritual ghetto of twelve-step programs. It recreates yet another self-serving, very impoverished view of people, which cheats addicts out of the prospect of getting recovered. Twelve-step groups, being an isolated sub-culture, and the isolating/blaming personality attributes of addicts or alcoholics, create the subtle and dangerous spiritual problem of being walled off from the community at large. Step Eight, and those that follow, require community participa-

---

[7] This phrase comes from the AA pamphlet *A Member's Eye View of Alcoholics Anonymous*. I imagine that if members of twelve-step programs spent less time blaming and accusing others of not caring, and stopped using derogatory terms like "Normies", then those other people who are being blamed might be somewhat more understanding and caring.

tion—going "out" to the larger community. This is where you find those people you harmed. But it's impossible to complete the steps beyond Seven while you are isolated from the larger community by arrogance and harsh judgments.

All addicts getting recovered in a twelve-step program have hurt people who aren't involved in twelve-step programs. Neither Step Eight, nor any of the steps following it, can be completed without confronting the demons that belittle and judge harshly those people who live their lives outside of meetings. If you have subtly created the Evil Blue Meanies (unsympathetic outsiders), you have manipulated your perceptions to justify avoiding the community at large. If you create this subtle and subtly vicious mindset, when you address Step Eight, there will be an underlying resistance to self-examination. You will therefore make only a minimum effort to amend harms outside of your "program" relationships. That's stultifying and defeats the point of the process. This is certainly contrary to spiritual principles, and is one of the main reasons that so many Step Eight lists are done half-heartedly (which makes any amends self-serving).

Another resistance to thoroughness stems from the refusal to accept addictions as a self-imposed crisis. If you don't believe this is a self-imposed crisis, you'll believe it's an "other-imposed" crisis (parents, foster parents, caregivers, police, brothers, sisters, relatives, teachers, priests, bullies): "They hurt me and that's partly why I became an addict." This reasoning is patently false, but with this belief, it's easy to avoid examining what harms you did to others. They hurt you—your struggles are their fault—and they're not doing anything to help, so (therefore) they don't deserve an amend. Irresponsibility is insidious.

––––––––

Many people who weren't alcoholics were instrumental in helping the co-founders of the original twelve-step group. *Alcoholics Anonymous* might never have been written, and AA might not exist, if it wasn't for the dedicated efforts of non-alcoholics: millionaires, priests, doctors, ministers, therapists, friends, spouses… . People who will help, or are willing to help, are out there by the millions. These "outsiders" are, for the most part, potential allies. It's up to you to find the kind ones, and regardless of how anyone treats you, respond to *every*one with consideration. When addicts make spiritual ghettos of twelve-step programs, everyone gets hurt.

When it comes to making a list of people you have harmed, whether they are still alive, or using, or drunk, or empathetic, or remember, or care, or don't care, or don't like you, is immaterial. Whether they understand is irrelevant. Whether they support you is irrelevant. Blaming others, being suspicious, denigrating their character, casting aspersions on their integrity, withholding compassion, are manifestations of your lack of spiritual commitment. Harboring these attitudes makes all program work beyond Step Seven ineffective.

Identifying the harms, eventually making amends, and maintaining a spiritual attitude doesn't imply you have to be friends with everyone. You voluntarily obligated yourself to abide by spiritual principles. Creating stereotypes that "they" can't, won't, or don't care defeats the purpose of the steps, and makes for a narrow, self-righteous version of spirituality, and a self-serving vision of God, by whatever name. If you're having trouble starting Step Eight, review four things: (i) the thoroughness of how you came to believe at Step Two; (ii) your decision to commit to a spiritual *life* at Step Three; (iii) your willingness and humility from Steps Six and Seven; and, (iv) the way you view other people—especially those outside your twelve-step program. If you find yourself less than willing to create a detailed list of harms you have caused, you've somewhere missed the spiritual point and may erroneously think Step Eight is an exercise in social atonement.

Passion

If you're passionate about something, and it doesn't matter what it is— painting a picture, cooking, wind surfing—you will probably go off and do it. It won't really matter at the beginning that you make mistakes, or that you're not very good, because your passion will push you to overcome the errors of the novice. Whether you're good at it is secondary to the desire to do it.[8]

In Step Seven... *"A great turning point in our lives came when we sought for humility as something we really wanted, rather than something we* must *have."*[9] Pursuing humility, and the desire to take responsibility, are attributes that you should be attracted to at this point. Willingness to care for the wellbeing of others (a part of Step Eight), and a desire for humility, are both associated with passion and love, and are at the core of spiritual heliotropism between Steps Seven and Eight.

If an activity like playing the guitar, or an attribute like humility, is attractive and perceived as valuable, it's easy to become committed to it. Seeing willingness and humility as valuable will allow you to be eager and interested in making amends, regardless of the inconvenience or cost. However, when humility is absent or is imposed out of fear and pain, as it was in the first few steps, you'll do Step Eight grudgingly. That means you've missed the point of humble service to God by caring for others. When you're quietly passionate about Spirituality[10], and if humility is good, then making the list of harms you caused will be a pleasure.

None of us are perfect and people flail away at life, temporarily forgetting the beauty of what they've learned within the twelve steps. When this happens, it's only a matter of gently nudging yourself back to spiritual principles. Too many people fumble around unnecessarily in the steps, interpreting spirituality as a matter of inconvenience. They miss the celebration of a Spiritual life in heartfelt amends.

---

[8] Don't confuse soulfully motivated passion with overachieving, anger, obsession, or a desire to impress others. In these latter scenarios, passion is rooted in insecurity.

[9] *Twelve Steps and Twelve Traditions*, p. 75.

[10] As with all virtues that manifest attendant to passion, caution is advised. Thomas Merton points to the disruptive danger of passion arising in a soul given over to human violence. *A Thomas Merton Reader,* Revised Edition, Edited by Thomas P. McDonnell, Image Books, 1996, p. 124. The relevant passage begins: *"The delicate sincerity...."* The section of the book entitled Sincerity is worth careful examination. The introduction to that book, written by M. Scott Peck, ©1996, contains many succinct observations about contemplative people which, by analogy, would be also worthy of contemplation by any twelve-step pilgrim who is sincere about a spiritual life. Passion that arises out of anger, arrogance, self-righteousness, or viewing a twelve-step path as superlative to other spiritual endeavors, always harms people, prohibits sincerity, and denies access to God.

Any time there's a struggle in any step-related work after Step Seven—if it's hard to write the list, make the amends or pray; or you're afraid, reluctant, or bitter, these are evidence that humility has become *un*attractive. Humility is to be willingly sought. That's the essential, crucial, fundamental, basic, unremarkable, unavoidable, and unalterable premise for the rest of the program. Being quietly passionate about humility makes *every*thing easier.

Misalliance of Commitment

Many people view the steps as "tools" to get through onerous and trying times—an acquired skill-set that facilitates a smoother life. This misperception arises when the greater focus is placed on psychology rather than spirituality. What follows is based on the many references in *Alcoholics Anonymous* and *Twelve Steps and Twelve Traditions* that clearly indicate that the solution to alcoholism [addictions] is spirituality, that serenity is dependent on a relationship with a higher power, and that no human power (intellect, willpower, science, psychology) is adequate for recovery.

None of the steps are designed to allow you to resolve psychological deficits. The steps, such as they are, are for the creation of a Spiritual life, not for the reorganization of your secular life. It's far too easy to get sidetracked off of spirituality onto psychology because as you complete the steps, there's obvious derivative social improvement and some psychological benefit. These are easier to see and appreciate than the spiritual benefits. The disastrous result of viewing the steps psychologically rather than spiritually is a Misalliance of Commitment. An unregenerate ego always chooses the easier, softer way (psychology). What follows is a rather long aside to Step Eight, but it is appropriate here because of the deceptively easy misinterpretation of the purpose of this step.

Precedent to abstinence and the steps—within any active addiction—addicts, for the most part, live with the illusion of unity and competence because while they are acting out, the sense of estrangement-from-self disappears. [Bear in mind, too, there is the other equally devastating illusion that spirituality and unity are present when suffering is absent.] The purpose of acting out is to achieve unity, but in acting out, the unity is an illusion and the actual result is self-annihilation.

Remember the five spiritual principles: respectful self-care—respect for the body-temple, veracity, secular and spiritual humility, charity, and responsibility and obedience (to these principles). And, recall the purpose of *Alcoholics Anonymous*, cited on page 45—to help you find a higher power that will solve your problem. The primary intent is spiritual, but there are also psychological/social benefits which, although not the primary goal, are easier to sense and appreciate. This means that each step has one goal or purpose—spirituality, but has two results: improved spirituality *and* some minimal psychological integration. This is where the misalliance of commitment is born.

251

Step One
Purpose: To begin to establish the first, second, and fifth spiritual principles.
Spiritual Result: Establish some respectful self-care (the reduction of blatant self-destruction), and the laying of the foundation for the second and third spiritual principles. This is the beginning of responsibility and obedience.
Psychological Result: Through and in abstinence, the obvious reduction of mental chaos, self-destruction, and conflict.

Step Two
Purpose: To completely reorganize (and lay the groundwork for future reorganizations of) your perceptions regarding the disease, spiritual corruption and its resolution, and to establish a new basis for Life: the commitment to spirituality.
Spiritual Result: The recognition that willpower directed towards recovery is ineffective; an increased interest in pursuing a spiritual life; a clear perception that the steps are the structure for the addict's pilgrimage to a higher power. These results altogether lay the groundwork for the third, fourth, and fifth spiritual principles.
Psychological Result: Experiencing success through social stability in "the fellowship", the reduction of social alienation, and the development of the illusion that "the program" is the solution.

Step Three
Purpose: To commit oneself to, and to marshal and focus personal willpower towards, an all-encompassing "higher-power" oriented lifestyle, in terms of both will and life.
Spiritual Result: The development of the second, third, and fifth spiritual principles.
Psychological Result: The experience of Life organized around a twelve-step social structure, which creates regular social interaction. Life becomes gradually less chaotic. The association between "sobriety" and "hanging around in the program" is an easily drawn conclusion.

Step Four
Purpose: To create an awareness and belief that misaligned and out-of-control instincts are exacerbated and not resolved by blame, resentment, or controlling others; to understand that addictions and the related crises are all self-imposed.
Spiritual Result: The ever-deepening awareness of the second, third, and fifth spiritual principles, and an increasing desire to experience spiritual grace (which solves problems). This lays additional groundwork for the fourth and fifth spiritual principles.

Psychological Result: New "self-insight and awareness" creates a determination to focus personal willpower on secular concerns. This misdirected energy encourages the addict to strive to "control" their own character defects, through a determined effort to get along better with others.[11]

Step Five
Purpose: To take complete responsibility during accurate self-disclosure, for the self-imposed crisis and defects of character; *and* to establish a style of self-disclosure that exonerates others and assumes personal responsibility at the public level.
Spiritual Result: A deeper awareness of humility and more practice of the second, fourth, and fifth spiritual principles. The proper context for petitionary prayer is established within this step.
Psychological Result: The experience of "acceptance" at a social level, through the interaction with the person chosen, which creates an experience of less guilt and shame. This is often described as "feeling stronger and more determined" (the illusion of psychological integration).

Step Six
Purpose: To create an inner spiritual atmosphere of personal willingness to remove character defects and to abandon old survival skills, which block the action of Grace in the pursuit of spiritual humility.
Spiritual Result: An actual shift in the perception of God, and a deeper entrenchment of spiritual principles two, three, and five. Additional groundwork is laid for the fourth spiritual principle.
Psychological Result: Superficial psychological integration: "I feel better and feel less guilty," which creates the illusion of spiritual commitment because life "conditions" are improving. This entrenches the idea that the steps are an acquired skill-set of tools for improving social relationships.

Step Seven
Purpose: To realign personal values, and especially to enhance devotion to a higher power through a willing search for humility, and beginning to see this search as the highest human good.
Spiritual Result: Sensing God as an evermore present and reliable source for the courage to transform; and expanding the principle of humility to include serving God in the context of human relation-

---

[11] In Step Four, the problem *appears* to be that you resent others and don't get along with people, but that isn't the problem. The addiction underneath the conflict is the problem, but that isn't really the problem, either. It's spiritual corruption and alienation from a sincere relationship with God through the absence of spiritual principles that's the problem.

ships. There's a dramatic increase in selflessness (which is intrinsic to the third and fifth spiritual principles) and more groundwork is laid for the fourth spiritual principle.

Psychological Result: Addicts "in recovery" appear to get along better with each other. This illusion of humility exists because they have become more selective about whom they associate with, and thusly appear to have fewer defects. This is Impression Management and not authentic humility, and entrenches further the illusion that step-work makes them happier.

Step Eight

Purpose: To identify harms done (and amends required) to all others; and to take complete responsibility for these harms, which is a clear demonstration of spiritual generosity on behalf of God;

Spiritual Result: A deeper intuition around the spiritual benefits of, and freedom inherent in, taking complete responsibility, regardless of the personal cost. There's much more acceptance of the spiritual principles, especially the first, second, and fifth.

Psychological Result: The anticipation of less social and inner-personal tension and less guilt through social atonement. This is often accompanied by a subtle motivation related to expectations of being forgiven. [This plays on the often unresolved confusion of "I'm bad" vs. "I'm sick".]

Step Nine

Purpose: To repair the harms done and damage caused, and to sincerely facilitate peace in the lives of other people; to demonstrate spiritual responsibility through social responsibility.

Spiritual Result: A deep and direct experience of the five spiritual principles, and a substantially different sense of freedom, in such a way that The Promises are now appreciated as the direct result of spiritual self-discipline.

Psychological Result: A sense of getting along better with other people; feeling more confident in personal/social situations, with a sense of self-congratulation for your own hard work: "*I'm* working *my* program." "*I'm* getting rid of my character defects."

Someone using these steps as a psychological process is successful only as long as Fate doesn't present calamity in too many big or successive doses, meaning one or several big things happening they don't like or can't control. [With an addict's propensity to drama, any misadventure can be turned into a calamity of magnificent proportion.] This is evident when they say things like: "I'm mad/scared/worried about __(insert circumstance)__ , so I'll do another Step Four." Or, "I just broke up with __(insert name)__ so I'll go to more meetings. That'll make me feel better." Or, "I'm fighting with __(insert circumstance or name)__ so I'll do another Step Eight-

and-Nine." All of these, and other, similar control tactics, are the result of a Misalliance of Commitment. These indicate the steps are used as situational problem-solving techniques, which is not what they are designed for.

The steps (to Nine) are the mechanics of transformation, which isn't "problem solving". Altogether they create the foundation for the maintenance steps—the ever-present, intrinsically interdependent themes of an ongoing spiritual lifestyle.

Steps Ten, Eleven and Twelve are not separate tasks that an addict completes to fix things. They reflect the on-going ambiance of a Spiritual life. As regards a Misalliance of Commitment, they are here examined together.

> Steps Ten, Eleven, and Twelve
> *Purpose*: To maintain being recovered, and to enhance and deepen
> a sincerely spiritual lifestyle in order to entrench spiritual integrity.
> These steps involve exerting your will on behalf of God, as you
> understand God, through the maintenance steps, which embody the
> five spiritual principles.
> *Spiritual Result*: A continuing and deeper awareness of spiritual
> grace, and a gradually increasing devotion to the five spiritual
> principles. This results in: (a) more consistent serenity, regardless
> of what events occur, (b) Life ceasing to have a personal/secular
> agenda, and taking on a spiritual agenda (the difference is pro-
> found), (c) a greater devotion to God; and (d) noticeably less
> meddling in the affairs of others. The adage of attraction rather
> than promotion will have a definable presence.
> *Psychological Result*: Addicts claim to get along better with peo-
> ple, especially inside the program, and establish a network of
> friends they turn to more than their higher power. Life is experi-
> enced as less chaotic. When it's chaotic, they avoid responsibility
> and blame "Life". Providing that Fate cooperates, they establish a
> lifestyle whereby they can tolerate their character defects and ra-
> tionalize various subtle harms and disrespect to others.

Many of these psychological benefits have some value because we do live "in" the world, but psychological benefits are ancillary to the spiritual intent of the twelve steps. It is easy to see in this age of technology and self-help how psychology can easily supplant spirituality. Psychology is more visible, socially easier to appreciate, easier to get compliments on, more accessible, doesn't "oppose" culture, and the successes are easier to use as a justification for the effort expended.[12]

However, not choosing the more difficult spiritual orientation to life leaves your abstinence at risk and your integrity dependent on the cooperation of Fate. A

---

[12] Obedience to universal spiritual principles, which usually invites social suspicion, is hard to justify in our culture. Put another way: "For years I've worked very hard at living by spiritual principles. That is my main desire." Other people wonder: "All that effort and for what? You can't afford a world cruise and your car's ten years old. Why bother?" The rewards of a spiritual lifestyle are held in low regard in this culture, especially in view of what those rewards cost.

misalignment of commitment is often demonstrated in unresolved moodiness, recurring bouts of depression or complaining, anger, general discontent, disregard for the emotional rights of others, belligerent or caustic behavior, justified deceitful behavior; and the ongoing presence of character defects or socially approved addictions.

Step Eight brings into focus the nature and degree of all the harm you did to others. When humility is a desired virtue, cataloguing the damage you did to everyone is an exercise in generosity, not an attempt to scramble for personal salvation. This is especially important when examining the very serious harms where the amends may place you in poverty or at legal risk. You may balk at including these in any detail on your Step Eight list, in which case I refer you to the paragraph that begins: *"Although these reparations... ."*[13]

The natural outcomes of devotion are willingness, love of spirituality [God], and a desire for humility. Only these can resolve the insecurity and reluctance about making amends where you are at risk of social sanctions, financial hardship, or long-term inconvenience.

Political arguments notwithstanding, rumor has it that Yeshua of Nazareth taught primarily two things: people should love God above all others (a process that begins in Step Two and comes to fruition in Step Eleven); and people should do unto others as they would have done unto themselves. How to "do unto others" (responsible, kind, charitable, etc.) is what's learned in the first nine steps and practiced and strengthened in Steps Ten, Eleven, and Twelve. In theory, realizing these two spiritual axioms are one end result of the transformation you experience in doing the steps.[14] This includes accepting responsibility and making amends for the harms you have done, with little consideration for the consequences to yourself, without keeping a secret scorecard of the wrongs done to you by others.

Humility is the premier prerequisite to being able to clearly and accurately identify what harm you've done. Without humility being attractive, you'll be caught up in various kinds of selfish justification that permits a half-hearted or begrudging effort here. Without humility as the primary, underlying principle at Step Eight, you'll not be able to see clearly what harm you've done. You will not, therefore, be able to clear up the wreckage of your past.[15]

The New Mandate

Here is the twelve-step spiritual pilgrim's new life mandate: *"Learning how to live in the greatest peace, partnership, and brotherhood with* all *men and women, of whatever description, is a moving and fascinating adventure."*[16] This sentence

---

[13] *Alcoholics Anonymous*, p. 79.

[14] As I've said before, I'm not advocating for Christian hegemony. The invisible spiritual philosophies; the underlying mysticism that informs any of the cultural religions, has equally subtle and beautiful applications within these steps.

[15] Without humility in Step Eight, the amends required will be inaccurate, or inadequate and insincere. To step for a moment into Step Nine, that will leave the amends themselves in spiritual misalliance, and a subtle sense of unfinished discomfort will remain after the amend. This contributes greatly to the need to repeat all the steps again, and again, and again...

[16] *Twelve Steps and Twelve Traditions*, p. 77, emphasis added.

outlines the task at hand, and defines the new focus for your behavior in all relation-ships—getting along graciously with *every*one. This is required because *"...defective relations with other human beings have nearly always been the immediate cause of our woes, including our alcoholism,* [and] *no field of investigation could yield more satisfying and valuable rewards than this one."*[17] Defective relations with others is self-generated, and is both a significant justification (through blaming and complain-ing) to act out, and a significant contributor to the entrenchment of addictions. If, in the maintenance steps, you are to become responsible and charitable (Steps Ten and Twelve), it follows that you must learn to be forever considerate of others. It is here, with your ever-deepening commitment to being responsible, that you begin to create that *"moving and fascinating adventure"* with others.

The twelve steps are presented in the only effective sequence that would enable an addict to reduce alienation from God. The first steps begin with creating new perceptions and altering the addict's interior life. This is an inner integration of disparate elements of awareness, and the resolution of dilemmas and distress. What-ever is corrupt in the interior life of an addict (or in anyone for that matter) manifests itself metaphorically in social distress and conflict. After establishing some inner harmony in the early steps, through the inculcation of spiritual principles, the later steps shift to resolving the disharmony in external life with spiritual behavior. With-out first largely resolving inner conflict, all attempts to resolve outer conflict are efforts in Impression Management, and layered over unaddressed inner corruption.

That's the "why" of working on yourself and your commitment to a higher power first. Any reorganization or re-sequencing of the steps, or combining them in a way other than they are exactly laid out, or recasting their content, or forcing a rela-tionship with a higher power through pious behavior or dramatic devotion, may look good, but will eventually prove ineffective.[18]

Prior to Step Eight you are (supposed to) have largely resolved your inner bewilderment, and have come to rely on your higher power. Only then are you ready to go away from "you" towards "others". Should you have created the Evil Blue Meanies, and done nothing to resolve that abusive stereotyping, it will be impossible for you to sincerely approach Step Eight—after all, if all those outsiders are mean and don't care, why should you make a sincere effort?

The primary goal of all twelve-step work is to establish an authentic and meaningful relationship with a higher power, and subsequent to that, a spiritual rela-

---

[17] *Twelve Steps and Twelve Traditions*, p. 80. This may appear to be at odds with several previous asser-tions that addictions aren't caused by abuse. This passage refers specifically to "defective relations with others", not to being abused. At Step Four it was clearly identified that alcoholics are responsible for their own conflict and resentments. In all defective relations, the addict is responsible. If, then, defective rela-tions cause alcoholism, and addicts are responsible for the defective relations, then "addicts" are causing their own alcoholism because they are never innocent of responsibility. The addict always contributes to defective relations, and therein lies the place of complete personal responsibility—for the defective rela-tions *and* all subsequent consequences. This is a self-imposed crisis.

[18] Re: Dramatic Devotion... For alcoholics and addicts, this is why short-term conflict-resolution strate-gies (like anger management courses and weekend-long conflict-reduction workshops) never offer more than very temporary relief, and do more harm than good: they entrench a need for a dramatic catharsis. The drama and adrenaline of the intensive workshop is addictive and falsely reassuring. Their popularity is evidence of their addictive nature and the quick-fix, disposable mindset of our culture. Have no doubt about the workshop junkies' vicious, vehemently denied, deep sense of failure.

tionship with *every*one else. Addicts are clearly told that henceforth, the general purpose is *"...that we may develop the best possible relations with every human being
we know."*[19] Obviously *"every human being"* is all-inclusive. There is no exception
for people whom you believe have hurt you badly (or other nasty scoundrels) and
have thereby meritoriously earned your scorn and disapproval.

The wholesale disregard of this requirements is demonstrated in racist and
sexist jokes, gossiping, breaking anonymity, being dismayed at the good fortune of
others, being pleased at the misfortune of people you don't like, practical jokes, teasing, and patronizing character assassination. These behaviors are done by people
who are working "their" program, but not working *the* program

How am I doing? I'm not sure.

Addiction is a disease of isolation. Addicts isolate from others and especially from themselves. Because of fear and shame, they don't have any insightful
way of judging how well they're doing. Having minimal and largely inaccurate insight about the truth of what is actually going on in their life results in significantly
skewed self-perceptions. They are generally afraid of the truth, confused, and bewildered. Until they are abstinent from *all* addictions, and are comfortable with sincere
spirituality, they have no reliable system of self-evaluation.

Defective relations with others always runs parallel to their inability to get
along with themselves. All of this requires an addict to stay out of relationships emotionally, but to seek them physically for the mood-altering experiences of romance,
sex, chaos, conflict, or receiving and dispensing all manner of self-righteous advice
or abuse. The relationship eventually fails, or remains in some form of habitual tension and deal-making. The lonely result is that no one ever really gets to know
addicts, and they fail to know themselves. When anyone asks them how they are
doing at a meaningful level, it's generally a guessing game. Until you live without
addictions, or at the minimum until you've got several years of solid abstinence and
are well along in spiritual self-discipline, you are a poor judge of how well you're
doing.

While sorting all this out, it doesn't mean that you can't create a new life, or
you can't have a relationship or be happy. It means you're a newcomer for a very
long time. The disease requires it. Do not think that a few years of sobriety and hanging around meetings for a while leaves you capable of accurate self-evaluation.

For an addict to achieve reasonable psychological-emotional health—the
ability to be respectfully assertive, and to become established in a responsible and
ethical lifestyle, takes *at least* five years of continuous abstinence, *including* at least
three years in well-conducted, weekly therapy, all the while working at understanding and completing the steps.[20] For people with additional, more complicated non-
addictions issues, having ten years of abstinence and spiritual work and six or seven

[19] *Twelve Steps and Twelve Traditions*, p. 77.
[20] Charles Whitfield, in his book *Co-dependence, Healing the Human Condition,* Health Communications
Inc., 1991, indicates that five years, and sometimes as much as eight years, of work is required to recreate
yourself out of codependence and addictions. "Work" implies much more than twelve-step participation,
and any therapy has to be with a non-addicted therapist who understands addictions.

years of devoted work in therapy is not uncommon.

Independent of psychological health, to attain true spiritual integrity beyond some arbitrary, self-defined standard of "good enough" requires probably ten years of abstinence after completing the first nine steps, and *regular, ongoing*, devoted spiritual prayer and meditation, including regular counsel from a bona fide spiritual advisor. This means someone far more insightful about spiritual defiance than the run-of-the-mill, old-timer sponsor. At the outset it's daunting, but it's worth it. Really.

Amends To Yourself?

Some people defend the idea it's acceptable to put yourself on your Step Eight list. From a spiritual perspective, if you do, you've missed the point of your own transformation. As I mentioned earlier, between Steps Seven and Eight there's a major reorientation—the focus changes.

When you look at the steps from a global perspective, you got the first seven. They're yours. It was during these steps you were to have made whatever "amends" to yourself you needed to make. The first seven steps allow you to fix whatever harm you did to yourself through the following actions: quitting your addictions, becoming abstinent, ceasing to hurt yourself through acting out, caring for yourself by developing self-respect, attaining gentle self-insight rather than caustic self-judgment, recovering physical health, ceasing to blame yourself for being stupid or weak-willed, developing and maintaining a relationship with a higher power, distancing yourself from people who hurt you, and associating with those who are respectful towards you. All of this is "making amends" to yourself, and should have been done by the time you get to Step Eight. Whatever amends that you owed to yourself should have been attended to by this time.

After Step Seven, you are no longer the primary focus of step work; other people are. Humility becomes active and now shows itself as behaviors of kindness, respect, caring, and responsibility *to others*. The direction of transformation changes from proper self-care and self-love (Steps One to Seven) to proper spiritual love for others and for God (Steps Eight to Twelve).

Including yourself on the list implies that you missed some aspect of self-care in the first seven steps, or are working with a misalliance of commitment. Any misalliance of commitment will act directly against the shift away from self and towards others and love of a higher power. Because the last five steps are other-oriented, putting yourself on your Step Eight list is clear evidence of misunderstanding what's to have transpired before you got to Step Eight, and would turn a selfless program into a selfish program.[21]

Some amends require that addicts put themselves into hardship: paying large bills, owning up to some crime, etc. Putting yourself on the list will create a conflict with the instructions contained in the paragraph that begins, *"Although these*

---

[21] By doing Steps Eight to Twelve in an other-oriented manner, the way they are intended, you indirectly make amends to yourself by working spiritually to reintegrate yourself into the community. This counteracts the harm of isolation and eliminates social dislocation.

reparations... ," which includes this phrase: *"...no matter what the personal conse-quences may be."*[22] If you believe you are to put yourself on your Step Eight list, you will naturally follow with the idea that you can't make amends "to yourself" if you harm yourself by putting yourself into hardship when making amends. By putting yourself on the list, you create what might be referred to as a contradiction of intent:

- Step Eight *intends* that you identify what amends to others are required, regardless of the consequences to yourself, which necessarily requires that you may have to cause hardship to yourself; but,
- If you include yourself at Step Eight, you cannot then harm yourself further, so you won't make amends where that will detract from your personal "comforts" (cause hardship).

If you create this contradiction of intent by placing yourself on the Step Eight list, whenever an amend causes yourself hardship, you'll always renege on the side of selfishness and your amends to others will be inadequate or entirely avoided.

It is authentic spirituality when someone is capable of depriving themselves of comfort and shiny things, and *willing* to place themselves in awkward circum-stances, in order to care for the wellbeing of others; others they may not know well, or care for, or when there is decidedly no advantage for themselves. Being spiritual necessarily requires that you put yourself through hard times.

There is much to gain from reflection about yourself—which is the focus of all that you have been doing up to Step Seven. The literature recognizes the *"...emotional harm we have done ourselves"*[23] might be great, but that *"making res-titution to others is paramount* [of overriding importance]."[24] The book establishes the priorities. In the chapter on Step Eight, there's no instruction or inference that you are to put your name on this list. You're already well on the way to developing the best possible relationship with yourself that you can. The goal here is to develop the best possible relations with every *other* human being.

"We are there to sweep off our side of the street..." "[Their] *faults are not discussed. We stick to our own."*[25]

Reflect on the depth and the breadth of *"...the best possible relation with every human being that you know."* It's all encompassing, and it can be frightening. It's an exercise in patience, determination, and thoroughness, and it's impossible to be spiritual while ignoring this instruction. And (almost finally), to be spiritually successful in negotiating through Step Eight three things are essential: (1) time: be patient with your own painstaking effort; (2) having a spiritual advisor who is very firmly grounded in spiritual responsibility; and, (3) having a higher power: be well-established in your relationship with one.

You learned and accepted that humility is good (Step Seven) and your char-

---

[22] *Alcoholics Anonymous*, p. 79.
[23] Ibid., p.79.
[24] Ibid., p 80.
[25] Ibid., p.77, 78.

acter defects of sloth[26] and fear have been regularly challenged by prayer, so the task of making a detailed list is, in fact, something you [should] enjoy. You're now *will-ingly* pursuing spirituality. It's of questionable benefit to anyone if this is not a labor of love. Being cheerfully compliant is essential to this task. Should you become discouraged, review Steps Six and Seven.

While making the list of harms done, addicts and alcoholics are crafty at hanging on to grievances. *"To escape looking at the wrongs we have done another, we resentfully focus on the wrong* [they have] *done to us."*[27] Your ego will remind you of the presumed transgressions of others as often as it can. Lingering over the harms you perceive that others did to you, whether real or imagined, results in:

- withholding thoroughness in identifying what harm you did to others. Step Eight will then be incomplete (which will render Step Nine ineffective); and,
- being irresponsible, where you avoid examining your own conduct and won't admit truths about yourself. This keeps your inner life in turmoil, and perpetuates external conflict.

Only through humility can you focus on personal responsibility; only that allows you to abandon grievances. Doing this is completely unselfish behavior. Your fellow human beings benefit, and being completely responsible is evidence of your devotion to your higher power. Anything less than a willing generosity of spirit towards those you have harmed results in superficial amends (which are probably worse than none at all—they add insult to injury).

Contracts & Reciprocity, Forgiveness & Covenants

Contracts, Reciprocity, Forgiveness, and Covenants are the operating principles that inform the paradigms of relationships. Altogether, they carry a very subtle spider's web of meanings and obligations. They each need to be closely examined in order to bring integrity and clarity to relationships. This is intricate, so go slow.

When a person forgives someone, apparently sincerely, people usually view this as evidence of spiritual soundness, i.e. forgiving someone for some crime or misdemeanor is "good". Forgiveness, in itself, is commonly understood to be a spiritual "last step" in conflict resolution, and certainly with a mindset of righteous judgment, it is. However, should the transgressor reappear after some absence, or should anyone discuss it or some other similar offense, it often follows that the memories are dragged out, the pain dredged up, the grievance aired yet again, and the moral high-ground claimed once more. This is contrary to the aggrieved person's claim of having forgiven the offender. In reliving the offense, the addict (who carries

---

[26] When undertaking such demanding spiritual endeavor as the original twelve steps, it's worthy to note an important definition of sloth. Sloth [*acedia*] means much more than generic laziness. *"For Dante, acedia was a central spiritual failure. It was the failure to be sufficiently active in the pursuit of The Recognized Good. It was to acknowledge Good, but without fervor."* From How To Read Dante, by John Ciardi, *The Divine Comedy*, by *Dante Alighieri*, translated by John Ciardi, New American Library, 2003, p. xiii.
[27] *Twelve Steps and Twelve Traditions*, p. 78.

the grudge) goes through the cycle again: offense, victimization, accusation, debt-obligation, benevolence, forgiveness, righteous indifference.

Outside of socially legislated culpability or contracted mercenary endeavor, the politics and impression management around forgiveness, the misunderstanding of its spiritual application, and the self-serving shortsightedness in viewing it as an ultimate good, are evidence of how unwilling people are to be truly spiritual.

Forgiveness is the saving grace in relationships with a higher power; however, in secular terms, it does nothing to address the underlying spiritual corruption in people who find it necessary to offer or seek forgiveness. If you become well-established in spiritual integrity, it's possible to render forgiveness unnecessary. What I'm about to offer is a perception of forgiveness, and an aspect of acceptance, that allows for Grace in the face of egregious personal calamity.

I am proposing that forgiveness is a second-best solution to human conflict. There's a more fulfilling alternative to aspire to. For this to make any sense it is dependent upon understanding that:

- Addiction is a self-imposed crisis.
- Acceptance of our fallibility (our humanness) is something to strive for, which prohibits all mean-spirited judgments.
- Whenever there's conflict, you are completely responsible for your participation in it. If you're involved, to *any* degree, you are completely responsible for the conflict.
- A spiritual objective defined by a higher power is preferred to a spiritual objective defined by you or your peer group.
- The five spiritual principles are beyond personalities and preferences. They are to be striven for, and are only of value if you adhere to them when it's inconvenient.
- Because something is difficult to understand, hard to achieve, or stands contrary to popular opinion, does not detract from its truth or worth. *"Some of us tried to hold on to our old ideas..."*

How involved anyone is in spiritual pursuits—their level of devotion, is always a matter of choice. Regardless of your position on the spectrum from theism to atheism, you assign your own position, *and* it's not something you can exempt yourself from. That's the ubiquitous and unique nature of spirituality—everyone believes something about it. Even atheism might be seen as participation in spirituality, in that an atheist must work at maintaining proof of the non-existence of deity, probably as much as the theist works at belief. Not everyone believes *in* God, but everyone believes something *about* God.

Some type of connection exists, *a priori,* between a person and the broad concept of Spiritual Deity. There's no exemption from having some value about spirituality. It's the same with sexuality and love. On the spectrum from sex is dirty/evil to sex is wonderful/spiritual, or that love is or isn't worth it, everyone has values and opinions.[28] Human nature requires that people have some opinion about God, Love, and Sex. This no-choice/obligatory aspect to the relationship between people and a deity mandates the very unique dynamic of it being a covenant. And, it's within the nature of "covenant" that lies the dynamic of forgiveness. Between people, however, their interactions are…

Relationship Contracts

All relationships between people, even the "strangers" you pass on the street or sit beside on the bus, are agreed-to deals of one sort or another. Every human relationship has a set of expectations attached to it: they are contracts, *not* covenants. Generally, the more significant the relationship, the greater are the overt and covert expectations. These expectations are the fine-print of the contract.

In human relationships, it's fairly assumed that, because a person participates voluntarily, each person is capable of doing what they imply they can do because they are "participating". Take the traditional Western view of marriage: fidelity, honesty, compassion, affection, care, support, etc.—that's "the deal". Your relationship with your best friend has many different expectations attached to it because of the designation "best friend". In a restaurant, you reasonably expect the other patrons to follow the restaurant-patron guidelines. There are implied or declared expectations in *all* human relationships. Generally, each person expects other people to deliver what's declared or implied in the relationship agreement. What arises when a person doesn't voluntarily follow the "best friend rules", the "marriage rules", the "theater-patron rules", the "house-guest rules", is the notion of breach of contract—someone not living up to their end of the deal.

When one person doesn't live up to, or fails to maintain, the conditions of the agreement, the aggrieved party thinks: "Hey, that's not right! Girlfriends or boyfriends, or commuter-train passengers, or whomever, aren't supposed to __(insert transgression)__." The aggrieved person in the relationship has convicted the "offender" of breaching the deal. This is immediately followed by a sense of entitlement. A debt has been created in the mind of the person who has decided they've been hurt. There's some subtle expectation of amends, restitution, apologies, or contriteness from the offender for the breach of the relationship rules. *It's the nature of all unregenerate human relationships that, declared or implied, expectations and rules are in play, and when the rules are broken, someone owes.*

To make it more confusing, everyone has subtly different rules, and the size of the debt owed "depends". Someone named A. promises to do something. They forget (creating a level of debt), or they deliberately change their mind without telling the other person (an increased level of debt: people "owe" more for rudeness than forgetfulness). Person A. didn't live up to the rules. Partner B. now expects one "I'm Sorry" and an act of contrition: A. has to do the dishes, or give them sex, or buy lunch. For the same offense, a different partner, C., might say, "Okay, we'll forget about it this time, but don't let it happen again." This is conditional forgiveness: a

---

[28] This is partly why so many problems related to relationships and Life manifest in expressions of sexuality and "religion", even when the problems don't originate there.

veiled threat and a suspended sentence that depends upon future good conduct (pro-bation). And another different partner, D., might expect a very sincere promise from A. that they'll *never, never ever* do it again, and A. will have to pay a token financial penalty: flowers, or theater tickets and dinner, or a summer home in the Caribbean.

This is the courtroom relationship. I know of situations where people kept written diaries of their partner's offenses, like a judge's notebook. A relationship, in these circumstances, isn't graceful or kind. It's based on reward and punishment, and whoever has the best memory (or takes the most detailed notes) wins. These con-tracts and have little to do with love.[29]

Expectations of Perfection

Relationship rules, declared or implied, cause no end of problems, espe-cially because of the way they lend themselves to the expectation of perfect behavior. Perfection in this context doesn't mean being a perfect person, it means doing *exactly* what you agreed to do, and the operative word here is *agree*. Whether the rules are particular to an individual or implied by social custom, you can tell when one person isn't following them, meaning abiding by the contract they said (or implied) they would. The person who didn't breach the contract (the rules and expec-tations), announces the infraction in a morally superior tone:

"You didn't phone. When you're late you're *supposed* to phone."

"*You* left the lid off the toothpaste."

"You're masturbating! When *I'm* in a committed relationship..."

These condemnations are about infractions of the clauses of the contract, i.e. Page Three, Paragraph F, subparagraph (ii): Changing Plans and Notification Thereof: We the undersigned, agree... . Or: Page Four, Paragraph J, subparagraph (iv): Parameters of Bathroom Etiquette and Moral Turpitude. Be it understood... .

Of course the responses from the offender are variously: "Oh, ya? Nobody told me." Or, "Who said so?" Or, "I didn't agree to that." The arguments that ensue are about the offender not adhering to "the rules" of the relationship contract for which they volunteered; rules which are contained in the expectations of the ag-grieved party. One person reasonably expected (trusted) the contract would go ahead according to their own rules, and when it didn't, they presumed they were *owed* something. In business, when someone breaks a contract, they owe. In roman-tic/sexual relationships, friendships, etc., the same paradigm of debt and obligation is activated when a rule gets broken.[30] All human relationships, regardless of their con-text, are styled on the basic premise of contracts: "I agree to do __*this*__ and you agree to do __*that*__."[31]

---

[29] I will explore this in more detail in *Facets of Personal Transformation*.

[30] In relationships of coercion (prisoners, hostages, sometimes spouses and children), the nature of the relationship establishes that ordinary rules of respect-commitment-courtesy don't apply. Regarding war, the Geneva Convention naively and foolishly tried to add a veneer of sophistication to the vicious brutality of war by assigning rules to murder and violence. Since prisoners and hostages aren't voluntary relation-ships in the usual sense, the usual rules don't apply, but there are still rules there, too.

[31] As regards an unregenerate ego: Poor relationship choices and willful blindness are always self-serving. Out of fear-driven reaction, desperate attempts to avoid loneliness, acting out in relationship addictions, or a need to recreate conflict, people are irresponsible about what they expect from whomever they get into

Reciprocity

In addition to a relationship being voluntary *and* contractual, people carry expectations of reciprocity. They may not contribute equal property, but within the contract (relationship), and especially in romantic, committed relationships, they expect (oftentimes foolishly expect) reciprocity of effort. There's no end to the arguing that goes on about this.

You can tell right away when reciprocity doesn't happen. One half of the agreement says to the other half of the agreement, and always with a tone of indignation or moral superiority: "You're not trying as hard as I am." Two obvious examples are: "I work all day, and I do the _insert extra effort_ and you don't even _insert examples of laziness_." And: "I'm going to therapy to save this relationship and you're not. I'm trying harder than you!" These identify the grievance of not following the rule of Reciprocity of Effort.

Thus far, there are these considerations: All human relationships are voluntary, with both declared and implied rules and expectations, which places them in the category of contracts. Failing to hold up "your end" of the deal activates debt and obligation. Reciprocity of Effort is expected, and is a source of chronic complaint.

Forgiveness

Forgive: verb 1. To excuse for a fault or an offense; pardon. 2. To renounce anger or resentment against. 3. To absolve from payment (of a debt, for example).[32]

To forgive someone means to give up some entitlement to personal compensation: grant others relief by abandoning any claim to recompense for some grievance/injury. In any transaction between people that's commonly called forgiveness, there are unspiritual preconditions that exist that are seldom, if ever, examined.

Guess Who's Late For Dinner?

You're invited to a dinner party. Of the dozen people there, you're acquainted with the host, and couple of the people are your friends. The others are strangers. You're noticeably late. The group delays dinner, waiting for you. When you arrive, there's some teasing about your being late. After dinner, the host, whom you've met only once before, approaches you and says quietly and seriously: "I know you said you had to work later than usual and were caught in traffic. I feel hurt that you didn't arrive on time or maybe didn't give my dinner party more of a priority. You could have at least phoned. I feel hurt by what you did, but I want you to know I forgive you."

---

relationships with, and are often willfully blind to the obvious. People are never innocent in the consequences of poor choices.

[32] Edited excerpt from *The American Heritage® Dictionary of the English Language, Third Edition,* © 1996, Houghton Mifflin Company. Electronic version.

You would probably have some reaction of indignance or affront for being forgiven for being late to a dinner party. Yet you were late, you didn't phone, the host did feel hurt, some people felt inconvenienced/annoyed (which was evident in the teasing), and the host forgave you. According to a strict definition of forgiveness, being forgiven by the host was appropriate to the circumstances, but it didn't feel right. Why is it so many people defend forgiveness and applaud its use in conflict resolution when, upon closer examination, they are often insulted by the temerity of anyone who forgives them?

The Forgiveness Transaction

To forgive someone indicates that in between the offense and the act of forgiveness, the offended person assumed they were entitled to claim a debt because the offender didn't try as hard as they should have, or they broke a rule. The injured person had a right, therefore, to blame the transgressor for their own unhappiness. That period of time between the commission of the offense and the act of forgiving, be it minutes, days, or years, was occupied with spiritual sloth and blaming: "You were late, had an affair, kicked the dog, didn't take your shoes off... and therefore I now feel... insulted, hurt, sad, angry, scared. You caused me... pain, hardship, trouble, more work. Now I'm *entitled* to get a gift, receive an apology, be offered contriteness from you because you did that bad thing to me. But it's okay... I forgive you." The subtext is: I forgive your debt (to me) for doing that bad thing (to me).

The magnitude of the crime has no bearing on this. Someone tells vicious lies and you're fired from your job, or someone steals the carrots from your garden: there was a transgression, an offender, an injured party, and the creation of a debt owed to you. You forgive the debt. The theme is identical to being late for the party.

Forgiveness is usually only thought of in relation to big transgressions, but if it's a principle of good conduct, it should apply to all offenses regardless of the circumstances. For the most part, people think it's spiritually sophisticated to forgive for big offenses, but almost invariably become indignant when forgiven for the little ones. In the big calamity people think forgiveness is nice, and in the small annoyance, people think it's pretentious. Apparently, we're not supposed to accept big offenses as a matter of course, we have to forgive for those; yet we're supposed to accept the tiny offenses, and be "above" forgiveness for them.

Who decides which crimes require, or which are exempt from, forgiveness? Our parents? The police constable? The minister? The bank manager? The therapist? The priest? Who decides? Of course, it's the aggrieved person who always decides what's forgivable and what isn't. Therein lies one major corruption when forgiveness is seen as the "spiritual" final step in conflict resolution. It's not uncommon to hear: "I'll never forgive them. Never!" And, neither is it uncommon to hear: "Oh, that's fine; don't worry, I'll get over it. But don't let it happen again." Both responses are entirely self-serving, based on the perceptions of the forgiver. (And never forget that receiving some token of regret from the offender like sex or movie tickets is always appreciated.)

If forgiveness is a principle, it can't be a convenience. For spiritual integrity, people must choose to either forgive for every harm, regardless of how slight and then appear pretentious, or to give up forgiving anyone, regardless of how horrific the offense. This is no small challenge—you are in the deep end of the spiritual pool here.

Regarding the five spiritual principles, the maintenance steps, and life in general: People are spiritually handicapped in that life can never be lived, and love can never be offered, perfectly. Knowing this full well, people still choose to deny their limitations and their humanness when they think that mistakes are optional. They're not. Forgiveness implies some particular "bad" thing shouldn't have happened (to you). Yet, being human requires bad things happen. If we know this, why would we condemn someone and expect they owe us something for being human?

As I offer this information, I know that it's risky to personify God. Sages throughout the centuries have observed that as soon as we create icons or personify God, regardless of the image we've created, it isn't "God". Truly, God is beyond anything we can conceive. However, being the mere humans that we are, it's necessary to speak about God in recognizable, human terms. Look at the moon, but do not mistake the image for the thing. Feel love in your heart, but know that it isn't love— it is the sensation-image of love.

Mystics, some monks, a very few writers and poets, and wiser spiritual pilgrims, know that we can never tell of Love *or* God. There is only metaphor and felt experience. Symbols are easily confusing and barely adequate; signs are pitfalls, and all words can offer are inadequate metaphors to tell of the transformation out of the spider's web of addictions into spirituality. Do not mistake my "picture" of spirituality for spirituality.[33]

Covenants

As I mentioned earlier: What requires that a relationship between a person and a deity (of whatever description) be completely different from *all* other relationships is the relationship is *not* voluntary. The relationship is mandated by the nature of our soul, and no one's exempt. Whether people affirm or refute the existence of an ever-present energy that informs the universe; whether they call *It* God, call *It* something else, or insist nothing is God—however they arrive at whatever their beliefs are, the intrinsic nature of people requires they have some style of relationship relative to *That Which Art.*

Atheism, in its argument for the proof of the non-existence of *That Which Art*, is still a relationship relative to it. Everyone has, in some context, a belief related to their perceptions of *Its* nature, or *Its* non-nature. Similarly, everyone has a belief or an opinion about sex. People can't not have an opinion because of the intrinsic nature of sex. The relationship with *That Which Art* is not voluntary, and so the usual rules of human relationships—expectations and reciprocity—don't apply. Human relationships are "voluntary" and that requires they be contracts. Any relationship that isn't voluntary, like the one with "God", can never be a contract; it's a covenant.

In what might be called old-fashioned, arranged marriages (i.e. not voluntary), it was common for the officiating authority to say something like: "In this covenant of marriage between this man and this woman, entered into before God...". Marriages were considered more as covenants than contracts. As marriages made the transition from local-custom pre-arranged public declarations in small communities, to religious rituals where self-appointed religious officials wanted to generate revenue and legislate sexual conduct, to free-choice agreements in politically complex industrial cultures, our view of them shifted from covenants to contracts.

This distinction is important. The rules and expectations for contracts are very different than for covenants, and these aren't interchangeable. When the rules for contracts (human relationships) are applied to covenants (relationships with a higher power), or vice versa, regardless of the social structure out of which the conception of God arises, they are doomed to inefficiency. The covenant with a higher power requires a completely different style of commitment and obligation than contract relationships between people. People enter into covenants with God and contracts with each other. (There are only two exceptions to the contracts-rule, which I'll mention in the next section.)

In a spiritual covenant with "God", your responsibility is to be the person you are, and you're required to do nothing but be human (which requires making mistakes). *From a Western perspective*, if Love is the closest word to describe the action of a deity towards people, your higher power loves you *because* of your shortcomings and humanness, whereas the opposite is true for people: we love each other *despite* our shortcomings. This is because "God" embraces our humanness, and people for the most part reject their humanness by expecting perfection. In relationships with a higher power, the unalterable and required *in*equality makes reciprocity impossible. Forgiveness is crucial in covenants and dangerous in contracts.

The Idea of Debt

In human relationships, if you don't harm others, invade their life to their detriment, or take anything from them, or if you live up to your end of whatever the deal is, you don't owe them anything. In the spiritual realm, it's different. People can't harm God, or ever take anything from God, and can't *not* live up to their end of the deal because their end of the deal is to be human. And in truth, "God" being what God is, by definition people cannot cast aspersions on God, but can (and do) cast aspersions on other people and their beliefs about God. In the vernacular, God isn't offended by different beliefs; people are. So, because people can't hurt or harm God, they're never indebted to God in the usual manner of human relationships.

Regarding people: We are what we are. People are their "good" parts and their "bad" parts. Everything that "I" am is me. In a general, symbolic interpretation, in the Eastern traditions, everything *is* God. In the Western traditions, everything *belongs* to God, and God is everywhere or *in* everything. In either perspective, since everything belongs to God or everything is God, then (from within the context of

---

[33] I expand upon signs and symbols later.

human interpretation), human shortcomings and harms caused are a part of God just as much as love or compassion are.

Calamity and misadventure are random. Death is inevitable. Pain is required. Suffering is optional. God cannot be indebted to people for their misfortune because people are the authors of their own misfortune. God never "owes". And, people cannot harm God, so people can never be indebted to God. There can never be indebtedness, either way, in true covenants.[34]

A general, intellectual perception of "God" holds the belief that God is ubiquitous and beyond comprehension, with the common implication being that God is beyond imperfection (but that would also make God beyond perfection, too). However, as regards people, because of the human limitations inherent in our being, imperfections are a given. This requires that the best we can conceive of is that God (by whatever name) must be beneficent and forgiving. Otherwise, all people would be forever condemned because we are forever making mistakes. This, and the unequal and non-voluntary relationship with God, requires it be a covenant.

An inadequate metaphor might be: An infant is attempting to drink juice from a glass. The infant spills the juice, drops the glass, and it breaks. The child has completely "failed" at the complicated task of drinking from a glass: juice spilled, glass broke, and the child never tasted any of it. Here, being inept is a condition of existence, not a moral deficit. A loving parent accepts this lack of perfection as a matter of course, is beneficent, and doesn't even think about "forgiving" the infant. The parent isn't hurt. The infant doesn't owe anything. In an uncommon perspective of this, forgiveness is the exact nature of the relationship. From the parents perspective, forgiveness is the context that embodies the entire relationship.

Consider the circumstance where you enter into an association with someone who is obviously mentally challenged. Whatever the relationship is, the usual expectations of relationships are automatically suspended. The mentally challenged person is incapable of meeting the usual standards of relationship. Many tasks will be beyond their capabilities to do well, or even to do at all, so there's a kindness of spirit in participating in their life, in taking pleasure in the fact that whatever they do is perfect and wonderful. That they can't do something well, or because they don't reciprocate with the correct amount of effort, is of no account.

These two examples of human relationships are thematic examples of the two exceptions to the contracts rule. Automatically forgiving *is* the "one way" transaction. In temporal terms (which are inadequate), humans fail miserably at being spiritual, but are perfect at being spiritual infants.[35] Forgiveness from God isn't a considered action that God does (like in a contract); it *is* what God *is* in the covenant.

In the spiritual realm, a higher power holds no IOUs. Forgiveness *is* the relationship, not a part of it. In secular terms, you cannot separate forgiveness from a

---

[34] Expressing gratitude in prayer is for the existing covenant with God. If the spiritual relationship were a contract, rather than a covenant, we'd all be dead or fired for not living up to our end of the deal. Prayer is to express gratitude for the state of forgiveness and grace, which allows for the appreciation of the implacable grandeur of the experience of our humanness through spiritual failure—not for the relief from the guilt of transgressions. I discuss this in more detail later.

[35] Reflect on the quote at the front of the book by Edwin Arlington Robinson.

higher power because that's what *It* is. Try it this way: You think—you can't not think. You may think about important things or trivia, you may think about thinking about nothing, but you are always thinking. Your mind hasn't stopped thinking (asleep or awake) from the instant it started. Thinking *is* you. You can't separate thinking from humanness. A higher power *is* Forgiveness.[36] No degree of obedience, misbehavior, or groveling can ever change that.

If spiritual forgiveness is the action of God in our covenant with God, regardless of our conduct, why bother with the five spiritual principles at all? Colloquially: If "God" automatically forgives the sinner, regardless of the transgression, why bother being good? God doesn't need anyone to act spiritual to(wards) God. God doesn't require people to act spiritual towards each other, either. But, in order to appreciate the implacable grandeur of life exactly as we have been given it, we need to be spiritual. Spiritual principles emanating out "from people" are what allow people to create heaven on earth.

Back to forgiveness: At the human level, in contracts, in order to forgive someone, in between the "transgression" and the "forgiveness", you first must hold a belief that you are owed something. In a subtle model of entitlement, you have judged that because they were bad or somehow negligent, they owe an apology, reparation, some money, a favor, or contriteness: you're entitled.

In the example of being late for the dinner party, the host viewed you as either rude, insensitive, or irresponsible (some degree of condemnation), and the host felt "entitled" to feel hurt. You, therefore, owed them something for the transgression of being late. They therefore had the authority to forgive "the debt", which they, themselves, created, which debt becomes theirs to collect. The host lives by relationship rules that allow them to condemn you for being the human that you are. For the host to presume that they're entitled to forgive you, or they're even capable of it, is arrogant and presumptuous. You're a person (it's what people do). Being condemned is tantamount to being condemned for being human, and therein lies the first major corruption when forgiveness is seen as the final step in conflict resolution.

Being human requires that mistakes, hurts, errors, harm, and transgressions *will* happen, caused by you and done to you. Attaching condemnation and forgiveness to these mandatory foibles is one source of dislocation that exemplifies and enables the wheel of suffering as described in Buddhism.[37] In the context of human forgiveness, preceding the belief that you can forgive someone for hurting you, is your belief that that person shouldn't have "hurt" you. When you're offended, it isn't their offense that causes your offendedness, but your interpretation of their behavior, and your presumption that they should have somehow been above their humanness. They owe you something for being human. Therein lies another major corruption

---

[36] From Alan Watts: People don't say: "I am beating my heart." Your beating heart is not a considered action of will; from *This Is It*, Vintage Books, 1973, p. 91. Similarly, people will say "I am thinking," as if thinking as a function of will. It isn't. And God's forgiveness isn't a considered action, either. It just *is*.

[37] The resolution of this is not to be perfect, but to change your attitude towards the fallible nature of people and the always self-serving nature of attachment. Regarding attachment, in the scenario of forgiveness it's attachment to entitlement, debt and obligation.

when forgiveness is seen as the spiritual final step in conflict resolution.

The condemnation of humanness leaves people perpetually prepared to feel hurt before anything happens: Victims in Waiting. The traditional stance of the victim is: "I have been hurt and the offender owes me." (This is the Two-Step Dance.[38]) When forgiveness is the transaction between people, at its core, one person is being condemned for being human and the other person is (at least temporarily) holding themselves above being human.

The Forgiven

When (if) people subscribe to the idea that forgiveness is the best resolution strategy, and then they, themselves, commit some offense, any subsequent amend they offer requires, at least in part, some contriteness for being human. Within the forgiveness transaction, the offender must include some apology for being human because that's what they are being condemned for. How damaging is that?[39]

This doesn't absolve addicts or alcoholics (or people in general) of the responsibility to be reasonably determined to not hurt others. And, all efforts must be made to amend any damage done, and to take responsibility for that. But at the same time, identifying the harm you caused in Step Eight does not carry any obligation to apologize for having shortcomings, or to defend the fact that you have an illness, or to be contrite about being human.

Because human relationships are contracts, they carry an expectation of reciprocity. Many people assume that when they're hurt, the ultimate spiritual response on their part—the reciprocity required of the aggrieved party—is forgiveness.[40] Additionally, when addicts are caught up in cultural confusion regarding relationship contracts, they often expect to be forgiven by the person they have hurt after they make an amend. These are evidence of a serious misalliance of commitment within a spiritual lifestyle, and defeat the task at hand.

Forgiveness is spiritually inefficient when it's offered in secular relationships. It implies condemnation for being human; is evidence of the Two-Step Dance; and assumes a debt is owed by the transgressor to the aggrieved person, when all that happened was someone was being human. It implies spiritual superiority on the part of the forgiver, and moral turpitude on the part of the forgiven. It implies *in*equality between the parties in the transaction.[41] There are seriously unspiritual aspects to believing that forgiveness is the highest spiritual solution to human problems.

---

[38] The Two-Step Dance is described in Chapter 8.

[39] This is one theme at the core of the Christian parable "Let those without sin cast the first stone." Since we are all "sinners" [sic] to some degree, the moment anyone condemns another for any human failing, regardless of its magnitude, there is hypocrisy. In addition to the hypocrisy, at a deeper level than the crime, the offender is being condemned for being human. None of us are above being human.

[40] Should a person think it's spiritually sound at the human level to forgive someone, then if they can forgive them, it implies they can also withhold forgiveness. People who believe in forgiveness will often withhold it until the offender is contrite enough to satisfy their wounded dignity. How spiritual is that?

[41] Wherever condemnation is present in any human relationship, in terms of the transaction of forgiveness, three of the five spiritual principles are subtly absent (respect for the body-temple, veracity, and responsi-

However, in a relationship between a deity and a human, the secular notions of reciprocity and equality don't apply. Forgiveness on the part of God, and prayer and meditation (worship) on the part of people, are what honor the inherent inequality of the relationship. Forgiveness for being human is God's covenant with people. Responsibility/acceptance for our human failings is your contract with people. Confusing these is disastrous to either relationship.

Getting Beyond Forgiveness

Before alcoholics, addicts, or people in general, can get beyond forgiveness to a more peaceful and fulfilling mindset, these beliefs are required:

- addictions, unmanageability, and related "Life" problems are self-imposed,
- absolute personal responsibility, and consistently examining yourself and not others, is the order of the day—every day,
- for spiritual pilgrims, regular, frequent, and properly focused prayer/worship/meditation with an adoption of non-angry moral responsibility; and for morally committed atheists, an adoption of non-angry moral responsibility, are crucial; and,
- for those getting recovered, diligent adherence to the original instructions throughout the steps (without editing or rewriting), and eventually living "in" the maintenance steps that embody the five spiritual principles, is the overall task at hand.

No one of these are any more important than the others. Any commitment to one of them is rendered meaningless without an equal commitment to the others. Alternately, an absence of commitment to one of them makes any commitment to the others political. Integrity requires equally sincere devotion to all of them.

For the self-proclaimed aggrieved party, notice that in between being hurt by someone and offering forgiveness to them, there is a period where they believe they're an Entitled Victim. Recall earlier discussions that self-examination and commitment to *uncompromising* personal responsibility are what takes a person out of being a victim and frees them from self-pity. These are also the fundamental conditions that allow them to go beyond forgiveness. What happens is, when people reeducate themselves through personal responsibility into a very deep level of self-acceptance regarding their own limitations, they achieve a wonderful sense of inner peace through compassion and gentleness towards themselves regarding their humanness. They (eventually) stop condemning themselves for anything.

As soon as they assume uncompromising personal responsibility and attain self-acceptance, they stop condemning others. When people accept their own humanness; when addicts and alcoholics accept their disease and themselves, without apology or guilt, exactly as they are, especially their imperfections, they are capable

---

bility and obedience), and two are flagrantly absent (humility and charity). Being in a relationship where one person has political advantage or legislated authority doesn't automatically mean there is inequality.

of offering that acceptance of "self" out to others, as true respect and egalitarianism, exactly as others are—even when others grievously hurt them. That sets other people free from being blamed and condemned, regardless of the transgression.

What the mystics and truly spiritual people accomplish by *microscopic* self-examination and complete responsibility is insightful *self*-acceptance, regarding their own frailties. They are then able to eliminate all condemnation and offer out love and acceptance. At the core of all spiritual discipline is challenging yourself, and taking complete responsibility, and thereby setting others free from your judgments and arrogance. This renders forgiveness unnecessary.

From a slightly different perspective: When you understand the necessity for accepting your own shortcomings, which is the accepting of your humanness, the truth is that your own ever-present frailties make a mockery of you ever forgiving anyone for anything. In this mindset you find authentic self-love. Then it's natural to love others because and in spite of their frailties, regardless of how grievously you are wounded or inconvenienced by them. This is only available with you believing in consistent, uncompromising devotion to veracity and personal responsibility. This is the key for going beyond the spiritually limiting place of forgiveness, to true accep-tance (which again, then renders forgiveness unnecessary).

———

Character defects are demonstrations of insecurity and fear. They allow you to avoid personal responsibility—that's what you've designed them for. More di-rectly: Every time you find it necessary to offer or seek forgiveness, that in itself is motivated by a character defect. In other words, Forgiveness is your Character De-fect Concealment Strategy—it conceals your own arrogance and harsh judgments. Going beyond forgiveness is dependent upon your ability to take complete responsi-bility for your character defects.

When you become *willing* at Step Six you gently reduce your insecurities. Without willingness, you sentence yourself to forever secretly managing your inse-curities as the top priority of your inner existence. But, whatever goes on inside, goes on outside. If you're managing your insecurities, that requires you to constantly, se-cretly, manage your human relationships. If you're stuck in managing yourself, you're stuck in managing others. With this, the cycle of forgiveness: offense, hurt, fault-finding, condemnation, recrimination, contrition, benevolence, forgiveness, and righteous indifference is all that's available to you. All of this work "managing" things leaves no time to appreciate that Life is monumentally spectacular and over-flowing with beauty—exactly as it exists.

Character defects are always self-serving. They magically magnify those circumstances where it appears you are "more right" than the other person. How many times have you thought you forgave someone and then found yourself, days or years later, in another fit of pique about the circumstance you had forgiven them for? Reliving the event occurs because character defects that conceal insecurity are them-selves, concealed under the transaction of forgiveness, and forgiving someone (yet again) allows you to reclaim the moral high ground. At the human level, when for-giveness is the ultimate good, that justifies condemnation of another, and leaves the arrogance and absence of humility underneath the forgiveness unchallenged.

Without accurate, sincere realizations about your selfish, self-destructive character (gained through to Step Seven), *and* a commitment to complete personal responsibility, *and* a willingness to become humble, forgiveness remains the necessary game of relationship politics. Absolution through forgiveness is an amazing vehicle through which you alleviate guilt and foster spiritual irresponsibility: People get to rush about, recreating their offenses. It does nothing at the human level to further the responsible pursuit of sincere spirituality. There's no serenity in the repetitious cycle of offense, hurt, fault-finding, condemnation, recrimination, contrition, benevolence, forgiveness, and righteous indifference.

Embrace both aspects of humility and embrace a deep acceptance of your own humanness. You will then sidestep the need to judge, condemn and forgive others. This is truly, serenity at its best.

The Foundation for Step Eight

To sort out all these subtleties, it's important that you have laid the proper foundation for Step Eight in the preceding steps. If you've not done them *exactly* as instructed, you will be incapable of emotional balance and responsibility when itemizing the harm you caused. Here is the foundation you have laid thus far, and its specific relation to Step Eight:

Step One: A significant reduction in culturally imposed guilt, along with a solid conviction that you are resolving a disease. Your soul doesn't need fixing; the phenomenon of addictions needs resolution. At Step Eight, this realization allows you to admit the harm and be responsible without being controlled by guilt and shame. You may still feel some of them, but you won't be controlled by them, and they won't undermine the integrity of your investigation into the harm you caused.

Step Two: The recognition that the solution to your addiction and the related insanity rests in your sincere alliance with spiritual principles and devotion to a higher power. At Step Eight you will then be focused on Spiritual integrity and service to God, rather than social atonement and service to yourself. This permits charity and thoroughness when identifying the harm done.

Step Three: The decision to turn your will and life over to the care of God (as you understand God) allows you to always be clear about your purpose: *being spiritual*. That decision, when you arrive at Step Eight, allows you to remain consistent in your devotion—ignoring any possible political advantages of amending one harm more thoroughly than another harm. The decision at Step Three entitles every incident of harm to equally thorough examination.

Step Four: The examination of your insecurities, fears, and sexual selfishness allowed you to be aware of the subtle ways you tried to control Life, and thereby blame and harm others. Step Four trained you to examine your fault and ignore the behavior of others. This extends itself into Step Eight, and allows you to see the harm you caused, and ignore the other person's participation.

Step Five: The honest admission of your insecurities, fears, and sexual selfishness facilitates two things at Step Eight. (1) It alleviates cultural guilt that will arise when you identify harms caused, and allows you to retain your integrity when you itemize harm. (2) Step Five is the crucial training experience for talking about your responsibility without blaming others. Honestly calling only yourself to account at Step Eight is only possible because of the exercise at Step Five.

Honestly identifying the harm you caused others at Step Eight is a natural extension of your discoveries in Step Four and admissions in Step Five—but only if you very specifically followed the instructions. Additionally, what sometimes comes up during Step Nine is, people you harmed may be curious about why it happened. Should the need to discuss your motivations for causing harm arise, practicing self-responsible, non-blaming disclosure at Step Five makes that discussion at Step Nine a non-threatening experience for the person receiving the amend.

Step Six: Here you became willing to make a necessary, fundamental change: giving up your survival skills and abandoning your character defects on behalf of God, not for personal contentment. This makes possible the elimination of the need for social atonement in later step-work, which is itself crucial for transforming your perspective of Life from social success to spiritual integrity. At Step Eight, this willingness counteracts any selfishness so it can't detrimentally influence the patience and thoroughness that's required.

Step Seven: You learned that humility is a desired virtue, and it's to be sought because it's inherently good. You're now able to transform without being motivated by shame and pain. After Step Seven, spirituality isn't self-serving, which means examining the harms you caused isn't self-serving to escape pain or guilt. "No pain, no gain" becomes unnecessary. Step Eight becomes charity in the form of spiritual responsibility, and has nothing to do with you.

Without devotion to humility and responsibility, Step Eight will be onerous and superficial. If your effort is without a sense of willingness and joy for the task at hand, go back to Step Two and reexamine your belief that a higher power is the solution. Then, review Steps Six and Seven until such time as you notice you're willing. That will clear up any begrudging attitude towards the huge amount of work that is necessary at Step Eight.[42]

In the final analysis, you cannot for long seek a spiritual life that's motivated by guilt or shame, otherwise, the resulting relationship with God is always self-serving. This renders spirituality selfish. When you were in your addiction there was no end of shame, pain, and self-destruction. These were what initially motivated your pursuit of transformation. When humility is a desired virtue, it makes microscopic truth-telling and personal responsibility a pleasure. Step Eight, and everything you do thereafter, is then a labor of love.

The Administration of Step Eight

Patience, thoroughness, and honesty are paramount to the task at hand: *"Made a list of all persons we had harmed, and became willing to make amends to them all.*"[43] Certainly, it's direct and to the point.

Retrieve the copy of the autobiographical list of everyone/everything in your life that I suggested you make at Step Four. Since this would have been months ago, reflect on your life since then and, if necessary, add to the list those new people you have met since you finished Step Four.

The guiding phrases are: "*...and really makes an accurate and unsparing survey...* , " "*...[we] ought to redouble [our] efforts to see how many people [we have] hurt... ,*" "*Calm, thoughtful reflection... ,*" "*ransack [your] memory...*".[44] There is no guideline about how this should actually be laid out on paper. My suggestion is to use a layout of three columns, similar to Step Four. The list you have retrieved, after some appropriate editing, will become Column One.

The instruction is: "*as year by year we walk back through our lives as far as memory will reach, we shall be bound to construct a long list of people who have, to some extent or other, been affected,*"[45] (meaning harmed). The wording implies the list is chronological—you would begin in the present and work back into the past; the list is thorough and long; the harm is either minor or major; and, the tone of the sentence, along with the phrase "*walking back,*" implies patience and thoughtfulness in the effort.[46]

The author(s) of *Twelve Steps and Twelve Traditions* were well aware of an alcoholic's [addict's] tendency to minimize the harm done by creating self-serving definitions of "harm", and thereby evading responsibility. They eliminate that loophole by defining harm as "*...the result of instincts in collision, which cause physical, mental, emotional, or spiritual damage to people.*"[47]

The next paragraphs outline the obvious forms of harm that addicts do, and provides a detailed list of the subtler forms of harm that you are to look for. Addicts may "*...lie and cheat [and thereby] deprive others; [or be] ...miserly, irresponsible, callous, ...cold, irritable, critical, impatient, and humorless; [or they may] ...lavish attention on one and neglect others; ...dominate the whole family by rule of iron or constant outpouring of minute directions; [or] ...wallow in depression, self pity oozing from every pore. Such a roster of harms done others... ".*[48] This identifies fifteen ways that addicts and alcoholics cause harm in relation to Step Eight. Yes, it may end up with you having to make some type of amend, large or small, to quite a few people. Remember, you have volunteered to go to any length for a spiritual experience, and you have acquired the willingness and humility to do that.

Examine your behavior in relation to every person on your autobiographical list. Ask yourself the following questions:

---

[42] Oftentimes, when spiritual self-discipline becomes difficult, pilgrims forget that they volunteered for it and can always choose to return to their addiction. There are always choices.

[43] *Alcoholics Anonymous*, p. 59, and *Twelve Steps and Twelve Traditions*, p. 77.

[44] Phrases from Step Eight in *Twelve Steps and Twelve Traditions*, pp. 77, 80, 81.

[45] Ibid., p. 81.

[46] Ibid. Be cautious with the phrase, "*as far as memory will reach.*" This is about your addictions. If you insist on examining your pre-addictions life for incidents where you harmed others, do this under the protective umbrella of well-conducted therapy. The propensity of addicts to oscillate between justifying their offences and debilitating self-blame for everything imaginable is to be kept in mind.

[47] Ibid., p. 80.

[48] Ibid., p. 81.

- Did I harm this person physically? Did I harm this person mentally? Did I harm this person emotionally? Did I harm this person spiritually?
- Was I miserly, irresponsible, callous, cold, irritable, critical, impatient, humorless?
- Did I lavish attention on one and neglect another? Did I dominate the whole family, constantly issuing minute directions?
- Did I wallow in depression or self pity?

The more you are thorough and responsible here, the greater your eventual sense of spiritual peace will be. <u>Nothing is free</u>. If you want deep and lasting contentment, then be meticulous and responsible in defining what harm you have caused. Be patient. Pray for willingness to do this on behalf of your higher power. Seek wise spiritual counsel. This *"is the beginning of the end of isolation from our fellows and from God."*[49]

After thoughtful reflection regarding each person on your list, and the broad definition of "harm" given in the AA literature (noted above), if you have not harmed them cross them off the list. Once you identify that you did harm them, write briefly what the harm was in a second column beside their name. Don't use ditto marks. When you have identified the harm you caused, in a third column identify what amends are appropriate. This can range from sending cards and letters, making a phone call, arranging a personal visit (plan what you will say), reporting yourself to the authorities (plan ahead), and paying off debts. Whenever you are in doubt, err on the side of responsibility, avoid blame, and seek wise spiritual counsel.[50]

This is a seldom-discussed, crucial exercise that you must participate in for any lasting change — the long, gently repeated exposure *of* yourself, *by* yourself, *to* yourself. There are several things about patient, responsible self-discipline that are *un*attractive to alcoholics and addicts getting recovered: it isn't dramatic, it isn't quick, it can be expensive, it requires concentration, it can be embarrassing, there's no one to blame, and it exposes you for exactly what you were (or are). This is awkward and difficult, which is why this aspect of spiritual transformation is presented after you have developed the willingness to see humility as desirable.

It takes a *long* time to become spiritual. While *en route* to "Spiritual Bliss" [sic], fall in love, change jobs, go to a movie, paint a picture, go back to school, make love, learn to play the trombone, sail a boat, do the tango (whatever) — continue living your life while you do your step work. Keep abstinence and spiritual principles as the higher priorities, and Live.

---

[49] *Twelve Steps and Twelve Traditions*, p. 82.

[50] Seeking wise spiritual counsel doesn't include jogging partners, the consensus of the people in your group, workmates, your spouse, or your sponsor if your sponsor is someone you call your friend and with whom you loiter about the coffee shops. The awkward truths, intimate details, and objectiveness required for wise counsel excludes all people who have a vested interest in the politics of your relationship with them. Demand of yourself to go outside of this comfort zone. Seek authentic counsel that seriously calls you to task regarding responsibility and spiritual principles. *"Hard on ourselves..."*, p. 74, *Alcoholics Anonymous*.

Sensitivity and Awareness

Many addicts end up with inordinately short lists of harms caused. Oftentimes this is because of a self-serving definition of harm and an arbitrary classification of which harms are important enough to pay attention to. This self-serving behavior isn't always deliberate. There are understandable reasons for alcoholics and addicts minimizing the harm caused, which are related to self-awareness and sensitivity.

When anyone is significantly out of touch with feelings (when subtle emotions are unknown to them), they're only aware of their major feelings. They're legitimately unaware of the small hurts and insults that might be experienced by people who are more sensitive to emotion. Yet others are *so* sensitive that all emotional experience is traumatic.

Accuracy and thoroughness at Step Eight are influenced by your own sensitivity. You may well be sincere, but not sensitive. Should you be noticeably unaware of emotional nuance within yourself, or have a limited view of a person's rights and freedoms, you'll be unable to accurately appreciate the nuance of emotional harm you caused. Notice these two conversations between Me and You regarding the same phone call. In the first example, Me is the more sensitive person, and in the second, You is more sensitive.

> Me: "Yesterday, on the phone, I was impatient with you. I regret the abrupt tone I used and how I ended the call. I'm going to make a sincere effort to not do that again. I'd understand if you felt hurt."
>
> You: "What? Rude? What're you talking about? It was fine."

Next is a conversation about the same phone call where You is the more sensitive person.

> You: "Listen, yesterday, on the phone, I felt a little rushed and, I guess, a little hurt that you seemed so abrupt. You sounded impatient and almost hung up on me. Are you upset with me?"
>
> Me: "What do you mean, abrupt? I didn't think I was. Really?"

Sometimes people are insensitive because they are deliberately unwilling to be responsible. They're afraid. Other people appear insensitive because they really are out of touch with their emotions and unable to understand emotional nuance in themselves *or* others.

From a psychological perspective, a person's response to being deliberately dismissed by a rude or mean person would be quite different from the response to a dismissal from someone who is sincere but insensitive to emotional nuance. Sometimes it's very difficult to tell which is which. In Step Eight, be sensitive. If you identify what harm you've caused with a "hard heart", or if you are still entrenched at all in blaming others, you'll have only seven people on your list. Reflect carefully on the broad definition of "harm" in the AA literature. Narrow definitions of "harm" are irresponsible. [The theme here is similar to an issue discussed at Step Four: avoiding responsibility by creating a narrow definition of resentments.]

Watch for indirect harm. For example: B. is making a list of harms. When in active addiction, B. would often manipulate K. into irresponsible, drunken behavior by intimidating, bragging, shaming, teasing, and flashing money. If B. had left K. alone, there would have been much less conflict in K.'s family. [Yes, K. might have said "No," but that's not the point. This is about B.] B. contributed to K.'s family conflict, even though B. didn't know K.'s family, and didn't harm them directly. In this spiritual endeavor, an amend *may* be in order from B. to K.'s family.[51]

———————

Earlier, I pointed out the regeneration steps must be viewed independently of each other. Thinking about any one step, while completing another, always contaminates the outcome. Here's one area where that's obvious...

At Step Nine, the original twelve-step literature identifies an exception to making amends when the amend would cause further harm. That's wise, but that applies to Step Nine, not Eight. While in the midst of Step Eight, if you debate whether or not you should make the amend because that may cause more harm, you will evade thoroughness in identifying what harm you actually did cause. In the midst of Step Eight, if you ruminate about Step Nine because you may not make an amend, you'll shirk the responsibility of a detailed examination of the harm caused. It's too easy to decide in Step Eight that dredging up old wounds "that are better left forgotten", or that reminding people of their hurt and anger at *your* past behavior, is causing harm. People being reminded of painful historical events *which you are responsible for,* does not necessarily qualify as them being harmed, and it never exempts you from examining the circumstance in detail.

Step Eight has nothing whatever to do with actually making the amend. It's only identifying in detail exactly what the harm was. Be very thorough in examining your harmful behavior, no matter how slight or egregious. You need the exercise in veracity, responsibility, and obedience in self-examination. Whether you make an amend later is entirely irrelevant when identifying the particular harm you caused.

There are different ways of evading honesty and thoroughness. You can make your list shorter than it needs to be due to unmanageable shame, fear, guilt, blame, or anger. You can make it too long by taking on too much responsibility and blaming yourself for all the conflict and harm everywhere. And, whether real or fancied, you may edit your examination by deciding no amend should be made because you will be harming others by dredging up the past.

Earlier I talked about newcomers being unable to judge how well they're doing. This is applicable in the process of closely examining your relationships for harm you have caused. It's crucial to have the counsel of a trusted sponsor, spiritual advisor, or therapist who is *well*-versed in the spiritual aspects of twelve-step pro-

———————

[51] *Twelve Steps and Twelve Traditions*, p. 79. The reference begins: *"There were cases, too, where... "*

grams, and has no investment in the politics of your life. They are "supposed to" gently, and firmly, and persistently, encourage a high standard of responsibility and spiritual commitment.

Don't Apologize Or Be Sorry

It's a given that practicing alcoholics and addicts are irresponsible. This is also apparent in unregenerate addicts-in-recovery who have invested only a superficial effort in spirituality. Nowhere is this as obvious as in their self-serving attempts to manipulate others by penitent declarations of "I'm sorry" and "I apologize". When deciding what must be done to amend the harm, do not consider apologizing.

Here are two definitions of apology: (1) a formal defense or vindication against an accusation; and, (2) a justification, an explanation, an excuse.[52] Certainly there are other interpretations of "apologize" that include an expression of regret or an acknowledgement of fault. However you define it, making an apology (i) carries some direct reference to extenuating circumstances: a defense, (ii) implies an expectation you'll be forgiven or that you're less accountable because of those extenuating circumstances; and, (iii) carries an implicit expectation that the aggrieved party should cooperate with the offender's effort at self-exoneration.

Any time you defend a harm you have caused by tendering reasons and justifications, it follows as an accepted principle of jurisprudence, if the reasons are good enough, you will be exonerated from accountability (meaning not held responsible). And, if you're held "less" responsible, then you may have done the deed but only minor accountability accrues to you. So, if you can justify it, you really don't have to change at all and, the icing on the cake you have baked is, you get to do it over again.

Apologies are not amends, and they make any amends patently self-serving and disrespectful to the aggrieved party. The offender is (yet again) trying to control the aggrieved person and the situation. We'll go through this in detail. It is crucial.

Apologize By Numbers

The instructions are: (a) Read through the options. (b) Using a pencil, check off/select one sentence-stem from each section, (1) through (6). (c) Then, from the beginning, read through your selections following the suggested inflections.

(1) **The Set Up**: (be *very* sincere)

( ) I'm *very* sorry that I …
( ) I *apologize* that I …

(2) **The Confession**: (contrite, minimized, and/or dramatic)

( ) had an affair.   ( ) hit the dog.
( ) slapped you.   ( ) didn't put gas in the car.

---

[52] *The New Shorter Oxford English Dictionary,* Clarendon Press, Oxford, 1993.

( ) wrecked the car.
( ) took the car.
( ) lied to you.
( ) didn't call.
( ) did call.
( ) left.
( ) spent the money.
( ) called you names.

( ) was ( ) one, ( ) two, ( ) eleven…
( ) hours, ( ) days, ( ) months,
( ) years, late.
( ) drank, ( ) used drugs.
( ) ate the ice cream.
( ) spilled the milk.
( ) didn't __(insert oversight)__.
( ) did __(insert misdemeanor)__.

(3) **The Exaggerated Self-Attack**: This is to elicit sympathetic disagreement and bolster the planned defense (for best results, be dramatically and sincerely contrite).

( ) I know I'm *terrible*.
( ) I'm such a *jerk*.
( ) I'm so… ( ) *horrible*, ( ) *disgusting*, ( ) *stupid*.
( ) How can you *stand* being with me?

(4) **The Defense**:   But, you see, ( ) **Dear**, ( ) **Sweetheart**, ( ) **Honey**,

( ) I'm in recovery.
( ) I'm under a lot of pressure…
( ) My foot was sore.
( ) I didn't mean to. I got carried away.
( ) The meeting was…
( ) I thought that…
( ) The bus was late.
( ) I missed the bus.
( ) I got hit by the bus.
( ) I had a headache.
( ) I couldn't find a taxi…
( ) I didn't think that…
( ) The guys insisted.
( ) I'm a drug addict and you knew that…
( ) The courier didn't…
( ) I'm an alcoholic and you knew that…
( ) The girls wanted me to…

( ) My… ( ) mother, ( ) father,
( ) priest, ( ) therapist.
( ) sister, ( ) uncle,
did (or didn't) _____.
( ) I was ( ) horny, ( ) lonely, ( ) angry,
( ) hungry, ( ) tired, ( ) sad.
( ) You *knew* I was like this when we met.
( ) When I was   ( ) in college…
( ) a child…
( ) at summer camp…
( ) away in Europe…
___insert sorrowful details___.
( ) My boss ( ) didn't
( ) couldn't
( ) wouldn't…
( ) It was ( ) snowing,
( ) raining, ( ) windy,
( ) hot, ( ) dark.
( ) You're *not* going to believe this, but… _____.
(insert your own unique excuse)

(5) **The Obsequious (Exception) Factor**: (said with *very* sincere conviction)

( ) but I *really* didn't mean it.
( ) but I *won't* do it again.
( ) but I'll *try* not to do it again.
( ) but it's really *not* as bad as it used to be. Right?
( ) ah, come on, I haven't done it for a *really* long time.

(6) **Shifting Responsibility**: (with a *dramatic* gesture):

( ) I'm *so* sorry, but *you've* got to understand.
( ) I'm *really* trying, and I hope *you'll* understand.
( ) I'm very, *very* sorry. *Please* forgive me.
( ) I apologize, so can I *please* get another chance?

By beginning the apology with a penitent declaration of how sorry you are, you begin to effectively shift the transaction away from the other person's hurt and onto your excuse. If you've enough good reasons (justifications) for your irresponsible or mean behavior (at 3 & 4), you won't have to change. *And,* if you can make your sorrow/regret (at 1 & 5) and your self-serving compassionate plea (at 6) "bigger" than their hurt, you get the empathy spotlight.

The end results are that you have minimized your own culpability, the "wrong" isn't fixed and, by shifting the focus at 6, the aggrieved person is made responsible for the outcome. Now it's entirely about you, and completely self-serving.

This is a controlling set-up for additional irresponsibility. If the aggrieved person doesn't "understand" or give you another chance (at 6), you get to think with self-absolution: "Well, this conflict is their fault because I apologized and they didn't accept it. I *told* them how bad I felt—what do they want, blood?"

The primary purpose of Step Eight is to identify where you were wrong (did harm) and decide exactly what you need to do to fix it. Throughout the Apologize by Numbers exercise, none of it addressed the harm that was done, and there was no action to actually repair the damage. In making amends, whatever you think may be a probable defense (at 4) is irrelevant. Amends must begin with sincere willingness and humility; otherwise, the exercise is motivated by selfishness and you'll portion out responsibility and offer excuses. Focus on the needs of the aggrieved person in relation to the harm you have done. Nothing else matters.

Don't be sorry or obsequious in responding to the circumstances of life. If you have an addiction, that's a bona fide reason for symptomatic behavior. People with narcolepsy fall asleep. It's not an excuse and it doesn't mitigate responsibility; it's just the reason for falling asleep. It's the disease that dictates the behavior, not your evil soul. Yes, there's a need to be completely responsible and, in identifying the harms, you may feel sad or regretful, however these are noticeably different from being sorry or obsequious, which are an attempt to elicit sympathy and minimize responsibility.[53]

There's no reference within the original twelve-step literature (personal stories excluded) that advises an apology or being sorry are amends. The implicit task is to decide what harm you caused, and as you do this, not to justify your irresponsibility or meanness. From a spiritual perspective, after the damage has been done, an amend is to repair the damage and re-establish some harmony in the life of the per-

---

[53] *"We should be sensible, tactful...,"* Alcoholics Anonymous, p. 83.

son you harmed.[54]

Inappropriate Compensation

The depth of spiritual responsibility that I am about to describe can carry a difficult demand that is laid on the conscience of those who were harmed by others. Being harmed by the misfortunes of life or by others, in our blame-oriented culture, has created a victim's game called Make Anyone Pay.

As a child, if you were abused, you were completely innocent. That childhood innocence does *not* carry itself over into adulthood as a justification for mean, irresponsible behavior. Only by extreme anger and other defects can you justify demanding reparation from people who didn't cause the harm. If you do, you're taking the role of persecutor—harming innocent people—an exact parallel to how, as a child, you were harmed. The victim becomes a persecutor. (I explored this earlier in The Ripple Effect of Irresponsibility, p.71).

Whomever hurt you as a child tore a hole in the spiritual fabric of the universe. That isn't mended by you punishing innocent people, a game called Make Anyone Pay, no matter how badly you were hurt. In a Spiritual world, nothing justifies violence or revenge. Making innocent people pay is both violent and vengeful. Morally self-righteous victims, and the professionals who aid and abet them, crash through our communities suing anybody they can, making anyone pay. Greed and vengeance masquerade as justice—viciousness clothed in judicial respectability.

It happens in intimate relationships all the time: partners inflict revenge on their spouse, their children, and friends, for harms done to them by others. Psychologically, Make Anyone Pay is our favorite national sport. The people who Make Anyone Pay are as harmful to others as were those who hurt them in the first place. Making anyone pay is insidious. "I was hurt by the priest so I'll sue The Church." "I was hurt by... a Jew, an African American, a white person, a cop, a woman, a man, an Asian, a teenager... (pick your own)... and now I can despise all of them!" The recreational pastime for Victims is: someone hurt me so I'll hurt anyone. This is grossly irresponsible, and the cycle of abuse continues.

Should you be a person who was hurt and at that time you were innocent, be cautious about how you attend to your healing. If "it's not fair" is the ambience of your attitude, it will turn into a grievance with the universe, and through vengeance ("make anyone pay") you'll initiate another cycle of abuse.

Spiritual Reasonableness

At Step Eight, you're going through the process of examining the harm you did to others. You have to take full responsibility for this without expecting any cooperation or support from the aggrieved person. Disregard whatever they might have done. This is being spiritually responsible. However, as you examine your behavior, that examination has to have some balance.

---

[54] *"Our real purpose is to fit ourselves..."* and *"...having the other one's happiness uppermost in mind."* *Alcoholics Anonymous*, p. 77 and p. 82, respectively.

However you amend whatever you did that was harmful, it must have a tone of what I call spiritual reasonableness. Enjoy frequent guidance from a mentor or sponsor who is spiritually principled, who is uncompromising in responsibility and fairness, and with whom you can discuss the details of each situation. This person must be cognizant of the requirements of the original twelve-step program. You need sage counsel that is uncompromising and accurate for you, and easy on others.[55]

The last phrase of Step Eight is: *"and became willing to make amends to them all."*[56] Recall that willingness was the primary teaching of Step Six. If you haven't commanded Step Six, then you will be unwilling at Step Eight and begrudge the amends. If Step Eight is difficult, go back to Six, and if Step Six is difficult, go back to Step Two.

Regeneration

All things generate from something. Plants originate from seeds, animals and people from parents; everything from the earth. Personalities also have a crucible of origin, which is made up of genetics, physiology, and environment (culture possibly more than family). And, of course, within every personality is willpower and character defects. For most people, willpower and character defects are of a garden variety, and people aren't particularly noticed for how they create their life.

However, some people stand out because of their character, including its defects, and their strong willful energy focused intensely on a specific thing. They are noticeably different and garner attention for this, which is witnessed at both a social and psychological level. Some people's character, including its defects and willful energy, is organized around committing crimes: serious career criminals. Other people's character (again including its defects) is organized around the relentless pursuit of wealth or fame; music or artistic endeavor, or writing. An addicted person's character embodies character defects and willful energy, but their character, and all that energy is organized around self-annihilation.[57]

It is long known that a problem can't be resolved on the same level that it manifests. We can't eliminate war with guns, or sexism with anger and privilege. Neither can we resolve addictions with psychology because an addiction shows itself as a psychology of self-annihilation. An addicted personality must therefore regenerate at a level underneath psychology. It must regenerate within the crucible of spirituality. The original twelve steps and spiritual principles are the method of self-introspection that allow an addict to go underneath "personality and psychology" where they can then experience transformation. The self-annihilation begins to stop at Step One; but abstinence and completing Step One aren't a change in personality:

---

[55] From *Alcoholics Anonymous*: *"...we resolutely looked for our own mistakes"* and *"tried to disregard the other person involved entirely,"* both p. 67; and this: *"...hard on ourselves but always considerate of others,"* p. 74. Then, from *Twelve Steps and Twelve Traditions*: *"...we had to drop the word 'blame' from our speech and thought."* p. 47.
[56] *Twelve Steps and Twelve Traditions*, p. 77.
[57] How this condition originates is the subject of much debate, and is not what's under discussion here. The resolution of addiction is the matter at hand.

they're a change in behavior. Regeneration really begins at Step Two.[58]

The "*...Greater Mysteries discussed the principles of spiritual regeneration and revealed to initiates not only the simplest but also the most direct and complete method of liberating their higher natures from the bondage of material ignorance.*"[59] Material ignorance, in this case, is bondage to self-annihilation and addictions. Unregenerate means living as a practicing addict, or as a "sober" but unspiritual addict where nothing has changed, or where the change is only political. Regenerate means to resolve dislocation by re-growing and reorganizing your personality within a sound spiritual paradigm.

Many people in twelve-step programs do just enough to get by. They're only as charitable as their guilt requires, only as kind as the image requires, only as industrious as they need to be, and are honest only so long as it's convenient. Honesty as a default behavior because of ineffective lying skills isn't spiritual in any sense of the word. These people smoke, curse and swear; are sexist, irresponsible, or mean in relationships; and cut corners on everything from downloading pirated software and stealing copyright-protected music, to completing Step Eight. They look like they are acting differently, but other than abstinence, nothing has really changed.

In order to be recovered, the requirements of Spirituality and the tenacity of addictions won't allow for cutting corners, substitutions, or half-hearted efforts. There are two reasons for this: one is because of the spiritually corrupt and incredibly complicated nature of addicted personalities. Addictions are rigidly constructed and unyielding. The other is because: "*The unfolding of man's spiritual nature is as much an exact science as medicine* [or] *astronomy... .*"[60] Surgeons or auto mechanics can't change the rules of their craft because they don't like them, and neither can addicts or alcoholics wanting to get recovered. Addicted personalities can only successfully regenerate within a firmly structured paradigm. An all-encompassing demand for obedience, detail, and commitment are what makes solid that place out of which your spiritual personality will grow.

By following the instructions thus far, you should be fairly aware of the rudiments of Spirituality. However, if you find yourself at Step Eight and are confused about the role of God in your life; if your praying is sporadic; if you're in conscious ethical turmoil about anything in your life; if you're consciously neglectful of your health in emotional or physical matters; if you're willfully lying to anyone about anything, then these behaviors are evidence of either (a) the presence of unaddressed addictions, or (b) a commitment to spirituality that is misaligned and rooted in convenience. There has been no significant regeneration in your personality.

Alcoholics Anonymous advises that in the final analysis, it is deep down

---

[58] Regardless of how long someone has been abstinent, if they still act like a sober drunk — angry, rude, insensitive, sexist, manipulate for attention, blame, gossip, are racist, etc. — they have only really done Step One, and have not completed any of the other steps, even though they claim otherwise. Step One requires a specific change in behavior (sobriety); all the others require a change in personality.

[59] *The Secret Teachings of All Ages,* by Manly P. Hall, Reader's Edition, Jeremy P. Tarcher/Penguin, 2003, p. 71. Also: See the quote from *Isis Unveiled,* H.P. Blavatsky, cited at p. 5.

[60] Ibid., p. 120.

within us that we find the Great Reality.[61] That means some subtle nature of "God" exists in each of us, politics and personality notwithstanding. In order to regenerate yourself, you must be completely aware and absolutely convinced of what is required at Step Two. Otherwise, you will be at loose ends and cutting corners, wandering haphazardly or repetitively through the steps. If you are still like this at Step Eight, you've worked outside of the crucible of transformation.

Addicts act out at the expense of other people. They must not get recovered at the expense of other people. They have to pay for their own recovery. Step Eight is about being willing to be socially responsible—being willing to be called to account for your former irresponsible behavior: "I did this harmful thing and I'll own up." Regeneration into spiritual peace is expensive.

———

It's too convenient and superficial to dismiss an addict's lack of accomplishment as a fear of success. It's much more complicated than that. It often bears out that addicts are more afraid of accountability and the responsibility that goes with success, than the success itself.[62] They may be petulant about the hard work that goes into being successful; or are unable to be a success because of the all-encompassing demands of unaddressed addictions; or avoid success because of an uncanny ability to avoid the resentment of others.[63] The most likely time for an addicts to avoid success by relapsing, quitting therapy, or quitting a support group (or a job) is when they sense the impending arrival of responsibility or truth.

With a self-imposed crisis (addiction), only a self-imposed solution (spirituality) will work. Self-responsibility, individuation, and assertiveness are crucial to spiritual endeavor. Self-help jargon includes the phrase "back doors". A back door is a subtle way to avoid accountability or responsibility. The focus of Step Eight is figuring out exactly what you did that was damaging and harmful to others and being willing to fix it, *after* having slammed shut all the back doors that permit irresponsibility. Some back doors that avoid responsibility at Step Eight are:

- No one will ever know.
- I was stealing from criminals.
- They did bad things, too.
- They hurt me more than I hurt them.
- They don't remember.
- There's no point, they won't understand.
- They were too little to understand.
- I kind-of already made an amend by getting sober/clean/abstinent.
- Everyone else was doing it.

Here are four quotations regarding Step Eight that I refer you to: *"This is a very large order,"* and *"We should avoid extreme judgments, both of ourselves and*

---

[61] *Alcoholics Anonymous*, p. 55.
[62] To be generally successful usually requires individuation and self-defined assertiveness, which many addicts [people] lack.
[63] Aspects of this are discussed at length in *Resentment Against Achievement*, by Robert Sheaffer, Prometheus Books, 1988.

of others."[64] *"We are there to sweep off our side of the street,"* and *"His* [Her] *faults are not discussed,"*[65] These are "why" you need spiritually wise counsel that is hard on you and easy on others, ample time, and much willingness and humility through your relationship with a higher power, to accomplish Step Eight.

For those of you who have been around "recovery" for a while, you've no doubt attended meetings, feel like you belong, and everybody knows your first name (many people know your last name, too). You've attended the summer barbecue, the Christmas party, all the "cakes", and the round-up. You're generally well liked. You've been the group secretary and chaired meetings. But when you're in bed at night, in those quiet moments when you're all alone with your very-secret thoughts, there's a tiny, noticeable loneliness that you avoid. You wonder if they knew the *real* truth, would they still like you? *"Whenever our pencil falters, we can fortify and cheer ourselves by remembering what AA experience in this Step has meant for others. It is the beginning of the end of isolation from our fellows and from God."*[66]

In spite of all the work you've done to this point, you won't begin to lose that deep sense of isolation until you become completely responsible for the harm you've caused. It's this heretofore unexamined core of irresponsibility and harm caused that perpetuates that subtle, painful isolation that sneaks up on you when you least expect it, and it's always present in those quiet moments—if you look for it.

Irresponsibility manifests in many different ways: greediness, small manipulations, subtle exaggeration, tiny dishonesty, subtle withholding, silent blaming or anger, subtle or silent racism or sexism, petulance, and envy. Out of character defect-driven irresponsibility comes isolation. If you're irresponsible in any manner, and conceal this, you're lonely and not loved for who you are—you're loved for the image you project (to conceal the corruption). Therein lies the loneliness.

"Learning how to live in the greatest peace, partnership, and brotherhood with all men and women, of whatever description, is a moving and fascinating adventure."[67] First, it's worthy of note that this effort is described as a moving and fascinating adventure; not something arduous or painful. If this isn't a moving and fascinating adventure, go back to Steps Six and Seven and figure out where your willingness and humility went. Second, at this point, learning how to make your life a moving and fascinating adventure has nothing to do with learning about other people. It's always about learning about yourself and deepening your relationship with God, as you understand God, vis-à-vis the maintenance steps.

When you become microscopically responsible[68] in all aspects of your life, you will noticeably and gradually lose your isolation from God. If you don't do Step Eight in this manner, you will forever cover up the loneliness with politics. Why do people with five and fifteen and thirty years abstinence step up to the podium, tell

---

[64] *Twelve Steps and Twelve Traditions*, pp. 77 and 82, respectively.
[65] *Alcoholics Anonymous*, pp. 77 and 78, respectively.
[66] *Twelve Steps and Twelve Traditions*, p. 82.
[67] Ibid., p. 77.
[68] Being microscopically responsible can only happen with microscopic truth-telling. This perspective of honesty, which is crucial to recovery from addictions, is found in *Conscious Loving*, Gay Hendricks, Ph.D., & Kathlyn Hendricks, Ph.D., Bantam Books, 1992.

ribald drunk-a-logue stories, curse and swear like they're still in a bar, break anonymity, or brag about their program and the people they sponsor? They're scared, lonely, irresponsible, and hiding it. This is what breeds a carnival-like atmosphere in many meetings; none of it is spiritual.

"Since defective relations with other human beings have nearly always been the immediate cause of our woes, including our alcoholism, no field of investigation could yield more satisfying and valuable rewards than [repairing harms caused]."[69] Intimacy and fulfillment cannot coexist with exaggeration, deceit, withholding (even a little bit), manipulation, or shirking responsibility. Backtrack and make an accurate and unsparing survey of the wreckage of your past.[70] Redouble your efforts to identify those you have hurt.[71]

Step Nine

"Made direct amends to such people wherever possible, except when to do so would injure them or others."[72] The actual wording of Step Nine, and the chapter regarding Step Nine in *Twelve Steps and Twelve Traditions*, don't contain the word "sorry". In *Alcoholics Anonymous* we find the word "sorry" used twice. On page 78: *"Arranging the best deal we can we let these people know we are sorry."* This passage refers to debts of money. Within that paragraph it very clearly implies that arranging the best deal for repayment is the way we demonstrate that we are sorry. There is no reference to saying the word, it's demonstrating being sorry by arranging the best deal we can. The other is on page 83: *"A remorseful mumbling that we are sorry won't fill the bill at all."* This needs no explanation.

It's worthwhile to closely examine why people, in most discussions regarding amends, and in the routine of everyday failings, include some notable reference to the transgressor being sorry or apologizing. To amend anything is to repair it, to change it for the better, or to improve it. That's the focus of the work required—to change the situation for the better and to repair the damage. There are *un*spiritual reasons why people say they are sorry within the context of Step Nine.

As described in Apologizing by Numbers, To say "I'm sorry," when making an amend, blurs the transaction by shifting the focus away from the person you hurt onto you. How could anyone be mad at you, or not forgive you, or wish to do anything but understand, because you feel *so sorry* about the mess you created? Your feeling sorry is exactly where the focus should not be.

You are not the harmed person. The amend isn't supposed to be about you, so don't make it about you. The Spiritual truth of the matter is that your feeling sorry really doesn't matter at this point. Feeling sorry doesn't fix anything. At some much later point, after the amend is complete, and you have sincerely acknowledged the harm you did, *and* have taken complete responsibility for it, only then, (maybe) make a sincere and simple statement of your regret. Nothing more.

---

[69] *Twelve Steps and Twelve Traditions*, p. 80.
[70] Ibid., p. 77.
[71] Ibid.
[72] Ibid., p. 83.

Please-Sorry-Thank You

If you practice chanting, there's an insightful experience within the mantra: "please-sorry-thank you".[73] As Westerners, in our insecure passion for wealth and power (they're the same), and an insecure need to win (competition), we're so inculcated with guilt, servility, envy, and irresponsibility that we've become jesters in the Court of Spiritual Integrity. Many of us wander through our entire lives offering a polite and continuous apology for the effrontery of our own existence. This is hard to escape since it's inculcated in our culture. It takes years of work to understand that *"As God's people we stand on our feet; we don't crawl before anyone."*[74]

In Step Nine, getting recovered is about generously undertaking the adventure of creating the best possible relations you can with everyone, willingly admitting where you have harmed people, and then repairing that damage, regardless of the cost to yourself. You being sorry, or you being offered forgiveness from people for the harm you caused, are very distant, generally unrelated concerns to actually making amends. Step Nine is the training ground for charity of spirit.

Being spiritual and recovered is not some sober retrenchment or reorganization of inculcated religious and cultural guilt. The steps are intended to achieve the opposite: authentic freedom. When making amends, servile invitations to please understand; abject or grandiose declarations of being sorry; a droning, mumbled thank you to avoid imprecation; and struggling to absolve yourself of your own human condition, have no place in a Spiritual life.

When you admit that you were wrong, without giving a detailed explanation about the extenuating circumstances, and you repair the damage, the aggrieved party will be left to feel about you as they will. Don't underestimate your ability to disguise an irresponsible agenda under some apparently benevolent behavior (like apologizing). This is self-serving in the extreme. There are literally millions of examples of this, and many of them are quite complicated. Here's one example:

Kim and Terry are going away for the weekend. Kim, who has to work on the day they leave, promises to leave work early, be home by 4:00, and help Terry with preparations so they can be gone by 5:00. Kim tells Terry to depend on it. Kim goes to work and doesn't get home until 6:00. Terry is quite upset and says so. Kim replies sincerely: "I'm really sorry I'm late. I apologize, but my boss wouldn't let me leave early." Kim's sorrow and the reason given, both of which are true, should, according to Kim, end the matter. Kim expects, by implication, that Terry should understand and not be mad. Kim's declaration of sorrow and the reasons for being late, are intended to exonerate Kim from accountability. Terry's feelings and concern are (technically) no longer a part of the transaction.

Terry is hurt and after the apology from Kim, Terry somehow senses being insulted but can't pinpoint what happened. If Terry responds with anything other than: "I understand, it's okay," Terry will appear as unsympathetic and selfish. Kim could then say some variation of: "But I had to work! Don't you understand? Do you

[73] *The Only Dance There Is,* by Ram Dass, Anchor Books, 1973, pp. 92, 93.
[74] *Alcoholics Anonymous,* p. 83.

want me to quit my job? I was working. I couldn't phone. Hey, I'm *really* sorry! I apologize. I'm *really* sorry. What more do you want?"

After this exchange, if Terry is still dissatisfied or hurt, according to Kim the conflict is now Terry's fault for being unreasonable and unsympathetic. Kim explained it away by professing great sorrow and presenting "good" reasons (and thereby shifted the responsibility onto Terry). Kim has made a defense, not an amend, and has taken no responsibility. The apology addresses nothing substantive, and if Kim's irresponsible blaming goes unchallenged, their relationship will remain in turmoil. But in the face of Kim's "good reasons" and "deep sorrow", it's hard for Terry to challenge Kim's irresponsibility without appearing unsympathetic.[75]

The underlying issue—the error, if you will—is Kim made a sincere promise which Kim could not guarantee with reasonable certainty, and yet declared that Terry could depend on the promise. Terry did depend on the promise, which was appropriate to the manner of Kim's promise. The contract went sour when Kim took no responsibility for having made an unreliable promise. Kim immediately defended the irresponsibility by blaming "the boss", and focusing on being sorry rather than on what Terry was feeling. Terry's subtle sense of insult is related to the disrespect shown by Kim for Terry's feelings and sensibilities. To fix it, Kim... (i) is required to be responsible for commitments and promises, (ii) must stop blaming the boss and Terry for being unsympathetic, (iii) should accept and honor whatever it is that Terry feels; and, (iv) must make every attempt to not repeat the behavior.

This will seem pedantic on paper: Kim's amend should be similar to this: "You're right, and I understand that you feel angry and hurt. I made a commitment that I didn't live up to. You depended on me because I told you you could. I'll have to be more clear and responsible about the commitments I make. I was wrong." Kim must recognize and accept Terry's feelings exactly as they are, and demonstrate a resolve to not do it again. In this circumstance, the measure of sincerity is in respecting Terry and not repeating the irresponsible behavior. Sincerity, like honesty, isn't a matter of convenience. Being recovered means bringing a measure of wisdom to commitments—people make decisions based on what they're told.

To argue on behalf of popular opinion—that apologizing and saying sorry is acceptable—is to argue on behalf of irresponsibility and selfishness. It's irresponsible to make excuses, and selfish to shift the emotional content away from the person you harmed onto yourself. Regarding the accurate meaning of apology, I'm someone who defends, by considered reflection, a twelve-step perspective that would not include saying sorry or apologizing. I'm an apologist on behalf of not apologizing for harm done.

What follows is an edited and very compressed version of a true story. A

---

[75] The emotional manipulation is the offender making their "sorrow" bigger than the offense, or bigger than how badly the other person feels. In this way the person hurt or "wronged" is manipulated into compassion for the offender, and then the hurt person feels guilty for expecting compensation or being angry at what was done to themselves. If the person who is hurt allows the offender to "get away" with this manipulation, they are relationship addicts (codependent), and are putting the offender's selfish manipulation ahead of their own dignity and self-respect.

person had been saying unkind and untrue things about Lee. Some time later they admitted this to Lee: "I realized I've been slandering you to some people and I'm really sorry about that." Lee said, "I don't care that you're sorry." They said, "What? I'm making an amend." Lee said, "No, you're not, and I don't care that you're sorry. There are people wandering around with misinformation that's harmful to me, and your being sorry doesn't fix it." The person asked, "What can I do to fix it?" Lee said, "Examine carefully what fear and insecurity caused you to say these untrue things about me. If you are sincere about making amends, speak personally with *everyone* to whom you lied about me. Tell each of them your fear, and that you lied, and that you were wrong in what you said." The person then did just that.

Attending to Step Nine with glib and self-serving interpretations of amends is, from one perspective, worse than making no amends—it adds insult to injury. Be cheerfully disposed (willing), and completely devoted (sincere), and interested in the adventure of establishing the best possible relations with *everyone* that you know. Here are a few indications of what's required:

- *"We must lose our fear of creditors no matter how far we have to go,"*
- *"Reminding ourselves that we have decided to go to any lengths..."*
- *"...[we must] do the right thing, no matter what the personal consequences may be,"*
- *"We must not shrink at anything,"*
- *"[if a] drastic step is indicated we must not shrink,"*
- *"A remorseful mumbling... we are sorry won't fill the bill at all..."*
- *"The spiritual life is not a theory. We have to live it,"*[76]
- *"...[we must] take the full consequences of our past acts, and... take responsibility for the well-being of others."* [77]

None of these statements leave any doubt about the detail, the level of commitment, or the thoroughness required.

When making amends, it's important to set yourself up for success. Here's another edited/compressed, true story: D. lived on the west coast and had unresolved legal issues on the east coast. It was serious and certainly appeared that jail time would be in the offing. D. was determined to follow the program guidelines. While in the west, D. had become well-established in sobriety, had started seeing a therapist regularly, was involved in his community, and after two years of therapy, hired a lawyer in the west, who on behalf of D. hired a lawyer in the east. Seeing that their client had evidence to prove his sincerity, and had extensive professional support, the lawyers worked with the authorities. D. went back east and dealt with his past.

D. achieved extended sobriety, worked at prayer and meditation, became established in a career and in the community, had references, enlisted the aid of

---

[76] These appear in *Alcoholics Anonymous*, pp. 78, 79, 80, 83.
[77] *Twelve Steps and Twelve Traditions*, p. 87.

therapists and lawyers, paid for it all without complaining, and followed the rules (of our culture and of the original twelve-step program). There was no relapse, amends were made, and the obligations inherent in a Spiritual life were met. If you work hard, use common sense, get help from professionals, plan carefully, be responsible, and trust in God, you can clean house.

Yes, some addicts have done some pretty nefarious things they are reluctant to address. Only you can decide how much responsibility (and irresponsibility and secrecy) you're prepared to live with. It's a personal choice. If you think you can live a comfortable, safe life and not make some particular amend, or can conceal some particular harm you caused, then live with that. Even though *Alcoholics Anonymous* is rather clear that people must be willing to go to any lengths to make amends, we all live at some personally chosen level of spiritual responsibility.

Sponsors, spiritual advisors, therapists, can only interpret *Alcoholics Anonymous* and encourage you as they think best. Regardless of any advice given, it will always reduce itself to your having to decide for yourself. You are responsible for the quality of your life. There is never anyone to blame.

Living By Consensus

A man approached me for professional counsel. He was in a chaotic, conflicted relationship with almost constant arguing, betrayals, and lies. He explained it all and concluded his tale with this (which I relate almost verbatim): "Before you tell me what I should do, I want you to know that I've spoken to several other people and the consensus is I should leave my relationship. What do you think I should do?"

Examples this blatant aren't common, but examples of living by popular opinion are legion. Living by consensus evades hard work, avoids criticism or rejection of you by others, and guarantees you'll always have someone to blame. It may not be as physically destructive as acting out, but it's emotionally destructive and just as unfulfilling. Far too many otherwise capable people, live their lives out of a ballot box: obedient to popular opinion, just good enough to get by, and always with something to complain about.

D., in the preceding example, willingly returned to the east coast to face a shortened jail term. This met with a great deal of criticism and some derision from many of his twelve-step peers. D. was called a fanatic, a perfectionist, arrogant, and foolish. Those that criticized him lived "good enough" lives. Good enough wasn't good enough for D., who wanted a spiritual life. *Nothing is free.*

Get a few years of years of abstinence; get a good sponsor—spiritual, gently assertive, and responsible; get into well-conducted, long-term, weekly therapy; get a spiritual advisor; get a lawyer if you need one; and get a job. Force yourself to live by the five spiritual principles—do whatever it takes—and deal with your past. Your freedom and serenity depend on it.[78]

---

[78] By doing these things, and adhering to this lifestyle, you will remove the sense of dislocation and alienation you experienced in your addiction. Only this allows you to create a soulful lifestyle and live with a sense of belonging and purpose.

Discernment

The first sentence in the Step Nine chapter is: *"Good judgment, a careful sense of timing, courage, and prudence—these are the qualities we shall need when we take Step Nine."*[79] The first sentence of Step Nine requires you should make judgments. What about the all too-common admonition, from so many people, instructing others to not make judgments?

Why did you pick this book to read? Why do you choose this person rather than that person for a sponsor? You made a judgment. Life is a judgment call. You made a judgment to attend this movie over that one. You picked a brown jacket over a blue jacket. You joined this group rather than that group. You chose this therapist rather than that therapist. You picked this sexual partner over some other one, and this person for a close friend rather than another one. These are all judgments, and judgments reflect values. Outside of obviously cruel judgments, there is nothing wrong with judgments *per se*—it's more how they're arrived at and what you do within them that needs examination.

You must develop the ability to evaluate circumstances from a spiritual rather than a racist, sexist, angry, addicted perspective; from a humanitarian-humble rather than arrogant/victim point of view. Examine carefully how you spend your life and make respectful, prudent judgments because you are trying to both save, and recreate, your life. An addict's history of self-abuse proves, beyond any doubt whatsoever, what addictions and poor judgments can do. Establish ethical criteria, make judgments, and live with the consequences.

Once you have judged that you would rather do this than that, or be with this person rather than that person, do not proclaim your criteria: "I dated A. rather than B. because B. is a jerk. Let me tell you why B. is a jerk... ." In relation to judgments, what you're required to do is: act on the circumstances you deem more acceptable to you, and say nothing about whatever you decided against.

I recall an adamant and very angry person who insisted loudly that no one had the right to be the arbiter of anyone's sex conduct. It was an accurate, but very self-righteous quoting of p. 69 of *Alcoholics Anonymous*. In the next breath, they loudly condemned someone for asking a newcomer on a date. The hypocrisy escaped them completely. It is your task to make discerning choices, that you decide are to *your* advantage (good judgments), and to never condemn, malign, gossip about, or slander anyone. Investigate wisely, decide accordingly, act quietly, don't gossip or slander, and kindly mind your own business.

It is possible to ignore truths, but with a guarantee that harmful consequences will follow. It is not possible to not make judgments. Trying to force yourself to make no judgments, at the insistence of someone else, is judging that you should live by someone else's judgments. Living your life by others' judgments will consistently lead to calamity, yet a common twelve-step admonition seems to be to not make judgments (which is, in itself, a judgment judging that judgments are bad). Without judgment there's no discernment. Without discernment, life becomes inordinately dangerous.

Where will you learn about good judgment, a careful sense of timing, courage and prudence—the necessary attributes for completing Step Nine? You will learn these by being with people who graciously demonstrate these as natural parts of their lives. You learn about courage, prudence, good judgment, and timing by associating with, and paying attention to, spiritual people: people who aren't mean or sarcastic; people who are responsible and live to evince spiritual principles.

You cannot learn these from tough, crude sponsors who "kick your butt". Emotionally abusive, dictatorial sponsorship reinforces alienation. There is no place for that type of behavior in a spiritual pilgrimage. Spiritual people don't emotionally knock others around. They treat people gently, with dignity, regardless of the other person's beliefs or behavior, and they remember their responsibility and commitment to spiritual principles. The only way that you can learn the four attributes essential to Step Nine is by associating with kind, gentle people who are wise about the spiritual philosophy and intent of the original twelve-step program.

Once you've completed Step Eight, and have a fair grasp of these qualities, begin attending to Step Nine. You've probably made some amends throughout your recovery thus far, but this is where you formally begin. You'll now have clarity and direction—knowing exactly what you have to do, and with whom.

As an aside: Since you've achieved abstinence, you've probably become more considerate by not forgetting birthdays, showing up for Christmas, and making an effort to remember and respond to the important events in the lives of people you care about. Etiquette and courtesy go a long way towards establishing trust and respect, but being considerate of others is something that happens *now* and making an amend is repairing the harm from past inconsiderate behavior.

There are four categories of amends. **The first** category addresses situations of harm where there are no mitigating circumstances: You hurt someone, you fix it. By the time you get to Step Nine, you may have been abstinent for two or three years and you will already have made amends to various people along the way. It is certainly wise to review these with the clearer eyes of longer abstinence, but it isn't necessary to repeat the amends if nothing has been overlooked.

The second category is making partial amends, or in *rare* circumstances, no amend, to avoid harming others. Here's a story to illustrate this potential scenario:

> Heading home drunk from an after-hours club at the top of the hill, Jack falls down and breaks his crown, and Jill comes tumbling after. They spend some time as in-patients at the hospital and a few weeks later, all is well. Jack and Jill have a notorious party to celebrate their discharge from hospital. It's near dawn. Jack has passed out. Jill's pretty stoned, and Miss Muffett entices her into a brief sexual encounter. Then Miss Muffett takes Jack's car (without permission), and drives over to her ex-boyfriend's, Jack, The Giant Killer. They argue and Miss Muffett drives off in a fury in the first Jack's car, crashes through a garden into her ex-boyfriend's beanstalk, abandons the car, and the next morning leaves town. Only Miss Muffett remembers what happened.
>
> Five years later, Miss Muffett has made it to *12 Steps for Fairy Tale*

---

[79] *Twelve Steps and Twelve Traditions*, p. 83.

Creatures (a very closed group—it's hard to find). Everyone's older and wiser and settled down. There's a new edition of nursery rhymes out—hard-cover, glossy pages, and full-color artwork—and everyone's prosperous off the royalties. Jack and Jill have straightened out their lives, moved to the flats, and installed indoor running water. They're making a go of their relationship. Miss Muffett isn't frightened of arachnids now (from good therapy and a few years of abstinence), and she's at Step Nine. Imagine that Jack and Jill, who remember nothing, one day get an unexpected letter:

Dear Jack and Jill:

   Surprise! Remember the big bash five years ago after Jack's crown got better? Well, Jill, I was wrong for pressuring you into having sex with me. At the time I was jealous because my boyfriend Jack the Giant Killer was flirting with The Green Fairy, so I had sex with you, Jill, stole (your) Jack's car, and then bragged about it to (my ex-boyfriend) Jack the Giant Killer. We got in a fight, and I took out his beanstalk with your car, Jack. I abandoned it in a ditch, and hence the damage.

   Jill, I don't think you remember having sex with me, and (your) Jack doesn't know I'm the one who wrecked his car. I really feel sorry about the whole thing. Here's some money (cheque enclosed). Hope you're both doing well.

   Do you know if Jack the Giant Killer still lives with his mother at the old cottage? Apparently I took out her flower bed before I ploughed into his beanstalk. I owe her an amend for gardening expenses. You know, I had to replace the beanstalk and that cost a tuffett full of money... magic beans are expensive. I'm doing well on the coast and feel much better since I got sober and went vegan.

Sincerely,
Miss Muffett

P.S. Did I mention I had herpes? I'm really happy it's been in remission since I got sober. Do you know where The Old Woman Who Lives in A Shoe is? Is she still in the shoe? I've got to find her and sort out something about my family of origin. Apparently Peter Peter Pumpkin Eater is involved. Drop me a note if you can help. Thanks. M. M.

   How Miss Muffett should conduct herself, within these circumstances, is not with this irresponsible disclosure. Other fairy-tale creatures will be hurt. Alcoholics and addicts must not get recovered at the expense of others. To negotiate yourself into being recovered, and maintaining that spiritual perception of Life, requires a sponsor, a spiritual advisor, and very likely a therapist, all of whom understand the nuance of twelve-step programs and the tremendous commitment and responsibility required of spiritual people. If it's wise to make no amend, or a partial one, and your advisors concur, you may have to carry some guilt within yourself and be responsible silently. Seek wise counsel.

   The third category is amends you may postpone if there's a good reason. Your own fear isn't a good reason. If you have noticeable fear in making amends, you've missed the point of willingness—go back to Step Six and sort that out.

   Let's assume you need to make an amend to someone who lives in another city. You're planning a trip there in a few months. Do you write a letter? Do you phone? Do you wait until you get there to make the amend in person? If you wish to delay the amend, discuss the matter with your advisor and examine your motives.

The fourth category are those amends that cannot be made: to people you don't know, or to people who are dead. This includes a subcategory where you have to make an amend, but the harm you caused is so grievous and irrevocable that any amend seems entirely insufficient.

What do you do when the amend is to someone who'is dead or untraceable? I've heard many suggested solutions: write a letter, pray, visit the grave, never repeat the behavior that caused the harm, make a donation to some charity. These are all rituals that may or may not be an acceptable substitute for the amend. Any substitution: prayers, letters, visits to the grave, etc., are a minor consideration in the process.

It's easy to write a letter of amend to someone who's dead or untraceable — there's no emotional risk, potential loss, or impending inconvenience. It's easy to fulfill the requirements of Step Nine by writing a letter of amend to a nameless stranger — there's no risk. Ask yourself, if you knew who or where they were, if they were alive, how willing would you be?

Imagine you have a major amend to make to someone who's dead. You claim to be willing. If that person walked in the door right now, would you be eagerly and pleasantly disposed to be completely responsible, and to create the best possible relations with them if they were standing in front of you right now?

Imagine having to make an amend to someone who, years earlier, you had seriously injured and they've been physically affected ever since, because of something you did. This amend begins when they hear in the tone of your voice, and see in your demeanor, complete willingness and sincerity. This doesn't mean anything stupid or grandiose, like, "Oh, I'd cut off my right arm if only... ." That's theatrical nonsense. The key is the sincerity and willingness underneath the words. In this category, as with all amends, that is the vital test: whether or not you're sincerely willing. The key to any amend is always rooted in your willingness to be responsible, which is directly related to being humble on behalf of your higher power.

How often have people said "I'm sorry," or made some apology, or made an amend grudgingly, and by the time they got to the third word, you knew their "amend" was meaningless? The insincerity was obvious, and even though they said the correct words, it was for their benefit, not yours. If you've got to make amends to someone and they're dead, you can't find them, or it's for some irreparable harm that you caused, the underlying spiritual attitude is what makes the amend sincere.

In some complicated situations, or with people you haven't spoken to for a long time, there are ways to proceed through the actual making of an amend. First, very *briefly* describe the incident and what the harm done was. State your responsibility to fix the damage, and then offer what you propose to do. In some situations it may be appropriate to ask what they think you might do to fix the harm. If the aggrieved person expresses emotions, or offers any comment, spend time listening to how the harm affected them. Make a sincere effort to understand what they say, from their point of view, without defending yourself. Fix the damage you caused. Be emotionally responsible and spiritually generous.

Only if they ask, and only if it seems appropriate, briefly and quietly explain what happened, or why you harmed them. The reason will be some aspect of your fears and instincts gone awry. You learned this in your Step Four. You didn't do the harm because of anything this person did to you, or because of anything that anyone else did. You did it because you wrongly handled your insecurities by hurting them.

Some people will be curious and interested; others won't. Each situation will be different. Remember that sorry and thank you are worn out, misused words in our culture. Avoid self-serving interest in others like trying to get them to forgive you or to give you a break. Limit yourself to making the amend and only go beyond that if the tone of the conversation invites it. At the end thank them for hearing you—*be gracious regardless of their attitude*—and if it seems appropriate, sincerely (briefly) offer that you *regret* the pain (or hardship or extra work) your irresponsibility caused them.

Compassion and Self-Awareness

By the time you get this far in your pilgrimage, you should be somewhat in touch with your own emotions and appreciative of your fears and insecurities. This is important: It's only when you are in touch with your own emotions that you can hear clearly how you hurt someone else (since you can now appreciate both the feelings you have and the damage you caused yourself within yourself).

People who are violent or mean, and those who lack compassion, are significantly out of touch with their own humanity and emotions. They can't appreciate the consequences of what they do because they can't experience their own frailty and pain. When they (hopefully, eventually) sincerely appreciate and experience their own pain and loneliness, especially the unresolved ancient pain they've been carrying for years, they stop hurting others.[80]

At Step Nine, if you appreciate your own pain, and are truly aware of your humanity and feelings, you will be able to sincerely listen to, and appreciate, what others tell you about the pain they experienced as a result of your addiction. Your appreciation of this is the emotional insurance policy that goes a long way towards your not repeating the harm again. You'll be left with a really clear sense of how harmful you were in interpersonal relationships.

You may occasionally offer an amend where the other person is completely surprised. You believe you did cause them harm, but the other person asks: "Whatever are you talking about?" They're truly surprised and don't remember the incident as harmful. Some may not even remember the incident at all.

The presence of guilt in you; the fact that you feel guilty or ashamed, is not necessarily evidence of wrongdoing. Addicts and alcoholics, depending on the "outside issues" they have to deal with, and because of the possibility of unresolved trauma, can feel guilty in circumstances where none need exist. This is through an

---

[80] Again, use common sense. This is in the realm of general human conduct and not in the twilight zone of sociopathology.

over-coupling or fusion of emotional experiences and traumatic circumstances, or the globalization of an emotion into unrelated facets of your personality. This is very complicated psychology. [Now that I've said this, don't use this to avoid responsibility. Your sense of guilt and the obvious harm will, for the vast majority of cases, require an amend. Feeling guilty or ashamed is always reason to examine the circumstances, but it is not a guaranteed indicator of harm done. Seek wise counsel.]

Also, people have different values and assess life's vicissitudes differently. They may sincerely believe no harm was done, or that circumstances were *quid pro quo,* and therefore finished. In either case, discuss it with the person, but don't force your point of view on them. If they appear to be sincerely satisfied that no harm was done, your argument that your assessment of the incident is more accurate than theirs can be insulting (and you'll have to make an amend for that). Thank them sincerely for their time, and then seek wise counsel. It may well be that there was no harm done, and your ego is blaming you for some imagined wrong (which again could be over-coupling, fusion, globalization of affect, or an introjected family of origin script). Very often, this can only be modified through therapy.[81] It's complicated.

The inherent value and subtle wisdom of any step is only clearly seen in hindsight. This is another reason why it's so important to do exactly what is suggested in the original literature. You won't understand the power and the beauty of any one step until you've gone beyond it. As you move into Step Nine, reflect on the close relationship between willingness and humility when making amends.

Be diligent and persevering, and resist the impulse to rush. If you've to make an amend that is particularly sensitive, have your sponsor or a program friend meet you immediately afterwards. Set yourself up for success. Practice prudence rather than evasion. Don't avoid amends—any of them, ever.

The Promises

The Promises are not gifts purely from God. In getting recovered, you don't get The Promises because you did a good Step Three, or because you chair meetings and make coffee. You do not start to experience what The Promises offer because you're staying abstinent. You may get glimmers of them as you complete the first few steps; however, they only arise substantively because of an exceptional effort at Step Nine. They may be perceived as spiritual "gifts" but they are behaviorist-oriented. Yes, a higher power and Providence participate in the uncanny manifestation of courage and strength to be humble and honest; and yes, faith marshals the energy for you to be sincere and willing, but it's from thoroughly attending to the details of Step Nine that The Promises are created. [And, it is only by rigorously adhering to the requirements of the maintenance steps that they remain.]

"If we are painstaking about this phase of our development, we will be amazed before we are halfway through."[82] Some people ask: "Halfway through what?" This question arises because of the decided tendency of addicts to take things

---

[81] I will explore this in some detail in *Facets of Personal Transformation.*
[82] *Alcoholics Anonymous,* p. 83.

out of context. You will be amazed before you are halfway through Step Nine; however, the qualifying precondition is *painstaking*. If you aren't painstaking, you won't be amazed. I imagine anyone could find several dozen references to *painstaking, thorough, detailed,* or *rigorous* if they made a careful search of *Alcoholics Anonymous* and *Twelve Steps and Twelve Traditions.*

Personifying God, even as much as calling *It* "energy"; claiming divine influence in the trivia of life; confusing a decision with an accomplishment or an intent with an action, are fatal to realizing The Promises. Here they are, explained as the result of detailed amends and hard work.

"We are going to know a new freedom and a new happiness."[83] Before alcoholics make amends, they hide from, and avoid, some people, situations, and places. They'll be subtly cautious as they go through life, consciously or subconsciously anxious about the possibility of meeting some person that they owe something to because of a harm or a debt. Their social and emotional freedom is restricted because of that anxiety, and their anxiety is managed by (1) avoiding people, places and circumstances; or (2) by controlling others, like friends or lovers, to prevent those others from doing things that they, themselves, are discomfited by. Once they understand exactly who they owe what to, and address it, or carry the Spiritual willingness to address it at the first opportunity, they know a new freedom. This creates the liberty to go where they want, and to encounter anyone, without anxiety. A new freedom and a new happiness comes from the absence of anxiety that results from addicts making amends responsibly.

"We will not regret the past nor wish to shut the door on it." To regret is to feel disappointed or distressed about something, and to remember it with a feeling of loss and sadness. There's regret and shame at the harm addicts have caused others. This regret persists because of "hiding" the past by avoiding memories. When there's regret about the past, joy about the present is not available. When addicts responsibly and willingly make amends, the regret disappears.

"We will comprehend the word serenity and we will know peace." Serenity isn't the absence of conflict, it's that abiding sense of confidence and trust that you can handle the vicissitudes of Life. Through making amends, which is the solving of your own previously, repeatedly-ignored, repetitive problems, you develop confidence that you know how to handle awkward situations that arise in your life.

Invariably, solving problems entails being honest, unselfish, and responsible. When you have faith in your higher power, and feel confident in your own ability to respond to Life, the more competent you will feel about handling any situation. The result is you'll comprehend serenity. Here, comprehending has three perspectives: (i) understanding the process of how you created conflict and harmed others, rooted in blame, deceit, and irresponsibility, (ii) understanding the method to resolve conflict and prevent harm; and (iii) to comprehend the experience of serenity.

---

[83] This, and the following quotations, are "The Promises," *Alcoholics Anonymous,* pp.83-84.

One of the things addicts usually don't get told is that spiritual serenity is accompanied by a gentle and lovely loneliness. For the spiritually *un*regenerate person, Life is hard because it is dislocated from its spiritual potential. When you learn, by making (often repetitive) amends, how all-encompassing was the harm you did to others, and remain determined to be humble through spiritual self-discipline, you acquire an ability to rein in your character defects. Few things, if any, will remain more important than not hurting others. This fosters serenity and peace, and allows insights into the loneliness of the human condition. In the final analysis, we're alone in this, which isn't bad in and of itself.

"No matter how far down the scale we have gone, we will see how our experience can benefit others." The "experience" referred to in this promise isn't only the experience of the harm caused, it's the experience of making amends. There are three parts to benefiting others. Imagine someone owes you $375.00. This has gone on for several years. You've mentioned it casually a few times, but they've been evasive and vague or rude about paying it back. Your telephone rings right now. It's them. The instant you recognize their voice, something unpleasant hits you: They owe! They say, "I'd like to come over and pay what I owe you." Your annoyance and resentment immediately switches to hope and suspicion: "Oh, really? Yeah, that'd be nice." It's been years, but maybe it's true. You wait.

They arrive and pay you the money. They admit their irresponsibility, and graciously include an extra $50.00 so you can have lunch on them—a token condolence for the trouble they caused. They don't demand any favors, ask for any special consideration, or expect gratitude. They leave. You feel happy. *You* have certainly benefited by the experience of that person making an amend to you.

Now switch roles. You're the person who's just paid the debt. By your making amends—the way they're outlined in *Alcoholics Anonymous*—your experience has benefited the person you paid back, but it will also benefit people in your life and twelve-step program in two ways. One is from your deepening serenity and quiet, responsible nature. This is a powerful role-model for everyone. And, the other is you can now guide others in how to make amends, and wisely encourage them to make amends exactly as the original literature describes. No matter how far down the scale of destruction and harms caused you've gone, you'll see how your experience of making amends will benefit others. The people you hurt get some peace, people in the program get a good role-model, you may become a wiser spiritual mentor, you bring serenity to people in your private life, *and* your higher power gets all the credit. Everyone benefits.

While you are making amends, the subject of "why" may come up. Don't blame your addiction. A quiet, simple explanation regarding the mishandling of your fear and insecurity, and your new spiritual responsibility, is all that's required. Without advertising, or forcing your opinion on anyone, you present spirituality as an attractive lifestyle.

"That feeling of uselessness and self pity will disappear." Useless means "having no value". By seeing what you are now contributing to the world—the bene-

fits to everyone noted above, you acquire an increased sense of personal value. You're now able to contribute to life in new, very useful ways. When you benefit others, you no longer feel useless.

Self-pity, as I wrote earlier, always contains an element of feeling so flawed and defective that you really can't help yourself, or help others for that matter. Thoroughly addressing each amend demonstrates you are changing. You aren't hopeless or doomed to perpetual guilt and misery. You're realizing various positive changes in yourself. Self-pity disappears.

"We will lose interest in selfish things and gain interest in our fellows." Understanding this is closely related to the next promise: *"Self seeking will slip away."* Here's an example: Kim has been in a program for a while and has not yet made any amends. Kim was born and raised in the west end of a large city, drank and used in the west end, and knows hundreds of people there. Kim hides from the past, and controls the anxiety from *un*made amends by altogether avoiding the west end.

Kim meets Terry. Terry is interested in spending an evening with Kim so Terry invites Kim to dinner and a movie in the west end. There's a great restaurant there, and the west end is the only place that some particular movie is showing. Now Kim has a problem: Kim is very interested in spending time with Terry, but Kim has to be evasive about going to the west end. In order to deal with the anxiety, and because amends haven't been made yet, the west end is unsafe for Kim.

Kim hides this insecurity and anxiety by manipulating Terry: "Oh, it's hard to find parking, and the west end is so crowded, and we both live way out here in the east end, and we have to drive *all* that way. Maybe the movie's on video. There's good restaurants in the east end, too." This is selfish self-interest and manipulation. Kim can't be generous with Terry. If Terry is persistent, Kim may go, hoping not to meet anyone, but the subtle anxiety during the date will detract from the joy and pleasure they might otherwise have had. Terry will probably sense the discomfort in Kim and silently wonder what's wrong.

Change the scenario. Kim has made amends to dozens of people in the west end. Debts are, or are being, paid and Kim is completely willing to make amends whenever and wherever that's required. When Terry suggests dinner and a movie in the west end, Kim can gracefully agree. There's no selfish self-interest on Kim's part, and Kim can easily gain interest in what Terry would like do. Kim is graceful and generous because there's no hiding. Self-seeking has slipped away.

This scenario applies in all areas of the unregenerate addict's life: at work, where they socialize, where they live, what meetings they attend, their recreation and leisure, where they go on vacations, and where, when, and which family members they visit. The avoiding of emotions, places, or people by manipulating others is rampant in the personalities of addicts. Self-deceit and manipulation are standard operating procedures.

A sincere and detailed application of the twelve steps may be sufficient to eliminate controlling behaviors. However, some addicts were entrenched in destructive manipulation as a survival skill in their childhoods. Therapy, in addition to the original twelve steps, is often required for any significant resolution of this isolating behavior.[84]

"Our whole attitude and outlook upon life will change." For addicts, a good life, in a spiritual sense, is dependent upon adhering to the five spiritual principles. To the extent that they amend the harms which they caused, they (with authentic integrity) gradually view themselves as capable of repairing damage, being of benefit to others, and no longer feeling useless or selfish (through the previous promises). Altogether, they experience significantly less anxiety in life. People, especially in interpersonal relationships, are easier to be around, and the addict begins to experience spiritual competence at a social level. Their whole attitude and outlook upon life changes as the result of their hard work in making amends.

"Fear of people and of economic insecurity will leave us." There are two types of fear. (1) These fears are generally existential or "spiritual" in nature, i.e. fear of death or of having no human value. Ever deepening spirituality *and* your upcoming work at Step Eleven will address these anxieties. Or (2), fears are cultural or social in nature: You may be afraid you're not good looking enough, tall enough, wealthy enough, or that the line-up will be too long, the plane will be late, or there won't be enough mashed potatoes. These are all ego-constructed/cultural fears. What follows is subtle and complex...

Perseverance in making thorough amends initiates a chain reaction. When you are *consistently* responsible, over a *long* period of time, people begin to trust you. As people begin to trust you, they will help and support you. People will enjoy being around you, and they'll believe what you say about yourself. People will offer you opportunities to participate in their life. Having other people, over a long period of time, sincerely participate in your life, allows you to slowly create a different self-concept, a different concept of others, and a different concept of relationships.

Several things will happen. As you feel more confident about being able to respond to misunderstandings in personal relationships; as you gracefully assume complete personal responsibility; as others become more trusting of you because of your non-blaming, responsible nature, you will be less afraid of people. This will allow you to interact with people in a way that you hadn't before. Through making detailed amends, your relationships will eventually embody respect and integrity rather than manipulation and power struggles. They become a resource for celebrating joys and managing hard times.

Thus far you will have established a true and sincere relationship with God (spiritual trust and commitment), and relationships with people that are guided by the five spiritual principles. The relationship with God, primary; the relationship with people, secondary. At a spiritual level, you finally "get it" that experiencing joy, celebrating life, and coping with hardship aren't about successful economic strategies. You *know* that life is really about love, spirituality, and companionship. All else becomes less important, and you will not be afraid of people.

Fear of economic insecurity arises from an erroneous and entrenched belief

---

[84] This will be explored in *Facets of Personal Transformation.*

that fulfillment is based on wealth and the accumulation of shiny things. The associated illusion is that money (power) ensures happiness. Having a fear of economic insecurity, therefore, is rooted in the cultural illusion that money is the prime source of happiness and abundance. When you lose your fear of people, through responsible and meticulous amends, *and* you establish an authentic relationship with God, you appreciate the non-importance of money in the attainment of peace and joy. You will have then removed "economics" from the recipe for fulfillment. It soon follows that there won't be fear of economic insecurity.

"We will intuitively know how to handle situations which used to baffle us." If, over the course of one or two years, you make 357 amends, and understand and resolve the problems from your past, you will learn how to handle situations which used to baffle you. You will learn how to confidently address problems that you previously avoided. Problem-solving "intuition" doesn't come from God, it comes from solving 357 problems from your past. Now, in the present, when faced with a situation that is potentially a problem, you will know how to handle it—probably in some manner approximating the six-dozen other, similar solved problems from your past.

What's equally important to having solved all your old problems is that you have now become skilled at preventing new ones. If you've been reflecting on the reasons you continuously ended up in conflict, and thereby hurt others, and have conscientiously made detailed amends, all that hard work is intuition in the making. Trust this: The five spiritual principles, used repeatedly and sincerely in your life, will solve every problem you could ever encounter.[85]

"We will suddenly realize that God is doing for us what we could not do for ourselves." Usually what dawns on you is that you're accomplishing things you only heretofore dreamed about. The realization is, through your effort and devotion to appropriate prayer and meditation, you have received two things. The first is the attributes of courage, willingness, prudence, perseverance, and faith. [Addicts only get these attributes in sufficient abundance to complete their Step Nine, or any of the other steps, from a higher power.] The second is: In as much as you may have thought you and "your program" (sponsor, steps, meetings, etc.) were the substantive force of change, you appreciate at a deeper level that in getting recovered, God, as you understand God, was and is the source and resource for transformation.

The spiritual attributes of faith and humility (which allow people to depend on God), allow an addict to find a spiritual solution to human problems.[86] The perseverance and courage to embrace transformation comes from God. There is a deeper appreciation for the sentence on page 45 of *Alcoholics Anonymous* about the purpose of that book being to find a higher power.

"Are these extravagant promises? We think not. They are being fulfilled among us— sometimes quickly, sometimes slowly," which leads into the most impor-

---

[85] *Alcoholics Anonymous*, p. 42.
[86] I often remind myself of the ancient Arabian proverb: Trust in Allah, but tie your camel.

tant and final promise: *"They will always materialize if we work for them."*[87] That's a guarantee. The work referred to is the labor of prayer and meditation (this being the proper use of willpower) directed towards being meticulous and responsible in doing Step Nine.[88] The rewards embodied in The Promises are only as profound as you are responsible and "other directed" in a humble manner. If The Promises are fleeting, intermittent, or vague, then so is your commitment to God and the process.

The closing paragraph of Step Nine clearly identifies two themes.[89] The first is being personally and completely responsible, and willing to take the full consequences for your past behavior. The second is to take responsibility for the well-being of others. That's a hard, bitter pill to swallow for those who haven't properly done the prerequisite work. The prerequisite work is, of course, the preceding steps.

Through willingness and humility, you take full responsibility for yourself, your behavior, and the harm you've caused, and fix it. There are no exceptions to the instruction to *"develop the best possible relations with every human being we know."*[90] Being humble and responsible for the well-being of others, in the context of spiritually based, interpersonal relationships, is the underlying philosophy of Step Nine, and one of the predominant themes of relapse prevention.

What started as a travail has ended as an adventure. You are now recovered — not cured, but recovered. Now what?

---

[87] *Alcoholics Anonymous*, p. 84, emphasis added.
[88] An interesting parallel is on page 163 of *Alcoholics Anonymous*. *"To duplicate, with such backing, what we have accomplished is only a matter of willingness, patience, and labor."* Nowhere else have I ever found such a global guarantee about healing from addictions.
[89] *Twelve Steps and Twelve Traditions*, p. 85.
[90] Ibid., p. 77.

7

Being Recovered: The Spiritual Life (Where This Ends Up)

The state of being recovered is referred to many times in the original twelve-step literature. Here are two instances:

- *"We... are more than one hundred men and women who have recovered... "*
- *"...clear-cut directions are given showing how we recovered."*[1]

These two quotations, and many others like them, clearly point out that people don't have to stay sick or in recovery. This implies that the object of being in a twelve-step program is to get recovered (which means to be spiritual). It is viable, and from the outset, it is the point of the entire exercise. Appreciating the complexity of what happens in getting recovered requires the coalescence of ideas from apparently unrelated disciplines, but it really does all fit together.

Having said this, what appears to be very threatening to many people in twelve-step programs is the fact that when they do the steps, the way that they are presented in the original literature, they can't help but become recovered. It would appear this fear exists because they lack spiritual commitment and/or are still acting out in some other addiction.

Should you have meticulously followed the instructions thus far, and are absent of addictions, you will have sufficiently qualified yourself to be recovered. You are, at a basic level, living by spiritual principles. The task now is to enhance them—which is the function of the maintenance steps—for the rest of your life. The next chapter (Chapter 8) will focus on the importance of ongoing self-monitoring and responsibility (admitting wrongs); Chapter 9 on prayer (don't confuse God with Santa Claus), and meditation (spiritual humility through open-mindedness); and, Chapter 10 on the art of discussing spiritual transformation, which is authentic twelve-step work (humility in carrying the message).

Lao Tse (c. 580-500 BCE) advised that to venerate without understanding or to worship without inner vision would be blasphemous and vain. Regarding veneration, which is a heartfelt deference for someone or something, the observation implies for twelve-step participants that to hold their "program" in authentic reverence, they must understand it to a significant degree. According to him, anything less

---

[1] *Alcoholics Anonymous,* pp. xiii and 29, respectively.

would be blasphemous vanity.[2] What I will be addressing in the following discussion is the apparent, general lack of understanding of how all-encompassing being recovered is, from the perspective of completing the original twelve-steps.

There's a subtle parallel in M.C. Richards' observation cited earlier: *"Let no one be deluded that knowledge of the path can be substituted for putting one foot in front of the other."* Intellectual astuteness, precocious or otherwise, does not imply understanding, which was explained by example in the section 811 Facts About Rigorous Honesty in Chapter 2. Nothing can substitute for the discipline and hard work of actual spiritual transformation. By completing these steps in the manner the AA texts describe, you put one foot in front of the other. That eventually gives you an experience of "the path" that integrates emotional, physical, and spiritual awareness. From within this integrity, there can be authentic veneration.

Twelve-step meetings are full of politics and glib clichés: stultiloquy at its best.[3] People walk into a meeting and the switch flips on, and out comes the rhetoric; they walk out of the meeting, the switch flips off. At home they yell at their kids, lie to their partners, tell racist/sexist jokes "for fun", smoke, cheat on their taxes, pirate software and music and movies off the internet, slander and gossip, complain (about anything), and still, at meetings, spew out empty rhetoric about honesty and spirituality. Living without authentic awareness, constantly recreating petty conflict (samsara for the Buddhist[4]), they live a dislocated and defiant existence, but without the blatant self-destruction of gross addiction. The harm is now more subtle. They've done little beyond learning how not to drink or use, and continue their self-annihilation in well-concealed, quiet desperation.[5]

Out of my own experience of the consequences of shallow commitment, I will not participate in any circumstance or relationship that is morally or ethically squalid (unspiritual) for the suffocating and dangerous "advantage" of popularity, sex, convenience, or financial reward. When I begin an association with a person who declares a desire to live by spiritual principles, and who appears to be doing so, and then later they willfully, repeatedly choose politics or personal advantage, or don't challenge their own defects of character, they are demonstrating that integrity and spirituality are only a matter of convenience. Eventually that will be turned on me, so I quietly distance myself from them.

I have often ended relationships because the other person continued to deliberately ignore some principle of spirituality. Misdemeanors of ignorance or naiveté are entirely different from deliberate non-spiritual conduct. Each of these people were important to me, and in some way contributed to the quality of my life. However, their *deliberate* participation in some behavior that was spiritually untenable was, by association, spiritually costly to me. Long ago I realized that I could not

---

[2] The other clause from Lao Tse, *"...to worship without inner vision... "* is explored in Chapter 9 at Meditations on Wisdom.

[3] *"Stultiloquy: n. An instance of speaking foolishly; foolish* [or senseless] *babbling."* The New Shorter Oxford English Dictionary, Clarendon Press, Oxford, 1993.

[4] *Samsara* is sometimes translated as "perpetual wandering", which results in dislocation and misery.

[5] In *Huxley and God, Essays*, by Aldous Huxley, edited by Jacqueline Hazard Bridgeman, HarperSanFrancisco, 1992, the chapter Knowledge and Understanding is well worth extensive meditation.

afford to evade my commitment to the five spiritual principles by ignoring someone else's non-compliance, when it affected me. This is the standard I set in my adherence to a long-known truth, especially in Buddhism, regarding Right Association.[6]

Spiritual integrity requires that you attain a clear understanding of the inherent importance of the five spiritual principles, *and* that with observable success, you direct your will towards adhering to them within the maintenance steps. After following the specific instructions, and finding yourself at Step Ten, it implies you will have acquired some integrity. This means you think, feel, and act spiritually in your behaviors. In falling short of that, your effort was at least well-intended: you amend any harm, and you adjust future efforts to become as you proclaim you desire to be—spiritual.

Being Recovered: The Preliminaries

Throughout this process I assume:

- You are willing to accept, at face value, the statement that: *"…you had better use everyday language to describe spiritual principles."*[7] There is nothing convoluted or particularly esoteric about the language used. Be cautious of people who apply self-serving definitions and interpretations to words. Do not allow yourself to do this.
- You have followed the instructions in both *Twelve Steps and Twelve Traditions,* and *Alcoholics Anonymous,* from the beginning of the book to the end of Step Nine (p. 84), as well as Appendix II, <u>Spiritual Experience</u>. You did not use step guides from other sources.[8]
- You've completed each step, up to and including Step Nine, in sequence, slowly and thoroughly, while being dedicated to understanding the nuance of each instruction in the original literature. You stayed on each particular step until you realized the spiritual principles inherent within it, and understood the spiritual connection to the step before it.[9] You've not done any

---

[6] Huston Smith in *The World's Religions*, HarperSanFrancisco, 1991, pp. 104-105, discusses Right Association. Although not stated specifically as part of The Four Noble Truths of Buddhism, Right Association is a cornerstone of all spiritual action, and a given in all forms of human endeavor. People naturally understand, without explanation or instruction, that to aspire to anything contains within it the necessary requirement to reorganize their conduct to associate with people who evince similar aspirations, and/or to distance themselves from people who have a strong contradictory intent. Right Association is imperative in spiritual transformation, and especially so in a twelve-step pilgrimage.

[7] *Alcoholics Anonymous,* p. 93. "Everyday language" does not limit people to using words of only one or two syllables. Use a dictionary.

[8] No one needs to write personalized step guides: the best one has already been written.

[9] Earlier, I advised you to keep each step independent of all the others, and here I advise that you must understand their connection. As an exercise that you complete, each step is entirely independent of any other step. However, each step has a spiritual content that directly or indirectly relates to each of the five spiritual principles; *and* each step is connected to all the other steps through these principles. Note that although unstated, the first, second, and fifth spiritual principles are implied at Step One. There is a spiritual connection between Step One and your earlier, addicted, destructive life. The connection is the…

step in a pressured, impatient manner (which is evidence of fear and results in having more complications than you started with).

Learn these definitions:

- *re•cov•er (ri kuv'ér) v. -ered, v.t. 1. to get back or regain (something lost or taken away). 2. to regain the strength, composure, balance, or the like, of (oneself). 3. to reclaim from a bad state, practice, etc. v.i. 4. to regain one's health, strength, composure, balance, etc., after illness, trouble, disturbance, or the like (sometimes fol. by from): to recover from the flu to regain a former and better state or condition.*
- *pre•cise (pri sís') adj. 1. definitely or strictly stated, defined, or fixed: precise directions. 2. being that one and no other. 3. exact. 4. carefully distinct.*
- *so•lu•tion (sé l°Ω'shén) n. 1. the act or process of solving a problem. 2. the state of being solved.* [10]

Some References to "Recovered"

These following quotations are from *Alcoholics Anonymous*:

- *"We, of Alcoholics Anonymous, are more than one hundred men and women who have recovered from a seemingly hopeless state of mind and body. To show other alcoholics* precisely *how we have recovered is the main purpose of this book."* (emphasis theirs, p. xiii).
- *"...we work out our solution on the spiritual as well as an altruistic plane... "* (p. xxiv).
- *"Nearly all have recovered."* And: *"The tremendous fact for every one of us is that we have discovered a common solution."* (p. 17).
- *"There is a solution." "When, therefore, we were approached by those in whom the problem had been solved..."* (p. 25).
- *"Further on, clear cut directions are given showing how we recovered."* (p. 29).
- Regarding the book *Alcoholics Anonymous*: *"Its main object is to enable you to find a Power greater than yourself which will solve your problem."* (p. 45).

---

glaring relationship between relentless suffering/self-annihilation and the complete absence of spirituality. Through the continued abstinence you initiate in Step One, you develop an awareness of the complete absence of spiritual content in your life.

[10] These are taken from *The American Heritage® Dictionary of the English Language, Third Edition,* © 1996, Houghton Mifflin Company. Electronic version.

- *"...the problem has been removed. It does not exist for us."* (p. 85).
- *"...others, who have since recovered... "* (p. 96).

Notice, also, there is an entire chapter entitled <u>There Is A Solution</u> (p. 17). There is an undeniable confidence in these quotations—no half measures. The author(s) of *Alcoholics Anonymous* were very sure (were convinced) that these steps allowed alcoholics to become recovered.

There's a qualifying requirement that relates to the effort you invest in all of the work you do, which in turn relates back to the state of being recovered. This requirement is found in <u>How It Works</u> on page 59 of *Alcoholics Anonymous*: *"Half measures availed us nothing."* It would appear that being forever "in recovery" is a half-measure.

"In Recovery": The Mediocre Solution

Addicts and alcoholics are told that they can get recovered, and these are people who don't like to do what they're told. Unregenerate alcoholics and addicts don't want responsibility put on them, and being responsible is a mandatory part of getting recovered. When an addict or an alcoholic argues that they can only be forever in recovery, they're trying to justify their own fearful half-measures.

People who live in desperate mediocrity, or continue to fail away at Life, are too easily, glibly labeled as being afraid of success. The reasons for "failure" are much more complicated. In addition to those I mentioned earlier, here are some other possibilities... People underachieve because (1) they're angry, and underachieving is one way to punish and keep disappointed those people who love them—people at whom they, the underachievers, are mad at; or (2) it's an expression of self-loathing. (3) Being a failure prevents caregivers who were mean to them (that the underachiever may subconsciously wish to punish) from taking some credit for, or taking pride in, any success. As a success: (4) Their own introjected, self-critical scripts will have nothing to berate them for; (5) they'll be resented by other underachievers, and so they avoid being resented; (6) they'll be held accountable—no more hiding. (7) If they become a success they'll have to leave their underachieving comfort zone and create a new social circle. (8) Being spiritually successful is *very* hard work. It takes much less effort and little discipline to be mediocre or fail.

The five principles of spirituality are the antithesis of the five main symptom-constellations of the disease of addictions: (i) self- or other-destructive behavior, (ii) deceit and dishonesty, (iii) arrogance, self-righteousness, and pride, (iv) greed and selfish behavior; and, (iv) irresponsibility and defiance. Being "in recovery" allows you to be mean or irresponsible and to justify it. You present the big excuse and demand compassion for your never ending struggle of continuous healing: "So I told a lie. What'd you expect? I'm in recovery. I'm *trying*."[11] Being "in recovery" doesn't sound like a solution; it sounds like petulant purgatory.

Regardless of how long you've been sober—three years or three decades—if you're always "in recovery", after you claim to have done all of the steps (several times) you still get to act like an addict: harm yourself, hurt others, lie, be arrogant, selfish, rude, disobedient, and irresponsible, and when challenged on any unspiritual behavior, you're able to invoke the defensive In Recovery Irresponsibility Clause, "I'm in recovery. I'm *trying*." Instant exoneration, and who can argue with that? Remember the perfect in-recovery prayer: "Please God, let me be honest and humble (but not yet)."[12] Being recovered is threatening to the spiritually unfit because it requires an ongoing posture of no excuses.

Being recovered doesn't mean that life will become a conflict-free, love-zone of bliss. When recovered, there are still times when Life is demanding, and probably more so for the truly spiritually minded. This may cause you to wonder if spirituality is so expensive, and if there's going to be hardship anyway, why bother going through the struggle to be spiritual? Why not give up, settle for mediocrity, and take it easy? There are three reasons.

The first reason is that the addict that's abstinent but forever "in recovery" endures perpetual pain, loneliness, and isolation, and it never gets better. **The second** is that the fear and anxiety during step work is constantly re-experienced and cannot be resolved. **The third** reason is that all that's available in social situations is commiseration, and a gossiping interaction of comparison and one-upmanship. Authentic intimacy and love are forever absent. However, for the person who is spiritually determined, the pains of life are never carried alone; they aren't re-created, and they can be resolved. Life always gets better. Only the truly spiritual person can celebrate the implacable grandeur of life in the midst of calamity and misadventure.

Too many people, regardless of abstinence seniority, hide in twelve-step meetings, making enemies of people unlike themselves. They refuse to believe, or haven't been shown, what's available through the original steps. Many twelve-step participants fail to (first) closely examine the original literature, and (then) therefore cannot explore spirituality at a depth sufficient enough to permit the detailed self-examination that is required. They are unable and unwilling to call themselves to task. Defending against being recovered is one manifestation of a fear of being responsible, and is evidence of a lack of spiritual commitment.

"We... have recovered from a seemingly hopeless state of mind and body."[13] If you don't believe this is possible, then you are disbelieving of *Alcoholics Anonymous* and lacking in faith. It appears too self-evident to require articulation, but there is a direct correlation between being spiritual (recovered) and the effort you

---

[11] Take some small object and set it on the floor in front of you. Now try to pick it up. Don't pick it up, just *try*. In definable (absolute) areas like honesty, you either are or you aren't. You care or you don't. "Trying" is very often a petulant excuse for irresponsibility and a plea for unearned leniency.

[12] This is a variation of an observation made by St. Augustine.

[13] *Alcoholics Anonymous*, p. xiii.

invest in spirituality. When the author(s) entitle a chapter <u>There Is a Solution</u>[14], who is it, within twelve-step programs, that thinks there isn't one? It doesn't say that there is an almost-solution. It says: *"...we have discovered a common solution."*[15] And, *"...clear-cut directions are given showing how we recovered."*[16] What is it, exactly, that's unclear?

If a person has cancer, the flu, or a broken leg, the goal is to get recovered, not to almost get better and stay in recovery. By that logic, from the moment a person becomes abstinent, the goal should be to get recovered, not to "stay in recovery". This is equally true and equally possible for any of the abstinence not-available addictions like sex, work or relationships. Believing that an addict cannot get recovered is an issue of investigation, commitment, and faith, not representative of fact.

Being "in recovery" implies you are in the process of getting out of a disease, not that you are out of it. To be recovered must mean you are no longer *in* recovery and have finished recovering. However, this does not mean that you are cured, can "act out" safely, or that you are spiritually perfect. It means you are living within the five spiritual principles, in the maintenance steps, without addictions, and are consistently accountable for your behavior—responsible with no excuses.

Without a sincere spiritual purpose, all step-work is only an exercise in Impression Management. That is sufficient for remaining in recovery, but insufficient for those who actually intend to become recovered and experience spiritual joy.

Understand how the spiritual principles are embodied in each step, and how these principles connect the steps together. Understand how obedience to spiritual principles will eliminate the symptoms and eliminate addictions. This will inform your inner vision of a higher power and establish its relationship to your life. Be determined, patient, and obedient, and you'll become recovered.

Recovered and Step Two

The potential to eventually be recovered is born in Step Two. *"Came to believe that a power greater than ourselves could restore us to sanity."*[17] If addicts believe that being in recovery is the best that's available, they lack faith in the program and in a higher power, and have missed the point of Step Two. By definition:

- *be•lieve (bi lêv') v.i. 1. to have confidence in the truth or existence of something. 2. to have religious faith. v.t. 3. to have confidence or faith in the truth of;*
- *re•store (ri stôr') v.t. -stored, 1. to bring back into existence, use, or the like; reestablish. 2. to bring back to a former, more desirable condition. 3. to bring back to a state of health, soundness, or vigor; and,*

---

[14] *Alcoholics Anonymous*, p. 17.
[15] Ibid.
[16] Ibid., p. 29.
[17] Ibid., p. 59.

- *san·i·ty (sàn 'î-tê) noun 1. The quality or condition of being sane; soundness of mind. 2. Soundness of judgment or reason.*[18]

Step Two doesn't read: "Came to believe that a power greater than ourselves could keep us in recovery." Step Two is a whole-measure, not a half-measure. Don't settle for mediocre commitment and partial responsibility, which are all that's available when you create a psychological orientation within a spiritually structured process. Remember to avoid the Misalliance of Commitment (p. 251).

One Item of Twelve-Step Jargon

In twelve-step programs, no one refers to the first nine steps as Maintenance Steps. That label is reserved for Steps Ten through Twelve. To "maintain" is: [v.t.] *1. to keep in existence or continuance; preserve. 2. to keep in due condition, operation, or force. 3. to keep in a specified state, position, etc.*[19]

The implication is that the first nine steps enable you to attain something, and the last three allow you to maintain it. What have you attained? The state of being recovered. If the best end result was to remain in recovery, the last three steps wouldn't be called maintenance steps. In fact, they'd be redundant. Through willingness, patience, and labor,[20] you achieve the same level of confidence that is evident in the original twelve-step literature — guarantees the cofounders discovered through spiritual devotion.[21]

---

[18] *The American Heritage® Dictionary of the English Language, Third Edition,* © 1996, Houghton Mifflin Company. Electronic version.

[19] Ibid.

[20] *Alcoholics Anonymous,* p. 163.

[21] There is a particular discontent in some quarters of some twelve-step groups and recovery programs. Demeaning comments and observations are made about the personalities and possible unspiritual behavior of a few of the original members and of the co-founders of AA. These views are expressed by professionals or twelve-step participants who appear to be seeking status, justification, or credibility for some unspiritual agenda, at the expense of the people whom they gossip about. This undermines the ability of newcomers to trust the integrity of the original written program, and it slanders and undermines the sincerity of the program founders. The comments and writings this author has been privy to, whether accurate or not, were unnecessary in context, and unspiritual in principle.

Regarding these unkind criticisms, these AA-text passages are relevant here: *"play the big shot...";* *"all people, including ourselves, are to some extent emotionally ill...";* *"our ancient enemy, rationalization...";* *"We 'constructively criticized' someone* [to] *hide a bad motive underneath a good one...";* all from *Twelve Steps and Twelve Traditions,* pp. 92 - 94. There are other relevant passages.

I have described elsewhere that the original AA texts are in that very small group of spiritual teachings that changed the world. They are arguably the most profound writings on spiritual transformation in 1500 years. They grew out of a very specific need to address the horrendous spiritual dislocation in addictions, and the related alienation in modern culture; which culture promotes and enables these unkind comments. The AA program texts stand independent of their author(s). The people who conceived of AA, and authored the books, were just "people" with the foibles common to humanity. That neither detracts from the integrity of what is written, nor detracts from their personal sincerity.

It is this simple: The co-founders were not perfect. So what's that got to do with anything besides the fact that they were people? They were devoted and sincere. What they wrote is true. It is spiritually profound *and,* it works. For these teachings, millions of addicts are grateful. That the original few people, themselves, didn't achieve spiritual perfection is of no account in the matter. The comments that demean their private lives speak more to the insecurities and fears of the purveyors of the gossip, and the malicious ambience of this culture, than anything else.

Six Perspectives of Being Recovered

What follows is an examination of "addiction" and "recovered" from six differing models or perspectives.[22] These general perspectives are from (1) the World Health Organization; (2) a mental-health model; (3) a medical or psychiatric model; (4) a psycho-social model; (5) a spiritual perspective; and, (6) the view of addiction presented within *Alcoholics Anonymous*. But first, I will present a problem, the discussion of which will establish the structure for what follows.

Imagine you see an old woman slouched up against the wall of a run-down tenement building. She's obviously very poor, in tattered clothes, emaciated, somewhat disoriented, in ill health, disheveled, dirty, and drunk. A committee is formed to address "the problem".

If you were a social worker, you might focus on finding adequate housing, getting medical attention, and accessing seniors' services. If you were a medical doctor, your resolution strategy might stress medication, hospital care, and diseases unique to gerontology. If you were a psychologist, you might tend to define the old woman's problems in terms of family systems, a psychological crisis of aging, and long-term de-compensation arising from any number of factors. A sociologist may find legitimate cause for the woman's problems in the midst of a highly mobile culture and the disintegration of the extended family. If you were a strongly opinioned feminist, you might view the woman's problems in relation to culture and the apparent social and political advantages available to men. If the old woman were a member of a visible minority, and you were a social activist, you might create a resolution strategy that identified racism or prejudice as a core issue. If you were an addictions counsellor, or a member of a twelve-step program, you might classify the woman as an alcoholic and argue that if she could get sober, many of her problems would be solved. A religious professional might categorize the old woman's problems in terms of an ineffective relationship with God, and point to evidence of lack of love and caring for old people in our culture.

Imagine these people on a committee: social worker, medical doctor, addictions counsellor, psychologist, sociologist, feminist, minorities advocate, someone from a twelve-step program, and a minister or priest. Whomever on the committee is given the authority to prioritize the problems determines the focus of the solution: different perspectives, different truths. All of these people are well-intentioned and probably right from their own particular point of view.[23]

---

[22] What I present here is not intended to imply that any professional, or layperson, or any organization, that is associated with addictions recovery, agrees with me. Neither am I representing that I am a doctor or psychologist. I am an addictions counsellor/therapist. The observations and perspectives presented here are intended only to suggest a more open awareness of the broad scope, and far-reaching possibilities, of the original twelve-step process of getting recovered from addictions.

[23] Should anyone whom you seek guidance from be spiritually unregenerate or noticeably struggling themselves, their insights to your problems will be particular to their needs and not in your best interests. Should your sponsor or mentor be one of your friends; someone you socialize and loiter about the neighborhood with, their counsel will be self-serving to their needs within the politics of their relationship with you. If you, personally, have a recurring problem, create a new view of the problem, and abandon the ineffective resolution strategy. Don't try harder, try different.

There are many views of addictions—different philosophies if you will—and each one covets definitions that dovetail with that particular view. They're all well-intentioned. Each of the six addiction-perspectives is slightly different from the others, and would necessarily have their own view of what it means to be recovered. The process outlined in the original twelve-step literature is so all-encompassing in its resolution of alcoholism [addiction], that achieving The Promises, being recovered, and being spiritual, not only addresses all the concerns of the other five perspectives, but goes far beyond anything offered anywhere else.

(1) The World Health Organization

The definition of addiction that seems to have the most universal credibility, and is most concise and universally applicable, is from the World Health Organization. An addiction is *"...a pathological relationship with a mood-altering experience that has life-damaging consequences."*[24] This compasses the symptom constellations and dynamics evident in this self-annihilating behavior. It's easily applicable to the abstinence not-available addictions (food, sex, anger, religion, relationships, etc.), the distraction/behavior addictions (television, work, exercise, gambling, etc.), and the substance addictions like alcohol, tobacco, adrenaline, and drugs.

Pathology is the scientific study of disease. A pathological relationship would be diseased: a destructive and unhealthy condition (ingestion of a substance, or some other behavior) that is mood-altering (changes one's state of mind or emotion), where the behavior or consequences of the experience are life damaging and the person cannot "stop" (which is what makes it pathological).

Within the original twelve-step program, a loss of the obsession or compulsion occurs through continued abstinence and sincere self-application to the twelve-steps. There is no mood altering through acting out, and the pathological relationship ceases to exist. With continued twelve-step work and abstinence, life-damaging consequences cease. Making amends addresses the consequences and harm done to others. Taken altogether, abstinence and authentic step-work resolves each component of the World Health Organization's definition. Within this particular perspective, an addict could become recovered through the original twelve steps.

(2) Mental Health

A mental health worker might define alcoholism or addiction as a mental obsession, that causes a person to repeatedly engage in a self-destructive lifestyle, with various attendant emotional problems, and social isolation. When addicts arrive at the threshold of Step One these problems are evident. Accordingly, then, to be recovered an addict would have to address these four constellations of issues: mental obsession, destructive lifestyle, emotional problems, and social isolation.

Alcoholics Anonymous advises: *"The feeling that the drink problem* [obsession] *has disappeared will often come strongly,"* (p. 75); *"We are not fighting it,*

---

[24] Life-damaging consequences are discussed in detail in Chapter 2, under Symptoms.

neither are we avoiding... " [and] *"...the problem has been removed,"* (both p. 85); *"For by this time sanity will have returned,"* (p. 84). The obsession to act out, with the related insane thinking and destructive behavior are resolved.

Additionally, within a twelve-step program lifestyle, social isolation is eliminated and, though there may be emotional problems, these are modified or reduced in the majority of cases to manageable or treatable levels. Even in the situation of dual-diagnosis, the mental-health issue that is attendant to the addiction *isn't* an issue of addiction. Life may not be a text book version of peace and harmony, but should the non-addiction part of the diagnosis remain evident, that wouldn't negate the resolution of the addiction itself. Through the twelve steps the addict would qualify as recovered.

(3) Medical / Psychiatric

The following criteria for the categories of Dependence and Abuse are edited here, and found in the DSM-IV.[25] My intent is to capture the themes of the issues to enable some observations about being recovered, not to provide medical advice. Distraction and behavior addictions can be substituted for "substance" to provide insight into assessing other addictive behavior. The DSM-IV requires a one year period for the presence of symptoms for either classification to be valid. In order to err on the side of caution, I have arbitrarily chosen a two year period of abstinence as a baseline for the consideration of being recovered.

Criteria for Substance Dependence[26]

Clinically significant impairment or distress from a maladaptive pattern of substance use, evidenced by three (or more) of the following symptoms occurring at any time in the same twelve-month period:

- Tolerance by either markedly increased amounts to achieve intoxication or to achieve the desired effect, or having a diminished effect with continued use of the same amount.
- Withdrawal symptoms appear when the substance is removed, or some other similar substance is used to avoid withdrawal symptoms.
- Substance is taken in larger amounts over longer periods than was intended.
- A desire, or unsuccessful efforts, to reduce or control substance use.
- Significant time is given over to activities related to obtaining or using the substance.
- Important activities are reduced or given up because of the substance use.

---

[25] *Diagnostic and Statistical Manual of Mental Disorders,* Fourth Edition, American Psychiatric Association, 1994.
[26] Ibid., p. 181.

- Use is continued despite knowledge of problems stemming from the use or activity.

With two years of continued abstinence and participation in a twelve-step organization, the first five criteria (specific to using and acting out) become non-issues. Regarding the last two criteria: important activities would be resumed or new ones created, and there would be no problems from use or activity.

Criteria for Substance Abuse[27]

Clinically significant impairment or distress from a maladaptive pattern of substance use, as evidenced by one (or more) of the following symptoms occurring within a twelve-month period:

- Recurrent substance use resulting in a failure to fulfill obligations.
- Recurrent substance use in hazardous/harmful situations, including driving.
- Recurrent substance use resulting in legal problems.
- Continued substance use despite persistent or recurrent social or interpersonal problems arising from the effects of substance use.

The situation is basically identical here. After two years of abstinence and twelve-step work, there would be no impairment, no recurring hazardous situations or consequences, and no recurring distress or problems related to substance abuse. Hence: recovered.

From another medical perspective, two years of abstinence would allow time to address the physical/medical problems from use or abuse: physical health would be reestablished and stabilized; detoxification would be finished. General health would be largely regained within two years. Granted, there may be permanent complications like HIV or hepatitis, but two years of abstinence and responsible twelve-step participation would allow time for these to be properly assessed and managed. Continued commitment to abstinence and a twelve-step program would qualify as being recovered from the symptoms outlined within the DSM-IV.

(4) Psycho-Social

A general pattern of symptoms in a psycho-social model of addictions (closely related to the mental health perspective) might be:

- substance abuse and destructive or harmful behavior
- deceit
- arrogance and blaming
- selfishness
- noticeable irresponsibility

---

[27] *Diagnostic and Statistical Manual of Mental Disorders,* Fourth Edition, American Psychiatric Association, 1994, p. 182, 183.

These five would manifest in a consistently noticeable pattern, over an extended period of time, with increasing persistence or frequency. Therefore, in order to become recovered, addicts [alcoholics] must extricate themselves from, and eliminate, the symptoms in some permanent manner, over an extended period of time.

Assume, for at least two years, an addict participates in a twelve-step program, maintains abstinence, and sincerely follows instructions through Step Nine. Throughout this period, the substance abuse and self-harm cease; and deceit, arrogance, selfishness, blaming, and irresponsibility are reduced to within "socially acceptable" limits. There would be a generally non-destructive participation in life. In achieving all this, the addict in a twelve-step program would have eliminated all of these symptoms and demonstrated responsibility. This would qualify them as having recovered from addiction from a psycho-social viewpoint.

(5) Spiritual

For this point of view, I'll begin with the five spiritual principles: respect for the body-temple, veracity, humility, charity, and responsibility and obedience.[28]

The behaviors of a practicing addict are consistently these: self- and other-destructive acting out (causing harm and mood altering); dishonesty; arrogance; having pride to the detriment of themselves and others; selfishness in a way that detracts from the rights and well-being of others; and general irresponsibility and willfulness. These unspiritual behaviors are altogether the classic aspects of addiction. Maintaining abstinence and following precisely the original instructions eliminates the symptoms and enables and addict to live by spiritual attributes: from unspiritual (addict) to basically spiritual (recovered). *"Well, that's exactly what [Alcoholics Anonymous] is about. Its main object is to enable you to find a Power greater than yourself which will solve your problem."*[29]

The twelve steps don't "treat" addiction, they resolve spiritual corruption, and that makes the phenomenon of addictions disappear. The first nine steps, done meticulously, eliminate the symptoms of spiritual corruption (which was your addiction). Addicts would achieve a noticeably spiritual aspect to their life, which the maintenance steps are designed to enhance. From a spiritual perspective, completing the steps properly allows you to become recovered.

(6) The (Original) Twelve Steps

There are many references to being recovered, some of which are noted earlier in this chapter. The original twelve-step reference texts, in the midst of pages of explanation, advise that there are essentially two things to accomplish: overcoming the obsession to drink [act out], and eliminating the insane thinking.[30] By the time you finish Step Nine, these two general conditions are gone. Achieving a life with no

---

[28] See Appendix II.
[29] *Alcoholics Anonymous*, p. 45.
[30] This was discussed earlier at The Doctor's Opinion.

obsession and no insane thinking removes the five main traits of addiction (noted in the second paragraph of the spiritual model immediately above). Steps One to Nine allow you to become recovered. Steps Ten to Twelve allow you to maintain it.

————

It's easier to stay recovered than it is to get recovered, and within a few days of inattention to spiritual principles, it's easy to lose what progress you've made. Study the original reference texts—*extensively*. Practice doing what you are told rather than discussing "whys and wherefores". Wear out the books, and fill up many pads of paper with cross-referenced notes, all the while constantly focusing your willpower on creating a sincerely spiritual mindset. Tell no one that you are working so hard, and eventually, regardless of how you look at it, you will become recovered. You, and anyone who associates with you (children, work mates, partners, friends, family) will benefit.[31]

Responsibility in Spirituality (Being Recovered)

Many things prevent people from becoming recovered. One of the more prevalent obstacles, heretofore unstated, is contained in the unhealthy ego-posture of "perfectionism". Some people repeat the steps in an effort to get them done perfectly, believing their salvation depends upon not missing the minutest detail of any task. [Conversely: It is also true that many of the litanies of magnificent failure, and the grim determination to maintain a squalid life, are a dramatic twist on overachieving.]

For perfectionists, any level of achievement that's generally acceptable to the majority of their culture is *un*acceptable to them. Just because perfectionists don't believe they are recovered doesn't mean that they aren't; it means they're perfectionists. Being subjected to the tyranny of an inner, relentless, demand for perfection is often a mental health issue that's independent of addictions. There's a great deal of misdirected emotional energy in struggling to achieve perfection within the steps, which perpetuates the abysmal mind-set of self-castigation and failure.

Should you misunderstand what serenity means, or misperceive how the steps accomplish what they do, you may believe that today's turmoil or conflict is evidence of yesterday's "poorly completed" steps. In many cases this may be accurate; however, completing the steps with an attitude that demands perfection, doesn't allow for an eventually conflict-free life; it promotes conflict. "The Program" promises full recovery and serenity, but these do not imply an absence of error or misadventure. As a perfectionist, if any time you encounter turmoil, and are left with the sense (fleeting or otherwise) that somehow you didn't do something right within the steps, your perfectionism and insecurity will then prompt you to repeat them.

One aspect of serenity is feeling comfortable that, with help from a higher power, you are competent to respond spiritually to whatever Life throws at you. In the midst of turmoil and misadventure, there may well be indecision and disagree-

---

[31] By the same token, you, and anyone who associates with you, will be hurt by your half-measures. Everything costs something.

ment. However, you will carry an abiding faith that if you choose a humble, "main-tenance-step" orientation to life, meaning that you view Life spiritually and not temporally, you'll always succeed in being abstinent and serene, regardless of the outcome. Out of this mindset comes this truth: You don't have to be wise or power-ful—the maintenance steps are. You can therefore focus on obedience rather than dominance, and humility rather than self-importance. You never again have to figure out "how" to live, you only have to adhere to the five spiritual principles. [That's "how" to live, but what you actually do with your life is another matter entirely.]

Are They Good Enough?

When you went through school and passed from grade to grade, rarely did you get perfect marks in all subjects. Your range of marks were sufficient to progress into the next year. B's or C's may not have been sufficient for your caregivers or yourself, but they were sufficient for the educational system. As an adult, should you decide to return to school, I suspect you would not be required to repeat grade five in an effort to get perfect grades because you only managed a C+ when you were there before. The passing marks from years gone by were sufficient then, and they are still sufficient today.

So it is with the steps in the program. If Step Four rates a metaphysical B, so be it; if it rates an A, that's fine too. With willingness, patience, and labor, be thorough; make a sincere and honest effort; be diligent. Trust in the spiritual integrity of what's written in the original twelve-step literature, and in the firm, gentle guid-ance of a spiritually wise mentor. The maintenance steps are revealed in such a way that they compensate for our less-than-perfect (all too human) efforts. Struggle against perfection, which masks insecurity, and be satisfied with being confidently ordinary. Should you ever manage to live within the five spiritual principles, and be confidently ordinary, you'll be remarkable for that.

The first two sentences of Step Ten are: *"As we work the first nine Steps, we prepare ourselves for the adventure of a new life. But when we approach Step Ten we commence to put our AA way of living to practical use, day by day, in fair weather or foul."*[32] This points to the clear separation between getting recovered and being recovered. There is also this: *"We have entered the world of the spirit,"*[33] which implies that before Step Ten, you weren't "in" the world of the spirit, you were approaching it. At Step Ten, you've entered it. There are profound implications in these sentences regarding the major shift that occurs after Step Nine.[34]

---

[32] *Twelve Steps and Twelve Traditions*, p. 88.
[33] *Alcoholics Anonymous*, p. 84.
[34] In this book, in Chapter 9 on Step Eleven, I examine meditation in some detail. After reading that sec-tion, consider returning to this point and reflect again on what I offer here.

Being recovered and maintaining that spiritual state requires a steady, gentle, persistent effort towards responsibility and spiritual fitness. Living in the maintenance steps doesn't carry the requirement to be above your humanity.[35]

People make mistakes—it goes with being human. Being recovered entails living a life of ups and downs, and sometimes missing the mark of spiritual soundness. When success and misadventure befall you, compass your behavior with the maintenance steps and spiritual principles. Responsibly address any irresponsibility. Being recovered is frightening to many people because there is so much responsibility attached to it, but remember, you were [supposed to have been] trained for living responsibly through the process of meticulously doing the steps. Maintain your commitment to your higher power; seek trenchant, percipient guidance from a well-informed spiritual advisor; and be honest (about *every*thing). Being human doesn't remove your entitlement to being recovered.

In examining the invisible, perennial themes of spirituality, I've come to believe that for an addict to get to the maintenance steps is to attain only a very elementary competence in spiritual endeavor. Certainly, they are recovered, but that's only novice-level spirituality. Going beyond the maintenance steps to the next level of being Spiritual through true humility and devotion to God—becoming someone who is an insightful, wise, and humble spiritual advisor to other pilgrims, is another matter entirely. That's why there are so very few bona fide saints and spiritual gurus—it's such hard work. (But, from my reading, and from what I'm told, the rewards are legion and beyond anything an unregenerate person can imagine).

With willingness, patience and labor; with Right Effort, Right Association, Right Conduct, etc., and wise counsel, you can become and stay recovered (maintain spiritual integrity)—all within the guidelines of the original twelve-step program. *Alcoholics Anonymous* refers to drinking as only a small part of the problem. Drinking or acting out are only a symptom; character defects are only a symptom. The purpose of the original twelve steps appears to be to relieve you of your addiction and character defects; but not really. At a deeper level, they're to repair the spiritual corruption in your human condition, which will enable you to embrace a sincere relationship with God and enjoy Life.

As *Alcoholics Anonymous* leads into The Promises, you are advised: *"For by this time sanity will have returned."*[36] There is nothing unclear about that, but it's dependent upon the following observation: *"Rarely have we seen a person fail who has thoroughly followed our path."*[37] If you do a Step One from a recovery house, Steps Two and Three from some treatment center, and then an AA Step Four and Five; if you use the NA text for Steps Six and Seven, then a self-help book for Eight and Nine, I don't know what you'll end up with, but it won't be The Promises as outlined in *Alcoholics Anonymous*.

---

[35] What might serve us well is recognizing that our modern-day culture, which embraces fantasy, illusion, greed, power, violence, blaming, accumulation of shiny things, sexual dysfunction, status, fame, character assassination, notoriety, tabloid gossip, racism, and sexism, actually denies our humanity.

[36] *Alcoholics Anonymous*, p. 84.

[37] Ibid., p. 58, emphasis added,

Another observation about being recovered is this: Read The Promises several times, very slowly. Meditate on their *all*-encompassing nature. Reflect carefully on how they are the antithesis to any and all of the symptoms of addiction. They represent virtues and attributes that, with continued Right Effort, etc., will be present in *every* aspect of your existence from the first time you appreciate them to the moment you die. The Promises are universal in their scope and soulful in their depth. They contain respect, veracity, humility, charity, responsibility—the essence of spirituality—deep within the experience of them. Should you authentically achieve these promises, how could you not be recovered?

Maintaining a Spiritual Aspect to Life

Your exploration of your own three-dimensional spider's web (described in The Manner of Presentation[38]) has, in concert with the mysterious machinations of Providence, allowed you to acquire certain abilities. Acquiring these abilities, and learning in general, always follows these four stages, that I've explained by example:

- 1st Stage - *Unconscious Incompetence*
  A newborn baby doesn't know that bicycles exist (unconscious) and doesn't know it cannot ride one (incompetent).
- 2nd Stage - *Conscious Incompetence*
  One day, when still very young, the infant learns of the existence of bicycles, or sees a child riding a bike. It now knows there are bicycles (conscious), and realizes that it is incapable of riding one (incompetence).
- 3rd Stage - *Conscious Competence*
  When a little older, after diligent practice, by carefully concentrating on exactly what they're doing (conscious), the child can ride a bicycle (competence). They can't pay attention to the scenery or chat with friends as they ride along.
- 4th Stage - *Unconscious Competence*
  After years of riding a bicycle the child takes no notice of its skills and ability (unconscious), and is able to chat with friends and notice the scenery as it rides along (competence).

For a moment, consider playing the guitar. To play a guitar well requires a wide range of finger and arm movements, mastery over a certain amount of musical knowledge, and the ability to coordinate these things to achieve competence in this art form.[39] These various elements might be broken down into these categories:

- Notes: chord positions, octaves, scales, fret use.

---

[38] The Prologue to this book, p. 11.
[39] It is the same for all skills that have to be mastered, from acting (film or theatre) and music, through to performing surgery, teaching, pounding a nail, paddling a canoe, or making spaghetti sauce.

- Tuning and Strings: open tunings, number of strings (usually between four and seven), number of frets (usually between seventeen and twenty-four).
- Plucking: multiple string plucking, strumming, movement of fingers, using a plectrum, different kinds of plectra, slide bars, or any combination of these.
- Music Theory: playing melody lines, rhythm chords, lead lines, chord structures, riffs, chops, scales, "comping", harmonies, and arrangements.
- The Instrument: acoustic, electric, solid-body, hollow-body, semi-hollow body, wood, metal, synthetic, pickups, amplification systems.
- Music Genre: Jazz, Pop, Blues, Rock, Fusion, Country, Folk, Classical, Spanish, R & B, Grunge, Ska, Heavy Metal, Soul, Punk Rock, Blue Grass, etc.

Prior to their first lesson, want-to-be guitarists don't know what it is they don't know because they don't know. Unconscious Incompetence. As novices, guitar students are told and shown what the basic elements are, but they still can't do them. Conscious Incompetence. In other words, they now know some of what they don't know. This stage is always identified by the universal proclamation: "Hey! I can't do *that*!" Under expert guidance they are taught, and for a long time they select one skill and focus on it in isolation from other skills.

To focus in isolation is what happens when a guitar student concentrates on what their chord-hand is doing and ignores or forgets what their plectrum-hand is supposed to do. Or, they're concentrating on singing the lyrics and forget some chord change. They learn C, F, and G, and when asked about B-flat, they look puzzled as they count up the neck to find it. They have to concentrate on "one thing" in isolation from everything else they've learned until they command all of it. Then, one day, they play gracefully through a scale modulation or blues turn-around, and are thinking self-congratulatory thoughts—"Wow, I did it!"—and miss the tempo change two bars later. This is the beginning of Conscious Competence.

After years of study and practice, they multitask, and choose from many alternatives without thinking too specifically about any one of them—Unconscious Competence.

(1) Immediately *prior* to entering a twelve-step program, a newcomer doesn't know what it is they don't know about addictions, the steps, spiritual principles, or regeneration, nor do they know how to achieve any of this. They are unknowing of, and unable to live, a spiritually principled life. Unconscious Incompetence. (2) Shortly after their arrival in a twelve-step group, they [hopefully] observe recovered people behaving spiritually, but realize they're unable to do it themselves. Conscious Incompetence. (3) The steps, through to the end of nine, require an extraordinarily concentrated effort, to the exclusion of other spiritual tasks. Each step is focused on, and completed, in isolation from the others. The newcomer is working

towards a very basic, spiritual lifestyle. Conscious Competence is realized with the acquisition of The Promises—entry-level serenity. This requires a diligent, focused effort. Since they've become recovered through the completion of the first nine steps, they are then able to undertake the maintenance steps without too much discomfort—entry-level spirituality. (4) Years later, with continued devotion to the maintenance steps and the spiritual principles embodied therein, they really don't notice their willing obedience to a spiritually principled life. Unconscious Competence. [What I say next may sound like a contradiction, but it really isn't: Being truly spiritual is most often lived at the level of Conscious Competence.]

A New Perspective of the Maintenance Steps

There is a subtle and important perspective attendant to the last three steps, and how they arise in your personality, that's remarkably different from the first nine steps. This new perspective allows you to live *in* the integrated ambiance of a spiritual life. Without this, the maintenance steps will be ineffectively viewed as three somewhat independent spiritual exercises—independent of each other and of you.[40]

Steps Ten, Eleven, and Twelve are not independent of each other, they're *inter*dependent and completely *inner*-dependent—they happen together, in concert, at the same time, and inside you. Even though you'll be attending to one of them at any given moment of your life, the other two will be operating in the background. They are infused within each other and [should be] infused within you.

Another way of representing this truth is throughout the first nine regeneration steps, you acquired insight, and rudimentary spiritual discipline that, within those nine steps, were noticeably independent of each other. For example, what you learned in accomplishing Step Four was, in some clear way, independent of what you learned in accomplishing any other of those nine steps. The individual themes and tasks of each of the first nine steps—the regeneration steps—were completed as individual exercises, with spiritual insights peculiar to that step.

"Doing" the maintenance steps aren't each an independent, specific course of study in themselves. For example: You realize you must make an amend to someone and you do this promptly. Attendant to the amend, you're demonstrating each of the five spiritual principles (in the amend itself, you are respectful, honest, humble, charitable, responsible); *and* by making the amend, you are also practicing a meditation on the wisdom of others (Step Eleven), and practicing the principles in all your affairs (Step Twelve). This deep interconnectedness is equally true for the other two maintenance steps. Any one of the three embodies the other two, and each embodies all the spiritual principles, all at the same time.

The maintenance steps both preserve and enhance a spiritual way of life, the basics of which you've already established. In maintaining, you aren't learning any specific new thing. What you learned through Steps One to Nine merges together

---

[40] Even though the phrase may be worn out from overuse (psychobabble), we are human beings, not human doings. Spirituality is not a thing you do: it's actually a state of being. Seeing the maintenance steps as noticeably independent tasks leaves them splintered from each other, and leaves you with a subtly dislocated sense of spiritual unity. This results from an error of application—doing the maintenance steps instead of being them.

within the maintenance steps. You aren't so much learning about a spiritual life; you are a spiritual life.[41] [I referred to this from the perspective of language on p. 162.]

Here's a similar perspective regarding another behavior: Consider, for a moment, breathing. Only occasionally do people think about breathing. They simply breathe. In the midst of *extra*ordinary exertions, people notice their breathing, and probably concentrate on some aspect of it (depth, regularity, chest movement). But for the most part, most people don't notice their breathing. Spirituality, breathing, and loving never need to be taught. Truly spiritual people throw off (abandon and become unattached to) the selfish trappings of culture and addictions, and apprehend the reality that Spirituality naturally resides within them. In times of *extra*ordinary circumstances these people may have to concentrate more diligently on spiritual principles (it's how they get through trying times), but otherwise, being spiritual is simply the nature of their life.

The prominent themes of any one maintenance step are always noticeably influenced by the themes of the other two maintenance steps, which themes always hover in the background. Spiritually, you can do none of them independent unto themselves. Focusing your attention on any one of them naturally entails the visible presence of the spiritual elements of the other two. They are *inner*-dependent.

In *any* circumstance in your life, you can incorporate the themes of all three maintenance steps (the five spiritual principles) at the same time. In the midst of making love, eating dinner, resolving misunderstandings, paying taxes, driving a car, going through divorce, undergoing surgery, or dying, you can gracefully behave, speak, and *think* (which is the hard one because no one can see your thoughts and many of us are good actors) in a way that demonstrates the five principles. You will examine only your own behavior as it relates to the service of a higher power.

You evince a life of spiritual principle, and are devoted to God's will, without ever mentioning "God" or "Spirituality" or "maintenance steps". In the special circumstance of carrying the actual message of a spiritual awakening to another alcoholic or addict, there's the added responsibility of discussing specifically a higher power and the attendant spiritual work involved. Outside of that, however, you live by God's will, in the moment, in all the maintenance steps, evincing the spiritual principles, all at the same time, in every circumstance, and never mention spirituality at all.

This is what it means to *"...practice these principles in all our affairs."*[42] Simple, eh?

---

[41] *"...when they are logically related and interwoven, the result is an unshakable foundation for life."* *Twelve Steps and Twelve Traditions*, p. 98.
[42] *Alcoholics Anonymous*, p. 60, and *Twelve Steps and Twelve Traditions*, p. 106.

8

Step Ten: Responsible For Truth

"Everything I do for my private wellbeing adds another layer to my ego, and in thickening it insulates me more from God."
Huston Smith[1]

Be advised at the outset: Should you harm someone, in setting things right and repairing harms you caused, inconvenience to yourself in making it right is of no account in the matter. Step Ten: *"Continued to take personal inventory and when we were wrong promptly admitted it."*[2]

Throughout this step, a tone of immediacy prevails. This urgency comes from the words *continued*, which implies a gentle relentlessness, and *promptly*, which implies a gentle urgency. Taken together, these define the spontaneous immediacy of your ongoing personal inventory and your admissions of wrongs done. Within the framework of the step, there are two aspects to *continue*; one is to continue to take your own inventory, and the other is to continue to admit the results of that inventory regarding *your* character defects when you harm someone.

In regard to the spiritual principles contained within Step Ten, there is:

- Respect For The Body-Temple
  When others are wronged by you, emotionally or physically, it affects their physical well-being. To repair a harm done—to amend a wrong—shows respect and consideration for their body-temple. (And your subsequent inner peace contributes to your own physical health.)

- Veracity
  In circumstances where others have been harmed, to withhold the truth about your own accountability, aggravates relationships through suspicion, cynicism, and ill will. When people have been hurt, they'll often withhold kindness or gentleness, and become reluctant to be honest themselves. Suspicion by them for the harm you caused may be directed at innocent persons, and prejudices sometimes develop. Veracity is fostered

---

[1] *The World's Religions,* by Huston Smith, HarperSanFrancisco, p. 38.

and encouraged in others when you take responsibility for the harms you've caused.

- Humility
  In its aspect of being egalitarian, the decision to comply with Step Ten contains an admission of human ordinariness (imperfection) which is an element of humility. No one is above wrong-doing, and to honestly admit your humanity is an exercise in humility. The second aspect of humility, honoring a deity by whatever name or cultural manifestation, is evident in your continuous effort to "do God's will". Any sincere effort to amend harm, without any coercion to do so, demonstrates spiritual grace.

- Charity
  In its purest form, charity is enveloped by willingness. It's charitable to spread the bounty of the world, and so it is with promptly making amends—generously providing peace and serenity to others by smoothing the disruptions caused by your character defects. It is charity of spirit to admit wrongs.

- Responsibility & Obedience
  Responsibility is an obvious component of making amends, especially in never finding fault elsewhere, and the requirement to examine only your own conduct. Taking responsibility within Step Ten demonstrates obedience to spiritual principles and to the tenets of all the maintenance steps.

All five principles are clearly evident within the action of Step Ten. Over a long period of diligent application, it becomes easier to apprehend the depth of what's spiritually afoot here. It follows that the more continuous your personal inventory-taking is, the more graceful your admissions will be, and the less often you'll have to make amends.

Observations About Words and Phrases

"*Continued to take*" has a very straightforward meaning. In using everyday language to describe spiritual principles, "continued" means repetitive and ongoing, or extended without interruption.[3] Certainly, yes, if someone takes a personal inventory the first Saturday of every third month they could claim to be continuing to take a personal inventory. However, when you appreciate the tone of the suggestions, and the nature of spiritual principles, a *continuous* personal inventory, once every three

---

[2] *Alcoholics Anonymous*, p. 59, and *Twelve Steps and Twelve Traditions*, p. 88.
[3] *Merriam-Webster's Collegiate Dictionary*, Tenth Edition, ©1993.

months, doesn't fit with sincere commitment, or within the context of Step Ten, or fit with the word promptly.

This *"personal inventory"* is your own, never others', which reflects the previously established theme of taking responsibility for your self-imposed crisis. Step Ten demonstrates what was learned in Steps Four, Eight, and Nine. You repeatedly examine your insecurities, how you harmed others, and fix it... and leave *un*analyzed anything that anyone else is or isn't doing.

"...and when we... " This leaves no doubt that you will be wrong—the human factor. You are going to make mistakes. Humility is the virtue that allows for grace in accepting our own (and others') fallibility.

"...were wrong... " Wrong encompasses any conflict you participate in, any harm you cause, and any behavior or thought motivated by a character defect of yours. You learned, in Steps Four and Eight, the nature of character defects, how they arise in your personality, and the broad scope of harm. All of this applies here.

"promptly" Especially notice, the step does not say: "...and when we were wrong, promptly, provided we weren't too tired or too busy or too inconvenienced, admitted it." Promptly means what it means.

"...admitted it." Admitting you were wrong (and by association, amending any harm) is the task at hand. The step doesn't say to admit being sorry, sad, bad, mean, or angry. Neither does it advise you to announce any mitigating circumstances in your own defense, or to expound at all regarding the real or imagined character defects of the other person.[4]

"... there is a long period of reconstruction ahead. We must take the lead. A remorseful mumbling that we are sorry won't fill the bill at all."[5] This maintenance step does not allow you to rest on your laurels from the hard work of the first nine steps. Yes, you have completed the primary phase of major reconstruction, but, according to this sentence, there is still work to be done, and you must take the lead in this. Don't wait until you're caught in a defect by someone else; don't wait until calamity forces you to act. Take the lead; be proactive, not reactive.

Being sorry and apologizing are entirely insufficient. What lies ahead isn't only making amends and repairing damage. There is also reconstructing how you view apologies, amends, and responsibility; reconstructing how you interact with others, and how you view spiritual principles; and reconstructing your personality to embody this gracefully.

There are various kinds of inventories.[6] The focus here is: *"A spot-check inventory... aimed at our daily ups and downs, especially those where people or new events throw us off balance... ."*[7]

---

[4] All of this seems so straightforward, it's almost patronizing to explain it in this detail, yet the original author(s) found it necessary to write eight pages of explanation. (*Twelve Steps and Twelve Traditions*, pp. 88-95.) Why? Probably to identify and eliminate as many of the evasive strategies and excuses that unspiritual addicts can dream up.

[5] *Alcoholics Anonymous*, p. 83.

[6] See the paragraph: *"Although all inventories... ." Twelve Steps and Twelve Traditions*, p. 89.

[7] Ibid., pp. 90-91.

Take a few minutes right now and think about the last twenty people you interacted with: a person at the grocery store, a neighbor, a child, an accountant, a person selling something through a phone survey, a driver of another car, a loud person in the movie theater, your spouse, someone from your twelve-step group. Were you mean, harshly judgmental, disrespectful, or unkind? Did you take advantage of your authority? Were you unfair, abrupt, angry, or inconsiderate? Were you silently mean spirited, racist, or sexist, but overtly behaved otherwise? Have you gossiped? If *any* of these questions have a "yes" answer, regardless of who they are, whether or not they know it, how old they are, where they are, or how inconvenient or embarrassing it may be for you, an amend *may* be in order.[8]

Consider that if it takes you several hours or days to make an amend, you have all that time of irresponsibility and awkwardness building up, and both you and the person you harmed, lose serenity. This always impacts your conscious contact with God (as you understand God), and, if left unattended, subsequently jeopardizes your abstinence. Equally as important: When you are harming others, you cannot carry the vision of God's will into your life[9], and the other people in your life will affected by the meanness or cruelty of your character defects and your irresponsibility in not addressing your defects promptly.

"*...we need self-restraint, honest analysis of what is involved, a willingness to admit when the fault is ours....*"[10] Balking at continuous responsibility, or finding fault with this literal interpretation of the original instructions, means you aren't willing "*...to go to any length to get* [what we have]." Nor have you "*...decided to go to any lengths for a spiritual experience.*"[11]

Here are some related concepts that are difficult for many people to grasp:

- When you have hurt someone or wronged them, they are the injured party. The fact that you are sorry, or you think you have a "good" reason, or that you feel guilty about it, may not mean too much to them. The amend isn't about you: it's about them. Don't justify it—fix it.

---

[8] If your unspiritual behavior is *silent* harsh judgement, rage, racism, sexism, etc., but doesn't involve any overt demonstration of such, you might not have to make an amend to the other person. However, you must take the lead in resolving this spiritual corruption. You will be required to discuss this in honest detail with a therapist or spiritual advisor—with a single view to eliminating *your* unspiritual attitude. In this context, it is acceptable, when discussing your behavior in relation to another person, to make mention of someone else, including their (apparently) unspiritual behavior or character defects, *provided* it is done (1) in the strictest confidence, to only one person who themselves doesn't behave this way, and is wise enough to assist and facilitate your changing your behavior; (2) with the single view of challenging only yourself; (3) with someone who'll understand your intent; and, (4) with an advisor who is spiritual enough in their own character, and far enough removed from the circumstances, to not have their view of the third party affected by your disclosure. Discussing the misdemeanors of others, outside of these conditions, is gossip—unspiritual behavior, motivated by a character defect of yours, and facilitated by a character defect in anyone who'll listen to you, or anyone who promotes it. Being truly spiritual demands attention to detail. It is complicated, but once you have some self-discipline and an experience of humility, it's an enjoyable quest. You must do everything possible to avoid gossip and any hint of character assassination (your own or others') when trying to sort out your own unspiritual conduct.
[9] *Alcoholics Anonymous*, p. 85.
[10] *Twelve Steps and Twelve Traditions*, p. 91.
[11] *Alcoholics Anonymous*, pp. 58 and 79, respectively.

- Avoid telling them you are bad or stupid for what you did in the midst of making your amend. Don't demean yourself or apologize for your humanity.

- Don't, at any time, focus on whatever it is the other person may have done—it's irrelevant. Identify and focus on what you are responsible for in the conflict and harm done.

- Some people report they may be too angry to make an amend promptly. Take a Time Out[12] i.e. force yourself to temporarily excuse yourself and in the interlude, direct yourself to examine both what you did to cause the harm, *and* how you are irresponsible in being so angry. Being angry is a choice you make.

- In an anecdote related by Joseph Campbell to Bill Moyers, a Japanese Shinto priest was overheard offering this response to a question about ideology, theology, and life: *"I think we don't have ideology,"* the [Shinto] *priest said. "We don't have theology. We dance."*[13] Like people on a crowded dance floor, we move through Life to the song we hear, bumping into each other, interacting, and moving on. Sometimes we dance alone, sometimes with a partner, and sometimes our dance is to sit on the sidelines watching everyone else. Some people make up their own music, and others dance their whole life to someone else's song.

  The Two Step Dance is something my friend Leonard Shaw talks about.[14] Most people think that life is a Two-Step Dance. The first step is when something happens or doesn't happen, or when someone else does or doesn't do something. The second step is the reaction: the first person is upset, hurt, angry and they can't help it. Ask them and they'll emphatically tell you their reaction couldn't be helped.

  However, life is really a three-step dance. The <u>first</u> step is that something happens. The <u>second</u> step is an instant perception of the event, and the fact that the event is assigned *both* a meaning in terms of emotions (happy, sad, pleased, angry, bad, good, they deserved it, I didn't deserve it, etc.), and it's also assigned a value in intensity (i.e. low – medium – high). The <u>third</u> step is the person's visible reaction. They're upset or in some other emotional state that's related to the meaning and intensity they assigned at the second step.

---

[12] Time Out will be described in some detail in *Facets of Personal Transformation*.

[13] *The Power of Myth,* Joseph Campbell with Bill Moyers, Betty Sue Flowers, Editor, Doubleday, 1988, p. xix.

[14] Leonard Shaw, M.S.W., A.C.S.W., a therapist in Seattle, with whom I had the privilege to work, wrote a short and impactful book called *Love and Forgiveness*, available through Leonard Shaw, Seattle, WA, Ph. 206-322-5785.

The second step, of assigning perception and meaning, is always present, even if the person's unaware of it. The perceptions, values, and intensity assigned to a circumstance are always the responsibility of the one who's assigned them. If you don't want to be upset, take responsibility and change your perceptions at the second step.[15]

- The Four Noble Truths of Buddhism are the living philosophy of achieving non-attachment and of being responsible. According to this path of self-discipline, every time you are disturbed there is something wrong with you because of your attachment to some particular value or perception. *Twelve Steps and Twelve Traditions* advises, similarly, that *"...every time we are disturbed, no matter what the cause, there is something wrong with us."*[16] What's "wrong" is the meaning that is assigned at the second step of the dance.

Humility at Step Ten

Recall that Step Seven explored the importance and acquisition of humility. When humility is a desirable quality, and something you willingly pursue, the maintenance steps are graceful. At Step Ten, admitting wrongs will carry an element of spiritual joy when done in concert with humility. It's the absence of humility, specifically within Step Ten, that's one cause of twelve-step people ending up continuously repeating Step Four for the rest of their lives.

Here's a view of fear and irresponsibility which perpetuates repetitive step work. For ease in explanation, I've described completing the twelve steps in relation to a period of one calendar year.

In January a person does Steps One, Two, and Three. In February they do Steps Four and Five. In March they do Steps Six to Nine. In April they claim to be at the maintenance steps and appear to have recovered. However, this person was impatient and didn't really understand the spiritual requirements, and has completed the steps with a misalliance of commitment (described in Ch. 6). They missed the crucial importance of humility at Step Seven. This leaves them with a self-serving attitude towards amends—they are striving for personal exoneration (guilt reduction), will portion out accountability, and are neither in service to God nor living a spiritual lifestyle. When this person is wrong or harms others, they will then be lax in spiritual discipline. If they, themselves, aren't affected by the harm they caused others, the necessity of making an amend appears minor. They'll be wrongly focused more on what the other person did, and will then disregard *continued* and *promptly*.

---

[15] Changing expectations and perceptions about people was a major theme of the discussion in the section Contracts & Reciprocity, Forgiveness & Covenants, in Chapter 6. It's also discussed in Appendix IV regarding perception and filtering.

[16] *Twelve Steps and Twelve Traditions*, p. 90, emphasis theirs.

So, in May they hurt a dozen people and don't promptly take full responsibility for this. In June and July they harm twenty more people, and mumble an insufficient "I'm sorry." In August it may be twenty-five people, and they avoid admitting their wrongs and fixing the harm. In September they hurt a dozen more and in October, six others. By November, over the previous six months, they've wronged or harmed about seventy-five people—the accumulation since completing Step Nine in March. There is now another "wreckage of their past" that resulted from a superficial spiritual focus (*Acedia*; see fn. p. 261). Because they missed the profound import of humility, which was because of negligence in the earlier steps, they focus more on portioning out responsibility (blaming) and social atonement, than spiritual responsibility. This causes a rapid accumulation of harmed people.

If this person had valued humility, and done Step Ten *each* time they were selfish or mean from April to November, there would be no wreckage of their past. A misalliance of commitment when doing Steps One to Nine won't allow for spiritual integrity, so addicts cannot then incorporate *continued* and *promptly*. Their lack of spiritual accountability makes them incapable of maintaining the level of self-examination required. As a result, in November and December they have to repeat Steps Four through Nine to clean up the wreckage of their past (the seventy-five incidents from April to October); hence they "need" to repeat the steps, and start all over again (which reflects the Myth of Sisyphus). [17]

The Mechanics of Step Ten

Alcoholics Anonymous describes, in succinct detail, the mechanics of Step Ten where it begins: *"This thought brings us to* Step Ten... ."[18] All of the quotations immediately below come from that one paragraph.

"...continue to take personal inventory..." identifies the task at hand, which you learned at Steps Four and Eight.

"...continue to set right any new mistakes as we go along." This identifies how you are to do it—continuously: the gentle relentlessness needed for setting things right (amend making), which was practiced at Step Nine.

"...grow in understanding and effectiveness." This identifies the ongoing process which was explored from different perspectives at Steps Two, Four, Six, Seven, and Eight.

---

[17] Repetitive cycles of step completion are now-a-days almost standard procedure. This inefficiency results from an ineffective attempt to manage addictions through psychology (again, the misalliance of commitment). Regarding sponsors who encourage recycling through the steps, or who deny the possibility of being recovered, in addition to their own spiritual sloth, they camouflage their insecurity and lack of faith, and reassure themselves, by enrolling naïve newcomers into a complex system of ersatz spirituality. This creates more shame and results in all manner of spiritual dislocation. A grudging or intermittent effort at Step Ten is the direct result of an insincere or non-existent desire for humility. This will inevitably require a return to Step Four. In order to camouflage the shame that's generated from going "backwards" and repeating the steps (repetitive inadequacy), there's an automatic defiance to, and slick defenses against, being recovered. The only way to get off this merry-go-round of repetitive inadequacy (which generates shame) is to *plant* yourself in Step Two and stay there for a *very long* time.

[18] *Alcoholics Anonymous*, p. 84, emphasis theirs.

"Continue to watch for selfishness, dishonesty, resentment, and fear." This requires ongoing vigilance—being observant for the insecurities, fears, and sexual selfishness you identified in Step Four.

"When these crop up, we ask God at once to remove them." The ability to do this is a result of a thorough investigation at Step Two and a sincere decision at Step Three. It's also a variation of the theme of Step Seven, bringing you back to humility, which unites Steps Ten and Eleven.

"...discuss them with someone immediately..." Here is the experience of humble disclosure that you practiced in Step Five.

"...make amends quickly if we have harmed anyone." This is what you practiced at Step Nine. Notice: It's done quickly.

"...resolutely turn our thoughts to someone we can help." Here you incorporate charity of spirit and service work on behalf of a higher power, which unites Steps Ten and Twelve. "Someone" isn't limited to those in your recovery program.

"Love and tolerance of others is our code." Love and Tolerance are now two identified standards of conduct that you began to appreciate as far back as Step One, which are also attributes of humility.

This one paragraph describes the process of making amends during the normal course of your day. Doing "Step Ten" embodies the themes and practices of Steps Two to Nine, and is united with Steps Eleven and Twelve. With humility as the fundamental operating principle, and the degree of thoroughness that is described in these Step Ten instructions, what need is there to repeat the steps?

Here's a very true imaginary story:

The Story of Lee

"A long time ago, for a couple of years, Lee had been in a twelve-step program. Lee was divorced at the time, a single parent, and someone who seemed to be doing fine. I remember Lee being invited to some big AA house party. 'What?' Lee exclaimed, 'A party? Sober? Do people do this? What a concept!' We laughed. Lee was very nervous about meeting new people and socializing sober, but Lee went anyway.

"Apparently, at the party, Lee had noticed someone and asked them to dance, but they said: 'No thanks. I don't feel like dancing. Thank you for asking.' Lee told me about smiling awkwardly and feeling silly, and someone from the group sniggering and saying something sarcastic. Lee, apparently embarrassed, said something sarcastic to this other person and didn't stay much longer. The next morning Lee felt a little depressed and awkward, but didn't call anyone. At a twelve-step meeting the night after, as people were recalling how much fun they had at the party, Lee was quiet.

"On Monday morning, driving to work, Lee got cut off and was a little angry. At the office, Lee ignored the receptionist's greeting, and later, in a meeting, noticed people seemed quite reserved. Driving home, Lee thought: 'I don't know if I really like working at that place.' By the next weekend, Lee hadn't called anyone and couldn't find the energy to pick up the literature for the group. A few days later, while hurrying to work depressed and late, Lee got a speeding ticket. By that time Lee was hardly speaking with anyone.

"No one in the group knew anything about this. Lee hadn't told anyone, and was convinced that nobody really understood, and daydreamed a lot about the 'old days'. Lee's partner had left about a year earlier. Lee had been neglecting spirituality and prayer for a while and finally, quite fed up (I could see it coming), said: 'I've had it!' and bought a bottle of liquor.

"Lee only blacked out for a few hours, and only missed three or four days of work in the next month. Eventually, though, arriving late and hung over, one morning, Lee was fired, had to find another job (at half the salary), and had to give up the house. Lee's children went to live with their grandparents and six months later, Lee was down to casual employment and getting drunk several times a week.

"That's when Lee started getting picked up by the police—drunk, disorderly, shoplifting—and ended up sleeping in some tiny welfare-room. Last winter Lee caught double pneumonia and was found passed out on the sidewalk on Main Street. The police had to make an arrest. I guess Lee was covered with body ulcers, underweight, and almost dead then. When I was called a month later to identify Lee's body, I spoke with the constable who made that last arrest. Apparently, as Lee was being rolled into the back of the paddy-wagon, I guess the cop was puzzled by the whole thing—maybe a little disgusted—and apparently said: 'You're killing yourself. You're in <u>terrible</u> shape. What happened to you? What's wrong with your life?' The cop told me that Lee started to cry—just couldn't hide the shame and pain anymore. Through the crying and sobbing, Lee could only say: 'I was at a party two years ago and someone wouldn't dance with me.'

"It guess it was a nice funeral, but not too many people were there."

Many "in recovery" addicts interpret Step Ten so that it dovetails with their thinly disguised self-serving agendas. This is evident in people who do "a Step Ten" at night, only at the end of their day. These people examine their daily relationships in hindsight, many hours after the fact, and then decide which interactions require admissions of personal wrongdoing. There are three concerns with this.

First: An inventory at day's end, practiced over the long term, may satisfy the definition of "continued", but done at the end of the day prohibits an amend being made promptly. Consider what would happen if an addict has an interaction with someone early in the morning, they do harm in some manner, and then before bed that night realize an amend is required (if they remember the interaction at all). The person they have wronged fourteen hours before, would have been carrying the hurt all day. And now are added the complications of locating them, diffused memory, and explanations. Any commitment to doing an amend the next day may be minimally adequate in theory, but decidedly lacking in devotion and promptness.

Second: There is the added risk that the addict's late-evening, good intentions to make an amend the next day will get lost in the demands of a chaotic and busy new day. They will then accumulate another wreckage of their past, in spite of otherwise good intentions. In spirituality, good intentions don't count.

Third: Many twelve-step participants confuse Step Ten, i.e. continuously reviewing their behavior, identifying wrongdoings, and making prompt amends, with something similar, but is a specific part of Step Eleven. In *Alcoholics Anonymous,* on page 86, is a paragraph that begins *"When we retire at night, we constructively re-*

view...".[19] This Step Eleven paragraph encourages a meditative review of the *entire* day, and would include a review of amends that were made earlier that day, and possibly uncover harms that were missed. However, this Step Eleven daily, evening review would *also* include meditating on fears that were encountered and addressing them, noticing where indifference was practiced rather than love, noticing silent anger, racism, sexism, etc., *and* also observing the successes of the day. All of this requires attention, but it's a part of attending to Step Eleven, not Step Ten.

At the time I was personally discovering the complex beauty of this, I was employed in the traffic-monitoring, consumer-relations and complaints division in a large department of a municipal government. My spiritual advisor commented that, while at work, it would be a fine opportunity for me to practice this step. My immediate reaction was mildly defensive—I was at work and they were just complaints.

He observed there were probably times when I was sarcastic or belligerent when encountering an irate citizen. I shrugged, and vaguely allowed that I might possibly, sometimes, be only slightly less than considerate. He smiled and observed that Step Ten required promptness and was explicit about righting wrongs to everyone, meaning at work or not. Should I realize long after any interaction, that I had in some way harmed someone, been rude or inconsiderate, etc., it would be difficult for me to then contact the person to make an amend (which was clearly required if I were to thoroughly follow the instructions). He suggested I take a brief moment to examine my behavior at the conclusion of *each* encounter, with *every* person, during the course of my entire day. When I realized I was wrong or had harmed someone, I could immediately make an amend and start the next encounter with a fresh attitude. It was an obviously good idea, clearly within the suggestions of Step Ten, definitely in line with spiritual principles, and over time would make my life more graceful. So being the cooperative person I was at the time, I became evasive and thought it over for a week or so.

It soon came about that I would briefly examine my conduct at the conclusion of each interaction and make amends if required. In a matter of weeks, I had made progress in curbing my surly attitude and soon had to make amends less often. I was more considerate and sincere in my dealings with people. More importantly, I modified my interaction with people I didn't like, so the encounter was at least respectful. I was very much more aware of myself during each interaction, and no longer developing a wreckage of my past.

It didn't take too long for me to realize how much energy I had formerly invested in keeping my resentments at the forefront of my mind. Maintaining anger, rationalizing disrespect for others, and justifying blame, are exhausting. Over a period of weeks, as I explored the nuances of what was afoot, two profound realizations were (a) how much easier I could make other people's lives; and, (b) how much less exhausted I was at the end of the day. My life was subsequently more graceful, and I became less invested in controlling others and winning arguments.[20]

---

[19] *Alcoholics Anonymous*, p. 86.
[20] Arguments are either disagreements over facts: The longest river is... , The correct spelling is... , The population of Ireland is... ; or arguments are disagreements over opinions: Blue is a nicer color than red...

Whenever you make an amend right after you've harmed someone, you don't have to carry that queasy, upset-guilty feeling. Neither do you become inattentive or exhausted from constantly revisiting the memory and justifying your neglect of spiritual principles. You experience the serenity that comes from never having a wreckage of your past. The other person doesn't have to feel insulted or hurt, and they have no need to feel defensive. Certainly people get wrapped up in the chaos of a busy day, and at times some encounter isn't examined with the scrutiny that Spirituality requires. When you realize this omission, promptly address it. As the years go by, you will make amends more promptly and less often.

When you think an amend is in order and the other person sees the circumstance as being of no consequence, don't force the issue, and still live your life by your standards. Quietly and *politely* say something like: "Well, thanks for your generosity. I think I was a little _(insert defect)_, but maybe I wasn't. Thanks for talking about it," and then get on with the business at hand. Establish your own integrity and move on.[21]

Sometimes when making an amend the other person may reply with anger: "Yes, you're wrong. You're inconsiderate too... and nasty and mean! You're horrible." The spiritual task, at this moment, is for you to buy out of the conflict, thank them kindly for telling you what they think (*no* sarcasm), and get on with your business. Don't argue. If the business is concluded, politely excuse yourself (*no* sarcasm).

The spiritual rationale for not arguing is this: Their perspective of your behavior is a personal opinion. Their opinion is right—for them. It may or may not be accurate; you probably have a different opinion of your behavior. Trying to convince them (argue) that your view of your behavior is more right than their view of your behavior is pointless. It's what they believe.[22] To do this is going beyond forgiveness to acceptance and compassion.

The message in the first two paragraphs on page 88 of *Twelve Steps and Twelve Traditions* is obvious. A continuous inventory is frequent and without interruption. This requires a significant amount of focused, conscious energy, and can only be sustained with spiritual support. No longer can you slide through your day living in ignorance of the moment and hoping for wisdom in hindsight. Through Step Ten you will very quickly start living in the present, listening to others with less prejudice, and responding with acceptance. *"More experienced people, of course, in all times and*

---

no it's not. Asparagus tastes better than chocolate cake... no it doesn't. If it's an argument over a fact, don't argue, go to the library. If it's an argument over an opinion, it's an opinion, and so there's no point in arguing. A truly spiritual lifestyle can never justify arguing—over anything. Now I offer one exception from *How To Be A Gentleman*, by John Bridges, Rutledge Hill Press, 1998. On page 67, Mr. Bridges advises that a gentleman *"...argues only over an issue that could save a life."*

[21] Addicts generally find that life is more serene when they develop an expertise in taking their own inventory rather than honing their skills at taking others'. Too many addicts instantly calculate the "Conflict Responsibility Factor"—what percentage of the conflict is "their own fault" (49.5% or less is the desired amount) and what percentage is the other person's fault. In unregenerate people, the end result is decidedly self-serving.

[22] Keep this in context. If it's necessary to defend yourself legally, then do that. But, even then, don't engage in petty squabbles or name-calling. In the realm of personal relationships, however, what someone else thinks of you is none of your business. The more you try to debate people out of their cherished beliefs, the more they'll cling to them.

places have practiced unsparing self-survey and criticism. For the wise have always known that no one can make much of his [or her] life until self-searching becomes a regular habit... and until he [or she] patiently and persistently tries to correct what is wrong."[23]

One of the AA cofounders described his own early views of Christ: "*His moral teaching—most excellent. For myself, I had adopted those parts which seemed convenient and not too difficult; the rest I disregarded.*"[24] Many twelve-step people have a similar view regarding the moral and spiritual teachings of *Alcoholics Anonymous*[25]—selective convenience. What suggestions do you neatly avoid that go against your more cherished and justified prejudices? How do you slyly promote only those principles that do not entail too much social, emotional, or financial inconvenience? In my experience, sadly, most people in twelve-step programs are too busy with "social" things to be concerned with the nuances of continuous spiritual self-examination. Yet regarding human relations, the twelve-step pilgrim is clearly told:

- *"Learning how to live in the greatest peace, partnership, and brotherhood with all men and women, of whatever description, is a moving and fascinating adventure."*
- *"...no field of investigation could yield more satisfying and valuable rewards than this one."*
- *"...[no] need to wander morbidly around in the past; ...[strive for the] admission and correction of errors <u>now</u>; ...settle with the past; ...made peace with ourselves..."*
- *"Once this healthy practice has become grooved, it will be so interesting and profitable..."*
- *"...[to quiet] stormy emotions..."*
- *"...see what real love for our fellows actually means..."*
- *"...[express gratitude] for the blessings we have received..."*[26]

With all the popular and various declarations about peace, love, and gratitude, what is it that makes so few twelve-step pilgrims willing to eagerly seek these out? It's fear. So, they abandon a spiritual objective for the more easily attainable and popular social objective. When people other-examine rather than self-examine, and amend wrongs less than continuously, they miss out on the continuous serenity that arises from being spiritual in the moment (which, in turn, only arises from a sincere dedication to the well-being of others).

Many people in twelve-step programs blatantly ignore the responsibility in *continued* and *promptly,* but they don't relapse. However, they do stay mean, moody,

---

[23] *Twelve Steps and Twelve Traditions*, p. 88.
[24] *Alcoholics Anonymous*, p. 11.
[25] "*That means we have written a book...*" Ibid., p. 45.
[26] All taken from *Twelve Steps and Twelve Traditions*, pp. 77, 80, 89, 89, 90, 92, 95, respectively, emphasis theirs.

and miserable—and they're often secretly racist, spiteful, dishonest, sexist, etc.[27] Spiritual principles are remarkably absent, and various other addictions (work, sex, anger, violence, tobacco, relationships) are remarkably present. As a consequence, serenity will be forever distant, and then abstinence is dependent upon belligerence and the cooperation of Fate.

For the most part, addicts in recovery are excellent at surviving the big calamity and managing major crises. Such people don't relapse because their house burns down or war is declared; it's because someone didn't hang up their coat. They rise to the challenge of Armageddon, but don't anyone buy the wrong kind of toothpaste. Their personality traits, which accumulate petty annoyances and ignore their own wrongdoings, are exactly what's counteracted by *continued* and *promptly*. Step Ten, when approached with obedience to the spiritual principles it embodies, prevents everyday misdemeanors from escalating into relapse and death.

In order to live like this you will need *"In all... situations... self-restraint,* [an] *honest analysis of what is involved, a willingness to admit when the fault is* [yours], *and an equal willingness to forgive when the fault is elsewhere."*[28] You acquired the wherewithal to do this in Steps Four, Eight, and Nine, and the willingness and humility to be interested in doing this at Steps Six and Seven. You learned everything you needed before you arrived here.

Clues to Self-righteousness

There are four styles of behavior that demand careful scrutiny. Even though they may appear to be well intended, they actually conceal unspiritual/selfish motives. These self-righteous behaviors, and the common justifications for them, are:

- constructively criticizing someone who is present and who "needs" the criticism to help them understand their own character, when, in fact, we're trying to win a useless argument or to feel superior;
- constructively criticizing someone who isn't present, claiming we're trying to help others understand this person, or warning people so they won't be hurt, when, in fact, we're trying to feel superior, and hurt the person we are criticizing; or trying to endear ourselves to someone and collect allies;
- teaching someone a lesson and "helping" them to be smarter or wiser, when, in fact, we're only trying to punish them; and,
- telling others how we're sick, depressed, tired, or forced to contend with life's difficulties—"sharing"—when, in fact, we're trying to elicit sympathy and get attention.[29]

---

[27] It appears that many people automatically assume that sexism is the degradation of women by men. Sexism is as equally prolific regarding women towards men. For an important, although for some people a controversial perspective, see *The Myth of Male Power,* by Warren Farrell, Simon & Schuster, 1993.
[28] *Twelve Steps and Twelve Traditions,* p. 91.
[29] Ibid., p. 94.

The original literature is rather specific: *"...this perverse wish to hide a bad motive underneath* [an apparent] *good one, permeates human affairs from top to bottom. This subtle and elusive kind of self-righteousness can underlie the smallest act or thought."*[30] Your task, regardless of whatever anyone else is doing, is to eliminate this perverse trait from your character through diligent effort at Step Ten, and to discipline only yourself to be obedient to the spiritual principles.

Spirituality In Action

Step Ten is the realization of living within the mandate of the Step Seven prayer. Step Ten is actually what eliminates *"...that which stands in the way of my usefulness to you and my fellows."*[31] Step Ten keeps your defects out of the way so you can *"...carry the vision of God's will into all* [your] *activities."*[32] Humility is the crucible out of which you do God's work. Using your willpower to continue to promptly attend to Step Ten *"...is the proper use of the will."*[33] It's the most effective way of attracting rather than promoting a spiritual lifestyle.

Any benefits to yourself become secondary to taking responsibility for the well-being of others and carrying "God's vision" into your life. Yes, you may have a good day, but that's not the primary purpose of doing this. Besides, if you've done your homework, and approach this right, you won't really be interested in what you get out of it. If you insist on pinpointing a personal reward, it's this: Experiencing the essence of humility in making amends is winning the spiritual lottery. Making amends becomes easy, and self-searching becomes enjoyable. It's at this point that you begin to understand what Mr. Camus was referring to when he described appreciating the implacable grandeur of life exactly as we have been given it.[34]

When humility becomes more important than being right, making amends promptly is no trouble at all. When making amends promptly becomes no trouble at all, you never build up a wreckage of your past. When you never build up a wreckage of your past, you get to stay in the maintenance steps. When you stay in the maintenance steps, you stay recovered.

The original literature advises we're meant to be joyous and free, but not without taking responsibility, and we must still be human (and therefore make mistakes, and sometimes serious ones). How can we make mistakes and hurt others, and be hurt by others, and still be joyous and free? When we seek out humility in both its aspects. It is very simple. It is also very complicated and profound.

———

It is important to note the grammar and syntax of the following sentence: *"For the readiness to take the full consequences of our past acts, and to take respon-*

---

[30] *Twelve Steps and Twelve Traditions*, pp. 94, 95.
[31] Part of the Step Seven prayer, *Alcoholics Anonymous*, p. 76.
[32] Ibid., p. 85.
[33] Ibid.
[34] *The Myth of Sisyphus and Other Essays*, Albert Camus, Vintage Books, 1991.

sibility for the well-being of others at the same time, is the very spirit of Step Nine."[35]
Pay especial attention to the words *"at the same time"*. This is embodied in Step Ten,
which is, in fact, a combination of examining yourself for instincts gone awry (that
are evident in the harming of others through your character defects) and promptly
making amends (thereby taking responsibility for the wellbeing of others).

By using the phrase *"at the same time"* the author(s) of the original literature point out that these two apparently separate actions—taking the full
consequences of our acts, and taking responsibility for the well-being of others—
happen together. They're embodied entirely within each other, and within Step Ten.
It's rare that anyone could reasonably accomplish either of these with any amount of
sincerity, amongst all the resistance that is attendant to spiritual endeavor in this day
and age. But to have a formerly self-destructive, non-spiritual, selfish addict act this
way, and be able to do it at all gracefully, is rarer still. It's a great blessing to be able
to choose this as a way of life.

One subtle but devastating result that arises from being forever "in recovery" is the sense that you end up being on the road to recovery for so long that you
forget you're trying to get somewhere. An almost subconscious despair develops that
is too often interpreted as depression. Addicts struggle through getting abstinent,
through coming to believe, and then through an inventory that requires changing
values and making amends. The constant and repetitive effort of trying to heal, trying
to grow, trying to get through the steps, and then to start all over again, becomes a
frustrating, never-ending morass of minimal accomplishment.

One unstated and powerful derivative benefit of being recovered is that you
realize that you finally did "got somewhere". With the proper approach, at some unexpected moment in the middle of some amend, you will suddenly realize how
sincerely graceful and stable your life is. To regenerate yourself from active addiction into being recovered, and at the same time into being spiritual, allows you to
realize that you have actually become a different person. For a formerly practicing
alcoholic/addict to achieve any of this is profound. However, for them to achieve it
to the depth that is available, after only several years of very hard work, is true evidence of spiritual grace and the bounty of Providence. Your quest for spirituality has
become a comforting reality. *"But we must go further...."*[36]

---

[35] *Twelve Steps and Twelve Traditions*, p. 87, emphasis added.
[36] *Alcoholics Anonymous*, p. 85.

9

Step Eleven: Responsible For Humility

"There is a principle which... cannot fail to keep a [per-son] in everlasting ignorance—that principle is contempt prior to investigation."

Herbert Spencer[1]

"As we have seen, self-searching is the means by which we bring new vi-sion, action, and grace to bear upon the dark and negative side of our natures. It is a step in the development of that kind of humility that makes it possible for us to re-ceive God's help."[2] One implication is that the dark, negative side of your personality prevents deep inner awareness, which (in turn) prevents finding the Great Reality deep within you.[3] So, in order to be effective in prayer and meditation, you must first commit to continuously challenging your own dark nature (subtle self-righteousness, character defects, selfishness)—that's Step Ten. It will nurture the development of a special kind of humility that makes it possible to receive God's help through Step Eleven, which is: *"Sought through prayer and meditation to im-prove our conscious contact with God as we understood Him, praying only for knowledge of His will for us and the power to carry that out."*[4]

What this means is that anything you may accomplish by way of prayer and meditation, within Step Eleven, is directly dependent upon your willing and continu-ous *self*-examination within Step Ten. Should you believe that you are sincerely praying and meditating, a few times a day, on a regular basis, and over some months you notice that your spiritual serenity isn't slightly more apparent, then you are ei-ther not praying or meditating properly, or you're not diligent and relentless in self-examination.[5]

Regarding the spiritual principles contained within Step Eleven, there is...

---

[1] As quoted in *Alcoholics Anonymous*, p. 570.
[2] *Twelve Steps and Twelve Traditions*, p. 98.
[3] *Alcoholics Anonymous*, p. 55.
[4] Ibid., p. 59, and *Twelve Steps and Twelve Traditions*, p. 96, emphasis theirs.
[5] Should you have achieved a sincere spiritual ambience in your life, then become lax in self-examination, the defects-side of your character will increase its influence and eventually block your conscious relation-ship with your higher power. You will then begin to accumulate a wreckage of your past. Should this happen, until you reestablish diligent self-examination, your conscious contact with your higher power, and any effort at prayer and meditation, will be ineffective because you will be controlled by your charac-ter defects. The maintenance steps are linked to each other in incredibly intricate patterns. To not do any one of them is to prevent yourself from doing the others.

- Respect for the Body-Temple
  With frequent and regular prayer and meditation, your body will relax and carry less tension—healing benefits for your body. Your own reduced tension, through prayer and meditation, has a calming effect on people who associate with you. Prayer and meditation on your part shows respect for the place where God resides: the body-temple—your own and others'.[6]

- Veracity
  Veracity's aspect of honesty is strengthened through prayer by truth-telling to your higher power, and its aspect of gentle trustworthiness is enhanced through the nature of meditation.

- Humility
  Regarding the egalitarian aspect of humility: in prayer, you reveal your ordinary, fragile humanness (universal equality with all people); in meditation, you seek the wisdom of the spiritual masters (demonstrating that you are teachable). Regarding the spiritual aspect of humility: in both prayer and meditation, you recognize your dependence on a higher power, and demonstrate your desire to submit to God's will.

- Charity
  Charity is only a valid spiritual endeavor when it carries no pity, sorrow, self-advertisement, or other selfish ego-agenda.[7] During prayer and meditation you are actively reorganizing your personality to remove any selfish agenda. Without selfish agendas underneath charity, other people benefit because for them there's no obligation arising from your charity. All sincere prayer and meditation is charity to others before the fact.[8]

---

[6] Two related views of God residing within us are found in *Mysticism In Religion,* by Rev. W.R. Inge, University of Chicago Press, 1948. In Chapter 3, p. 35, attributed to St. Paul, Rev. Inge offers: *"...the Spirit dwelling in us, or of our bodies as the temple of God...,"* and *"'the body' as the 'tabernacle' of the soul while we live here."* And, from Rev Inge, himself: *"The body must be reverenced and preserved from defilement because it is the temple of the Holy Spirit."* Many other, similar perspectives are found in all the major religious philosophies.

[7] *"The* [pilgrim] *should also bestow* [charity], *uninfluenced by any preconceived thoughts as to self and other selves and for the sole purpose of benefiting sentient beings"*; and *"...in* [the] *practice of charity* [have] *no arbitrary conceptions of the attainment of the blessing and merit which* [you will] *will attain by such practice...".* *A Buddhist Bible,* edited by Dwight Goddard, Beacon Press, 1994, pp. 90-91.

[8] My observation is dependent upon your prayer and meditation being absent of selfishness, righteousness, and self-serving rationalization.

- Responsibility & Obedience
  The continuous seeking of God's will through Step Eleven demonstrates both of these attributes at the same time. Responsibility is inherent in prayer and meditation, and these are the actual crucibles out of which greater responsibilities arise and expand into your life. Obedience has two aspects within Step Eleven. One is being obedient to the principle of prayer and meditation, and the other is being obedient to the spiritual obligations that arise *from* your prayer and meditation. Should you regularly pray and meditate, over time, you will be rewarded with spiritual tasks that require greater responsibility and obedience.

All of the spiritual principles are evident within the action of Step Eleven. Over a *long* period of diligent application, it becomes easier to apprehend what's spiritually afoot here. The more continuous your prayer and meditation is, the more graceful your life will be. The more graceful your life is, the less often you'll face indecision or turmoil. Thusly, the more aware you'll be about what God's will is for you, and you will receive the power to carry that out.

Observations About Words and Phrases

"*Sought...*" [Seek]: *1. To attempt to locate or discover; search for. 2. To endeavor to obtain or reach: seek a* [higher power]. *3. To inquire for; request: to seek direction* [from a spiritual advisor].[9] The central theme of these definitions involves making an effort to find something. Sought is an action word that has within it a sense similar to "continued" in Step Ten—expend energy in an ongoing (continuing) effort to find something. Sought implies a gentle relentlessness.

If you are a person who likes to refinish old furniture, you first have to find the old furniture. *How* do you look—drive around, read newspaper ads, telephone friends? *Where* do you look: newspaper ads, yard sales, retail stores, garage sales, estate sales, auctions? Which of these alternatives of "How" and "Where" provide the best results for getting old furniture? In Step Eleven you are advised "How" to seek—through prayer and meditation. At other places in the literature, you are advised "Where" to seek:

- *We found the Great Reality deep down within us;*"[10] and,
- We reduce the influence of our defects and enable prayer by self-examination. In other words, we look inside ourselves.[11]

---

[9] Excerpted and abridged from *The American Heritage® Dictionary of the English Language, Third Edition,* © 1996, Houghton Mifflin Company. Electronic version.
[10] *Alcoholics Anonymous*, p. 55.
[11] *Twelve Steps and Twelve Traditions*, p. 98. The relevant passage begins, "*As we have seen...* ".

So, "where" to look is inside yourself. How to look is by first doing Step Ten—eliminating defects, which enables spiritual insight; and then, "how" you look is through Step Eleven—prayer and meditation, which are explained later in this chapter. This has proven to be the most effective process for the recovered alcoholic.

These instructions, regarding effective spiritual endeavor, prevent you from becoming frustrated with ineffective or otherwise scattered efforts such as doing service work, being a circuit speaker, chairing meetings, or having a good sponsor (which are all inadequate for the task at hand). Do not permit yourself to seek easier ways that suit your fancy, meaning light-hearted efforts that look and sound good, but accomplish little. A higher power is like honesty: It may be appreciated in others, but only found within yourself.[12]

If you've been in a twelve-step program for some period of time, and you aren't making a regular, noticeable effort to pray and meditate in some fashion approximating what you've been advised through the literature, you're cheating yourself. Years ago, I was annoyed that a mentor had kindly pointed out this truth about me. I responded with irritation. At that point, he gently informed me that he was more interested in saving my life than in whether or not I liked what he had to tell me.

For an addict/alcoholic to recover and achieve sincere personal fulfillment, the phenomenon of addictions has taken away any other options, other than spirituality, that they might have had in the some-time distant past. Their addiction may well require that they obey the original twelve-step instructions or die.

"*...to improve...*" is the goal. At the beginning, you had to eliminate your acting out, and then later, your character defects, selfishness, and irresponsibility, in order to let God work within you. You did this through to Step Nine, and developed a very basic relationship with God (and a rudimentary understanding of what God's will is for you). By the time you finished Step Nine, you should have created a very basic spiritual tone to your life. Here, within the maintenance steps, you're not creating a belief about whether or not God exists, or creating a conscious contact with God: you should have already done these. At Step Eleven, the orientation of effort is to improve this foundation, not to establish it.

"*...conscious contact...*" does not mean that God is going to appear to you personally. Conscious, in this context, means awake and deliberate, not haphazard or accidental, on *your* part. An analogy may be that you can wander aimlessly in the wilderness and accidentally see a bear, or you can study the bear's habits, the terrain, and then walk quietly and carefully searching for it. One event is not conscious or deliberate; the other one is. A deliberate search will have decidedly better results than a haphazard one; hence, *conscious* contact.

---

[12] Some spiritual philosophies suggest that personal transformation is primarily by meditation—stressing meditation more than deliberate self-examination. Choosing this more "eastern" approach (rather than the specific AA approach: detailed self-examination independent of meditation and prayer, and then contemplation of the wisdom of others), doesn't appear to be an effective substitution for addictions recovery. General meditation practices are designed for everyone. Addicts/alcoholics have very specific needs that are dictated by addictions, which addictions preclude generic approaches.

How you ended up in a twelve-step program in the first place, when you were blinded by your addictions and still in monumental denial, indicates there was some (forever unknowable) unconscious relationship with a higher power. Providence, it seems, without your conscious intention, rolled over in your favor. Early in your pilgrimage, contact with a higher power was largely unconscious and sporadic. Step Eleven is intended to eliminate this haphazard relationship with a deity and to create a conscious, deliberate one. This doesn't imply that you will be conscious of God in your life like you are conscious of someone walking into a room.

Conscious contact with God can only arise from a regular and continuous effort. Through self-discipline, ritual, and regular wise counsel, you become capable of noticing subtle, unexplainable shifts that enhance virtue and make you mindful of spiritual principles. Sensing these shifts is your conscious contact, and they enhance trust in a higher power. This is never noticeable in sporadic effort, or in a life with addictions or chaos, or if your recovery efforts are psychologically oriented. It only arises and is appreciated out of a continuous, sincere, and properly focused effort in prayer and meditation. This is rooted in a deliberate and planned effort on your part, hence, "conscious". Because of the propensity of addicts to create drama and chaos, only ongoing rituals of prayer, meditation, and wise counsel allow you to develop a mindset where you can be aware of God's influence without seeing *or needing to see* God.

"*...as we understood* [God]*...*" Understood is past tense. This relates back to how you came to understand and believe at Step Two. The chapter on Step Two in *Twelve Steps and Twelve Traditions* ends in the present tense with: "*...is the rallying point,*" and "*...we can stand...*". At Step Three, and thereafter, the grammatical tense in relation to God changes from present to past: it becomes under*stood*. When you reach Step Eleven, you completed Step Two a while ago, and so at Eleven it is how you under*stood* God. This again points to the idea that at Step Eleven, you aren't creating the relationship; you're enhancing it.

Step Eleven in particular, and the original twelve-step program in general, allow you complete freedom in identifying the symbols around which you organize your beliefs. The image of *That Which Art* that appears in your mind, the name you assign, the metaphors you employ, are how this higher power manifests in your consciousness. This is particular to you. There is this caution: Beware of idolatry. Our minds, restricted by Time and Space, must perceive everything, including a higher power, in some image, but when the image (or concept or picture or statue) is itself imbued with spiritual power, that's idolatry.

Carl Jung differentiated between *symbol* and *sign*. A *symbol* is a thing, or an image, that represents a link to deity: one part here in Time and Space, connected to the other part in the unknowable realm, transcendent of Time and Space. A symbol represents a way that people can conceive of something that, by definition, is beyond conception. A *sign,* however, doesn't transcend—it's something here, concrete and knowable. The wise spiritual pilgrim is ever mindful that the image is not God, it's a symbolic conception of God, only linking Time and Space to The Transcendent. When you imbue any image or thing with God-like powers, or attempt to organize

God's "powers" around any logical or rational construct (meaning within Time and Space), there is idolatry, and all manner of spiritual misadventure results.[13]

Beware of getting caught in the self-aggrandizing posture of superlative comparisons: my God is better than your God, or my path to God is better than your path to God. Any time you hear anyone talk about people needing to find "the one true way", trouble is brewing. Having one true way for you alone is quite acceptable, but don't adorn your path with righteous superlatives. This builds *you* up and not God.[14] Also beware of clinging to temporal or social constructions of a higher power: your cat, your support group, Nature. These are all finite and limited, leaving you at the mercy of charismatic people and Fate.

Some personal religious views may suggest that temporal realities, like your cat, a sunset, or Nature, contain some manifestation of God or Godlike attributes. Should this be the case, those people are then imbuing signs with Godlike powers, and that's idolatry. At another level, yes, your children are some genetic extension of you; or your home that you decorated entirely by *your*self may be an extension of your personality; but these are not you. Nature may be God's handiwork, but Nature isn't God.[15]

There is compassionate guidance offered in this matter in the original twelve-step literature. *"To certain newcomers and to those one-time agnostics who still cling to the A.A. group as their higher power, claims for the power of prayer may... still be unconvincing or objectionable. Those of us who once felt this way can certainly understand and sympathize. We well remember... rebelling against the idea of bowing before any God."* The next paragraph encourages going beyond clinging to a group as a higher power and includes this passage: *"almost the only scoffers at prayer are those who never tried it enough."*[16] This statement tells any twelve-step participant, without a specific reference to the definitions of sign and symbol noted earlier, that with the right effort and concentration, they can go beyond a sign (the AA group) to a symbol of God, and thereby create a more dependable relationship with a higher power.[17]

---

[13] *Man and his Symbols,* Carl G. Jung, Anchor Books (Doubleday), 1964, pp. 20-21, p. 55. This delineation is also important in understanding mythology—cf. *Transformation of Myth Through Time,* Joseph Campbell, Harper and Row, Publishers, 1990, p. 132. This concept was apprehended 2500 years ago, and, in a slightly different sense, is referred to in The Diamond Sutra, as translated in *A Buddhist Bible,* edited by Dwight Goddard, Beacon Press, 1994 edition, p. 89. The Buddha's words are figures of speech. The metaphors are symbols, not signs. And elsewhere, the chapter Idolatry, in *Huxley and God, Essays,* cited at an earlier footnote, is well worth extensive meditation.

[14] There is a succinct and related perspective to this written by Thich Nhat Hanh in the Introduction to *Contemplative Prayer,* by Thomas Merton, Image Books (Doubleday), 1996, p. 6. The paragraph begins: *"But many Christians and many Buddhists... ."*

[15] In *The Bhagavad-Gita,* Lord Krishna says to Arjuna: *"The whole universe is pervaded / by my unmanifest form; / all creatures exist in me, / but I do not exist in them." The Bhagavad-Gita,* The Ninth Teaching / The Sublime Mystery, Translated by Barbara Stoler Miller, Bantam Books, 1986, p. 83.

[16] *Twelve Steps and Twelve Traditions,* pp. 96-97.

[17] If you struggle with imagery and are fearful in this regard, it may be wise to choose a neutral image when praying. Review the information on a "limitless blue-black nothingness" in Chapter 3. When addressing religious addictions, it is necessary to help addicts deconstruct the *signs* of God they use that are imbued with power, and help them create symbols that can transcend secular or temporal limits. This is incredibly complex cross-over work.

The original twelve-step program does offer complete freedom by encouraging you to choose your own personal understanding of God, when you choose to submit yourself to that spiritual pilgrimage. But, as with all freedoms, there are dangerous pitfalls. Be alert to the ones noted above.

"*...praying only for knowledge of* [God's] *will for us...*" The purpose of prayer is quite limited in this context. You pray for only that one thing, which, of course, begs the question: "What is God's will for me?" There is endless and pointless debate about "God's will" in twelve-step meetings. Here are ten phrases from the original twelve-step literature that suggest what God's will is, as it manifests in the process of getting recovered. These aren't specifically cited within Step Eleven; they're taken at random from *Alcoholics Anonymous*.

- "*...to perfect and enlarge* [your] *spiritual life through work and self-sacrifice for others...*"
- "*...tolerance of other people's shortcomings and viewpoints and a respect for their opinions...*"
- "*...constant thought of others and how we may help meet their needs.*"
- "*...to be of maximum service to God and the people about us.*"
- "*...to do the right thing, no matter what the personal consequences may be.*"
- "*Helping others is the foundation stone...*"
- "*...to be at the place where you may be of maximum helpfulness to others...*"
- "*...to think of what you can put into life instead of how much you can take out.*"
- "*Giving, rather than getting, will become the guiding principle.*"
- "*...transcended by the happiness they found in giving themselves for others. They shared...*"[18]

It would appear that social status, sexual relationships, wealth, and collecting shiny things, aren't a part of "God's" will. But, to debate at all what God's will is (or isn't) is certainly an expression of what your will is. According to these quotations, neither is it God's will for addicts to agonize in dubious intellectual battle about the efficacy or credibility of God's design—it's beyond our comprehension, just as God is. [Recall the analogy at the end of Chapter 5 about The President and The Janitor. The janitor is incapable of understanding anything the CEO is doing, and, quite possibly, the CEO doesn't understand much about floor cleaners.]

Debating the designs of God is rooted in a lack of faith and absence of humility. So many people in twelve-step programs (and in the world) spend *so* much time trying to "figure out" either what God's will is for them, or what The Grand Plan of the Universe is (and, of course, what they disapprove of and how they'd im-

---

[18] *Alcoholics Anonymous*, pp. 14-15, 19, 20, 77, 79, 97, 102, 120, 128, and 159, respectively.

prove it), they have scarcely any time to pray for the courage to challenge their short-comings and racism, or to acquire simple virtues. However, in a spirit of fairness, since *no one* has verifiable direct access to God Transcendent of Time and Space, I concede that for some people, God's will may be:

- to accumulate vast wealth and power, with a caravan of ser-vants, in a blissful fulfilling relationship, growing old gracefully, in a magnificent palace, on a huge tropical planta-tion (with no mosquitoes), forever free from pain in paradise; or God's will may be...
- to rise above being merely mortal and act as God's personal advisor on how to improve the general conditions of human existence. Or, if not that, to at least advise everyone on which of the religious and political views [in certain geographical ar-eas] are, according to them, rooted in lunacy and deserving of immediate eradication.

Either of these could be God's will for some people, but I'm skeptical. Of course, my exaggerations were facetious; however, do *not* be fooled by the excess. The defects of spiritual racism, greed hidden under charity, arrogance in prayer, and religious elitism, are rampant in the routines of everyday twelve-step and spiritual life.

From the experience and wisdom of the ages, it would appear that fiscal concerns and social advantage are at odds with the benefits and blessings of authen-tic spiritual endeavor. I'm not intending this as a criticism of people who have significant financial resources or social influence. Nothing in and of itself makes these wrong. There are, however, important considerations and implications regard-ing power and wealth if your desire is to be sincerely spiritual.[19]

There is yet another important caution for those on a spiritual pilgrimage. Too many times, abuse, violence, punishment, spiritual elitism, gossip, racism, ho-mophobia, greed, etc., are perpetrated and justified as "God's will" by fanatics and neurotics. This abuse arises from all manner of fear and insecurity, and often indi-cates an addiction to religion (distraction) and self-righteousness (adrenaline).

Notice: *"Quite often, however, the thoughts that* seem *to come from God are... well-intentioned unconscious rationalizations."* And: "[there is] *...the possibil-ity that* [a person's] *own wishful thinking and the human tendency to rationalize have distorted* [their] *so-called guidance."* Asking for things via petitionary prayers *"...[is] based upon a supposition that we know God's will..."*.[20] Be especially cau-

---

[19] Yes, it would be spiritually corrupt to be powerful or wealthy and claim more entitlement to Life than others because of this. However, it's equally corrupt to claim you're spiritual, and to be arrogant in prayer and meditation, claiming you're better or wiser than those who aren't (spiritual). This hypocrisy, con-cealed in elitism and righteousness, and stemming from fear/envy and/or lack of humility, is often prevalent when twelve-step people discuss how "their way" is what the world needs, and how much nicer it would be if everybody did what they're doing. This dynamic is evident in most religions.

[20] *Twelve Steps and Twelve Traditions*, pp. 103, 104, emphasis theirs.

tious and reserved about what you think God's will is for you if it falls outside of the original literature's guidelines, or what you think it is for others in any circumstance.

Alcoholics Anonymous offers specific counsel about what God's will is for twelve-step pilgrims. Meditate less on what God's will may or may not be for you, and more on how you can be more generous and kind, and less inclined to selfish petulance, annoyance, and gossip. Pray frequently for the courage and perseverance to challenge your own unspiritual behavior, and everyone around you will benefit.[21] (Maybe this is all that God's will needs to be.)

"...and the power to carry that out." Earlier I explored the relationship between an increase in honesty and spiritual help. There is abundant anecdotal evidence from millions of twelve-step pilgrims that a higher power and the relationship therewith are the sources of change. Having only good intentions from the addict, although laudable, are insufficient to the task of getting recovered.

The phenomenon of addictions precludes sincere recovery without spiritual assistance. Within the context of Step Eleven, *"...and the power to carry that out,"* is a request of God, as you understand God, to provide the strength or perseverance or "power" to enable you to heal from addictions and live by spiritual principles. This is of long-term and permanent benefit to everyone around you.

There's an interesting book which identifies an insidious hypocrisy in Western culture. *Resentment Against Achievement*[22] advises that as much as we encourage and applaud the acquisition and possession of wealth, influence, power, beauty, and fame, those who acquire it are resented. This applies also to those people, without fame or wealth, who are decidedly assertive and live life by their own values, caring little for popular sentiment. The *"...one thing that enrages people trapped by their lives is the flaunted freedom of outsiders."*[23]

Out of this resentment arises the popularity of tabloid papers, magazines, TV shows, and entire books, in some cases, that smear the characters, demean the accomplishments, and exaggerate into character assassination the ordinary foibles of famous or powerful people. It's a manifestation of resentment and bitterness against assertive, passionate, successful people who aren't necessarily flaunting anything, but who are just being successful. Our culture is overloaded with insecure people — successful or not. This underlies the power of peer pressure and the neurotic need for compliance. Those who aren't compliant are envied and resented.[24]

---

[21] *"Every active force produces more than one change—every cause produces more than one effect." Herbert Spencer on Social Evolution,* Herbert Spencer, Edited by J.D.Y. Peel, The University of Chicago Press, 1972, p. 47. Prayer and meditation have a ripple effect; so do character defects.

[22] *Resentment Against Achievement – Understanding the Assault Upon Ability,* Robert Sheaffer, Prometheus Books, 1988.

[23] This quote is taken from *The Great Movies,* by William Bayer, The Ridge Press, Inc., and Grosset & Dunlap, Inc., 1973, p. 161. It was related to an insightful and well-merited classification of *Easy Rider* (directed by Dennis Hopper and released by Columbia Pictures, 1969), as a great film.

[24] This works both ways. I also write screenplays. Years ago, I offered two film scripts to two different director/producers. These producers were successful by cultural standards, known in the industry, and often resented for their success: They were the subject of tabloid/coffee-room gossip. Each producer wanted to develop the script I had given them, but they also wanted the endings changed as a condition of development. What one described as a too-bleak ending about families in one script, and the other a too-macabre ending about mothers and sons in the other script, were to me only realities of the plots and ex-

It's the same in twelve-step programs. Be advised: Should you go beyond the social comfort zone, diligently pursue spirituality, and seek the courage to practice God's will in *all* your affairs, you will be successful at it, and soon stand apart from the crowd. You will then be resented. People will gossip about you and malign your integrity. If you're truly spiritual, it won't bother you beyond a poignant sadness, but it will affect how you act in the world, and how you are treated.

The Myth of Ego Reduction as Humility[25]

Historically, a desire for political power, religious arrogance, and social or cultural factors, have allowed insecure religious leaders, and more recently "health gurus", to present self-serving interpretations of spiritual principles and religious doctrine. This includes people misrepresenting what the bona fide spiritual masters tried to teach (which is very common), and people who amend the original twelve steps to suit their convenience (financial or otherwise). Challenging the status quo established by the religious or social power-elite is dangerous business.

George Santayana recognized this self-serving nature of politics in religion:

> *"My atheism is true piety towards the universe and denies only gods fashioned by men in their own image, to be servants of their human interests."*
>
> George Santayana

In the last thirty years, it's generally represented that a spiritual pilgrim, people in therapy, and people in relationship "power struggles" have to knock their egos down to size to be healthy, content, humble, or spiritual. Variations of the following statements are made all the time: "He's got a big ego; that's his problem." "She's got to get her ego in check, otherwise, she'll never be happy." "You've got to get your ego down to size." And then there's the professional observation: "If you really want to become more spiritual (or serene or content)," said by the therapist (or doctor or minister or sponsor), with a quiet tone of rebuke or a patronizing air of superior insight, "you'll have to get rid of your ego. It's too big."[26]

These often indicate the person who made the judgment is either threatened by strong-willed people; or they're at a loss for how to respectfully counsel the pil-

---

tensions of the characters. Both producers told me I'd probably do well in the film industry. However, because of their insistence on drastically revised endings, I politely turned down both offers. The endings stayed as written and the film scripts sit on my shelf today, still undeveloped. I don't know that's what I'd decide today, but that's what I did then.

Here's the point: Both producers were resentful that I said no to the deals they offered. By *their* standards, I chose "non-success" when I was offered "success" in the form of being a (compliant) working scriptwriter, receiving a sizable amount of money, having a lucrative income, and the opportunity to become established in the film industry. Be advised: Anyone in our culture of compliance who assertively insists on adhering to a personally established code of conduct, with polite disregard for the sensibilities of others, will meet with resentment and end up as tabloid-gossip for insecure people.

[25] It may be appropriate to review Appendix IV.

[26] The place someone is assigned to on the spectrum "Passive -> Assertive -> Aggressive" is influenced by the ego-posture of the person doing the assigning. i.e. An aggressive person will probably be labeled a variation of mean/nasty/frightening by a decidedly passive person; and they may view an assertive person as "safer" but possibly somewhat bossy. A decidedly assertive person would have a different view of the same aggressive person. It's all relative.

grim by utilizing the focus of their will power. Making this judgment immediately creates an inner power struggle. It also implies that "small" egos are present in humble/spiritual people, and significant ego-reduction always contributes greatly to spiritual or psychological health. These are patently false. It's a myth that becoming truly spiritual (or healthy) is an exercise in ego reduction or ego annihilation.

Consider a person who's independent and decidedly assertive; they refuse to be manipulated. They could easily be labeled as having a big ego. From the rationale of "get rid of your ego", it appears that assertive, independent people can not then be spiritual or happy because they're willful and have "big" egos. Yet, on the flip side, other people who are passive, and "helplessly victimized", or manipulated by predators, are told to get independent, get strong, get assertive, be more willful or bold... which could be easily construed to mean "get a bigger ego".

My own investigation repeatedly reveals that any great saint or spiritual leader who evinces humility has an ego that is "comparatively at par" with any tyrant or ruthless dictator who's the model of arrogance. (Don't get caught up in arguing with this just yet.) The difference between the saint and the tyrant is not in the size of their egos, or the force of their willpower, but what their egos and willpower are directed towards. One of these people has their ego and all their considerable willpower set on the five spiritual principles and serving God. The other, equally strong "personality" is focused on selfishness, anger, and domination.

This interpretation applies to anyone. What any individual focuses on: sex, winning, harmony, righteousness, humility, dominance, money, being right, passivity, is what they present to the world. The character traits people consistently display and defend represent an accurate reflection of the focus of their ego. Since, (i) our instinct for survival naturally resists annihilation; and (ii) our willpower/ego exists to facilitate survival, it is more effective to applaud our ego's strength and get it focused differently, rather than eliminate it (which is impossible, anyway).

If your ego—if *you,* they're the same thing, believe that spirituality and, attendant to that, humility, is dependent upon chopping your ego down to size, then praying and being humble will always be subconsciously threatening (an inner struggle). I've seen time and again that people resist "ego reduction".

I know many people who, after years of being a therapist or spiritual advisor (minister, priest, etc.), or after years of therapy as a client, still talk like the death of their ego is the ultimate objective. They batter themselves with recrimination for not annihilating, subduing, reducing, eliminating, killing, whittling down, chopping up, shrinking, or erasing their ego. Attempts at ego reduction in the pursuit of spirituality, humility, or health, should that ego reduction actually happen (which, by the way, I've never seen any evidence of), would leave the person at the mercy of tyrants, predators, and abusive partners because of the weakening of their ego boundaries. Mental-health professionals are long familiar with the theories that refer to the development of strong ego boundaries.

Nowhere in Step Seven does it say that you are required to annihilate or even reduce your ego. Addicts are told they will have to get rid of arrogance and the like, and adopt spiritual virtues, but that doesn't require killing your ego. By adhering to the theory of ego reduction, spiritual pilgrims will forever have to drag themselves kicking and screaming to the alters of humility, prayer, and meditation. The original program advises, in many places, that these are only sincerely available to people with a strong and devoted commitment to a spiritual lifestyle. How, then, could someone with weak ego boundaries, or a "small" ego, accomplish this?

The traditional, popular theories almost invariably present that strong or "big" egos are fatal to serene health or spirituality. And yet, I have met, or have had the privilege to be instructed by people whom I consider to be authentically Spiritual. These women and men, who were obviously living deep within the five spiritual principles, each had a strong, fine character. There was nothing weak or small about their egos. This also appears to be true in the writings of the spiritual masters. In fact, it appears to me that through prayer, meditation, and devotion, these spiritual pilgrims actually strengthen their character, and develop a strong ego focused on spiritual pursuits. Strong ego boundaries are what keeps them spiritually on track.

This isn't semantics. The "small/reduced ego" views on health and spirituality, and that theory's place in therapy and transformation, are seriously at odds with human nature and the dynamics of spirituality. Being truly spiritual exists at the core of human nature. Becoming spiritual must therefore be (somehow) consistent with health. If I am told that a strong/big ego prevents emotional or relationship harmony and bliss, and at another time I am told to have a strong, well-defined ego for self protection (to be assertive and independent for personal fulfillment), there are subtle and confusing contradictions that must be examined closely.

Our culture embodies everything unspiritual. It denigrates compassion, love, and humility, and encourages racism, wealth and privilege, religious elitism, greed, violence, and sexism. How can anyone be truly spiritual, or emotionally "balanced", or maintain inner-harmony in this culture, without a strong and well-focused ego? It's hard enough to stand up to addictions, but to live spiritually is to be generally opposed to modern culture. This requires tremendous ego strength. When I add to this my observations and learning about the characters of the bona fide spiritual masters, and the strong characters of recognized peace-oriented leaders of the world, the theory of "small egos for bliss and humility" is untenable.

I have yet to hear anyone, other than myself, say that becoming humble and spiritual, or sincerely loving someone (especially romantic loving) requires a strong, well-defined ego. In our culture, there is so little that supports the significant commitment and effort needed for truly spiritual endeavor, that it couldn't be accomplished by anyone with a "small" ego. Authentic transformation (spiritual or emotional), that must stand against addictions and culture, requires a strong ego for a fulfilled life of love, spirituality, and serenity.

Recognizing this truth has allowed three changes for me. The first is that all of the contradictions and puzzles I had regarding ego theories and transformation immediately evaporated. The second is that my own inner life and spiritual work (such as it is) became smoother. The third is that my work helping others (and their experience of themselves) became clearer; not necessarily easier, but less tangled.

Here it is in a nutshell: It's not necessary to change the size of your ego to become healthy or spiritual. This perspective has profound implications for the generally accepted views of personality, humility, love, relationship contentment, individuation, and personal change. Within the crucibles of genetics, family, personal temperament, intellect, and culture (social rituals, education, politics, religion), we adopt values. Those values, about *every*thing, which are very delicately balanced and carefully prioritized, are the manifestation of our egos. This forms the core of our perceptions. At a conscious level, this shows up as the organization of our personality, and governs what we focus our considerable willpower upon.

One person focuses their ego-willpower on passive behavior, another on charitable works, another on the acquisition of fame or wealth, yet another on dominating others or violence. People who are extremely passive actually dominate those around them with their ego's powerful focus on passive behavior. Their egos are the same size [sic], but are focused differently. Investing all your creative energy, intellect, and willpower, in music or painting isn't that much different than investing it in creative bank robbing, or creative stock swindling. The purpose of Steps Two, Six, and Seven (probably the least talked about steps), is to change the most basic thing about an addict's personality: the focus of their values and perceptions — their ego.

So, what's this got to do with praying? Strong ego boundaries are important to a fulfilling life. People instinctively resist ego-reduction ("ego-death"). At a very deep level, ego "annihilation" leaves a person at risk, and our psyches resist this. If you even remotely believe that humility requires an elimination of your ego, and praying does require humility, you'll resist prayer. If you have a hard time praying or approaching humility, part of that difficulty may be concealed in the belief that you need to "chop" your ego down to size (akin to self-annihilation) as a prerequisite to being humble or spiritual.

————

Many mystics and spiritual masters write of self-mortification and "the self" dying to the will of God. Reading these works as prose (literally), not as poetry (metaphorically), is one source of major corruption. The metaphor implies changing yourself so that your values are prioritized differently. Look at self-mortification ("dying" to the will of God) this way: Notice the powerful focus of energy on "self" and "selfishness", and with the same intensity, refocus that energy on service to a higher power. The "I" of selfishness "dies" — self-mortification — in a *symbolic* way, and ego-willpower stays strong, but is directed elsewhere. It's not about ego death, it's about ego redirection.

Monks, saints, Gandhi, Jesus (Yeshua) of Nazareth, Mohammad, and thousands of others, who proved themselves to be humble and spiritual, were strongly opinionated, *and* had powerful personalities (strong egos). Many were murdered rather than abandon their commitment to God or spirituality. There is no evidence of weak or small egos. These people had powerful egos directed at spiritual things.

Great humility is the direct result of an ego's unrelenting focus on spiritual principles.[27] The task of an addict/alcoholic becoming recovered is changing the focus of their ego from self-destructive, non-spiritual behavior to devoted obedience to the five spiritual principles. *"Every day is a day when we must carry the vision of God's will into all of our activities. 'How can I best serve Thee—Thy will (not mine) be done.' ...We can exercise our willpower along this line all we wish. It is the proper use of the will."*[28] It would require a well-organized and willful ego to comply with this guideline.

Should you be able to do this in some way similar to what the spiritual masters did (which encapsulates the themes of Steps Two, Six, and Seven: reprioritizing your values so that spiritual principles are at the top of the list), you will never again have to *force* yourself to pray or meditate. Ever. And your ego will be just as big as it ever was.

Prayer

Addicts getting recovered often experience an automatic belligerence towards prayer. Sometimes it's vicious enough to prohibit them from praying, and they relapse and die because of their refusal to pursue spirituality. Very often, however, addicts in recovery stay just on the very edge of spirituality, only dipping their toes in the waters of prayer (and meditation). This reluctance to pray, or demonstrating an intermittent effort, is evident in all manner of mediocre recovery and socially approved addictions like sex, shopping, relationships, exercise; and in long bouts of depression, irresponsibility, moodiness, and petulant complaining.

Prayer is: *1. a. A reverent petition made to God or another object of worship. b. The act of making a reverent petition to God or another object of worship. 2. An act of communion with God or another object of worship, such as in devotion, confession, praise, or thanksgiving. 3. A specially worded form used to address God or another object of worship.*[29] In order to explore prayer, it is important to start from a place of grounded orientation. I've (arbitrarily) divided prayer into three broad classifications to provide a basic sense of structure for the twelve-step pilgrim, so that the student at prayer can more wisely choose a focus for their interior life. The three classifications are Prayers of Petition, Contemplation, and Gratitude.

Prayers of Petition

Dear God:
Because of __insert circumstance__, and these itemized, righteous "good" reasons: __insert one or more justifications__, may I (and/or

---

[27] In counselling, I work at having clients develop not small, whittled-down egos, but powerful egos focused on truly ethical, spiritual endeavor. In this manner, much resistance to the idea of spirituality decreases because the ego isn't threatened with annihilation.

[28] *Alcoholics Anonymous*, p. 85.

[29] *The American Heritage® Dictionary of the English Language, Third Edition*, © 1996, Houghton Mifflin Company. Electronic version.

___ insert name___) *please have* ___insert desired gift(s)___.*"*

Thank you very much,

*_(insert name & address)_*

These are styled after the suppliant asking their higher power for specific things. It's a one sided conversation with requests. *"Our immediate temptation will be to ask for specific solutions to specific problems, and for the ability to help other people as we have already thought they should be helped."*[30] Even with devotion to God, and integrity based in the five spiritual principles, all petitionary prayer, even though necessary in one convoluted context, runs the risk of complications.

There are many drawbacks to petitionary prayer. If you "miraculously" get what you want, it tends to lead you to be self-righteous and self-congratulatory, and for you to then rest on your laurels or become greedy. If you pray and don't get what you want, it tends to lead into feeling forsaken; that you're doing something wrong; that God is punishing you, or God likes others more (those others who hint or brag their prayers were answered). This undermines faith, and may lead to abandoning God and pouting: "I'm not praying any more. I never get what I want," or increasing your efforts to the point of being obsessive: "When I get this prayer-thing perfect, then I'll get what I want," or "When I finally get rid of all my character defects, then God will listen to me." Any time you superimpose God on Santa Claus, you set yourself up to flatter your selfishness or slander your own character.

"In [asking for specific solutions] *we are asking God to do it* our *way. Therefore, we ought to consider each request carefully to see what its real merit is."*[31] Any petition to God (whether sign or symbol) contains your suggested solution for some situation you've assumed is a problem: your uncle gets over the cancer, your friend gets through the housing crisis, the little twins have a nice camping trip, your spouse comes home safely. Or, you seek some message from "God", to you personally, that you should or shouldn't move, quit, marry, divorce, leave, stay, hide, run, or buy something.[32] These petitions are a grocery list for God's Supermarket. You're asking the deity of your choice to intervene on your personal behalf, to keep you out of pain, or in happiness, or to rescue you out of responsibility.[33]

The moral value, often rooted in fear, embodied within the petition, lies at the core of this risky style of prayer. Within that moral value is the trap you set for yourself in how you righteously justify your prayer wish-list, and praying righteously is always spiritually dangerous. Praying that someone dies in a fiery car crash because they were late for your party would be a morally "bad" thing; you can't justify it. Praying it doesn't rain on the day of the orphans' picnic has an ambience of moral

---

[30] *Twelve Steps and Twelve Traditions*, p. 102.

[31] Ibid.

[32] In a truly spiritual life, there are no problems: there are only opportunities to work on humility. (Remember the Two-Step Dance.)

[33] The motivation for most petitionary prayer, albeit well disguised, is rooted in selfishness. It is the same with pursuing a relationship with The Divine Spirit, or the desire to acquire faith—both are most often rooted in selfishness. *"Some believe that spiritual achievement will bestow temporal authority; others, that it will compensate for weaknesses of character; and still others, that it will make available to them...*

uprightness—unless you're the farmer in the next field who's praying for rain for his crops. Praying a child recover from cancer is easily justifiable—it's "righteous". A perceived or justified moral correctness rationalizes petitions to God.

Petitionary prayer isn't necessarily wrong. However: Twelve-step participants, and those with weak faith, righteous spiritual intent, or pronounced character defects, need to be very cautious regarding its use. It's often a compensation for temporal laziness, or an effort to thwart disappointment and control Life. All petitionary prayer is to some degree self-serving, regardless of any apparently ethical or altruistic agenda.

———

The novice at prayer sometimes misperceives prayer-time with God as similar to an audience with royalty, or a job interview with the head of the corporation: have your shoes shined, fingernails clean, hair combed, and be on top of the agenda—get it right. Don't make mistakes and don't waste time: God's busy. This is indicative of God being seen as a sign: the CEO of the Universe, and not a symbol. This creates needless anxiety and all manner of corruption in prayer.

Many well-intentioned people live in perpetual dislocation within the disciplines of prayer and meditation. They end up confused, living with doubt, and worrying that they weren't eloquent or might have said the wrong things to God. I remember speaking about this with a monk. I was living in a monastery at the time, and we were walking along a trail in the woods on the monastery grounds. I told him of my anxiety about not getting my prayers "right". I remember him smiling reassuringly. He was kind, and as I recall it today, ten years after it happened, this is my perspective of what he taught me:

> Be kind to yourself. Accept your limitations as an important part of the unfolding of the universe, and graciously stop trying to understand God. God isn't anything that I can conceive of, ever, and neither can you. There are only metaphors and symbols that are always inadequate, and can never do more than magnificently misrepresent whatever is God's true nature. You don't accept this yet.
>
> Experiencing gratitude and love are gifts from God that become our prayers to God. For myself, I wish to become a total prayer to God; that my whole being and existence is the prayer. And so, when I experience doubt or confusion or anxiety, that is my prayer to God, too.
>
> Pray your confusion and your anxiety to God just as sincerely as your love and gratitude. These are as important as anything else we offer God. Contained within this is humility, and your faith and trust that God will understand your prayer as you giving yourself completely. The greatest gift we can offer God is everything.

———

the material objects of their desires. While such ulterior motives are present, true faith is not possible."
The Mystical Christ, Manly P. Hall, The Philosophical Research Society, Inc., 1993, p. 17.

In Life, and especially in the midst of your prayer, should you become lost or anxious, then *that* becomes your prayer. Pray your confusion to God too. In prayer, don't search for fancy words—that's Impression Management, and insincere. If you're angry with God because you've misperceived God's "participation" in your life, offer that too. Should you have turned your will *and life* over to the care of God, all of these are in your prayers because they are you.

If a twelve-step participant prays for reduced character defects or another day of sobriety and abstinence so they can have a peaceful life (both petitions for gifts), they have recast God as Santa Claus. What is spiritually more appropriate is requesting these "gifts" so as to be of service to God, to thereby reduce or eliminate the chaos and pain you inflict on others. In this second motive for prayer, certainly one side effect will be serenity for you. That serenity is not for your personal pleasure, it's so you can help bring peace to other troubled souls. When deciding to petition your higher power for *any*thing, do *every*thing to ensure that it is from humility, and of primary benefit to others, and little benefit to yourself.

Prayers of Contemplation

This style of prayer is sometimes called Prayer of Quiet, where suppliants become still within their heart, and peaceful in reverence. They communicate to God *without doing*. Taoism might describe it as *Wu Wei* in prayer—accomplishing without action; acting deliberately but with deliberate non-purpose. This unique, prayerful meditation takes you to rest with the knowing of God.[34]

Prayers of Gratitude

These are [supposed to be] a communication from a person to their higher power offering gratitude and praise, and asking for nothing for themselves. In the perspectives that superimpose God and Santa Clause, when something "nice" happens, like your drunken relative is well behaved at the wedding reception, or someone survives their surgery... well, you've received "a present" and polite people say thank you. As regards this particular type of prayer, you're essentially telling God you're pleased for getting your own way. There is no humility in these prayers.

For people with a different spiritual nature, prayers of gratitude mean gratitude for everything, including "hardship" (which is only an arbitrary, self-serving interpretation of some circumstance). In Chapter 11, there is reference to Boethius, and his view of spiritually "troubled" times, which applies here. Prayers of gratitude are an active recognition for the perpetually-available state of love and grace, and an appreciation for the implacable grandeur of the experience of our humanness through spirituality, regardless of the circumstance. This embodies humility.

Incidental to this, the more a person submits to humility on behalf of the God of their own understanding, the *less* emotional pain they will feel, regardless of

---

[34] *Contemplative Prayer*, by Thomas Merton, Image Books, Doubleday, 1996, although sometimes esoteric, is a valuable guide to contemplative prayer, which makes it a fine volume for learning about prayer through Meditations on Wisdom (which is discussed in the next section).

what happens. The realization of a true spiritual state of being is through devoted, humble service to "God". If stated in non-theological terms, this touches the essence of Buddhism: the absence of dukkha (dislocation) through humble non-attachment.

When prayers are primarily of contemplation and gratitude, you eventually pray only because God is worthy of being prayed to. Consider reducing petitionary prayer and increasing prayers of contemplation and gratitude, which are closer to the heart of sound spiritual endeavor. When assessing your commitment to prayer, ask yourself: "Do prayers interrupt my life, or does life interrupt my prayers?"

Meditation

Meditate: 1. To reflect on; contemplate. 2. To consider or reflect at length. 3. To engage in contemplation, especially of a spiritual or devotional nature.[35]

I've arbitrarily divided meditation into two broad categories: (i) Meditations *of* Transcendence (there are two subtypes: Intellectual and Physical), and (ii) Meditations *on* Wisdom. These general categories are only to help clarify the issues of meditation within Step Eleven, and to enable you to more clearly appreciate what the original twelve-step program advises.

It's important to remember: As you explore meditation in the context of the original twelve-step literature, that literature was written long *before* North American culture experienced any noticeable presence of Eastern philosophy. Step Eleven, written c. 1937, was at least twenty years before the work of Alan Watts, Ram Dass, Aldous Huxley, D.T. Suzuki, Thomas Cleary, Dwight Goddard, and many others fostered a conscious presence of Eastern philosophy in North America. Further: The TM movement that took root in the 1960's was at least twenty-five years after the meditation instructions for Step Eleven were written.

(i) *Meditations of Transcendence*

Transcendence, as a meditation, originates out of the Eastern religious philosophies of Hinduism and ancient Asian disciplines similar to Taoism. Generally, Transcendental Meditation (TM) is to rise above, and, at the same time disable, the distractions of mind-stuff and sentient chaos. When done effectively, this takes you beyond your pain or above the dislocation of your life, to achieve a state of "blissful absence". TM, in one way, is intended to create harmony in the broken images of truth. There are two basic approaches to TM... Intellectual and Physical.

TM — Intellectual: These would be those meditations that require no movement and much intellectual concentration: sitting quietly, generally immobile, concentrating on breathing, and/or concentrating on *OM* or other mantras, and chant-

---

[35] *The American Heritage® Dictionary of the English Language, Third Edition,* © 1996, Houghton Mifflin Company. Electronic version.

ing. With years of due diligence, the meditator achieves transcendence. This would include some types of yoga.

Mantras and intellectual meditation are to replace the chaos and broken images of thought-truth with a rhythm of focused awareness. The rhythm is established within the mantra or the pattern of concentration. Depending on the skill and intent of the meditator, and the style and rhythm of the mantra, it can elevate you into transcendence, *but* you may also just remain at the level of rhythmic, focused awareness.

TM — Physical: In this group are Tai Chi and those types of Yoga that incorporate movement and balance. Sometimes these include silent mantras. These disciplines aren't necessarily intended to transcend the spontaneous mind-chaos (which is the specific intent of the intellectual style of TM). They are to bring harmony and grace to our physical *and* mental condition. [And, too, some TM can be a justified-by-righteousness, mind-altering experience that isn't spiritual—it depends.]

When you practice TM or any similar discipline, with wise devotion, there's a "leaving" from what you are at the beginning, and a "going" to another conscious state. When the physical or intellectual meditation is over, you most often return to the previous state, where you were before you left. Sometimes the only thing that's really accomplished is a short vacation from yourself (which is a glib metaphor for what addicts tried to do in their addictions).[36]

Since the 1960s, Transcendental Meditation and mantra work have become very well known, and these are what people usually think of when someone speaks of meditation. However, the original twelve-step literature teaches a uniquely different style of meditation, which is rarely appreciated, because of the more popular awareness of TM. Not all meditation is transcendental. TM is valuable, but it should not (in fact, cannot) substitute for what is suggested in Step Eleven. Addicts have to transform their personalities, not transcend them.

What needs to be clarified for twelve-step pilgrims is the meditation suggested within the original Step Eleven is a Meditation *on* Wisdom (not TM) which is a crucial practice that challenges the recovered addict's self-limiting beliefs and prejudices. If recovered addicts are to reduce their defects of character, and enhance their spirituality, so they can improve their conscious contact with their higher power, they must *consciously* let go of their old ideas. This is accomplished by forcing themselves to appreciate the wisdom of others, through Meditations *on* Wisdom, not TM. Transcendental Meditation is also important—but in a different context.

(ii) *Meditations on Wisdom*

Rather than transcending the human condition, Step Eleven advises to *"improve our conscious contact..."* — to deliberately develop an awareness that promotes

---

[36] This is one aspect of a subtle corruption that is sometimes present in "spiritually minded" people—their spiritual endeavors are brief vacations from their greed or selfishness. They go to a church, a meeting, a therapist, a meditation retreat, thereby escaping their guilt and corruption and feel good about the impression they're making (mostly on themselves), and then return from the spiritual outing (like a picnic), to be themselves again, changing nothing. There is a well-concealed and self-righteous Impression Management scheme operating in this lifestyle. Challenging this widespread behavior is incredibly complicated.

insight and humility. This is how addicts detach from self-limiting ideas, dismantle old defense mechanisms, and alter perceptions. It's a spiritually focused, deliberate, self-initiated reorganizing of themselves through the wisdom of others. Meditations on Wisdom are active humility, which creates inner vision.

The original twelve-step literature teaches what a Meditation on Wisdom is by providing an example and offering instructions at the same time. There isn't a Step Eleven prayer, *per se*. The author(s) chose a prayer written by St. Francis of Assisi to demonstrate the technique of a Meditation on Wisdom.

The Instructions for Meditations on Wisdom

"Well, we might start like this. First let's look at a really good prayer. We won't have far to seek... ." And, *"The world's libraries and places of worship are a treasure trove for all seekers."*[37] First: find a prayer or spiritual writing that attracts you, and then *"As beginners in meditation... "* (Here are the instructions...)

"...reread [it] *several times very slowly..."*
"...savoring every word..."
"...trying to take in the deep meaning of each phrase and idea..."
"...drop all resistance..."
"...debate has no place."
"...rest quietly with the thoughts of someone who knows..."
"...ponder what its mystery is."
"...seek all those wonders still unseen..."

The goal is to *"...experience and learn* [and to]... *be strengthened and lifted up,"*[38] which has little in common with TM, and much to do with re-education and being open-minded. (Again, this creates inner vision. [39])

"It is to be hoped that every A.A. who has a religious connection which emphasizes meditation will return to the practice of that devotion as never before."[40] Many addicts, prior to joining a twelve-step group, may not have a religious connection that encourages meditation. Regarding this quote, however, there is this perspective: For those addicts without a prior religious connection, being both a twelve-step pilgrim and a member of a twelve-step program, places them inside an organization that strongly emphasizes a connection to God and encourages meditation. Regardless of whether or not they ever had a previous religious association that encouraged meditation, they have one now.

---

[37] Excerpts from *Twelve Steps and Twelve Traditions*, pp. 98, 99.
[38] These, and the preceding phrases, are taken from *Twelve Steps and Twelve Traditions*, pp. 99-100.
[39] Thich Nhat Hanh describes this regarding the writing of Thomas Merton: *"I hope you will read the words of this wise visionary slowly and mindfully, in a way that your reading will itself be a contemplation, a meditation, a prayer of the heart."* The Introduction, by Thich Nhat Hanh, in *Contemplative Prayer*, by Thomas Merton, Image Books (Doubleday), 1996, p. 7.
[40] Ibid., p. 98.

The Example for a Meditation on Wisdom

"The actual experience of meditation and prayer across the centuries is... immense."[41] The original literature offers an example of a prayer and explains how to apply this style of meditation to your spiritual life—which *is* your life. The example, from St. Francis of Assisi, begins: "Lord, make me a channel of thy peace... "

After quoting that prayer, *Twelve Steps and Twelve Traditions* applies to it the instructions for meditations on wisdom (noted above). The book advises that you reread it several times, savor each word, take in the deep meaning, drop resistance, relax, be strengthened, use constructive imagination, focus undisturbed, find the inner essence, take a good look at where you stand now, try to glimpse the ideal, and decide what would happen if you moved closer to that ideal. The text refers to all of this as "...a fragment of what is called meditation."[42] By doing all of this you are meditating *on* the wisdom of a spiritual master. (Simple, eh?)

Meditation on any spiritual/philosophical writing that pushes you to challenge your self-limiting thoughts tends to draw you closer to God (as you understand God). That's a Meditation on Wisdom, and how you abandon and replace your old ideas and secret prejudices. Learn about yourself and about spirituality. What do the spiritual masters (from any spiritual tradition) know that you don't know? According to Step Eleven, you are charged with the responsibility to find out.

Consider how these instructions for meditation apply in the context of understanding great artistic endeavor: Meditate on the applicability of what I am about to offer. Great actors, musicians, philosophers, writers, poets, painters, dancers, social activists, sculptors, etc., contain, within their work, some symbolic connection to humanity at large *and* to the transcendent. This isn't always easily visible in their work, but there's a symbolic connection to transcendence for the meditative observer, and that connection is its quality of greatness.[43]

When people witness great creativity, or hear a profound spiritual insight they don't understand, oftentimes there's an immediate tendency to dismiss it. They create a shallow argument to conceal their ignorance or laziness; or dismiss the artist through racism, sexism, or character assassination. The task for a twelve-step spiritual pilgrim is to not do this. At the minimum, be accepting, and if you're interested then listen, study, call yourself to task, discover, and savor the transforming connection. Rest quietly with the insight of someone who knows. Ask, "What are they teaching me?" Do not lose the opportunity to be enlarged by humility.

> "When there's something you don't understand, you have to go humbly to it. You don't go to school and sit down and say 'I know what you're getting ready to teach me.' You sit there and you learn. You open your mind. You absorb. But you have to be quiet,

---

[41] *Twelve Steps and Twelve Traditions*, p. 98.
[42] Ibid., pp. 99-101, emphasis added.
[43] The list of endeavors stated here is certainly incomplete. As I encourage you to meditate on endeavors of great merit, I do not endorse consuming gratuitous violence, pornography, hate literature, strident religious elitism, and the like.

you have to be still."
John Coltrane, Musician[44]

Lao Tse is reported to have said: *"To venerate without understanding, to worship without inner vision, is blasphemy and vain."* Creating inner vision is through Step Eleven meditation and is enabled by devoted self-examination at Step Ten. Step Eleven meditation is not to transcend the human condition (which most addicts tried to do in acting out), but to deepen your awareness and commitment to a spiritual life by absorbing the wisdom of others. Through this, you plumb the depths of your own character, and go past "yourself" into the universal soul that resides within you. This takes... *devotion: 1. Ardent, often selfless affection and dedication, as to a person (or a process). Sometimes a synonym for love. 2. Religious ardor or zeal; piety. 3. Often: devotions: acts of religious observance or prayer.*[45]

Seven Odds and Ends

(1) Meditate on the Step Eleven instructions for meditation.

(2) In the pilgrimage from Steps One to Nine, the process of understanding and completing those nine steps actually involves doing Meditations on Wisdom on each step. At Step Eleven, the recovered addict is instructed to meditate on the wisdom of the spiritual masters, whose insights will enhance but may not necessarily be particular to, the original twelve-step philosophy.

(3) Include some meditation on those points of view you see as different from yours. Contemplate the other view *from* the other point of view. For example, if you're a Muslim, study Christianity; if Jewish, study Buddhism for a while; and likewise for Christians—be respectfully informed about other religious perspectives. Work to appreciate the wisdom of the parallel. There are no opposites, there are only parallels. *"Be quick to see where religious people are right."*[46] This is not to convert yourself to another belief: it's to temper any prejudice with compassion and awareness. This is difficult. Belligerent, out-of-hand rejection of a different viewpoint is arrogant. At the level of mystic, there are no religious enemies.

It's easy to attend lectures and read books by people who agree with you, but that practice is disastrously limiting. Joseph Conrad wrote: "[people] *learn wisdom with extreme slowness, and are always ready to believe promises that flatter their secret hopes... ,"*[47] and I add: and they prefer to cater to their coveted prejudices. Meditations on Wisdom in Step Eleven counteract this dangerous tendency.

(4) To proselytize without invitation advertises arrogance and insecurity. Avoid offering opinions unless they're invited, and only then if they can be offered

---

[44] Years ago I clipped this out of a magazine, and have only a small piece of glossy paper with this quote on it. It appears to be from a mail-order club of some description, but I don't know which one. To the editor who included it in the magazine, thank you.

[45] *The American Heritage® Dictionary of the English Language, Third Edition,* © 1996, Houghton Mifflin Company. Electronic version.

[46] *Alcoholics Anonymous,* p. 87. Also, regarding spiritual principles and faith, on p. 48 is this: *"...we often found ourselves handicapped by obstinacy, sensitiveness, and unreasoning prejudice* [and] *...spiritual things made us bristle with antagonism. This sort of thinking had to be abandoned."*

[47] The quote is from Part III of *Nostromo,* by Joseph Conrad, Wordsworth Classics, 1996 edition.

without belligerence, *and only* if you aren't benignly indifferent to having others agree or disagree with you.

(5) Twelve-step people often suggest that praying is talking to God and meditating is listening for an answer. According to Step Eleven, Meditations on Wisdom are to seek the spiritual wisdom of others, not to listen for the voice of God. In Transcendental Meditation people seek the bliss of nirvana or peaceful-nothingness. Either way, hearing the voice of God isn't a part of meditation. A person can wait for an awfully long time to hear God, and besides, waiting and listening isn't seeking.

(6) Create a meditation place for yourself. Because of preconceived ideas about meditation in the Eastern traditions i.e. the lotus position, mudras, incense, and sitting on a cushion or a floor mat, what I suggest will be remarkably different from what many people might think a meditation place is.

Step Eleven meditation is quietly contemplating the wisdom of the insights and philosophies of the spiritual masters. You will need a comfortable chair—but not too comfortable, you don't want to fall asleep; a decent reading lamp, a nearby bookshelf, at least one large dictionary (with etymology), some writing paper, writing implements, and several spiritually oriented books, the content of which you would like to explore and meditate on.

If you want to meditate on *The Bhagavad-Gita, The Koran, The Upanishads*, or any other translated writing, get two different translations (at least a decade apart in terms of the publication date) and compare them. That's a part of acquiring wisdom—the wisdom of the writing, and of the translator. If you're meditating on the writings of T. Merton, F. Nietzsche, C. Jung, or some other similar author, consider beginning with a "Best of..." collection. Create a meditation place for Step Eleven and allow yourself to be taught.

(7) You entered a twelve-step program blind to the spiritual machinations that placed you there. After a few months of abstinence and participation, should you think you are still "in" your group because your higher power put you there, you are externalizing responsibility and, in a sense, holding God accountable for yourself.

Recognize that at some point after arriving, it was *you* who decided to stay. You may have asked for spiritual help, but it was you who decided to ask. As you make progress, there are those moments you cannot explain, that you may interpret as the hand of Providence, but it is you who decided to notice them. An appropriate self-respect arises from the spiritual choices you've made.

Often I've written that you are completely responsible for the chaos and turmoil in your life. You also choose to pray and meditate. Inherent in this is the responsibility of choice. Consider breathing and thinking. You don't necessarily take pride in these behaviors; however, you can choose to be reasonably physically fit and thus choose how you breathe, or through devotion to spirituality, you can choose how you think. Wise choices are the seeds of healthy self-respect.

———

Step Eleven is specifically designed to enhance your intimate relationship with *That Which Art*.[48] And, with Step Eleven, you continuously challenge whatever level of spiritual fitness you find yourself at. Its design is to establish a standard set by God and not by you. It will also maintain, within you, a consistent, conscious awareness of God beyond what you might otherwise, accidentally comprehend.[49] If you let it, it will take you out of yourself and put you into the spiritual wisdom of the ages. Prayers of Contemplation and Gratitude, and Meditations *on* Wisdom, lead and cause you to descend into a soulful awareness of God.

Through these manners of prayer and meditation you *"...let go of old ideas,"*[50] and rest quietly with the thoughts of someone (else) who knows. There are no accidents in authentic spiritual enlightenment.

Prayer and meditation require significant self-discipline, especially in the beginning. You will struggle. Your addicted, self-centered personality will categorize these new and unfamiliar practices as decidedly threatening. Why bother? The end of Step Eleven reads: *"Perhaps one of the greatest rewards of meditation* [on the wisdom of others] *and prayer is the sense of belonging that comes to us."*[51] This is not about belonging in your family, belonging in your meeting, or belonging in your workplace. It's about you belonging *in* the world and *to* God.

From a different perspective, but with a similar sense, Ram Dass represented this nicely in *The Only Dance There Is*. Regarding the concept of "home", he relates that during a road trip, he met a man at a gas station and unexpectedly ended up visiting with the man and his family. Ram Dass writes: *"So I stay for lunch... and we're all settling in, and we've all got our feet up and we're all home. I realize this is my home. Am I going to say, 'Well, I gotta go home?' ...we're all here."*[52] One of many interpretations of his book revolves around the implication that *everyone* is our family. Throughout the book, Ram Dass describes a spiritual mindset where the universe is our home, not some geographical location behind an imaginary, politically defined boundary. By doing Prayer and Meditations on Wisdom, in the manner suggested, you will recognize your membership in this universal family.

The vast scope of what can be accomplished within Step Eleven is a testament to the devotion and insight of the cofounders of the original twelve-step program. The reference texts of AA impart effective guidance and direction regarding the nature of transformation, prayer, meditation, conscious contact with God, knowledge of God's will for you (which carries a special set of concerns), and the power to carry out the will of God. At the best of times, too many people see these as contentious, which is only the result of their own Two-Step Dance.[53]

---

[48] *That Which Art* is a representation, in the symbolism of words, for the Great Reality, the Animating Principle, the Ground of All Being, the Clear Light of the Void... and a thousand other names.
[49] After twelve-step pilgrims become firmly rooted in the practices of Prayer and Meditations on Wisdom, Meditation of Transcendence will be easier to master. For twelve-step pilgrims: It may be judicious to spend more time trying to change your limiting defects rather than trying to transcend them.
[50] From How It Works, *Alcoholics Anonymous*, p. 58.
[51] *Twelve Steps and Twelve Tradition*, p. 105, emphasis added.
[52] *The Only Dance There Is*, Ram Dass, Anchor Books (Doubleday), 1973, pp. 7, 8.
[53] The Two-Step Dance was discussed in Chapter 8.

An Existential Summary

Life, to me, often seems to be a reality-based mirage that envelops people through the eternity between birth and death. It's real because we exist, but a mirage because nothing is ever as it seems. Spiritual pilgrims enlist God, through prayer and meditation, to assist them in their passage through this temporary existence. To apprehend the passage through this reality-based mirage with serenity—with love—is the result of obedience to spiritual principles.

At Step Eleven, Prayer and Meditations on Wisdom are nourishment to the life of your soul exactly as food and exercise are nourishment to the life of your body. Recovered addicts/alcoholics have a purpose now, and it's a great purpose: to pray and meditate to improve their conscious contact with their higher power. This is what brings peace to other troubled souls. For a formerly self-destructive, selfish, frightened addict to have a great purpose, and to embrace it in a way that brings harmony to the world, is a magnificent accomplishment.

> *"But, this is not all... there is more*
> *action. Faith without works is dead."* [54]

---

[54] *Alcoholics Anonymous*, p. 88.

10

Step Twelve: Responsible for Charity of Spirit

Discussing Spiritual Transformation: Art Form or Proselytizing?

"Having had a spiritual awakening as the result of these steps, we tried to carry this message to alcoholics, and to practice these principles in all our affairs."[1]

What points to Step Twelve's importance is that it's the only step within *Alcoholics Anonymous* that has an entire chapter devoted to itself. This would seem to be consistent with the frequency of various phrases that appear throughout the writing indicating that "God's will" for people in twelve-step programs is to primarily be of service to others. However, this is not a blanket injunction, there are some very specific limitations.

Within Step Twelve there are two different contexts within which you are to demonstrate spirituality: "carrying the message" and "in all your affairs". And, of course, in either context, the primary requirement is to role-model and actually practice spiritual behavior. Your devotion to spiritual principles within this step comprises the underlying philosophy of "carrying the message".

- Respect for the Body-Temple
  An obvious observation is there are two perspectives to this — respect for your own body-temple, and respect for others'. Being attentive to your own physical well-being, carrying the message, and practicing these principles in a responsible manner, allows you to peacefully integrate sensation, emotion, and wisdom within yourself.[2] When sharing your experience, strength, and hope, this balance (in you) is evident in your demeanor and tends to have a calming affect on others. This avoids causing others undue stress, and makes their lives more peaceful; hence you are respectful of their body-temple.

- Veracity
  If you embody honesty and gentle trustworthiness in all your affairs, whether carrying the message or not, you will present yourself as being sincere. These three — honesty, gentle trust-

---

[1] *Alcoholics Anonymous*, p. 60, and *Twelve Steps and Twelve Traditions*, p. 106.
[2] Being appropriately attentive to diet and health is essential to a well-rounded life. From a Buddhist perspective, the path is moderation: The Middle Way.

worthiness, and sincerity—will arguably become the most apparent qualities in your character, whether anyone knows about your obedience to spiritual principles or not.[3] When acting in the capacity of carrying the message, these qualities allow others greater ease in making choices.

- Humility
  There are two aspects to humility: egalitarian and spiritual, and two aspects to Step Twelve: carrying the message of a spiritual awakening, and practicing [spiritual] principles in all your affairs. By adhering to the egalitarian aspect of humility in all your affairs, which includes carrying the message, everyone you encounter will feel respected. This allows them to relax and, regardless of the social circumstance, they can retain their dignity and not feel demeaned or controlled. Their life will be graceful in their association with you.

  If the spiritual aspect of humility isn't offered in carrying the message then it becomes proselytizing; that's promotion not attraction. The newer person will feel patronized and demeaned (even if they can't articulate it, it will be there). Spiritual humility, in whomever carries the message, allows others freedom in choosing their conception of God, freedom in adopting the style of relationship with God that appeals to them, and leaves them the sense that access to God isn't dependent on obedience to someone else.

- Charity
  Step Twelve is the second of two never-ending exercises in being generous and graceful. (The first is Step Ten.) Giving away your hard-won wisdom and knowledge about the steps and spirituality, and offering serenity and acceptance, benefits everyone: authentic charity of spirit. Charity is "distributed" by your abiding by the spiritual principles, regardless of whom you come into contact with. If, in carrying the message, or in any of your affairs, there is a selfish agenda (seeking gratitude, living up to a reputation, collecting salvation points, impressing others with your devotion) you defeat charity.

---

[3] Some people see "truth" as a method to correct someone's behavior, to justify meanness, to manipulate people, or to autocratically impose values and limitations on others. This is using truth as a weapon to control others, or to establish some pecking order of entitlement, which prohibits veracity. The offering of truth will be seen as trustworthy when you're not trying to maneuver some situation to your own advantage, and you speak the truth without any manipulation. *Your truths must be presented as a lonely effort to develop your own integrity,* not as a tactic to gain external reward or control. Only then is your truth trustworthy, because it applies only to you, and can be heard by others without threat. This will be discussed at length in *Facets of Personal Transformation* regarding communication skills.

- Responsibility & Obedience
  In making an effort to be spiritual all the time—practicing spirituality in all your affairs, you would be exercising and demonstrating responsibility as you participate in Life. When you are responsible, regardless of the inconvenience to yourself, you demonstrate obedience to spiritual principles.

As with the other two maintenance steps, a long period of diligent application is necessary to be able to apprehend what's spiritually afoot here. The more consistently you devote yourself to practicing the principles in *all* your affairs, the more graceful Life will be. You'll rarely (if ever) face indecision or turmoil. You'll be very clear about what God's will is for you, and without realizing it, you'll create opportunities for other people to bring harmony to their world.

Observations About Words and Phrases

"Having had..." I've discussed that becoming recovered happened in the first nine steps. Therefore, by Step Twelve, a substantive personality change should have already occurred. Step Twelve facilitates having the already established changes improved upon. Similarly, "continued" from Step Ten and "improve" from Step Eleven also refer to something that has already happened. In Step Twelve, *"Having had"* is consistent in that it, too, refers to spiritual awakenings and religious experiences that have already happened.

"...a spiritual awakening..." When reading the first printing of the first edition of *Alcoholics Anonymous,* many people got the impression that there had to be some sudden, profound awareness of God; otherwise, they weren't doing it right. This misperception was corrected in the subsequent printings by the addition of the appendix Spiritual Experience.[4] A spiritual awakening is any change in your personality, *however small,* sufficient to bring about recovery from addictions. There isn't anything noteworthy or spectacular in the subtle, slow, small changes that are overlooked in the face of a busy, spiritually oriented lifestyle.

Your spiritual experiences are most often revealed in the fact that you are a little bit more willing to be honest, a tiny bit more willing to give charitably, and a little more willing to pray or meditate. They are usually noticed weeks (or months) after the fact: spiritual awakenings all, and primarily the slow, transformative type.[5]

If you're not praying and meditating regularly, there won't be slow, subtle changes; there'll be no changes. But out of arrogance and pride (fear), and almost subconsciously, you'll act as if there are changes to keep your reputation abreast of your abstinence seniority. It's pretty hard to attract people to sponsor, or have any

---

[4] *Alcoholics Anonymous,* p. 569.
[5] This is referred to as a conversion experience, detailed in *The Varieties of Religious Experience,* Lecture IX, by William James, The Modern Library, Random House, 1994. *"In the volitional type the regenerative change is usually gradual... ,"* p. 228. The second type is *"...the type by self surrender... ,"* which, although much less common, is, as a rule, startling and much more interesting. It isn't difficult to appreciate that addicts of any stripe, having a decided tendency to live in drama, ignore the slow and look (or wait impatiently) for the startling conversion experience.

influence in your peer group, or be taken seriously, if you're five or fifteen years sober and still acting like a newcomer. Impression Management hides neglect of spiritual principles. If you aren't regularly praying and meditating as suggested, there are no spiritual experiences. You're just pretending there are.

"...*as the result*..." There is only one result—the spiritual awakening—not the job, the relationship, the new furniture, or getting your name in the phonebook. These things do appear in a sober life, but however pleased you may be with social success, these self-satisfying accomplishments are not the intent of ethical step work.

"...*of these steps*..." The result isn't from any steps, or some steps, it's from *these* steps. Treatment centers, self-help books, therapists, sponsors, your own personal reorganizations of these steps, and any variation of these steps, aren't *these* steps. Becoming recovered isn't a matter of rocket science or creative genius; it's a matter of obedience (to *these* steps).[6]

"...*we*..." Throughout this book, I've suggested that the "we" and "our" in the original literature are only a grammatical representation of what each individual did (or must do). Here, the same grammatical representation applies. Under most circumstances, it is spiritually correct to interpret "we" as you who are being charged with the responsibility of carrying the message and practicing the principles. However, there is this advisory:

In the instance of your speaking to a raw newcomer, in the first few encounters, it's wise to attend those discussions with someone else. Should two people attend the twelve-step call, or even three, there's a greater opportunity for the new person to relate to the information presented.

In the situation where you attend to yet another one of the several relapses of a person you've sponsored for some time, how effective is it to rehash the same issues you've both discussed so many times before? Obviously, what you both are doing isn't working. Encourage them to seek a fresh approach with someone else. Do not get caught up in the underlying drama (yours or theirs).[7]

It takes experience and humility to know when it's more effective to "carry the message" alone, when to insist on bringing someone, or when to excuse yourself entirely from someone else's life. If you're ever in doubt, err of the side of humility and seek wise spiritual counsel. Bear in mind, too, if the person doesn't want what you have, even though they proclaim otherwise, nothing you say or do will work.

From what I've seen, not often enough do helpers excuse themselves from the drama of someone else's life. It takes great humility to recognize that you, the sponsor (or counsellor), are at the end of your own dead-end street, and that you must set someone free from your own limitations.

---

[6] I spoke to this idea regarding The Promises: to get these promises, you must complete *these* steps.

[7] Almost invariably, in these situations, the helper, sponsor, or family member has taken a willing but unwitting role in the drama of the person who continuously relapses. The helper or sponsor (or sometimes therapist) may have taken a martyr role, or have subtly defined themselves as a hero/savior. This is an enabling role in the melodrama of the practicing addict's life. To exit this style of relationship requires a very deep self-examination on the part of the helper, compassion without pity, and often a kind, firm exit from the drama. Here are two important references to this aspect of the helper-relationship: *The Only Dance There Is,* Ram Dass, Anchor Books, 1973, p. 73; and *Back To One, A Practical Guide for Psychotherapists,* Sheldon Kopp, Science and Behavior Books, 1977, p. 113.

"...tried to carry..." It doesn't say succeeded, it says tried. It's very clearly written that you *"...don't waste time trying to persuade* [them]." *"If* [they are] *not interested in your solution... ,"* or *"If* [they think they] *can do the job in some other way,"* Note: *"We find it a waste of time to keep chasing* [someone]... ".[8]

If someone doesn't want some reasonably close approximation of sobriety by taking the spiritual twelve-step path, move on. A newcomer, or someone return-ing after one of many relapses, may certainly want what you have, but is determined to attain it by some other means, which is fine (for them). They may die in the effort, but that isn't your concern, it's theirs. As advised in the original literature, invite them to try some controlled drinking or acting out.[9] I have often invited obviously unwilling people to try some controlled acting out, quietly adding: "I hope, however, that you don't die in the experiment, or even worse, kill someone else."

Over-explaining, cajoling, brow-beating, lecturing, threatening, hinting, dramatically declaring, arguing, entreating, or giving ultimatums, is entirely unspiri-tual behavior on your part. If they don't want *both* what you have and how you got it, move on. Some people are shocked by my apparently calloused approach to this. *Alcoholics Anonymous* advises this course of action. People who disregard it are themselves relationship addicts. They're overly invested in saving souls to hide inse-curity, look good, and collect social or spiritual brownie points.

"...this message..." The message you are to carry is specific: *"Having had a spiritual awakening as the result of these steps... ".* If you carry the message that meetings are fun, or people get a good life, or people get to have sober sex, or get their family back, then (according to Step Twelve) you're not carrying the message. Bragging about these social accomplishments has a very subversive effect on getting recovered. It creates a misalliance of commitment—switching the theme of step work from spirituality to psychology and social success.

Yes, people enjoy twelve-step meetings (usually), and it's fine to talk about the pleasure of your fellowship, and it *is* important to socialize within your fellow-ship. I do not quarrel with these truths. However, the primary message to convey is that if addicts [alcoholics] become spiritual, they will heal and become recovered from the seemingly hopeless state of mind and body that is destroying them. There's a significant number of sober/abstinent addicts who are still being destroyed by a hopeless state of mind and body, *and* are completely unaware that (a) this is optional; and (b) that it can be resolved by sincere spiritual self-discipline.

"Carrying the message" means discussing spirituality in friendly, attractive terms. If you think you're going to scare a newcomer away with spiritual talk, their acting-out will scare them back (if it doesn't kill them). How they respond to you, when you quietly and respectfully speak about spirituality, is not your concern. Be-sides, if you don't tell them about spirituality, and its preeminent position within the steps, you're dishonest, which means the newcomer's first twelve-step encounter is with a liar, and how spiritual is that? *"Stress the spiritual feature freely."*[10]

---

[8] *Alcoholics Anonymous*, pp. 90, 95, 95, 96, respectively.
[9] Ibid., p. 31.
[10] Ibid., p. 93.

"...to alcoholics [addicts]*..."* The Program and the twelve-step spiritual process are for alcoholics and addicts. It doesn't say we tried to carry this message to schizophrenics, abusive partners, terrorists, or corrupt politicians. The treatment for the phenomenon of addictions is twelve-step spirituality. The treatment for other "issues" is something else. Carrying this message is not for...

Saving the World

It's often apparent that some twelve-step participants believe that the world would benefit from what twelve-step programs offer: peace, serenity, love, tolerance, honesty, etc. They've decided the world is sadly lacking in virtue, and is in horrific trouble because of this. Getting this wonderful twelve-step message out to everyone would save the world for our side. Hooray! Regardless of how laudable the intent, it's arrogant to view this twelve-step process as applicable or superlative to other lifestyles, regardless of whether they harbor addictions. Should you proclaim that everyone be given this to better their world, that's uninvited proselytizing.[11] However true it may be that the world is in dire straits, it certainly requires arrogance to view these twelve steps as the panacea for the human race.

I admit there's violence we could well do without, but is there a shortage of love and harmony, or a shortage of press coverage? "Bad" people and violent sports get the front page; "saints" get Section Three, Page Two, Column Four. The public reads the front page. That's what they [you?] want to read, so that's what they get. If you change your personality, you change the front page of your own newspaper.

Remember: The treatment for the phenomenon of addictions is twelve-step spirituality. The treatment for other "issues" is something else.

"...and," There are two assignments within Step Twelve. There is carrying the message (the first assignment) and practicing the principles in all your affairs (the second assignment). Since carrying the message is now a part of your affairs, it means that practicing the principles will be done all the time.

"...to practice..." *Practice (verb): 1. To do or perform habitually or customarily; make a habit of. 2. To do or perform (something) repeatedly in order to acquire or polish a skill: practice a dance step. 3. To work at, especially as a profession: practice law. 4. To carry out in action; observe: She practices her* [meditation] *regularly.*[12] In practice, you are charged with the responsibility of demonstrating...

---

[11] Consider these points: (i) Racism, sexism, acrimony, resentments, and many of the abstinence not-available addictions, are rampant in many twelve-step meetings, or in group business meetings, or at service committee meetings... all of which are often very feisty. If there's such a lack of spiritual focus in meetings supposedly devoted to spiritual principles, there isn't much possibility of saving the world. (ii) The original twelve-step process is only effective for addictions. If a significant portion of our population is addicted, and addictions are increasing (both of which are true), then twelve-step programs may "change the world" (sic); but not because they are a panacea for all human ills, but because of the huge number of addicts. (iii) Because you see a value for yourself in this process does not mean it is of value to everyone. To impose what you value (The Program) on others, is abusive—no different from your sponsor or your parents imposing something "that's good for you" onto you, that you don't believe in.

[12] From *The American Heritage® Dictionary of the English Language, Third Edition,* © 1996, Houghton Mifflin Company. Electronic version.

"*...these principles...*" In relation to sharing and carrying the message, don't practice the principles of good storytelling, or of a good comedy routine. Don't hone your debating skills or social skills. Practice the maintenance steps and the spiritual principles which are embodied within them.[13]

As I've discussed elsewhere, there are many contentious discussions about what spiritual principles actually are, and also about how these should, or should not, be spoken about when working with new people. *Alcoholics Anonymous* advises: "*Stress the spiritual feature freely,*" and that the main object of that book "*is to enable you to find a Power greater than yourself which will solve your problem.*"[14] This doesn't leave too much room for debate.

"*...in all our affairs.*" This is about being spiritual in the check-out line at the store, in the movie theater, at the party, at the dentist's office, when someone interrupts your movie with a telephone survey, when someone you don't like wins the lottery, when dinner is late, and when you're late. In all your affairs includes when your spouse has an affair *and* during the ensuing divorce or reconciliation. Being spiritual is required in snowstorms, rainstorms, traffic jams, and mismanaged hotel reservations. Practicing spiritual principles is also required when you lose your investments, your job, your parking spot, your dog, or your wallet; and when you get a speeding ticket, a sunburn, the flu, or a tax notice. Spiritual principles should be evident when you share at your twelve-step meeting, miss your plane, get fired, get hired, get laid (or don't); and especially when you don't get your own way.

Being spiritual "*in all* [your] *affairs*" is no mean feat. Twelve-step people cannot give friends and lovers preferential treatment. It's easy to be spiritual towards someone when that someone is being nice. Twelve-step people are to carry the principles of spirituality out to the world, regardless of what the world and the people in it are doing to them. They may be the only version of *Alcoholics Anonymous* that anybody ever sees, so let's hope it's the spiritual version and not the victim/social version. By investigating and volunteering for a spiritual life (respectively Steps Two and Three) twelve-step participants take on a great responsibility and have a great purpose: to be an attractive advertisement for a spiritual life, all the time.

The Especially Unique Person

We've all seen characters in movies, heard of, or witnessed first-hand people who exhibit rare talent. The brilliant, unique jewel thief must be caught by the uniquely quirky and tenacious detective. Someone has an especially complex problem, so they track down and hire the uniquely trained and especially talented therapist, accountant, doctor, carpenter, business consultant, meditation guru, or mountain climber who is their last hope. Everyone cheers when the Especially Unique Person ("EUP") saves... the town, the puppy, the children, the beautiful girl,

---

[13] Elsewhere I have remarked that the steps are not principles, they are tasks to be performed. I have also observed that maintenance steps are remarkably different in context from the regeneration steps. The regeneration steps are the on-the-job apprenticeship that train you how to apply spiritual principles to your life. The maintenance steps are the graceful and practical embodiment of spiritual principles.

[14] *Alcoholics Anonymous*, pp. 93 and 45, respectively.

the space ship, the friendly alien, or the treasure map. We all understand that the fate of democracy, the world, the relationship, and the skier lost in the avalanche depends on some EUP, somewhere, who will make sure that the ship doesn't sink, the skier doesn't freeze to death (they just get very cold), the town isn't flooded, the mad scientist is thwarted, the criminal is arrested, the secret code is broken, and... the bridegroom makes it to the church on time! Thank goodness for the Especially Unique Person—wherever would we be without them? However, being an EUP can carry a tremendous burden.

If the EUP doesn't deliver the goods, thwart the evil plot, save the day, find the kitty cat, defuse the bomb, or deliver the computer chip, then someone dies, the house burns down, the evil-doers get the secret formula, and the world blows up— not nice prospects. And, *of course,* it's always better if they save it, her, him, them, or us at the last possible moment. (Is there any other time to be saved?) If "we" were saved at the first possible moment, many feature films would be seven minutes long. Everyone cheers except the cynics, who are often only jealous because they aren't the EUP (hence, the birth of the critic). Being an Especially Unique Person means you automatically take a place of importance in the lives of others. The more unique an EUP is, the more good they can do, but the more harm they can also do, too. [15]

Sponsorship

"So cooperate; never criticize,"[16] which is a pretty tall order for addicts, even sponsors, whom, I suspect, are to share only their experience, strength, and hope (which precludes making up rules and imposing values). It's amazing how, in the midst of a friendly social conversation that is called "fellowship" or sponsorship, so many people conveniently forget the injunction to never criticize. Along with the injunction to never criticize, there is this observation: *"...because of your own drinking experience you can be uniquely useful to other alcoholics* [addicts]*."*[17]

A sponsor is an especially unique person, who is supposed to do special and important work, called sponsorship, with a charitable spirit, on behalf of a higher

---

[15] Being especially unique or having great talent or devotion isn't always to be appreciated in relation to calamity or misadventure. It is to be noticed and valued elsewhere. In acting: Richard Burton and Elizabeth Taylor in *Who's Afraid of Virginia Woolf;* Nicole Kidman in *Moulin Rouge;* Sidney Poitier in *In The Heat of The Night;* Bruno Ganz in *Downfall;* there are *many* others. In medicine: Louis Pasteur or Marie Curie. In politics and civil rights: Nelson Mandela, Gandhi, Dr. Martin Luther King, Jr., Rosa Parks, Malcolm X, James Reeb; there are *many* others. In music: Bach, Mozart, Louis Armstrong, Charlie Parker, Miles Davis, Ella Fitzgerald, Lenny Breau, and Eric Clapton. Mr. Clapton offered a personal perspective of his life and playing blues music that relates to this theme: *"I have tried to play folk music, play country and western, play even jazz, and a lot of pop music, but I don't do it well. I* [play the blues] *best and that's been given me to do. And as much as I've questioned it, and railed against it, and been stubborn about my path, I'm back on it. For better or for worse. I'm happier doing this."* From *The Rehearsal* (video) ©Drumlin Ltd., New York, NY, 1994. Mr. Clapton's unique ability is in music, and according to him, even though he has resisted it at times, it is most apparent within blues music; and again, there are *many* others. This is equally evident in religion, art, dance, literature, teaching, parenting, and in expressions of great love: Heloise & Abelard for example. And, Bill Wilson and Dr. Bob Smith qualify for being especially unique. At some time or other, the burden of being an Especially Unique Person—and it can be a burden—falls on each of us. Our talents or devotion may not be witnessed or appreciated on a grand scale, but the magic of the human condition is that we all harbor greatness.
[16] *Alcoholics Anonymous*, p. 89.
[17] Ibid.

power, and without fanfare. It would appear logical that sponsors would willingly adhere to the tenets of the twelve steps, and encourage but never demand similar behavior from those they help. Sponsors, and twelve-step pilgrims in general, are EUPs: *"You can help when no one else can." "You can secure their confidence when others fail." "...you can be uniquely useful to other alcoholics."*[18]

This unique ability to help carries with it an important caution, and a significant obligation. Because of being especially unique and useful, sponsors must strive for genuine integrity; otherwise, those they help will become an extension of the unspiritual impression management schemes at play in the sponsor. When a sponsor, or a therapist or helper, lives with conflicted values and spiritual negligence, is unethical, or in any addiction, those they help will not be able to get recovered. It's difficult enough to face abstinence, the steps, and spirituality without having to negotiate through any hypocrisy in people who hold themselves out as helpers. In these circumstances, to blame or hold the client/newcomer responsible for all their difficulty is reprehensible, and ignores the program injunction to never blame.[19]

Yes, sponsors/therapists are human; and certainly everyone is completely responsible for their own abstinence, confusion, and relapses. We *must* each attend to our own disease, and above all, attend to it without blaming anyone or anything. But none of that absolves a helper from the responsibility to demonstrate devotion to spiritual integrity, to do no harm, and to make a noticeable effort to not impose or inject their own chaos and insanity into the lives of others.

As a sponsor, share your experience, strength, and hope, not your opinions. Rather than dispensing advice, demonstrate obedience to spiritual principles. Never demand obedience from anyone. When you offer advice and create rules, you go from sponsor to parent/personality consultant. This, indirectly and subtly, leads you to assume the role of rescuer, which demonstrates that you have an emotional investment in them getting recovered, which is entirely unwise.

When a sponsor shares their experience, strength, and hope, they remain a sponsor. Sponsors can't really go wrong if they follow the instructions, sponsor people "out of the book", and relate all discussions and struggles back to spirituality and spiritual principles—some relevant passage from the AA reference texts. It's not up to the sponsor to solve the newcomer's problems; that's the newcomer's job. A sponsor doesn't have to be precocious, prescient, wise, powerful, or amazing; they have to be humble and willing to follow the instructions. The sponsor's "job" is to (a) demonstrate spiritually-focused problem solving, and (b) to teach those they help how to identify any passages in the original twelve-step literature that relate to any "problem". This means sponsors teach other people to depend on the original literature and on their own (the other person's) higher power—on spiritual principles embodied in the maintenance steps, and not to depend on the sponsor.

There's no place at all for arguing when carrying the message. None. You demonstrate sincere spirituality, and share your experience, strength, and hope. The other person either wants what you have, or they don't. What's to argue?

---

[18] *Alcoholics Anonymous*, p. 89.
[19] *Twelve Steps and Twelve Tradition*, p. 47.

"Practical experience shows that nothing will so much insure immunity from drinking as intensive work with other alcoholics [addicts]. *It works when all other activities fail."*[20] It's important to notice that this statement insures immunity from drinking (insures abstinence), but doesn't insure a meaningful relationship with a higher power. A relationship with a higher power is developed by Prayer and Meditations on Wisdom, not carrying the message. Working with other addicts will keep you sober; it won't get you spiritual. If you want to guarantee your abstinence, work with other addicts—not just ordinary work: intensive work. However, "intensive work" isn't arguing with people who don't want what you have, or intensely trying to persuade those who aren't convinced (that's browbeating and debating). Intensive work is being available, charitable, accepting, dependable, generous with your time, and patient: being a spiritual role-model.

————

From infancy we are taught by example that what we love is what we give our time to. If you play with your dog more than you watch TV, or talk about sports more than about spirituality, you demonstrate your priorities of affection.[21] If you don't have time to commit to sponsorship (and some people don't), then don't say yes to it. If you're chaotic and undisciplined in your life when it comes to commitments, prayer, honesty, meditation, attending meetings, etc., give someone the gift of not making their life more awkward than it already is by not introducing your insanity into their life. Don't let them sense they are not cared for by your lack of attention, negligence, or unavailability. Do them a favor and say no to the relationship. Charity and kindness is keeping your insanity out of their life.

Should your sponsor have little group-meetings of all their sponsees[22], take you all through the steps *en masse*, dispense advice and opinions, enforce rules, or promote or use various outside step-guides for everyone's edification, then everyone's in trouble, especially your sponsor. You'll end up with a pocketful of clichés that you don't really understand, with no clear sense of yourself, of God, or of how the steps apply to you personally.

If you attend meetings flirting with newcomers to try to collect people to sponsor, you're in trouble. If you're asked to be someone's sponsor, and you agree to create that relationship, you'd better pay attention to this: By saying "Yes," you have held yourself out to be caring, interested in another's welfare, available, generous of

---

[20] *Alcoholics Anonymous*, p. 89.

[21] I will go into this in some detail in *Facets of Personal Transformation*.

[22] *Sponsees,* a term that has come into twelve-step vogue in the last decade or so, refers to people that someone sponsors: people with less abstinence and more naiveté, whom are offered help, and mentored into a twelve-step lifestyle. The help appears to be predominately concerned with indoctrinating them into the social etiquette, psychological jargon, and political correctness that prevails in meetings. Sponsors often speak about their sponsees—how many they have, how hard they work on their sponsees' behalf, how strict they are with sponsees, how wise they are in the rules they impose, how foolish their sponsees are for not complying, and flagrantly breach their sponsees anonymity by sharing details of their struggles and stories—all in tones of self-importance and phony humility. The term sponsees always seems to be used in a subtly pejorative sense (like *Normies*, which was discussed earlier), and designed to self-

spirit, willing to help, somewhat knowledgeable about the program and spirituality, and respectful. You should be capable of demonstrating a visible presence of program spirituality, and capable of minding your own business. This is what you imply by saying "yes" to sponsorship.

Being a sponsor is *not* being a therapist, a personality consultant, a relationship counsellor, a financial advisor, or the sobriety police. Don't betray the person who puts their trust in you, or misrepresent the twelve steps, or avoid spirituality. Especially do not betray whatever limited faith the newer person has in the program or in you by being a flake about your sponsorship commitment. The cost is too great. You may not relapse, but they almost certainly will.

———

I was a passenger in a car in a large parkade one Christmastime in the early 1980s. The driver was a person who sometimes promoted himself as being quite peaceful, and who often spoke of his own spirituality. We were slowly exiting the parkade because of the heavy holiday traffic. I observed the driver demonstrating impatience, anger, and racism. We got out of the parkade in about fifteen minutes, but with the driver's belligerence and mean spirit, it seemed an hour. Coincidentally, later that same week, I was in the same circumstances, in the same parkade, with someone else driving. This second driver was letting people in, waving and smiling, chatting with me about something festive, and simply appreciating a spiritual/sober life in the busy holiday season. It seemed like we got out of the same parkade, in the same heavy traffic, in no time at all.

In remembering the first driver, I asked the second driver what he did to have such an attitude. He quietly shrugged and we started talking about kindness, and meditating, and expectations, and following spiritual principles. That's sponsorship.[23]

> *"Setting an example isn't the main means to influence others, it's the only means."*
>
> Albert Einstein[24]

---

advertise and self-promote the sponsor at the expense of newer members. From a spiritual perspective, I can see no reason for someone to ever say anything about anyone they sponsor.

[23] Ram Dass describes a different scenario that has a similar theme to this, in *The Only Dance There Is,* Anchor Books, 1973, p. 1. The reference begins: *"But there is the story of a monk...."*

[24] This quote was told to me by an acquaintance. It may be apocryphal; I've been unable to find a reliable reference source.

Epilogue on "Maintenance"

There is a healthy process in the acquisition of values. In brief, it is this: Out of your rights and freedoms, discussed briefly in Chapter 2, you choose what you value. You choose it from alternatives, and when making choices, you have some knowledge of what each alternative entails. You choose values freely and voluntarily. What makes a value authentic is when appropriate, you announce or proclaim what you value and live by it. You are prepared to adhere to the value in the face of opposition and personal consequence. If you aren't willing to pay for it, it isn't a value, it's a political convenience.

Since you began these steps, and especially while completing the first nine steps, you've been transforming your values. You've adopted the spiritual principles that are embodied in the maintenance steps, in (roughly) the process I outlined above. However, *"Principles only mean something if you stick by them when they're inconvenient."*[1]

———

The maintenance steps are in a particular order for a particular reason. In maintenance, self-examination (Step Ten) must come first. All spiritual transformation begins, and deepens, with self-awareness and responsibility by first clearing the blockages to your inner spiritual nature, which blockages were created *by* your character *in* your character. Only then can you access a higher power through prayer and meditation—Step Eleven. And with both of these well established, you're now capable of imparting (a) something of spiritual substance to a fellow pilgrim, and (b) able to practice these principles in all your affairs—Step Twelve.

Notice the similarity of themes in the way the first nine steps are sequenced, as compared to the way the maintenance steps are sequenced:

- Steps One to Five are concerned with your character and the blockages to inner awareness: One is personality and addiction. Two is recognizing the limitations of your personality and your own willpower. Three is deciding to change the focus of your personality. Four is identifying inner defects, fears, and selfishness, and taking responsibility for them. Five is sharing information about yourself. (All this is represented in Step Ten: being aware of your character defects, admitting them, and being responsible for them.)
- Steps Six and Seven develop your willingness and humility in relation to your higher power: deepening your trust of, and dependence upon, God. (Represented in Step Eleven: Prayer and Meditations on Wisdom to develop faith.)

---

[1] This line is a quote from the feature film, *The Contender*, written and directed by Rod Lurie, © Cinecontender Internationale, 2000.

- Steps Eight and Nine are focusing on caring for the well-being of others, charity of spirit, and responsibility. (Represented in Step Twelve: practicing the principles and sponsorship.)[2]

Steps Ten, Eleven, and Twelve are designed to both maintain and deepen the spiritual orientation to your life, that you've supposedly established in the first nine steps. Your devotion to them is a reflection of how highly you value your relationship with your higher power.

A Fable

"Once upon a time there dwelt an old king in a palace. In the center of a golden table in the main hall, there shone a large and magnificent jewel. Each day of the King's life, the jewel shone more resplendently.

One day a thief stole the jewel and ran from the palace, hiding in a forest. As he stared with deep joy at the stone, to his amazement the image of the King appeared in it.

'I have come to thank you,' said the King. 'You have released me from my attachment to Earth. I thought I was freed when I acquired the jewel, but then I learned that I would only be released when I passed it on, with a pure heart, to another.

'Each day of my life I polished that stone, until finally this day arrived, when the jewel became so beautiful that you stole it, and I have passed it on, and am released.

'The jewel you hold is Understanding. You cannot add to its beauty by hiding it and hinting that you have it, nor yet by wearing it with vanity. Its beauty comes of the consciousness that others have of it. Honor that which gives it beauty.'"[3]

Make spirituality so beautiful that others will want to steal it from you; there's plenty to go around.

Having spiritual values like believing in kindness, not participating in or supporting violence or racism, adhering to the spiritual principles, and believing in God, are meaningless unless you're willing to face the consequences of adhering to those values without complaint (because they were freely chosen). Yes, being spiritual is very demanding, and expensive to your pride, and it does take a *very* long time to achieve. In active addiction, the disease required that you pay with your life, and being spiritual requires that you volunteer to give your life. All of it.

Everything costs something.

---

[2] This theme will be picked up again in the next chapter "Relapse Prevention."
[3] *The Lazy Man's Guide to Enlightenment*, Thaddeus Golas, Bantam Books, 1981, p. 78.

11

Relapse Prevention:
The Routine Of Spiritual Commitment

Understanding why Relapse Prevention is so simple is rather complicated. (i) There is relapse. (ii) There is relapse prevention. (iii) As you attain a deeper commitment to spirituality, and enhance your spiritual integrity, what constitutes relapse and what is required for relapse prevention will change from what is required in the first nine steps to what is required in the last three steps. Should addicts getting recovered not appreciate this difference, they may attempt the maintenance steps but always be living in addiction, and therefore stymie all their efforts to be spiritual.

- *Relapse: verb (relapsed, relapsing, relapses) 1. To fall or slide back into a former state. 2. To regress after partial recovery from illness. 3. To slip back into bad ways; backslide.*[1]

Relapse is to go "backwards" to such a degree that the symptoms of addiction reappear, which is usually thought of, but not limited to, overt acting out.

- *Prevent: verb (prevented, preventing, prevents) 1. To keep from happening: took steps to prevent the [relapse]. 2. To keep (someone) from doing something; impede: prevented [me] from [cheating].*
- *Prevention: noun 1. The act of preventing or impeding. 2. A hindrance; an obstacle.*

From these definitions it would follow that Relapse Prevention is work or effort directed towards stopping the symptoms of addiction from returning. In Chapter 2, the symptoms of an addiction were identified as acting out and life-damaging consequences, neurosis, denial, disproportionate fear, repression, isolation (from self and others), assumptions, shame, dishonesty/withholding, selfishness, irresponsibility, arrogance, and cynicism—all chronic and entrenched, and addicts are largely blind to them. Relapse Prevention is a deliberately focused effort, on your part, to stop these symptoms from returning. Ultimately, Relapse Prevention is an inside job—nudging yourself into obedience to the proven principles of spiritual behavior.

Someone has pneumonia. The doctor advises medication (six pills a day for fourteen days), and to also do this, and that, and some other thing. A week later, the

---

[1] Remind yourself to use the ordinary definitions of ordinary words when describing spiritual principles. The three definitions on this page are taken from *The American Heritage® Dictionary of the English Language, Third Edition,* © 1996, Houghton Mifflin Company. Electronic version.

person feels much better, becomes less diligent about following the doctor's instructions, and soon the pneumonia returns. This isn't a matter of "slipping". It's defiance or irresponsible neglect. The doctor gave reliable advice about the treatment of pneumonia and the patient didn't follow instructions. It isn't a slip, it's "a deliberate". If the patient ignores any of the physician's instructions, they invite relapse. Why aren't doctors surprised in these situations? Because they know.

In the same manner, *Alcoholics Anonymous* knows. Once you're advised that the recovery strategy is spirituality, and come to reasonably believe this at Step Two, if you subsequently ignore spirituality any relapse isn't a slip, implying an accident: It's "a deliberate". A decision to ignore spiritual principles, or to ignore the step instructions, is a decision to not recover. A decision to not embrace frequent, sincere prayer and meditation is a decision to embrace addictions and turmoil.

Think about what irresponsibility is concealed by using the word slip. You have manifested the phenomenon of addictions. If you are obedient to spiritual principles, which, according to *Alcoholics Anonymous* is the proven remedy, the symptoms will not return. There's nothing magic about Relapse Prevention.

Relapse Prevention Plans

Treatment centers and recovery houses are proliferating, and to my knowledge, virtually all of them have some document or treatment protocol that comes under the general heading of a Discharge Plan, or a Relapse Prevention Outline. Too often these plans set up confusion, create unnecessary burdens, promote misdirection, and actually contribute to relapse. As you read this, bear in mind that:

- Addict/alcoholic newcomers are desperate, and will necessarily place great stock in their counsellors and sponsors; and,
- Caregivers in general (counsellors, doctors, psychiatrists, therapists, gurus, ministers, priests, rabbis, and especially sponsors) carry an air of mystery and authority. They *apparently* have what the newcomer wants—the insight, knowledge, and experience which contain the keys to a new life.

Caregivers and treatment programs have great influence. Not only must they have integrity, they must be seen to have integrity. Whatever they propose, like Relapse Prevention Plans, must stand up under scrutiny. The following five examples that that I comment on are culled from the dozens I've seen over the years. I chose these not because they are the worst (they're not), but because they reflect the more common, confusing themes present in many treatment-discharge plans.

Relapse Prevention Plan #1

This plan begins with general statistics that break down, into various categories, the projected 95 percent relapse rate after discharge from treatment. It takes the position, and not subtly, that relapse will occur, and largely ignores the possibility that newcomers may remain abstinent. It contains considerable explanation about there being no shame when you relapse; it's an expected part of the "recovery". This plan focuses almost exclusively on the steps to take after a relapse happens, making it an emergency response to relapse rather than a relapse prevention plan. (Relapses aren't earthquakes; they're preventable.) Newcomers are told that after a relapse. they are to never give up hope, to return to meetings, return to treatment, and to believe that eventually something will happen: they'll "catch on".

This plan is seven pages long and advises, several times, that to err is human (it is), and to return to acting out is akin to making a mistake (it isn't). I agree that relapse by someone very early in their pilgrimage may simply be an error out of confused ignorance; but the sentence *"Rarely have we seen a person fail who has thoroughly followed our path,"*[2] implies that relapse is optional. Once a person is established in abstinence beyond a few weeks, relapse isn't about mistakes, and it certainly isn't inevitable.

Getting recovered isn't as haphazard as this plan implies. It isn't a matter of chance; it's a matter of well-informed counsel, proper support, and determined effort. What attitude must there be in whoever wrote this plan, that sees newcomers as bound to relapse, and spirituality as a matter of luck? Aside from the obvious cynicism, they've implied relapse is nothing more than an inevitable mistake. It isn't.

Newcomers are desperate. They'll believe what they are told. If they are told relapse is in their destiny by someone who is seen to be knowledgeable, it will be. Reporting that addicts are bound to fail, regardless of their efforts, is cynical and mean-spirited. It foments discouragement. This perspective allows an addict to blame the machinations of the universe, and conveniently ignore their own defiance and irresponsibility in the face of spiritual truths.

Relapse Prevention Plan #2

Here newcomers are advised to not intellectualize. Over the first two pages there is a lengthy discourse against "intellectualizing". Then, over the last four pages, newcomers are instructed, *in noticeable detail*, to understand their denial; analyze their minimizing; examine closely their blaming; understand their rationalizations, justifications, and diversions; and through self-monitoring, think about what pain they are avoiding through their fantasies.

Overall, there are two pages telling addicts to not intellectualize, and four pages teaching them how to do just that. With no explanation offered for this contradiction, clients can't follow the advice for relapse prevention (don't intellectualize) without ignoring the guidelines to prevent relapse (intellectual analysis)—a double bind.

---

[2] *Alcoholics Anonymous*, p. 58.

Relapse Prevention Plan #3

In this example, the plan strongly counsels clients to avoid being obsessive and preoccupied about any one area of their life. It is explained this could set up an easy segue into being obsessive about acting out and lead to relapse.

On the other side of the same page, and continuing for five pages, it advises them to: (i) talk as often as possible to people who are supportive of their relapse prevention, (ii) express as much as they can about what they're feeling, (iii) stay focused on relapse prevention by asking questions of others so they can understand their own denial and behavior, (iv) contemplate their relapse prevention strategies at preset times each day, (v) examine their own non-compliance with these strategies, (vi) analyze anything that didn't work well to learn what other options they might consider in the future in similar circumstances, (vii) to do all of this regularly throughout the day; and, (viii) it concludes with this evening exercise: Write an overall summary of their day: how they feel about it, what they might have missed, and what they might do to improve on the following day.

As with plan #2, this one sets up another double bind: Being advised not to be preoccupied, followed immediately by extensive instruction that creates preoccupation. The final page refers, in one paragraph, to twelve-step meetings, sponsorship, and spirituality.

Relapse Prevention Plan #4

In this one, newcomers are told that minor depression, daydreaming, and wishful thinking are indicative of pending relapse. These newly discharged clients are warned against defensiveness; tendencies towards loneliness (What's a *tendency* towards loneliness?), and loneliness itself; idle daydreaming (as opposed to active daydreaming? There's no clarification.); an immature wish to be happy (with no description of what a mature wish to be happy is); periods of confusion; irregular eating patterns; irregular sleep; wishful thinking; dissatisfaction with life; experiencing self-pity; and having unreasonable resentments. [Considering the general twelve-step caution against having any resentments, what would a reasonable resentment be?] There is minimal explanation about any of this, and the inference to people reading this plan is that (a) these behaviors or feelings are optional, and (b) if you have them, you're in trouble.

To varying degrees, during an addict's early transformation struggles, the experiences of defensiveness, loneliness, idle daydreaming, wishing to be happy, confusion, irregular eating and sleeping patterns, dissatisfaction, some self-pity, and resentments, are not optional. Experiencing these is a necessary part of getting recovered. To instill a fear of imminent relapse regarding these routine experiences of early recovery creates problems. What's needed is to normalize these experiences, because they are normal, to encourage perseverance, and to teach response strategies.

The center that uses this particular plan advertises that it is based on a twelve-step model of treatment. At the end of their relapse prevention plan they advise that should the newcomer begin the controlled use of any drug or alcohol, relapse is imminent. In twelve-step programs, where abstinence is vigorously encouraged, controlled use of chemicals isn't a warning sign of relapse—it is relapse.

Relapse Prevention Plan #5

This example is twenty-five pages long. There are instructions for finding a therapist, sitting in yoga postures, and meditating for relaxation (four pages). There's a list of twenty-three emotions, why people have them, and why they shouldn't have some of them (two pages). There are three pages of advice on diet and exercise. Spirituality and twelve-step meetings are encapsulated on one page. Sexual relationships are discouraged (one page). The plan insists all families are blatantly dysfunctional, with flow charts and stick-figures to prove it (two pages). It also requires writing a Personal Recovery Timetable Chart, which plots moods, emotions, and conflicts at two-hour intervals throughout the day; using extra paper if needed (one page). The newcomer is advised to carry the plan with them as much as possible and to refer to it frequently (one page).

The client is strongly warned that over the coming year, there will be seven predictable times of probable relapse. These are: just after leaving treatment, birthday, twelve-step anniversary, Christmas, family occasions, sexual encounters, and changing jobs or residences. Each situation gets its own page of analysis, with space to start immediately writing plans for these impending dangerous times.

The final three-column exercise is in three phases (one page per phase). The client is instructed to enter the calendar dates of the first twenty-one days of their abstinence in Column One. In Column Three, they're to enter the dates for the twenty-one days between day one of week six and day seven of week eight of their abstinence. The assignment is to write in Column Two a day-by-day comparative analysis of these two three-week periods of their abstinence. They are told that *if* they make it to six months abstinence, they are then to repeat this exercise, comparing and analyzing the first twenty-one day period of the sixth month of abstinence and the twenty-one days at the end of the second month; and then again (*if* they remain abstinent for ten months), comparing the first twenty-one days of the tenth month to the sixth month's twenty-one days.

This plan contains far too many assumptions, has no direct association with being spiritual, and firmly entrenches a misalliance of commitment in the life of a newcomer. It would prove a burden to a seasoned client in therapy, let alone an addict with a few days of abstinence. Additionally, a newcomer wouldn't have the insight to accurately self-observe, and is therefore encouraged to invest energy in a daunting relapse prevention exercise that has no chance of success.

In these "relapse prevention plans", clients are not supported in responding to their own fears and experience (whatever these may be). They're indoctrinated into the fears and misalliance of commitment harbored by the authors and the treatment centers who present them. Each of these five plans are complicated psychological instruments of very questionable merit. The people who wrote them apparently have little understanding of twelve-step programs and little faith in spirituality. Spirituality and spiritual advisors are only very briefly mentioned, even though each program claims to be based on "a twelve-step model of treatment".

The original twelve-step program is overwhelmingly rooted in spirituality. These programs and relapse prevention plans obviously aren't. They decidedly down-play or ignore: *"...being willing to believe in a Power greater than myself. Nothing more was required..."*, *"...to accept spiritual help"*, *"...they outlined the spiritual answer..."*, *"*[Your] *defense must come from a higher power."* *"...a Power greater than yourself which will solve your problem."* *"Our ideas did not work. But the God idea did."*[3]

These plans are a poorly disguised rehashing of ideas that don't work. In spite of their faults, and offering the benefit of the doubt, the authors are sincere; however, they are trapped in a psychological orientation (misalignment of commitment). At some level they think they're wiser than the original program. This invites, rather than prevents, relapse. According to Dr. Silkworth, Dr. Jung, Dr. Tiebout, the cofounders of AA, and the tenets of the original twelve-step program (that, in its first three decades reported a remarkable 50% of new people stayed sober at the first serious attempt), human oriented efforts are not effective and insufficient.

Dr. Harry Tiebout (a psychiatrist) was a specialist in addictions treatment, who was closely associated with Alcoholics Anonymous in its early years. He wrote and published a pamphlet: *Conversion as a Psychological Phenomenon.*[4] In it, Dr. Tiebout described a conversion experience, in a manner similar to what William James described 25 years earlier.

A conversion experience would be that personal transformative moment, sometimes dramatic or sudden, but most often slow and hardly noticeable, that originates in relation to spirituality, and embodies a healing change in an addict. With continued right effort and concentration, it facilitates a theretofore unavailable new perspective that makes recovery from addiction possible. Regarding a conversion experience, Dr Tiebout offered it was a *"...communion with God, man, and all the creative forces of the universe."*

In his pamphlet, he quoted one of his alcoholic patients as saying: *"Something has taken place in me. I cannot put my finger on it... I am grateful that my mind is able to accept the necessity of treatment that logically I cannot understand."* In the tone of the article, the patient was implying a spiritual connotation. These next quotes are also from Dr Tiebout's pamphlet:

- *"...religion provides the cultural media to the attainment of the affirmative outlook upon life."*

---

[3] *Alcoholics Anonymous*, pp. 12, 25, 42, 43, 45, 52, respectively.
[4] *Conversion As A Psychological Phenomenon*, a pamphlet, ©Dr. Harry M. Tiebout, M.D., The National Council on Alcoholism, Inc., New York (c. 1943). The pamphlet was read before the New York Psychiatric Society, April 11, 1944. In it Dr. Tiebout made these observations about the characteristics of an alcoholic: *"(1) Tense and depressed, (2) Aggressive, or at least quietly stubborn, (3) Oppressed with a sense of inferiority, at the same time secretly harboring feelings of superior worth, (4) Perfectionistic and rigidly idealistic, (5) Weighed down by an overpowering sense of loneliness and isolation, (6) Egocentric and all that implies in the way of a basically self-centered orientation, (7) Defiant, either consciously or unconsciously; and, (8) Walled off and dwelling, to a large extent, in a world apart from others."*

- *"Religion should function so as to permit the budding and flowering of the positive potential which resides in the deep unconscious..."*
- *"Too often religion has been identified with its dogma and not with its essence of spirituality."*
- *"Because religion often fails signally in its function is no reason to deny that that function exists, or with that denial of function to deny the existence of the inner forces which religion is designed to set in motion."*
- *"...we as psychiatrists* [or counsellors or therapists or sponsors] *must always be alert to the constructive forces residing in every individual. I am sure that without them, we... can do nothing."*

Reread The Doctor's Opinion. Notice where Dr. Silkworth describes how the best efforts of medicine and psychiatry *didn't* work. Reread the passage where Dr. Jung advises *"a certain American business man"* that it is hopeless unless there is a *"...vital spiritual experience..."*.[5] The passage goes on to explain what Dr. Jung meant. There are additional worthwhile expositions of this view by Dr. Silkworth and Dr. Tiebout in the appendices to *Alcoholics Anonymous Comes of Age*.[6] Be advised: Psychological endeavor has no long-term substantive value in resolving *addictions* issues. Psychology does not and cannot prevent relapse.

Do not let your recovery efforts be diverted away from spirituality because someone's extensive education in psychology or medicine presents a powerful looking relapse prevention scheme that isn't spiritually oriented. Do not be fooled into believing that modern, "human-oriented" ideas are any more effective in combating addictions today than they were seventy years ago.

For addressing addictions, nothing that's been tried thus far is an improvement on spirituality. It's hard for most people to accept the idea that as far as addiction is concerned (not the psychological symptoms that manifest out of it, but the addiction itself), psychology is impotent to affect recovery. The best plan you can have is to be determined to enhance your conscious contact with God. Entrench a spiritual attitude that makes the spiritual principles living things, and you'll be fine (as far as addiction goes). Be ever mindful of *"...the discovery that spiritual principles would solve all* [your addiction] *problems."*[7]

> *"My Lord God, I have no idea where I'm going. ...the fact that I think I am following your will does not mean that I am actually doing so... But I believe that the desire to please you does in fact please you. I will trust you always though I may seem to be lost and in the shadow of death."* [I add: or in the shadow of relapse.]
>
> Thomas Merton[8]

---

[5] *Alcoholics Anonymous*, The Doctor's Opinion, p. xxiii, and the reference to Dr. Jung, p. 26-27.
[6] *Alcoholics Anonymous Comes of Age*, Alcoholics Anonymous Publishing, Inc., 7th printing, 1977, pp. 302 and 309.
[7] *Alcoholics Anonymous*, p. 42.
[8] An excerpt from a prayer in *Thoughts in Solitude,* Thomas Merton, The Noonday Press, 1996, p. 83.

The Process of Relapse

One of the symptoms of addiction that operates in concert with denial is that you don't know you're sick. One of the goals, then, is to get yourself to the point where you know: "I am sick," and you *believe* it. Only then are you capable of relapse, and not before. Because of the profound difference between getting recovered and being recovered, which I've referred to many times, relapse prevention when completing the first nine steps is remarkably different from relapse prevention that relates to the maintenance steps.

Relapse Prevention: Steps One to Nine

In early recovery, relapse prevention is a matter of exerting your willpower to do what you're told as far as the original twelve-step program advises: get involved, pray for sobriety and the determination to be spiritual, study *Alcoholics Anonymous* and *Twelve Steps and Twelve Traditions* (often), and don't act out one day (or one minute) at a time. Because of what you became convinced of at Step Two, you should be taking the literature at face value. If you debate at all the importance of being thorough, or are doing other than those steps, or fail to maintain a relationship with God, as you understand God, as *the* priority, then (i) you never came to believe, or (ii) you do believe, but for whatever reasons, don't care enough to work hard, or (iii) you're defiant and searching for an easier way and hiding in psychology, or (iv) have other addictions you're refusing to address.

Recall at Step One the discussion about "admitting" or "accepting", and a newcomer's limitations on acceptance which are imposed by their defects. There's a similar limitation regarding "understanding" spirituality. During the first nine steps, and especially in the first four, a person's self-insight is drastically limited because their character defects are prominent. This doesn't allow for a deep understanding of anything, especially the nuance of spiritual awakenings.

Trying to understand the spiritual nuances of the instructions—their "enlightened" deep meaning, prior to Step Seven, is futile because character defects stand in the way. Granted, defects are [supposed to be] gradually reduced over the course of completing the steps; however, the strong presence of defects is what renders ineffective a newcomer's attempts to "understand" the deep meaning of the original literature. This is no reflection on character or intellectual astuteness, it's the truth of addictions.

Until there is reasonable proficiency at continuous *self*-examination (Step Ten), and regular consistency at prayer and meditations on wisdom (Step Eleven), relapse prevention is largely limited to taking responsibility, identifying and following the twelve-step instructions, and identifying and reducing spiritual defiance.

Trust, obedience, and determination are the primary requirements of relapse prevention for the early (up to Step Five) and middle (Steps Six to Nine) phases of all spiritual pilgrimages because of the defect-imposed inability to understand the nuance and depth of authentic spiritual practice. Only after someone is well established in the maintenance steps, and has several *years* of consistent effort, can one achieve deep spiritual insight.[9]

Through to Step Nine, the purpose of attending a twelve-step literature study-group (which is itself relapse prevention) is to clarify what the exact assignments are, and to complete them.[10] When you notice you *didn't* do whatever you were advised to do, ask yourself "Why am I not doing what I am told?" rather than "Why do they want me to do this?" Challenge your resistance, not the instructions. Should you be challenging the instructions, you never came to believe. In this way, your studying never becomes an opportunity to memorize knowledge and act precocious; it remains an exercise in obedience and faith (which is humility).

In early recovery, relapse means simply returning to overt acting out. Relapse Prevention is limited to the following: don't drink, go to meetings, get honest, force yourself to pray, breathe in, breathe out, don't act out. Between Steps One and Nine, relapse prevention is obedience to the suggestions. Exert your willpower to complete the steps as they are written; pray; and reduce your dishonesty, pride, greed, irresponsibility, and selfishness. The result will be the acquisition of virtues by default; it's the only way to acquire spiritual virtues.

By the time you arrive at Step Ten, you're told in the original literature that insane thinking has been removed and alcohol, drugs, etc., are no longer a problem. It follows after Step Nine, then, if these problems have been removed, relapse, and its prevention, must be something different than just not acting out.

"Some of us have tried to hold on to our old ideas and the result was nil until we let go absolutely."[11] Among other things, this refers to old ideas about relapse.

Relapse Prevention: Steps Ten, Eleven, and Twelve

First, something about enlightenment: As discussed earlier, denial is an ego-defense mechanism and a subconscious dynamic for surviving trauma. Too many people think that awareness resolves denial. Even though people report they are aware (meaning well-informed about psychology and their own personal history), debilitating and controlling defects still flare up, and repetitive, destructive behavior is often still prevalent. They'll be facing some other calamity in a few months. How many times have you heard (or said) after some calamity: "I'll find a book or go to therapy for a few sessions. I'll increase my meetings for a while." Over time, the

---

[9] An analogy: When a child is being taught addition, they are not also taught the theories of the relationships between the signs that represent quantitative value (Numbers Theory). Children have to master the basics like adding and subtracting first, otherwise, they will never understand advanced theory. Obedience first, insight second. It's the same here. Up to Step Nine a spiritual novice *cannot* understand the spiritual philosophy of regeneration that lies underneath the instructions—they aren't yet spiritually fit enough. Your work to Step Nine is the "adding and subtracting" of spirituality. That's why the instructions for Meditations on Wisdom (which is the on-going homework assignment for understanding spiritual theory) come after you've developed some mastery over the basics, meaning the first nine steps. Only after a long and persistent effort at Step Ten are twelve-step people reasonably successful at Meditations on Wisdom, because by then they will have completed the prerequisite work.

[10] I discussed this in Chapter 3, and is part of what's meant by *"...thoroughly followed our path." Alcoholics Anonymous,* p. 58.

[11] Ibid.

pain slowly hides itself, but there is rarely any substantive change to the person's inner nature—except for the addition of another layer of emotional scar tissue.

Twelve-step programs are full of people who've skimmed dozens of self-help books, attended many treatment centers, participated in insight-oriented workshops, and gone to a thousand meetings. They're aware and repeat the rhetoric flawlessly. Under close examination, they still participate in subtle addicted or symptomatic behavior. People who struggle with addictions may be aware that their life is erratic and painful, aware of shame, and know about their "family issues", yet they continue to act out, evince little joy, and evade spiritual principles. This all proves that awareness and insight, and "getting in touch with your feelings" are inadequate solutions to addictions. Being aware of the content of your "dark side" isn't the same as turning the light on.[12]

The true antidote to addictions is spiritual enlightenment. Once enlightened, the denial that concealed whatever you realized through the enlightened moment is eliminated. Once addicts transcend, with enlightened awareness, the denial that concealed some aspect of painful reality, transformation becomes possible. For the addict, only spiritual enlightenment guarantees recovery.[13]

One particular Buddhist discourse explores the task of delivering sentient beings from delusion. Hui-Neng (c. 550 CE) taught that: *"The false will be delivered by truthfulness; the delusive by enlightenment; the ignorant by wisdom... such is genuine deliverance."*[14] Very generally: Delusion is subscribing to a persistent false belief about ourselves, presented from the inside out. Delusion is an inside job (like denial), that conceals some unbearable or unacceptable reality. Addiction embodies the delusion that addiction is caused by outside factors, and the delusion that "addiction" is the problem. Both of these delusions conceal the reality that spiritual dislocation is actually the problem. Enlightenment is associated with spiritual integrity not psychological astuteness.

Once spiritual integrity exists within you (and the rudiments of that integrity are obtained by completing the first nine steps), you will apprehend a new perspective of relapse. It will be this: When you knowingly allow your character defects to harm or importune another, you are in relapse. Being intentionally dishonest, mean, selfish, blaming, arrogant, irresponsible, etc., are evidence that you are *in* relapse. Once you are willingly committed to spirituality, which is as much your effort to be

---

[12] Dark sides, light sides, masculine and feminine sides, inner children, inner critics, inner warriors, inner parents, [I've known people who created inner babysitters and inner pets], and various other similar metaphors, are only metaphors. Everyone is unified; there are no sides, and we are each an indivisible 'It'. These metaphors represent incredibly complex, and often self-serving interpretations of personality dynamics; they are symbols. When these are used in character analysis as signs rather than symbols, as labels in trendy workshops, or in coffee table/lunch room conversations, complex problems are created. Their over-use and misapplication have rendered them ineffective to the point of being dangerous.

[13] Be mindful of the difference between denial and belligerence which was discussed earlier. Here, belligerence i.e. intellectual arguing, is the antithesis to "surrender". And Meditations on Wisdom is the vehicle to surrender. Many therapists are skilled at fostering awareness and insight, but laying the groundwork for enlightenment is another matter entirely. This is the stumbling-block / inadequacy of most well-intentioned addictions-related therapy.

[14] Sutra Spoken by the Sixth Patriarch, *A Buddhist Bible*, edited by Dwight Goddard, Beacon Press, 1994, p. 510.

spiritual as it is your actually embodying the principles, any non-spiritual behavior will then be experienced as relapse.

Spiritual integrity, for a recovered addict, means in part to accept that to knowingly ignore character defects is to relapse. To accept this as truth takes many years of devoted attention to spiritual principles under the intimate guidance of a wise spiritual mentor. For anyone to attempt to describe how wonderful and reward-ing this level of willingness is, would be ill-advised promotion rather than attraction. Either you'll believe this and willingly pursue it (because you came to believe), or you won't. Either way, there's a high price tag attached.

When you're recovered and solidly in the maintenance steps, the purpose of then studying the literature, which in itself would constitute Relapse Prevention, be-comes two-fold: (1) to remind yourself to do what you are told; and (2) to engage in an exercise of Meditation on Wisdom that will enable you to reflect on the deep spiritual nuance of the literature. In this way, studying the original literature becomes both an exercise in faith and obedience (which is humility), and an exercise in sur-rendering to the wisdom of others (which is also humility).

After you become recovered (spiritual), relapse occurs when you don't gen-tly challenge your indifference to your own character defects, or when you're not abiding by spiritual principles. Relapse Prevention becomes, with due vigilance, con-forming to the five spiritual principles as embodied in the maintenance steps, with Meditations on Wisdom and prayer being a noticeable part of your routine.

When In Doubt, Start Inside

As I wrote in the Epilogue On "Maintenance", p. 376, all spiritual transfor-mation begins and deepens with self-awareness and personal responsibility — clearing away character defects that block access to our inner spiritual nature. Step Ten comes first. Only thereafter can there be access to a higher power through prayer and meditation — Step Eleven. Once these two practices are established, you are then capable of imparting something of spiritual substance to a fellow pilgrim, and can practice spiritual principles in all your affairs — Step Twelve.

When you're spiritually lost, often the impulse will be to pray harder, take a course, or attend a spiritual retreat. You may impress yourself with your willingness to "spend thousands" and sit in a cave in the mountains or at a silent retreat spa with a hot tub and vegetarian meals. But for addicts, without forcing yourself to be more diligent about Step Ten, it's only impression management. For the addict (for any-one, actually) they must *first* identify their dishonesty, their spiritually-crippling sense of entitlement, and various defects related to pride, and amend any and all wrongs and misdemeanors they've left unattended. (And there will be many.)

Self-examination is the initial and primary exercise in establishing and maintaining abstinence. Self-examination and amends always come first in maintain-ing spiritual fitness. *It is never external conditions that initiate spiritual sloth or relapse; it's always internal conditions and lack of due diligence regarding defects and amends.*

More on the Advanced View of Relapse

To establish a context for the advanced view of relapse, I will make some observations about the secular concerns of careers and ethics. In order to become a professional in some endeavor, a person must achieve some pre-established level of education and proficiency. Police academies, law schools, teacher's colleges—all professions—set basic qualifications. When these are met, people would then enter their chosen profession and be entitled to call themselves a chiropractor, a dental technician, a librarian (whatever it is they've trained for). Professional associations also establish ethical standards. Usually there are committees, or governing bodies to oversee their members' conduct, and because they've been trained, the members know what behavior is expected of them. Consider these parallels…

When acting out in your addictions, you were (unknowingly) completing the entrance requirements to a twelve-step program. You were paying your admission fee before you joined. *After* you joined a twelve-step program [the "Academy of Getting Recovered"], you started your spiritual basic training. By meticulously completing the regeneration steps, you became informed about the basics of spiritual principles, responsibility, self-examination, and amends. You completed this basic training, and thereby earned the right to qualify as recovered—a new member of the "Recovered Spiritual Pilgrim's Association".

However, in this particular spiritual pilgrim's association, unlike most professional or spiritual associations, there's no ethics committee or religious official to monitor your conduct (which is good). You can interpret your twelve-step program any way you want and you can't be fined, excommunicated, ordered to do penance, or denied membership. Only you can demand of yourself your own standard of spiritual integrity. No one has the authority to impose, nor are they to "suggest" rules for relationships, sexual conduct, step completion, meeting attendance, sharing, praying, bed-time, making decisions, diet, or anything else. Regardless of how articulately they state whatever their authority is for trying to impose rules and opinions, they have no authority. The dynamic of sponsorship is role-modeling. The AA literature (and this book) is to advise on what appears to be the most effective procedure to get recovered. The choice is yours. In twelve-step programs, the right to a *self*-assigned standard of behavior is inalienable.

Knowing the alcoholic's (addict's) penchant for resistance and sloth in spiritual matters, however, and by way of offering wise counsel, the original twelve-step program advises members to aspire to a standard set by God, and not by themselves. The higher the spiritual standard you aspire to, the more you demonstrate your devotion to God, and the better off you'll be. Ask yourself this, and meditate on the answer: "Is my level of spirituality enough to stay sober and be popular, or is it high enough to rate as truly spiritual?" The upshot of this is: You are your own twelve-step (spiritual) ethics committee, and no one else's, which is good.

Being a month sober and not acting out is something to be proud of. It's easy to notice what requires attention when you wake up in bed with a stranger, drive drunk, buy prostitutes, or gamble with the rent money. Once you've accumulated a few years of abstinence, however, should you still think relapse is simply a matter of returning to blatant acting out (drinking, drugs, sex), you live with the mentality of a newcomer. With this view, you've given yourself permission to ignore spiritual principles. Even after years of sobriety, your character defects will be hurting others, but you'll perceive yourself as not being in relapse. But you are — all the symptoms, including some self-destructive behavior, will be present.

Self-assigned spiritual standards are rooted in, and maintained by, fear and arrogance. Self-assigned standards leave coveted prejudices, anger, defects, pride, etc., unchallenged. For someone with long-term abstinence, they often act like a new-comer, but aren't seen as one because long-term abstinence is seen as "proof" of their being spiritual, but being sober for a long time only means long-term sobriety. People who don't maintain a high standard of spiritual behavior, within the maintenance steps, live with their character defects controlling themselves and harming others. This is always the result of belligerence towards spiritual principles.

When you do the steps as advised in *Alcoholics Anonymous*, you willingly (voluntarily) assume responsibility for always striving for deeper spirituality. This is the ever-present, underlying condition of the decision made at Step Three. The responsibility attendant to being spiritual becomes ever more intricate.

Through devotion to Steps Ten and Eleven, you'll notice minute spiritual impurities like tiny lies and exaggerations; small incidents of showing off; subtle sarcastic thoughts about all manner of things; and the invisible-to-others, silent ways you're arrogant or righteous. You need to maintain an Impression Management scheme to keep yourself looking good.

By the time you reach the maintenance steps, you should have trained yourself to realize that any time you ignore a spiritual principle, you're in relapse. Deliberate dishonesty, arrogance, selfishness, and the like, are all relapse. Once recovered, what constitutes "relapse" has a much greater scope than the early-abstinence idea of just acting out.

Your concept of relapse and its prevention will reflect your spiritual condition. You have to gently nudge yourself into deeper levels of accountability. Everything you say, think, or do is up for detailed scrutiny. You are your own ethics committee and, as you gently, firmly, and kindly drag yourself into embracing new truths, you must also reorganize your definitions of relapse to match new levels of spiritual insight. The shades and shadows of spiritual corruption are astonishingly subtle. That's why you must ever increasingly turn to God—the source of enlightenment and courage—in order to go deeper into spiritual principles.

Newcomers vs. Old-timers

Here, I refer to those [probably rather] rare twelve-step old-timers who are *authentically,* spiritually self-disciplined. Consider that newcomers and old-timers are both supposed to go to meetings, read the literature, be abstinent one day at a time, meditate and pray, and otherwise endeavor to be spiritual. Even though these basic requirements and obligations are remarkably similar, there are two main differences between newcomers and authentically spiritual old-timers.

The first difference is a matter of faith. Someone with a few months of abstinence who reads the original twelve-step literature will wonder: "Will spirituality really keep me sober through *every*thing: divorce, unemployment, sex, deaths, illnesses, dancing, dentists' appointments, blind dates, flat tires?" Unlike newcomers, these old-timers *know* that spirituality works—they have faith.

To develop faith in spiritual principles, newcomers have to test and examine them. They can't acquire faith in *Alcoholics Anonymous* and *Twelve Steps and Twelve Traditions,* which teach the process of how to acquire faith, if they do some treatment center's or recovery house's version of the steps, or if they make half-hearted (or psychologically-oriented) efforts. Not only must newcomers follow the original instructions, they must painstakingly follow them. Developing a strong faith is hard work; it isn't accidental. Without apparent rhyme or reason, the Spirit Of The Universe may have put a new person *in* some twelve-step program, but that person has to work to stay in it.

People "in recovery" will experience The Promises weakly or intermittently because they resist spiritual obedience. If they recycle through the steps, they have little faith. They made ill-advised step-substitutions or didn't work exactly as is suggested. No matter who designed the in-depth, important-looking, step guides, they aren't the real deal. Do them if you must, but realize that for disobedience to spiritual principles it may be you who pays with your life, not whomever wrote them. If you don't follow the instructions in the original literature, you may stay sober, but while you're harming others with substitute addictions, are burdened with ongoing character defects, and live a narrowly circumscribed life, you'll get to petulantly claim that spirituality doesn't work. Unlike newcomers, old-timers *know* that spirituality works—they have faith without belligerence.

The second difference between a spiritual old-timer and a newcomer is that an old-timer who regularly practices prayer and meditations on wisdom is often sensitive to the appearance of their character defects (a relapse out of spirituality), well before they actually cause harm. If people with any length of sobriety are mean-spirited, brag, gossip, curse and swear routinely, are racist or sexist, smoke, are demanding or intrusive, or are dishonest in any way, they cannot be sensitive to impending trouble.

Truly spiritual people can sense in advance when to be careful, and can govern themselves accordingly. Newcomers aren't sensitive to impending emotional calamity; they "wake up" in trouble and wonder how they got there. A newcomer has only hindsight. Spiritually-oriented old-timers have hindsight, insight, *and* foresight (about themselves).

Mental Relapse Patterns

In addition to the given condition that prior to relapse, an addict/alcoholic will have been dishonest, there are recognizable and identifiable thinking patterns that set up any relapse. When you are aware of these, and can notice them in yourself, it's easier to maintain a fit spiritual condition. Said in "self-help" jargon, this means that by having done the prerequisite inner-homework, you will be able to recognize and change whatever destructive trajectory you may have placed yourself on because of some passing thought or misadventure, *before* it damages you or someone else. These mental set-ups for relapse are in two main categories: *Falling From Grace* (a four step process) and *Isolation Thinking* (four different types).

Falling From Grace... Relapsing

By definition, this would be that process of losing whatever self-determined level of spiritual fitness you have established. In present-day, traditional religious terms, "sinning" implies some breach of religious or moral law. Several hundred years ago it found favor as an archery term meaning "to miss the mark". When you aim for some standard or goal, and fall short or miss the mark, you have "sinned". Granted, sinning is associated with religion, but it's important to balance the present-day sense of moral turpitude with the idea of missing the mark.

In an effort to legislate behavior and codify punishment for "missing the mark", some religions that incorporate the concept of sin have categorized sins this way: regarding religious endeavor, they are cardinal (big), or ordinal (little); and regarding mercenary-social endeavor, they are venal. Defining sin, and legislating the appropriate ecclesiastical punishment, is complicated and arbitrary at the best of times.[15]

In your desire to be spiritual, you would aspire to evince certain virtues like humility, kindness, charity, etc.[16] In a purist sense, should you fail to achieve or maintain these (i.e. miss the mark) you've "sinned". However, because you miss the mark of perfect virtue, which in absolute terms is sinning, it doesn't mean that contrition or penance is required. In a gentler view of spirituality, it isn't necessary to do penance for being human; it's only necessary to fix any harm caused. Being deliberately negligent or cruel on the other hand, is something altogether different.

After achieving enough "virtue" to be recovered, by living *in* the maintenance steps, you need only remain gently vigilant in order to avoid falling from grace (relapsing). Falling From Grace is that mental process of...

Thought, Form, Fascination, Fall

Thought: Initially you have a thought that falls short of integrity or fidelity—a fleeting idea of something *un*spiritual. In the midst of an ordinary day, at

---

[15] The related and important discussion of why self-appointed religious authorities (they're all self-appointed) need to punish people, is left for another time. And, for those of a more discerning temperament, it's worthy to note that the presence of guilt isn't necessarily evidence of sin or wrong-doing.

[16] Humility, kindness, and charity are attributes that might be referred to as virtues—laudable personality traits that govern and guide conduct. From an uncomplicated perspective, virtues would be generally opposite to the seven deadly sins (listed in *Twelve Steps and Twelve Traditions,* p. 48). The Catholic-Christian view of virtues is that there are two main categories: Cardinal (or Human) Virtues: prudence, justice, fortitude, and temperance; and Theological Virtues: faith, hope, and charity. [*Catechism of the Catholic Church*, Publication Services, Canadian Conference of Catholic Bishops, 1994, beginning at p. 381.] Cardinal virtues are to orient thoughts and behavior in relation to other people and the world, while theological virtues orient thoughts and behavior in relation to The Church and God. In *being* virtuous, the test is to act thusly in difficult times. (See Boethius, p. 428-429 this book.)

some inconsequential moment, the corrupt idea might be to steal something, have an affair, cheat, lie, go on a shopping spree, or get drunk.

Kim has been pleasantly married / living with someone for a few years. Kim is walking home from work and notices their new neighbor, Lee, and stops to say hello. Lee is rather attractive—really quite sexy. Kim wonders what it would be like to have sex with Lee, and their social talk continues for a few minutes.

There's the fleeting thought: the hit. Next comes...

Form: The passing thought gets stuck in your mind. For any number of reasons, summed up in your not doing enlightened inner work on insecurities, denial, and spiritual values, the fleeting unspiritual/corrupt thought is held onto. By thinking about it, it's given structure and Form. The passing thought becomes a presence.

Kim thinks: "I never noticed our new neighbors. They live just down the block. Nice body. I wonder what they do for a living?"

The initial thought of sexiness persists, but it's gently obscured and hidden in the Form of "being a good neighbor"—which is a ruse. In any casual conversation about the new neighbor there will be dishonesty.

Lee and Lee's spouse have a housewarming party and invite their new neighbors. Kim and Kim's spouse attend. When leaving, Kim will conveniently forget a jacket or scarf, or make some subtly unnecessary offer of "friendship" (a ruse) and will soon call Lee and make the necessary arrangements. In their conversation there will be a subtle sexual or romantic innuendo, some dishonesty about their respective situations, and/or compliments and too-personal personal disclosure—flirting—that can be easily defended as "friendly conversation".

Kim camouflages the desire and flirting within the form of being neighborly, friendly, and socially curious. Kim is incapable of challenging this ruse, and the original sexual thoughts are left unexamined. Kim's unaware of the illicit, destructive trajectory that's now been established.

Recall the World Health Organization's definition of addiction: *"A pathological relationship with a mood altering experience that has life damaging consequences."* The excitement and impending illicit romance/sex is the mood altering experience. Some need, concealed by denial and repression, has triggered this behavior, and is holding Kim captive in the destructive path that is now established. This is the visible beginning of Kim being manipulated by mood-altering, *un*examined subconscious issues, which lead to...

Fascination and Fantasy: The form (that was built around the original destructive thought) escalates to Fascination and Fantasy. There'll be preoccupation, anticipation, dishonesty, intrigue, and allure. Fascination will be a noticeable part of conscious thought, with justifications for the destructive path that's been established. These justifications will be relative to other life circumstances and rooted in blaming, a false sense of entitlement, an exaggerated/romanticized sense of unhappiness, and irresponsibility. Fascination and fantasy are designed to, and will always, minimize the harmful consequences, romanticize and exaggerate the expected pleasure, and categorize the situation as harmless, or worth it, or manageable. At this stage, people convince themselves they don't care (they always do), and especially that they can control the outcome (they can't).

Self-destructive behavior is designed to serve some unknown (but with proper work, knowable) need the behavior is compensating for. This oversimplified diagram may make you aware of this process, but remember that awareness isn't healing.

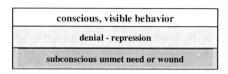

conscious, visible behavior
denial - repression
subconscious unmet need or wound

Some dormant need or wound has been activated underneath denial. A person living with unhealed wounds *must* compensate for them. The visible, compensating behavior is always a metaphor for what the problem actually is. Fascination is what mood-alters and compensates for the subconscious unmet need or unhealed wound. The fantasy-scenario cannot be understood by the person trapped in this cycle (they aren't smart enough for their own good) because it's origin is subconscious, but for some unexplainable reason it feels necessary and offers relief. [17]

Kim creates fantasies (about Lee's character, having sex, romantic dinners, getting away with it, or that it's of no consequence) and may suspect they aren't wise, but there's a silent, unavoidable need to ignore this suspicion. Kim justifies and rationalizes this by dredging up "reasons" from the past, creating illusions about the present, and forming various fantasies about the future. Kim's method of self-reassurance is to naively classify the fantasies as controllable. Kim remains powerfully preoccupied and is thereby forced into calamity.

If, in this scenario, Lee participates at all, Lee has also established some similar destructive trajectory. If Lee refuses to participate, Kim will continue wandering around in Life trying to create another scenario and be unaware of what's happening.

The subconscious machinations the person is blind to are what give fantasies their power. At this point, they are entirely incapable of preventing disaster. Whatever is hidden by repression and denial is in charge and, because the motivation for the behavior exists underneath denial and repression, it can't be challenged at a conscious level.[18]

The impending calamity isn't always horrific, but it is always damaging, emotionally expensive, and unavoidable. The actual fall from grace (the calamity) is only a matter of time and circumstance. It always appears outrageous or unnecessary because the motivation exists subconsciously, underneath denial, and no one, especially the person trapped in this relapse pattern, can understand why.

---

[17] The example I use here, for destructive behavior, is sexual, but it could be spending, eating, gambling, substances, violence... whatever. Also: The destructive behavior is rarely a direct reflection of the nature of the unmet need or wound. In the process of being externalized from unconscious to conscious, the need is transformed and reframed into something else.

[18] Recall the earlier discussion about Unconscious Incompetence. This is it in a destructive form.

Fall: *Kim will retrieve the "forgotten" item when Lee is home alone. If not that, some other "innocent" meeting scenario will be orchestrated, pushed by whatever is under the denial.* [By now it's too late, and the puppet plunges into disaster.[19]] *Sex "just happens" between Kim and Lee.*

The Fantasy will collapse in the self-destructive behavior; be that binge eating, pornography, shopping sprees (from CDs and clothes to cars and houses), affairs, adultery, impulsive marriages, divorces, violence, cruelty, substances, or crime. These are the visible consequences of the un-examined interior life.

Don't be fooled into a false sense of security because this example of adultery appears outrageous to your values. The destructive behavior is unique to each person and can be as innocuous as committing to a diet and then going grocery shopping, and coming home with $75.00 worth of junk food; or going into a book store to buy one book and walking out with seven you didn't plan on buying. It can be needing only new ski boots and leaving the store with $3,000 worth of new gear; or wanting one CD and buying ten; or planning to watch TV for one hour and later realizing you've watched TV for five hours and accomplished nothing. Immediately after the behavior ends, there'll be fused realizations of fear, shame, and guilt.

Fate and circumstance will act in concert with an unexamined life to abet Thought, Form, Fascination, Fall. Our culture of consumerism and disposability foments spiritual alienation (a crucial element of this). That's why there's so much calamity and misadventure in personal relationships in modern culture. People cannot change or control fate or circumstances, they can only become enlightened unto themselves, and thereby reasonably influence their destiny in non-harmful ways.

Thought, Form, Fascination, Fall can happen in the span of a minute, a month, or a year. The time-frame depends upon how available the opportunity is, how elaborate the ruse needs to be in order for it to appear harmless or controllable, and the "power" of the subconscious wound. The prerequisite conditions for this cycle of self-destruction were established long before the actual event.

People's *un*preparedness for commitment to an ethical or compassionate life through unresolved shame, a need for revenge, insecurity that demands power over others, greed, a self-destructive orientation, or an exaggerated view of entitlement, is all too common. People are responsible for the calamities they orchestrate, but will be confused about their culpability, and be incapable of preventing disaster. Without proper, long-term work, they're perpetually blind to their irresponsibility. Ending up in calamity, not knowing what happened, blaming someone else, and deflecting responsibility, are so entrenched as normal that people don't consider there might be alternatives, let alone the disasters can be successfully challenged and stopped.

Many people are in committed and notoriously unfulfilling relationships as a consequence of living an unexamined life. This is absolutely true for *un*spiritual addicts, alcoholics, and people in related programs like Alanon, Naranon, CODA and

---

[19] Consider further the metaphor of a puppet: A puppet isn't conscious and is controlled by strings it's unaware of: helpless to respond independently of the puppet master. An unenlightened person is unaware of the disasters they create which control their destiny.

ACOA. The degree of calamity is irrelevant. The poignancy of this all too-common situation is that whatever the disaster is, it's perceived as "the way life is".

This pattern is portrayed astonishingly well in the film *Unfaithful*.[20] The lead character, Connie Sumner (played by Diane Lane), without having done the prerequisite inner work, is trapped in this specific process of Falling From Grace (losing integrity, committing adultery—call it what you will), as is her husband, Edward Sumner (played by Richard Gere). The reality of this process is poignant in the excellent writing and both actors' excellent portrayals of their characters' blind helplessness, and the resulting crises. On the commentary track of the DVD-release of the film, Diane Lane offers these observations:

> *"When you know your own boundaries and what you're capable of being around or not being around,* [you can extricate yourself] *long before* [the character] *Connie did. Why is she capable of this affair? Because a lot of homework has not been done in their relationship. When you find yourself stymied because of what you are discovering...* [about] *betraying the person you are with... it's too late to go back and do the homework.*
>
> *"It's very funny because it can be an umbrella you leave at somebody's house. It can be muffins that you say you're bringing. It's a ruse. Your subconscious is ruling you. If you want to know what people are up to, look at the end result. Don't even look at the end result, look at the trajectory you're on. You're drawing closer to someone or you're pulling away from someone. Period.*
>
> *"There's a lot of denial. There's something to hide. The feelings are a betrayal to the inner church of what a relationship is founded on. Once you start to wander—once you start to allow yourself that on a daydream level—then you've already done it."* [21]
>
> *"[It's by] not doing your homework on your inner life in your relationship that you're vulnerable to an invasion."* [22]
>
> Diane Lane

The consequences to any cycle of Thought, Form, Fascination, Fall may appear outrageous to the extant circumstances, or they may appear to be inconsequential. The consequences are never outrageous or inconsequential. They only appear so because of the absence of enlightened awareness, which allows people's

[20] *Unfaithful*, directed by Adrian Lyne, ©2002 "Unfaithful" Film Produktion Co. and Twentieth Century Fox Film Corp. The film is an uncanny representation of the psychology that's under examination here. It's worthy of note that both main characters go through two cycles of Thought, Form, Fascination, Fall within the film, although from different perspectives and with different motivations.
[21] Diane Lane's comments quoted here were part of her commentary track on the *Unfaithful* DVD. I've used what's pertinent to the topic at hand.
[22] This last observation is on the *Unfaithful* DVD, in the interview with Charlie Rose, ©CharlieRose.com Inc., ©2000.

lives to be completely manipulated by whatever "unfinished business" lurks beneath their conscious awareness.

> *"Perhaps your definition of your self-system lacks authentic boundaries. You've erected a precarious structure of personality on unconscious factors over which you have no control."*[23]

The dynamic of Thought, Form, Fascination, Fall, as described by Diane Lane and portrayed in the movie, is also a parallel to falling out of a relationship with your higher power, and finding that you have relapsed.

If you are caught in the cycle of Thought, Form, Fascination, Fall, there will be a deeply entrenched Impression Management scheme.[24] Integrity and abstinence are then dependent upon Fate not presenting circumstances that hook into any unresolved needs. For recovering/recovered addicts, this is always the result of not doing inner-work: the steps exactly as suggested, living by the five spiritual principles, and seeking authentic long-term therapeutic and spiritual guidance.[25]

Life is ongoing change, and as life changes, so must you. Ongoing vigilance and commitment must keep spiritual integrity abreast of change and circumstance. If not, a person will be at risk of being impelled into destructive behavior because of resistance to ever-changing circumstances. This is why ongoing participation in spiritual counsel is wise. Even though some spiritual pilgrims have thoroughly and sincerely done their inner-homework, should they not continue to be gently vigilant, they'll slowly lose whatever integrity they've gained.

The Dance	gentle vigilance to integrity and
	abandon concern for success.
	disgrace lurks in shadows of negligence;
	in the illusion of preparedness
	Calamity smiles
	dislocated mysteries, deeply layered.
	the Abyss
	at the edge the pilgrim dances
	never hearing music
	parading fragrant ignorance.
	Disaster floats patiently

Thought, Form, Fascination, Fall, is a process that results in "waking up" in the middle of disaster or relapse—falling into the abyss and never knowing you were

---

[23] *UBIK*, Philip K. Dick, Bantam (Science Fiction), 1977, p. 45.

[24] Impression Management, which I've referred to several times, operates on two levels. At the conscious level, it could be as simple as getting dressed up, using fancy words, and acting other than as you are, in order to manipulate (impress) people. At the unconscious level, it's automatic behaviors that you are unaware of that are unconsciously created to compensate and maintain denial and repression.

[25] With the dramatic increase of abstinence not-available addictions. it would appear that seeking out well-conducted, long-term therapy is now, more than ever before, necessary. As cultural dislocation increases, so does that affect the quality of therapy that is readily available since many therapists are not as divorced from cultural insanity as they would like to think. (See cross-over work, Fn, p. 17-18)

standing on the edge. In what seems like a puzzling mess, and all too fast, once again you're buying sex, smoking, calling your drug dealer, spending money you don't have, waking up in bed with a stranger, getting drunk, binging on junk food, using pornography, getting married, getting divorced, or betraying your spouse.

There are two conditions which will exist prior to and during Falling From Grace. The first is you will have been dishonest. You will not remember when the dishonesty actually started, but you cannot relapse out of being recovered without being dishonest.[26] The second condition, and probably the most destructive trap there is for defeating spirituality, is the belief that you can handle it yourself (the justification for non-disclosure and dishonesty). You will cling to the devastating delusion that you are smart enough for your own good.

Jackson Pollock, the American abstract painter, said of abstract painting that for him there were no accidents. He believed that, even though he, the artist (or the recovered addict, or the two main characters in the movie *Unfaithful*) may not understand what's happening, there's an unconscious structure to it. Mr. Pollock "denied" the accident. There are no accidents in relapse, either.

Spiritual fitness, embodied in a commitment to the maintenance steps and the five spiritual principles, *and* a requisite amount of well conducted therapy, will prevent *un*spiritual transient thoughts from going farther than being transient. You'll never be free of troublesome thoughts, but you'll certainly have fewer of them, they will be less intense, and they'll always be manageable before they lead to disaster.

Isolation Thinking

Isolation Thinking is the other common process for relapsing out of being recovered, back to being "in recovery", and then from "in recovery" (without much effort), back into overt addiction.

To start: One simplified perspective of spiritual regeneration might be that it's a four-fold task: overcome isolation-from-self and eliminate self-destruction; appreciate and achieve individuality; continuously honor and respect another's individuality; revere the spiritual unity that underlies everything beyond Time and Space. Mystics and spiritual masters advise that beyond the limits of consciousness, we are all *That Which Art*. At the same time, the nature of our conscious existence within Time and Space requires that we each strive for independence. We are, within Time and Space, required to be "an individual" and must stand alone. In your present manifestation as "*I*", you're unique, and this, coupled with the phenomenon of addictions, both enables and entrenches destructive isolation.

---

[26] In *all* relationships: those that are some manifestation of addiction, those that are symbiotic, and those that appear for the most part to be truly stable and intimate, the partner that isn't first captured by Thought, Form, Fascination, Fall, will sense something is amiss as their partner descends into calamity. In addictive and symbiotic relationships the partner who isn't first caught in the Thought Form Fascination Fall cycle (the non-instigating one), will be triggered into their own destructive trajectory by their sensing that something is amiss in their partner, but will be unable to address it. Only in the truly intimate, trusting relationship, where the inner work has been done, will either person be able to bring either the "thought" *or* the sense that something is amiss out for discussion soon enough to prevent the calamity.

Unregenerate addicts isolate from themselves, from others, and from God, both (i) consciously, in a deliberate attempt to conceal things, and (ii) unconsciously—motivated by some compensation strategy underneath repression and denial. In addition to these dynamics of isolation, with all relapse there'll be two other associated conditions. (a) The person will have been dishonest; and (b) they'll think they are smart enough for their own good.

There are four types of Isolation Thinking that set up relapse.

(1) *Isolation Through Mental Arguing*

You'll be sitting in a meeting, listening to someone at a lecture, or talking with a friend or your partner, and you'll think: "You're wrong," or "That's stupid," and leave the accusation silent and yourself unchallenged. Anything like this represents mental belligerence—mental arguing—and separates you from others. The resulting isolation is not about the other person's behavior: it's about the attitude through which you filter their behavior.[27] What insecurity motivated you to need to be right or condemn them, and thereby leave yourself silently isolated? In one way, condemnation, racism, sexism, prejudice, etc., are all isolation tactics.

Even though you may be convinced that your view is true, or more spiritually tenable, it's your condemnation and overt rejection (of others) that isolates you. Your "silence" indicates extremely manipulative behavior. You're self-righteous about your own perceptions and, whether vocal or not, the mental argument itself will leave you separated from others. This applies equally when someone silently justifies their own obviously unspiritual behavior like violence or smoking, or some character flaw like greed or arrogance.

The point of noticing your mental arguing isn't to encourage you to voice all your disagreements with everyone. Addicts/alcoholics can be rather argumentative. It's oftentimes wiser to say nothing (otherwise many addicts would be arguing with everyone all the time). It is, however, very important to discuss this belligerence with a mentor, or better still a good therapist, if it's particularly frequent, and to eventually eliminate it through self-disciplined commitment to spiritual principles.

(2) *Isolation Through Unique Suffering*

"If they had *my* problems," or "Nobody understands!" are isolation tactics, and of the four isolating attitudes presented here, Unique Suffering is the most easily justified. The truth is, regardless of the degree of anyone's compassion and empathy, no one can ever truly understand the *exact* depth of another's pain (and this is especially so for The Suffering Victim). Nevertheless, understanding and compassion are available. As soon as you insist that no one could ever understand, or that no one cares, you place a glass wall of defiance between you and everyone else. You're in the world on your own, completely alone.

The Tree of Sorrows is an Hasidic tale about how, on the Day of Judgment, we each place our sorrows in a bag and hang our bag of sorrows from the Sorrow

---

[27] This will be discussed in detail in <u>Emotions and Communications</u> in *Facets of Personal Transformation*, and is discussed in this book in both Appendix IV, and <u>The Two-Step Dance</u> in Chapter 8.

Tree's branches. Everyone then walks slowly around the tree looking for another set of problems that appeals more than their own. The story goes that, at day's end, everyone takes back their own sorrows.[28] Sorrows are uniquely our own.

When you describe your problems as unique, you're accurate. Circumstances may be similar, but our personalities make them unique. Compassion for others must necessarily have a personal slant. However, when you introduce drama, and claim that your problems are *so* unique that *no one* could understand, or no one ever experienced these before, or that no one cares, you're wrong and you live isolated.

(3) *Isolation Through Superlative Comparisons*

"I'm sicker than they are," or "They're sicker than I am," or "I'm the sickest person in the room." And, for the self-righteous, there's the vicious game of silently comparing newcomers and deciding who are the sickest, and which ones will make it and which ones won't.

Many people in twelve-step programs live with the idea that, as far as addictions are concerned, some people are sicker than others. That *may* be so; however, there's a dangerous potential in that line of reasoning. As soon as you decide you're sicker than anyone else, or that others are decidedly sicker than you, there's a character defect in you arising out of insecurity that needs to be addressed. In the face of harsh judgments about who's the sickest, there's isolation.

Some people do have grave emotional and mental disorders, but they are able to recover (from addictions) if they have the capacity to be honest.[29] Helping them discover their capacity to be honest requires extra compassion and empathy from others. Does that make them "sicker" as far as addiction goes, or simply place a greater demand on you for spiritual behavior? They may appear to be "the sickest" because no one has ever offered them compassion, or you may classify them as sicker because you have to offer compassion when you're feeling tired, lazy or selfish. You're in charge of how accepting you are of others, so you therefore have the ability to enable and encourage honesty in others by offering acceptance. That makes it easier for others to be honest, and to therefore get recovered.

People may not be as far along in their pilgrimage as you, but does that make them sicker, or just not in the same place as you? Addicts are notorious for isolating themselves by creating a sick-sicker-sickest mentality.[30]

(4) *Isolation Through Withholding*

People will attend therapy and talk for a long time. They won't disclose everything that's going on, which guarantees that the therapy will be ineffective, then they quit therapy and blame the therapist. It's the same with physical fitness, relationships, almost any endeavor—especially a spiritual one: Your success will be commensurate with your commitment and emotional investment. Blaming anyone

---

[28] *If You Meet The Buddha on The Road, Kill Him,* Sheldon Kopp, Bantam Books, p. 17.
[29] *Alcoholics Anonymous,* p. 58.
[30] This superlative-comparison thought process relates to the exaggerated tales of one-upmanship and bragging that happens during "sharing" at meetings, which was discussed earlier.

other than yourself for your mundane accomplishments, in the face of your own half-hearted efforts, or blaming inefficiency or conflict on others and concealing your own mistakes or defects, is grossly irresponsible. Withholding constitutes a half-hearted effort in and of itself. It will ensure that you maintain whatever sense of isolation you are experiencing, and enable you to justify cynicism.

Mental arguing, claiming unique suffering, being self-righteous, living with "comparison recovery", and withholding, guarantee that relapse will forever be near to hand. These are partly what motivates an exaggerated and belligerent participation in meetings. Addictions wait patiently, and are nurtured in Isolation Thinking.

Alcoholics Anonymous points out *"...some of the mental states that precede a relapse... ,"* and *"What sort of thinking dominates... "* prior to relapse.[31] Be aware of thoughts and feelings that dominate your attitude. Relapse Prevention is an "inside job", and ultimately begins and ends within you. On a conscious level:

- Be vigilant for Thought, Form, Fascination, Fall—those persisting thoughts and fantasies about unspiritual/acting out behavior that set up a cycle leading to calamity. Seek wise counsel to discuss these.
- Notice and challenge your own Isolation Thinking.
- Be very wary of the ultimate arrogance: believing you are smart enough for your own good; and,
- Undertake whatever course of action is necessary to maintain a commitment to spiritual principles.

Six "Simple" Things

On a conscious level, there are six things you can do to make it easier to challenge how you think.

1) Obedience: The original twelve-step literature provides precise instructions on how to get recovered. There are guarantees and promises that, if you painstakingly do what you're told, you'll become recovered. Willingness, patience, and labor, under the umbrella of obedience, are all that's required. Doing what you're told within *Alcoholics Anonymous* and *Twelve Steps and Twelve Traditions* is relapse prevention. Don't follow any instructions—follow *those* instructions. Go to the source. This is difficult. Do it anyway.

2) Spirituality: Make a visible effort to live by spiritual principles embodied in the maintenance steps. Someone's late for an appointment—as they rush out the door they're abrupt, short-tempered, and drive dangerously cutting people off and speeding to get somewhere. The line is long and you don't get into the movie. Your hair isn't cut exactly how you want it. Someone forgets your anniversary or birthday. Someone you love dies. You can petulantly crash around making life worse or you can abide by spiritual principles. This is difficult. Be determined.

3) <u>Commit to Integrity</u>: Seek guidance from, and desire to become, a spiri-tually-oriented person. Attend meetings quietly. Don't show off. Be respectful. Don't lie—ever. Seek wise *long*-term spiritual counsel. Consider well-conducted long-term therapy, and pay for it yourself. Do it.

4) <u>Prioritize</u>: If spirituality and establishing a relationship with a higher power (via the steps) isn't first on your list of priorities, you've missed the point of the whole exercise. Establish your priorities and maintain them. This is very difficult.

5) <u>Never Blame/Stop Complaining</u>: These imply you can only become happy or recovered if "they" or "it" changes. If you're blaming anyone for anything, then getting recovered or being joyous is dependent on them. Maybe someday they'll agree that your misery is their fault, and they'll give you money, move away, be sorry, or do an act of contrition, thereby allowing you to finally become happy. You may think: "Yes, I shouldn't blame, but in *my* case, it was *so* horrific that it *is* partly their fault that I'm unhappy/unfulfilled/miserable." No, it isn't.

Your addictions, or bad moods, or anger, or petulance, or divorces, or bad marriages, or stupid jobs, or unhappiness, or lack of fulfilling sex is *your* fault. It's completely self-defeating, and totally ineffective to put someone else in charge of any aspect of your life. In our culture, it is difficult to never blame anyone for any-thing. We are advised in the original literature that we are to drop the word blame from our speech and thought.[32] Don't ever blame.

As far as complaining goes, any twelve-step spiritual pilgrim volunteered for this work at Step Three. Spirituality, honesty, Step Eight... whatever, may be difficult but there is never grounds for complaint. You volunteered. You may need extensive therapy to figure out how not to complain or blame—even then, don't complain, you will have volunteered for that, too.

"So a wise [person] *ought no more to take it ill when* [they] *clash with for-tune than a brave* [person] *ought to be upset by the sound of battle. For both of them their very distress is an opportunity, for the one to gain glory and the other to strengthen* [their] *wisdom. This is why virtue gets its name, because it is firm in strength and unconquered by adversity."*[33] This theme applies to spirituality as well. Any perceived difficulty is only an opportunity to celebrate your spiritual life. That was Boethius' point.

6) <u>The Declarations</u>: Review, and abide by, Declaration II, which is dis-cussed in Chapter 3, p. 132.

Some Odds and Ends

We all have complicated problems, get mixed messages, and live with con-flict. Albert Camus, in *The Myth of Sisyphus*, wrote about the absurdity of life. At times we're overwhelmed and confused. Not everyone will understand or care about your pilgrimage. Life appears tough. Sometimes. But when you're authentically spiritual, the difficulty vanishes and life becomes a place of grandeur.

[31] *Alcoholics Anonymous,* p. 35.
[32] Twelve Steps and Twelve Traditions, p. 47.
[33] *The Consolation of Philosophy*, Boethius, translated by V.E. Watts, Penguin Books, 1969, p. 144.

By being spiritual, you offer people in your life the special gift of not making their life worse by imposing your defects on them. This kindness will set you apart, and you'll be cherished by some and resented by others. Being spiritual in all circumstances doesn't mean that calamity will pass you by. People die, break legs, get cancer, and lose jobs. Big chunks of Life happen to everyone in particular, and some people deeply resent that Life takes up so much of their time. We're all susceptible to missing the mark and mishandling the daily ups and downs of life.

People can't develop habits of devotion when they're in crisis; and neither can they complete the subtle therapeutic work that signals permanent change when they're in calamity. In times of relative peace, maintain deeply committed routines of prayer and meditation, and seek out well-conducted therapy. If you don't, then spirituality and therapy become crisis management tools. If you think spirituality is expensive, try addictions. If you think therapy is expensive, try adultery, divorce, abuse, anger, denial... .[34] Force yourself to participate in wise and insightful counsel, and stay in it for a *very* long time.

Addictions and Life are cunning, baffling, and powerful. Being Spiritual offers you a gift—it disarms whatever is cunning, baffling, and powerful, and allows an appreciation for the grandeur of Life exactly as you have been given it. Be always sensitive to, and curious about, the beauty and powerful nature of a Spiritual lifestyle.

Being recovered and living in the maintenance steps doesn't mean you're not at risk of being dishonest, mean, arrogant, proud, selfish, etc. It does mean that moments of indecision are easily resolved in favor of spirituality, and you will therefore stay out of relapse. Indecision about how to conduct yourself doesn't happen when you're entrenched in sound spiritual principles.

Initially, while searching for peace and looking for God, newcomers will wander through their personality like it's a foreign, hostile territory. Getting recovered is possible and insanity is optional, but we never know beforehand how difficult the job of getting recovered is actually going to be. We are to be congratulated for this undertaking. The more senior, spiritual members of twelve-step programs should take some time to gently inform others about this truth.

"*Furthermore, we have not even to risk the adventure alone, for the heroes of all time have gone before us. The labyrinth is thoroughly known. We have only to follow the thread of the hero path, and where we had thought to find an abomination, we shall find a god. And where we had thought to slay another, we shall slay ourselves. Where we had thought to*

---

[34] These are my modification of a quote from Derek Bok, former President of Harvard University, who said: "*If you think education is expensive, try ignorance.*" As reported in *1,911 Best Things Anybody Ever Said*, compiled by Robert Byrne, Fawcett Columbine, 1988, p. 158. Regarding therapy and spirituality becoming crisis management tools: That is not what they are best suited for and using them thusly renders them ineffective.

travel outward, we will come to the center of our own existence. And where we had thought to be alone, we will be with all the world."

Joseph Campbell[35]

At the outset this is very difficult, but you volunteered, so don't complain (too much), and do it anyway. Persevere.

The Addict's Secret Desire

How many times have you thought: "When am I going to be normal? I just want to be normal." This desire isn't limited to addicts or alcoholics, and has nothing to do with gender, sexual orientation, religion, or culture. Quentin Crisp wrote:

> *"From time to time, every mature homosexual man should issue a solemn warning to all his young gay friends that they must never adopt, even unconsciously, an exile's view of normality. To this day, in spite of all that gay pride stuff, many of us who stand in the street, knee-deep in the snows of rejection, press our noses to the cold windowpanes of establishment and imagine that the carpet slipper setup that we see dimly on the other side of the glass is permanent, cozy, and peaceful.*
> *In fact, those who are on the inside are frantically trying to get out."*[36]

Many addicts in recovery talk about the twelve steps like they are a treasure map—secretly coded directions to the lost city of Normal. Addicts and alcoholics naively hope for "normal". Like other misunderstood or oppressed members of sub-cultures, alcoholics and addicts too often make the big assumption: getting recovered is getting to Normal (some vague place or state that they're supposed to arrive at). In the first place, Normal doesn't exist. In the second place, anything that a recovering addict could conceive of as normal, isn't.

People trapped in mediocrity often resent the flaunted freedom of outsiders.[37] As implausible as it sounds, the flamboyance of some addicts and alcoholics is envied by people who interpret reckless self-destruction as freedom (the antidote to their own desperation). Pining away, waiting for admission to Normal, is often the deeply-secret emotional posture of members of any troubled subculture like recovering addicts. They idealize the establishment from the outside-in. As Quentin Crisp says, we *"...press our noses to the cold windowpanes of establishment..."*.

Avoid the destructive assumption that becoming normal is the goal. Don't be normal: be sincerely spiritual, which, in this culture, is clearly abnormal. Ask: "What is 'normal' and, if I could figure out what that is, do I really want it? Is there within me a creative, spiritual person whom I will suffocate by being normal?"

Oftentimes I'm seen as a malcontent, a social outcast if you will, within the culture at large and within twelve-step programs. And yet, all I do is politely ignore

[35] *The Power of Myth*, Joseph Campbell with Bill Moyers, Sue Flowers, Editor, Doubleday, 1988, p. 123.
[36] *How To Go To The Movies*, Quentin Crisp, St. Martin's Press, 1988, p. 127.
[37] This refers to the quote, noted earlier, of William Bayer about the film *Easy Rider* (directed by Dennis Hopper), in *Great Movies*, The Ridge Press, Inc., Grosset & Dunlap, Inc., 1973, p. 161.

peer pressure and live by applying the five spiritual principles to *my* values, *my* desires, and *my* preferences. I've received no end of condemnation for this. And yet, I've no intention of surrendering me to them. I've worked too hard for too long, and I'm too precious to give up "me" for popular approval.

The original twelve-step program isn't designed to make you normal. It's designed to make you spiritual. The more spiritual you are, the less normal you'll be. Inherently, we all know this. But carbon-based life forms that are blessed with intellect and inundated with technology, cherish their preoccupation with mood-altering experiences, fornication, and shiny things.

Insecure people often live with the illusion that compliance with popular opinion will someday be fulfilling or meaningful. This is because they have decided social success and obedience to cultural values equals fulfillment. Within this faulty perception, they will have labeled relationship addiction as normal, violence as acceptable, greed as good, people as disposable, and sexuality as dirty, bad, or *un*spiritual. They know they'll be ostracized for being truly unique.

> *"Difficulty at the beginning works supreme success.*
> *Furthering through perseverance.*
> *Nothing should be undertaken*
> *It furthers one to appoint helpers."*

> *"No plain not followed by a slope.*
> *No going not followed by a return.*
> *He who remains persevering in danger*
> *Is without blame.*
> *Do not complain about this truth;*
> *Enjoy the good fortune you still possess."* [38]

After years of self-annihilation and active addiction, some addicts getting recovered take life very seriously. At the outset, they should. But that often extends itself into a permanent mindset that everything's a chore and it's all hard work. Yet, others make light of everything, and refuse to appreciate the life-or-death nature of addictions. After years of hard work and self-discipline, when addicts have finally recovered and are spiritual, they end up being able to evince a spiritual harmony; a benign indifference and joy, in any life circumstance. We can't take it too seriously, after all, it's just life. And for addicts, Life is easiest to manage when it's devoted to spiritual principles.

---

[38] These poetic aphorisms are taken from *If You Meet The Buddha on The Road, Kill Him*, Sheldon Kopp, Bantam Books, pp. 3 and 187 respectively. The original translation is by Cary F. Baynes, *The I Ching or Book of Changes*, Princeton University Press, 1950, pp. 16 and 116.

Appendix I

Traditions

"If a man does away with his traditional way of living and throws away his good customs, he had better first make certain that he has something of value to replace them."

Basuto Proverb[1]

There are two general purposes for this Appendix. The first is to enable you to understand how to examine and challenge traditions. You may find yourself experiencing guilt, or a sense of failure, and be unable to establish its origin. Unless spiritual pilgrims, who are exiting addictions, understand the double bind that often arises from conflict between new emerging value systems and established traditions, they'll relapse, and often stay rooted in a cycle that approximates: Desire – Action – Guilt – Aversion – Regression (explained at p. 410).

The second purpose is to provide a *brief* over-view of the two main temperance philosophies that predate AA. This will accompany some discussion about the short-sighted perceptions, within some twelve-step groups, that traditions exist only for the organizing of groups. At first look, this is what they appear to be for, but this categorizes the AA traditions as abstract concepts, separate from the individual member (which actually renders them ineffective). I hope to establish the basis for an alternate view of the AA traditions; a view that perceives them more as an expression of the five principles of spirituality. The AA traditions actually represent how to conduct yourself spiritually, in the context of community, anywhere in your life.

Forming Traditions

There are two basic ways that traditions originate. The first is from the collective experience of the people involved. The Hindu and Aboriginal religious traditions evolved over a few thousand years and were formed out of *both* the evolving mythology and the experience of people in the communities, without the dominant influence of any single leader; the result of a collective experience over a *long* time. The other way that traditions begin is when they're formed around the charisma of an inspired teacher like Buddha, Jesus, or Mohammed. Some individual's powerful philosophy motivates people to rally around them. This group then traditionally celebrates the insights and anniversaries that arise from identifiable, specific inspired events.

---

[1] *Something of Value*, Robert Ruark, Doubleday & Company, Inc., 1955.

A newly married couple will negotiate how to celebrate birthdays, Halloween, etc. Their traditions will evolve and often become some collaboration of what they've each done in the past. Over the course of five or ten years the new couple develops a collective experience of how to celebrate their life—from sharing food and lovemaking to anniversaries and funerals. This takes a long time.

The overall difficulty in surrendering to spiritual principles (which are new "traditions" for addicts) arises from being unsure of their viability. This is similar to becoming willing to let go of character defects at Step Six. It's hard to let go of, or modify, your old traditions if you don't trust they'll be replaced with something of value. Addicts getting recovered too often get trapped in debilitating limbo between the old and new ways. Here are two definitions (abridged for this discussion):

Tradition: 1. The passing down of elements of a culture from generation to generation, especially by oral communication. 2. a. A mode of thought or behavior followed by a people continuously from generation to generation; a custom or usage. b. A set of such customs and usages viewed as a coherent body of precedents influencing the present: followed family tradition in dress and manners. 3. A time-honored practice or set of such practices.

Custom: 1. A practice followed by people of a particular group or region. 2. A habitual practice of a person: my custom of reading a little before sleep. 3. Law. A common tradition or usage so long established that it has the force or validity of law. [2]

What's the point of having traditions?

- They create structure and cohesiveness in groups.
- They bring people together and create unity.
- They can be used for problem-solving: If you don't know what to do in a given situation, do the traditional thing.
- They can offer both a personal and a collective identity.
- Life, and the calamities it presents, are bigger than any individual. Traditions, within families and communities, allow people to face the enormity of life with more expectation of success.

Mom's Birthday

The family next door religiously gathers together to celebrate Mom's birthday (just like they did for Grandmother's birthday). Mom expects it, and Dad says so. It's so entrenched it seems like it has parliamentary approval, and besides, it's a tradition—everyone just always does it.

---

[2] Both from *The American Heritage® Dictionary of the English Language, Third Edition,* © 1996, Houghton Mifflin Company. Electronic version.

A week before Mom's birthday, two of her adult children get in a very nasty argument. One decides they're never talking to the other again. Ever. Period! Dad hears about the fight and phones each one. He says: "Mom's birthday is coming up. I'm looking forward to seeing you at the party." Each of the adult-children protests. Dad says: "Patch it up for the party. You can continue your fight after. I'll see you next Sunday at noon. It's *Mom's birthday*." The kids show up. (If one or both of them don't, there will be a heavy price to pay.)

Granted, rigidly adhering to tradition can be unwise. But clearly, tradition can often be used to foster harmony and resolve conflict.

Traditions operate on different levels: nuclear family, social, corporate, community, province, state, country, and international. They operate from many different perspectives: ethnic heritage, gender, geographic area, political association, and religious denomination. Family and local customs vary, i.e. Christmas in rural Quebec is very different from Christmas in California or Scotland; a grandparent's birthday celebration is different from a grandchild's. As you read the following short list of traditions, realize that as much as they operate on social levels and from different cultural perspectives, they are also uniquely personalized.

- birthdays, opening presents, eating and food customs,
- funerals, memorial services, anniversaries, weddings, stags, stagettes, graduations, class reunions, vacations, holidays, summer camp, spring break, visiting relatives,
- special-interest group celebrations, business conventions, Stonewall, Halloween, Valentine's Day, Labor Day, New Year's Eve, Independence Day, Canada Day, Remembrance Day, Armistice Day, Women's Day, awards ceremonies, Gay Pride, community festivals, pageants,
- celebrations in agriculture, technology, beauty, strength, art, any of the four seasons, amateur sports, theater, music, animal husbandry, hobbies, swap-meets, rodeos,
- family: Dad's chair, Mom's chair, Dad at the head of the table, TV rituals, chores, responsibilities, codes of family loyalty, codes of conduct, manners, the division of work,
- celebrations of the life, work, or death of famous people,
- rituals and traditions at mosque, synagogue, cathedral, monastery, retreat center, cloister, temple, sweat lodge, feast, coven, or church (any denomination),
- Hockey Night in Canada, World Cup Soccer, Monday Night Football, Kentucky Derby, The World Series, Grand Prix.

Traditions and customs carry tremendous influence and have powerful expectations regarding their celebration. One result of them remaining unexamined is they often end up having the force and validity of law, but they really aren't anything more than tradition. People know that if they want to stay out of trouble, they should do the traditional thing. As soon as people start breaking traditions, other people give them a hard time (and can be quite vicious), so people comply with tradition to avoid rejection or mistreatment. They'll be "accepted" and fit in, even though it may be against one of their secret beliefs; they'll comply, but at what cost?

Here's an awareness exercise: On paper, list thirty traditions/customs that affect your life. Now reflect carefully and evaluate each one for Participation/Interest, and then again separately for Spiritual Conflict.

Participation/Interest	Spiritual Conflict
• enjoy the tradition; look forward to it and participate eagerly: + 10	• the tradition embodies spiritual integrity and offers support: + 10
• pleasantly involved but not eager: + 5	• some spiritual value but not a lot: + 5
• not affected; notice it only in passing: 0	• no noticeable spiritual value, but nothing contrary to spiritual principles: 0
• dislike it and participate because of pressure to comply; reluctantly go along and put on a happy face: - 5	• noticeable, but not severely detrimental effect on spirituality: - 5
• strong dislike and participate with concealed disdain and anger: - 10	• decidedly contradicts spiritual principles; obviously detrimental: - 10

Reflect carefully on each of the thirty traditions you identified. Evaluate how each one does or does not conflict with your emotional well-being in getting recovered. What's your level of interest? Be aware of how it may or may not be in conflict with spiritual principles and getting recovered.

Guilt and Tyranny Under Tradition

Fear and shame are respectively, the predominant emotional characteristics of the first and second stages of childhood development. Fear and shame are primarily associated with pre-verbal developmental issues. Guilt (predominant in the third stage) is the major emotional consideration when children become capable of talking in sentences. Guilt is post-verbal.

For a person to understand the relationship between rules and behavior and feelings of guilt, it's necessary to be able to articulate ideas—a function of words and sentences (the intellect). Being able to articulate ideas requires a certain level of intellectual-verbal acuity; only then can rules be understood. Once rules are understood as a situational preference of the authority figure, the transgression of rules is understood as specific to some usually arbitrary circumstance. Guilt is the sensation that arises when rules are broken. When you feel *guilty*, you've broken a rule.[3]

Rules are abstract and arbitrary. Language is also abstract. Children must be able to "think" before they can negotiate and comprehend rules. When children can articulate simple word ideas they can comprehend simple rules. But, when children are forced to appreciate the consequences of breaking or adhering to rules *before* they are capable of understanding the concept of rules, then shame and fearful confu-

---

[3] There are other considerations which will be explored in *Facets of Personal Transformation*, but for this discussion, these generalities are sufficient.

sion are the result. Punishing people for not following or appreciating rules, before they can understand the nature of rules, is shaming, frightening and harmful.

As a *non-*addict adult, if you feel shame and/or fear when you unknowingly or *un*intentionally break a rule, there's more than likely a developmental dislocation present. In addicts, they'll feel shame and fear when they unintentionally break a rule. In addicts, however, this may be indicative of childhood development problems (just as it is with non-addict people who have unresolved developmental issues), and it will *also* be derivative of their addiction—from the fusion of emotional experiences and breaking rules in their self-annihilating acting out. Aside from any personal dynamics and their acting out, this "addict double-jeopardy" is also related to culturally imposed guilt which I spoke to earlier. It's very complicated.

The value of a rule is relative to the circumstance it governs. The rule may be a good rule, like honesty; but to a thief, honesty is a bad rule (in relation to thievery). If your family tradition is blood-loyalty and codes of silence, should you become open and honest about family secrets, you'll feel guilty because you're breaking the established family tradition. In the transition from addicted, dysfunctional traditions (like codes of silence or dishonesty) to the spiritual principle of veracity, you'll feel guilty for being honest until you've properly oriented yourself to the new rules of conduct. This takes a *long* time.

Earlier I mentioned the cycle of **Desire – Action – Guilt – Aversion – Regression**. It is here this comes into play.

(1) Desire (to heal): I'm sick and exhausted. I'm dying. I want to change my life. I want to get recovered. I'm really going to do it this time. I'm serious.

(2) Action (towards the desire): I'll quit acting out, stop attending addictive social events, change social groups, go to meetings (do whatever). I'll tell the truth. I will *not* attend events where there is drug use, heavy alcohol use, disrespect, etc. This may require I leave an abusive or addicted relationship, change jobs, and/or not attend family or social events. These are difficult changes with noticeable consequences (guilt, punishment, shame, fear) but I'll do them. I'm determined.

(3) Guilt/Fear (about breaking tradition): I'm not going home for Christmas. (I feel ashamed and guilty.) I'm not going to my best friend's birthday. (I feel guilty.) I'm not attending the company summer picnic. (I feel afraid and guilty.) I have to leave my spouse. (I feel stupid, ashamed, guilty.)

(4) Aversion (to #3, the guilt, fear, and shame): Getting recovered, not acting out, being honest, is *too* hard. What about my family? friends? career? social life? reputation? I can't handle recovery; meaning can't handle the fear, guilt, shame, and other consequences of new behavior.

(5) Regression: Abandon the original desire for healing, spirituality, honesty, integrity (at #1) to avoid the struggle/pain of changing rules and traditions at #s 2 & 3: Therapy is too expensive. I'll wait until after the party. I'll give my boyfriend-girlfriend-spouse-boss another chance. I'll wait until my parents die. I'll start after Christmas. I'll quit after I've pirated all the software I need; *then* I'll be honest. Next month I'll... leave, grow up, throw away the porn, quit the affair, stop stealing, get sober, move, or confess. I'll try again, after the snow melts. I will. Honest.

The experience of failure (regression at #5) becomes an additional, invisible burden—another layer of emotional scar tissue. This is associated with a perceived double-bind—feeling guilty for participating in some activity because they're breaking program/spiritual principles; or feeling guilty for adhering to spiritual principles and refusing to participate in established (but unhealthy) traditions.

They're now more deeply entrenched in self-annihilation. They'll invariably relapse. Time passes and they experience another desperate desire to change. The cycle starts over and they develop a fatalistic acceptance of recidivism and relapse. The mindset of repetitive inadequacy becomes entrenched in "recovery", which is partly rooted in the difficulty of abandoning old rituals and traditions.[4]

In many families, the dominant authority figure imposes the family's traditions by edict. Conflict often results, especially when either the authority figure or the traditions are perceived as restrictive by "underlings" seeking autonomy. The more restricting the traditions or autocratic the authority, the more likely the revolt.

Families that are molded on dictatorships (benevolent or otherwise) always carry an element of tyranny.[5] In these closed systems, saying No to any tradition because "you don't want to", meaning trying to assert personal preference, is never sufficient reason to excuse yourself from participation. These autocratic environments, where children are not allowed to say No, often extend into adulthood. People end up participating in certain marriages, careers, and lifestyles, even though they really don't want to. This has all manner of consequences from trivial to horrific.

When addicts in recovery are unable to say No in a way that establishes boundaries or appropriate levels of participation, it's too quickly assumed this is a family or pre-addictions issue. But, addicts often have periods of intellectual acuity in their addiction and realize they "want" to say no to their addiction, but cannot. To personify this: The addiction is the dominant authority figure of the addict's life and the addict wanting to say 'No' (assert personal preference) is insufficient.

The repetitive inability to say No in addiction is a condition that may appear to have its origin in childhood, that was then carried through their addiction and into recovery. This isn't necessarily so. Yes, this may have originated in childhood; it *will* have some origin in addiction. Regardless, the resulting behavior and consequences are the same. Do not too-quickly assume the cause of "poor boundaries" is a developmental/pre-addiction concern. [Note: For abstinence-available addictions (p. 16) this dynamic is a seriously complicating factor in maintaining abstinence.]

Society makes demands on everyone. As much as there may be comfort in knowing that many people do as you do, and that democracy may be the best form of government for trying to get it right most of the time, "majority rule" is risky. Popu-

---

[4] In Chapter 11, I spoke about Relapse Prevention Plans. Plan #1 presented relapse as almost inevitable. This cycle is very often the dynamic that has set up that particular fatalistic view of recovery.
[5] This is not meant to include age-appropriate prohibitions that speak to the considered safety of children.

larity is nothing more than a guarantee of popularity. Democracy ends up with whatever most people think is right (the popular perspective) being imposed on those who differ, both in and outside of the majority view. As soon as most people in a group do a given thing, there's the very real possibility of tyranny of the majority.[6]

A tradition is self-perpetuating, and is proof only of itself. The assumption that traditional behavior is right is what justifies exorbitant peer pressure to ensure compliance and punishment for non-compliance. Should someone surrender to peer pressure and participate in a tradition they'd rather not (or participate differently than the power brokers would prefer), there's resentment about doing the traditional thing. Bitterness that underlies begrudging compliance with tradition can motivate all manner of cruelty towards others.

Regarding participation in traditions, there are these two considerations: (1) If you suddenly stop doing something you've done for a long time, it may seriously disrupt your family, friends, or coworkers. It will have a major impact on others and on yourself. If you're going to change your life, be considerate when the change will be an imposition on other people.[7] Expect long periods of adjustment. (2) Carefully examine your motives for not participating in some tradition. Sometimes "I will not" is defiance for its own sake (dysfunctional independence). This declaration may be an unkind cover-up for something else.

It's important that you understand which traditions you're interested in, which ones you're not, and what motivates you to participate in them (or not). Knowing this information allows you to evaluate the spiritual, emotional, and social cost of participation or abstention, and to choose accordingly.

Traditions embody rules. Guilt arises from breaking rules. To resolve guilt, examine *both* the tradition (the rule) that you broke, *and* your behavior. Decide which you need to change: the rule, or your behavior. If it's a good rule (or tradition), stop breaking it; if it's a dysfunctional rule, change your rule (do not participate in the tradition). This is the process, but it is a lot more arduous and complicated than the simple equation presented here. It may be wise to consider well-conducted long-term therapy when challenging traditions.

Following a tradition fosters acceptance and popularity. Defying a tradition foments rejection, but may be what is necessary to acquire spiritual integrity.

Faith and Trust

Faith: 1. Confident belief in the truth, value, or trustworthiness of
a person, an idea, or a thing. 2. Belief that does not rest on logical
proof or material evidence. 3. Loyalty to a person or thing; allegiance. 4. The theological virtue defined as secure belief in God
and a trusting acceptance of God's will.

---

[6] For a slightly different perspective see *Blues ain't nothing but a good soul feeling bad*, Sheldon Kopp, Fireside/Simon&Schuster, 1992, entry for Dec 6.

[7] Adherence to spiritual principles requires this to be true: I cannot "succeed" in any endeavor when my success is built on abuse, dishonesty, or detracts from another's dignity.

Trust (noun): 1. Firm reliance on the integrity, ability, or charac-ter of a person or thing. 2. Reliance on something: in the future; in another's character.
Trusted (verb): 1. To have or place reliance; depend upon: Trust in... the Lord, destiny. 2. To be confident; hope. 3. To expect with assurance; assume: I trust that you will be on time.[8]

There are three ways that people acquire faith. One is to adopt the procla-mations of some higher authority who says: "This is good (or bad or right or wrong).", and to have faith because of who said it. This can prove to be a weak basis for faith because as soon as some more impressive authority-figure appears on the scene, faith can be undermined and confusion results. The second way faith is ac-quired is by personal experience and research—individual trial and effort, and the rejection of all outside authority. The resulting values and beliefs are valid, but for one person. They very often defeat community participation. Charity and egalitarian-ism are unavailable. The third, and what appears to be the most reliable and satisfying avenue to faith and belief, is by combining historical tradition and personal experience. This third way establishes the context for the traditions of AA.

"Henceforth we would have to rely upon spiritual principles, as set forth in the Twelve Traditions."[9] Why rely on these traditions? There are four sources of per-sonal experience which altogether make the AA traditions a dependable and reliable basis for transformation out of addictions.

1) The experience of active addiction—self-destruction, shame, pain; your awareness of the continuous and consistent results of acting out, proves acting out was unreliable for life-management. You may not know what to do to make your life better, but you certainly know what will make it worse. That experience is something you can rely on, and is included in molding your needs to the AA traditions.

2) The subtle changes you notice in yourself as you painstakingly complete the steps, those consistent personal changes, are an "authority" that you can rely on. What you're doing is not just "the steps". What you're doing is, by completing the steps and adhering to principles, you are learning the importance of these traditions.

3) Notice the improvement in others who are behaving according to the steps and traditions, and notice also the absence of improvement in those who aren't applying themselves to this. This promotes Right Association and through observa-tion of others, you come to rely on traditions that have spiritual integrity.

4) As you complete this work, and progress beyond the level of spiritual newcomer, there's an intrinsic realization of the obvious universal value of the tradi-tions which embody the five spiritual principles. You can rely on the innate truth about the inherent good that is beyond any person or personal ideology. Once you accesses this *a priori* knowledge through experience and meditation, it becomes an authority you can rely on.

---

[8] Abridged definitions from *The American Heritage® Dictionary of the English Language, Third Edition,* © 1996, Houghton Mifflin Company. Electronic version.
[9] *Alcoholics Anonymous Comes of Age*, Alcoholics Anonymous Publishing, Inc., 1977, p. 213.

These four sources of authority are actually a delicate combination of personal and social traditional experience, that was outlined (three paragraphs above) as the third option for acquiring faith and belief. With these, your faith will become quite unshakable and you'll come to rely on spiritual principles in the traditions.

Values & Tradition

Here's a situation: *Lou is well known in a twelve-step program, has years of abstinence, and talks about God, prayer, and the importance of honesty and respect for others. Lou (and Lou's spouse) are friends with another married couple. One member of the other couple tells Lou privately they're having an extramarital affair. Lou is now privy to the lying, manipulation, and betrayal in the other couple's relationship. Several days later, when Lou's spouse notices an unexplained tension and initiates a private conversation with Lou about this, Lou is evasive. Lou's spouse now becomes quietly anxious. Lou doesn't confront the adulterer, doesn't say anything to the betrayed spouse who is also a friend; Lou's spouse remains noticeably troubled by the mysterious tension. Lou continues to share at meetings about the importance of rigorous honesty, respect, and spiritual principles.*

What identifies spiritual people is not only that they value spiritual principles, but abide by them in the face of personal cost. Values are a belief about the worthiness of something or somebody. If a person doesn't adhere to their values; if there's no personal investment in upholding the "value", it's not a value, it's a convenience. Addicts who remain "in recovery" are long on conveniences and short on values. People cannot proclaim that honesty is of high value, and maintain integrity, while they continue to lie or participate in behavior that's deceitful; or where deceit affects their life, to allow that dishonesty or disrespect to go unchallenged.

To identify what you value, notice what you give your time to, how tenaciously you defend some behaviors, or the discrepancy between your thoughts and private behavior, and what you present to others. On any day of leisure, should you spend four hours on the golf course, two hours watching sports, twenty minutes playing with your children, and three minutes praying, you've identified your values and priorities. No amount of protest will alter the truth of this statement: What you love is what you give your time to; or what you love is what captures your energy. Your behavior, including your words and thoughts, are a reflection of what you value.

What fear causes you to be duplicitous? What addiction causes you to deceive others about the values you claim to embrace? These questions are worthy of careful examination so you can challenge yourself, and thereby develop integrity.

Addictions and Traditions

What I'm going to describe next aren't traditions in a sociological sense. I'm going to describe addictive, symptomatic behavior as "traditional", using that as a metaphor to create some clarity about one aspect of the task that awaits an addict getting recovered. There is a group of standard, "traditional" behaviors that addicts or alcoholics display, which represent the symptoms of the disease. A successful alcoholic/addict will act out, drink or use, lie, cheat, intimidate, manipulate, be violent, defiant, or compliant, and sound convincing as they blame others so as to extricate themselves from responsibility. These comprise the social behaviors that addicts traditionally display.

The more a person participates in these "traditional" addictive behaviors, the more they are successful at self-annihilation. It takes a lot of practice, talent, and determination for addicts to beat themselves into the all-encompassing mess that they do, and to blame others for the mess they, themselves, create.

The goal of getting recovered is to live with less personal cost and greater spiritual rewards—to abandon traditional/addictive behaviors and adopt spiritual behaviors. As addicts transform through their own hard work, they come to have faith in new principles and values, that are reflected in behaviors that are traditionally spiritual in nature. Only then can they confidently abandon their old lifestyle, because they have something of value with which to replace it.

Washington Temperance Society

The temperance movement in the United States (c. 1826 – 1836) was focused entirely on alcoholism and drunkenness, and generally geared toward keeping drinkers away from alcohol. Already-practicing alcoholics were believed to be doomed sinners unless they completely and vigorously immersed themselves in the more fundamental, Protestant-Christian values.

The Washington Temperance Society ("The Washingtonians"[10]) started in April, 1840, in Baltimore, Maryland, to prove that a drunk could, in fact, be saved. It was *"...in a spirit of fun to challenge the now waning temperance movement... ,"*[11] that six men (while drinking in a local tavern) formed a group, and, on the spot, paid twenty-five cents in dues, elected officers, and each agreed to bring a new person to the meeting they planned for the following week. They each signed a pledge to create *"...a society for our mutual benefit, and to guard against a pernicious practice which is injurious to our health, standing, and families, and do pledge ourselves as gentlemen that we will not drink any spiritous or malt liquors, wine, or cider."*[12]

By the first anniversary, there were about 1,000 *"reformed drunkards"* and 5,000 other members and friends. In three years, their membership grew to between 100,000 and 600,000 *"...recovered sots"*. Splinter organizations sprang up with varied political or temperance-related agendas. However, according to Dr. Milton Maxwell, the movement declined quickly because its *"membership, purposes and ideology were inextricably mixed with those of the temperance movement, and it turned into something it did not start out to be. ...the original purpose of rehabilitat-*

---

[10] The Washingtonians are referred to in *Alcoholics Anonymous Comes of Age*, Alcoholics Anonymous Publishing, Inc., 1977, p. 124.

[11] From the AA newsletter, *Box 459*, Vol. 34, No. 5 / October-November 1987; Fate of Washingtonians..., p. 6. That article uses as its source a monograph by Milton A. Maxwell, Ph.D., former chairperson of the AA General Service Board, and professor of sociology, Center of Alcohol Studies, Rutgers University, New Jersey.

[12] Ibid.

ing alcoholics was lost to sight."[13] By 1845 the Washingtonian movement had largely disappeared.

The article in *Box 459* goes on to point out these five distinct differences between the Washingtonians and AA, which allow AA to remain effective: *"1. Exclusively alcoholic membership. 2. Singleness of purpose. 3. An adequate, clear-cut program of recovery. 4. Anonymity. 5. Hazard-avoiding Traditions."*[14]

From the Washingtonians in 1845, leap ahead about 80 years to England.

The Oxford Group

The Oxford Group embodied *"...a campaign for the renaissance of the practice among men of the truths of simple Christianity..."*.[15] It was in a large part focused on alcoholism, but anything under the general heading of "sin" was included. The Oxford Group began with a Lutheran minister, Dr. Frank Buchman (twice nominated for the Nobel Peace Prize). Dr. Buchman was in England in 1908 when *"he caught a vision of a Christ-led world untrammeled by Sin."*[16] Dr. Buchman then traveled the world carrying this message. Eventually, in England, at Oxford, his message found energetic support. In the mid-1920's his vision caught on and expanded rapidly from there.

The Oxford Group adhered adamantly to the view that Christianity, through Jesus Christ, was the only acceptable avenue to redemption. Redemption, here, means to recover a Christian soul that was pawned or mortgaged for the pleasures in sin. [Sin in this context contains some Christian righteousness and prohibitions regarding morality. Here, it's much more than simply "missing the mark" as discussed earlier.]

The four points of the Oxford Group were *"1. Absolute Honesty. 2. Absolute Purity. 3. Absolute Unselfishness. 4. Absolute Love."*[17] These four points were to be demonstrated in *"four practical spiritual activities: (1) The sharing of our sins and temptations with another... ; (2) Surrender of our life, past, present, and future... ; (3) Restitution to all whom we have wronged directly or indirectly... ; and, (4) Listening to, accepting, relying on God's Guidance and carrying it out in everything we do or say, great or small."*[18]

The Oxford Group's four points and the related spiritual activities (although from a traditional Christian perspective, and adamant about the hegemony of Christianity) have an unmistakable thematic similarity to the Twelve Steps. The *"early A.A. got its ideas... straight from the Oxford Groups and directly from Sam Shoemaker, their former leader in America, and from nowhere else."*[19]

"At the [1955 AA] *Convention it was widely appreciated for the first time that nobody had* <u>invented</u> *Alcoholics Anonymous, that many streams of influence and*

---

[13] The AA newsletter: *Box 459*, Vol. 34, No. 5/October-November 1987; <u>Fate of Washingtonians</u>..., p. 6.
[14] Ibid., p. 7.
[15] *What Is The Oxford Group?*, by The Layman With A Notebook, Oxford University Press, 1933, p. 3.
[16] Ibid., p. 13.
[17] Ibid., p. 7.
[18] Ibid., p. 8-9.
[19] *Alcoholics Anonymous Comes of Age*, Alcoholics Anonymous Publishing, Inc., 7th printing, 1977, p. 39.

many people, some of them non-alcoholics, had helped, by the grace of God, to achieve AA's purpose."[20] That the cofounders didn't invent the AA process is not a criticism of AA or its cofounders, nor does it demean what they figured out or wrote. They, with much gracious help from non-alcoholics (and, it appears, some divine-like inspiration), made clear two things: (1) recovery from addictions depended upon achieving and maintaining a spiritually principled life; and, (2) the exact path that made recovery possible for the alcoholic [or addict] who really wanted it, *and* was willing to go to any lengths to get it.

Addicts struggle to make some kind of sense out of Life. They secretly despair at the senseless, destructive behavior they inflict on themselves, and search for some meaning to their apparently pointless existence—no differently than billions of other people over thousands of years. One truth that was made clear in 1935 was that while in any addiction, it is not possible to give meaning to Life. This can only be done when an addict is abstinent and participating in sound spiritual endeavor.

Unlike other people who wish to be spiritual, addicts have to start their pilgrimage from inside an addiction. This requires a different focus of effort and, at the outset, makes for a more arduous journey. *Alcoholics Anonymous* offers a path to transformation that [virtually] guarantees results. People with addictions are not pariahs; they too, belong in the world, but not all of them will find their way to a twelve-step program. And, sadly, many addicts in twelve-step programs never touch the true potential of what the original twelve steps have to offer.

Alcoholics Anonymous & Tradition

I offer only a few very brief comments on the development of the traditions of AA. This section is intended as neither an exposition of the origin of the traditions, nor an analysis of their obvious content. *Twelve Steps and Twelve Traditions* and *Alcoholics Anonymous Comes of Age* contain a wealth of information on the traditions' content and origin. Here, the purpose is to encourage Meditations on Wisdom in order to unveil the spiritual principles within the traditions themselves.

The traditions are presented as "rules for groups", which is important. However, they are much more than guidelines for group organization. They can also be perceived as a personal guide for spiritual living that manifests inside you, just like the steps—they're a way to create spiritual integrity in your behavior while participating in the communities that inform your world.

"Even as early as 1945, the solution to group problems by correspondence had put a large volume of work on [AA] Headquarters. ... The basic ideas for the Twelve Traditions of Alcoholics Anonymous came directly out of this vast correspondence."[21] Thousands of letters, over fifteen years or so, formed the basis of the Twelve Traditions. The collective, successful experiences of the members, which reflected the most effective ways to overcome addictions, be spiritual, and "carry the

---

[20] *Alcoholics Anonymous Comes of Age*, Alcoholics Anonymous Publishing, Inc., 7th printing, 1977, p. 2, emphasis theirs.
[21] Ibid., p. 203.

message" in a group—were distilled into guidelines for a successful spiritual *community* experience. [This is a compliment to the maintenance steps which are the guidelines for a successful spiritual *personal* experience.] In carrying the message to others, service to a higher power could now be demonstrated through the groups.

Throughout the AA twelve-step literature, there is never an obscuring of the truth that: *"Unless each A.A. member follows to the best of his ability the suggested Twelve Steps of recovery, he almost certainly signs his own death warrant." "We must obey certain principles or we die."*[22] *"The same stern threat applies to the group itself. Unless there is approximate conformity to A.A.'s Twelve Traditions, the group too can deteriorate and die. So we of A.A. do obey spiritual principles, first because we must and ultimately because we love the kind of life such obedience brings."*[23] This refers to spiritual principles inherent in the steps *and* the traditions.

The phrase *"...ultimately because we love..."* is a direct reference to the transformation of attitude regarding humility that happens at Step Seven. In this context, a love of obedience is rooted in humility. That passage also contains an implied reference to the difference between awareness and enlightenment. Awareness only allows humility to be perceived as a "must", and enlightenment through prayer and meditations on wisdom allows humility to become a cherished value.

Addicts who ignore any aspect of any tradition are acting in an *un*spiritual manner. Notice those who dominate business meetings or push personal agendas in twelve-step groups. With this happening, it's impossible for the group to carry the message of a spiritual awakening because the group becomes representative of the will of the dominant members, and not representative of spiritual principles.

Just as the maintenance steps keep individuals spiritual in their private relationship with God, the traditions keep individuals spiritual in their relationships with each other. The steps create spirituality inside you. The traditions create spirituality inside relationships and groups. The traditions are not "for the group"; they're for the people who are in the group.

"Implicit throughout A.A.'s Traditions is the confession that our fellowship has its sins ...these defects threaten us continually... But the twelve traditions also point straight at many of our individual defects... The Traditions guarantee the equality of all members and the independence of all groups."[24] How do you reconcile (a) the sins of the fellowship, (b) group-threatening defects, (c) individual defects, (d) equality of all members; and, (e) the independence of all groups? Through obedience to the spiritual principles that are embodied in the traditions.

"Henceforth we would have to rely upon spiritual principles, as set forth in the twelve traditions."[25] This doesn't mean there are twelve principles. Recall that a tradition is a guideline or a "rule of conduct" that carries authority because of its

[22] *Alcoholics Anonymous Comes of Age*, Alcoholics Anonymous Publishing, Inc., 1977, p. 119, emphasis theirs.
[23] Ibid., pp. 119-120.
[24] Ibid., p. 96, emphasis added. "...*the equality of all members*..." is egalitarianism. See App. II, Humility.
[25] Ibid., p. 213.

(apparent) historical efficiency in problem solving and its ability to create social harmony. There are five principles embodied in twelve traditions.

Recall that *Alcoholics Anonymous* advises that the purpose of that book is to help alcoholics find a power greater than themselves which will solve their problem (p. 45). Both the steps and the traditions are of a single view: to "train" an addict in how to become spiritual and maintain obedience to spiritual principles—but one is from an inner-personal perspective (the steps), and the other from a social perspective (the traditions). The traditions are designed to veto politics and impression management at the group level (relationships), and maintain a spiritual purpose in people, while they organize the group's chores and carry out its responsibilities.

Some Specifics

Each tradition, like each step, has specific tasks and conduct guidelines associated with it. The obvious intent is to harmonize the relationships within groups. However, immediately under the surface of the group's operation is the ever-present obligation to carry the message of a spiritual awakening. The traditions are guidelines that ensure the visible presence of spiritual principles. Each member is [supposed to be] representative of a spiritual awakening, which "should" be reflected in the group's organization and operation. Groups are a public forum for carrying the spiritual-awakening message of getting recovered (and no other message). A pleasant social life often results from group membership, but that's neither the message to carry, nor the goal of group membership. Every time a tradition is *not* followed in a group's operation, the message of a spiritual awakening is obscured, and politics and personality (impression management) are thereby placed above principle.

The AA traditions[26] are presented here for convenient reference. *Twelve Steps and Twelve Traditions* has a detailed explanation of their organizational intent.

> "*1. Our common welfare should come first; personal recovery depends upon A.A. unity.*
> *2. For our group purpose there is but one ultimate authority—a loving God as he may express himself in our group conscience. Our leaders are but trusted servants; they do not govern.*
> *3. The only requirement for A.A. membership is the desire to stop drinking.*
> *4. Each group should be autonomous except in matters affecting other groups or A.A. as a whole.*
> *5. Each group has but one primary purpose—to carry its message to the alcoholic who still suffers.*
> *6. An A.A. group ought never endorse, finance, or lend the A.A. name to any related facility or outside enterprise, lest problems of money, property, and prestige divert us from our primary purpose.*

---

[26] *Twelve Steps and Twelve Traditions*, Alcoholics Anonymous World Services, Inc., 1995, pp. 9-13.

7. Every A.A. group ought to be fully self supporting, declining outside contributions.

8. Alcoholics Anonymous should remain forever non-professional, but our service centers may employ special workers.

9. A.A. as such, ought never be organized; but we may create service boards or committees directly responsible to those they serve.

10. Alcoholics Anonymous has no opinion on outside issues; hence the A.A. name ought never be drawn into public controversy.

11. Our public relations policy is based on attraction rather than promotion; we need always maintain personal anonymity at the level of press, radio, and films.

12. Anonymity is the spiritual foundation of all of our traditions, ever reminding us to place principles before personalities."

Spiritual service to others reflects service to a higher power. It's humility in action; the foundation of all of AA's Traditions. With the work you've done to understand what Meditations on Wisdom are, it'll be fairly straightforward to study and discover which spiritual principles are prominent and which are subordinate within each tradition.

The five spiritual principles are demonstrated in relationships and groups by surrendering personal agendas to spiritual agendas. Twelve-step groups are too easily converted into drama clubs and soapbox arenas for spiritually undisciplined people.

In recent years, as devotion to personal spirituality has been disintegrating regarding the twelve steps, so has group integrity regarding the twelve traditions. This disintegration arises from a misalliance of commitment and an unhealthy influence of psychology. It's a variation of the idea of the Evil Blue Meanies that I spoke of earlier: No one outside AA can understand us. But… This is now manifesting inside twelve-step groups. i.e. Very few people inside "the program" can understand *me*, so I'll start my own special "recovery group", just for *my own* unique problems, because "that other kind of addict" can't understand (me) — an arrogant perception of terminal uniqueness.[27] This internal splintering can be stopped only by reliance upon, and obedience to, the traditions and the spiritual principles they embody.

The Myth of "The Movement"

One noticeable aspect of the mess that twelve-step programs are in is related to the subtle perception of many people that they are a "movement". A movement, in a sociological sense, is some organized effort or a series of organized

---

[27] (1) Earlier in this chapter, and in Ch.1, I discussed the shame and insecurity underneath flamboyant "sharing" of tales of excess and debauchery. Those dramatically expressed feelings of inferiority contribute to the group dislocation I describe here. (2) Recall the discussion of Four Important Topics in Ch. 4. In a psychologically oriented program, addiction of preference, acting-out and self-harm, detoxing, and abstinence remain important because of the grand "I". Within AA these create "regular AA" and "special-admission" groups for just old-times, only newcomers, only women or men or gays or lesbians, etc. Within NA there's regular NA, and Cocaine Anonymous, and Marijuana Anonymous. The creation of special admission twelve-step groups within twelve-step groups (internal splintering) is how disintegration and lack of spiritual commitment shows up.

activities where people promote some objective. The Suffragettes, Greenpeace, the Washingtonians, and Recycling are movements.

Twelve-step meetings are places where alcoholics or addicts can remind themselves of, and develop and enhance their own spiritual orientation to, Life. Meetings are [supposed] to provide a place to do this, or when invited, to help other people do this. Addicts getting recovered have [or should have] nothing to prove to anyone, and nothing to convince anyone of. They should work towards being spiritual, minding their own business, avoiding gossip, and not willfully debating the "issues". There's no planet to save, no axe to grind, no fundraising drives, no delegates to represent, no people to convert, no slogans to chant, and no morality to promote. Proselytizing is against the steps and the traditions.

Twelve-step programs are not movements. Thinking that they are assigns to them a political agenda that has no place in spiritual endeavor.

Self Supporting

Being financially self-supporting is the common assumption. Addicts getting recovered must pay their own way: rent, books, coffee, pamphlets, all by donations during twelve-step meetings. Certainly this is true; however, with the changes in our culture, "self-supporting" has become a more complex and much broader issue. What follows is subtle and worthy of careful consideration, especially regarding the first and fifth spiritual principles.

Modern government requires an important separation between church and state. Government grants are not awarded to organizations wanting to help people find God. Asking a government committee for money for spiritual pursuits will not be successful. However, asking for funding so people afflicted with the "medical disease" of addictions can become rehabilitated members of society (meaning law-abiding taxpayers) has proven successful, even though the success rate for rehabilitation is notoriously low. Receiving government/corporate money to treat alcoholics and addicts requires a significant suppression of spirituality in favor of psychology and social rehabilitation. The vague euphemism "a twelve-step model of treatment" hides all manner of reframing and misrepresentation to get money.

As a result, recovery houses and treatment centers that solicit government funding (whether it's applications for grants or for social allowance cheques), or that solicit corporate sponsorship, are political organizations. Government/corporate funding of "the twelve-step model of treatment" [sic] has now clearly established detoxification and treatment centers as powerful twelve-stepping agencies. These agencies, that must necessarily suppress spirituality to ensure financial support, have become a major disabling force to contend with in twelve-step groups.

Literally tens-of-thousands of rehab-clients are discharged each year from government, union, or corporate funded treatment centers straight into twelve-step programs. This process carries three subtle and powerful messages: (a) psychology is the main vehicle to recovery, (b) "rehabilitation" (implying recovery) should be paid for by someone else; and, (c) the time-consuming and frustrating work of early recovery will be handled by treatment centers and professionals. All three are sweet music to the irresponsible nature of addicts.

For those people already in twelve-step programs: Rather than the difficult job of role-modeling spirituality; rather than the difficult job of being held accountable for your disinterest; rather than being truly generous of spirit and accepting; rather than challenging your own impatience; rather than have your own life interrupted by some frightened, lonely, confused newcomer, when a new person relapses today, it's *far too easy* to deflect from your own lack of commitment by telling them they need to go to rehab. "Phone me back when you're done treatment." Click.

There are six profound influences at play: (1) The deification of self-help psychology. (2) The prevalence of a quick-fix mentality and disposable consumerism. (3) Outside professional agencies, funded by governments and corporations, are taking responsibility for carrying the message to newcomers, which by necessity must down-play spirituality. Corporations don't award grants for addicts to find God, they want tax-paying consumers—whomever pays the band calls the tune. (4) Medical experts aren't maintaining an only-supportive role in treating only the derivative physical damage/detoxing etc., which was the wisdom that assisted AA in it's first thirty years. There's the ever increasing takeover by medicine and science of "addictions treatment", which a massive profit from that treatment. (5) The increase of greed and dislocation in culture, the greater disparity in the distribution of wealth, the greater levels of consumerism and having the trinkets of psychology become status-jewelry, makes for "high-end" elitist treatment. And, (6) The drastic change in demographics in meetings.

Treatment centers are generally promoted by professionals in order to create patients, clients, and incomes. They're promoted to obtain government or corporate funding; and it's all endorsed by the addict's irresponsible nature. These altogether guarantee the internal splintering of twelve-step groups, and meetings are evolving into spiritually bereft social circles and dating agencies.

These dynamics of treatment and rehab require a disastrous realignment of priorities and a reduction of twelve-step group responsibility. Altogether, these have orchestrated an insidious shift in the mindset of people in recovery. Although much slower, and of an indirectly different focus (and slickly justified under the righteous declaration of "helping"), this is *exactly* what the Washingtonians and Oxford Groups succumbed to: political and corporate alliances.[28]

Treatment-center recovery that's primarily psychological, paid for by someone other than the addict, fostered in a Victim culture, *and* endorsed by irresponsible addicts in recovery, foments disaster. In twelve-step groups there are now

---

[28] This closely parallels the massive realignment of expectations regarding therapeutic services. As many therapists raise their rates and make their services inaccessible to the majority of our society, insurance companies, social and religious organizations, employee assistance programs, government agencies, etc., are in higher demand. It bears reflection as to why addicts in the midst of their self-imposed crisis should expect others to pay for any therapy that might be required. Additionally, since insurance/government plans have severely limited amounts that can be claimed for therapy, participants never have sufficient time to accomplish anything significant. This sets up a serpentine list of harmful expectations and consequences.

prominent but vaguely defined political alliances with recovery houses, detoxifica-tion centers, and treatment centers. Within this environment, there are many people, some with very marginal training, acting as professionals paid to do twelve-step work. Government and corporate funding largely controls the "twelve-step model" of helping newcomers; and altogether, there is an overwhelming misalliance of com-mitment (discussed in Chapter 6). This has clearly put twelve-step groups on a course that's parallel to The Washingtonians and The Oxford Groups: alliances with political and corporate agencies. As a result of all of this, twelve-step programs are glaringly less effective than in decades past, and rapidly getting worse.

The steps and traditions weren't designed to serve anyone in any social con-text, which is what a movement does. Government/corporate funding will not be awarded to help people "find God". It's a short step from there to the spiritually de-feating view that twelve-step programs are movements and recovery is a psychological issue. Now that "twelve-stepping" is largely paid for by someone else, and rehabilitation is the intent, twelve-step programs will (eventually) experience the fate of The Washingtonians and The Oxford Groups.

————

If you're an addict or an alcoholic getting recovered, consider carefully that twelve-step programs aren't designed to change the worldview of addictions, nor to change anyone's view of you. They're to change your inner perception of yourself, and to thereby enable you to create a devoted relationship with a power greater than yourself. There's nothing "social" about the intent or the process of twelve-step pro-grams. They were designed to teach you how to live by spiritual principles so you could rid yourself of addictions and humbly (anonymously) serve a higher power.

I'm not suggesting that twelve-step meetings aren't supposed to be friendly or enjoyable. Social occasions outside of meetings are important. I'm *not* suggesting that treatment agencies are necessarily wrong. They have a very important part to play. However, when (i) twelve-step meetings are social occasions, (ii) spiritually oriented traditions aren't the guiding authority; and, (iii) a non-spiritual approach to newcomers is underwritten with outside "rehab" agencies in control, meetings be-come dangerously ineffective.

Meditate on the wisdom of the AA traditions. See for yourself they're much more than rules that govern the operation of groups. Learn how the traditions em-body spiritual principles, and make them personal.

The traditions are guidelines for your attitude and behavior in all your group activities. [An intimate relationship is a group activity.] Interacting with your family, your lover, your leisure-activity companions, your friends, your coworkers, and your twelve-step associates are group activities. In your commitment to a spiritual way of life, the maintenance steps keep you in personal-spiritual harmony with God; the traditions keep you in social-spiritual harmony with people.

Appendix II

The Five Spiritual Principles

These are principles that appear to me, to govern ethical spiritual endeavor. And, as I understand it, underneath the complex beauty of parables, metaphors, and mysticism, Spirituality is very practical.

There are five universal principles that, when willingly complied with and taken together, create spiritual integrity in a spiritual pilgrim. These principles would also comprise the underlying, inherent qualities that would be required for an organization, or an applied philosophy, to be spiritually ethical. Again I refer to the Manly Hall quote cited at p. 197: *"The unfolding of a man's spiritual nature is as much as exact science as mathematics..."*. Yes, the varied manifestations of *The Ground of All Being* may be mysterious, and the debates and discussions may be esoteric, but the everyday application of spirituality is neither of these.

The Fundamental Qualities of a Principle

"Principles, unlike values [or rules], *are objective and external. They operate in obedience to natural laws, regardless of conditions."*[1]

A spiritual principle would be an authentic truth, and hold within itself a universal theme, that is applicable beyond personality or culture. It would also be the foundation out of which arise beliefs and attitudes that would enable a person to rise above (be spiritual), or descend below (be soulful), the ego-constructions of self-serving convenience—beyond psychology and the related, limited vision of personal insight. Additionally, a bona fide spiritual principle would be universal enough to embrace all of the generally recognized virtues, regardless of the folk-tradition through which they are perceived, and include (in this instance) whatever virtues recovering addicts would evince to be recovered. And finally: A spiritual principle would have to be authentic enough to hold up under close scrutiny.

The general chaos and confusion around spirituality occurs most often when people take something as fundamentally universal as "spirituality" or "God", slant interpretations to cater to their coveted prejudices and insecurities, then claim that their own personal interpretation is superior to others' interpretations. Spiritual principles must be broad and flexible enough to be available to everyone at a deeply personal level. Therefore, to allow some guideline to qualify as a spiritual principle (as opposed to a rule, which is secular and limited) is no mean feat. Each spiritual principle is exactly *what* it is because it is:

---

[1] *Principle-Centered Leadership,* Stephen R. Covey, A Fireside Book, Simon & Schuster, 1992, p. 19.

- <u>Universal</u> enough to accommodate and embrace all spiritual endeavor, beyond the narrow limits of culture,
- <u>Respectful</u> of any personal symbolism of deity,
- <u>Broad</u> enough to encompass the generally recognized virtues,
- <u>Restricted</u> enough to exclude the more universal vices,
- <u>Tested</u> enough over the centuries to be trusted,
- <u>Simple</u> enough to comprehend,
- <u>Complex</u> enough to perpetually require attention,
- <u>Demanding</u> enough to require continuous effort to evince it,
- <u>Idealistic</u> enough to be always worthy of respect, and just out of reach—to keep people humble in their pursuit of it,
- <u>Specific</u> enough that it can be approached with confidence,
- <u>Achievable</u> to a degree that people can demonstrate or realize personal progress; and,
- <u>Profound</u> enough to be above pettiness.

The five principles I recommend each satisfy each of the twelve qualifications noted above. Additionally, because there are only five, there are few enough of them so people can apprehend their interrelatedness. What may be more important is that these five allow the adherents of different faiths to peacefully interact, while maintaining different beliefs. These principles can be internalized and become the behaviors of truly spiritual people.

Regardless of the circumstances people find themselves in, they would aspire to demand of themselves adherence to these principles as non-negotiable standards of behavior. To the uninitiated, the principles are probably overwhelming, and for addicts they are often viewed with disbelief and thought to be literally untenable. However, with willingness, patience, and labor (or desire, devotion, and diligence), and Right Association, they are within reach of anyone who is desirous of a truly Spiritual way of life beyond the conventionally enlightened.[2] The five principles are:

Principle #1: Respect for the Body-Temple—Respectful Self-Care

It is long known in the perennial philosophies that the Atman-Brahmin resides within, and access to *It* is through ourselves.[3] Our souls, from one perspective,

---

[2] Marshall Frady, in his book *Martin Luther King, Jr.*, Viking/Penguin Books, 2002, p. 186, offered this observation about Dr. King: *"King was indeed passing now into that far country of all true prophets ultimately: that lonely region beyond the conventionally enlightened...."* People in twelve-step programs don't have to be prophets; however, the decision at Step Three has no limits attached to it. It was voluntary, and so the standard to aspire to is that set by "God" and not by mediocre social conventions (meaning socially acceptable levels of spiritual irresponsibility associated with twelve-step psychobabble). Go beyond the pale; it's worth it.

[3] According to *Alcoholics Anonymous*, in the final analysis, it is deep within us that the Great Reality is found (p. 55). Additionally, as was mentioned earlier, there are two similar views of God residing within us, found in *Mysticism In Religion*, by Rev. W.R. Inge, University of Chicago Press, 1948, Chapter 3: Attributed to St Paul: *"...the spirit dwelling in us, or of our bodies as the temple of God... 'the body' as the 'tabernacle' of the soul while we live here* [on earth]*."* And, from Rev Inge: *"The body must be reverenced and preserved from defilement... it is the temple of the Holy Spirit."* I do not intend Christian

are the access point to, and the residence place of, the dark void out of which we arise. From there, we are animated in a manner that allows integrity in two seemingly opposite directions. People can be drawn into a appreciation of the dark, sublime mysteries of primal life and love (soulful) or can rise above to the call of light and spirit (spiritual). Harmonizing these may the intended journey of Life.

Either way, the selfish trappings of personality and culture must be left behind. Being soulful is quite a bit different than being spiritual. Spirituality might be described as manifesting the action of a deity within each of us "out" towards the world. Soulfulness is sincerely demonstrating and honoring the strength, frailty, mystery, and power at the core of our being.

Because all access to "God" ultimately begins with challenging ourselves, and ends *within* ourselves, it is our bodies, our emotions, and our thoughts through which this deity acts. Our bodies are the temples within which the essence of God resides. Contact with the soul or the spirit *begins* through and within our own physical being. Your body is literally the home of your soul and spirit, as is everyone else's the home of their own. The "body-temple" must be cared for.

Respect for the body-temple, as demonstrated by respect and healthy caring for our physical being—for others as much as ourselves—is essential. Not damaging ourselves or others through squalid living, violence, addictions, greed, or physical or emotional abuse is crucial. Nurturing the residence of the spirit is the starting place for all spiritual transformation. If you're damaging or otherwise neglecting the care of the body-temple (your own or another's physical and emotional health), you are damaging the home of the Atman-Brahmin, and therefore cannot be spiritual.

Principle #2: Veracity

This is a style of presenting honesty, and describing your perception of truth, that incorporates gentle trustworthiness. For many years, with the advent of the social movement towards health and enlightenment in the 1960s, truth was quite rightly encouraged. "Let it all hang out" became a euphemism for honesty—blunt, brutal, or otherwise. Venting was the order of the day. However, being honest and presenting your truths without regard for others is cruel and not a part of veracity. Honest communication that is angry or without respect and consideration for others will be received as abusive. The speaker will be viewed as selfish or rude, and the truth will be held suspect because of the manner in which it's delivered.

Spiritual people always speak the truth—they are consistently and *gently* honest—with all people, in all situations, at all times, regardless of the cost to themselves. This disables Impression Management. In microscopic truth-telling they always offer respect, courtesy, and kindness to others, regardless of the nature of what needs to be told.[4] You cannot be spiritual and dishonest, *or* be spiritual and

---

hegemony in this. *The Kabalah* teaches similarly, that what we consume or use (good or not good), so it is that we become. Many other religious traditions, and Buddhism, promote respectful self-care with equal style and grace.

[4] Microscopic truth-telling is a descriptive phrase that I find particularly applicable. It is from *Conscious Loving,* Gay Hendricks, Ph.D., & Kathlyn Hendricks, Ph.D., Bantam Books, 1990, Chapter 4.

mean while being honest. Spirituality always requires gentleness, trustworthiness, and courtesy in microscopic truth-telling; no exceptions. That is veracity.

Principle #3: Humility

Often largely misunderstood, especially by people with addictions, humility is rare and elusive, and becoming ever more so. As soon as anyone talks about humility as a personal endeavor, it slips away. There are two aspects of humility that must be incorporated in both behavior and attitude in order for it to have integrity.

The **first** (too often ignored) requirement for humility involves adhering to a sincerely egalitarian philosophy as the foundation of all interaction. Being sincerely egalitarian, in attitude and outlook, must be universal, and operate generously and willingly regarding gender, age, health, ability, talent, culture, religion, politics and affluence; egalitarian about *every* category that people use to classify people and animals. [This extends out to other living things and the earth as a matter of respect and stewardship.]

Humility requires the fundamental prerequisite to all interaction be sincere egalitarianism. To interact with anything less than this fails to honor the universal truth of unity that underlies all intellectual categorizations of Life. An egalitarian philosophy for *all* of life is the spiritual issue at hand.

The **second** requirement for humility—which is the usual focus of any discussion about humility, which is itself an ego tactic to avoid egalitarianism—is participating in the sincere honoring of some form of deity, by whatever cultural manifestation. Recognizing that there is a universal spirit (by many names), and willingly incorporating a devoted and regular appreciation of *It* in your private and social behavior, is the second requirement.

Humility is the primary requisite for judicious participation in community. Humility requires a deeply willing participation in an egalitarian lifestyle *and* the regular and sincere appreciation of a Universal Cohesiveness that animates life, without regard to the inconvenience or awkwardness that this requires of you. As an aside: If you are truly humble, there is never any awkwardness or inconvenience.

Principle #4: Charity

Charity, common in the jargon of religious people, is generally understood to be some variation of "giving things away"—giving away your time, giving away money, volunteering your expertise, donating old clothes. What qualifies or disqualifies charity as having spiritual integrity is the ego-agenda underneath the "charitable" behavior (which agenda is often *in*visible to the individual in self-introspection).

When charity is offered as a social grace, or with any underlying agenda of personal advancement or salvation, then the charity lacks spiritual integrity. Yes, it's generous, but it's spiritually suspect. Charity, in other words, may be socially admirable but unspiritual when offered because the giver feels guilty; feels sorrow or pity for the recipient; tries to impress anyone (most often and especially themselves); rescues the recipient out of some responsibility that is the recipient's to meet; tries to collect salvation points with God; offers it with self-serving personal distinctions of who's worthy of charity and who isn't; offers charity to live up to other people's expectations (especially shadow-expectations from the past); or vies for social admiration through the charity. These unrecognized unspiritual ego-machinations that motivate "charity" are insidious.[5]

"*St. John of the Cross put the whole matter* [of charity] *in a single question and answer. Those who rush headlong into good works without having acquired through contemplation the power to act well—what do they accomplish? Little more than nothing, and sometimes nothing whatever, and sometimes even harm.*"[6] Within the giver of charity, without appropriate self-love/respect, veracity, and both aspects of humility (which are the first three spiritual principles), all as prerequisites to the charity, the charity is selfish and harmful to both the giver and the receiver.

Principle #5: Responsibility & Obedience

These two attributes, which together comprise the final spiritual principle, are usually abhorrent to addicts in general, to angry people, to Victims, and to social do-gooders. This principle doesn't harbor well in our culture of victim-hood, disposable consumerism, and greed. Certainly these two attributes are easily viewed as separate qualities, but in regards to spirituality they are so closely related and inter-dependent that I present them together.

If people value an idea, and are obedient to that value (uphold it), then they would be responsible in relation to it. And, if someone is responsible, then they would be willing to be held accountable for not following the values they proclaim they have.[7] For example: If people hold kindness as an important value, then they "should" be obedient to that. They would be kind. They would be responsible (to themselves) to offer kindness in trying or awkward circumstances. More importantly, they would hold themselves fully accountable if they weren't kind. If they were kind only when it was convenient, or only to certain people, or were unwilling to be taken to task when they weren't kind, then kindness wouldn't be a value; it would be only a convenience and used for Impression Management.

In Chapter 11, I referred to Boethius' statement that "*A wise* [person] *ought no more to take it ill when* [they] *clash with fortune than a brave* [person] *ought to be upset by the sound of battle.*"[8] And I add this: A person who willingly pursues a relationship with The Divine ought not to take it ill or complain when they clash with their human nature and defects. A spiritual pilgrim, who volunteered at Step Three, and became willing at Step Six, would view all inner-personal struggles with their unspiritual impulses only as an opportunity to be devoted—an opportunity to gain faith. "*This is why virtue gets its name, because it is firm in strength and unconquered by adversity.*" [Boethius]

---

[5] Joshua Loth Liebman, in his book *Peace of Mind,* Simon and Schuster, 1946, speaks to this in an anecdote about "victims of humility," pp. 38-39.
[6] *Huxley and God Essays,* Aldous Huxley, cited earlier, p. 175.
[7] Willingness is explored in detail in Chapter 5.
[8] *The Consolation of Philosophy*, Boethius, translated by V.E. Watts, Penguin Books, 1969, p. 144.

You are responsible for things that belong to you. If you are given a magnificent gift that you declare you value highly, you are [would be] responsible to take care of it. Your life was given to *You*. As an addict/alcoholic in recovery, your "recovery life" was also given to you, and not to anyone else. Your life, your health, your pilgrimage, belong to You, and only you are responsible to take care of them. And since you volunteered for the job of being spiritual (at Step Three), all the related responsibilities and hard work are all self-imposed.

Responsibility: Truly spiritual people are willingly and completely responsible for themselves, their conduct, their thoughts, and their feelings—for their very life, and everything in it—*without complaint.* Granted, at times you are not responsible for what is done to you (calamity is random), but you are responsible for cleaning up after it—again, without complaint. Always hold only yourself responsible for the entire state of affairs in your life, and never surrender this responsibility. Anything less prohibits your being Spiritual and denies you inner serenity.

Obedience: If you aspire or claim to be spiritual, then you will desire to adhere to these five principles, which are embodied within the maintenance steps of the original twelve-step program. Obedience is mandatory because it's obedience that proves you hold them of value and proves that you are spiritually responsible. Be completely responsible for yourself and obedient to the principles of spirituality; otherwise, you're not obedient, responsible, or spiritual.[9]

These five spiritual principles are applicable to every aspect of every situation and relationship in your life. Haphazard adherence to them is not evidence of spirituality, it's evidence of convenience and Impression Management. For addicts and alcoholics getting recovered, they are not negotiable or optional unless you're willing to embrace shallowness and hypocrisy. Then, in short order, your abstinence will be at risk. A person cannot disregard any part of any one of these principles and claim spiritual integrity.

A concomitant truth is whenever a spiritual pilgrim's own life is unsatisfying, conflicted, or lonely, they're not (consistently) living within these principles.[10] They're being ignored in favor of influence, affluence, petulance, sex, revenge, or power. That's the paradigm of the human condition. Being Spiritual seems monumentally difficult to many. Corruption appears easier, but that's an illusion, only because corruption is more popular and we're trained early to live that way. It's the transition into Spirituality that seems insurmountable. Once you are well on the way to achieving it, being Spiritual is much easier and more graceful than corruption.

It appears that these five principles are somehow innate and exist *a priori* to intellect. When children are allowed to be spontaneous, they eat when they're hun-

---

[9] St. Augustine wrote that Spirituality is not efficient. It is the most difficult journey that anyone can undertake. And, as explained by Aldous Huxley in *Huxley and God: The Essays* (cited at an earlier footnote), that's why there are so few saints..

[10] One of the more unique and exasperating facets of any addiction is the ego-posture that tells an addict their unhappiness or conflicted life is someone else's fault. In order to be Spiritual you will be required to willingly and definitively abandon this mindset.

gry, stop doing something when it hurts, and sleep when they're tired. The impulse to self-care and self-respect is innate. Honesty is natural and makes sense—it takes no effort. Truth is graceful and the facts are friendly.[11]

Children are taught how, why, and when to deceive. Many times I've heard an adult counselling a child to be dishonest and the child asks innocently: "But why can't I tell?" It's also natural to be egalitarian. People are taught racism, and all forms of prejudice. They're taught arrogance about culture and God: "My way is better and you're wrong." Likewise, people are taught to disbelieve the mysterious power of unity that underlies everything. Humility is natural; arrogance is cultural. Greed is taught. Responsibility is as natural as honesty: "Who did this?" "I did." Through fear, people learn how to blame others and minimize their accountability. It seems to me that being Spiritual is innate and doesn't really need to be taught.

Being Spiritual often generates insecurity in other people, especially regarding veracity. Rather than examine their own dishonesty, they justify their own insecurity and attack someone else. Be wary of the unregenerate person whose propensity to blame and disrespect others creates a dark labyrinth that keeps them off of the path of Spirituality, even though it appears (to them) that they're on it. Being spiritual is an all-encompassing lifestyle; a state of existence. You will miss the mark, which is the nature of being human, but you only have to make amends and diligently refocus your energy and intellect onto these principles. According to *Alcoholics Anonymous*, this is the proper exercise of willpower.

As I said in the Manner of Presentation: From wherever you are right now, at this immediate point in your own transformation, you are a newcomer to the rest of your life. This is the inherent uncertainty in Life. In the face of this uncertainty, in order to appreciate the implacable grandeur of Life, exactly as you have been given it, consistently and voluntarily demonstrate respect for the body-temple, veracity, humility, charity, and responsibility & obedience.[12]

---

[11] "The facts are friendly" is an expression attributed to the American psychotherapist Carl Rogers, referred to in an earlier footnote.

[12] As I reflect on how these five principles coalesced in my mind, I'm very aware of my gratitude to the monks, mystics, imams, priests, ministers, and rabbis I have the pleasure of knowing, who were *very* generous with their knowledge and wisdom. I'm also grateful to the authors of the many books I've studied; of these, especially to: William James, for his book *The Varieties of Religious Experience,* (various publishers)—my most recent edition is Modern Library Classics, 2002; to Huston Smith, for his book *The World's Religions,* HarperSanFrancisco, 1991; to Aldous Huxley, for two of his books: *The Perennial Philosophy,* recently by Harper Collins, 1994, and *Huxley and God Essays,* Jacqueline Hazard Bridgeman editor, HarperSanFrancisco, 1992; and to Gerald May, for his book *Will and Spirit,* Harper Collins, 1982.

Appendix III

Energy & Body Healing (A too-brief overview) *

In addition to the spiritual dislocation (which must be addressed), that un-derlies addictions, any acting-out may be an attempt to calm down a traumatized, dysregulated body-energy. This is evident when addicts achieve abstinence from socially disapproved-of addictions like pornography, alcohol, or drugs and make a quick transition to the socially-approved addictions like exercise, romance, relation-ships, greed, and work.[1] Because of the significant amount of trauma that's experienced during addiction, and the cravings associated with addictions, the energy treatments I describe here can be an incredibly valuable and effective part of any recovery/healing process. (*NOTE: Read the disclaimer at the end of this appendix.)

Trauma can be related to developmental concerns, emotional issues, abuse, or physical injury[2], and is often greatly complicated by toxins. Trauma, and subse-quent illness, occurs when body energy is disrupted and left out of balance — when a person is detrimentally (not necessarily overwhelmingly) impacted by some event.

(1) Some circumstance or event
that results in trauma or injury…

(4) A reestablished, balanced energy flow in the energy meridians, and a physiological homeostasis at an energy/cellular level — health.

(2) causes physiological dysregulation or disruption in the body's energy pat-terns — the generation of traumatic energy in body tissue and nerves, which is often complicated by toxins.

(3) A naturally occurring process (or formal treatment) "should" occur that compensates and rebalances the energy disruption.

If the process at 3 (above) is defeated before the body can reestablish proper energy patterns; if stress, trauma, and toxins are left unaddressed and on-going, and the body-energy isn't realigned through treatment, the energy disruption becomes

---

[1] Recall, in Chapter 2, the observation of Terry Kellogg that the most common solution to an addiction is another addiction. The attempt to self-regulate is one component of this.

[2] Developmental trauma (including fetal development) occurs when developmental or emotional needs are not met through physical or psychological abuse or neglect. Shock trauma occurs from some defined physical event like accidents, violence, surgery, and misadventure. Psychological trauma results from the other types of trauma *and* from illness, significant upheaval, significant loss, drastic change, etc. Some events aren't necessarily "bad" *per se,* but do cause trauma. i.e. There are harmful effects from undergoing a general anesthetic and surgery (which are both severe physiological shocks), even though surgery can be good and certainly saves lives, it still results in trauma. [*Note: This appendix is much too-brief an explana-tion of trauma and body-energy. This is only to provide a very general outline, to encourage curiosity, so readers will explore these aides to healing.*]

established as "normal". The longer this is left untreated, generally the more pronounced the subsequent symptoms of dysregulation are. This creates an *astonishing* array of health problems that range from chronic illnesses, panic attacks, phobias, and headaches to attention disorders, chronic pain, cancers, environmental illnesses, and addictions. Three approaches that are usually very effective are:

Self Regulation Therapy® (SRT) *

Clients are guided to a physiological awareness of unresolved trauma-energy within their body. Working with a trained professional, they're closely monitored and coached through a natural energy-healing process. For information, go to: www.cftre.com (Canadian Foundation for Trauma Research and Education)

Emotional Freedom Techniques (EFT) *

EFT balances body energy, similar in theory to acupressure or acupuncture, and is done by light, finger-tapping on energy meridians. People usually begin with assistance from a trained EFT practitioner. After an introductory period of treatment and/or acquiring basic skills, people are encouraged to self-administer EFT. For information, go to: www.emofree.com

Quantum Techniques Energy Medicine *

Using EFT and other energy treatments, the body's energy is rebalanced. While rebalancing, particular attention is paid to toxins, substance sensitivities, and environmental concerns. For information go to: www.quantumtechniques.com

At first view, especially with *EFT* and *Quantum Techniques,* because the methods are so unconventional, many people are suspicious and doubt their effectiveness. Energy balancing, although still considered by many to be in the experimental-research phase, demonstrates a remarkable success rate for chronic emotional, physical, and environmental illnesses. They are proving to be *very* effective aides to addicts getting recovered.

These treatments are respectful of a person's physiological and psychological needs and capabilities. They promote the body's natural ability to heal itself. When done in a skilled and persistent manner, in addition to the probable reduction or elimination of the original issues, there's a newly developed ability to self-monitor (especially with *EFT* and *Quantum Techniques*). This creates an enhanced level of sensation awareness, confidence, and physiological and emotional stability. *

* DISCLAIMER: These treatments do have an amazing record of success *and* are considered by many to be in experimental development. As with all therapeutic endeavors, and especially here, common sense is required. I'm not a physician or psychologist and I make no claims or guarantees as to these treatments' effectiveness, and make no guarantees of their success. Results vary. Both practitioners and the public must take complete personal responsibility and use judicious common sense in undertaking any body-energy treatment or therapy.

Appendix IV

The Ego — "I" Am It

There are many interpretations and definitions of what an ego is. I offer the following view not to imply other views are wrong, but to make The Ego a more tangible concept. This won't necessarily make becoming spiritual (or any personal transformation) easier, but it may prevent forays into unproductive ventures, and become more viable when "working with your ego" is no longer vague nor punitive.

Neutralizing the Self-Attack

It's common in discussions about spirituality, psychology, or self-help, to hear phrases similar to these: "She's got to get her ego down to size." "He's an ego-maniac and has got to get his ego under control." "You've got to get rid of that ego if you're going to be spiritual." "You've got to cut your ego down to size if you're going to be happy in your relationship." Among the many observations that might be made about these sentences, three are relevant here.

- They reflect the tendency of technological cultures to attach a negative connotation to words of neutral character (similar to the words "criticize" and "animosity").[1]
- These involve some element of attack or punitive judgment.[2] They're very non-accepting of "self". In this vein, egos are represented as bad.
- The self-rejecting nature of these perspectives; their disapproval of the human condition, makes them spiritually untenable. They're at odds with the first spiritual principle, and the aspect of egalitarianism in the third spiritual principle, and they do not embody charity.

---

[1] *Criticize* is to analyze or make observations on the value or worth of a thing. Paying compliments or giving praise is to criticize. *Animosity* originally meant having high spirits and great energy. Both of these words have taken on negative connotations, and so it is with *ego*. This negative perspective limits our perceptions, and limited perceptions are fatal to spirituality. (The observation on *animosity* is from *Brewer's Dictionary of Phrase & Fable,* Revised Edition, Edited by Ivor H. Evans, Cassell Ltd., 1981.)

[2] Whenever you're spiritually lost in character defects, you don't need to cut yourself down to size, or hack away at your ego, or slap yourself back into spirituality. Psychological violence, self-rejection, or harsh criticism implied rhetorically or otherwise, doesn't contribute to transformation—it prevents it. You simply need to recognize you're human (that's why you have an ego, and why you're off course), and lovingly nudge yourself in another direction.

Cutting your ego down to size, or any other euphemism that implies self-attack, isn't a loving nudge by any standard. Too often, our socially appointed mentors like doctors, therapists, teachers, priests, counsellors, parents, older siblings, religious leaders, or sponsors are themselves the purveyors of character assassination camouflaged as guidance or help. It's so often true that people pounce like jackals on the humanness of others, thinking that this cruelty will contribute to someone else's transformation.

In relation to alcoholics and addicts, and spirituality in general, neutralizing the commonly accepted negative connotation to "ego" enables a smoother transition into spirituality. In perceiving your ego as I am about to suggest, a spiritually based life becomes possible, and it becomes more palatable.

The Premise

Each person has two fundamental and non-modifiable realities to contend with. I call these the Matrix of the Soul and the Corporeal Universe.

The Matrix of the Soul is comprised of that inherent set of instinctual drives and emotions that are here generally categorized as fear, joy, sexuality, hunger, survival, social association, and some awareness of God (by whatever name). These exist "within our soul" and, altogether, are the mandatory, unconscious state of affairs in everyone. These exist like a multi-dimensional matrix, and whatever animates into life these aspects of our soul arrives from beyond, but exists in, Time and Space. The Matrix of the Soul is the unknown, animating energy of humanity — the "every person" in each person.

These attributes of the soul, at an unknowable level, collide and negotiate with each other. Fear, sexuality, social association, joy, survival (food/shelter), the dynamic of love, the essence and origin of life-energy, all interact *within* our souls.

The Matrix of the Soul constitutes that place from which we originate (collectively or individually). It's that lattice of interacting, fundamental life-energy which impels us to *be*. It cannot *not* exist. Everyone who is alive has and must respond to the nature of their own soul. It motivates Life — the never knowable source of our instincts and origin-point to our spiritual nature. The Matrix of the Soul exists beyond all quantifiable reality, and is one of the two experiences of reality.

The Corporeal Universe, which is the other experience of reality, is everything that isn't the Matrix of the Soul — literally *any*thing and *every*thing that can in any way be referred to as material, extant, or measurably present. The Corporeal Universe is other people, animals, and all material things of any description, and it includes your body, which is "external" to the Matrix of the Soul. Your own physical existence is not a part of what it is that impels you to *be*. Nerves and flesh and blood are only a container in which the Matrix of the Soul mysteriously resides.

Everything in the Corporeal Universe (all things outside of our soul) influences or negotiates with each other. The Corporeal Universe requires interaction within itself. There's an inherent imperative in and for relationship: fish and water; food and people; people with people; intellect and emotion; the environment and living things. Reality in the Corporeal Universe requires interaction. The Corporeal Universe is quantifiable reality, and is your other experience of that reality.

The Problem

The Matrix of the Soul and the Corporeal Universe are completely and mutually exclusive. They are each a different reality, with nothing in common. They each have independent aspects that negotiate within themselves, and these two realities must act upon each other. They often appear to be, and are often actually, at odds with each other, but Life demands they coexist. That mandatory coexistence, between The Matrix of the Soul and The Corporeal Universe, is where lies the problem of every individual.

In order for anyone to "be" or to exist, there must be an operating agent or system that facilitates the interaction and balancing of instinct and reality (The Matrix of the Soul vs. The Corporeal Universe). Your life, as you know it, is the result of the interaction between the Matrix of *Your* Soul and the Corporeal Universe. You, as a living person, must somehow negotiate between these two mutually exclusive realities. The job of balancing these two realities, falls to…

The Ego

The agency that coordinates that relationship, and creates harmony or disharmony between The Corporeal Universe and The Matrix of the Soul, is your ego. Your ego, encapsulated in your mind—which is an emergent property of "being"—is both a funnel and a teeter-totter: the filtering balance point where everything is organized and mediated. But… you can't see your ego, you can only see the results of it. Your ego is only visible in its derivations, and not in its reality. The end result of your ego's balancing act is your life.

Your ego is the organized conscious mediator between your unknowable, instinctual soul and all reality as it exists outside of your soul. Your ego is actually a solution to a problem. It's the solution to the existential problem of balancing the reality of your soul and the reality of the universe. The problem isn't your ego; it's how your ego balances the interaction of these two realities.

Matrix of the Soul	> **Ego** <	Corporeal Universe
	∧	
fear, joy, love, sexuality, hunger, survival, social association, and some awareness of God (by whatever name): the unknowable energy, beyond understanding, that animates life	**My Personality** the invisible mind-agency that negotiates, filters, and balances these two realities	*every*thing in reality, including your own physical being

Your interpretation of the reality you are exposed to is your ego at work. That interpretation is rooted in your ego's filtering and balancing, and was molded by your genetics, by your developmental stages, by how your caregivers influenced your perceptions of your own Matrix of the Soul and your own Corporeal Universe, by your temperament, and by the circumstances that befell you. Your ego was also molded by how your caregiver's egos manifested and organized their own balance in their own lives. It all combines to become You (your personality: your ego).

A soft generalization is the psychological problems that people experience, which are the content of most therapy, i.e. anxieties, neuroses, anger, despair, conflict, depression, unhappiness, and complaints about the unpleasantness of everyday life, is representative of this balancing act. Recall these earlier discussions: hopeless and helpless (Ch. 2); the committee that wants to help the old woman (Ch. 7); and, the overlooked middle step of the Two-Step Dance (Ch. 8). These are all representative of the ego's balancing and funneling.

Fill In the Blanks

- You're given $50,000 to spend so you _____.
- You get any book in a book store for free. You choose _____.
- Someone prays nine times a day and you think _____.
- Your favorite sexual position is _____.
- It's a warm summer day. An acquaintance stays inside *all* day, watches five movies, and eats popcorn. You think _____.
- You're late and stuck in heavy traffic behind a confused and timid driver, so you _____.
- You're *exhausted* and under *terrific* pressure at work. In the evening your spouse starts caressing and flirting. You _____.
- You have to spend the day by yourself, so you _____.
- Your idea of a physically attractive, sexy person is someone who looks just like the movie star _____.

Your answers represent the filtering and balancing of your ego. Your response to *any* circumstance is your ego in action, which is sometimes conscious (people act deliberately), or sometimes subconscious (people act without clear awareness). Perceived as evil or good, ordinary or magnificent, your ego is the solution to the problem of mediating between two unyielding, opposing realities. To try to eliminate or reduce it is akin to self-annihilation. Your spirit will resist, and transformation into spirituality will not be possible.

One crucial problem that addicts must address is their ego modifies and filters everything destructively. It negotiates and balances the relationship between these two realities *anti*-spiritually.[3]

Ego Comparison & Character Assassination

Personal Assassination of Self – the extra variable for addicts

Non-addicted people contend with themselves and with Life (two variables), and their view of themselves isn't separated from themselves. An addict, on the other hand, has to contend with Life, and with themselves, and an extra variable: an aspect of their mind that perceives "itself" as independent of itself. Their own

---

[3] When offering treatment strategies for addiction, if the addict's damage to other people is prioritized over *self*-damage, a socially-directed treatment plan is mandated. That would then be a reflection of a sentimental perspective that arises from relationship addiction (which is rampant in our culture). With addictions, "outer/socially-directed" treatment modalities always fail.

mind sees their own mind as independent or separate from the rest of themselves. An addict's mind, in the midst of their addicted life, has a very subtle way of excusing itself from reality. That part of the mind which values-and-judges, for an addict, embodies a curious and destructive characteristic: it views itself as not a part of the destruction, or capable of escaping unscathed. For addicts, it is thus: Their mind thinks it can kill them and still go on living.

The addict's mind thinks *to itself*, like a sub-conscious, internal dialogue, as if it's talking to the addict's body: "Go ahead, you can destroy yourself by acting out, but I'll get through this. I can force the reality of this to be different and not affect me." The addict's mind thinks it can continuously do destructive things to "the addict" and escape unscathed. (It's this aspect of addiction where rescuing plays it's destructive role. See *Facets of Personal Transformation.*)

People without addictions don't have this third aspect to their personality. For non-addicts, generally it's different: The part of their minds that views the nature of their personality, sees themselves as *not* independent of the part that judges.

Addicts often refer to themselves in the third person, which is indicative of this dynamic. [Other people may refer to themselves in the third person; for an addict it can have particularly sinister implications.]

In the mind (the ego) of an addict, there are these dynamics of perception operating: (i) perceptions of "other" (the corporeal universe), (ii) perceptions of "self" (matrix of the soul); and, (iii) that part of their mind that perceives itself as removed from the rest of the mind: a peculiar mindset which believes itself to be independent of the addict and the self-destruction. Eliminating this style of dissociation from the reality of their life is one crucial aspect to treating addictions.

Egos, Relationships & Comparative Character Assassination

Even though it often appears that one half of a couple is "healthier" than the other half, this isn't the truth of the matter. The appearance of one person being healthier than the other one is the end result of a mind game that I call Comparative Character Assassination.

Comparative Character Assassination is an ego gambit that goes like this: One half of a couple compares themselves to the other half of that couple and, for any number of reasons, decides, through assassinating the other person's character, that the other person is less "healthy" (whatever that means). This is announced at every reasonable opportunity, i.e. "I'm more in touch with my feelings than you because...", or "I'm more committed to the relationship than you because...", or "You're not as emotionally healthy as me because...".

Any partner that you're with, in any longer-term relationship, will have a mirroring ego-structure that compliments or "fits" with yours.[4] You will each have approximately the same capacity or incapacity to bring conflict, commitment, inti-

---

[4] Dating is actually that process of going "people shopping" for a complimentary ego structure. When you find the one that matches what your ego requires, that's the one you'll want. If you've asked eleven consecutive, different people out on a *second* date and they all say 'No,' your ego is deliberately (subconsciously) choosing these people because its balancing and mediation policy is rooted in rejection. Whatever you get is what you want, regardless of your verbal protestations to the contrary.

macy, or love to the relationship. If one person was actually and significantly more "emotionally healthy" than the other one, they wouldn't be in the relationship. Neither person is healthier than the other, even though it may appear otherwise. And, even if the *apparently* unhealthier person in the relationship agrees with the accusations of the "healthier" person, or if one half voluntarily condemns themselves as unhealthier, it still isn't true.

Many relationships are carefully pre-arranged, choreographed dances, and initiated as personal salvation strategies. They're compensations for unknown dislocation. This was very briefly touched upon in Thought, Form, Fascination, Fall (Ch. 11), and prohibits the capacity for intimacy and fulfillment.

If you select a mate who, over time, starts to love you more or differently than your own ego can accommodate; or if after the relationship is established, your partner (their ego) modifies the relationship contract (changes the dance) without your cooperation, i.e. changes the level of emotional disclosure or responsibility, without your ego making an accommodating, voluntary ego-shift, you'll not be able to tolerate or accept the change. You'll precipitate a struggle to change your partner back to the rules you agreed on. The machinations and needs of your personality will dominate the situation regardless of your intellectually good intentions.

There are traits that attract you to a person in the first place: He's so outgoing. She's so assertive and independent. He's so neat and tidy. She's so financially organized. These qualities will eventually be recast by your ego to be a source of complaint. The very qualities that were once attractive will become: He's a flirt. She's stubborn. He's a neat-freak. She's cheap.

All of this self-generated conflict was orchestrated before the fact, and may result in an end to the relationship. This brings immediate relief, but without significant inner work, the parties will sooner or later orchestrate another similar relationship scenario. Or, if they "can't" separate (another self-generated, self-serving perception), they'll remain in perpetual struggle, or completely smother and eradicate the vulnerable parts of their personality, eventually abandoning themselves and remaining forever unfulfilled.[5]

Self-condemnation that someone harbors, of which they are unaware, is so powerful that life situations and partners will be chosen so their relationships are a parallel reflection (a metaphor) of the unrealized self-condemnation. This is often reflected in parenting. All abuse [of children, or of anyone or anything] is never about the abused, it's always about the perpetrator.

These are all machinations of your ego—your personality. In relationships, nothing is accidental. People get exactly what they want, regardless of passionate speeches and public declarations to the contrary.

---

[5] Without expert help, many people can't change a situation that's intolerable, or separate from isolation, unfulfilling careers, conflict, or self-destruction. Their ego continues to choose these because of a subconscious contextual view that life *is* conflict, and/or an unresolved *self*-perception of unworthiness or personal incompetence, or because the perceived loneliness and fear attendant to being alone or independent is horrific. Without changing the underlying context, the possibility of a peaceful life is non-existent.

The Only Variable

Everyone has an instinctual soul that is what it is—the unalterable core of existence. Also: Everyone was born into reality, and reality is what it is—unyielding, resistant, and capricious. The only variable is how you negotiate between these unalterable realities—how you dance yourself through their interaction.

Your cooperation with or defiance to reality; your respect or disregard for others; the way you participate in life; and especially, the love or absence of love you have for your own authentic self, are all demonstrations of your ego. As an adult: your parents, your spouse, your job, your life, your childhood, your children, are not the problem, although to you it looks like they are. The problem may also appear to be the size of your ego, but even that isn't really the problem, it just looks that way because that's how other (insecure) egos have defined "the problem". The core issue is how your ego is organized, and how it funnels information between the matrix of your soul and the corporeal universe that you are exposed to.

Your own ego's balancing act; its interpretations and perceptions, are what generates your own psychological state of affairs. Your ego is the organizer of your psychology, be it passive, violent, spiritual, aggressive, submissive, rude, generous, charitable, selfish, kind, self-destructive, other-destructive, pompous, atheistic, kind, mean, chaste, dramatic, quiet, domineering, promiscuous... *whatever* (and any and all combinations and permutations of these attributes). Every thought you have, every emotion you experience, every word you utter, is some aspect of your ego.

The Solution

You can't change the Matrix of the Soul. You can't change the Corporeal Universe. You can't reduce or increase your ego. All attempts to do any of these only redefines the dynamics, and results in some new type of relationship, therapeutic, or spiritual disaster. The only effective, long-range plan is to modify the mandate of your ego—to adjust how it perceives and interprets information in the relationship between the matrix of your soul and your corporeal universe.

If you don't have a strong, well-defined ego that can harmonize and balance the relentless demands of these two realities, and have no doubt the demands are relentless, you will founder and become lost.[6] Weak or poorly defined egos cannot balance powerful forces like instincts and external reality. When you are lost, and foundering or unfulfilled (the manifestation of an external locus of control), you will attach yourself to strong, controlling egos like an abusive partner, a cult leader, or an overbearing counsellor, therapist, or sponsor. You may become involved in a rigid religious structure, or participate in a group with strong peer-pressure values, or simply abandon yourself to the whims and coincidences of the universe.

Your personality is actually a visible demonstration of the manner and pattern of your attempt to balance the matrix of *your* soul and the reality to which *you* are exposed. How your ego facilitates this interaction is "Life" as you know it, which

---

[6] For additional explanation see The Myth of Ego Reduction..., p. 349.

is the operational status of your personality. You are not your potential: you are you. You life is your ego in action.

Egos & Addiction & Relationships

People with addictions live in desperate spiritual dislocation. Regardless of how much they remember they were loved, or thought they were loved, or really were loved, or were not loved, or were abused, or were not abused, the fact is, they are attempting to solve their own spiritual dislocation through self-annihilation (called addiction). In a desperate reaction to Life to save themselves, they capture people—other addicts—in friendships, marriages, and sexual relationships.

These fractured relationships are an externalized metaphor to the addict's dislocated, interior life, and a skewed, holographic image of their ego. Along with the usual problems of sexually destructive/harmful behavior, power-struggles, anger, neglect, deceit, greed, a need to dominate or be victimized, betrayal, irresponsibility, etc., these relationships embody isolation and loneliness.

Life is Relationship. The addict approaches relationships as a game of blame, control, and manipulation, and Life is interpreted in such a way as to perpetuate alienation from others and God/Atman-Brahmin. If you resolve spiritual dislocation, you resolve addictions. If you're spiritual, that will become the paradigm for your relationships with people. Twelve-step programs are designed to reorganize and refocus your ego's focus, and thereby create spiritual integrity. Without spiritual integrity addicts and alcoholics remain unfulfilled.

The task in spiritual transformation is to deliberately modify your interpretations and perceptions of *both* how reality impacts on the components of your soul, and how your instincts interrelate and make demands on the universe. Spiritual integrity requires a well-defined, strong ego (not a reduced ego) that filters and balances these two opposing realities according to spiritual principles.[7]

Everyone is created without flaw, without prejudice or mean judgment, and capable of love in its purest form. However, at birth, that "purity" must be immediately abandoned on behalf of instinctual survival and obedience to the circumstances of the reality into which we are born. Over time, recapturing that spiritual essence is the task human beings are presented with—to reorganize their perceptions of the universe and to reclaim the spiritual principles that naturally exist within them. The original twelve steps have brought us (back) to an historical, subtle truth which was so succinctly stated by Aldous Huxley: *"God is. That is the primordial fact. It is in order that we may discover this fact for ourselves, by direct experience, that we exist."*[8]

---

[7] This is discussed in Chapter 9, in The Myth of Ego Reduction as Humility.

[8] *Huxley and God, Essays,* Aldous Huxley, Edited by Jacqueline Hazard Bridgeman, Harper San Francisco, 1992, p. 17, (quoted at the beginning of this book).

Epilogue

A Lot of Work to Go Not Very Far

It began with severe spiritual dislocation in you, and it really wasn't your fault that you ended up with an addiction, but neither was it anyone else's fault. Then Providence, in some mysterious machination, offered you the opportunity to recon-struct yourself. The condition attached to you achieving a fulfilling life was that it must be rooted in abstinence and authentic spirituality.

There was the realization that you were spiritually sick, and a decision to live by the will of God, as you came to understand God. As you slowly reorganized your life around spiritual principles, you realized that the crisis called "Your Life" was your fault, and admitted this. You abandoned willfulness and other destructive attributes you had formerly cherished, and sought willingness. Humility became a desired character trait, adopted not through fear but through appreciating its inherent beauty. Life was becoming graceful. It was with some eagerness, and no regret, that you examined your own life, and quietly made amends to repair the holes you tore in the fabric of the universe. You became truly responsible. You realized you had achieved what you were promised you could achieve, and volunteered to continually deepen your devotion to a spiritual way of life, which became your life.

In going from addicted to recovered, you've progressed along this approxi-mate spectrum of attitudes: hopeless, angry, despairing, angry, confused, suspicious, reluctant, resigned, curious, hopeful, interested, willing, serious, committed, devoted, and (finally) sincerely spiritual. If you painstakingly follow the original twelve-step instructions you end up with new values, new priorities, new traditions: a new life. And even after all that, nothing "out there" will have changed much. The three criti-cal decisions you made—to remain abstinent, to live by God's will, and to believe that humility is good, have altered your destiny. This is no mean feat.

According to Thomas Merton, Herakleitos the Obscure was of this view:

> *"The wise* [person] *must make tremendous efforts to grasp "the unexpected": that is to* say [they must keep themselves] *alert, and constantly* [seek for themselves] *and not fear to strive for the excellence that will make* [them] *an object of hatred and mistrust in the eyes of the conventional majority... ."*[1]

---

[1] *A Thomas Merton Reader,* Revised Edition, edited by Thomas P. McDonnell, Doubleday Image Books, 1974, p. 264.

"[Herakleitos] *preferred loneliness to the warm security of* [the] *collective illusion...*[2] *It takes humility to confront the prejudice and the contempt of all, in order to cling to an unpopular truth.*"[3]

For Spiritual Pilgrims

What I offer to spiritual pilgrims is this: Humans are very bitter-sweet, and people are not disposable.

A spiritual life is never about the result. It is never about getting some honesty "thing", or some prayer issue, or this relationship "problem" out of the way. If you don't fully explore it, understand it, or appreciate it, your life will end up being just good enough, and Life will never be satisfying or fulfilling. You will miss the meaning of your own life.

In spiritual endeavor, as in love, refuse to be restricted by time. What you love is what you give your time to. What you love is what captures your spiritual integrity. Don't walk away from some relationship, or some spiritual commitment, before you feel like you've really challenged yourself. Explore every avenue, every nuance, and then live your life based on that. Your time is the precious jewel that you offer to the world.

"So what's your life about?" "Where do you really want your life to end up?" "What are you doing with your life?" Smile gently and don't answer. Never justify yourself. Don't complain. Believe in something. Believe passionately in it. Devote yourself to it... completely, utterly.[4]

> "*Of all forms of caution, caution in love is perhaps most fatal to true happiness.*"[5]

The Movie Scene

Pretend you're watching a movie. The scene is set in 1937, in a cozy den. There are some worn, comfortable armchairs, bookshelves, a small fireplace, an oak desk and typewriter. Sitting at the desk is Bill Wilson. Sitting on the corner of the desk is Dr. Bob Smith. The cofounders of AA are wearing casual clothes, or maybe suits with their collars and ties loosened. It's late at night. The table lamps are on, and it's quiet. A clock ticks in the background.

Bill Wilson says: "Bob, what can we say to these people to give them hope?"

---

[2] *A Thomas Merton Reader,* Revised Edition, edited by Thomas P. McDonnell, Doubleday Image Books, 1974, p. p. 266.
[3] Ibid., p. 267.
[4] Here I have recast, from film-making to spirituality, the views expressed by Nicole Kidman that were discussed in Chapter 5.
[5] Bertrand Russell, as quoted in *The Blues ain't nothing but a good soul feeling bad,* Sheldon Kopp, Fireside Books, Simon & Schuster, 1992, entry for Sep. 17.

"I don't know exactly," Bob replies, "but I guess they'll have to at least do what we did. How do we get them to persevere?" They both shrug.

Bill Wilson shakes his head. "We're right at the end of the book. We've got to end it with something. But what?" He fiddles with a pencil on the desk.

Dr. Bob paces about the room, finally sitting in one of the armchairs. With his face in shadow, he asks Bill, "What was it that *we* wanted to know when we were all jittery and alone?" There's a long pause, and then Bob quietly asks, "What did you want, Bill? What did *you* want to know?"

Bill Wilson is startled by an idea. He shifts closer to the desk and types a few sentences, then pulls the paper out of the typewriter, and smiles at Bob, who's half hidden in the shadows. Bill turns to the camera and looks directly at you.

"Bob and I '...*know what you are thinking. You are saying to yourself: "I'm jittery and alone. I couldn't do that." But you can. You forgot that you have just now tapped a source of power much greater than yourself. To duplicate, with such backing, what we have accomplished is only a matter of willingness, patience and labor.*'"[6]

———

On this pilgrimage you have been required to make many difficult choices, often wandering into the hostile areas of your own personality, always on faith, always pushing yourself deeper into spiritual principles. This has not been easy. The author W. Somerset Maugham was reported to have said that if you refuse to settle for nothing but the best, you very often get it. What will you settle for?

Here we are at the end of this book but not of our pilgrimage. Love and fear are not the opposite of each other. They are parallel. People can lose their fears and that doesn't necessarily leave them experiencing love. People can stop loving and not necessarily end up experiencing fear. They are perfectly parallel paths of the same thing—Life.

> "*I shall be telling this with a sigh*
> *Somewhere ages and ages hence:*
> *Two roads diverged in a wood, and I—*
> *I took the one less traveled by,*
> *And that has made all the difference.*"[7]

The paths of Love and Fear are so close together you can change from one to the other and move nowhere. Becoming spiritual is accomplished through traversing that very short distance from fear to love, and staying there. You've worked hard and changed a great deal to accomplish this, and yet haven't gone very far at all.

M. Scott Peck was reported to have said that when future generations look back on the 20th century, it won't be nuclear fission they'll remark on; it will be Al-

---

[6] *Alcoholics Anonymous*, p. 163.
[7] The Road Not Taken, *The Poetry of Robert Frost*, Robert Frost; Edited By Edward Connery Lathem, Holt, Rinehart and Winston, 1969, p. 105.

coholics Anonymous. From my own perspective, it will be *Alcoholics Anonymous* and *Twelve Steps and Twelve Traditions*.

Remember: You are a sexual being, in a physical body, trying to be a spiritual entity, in a human context, within a limited but unknown segment of eternity. Even without dysfunction and abuse, or addictions and a destructively oriented ego, it's incredibly complicated.

As an addicted person now recovered, somehow realize within yourself that simply learning and doing will not guarantee your remaining Spiritual. Knowledge and action are not the solution. In its broadest sense, and by whatever name, God is. Labor with patience and devotion for many years. Live intimately with trusted loved ones. Have compassion and respect for the earth and all living things. Maintain an intimate, *long* relationship with a spiritually oriented mentor or therapist. And, in all of this, hold personal responsibility, truth, respect, humility, compassion, charity, and non-violence as the highest values. Labor with devotion and patience only to this end: Through the maintenance steps, be forever obedient to the five spiritual principles.

You will have crossed some ubiquitous line and sense in hindsight, and only by continuing to embrace your ever-present frailties, that you are recovered. Some might call you wise, many will resent you, and you'll smile gently because, for you, it will be sufficient to quietly repose in the safety of knowing that the mysterious machinations of Providence are beautiful.

Words cannot describe everything.
The heart's message cannot be delivered in words.
If one receives words literally, they will be lost.
If one tries to explain with words, they will not
attain enlightenment in this life.[8]

As for myself...

As I traverse the eternity between my own birth and death, I am forever encased in the *being* of my own life. I must remind myself that I unfold into only a supporting role. At my own last exit I will face a final curtain, the closing of which always comes before the end of the play. And as for encores, if there are any... probably none that I'll remember.

---

[8] *Zen Flesh, Zen Bones, A Collection of Zen and Pre-Zen Writings,* complied by Paul Reps, Anchor Books, 1989, p. 120, (quoted with minor editing of pronouns).

About the Author

Richard Clark was born in 1950, in Ontario, Canada. He wandered through the 1960s and college in a manner of 'protest and experimentation', and traveled widely throughout North America. He was known to lean heavily on a quote from William Blake: *"The road to excess leads to the palace of wisdom."* [9] Certainly the excess part was true, but some people might question where that excess led him. He's been a construction worker, miner, soldier, military policeman, security guard, driving instructor, police constable, seniors' outreach worker, teacher, writer, artist, musician, therapist, seminar leader, consultant, and counsellor.

Richard trained in addictions treatment and many of the issues related to addictions at Grant MacEwan College, the Alberta Alcohol and Drug Abuse Commission, the Justice Institute of B.C., the Human Potential Institute, and the Whole Person Recovery Center. He's a certified addictions counsellor (CAC II) through the Canadian Council of Professional Certification; certified in Self Regulation Therapy® through the Canadian Foundation for Trauma Research and Education; a certified life-skills coach and coach trainer; and trained in Emotional Freedom Techniques and in Swedish-relaxation massage.

He's offered seminars and lectures to over fifteen thousand people on topics that include addictions, sexuality, violence, relationships, change, stress and trauma, leadership, religion, spirituality, applied problem solving, gender issues, life skills, counselling, and interpersonal communications. As a therapist and educator, Richard's worked in colleges, First Nations' communities, the sales industry, prisons, monasteries, non-profit agencies, and treatment centers. He's offered seminars and lectures in Canada, the United States, and Russia, and has been a therapist and addictions counsellor since 1986. (**www.richardwclark.com**)

Facets of Personal Transformation

The first-draft, original text of this project counted in at close to 800 pages. In it, I had said all I wanted to say about addictions, twelve-step programs, personal transformation, and spirituality. When I talked about this with my friend Michael, to whom this book is dedicated, for various reasons he wisely suggested I divide the material into two volumes.

Addictions & Spiritual Transformation is the first book of a set. This book doesn't say all; there is more to discover about transformation, spirituality, and addictions.

Throughout this book there are many references to *Facets of Personal Transformation*. This will be the companion volume to this book. In it, I'll discuss family, personality, psychology, gender, the dynamics of relationships, applied personal problem solving, therapy, emotions, communications, ethics and values, religion, and spirituality. These topics will be of interest to people in general, but there will also be specific information for people getting recovered from addictions.

Facets of Personal Transformation is scheduled for publication in 2008. Together, these books will comprise a detailed examination of the dynamics and process of self-directed personal transformation and spirituality.

---

[9] This William Blake quote comes from <u>Proverbs of Hell</u>, which begins: *"In seed time learn, in harvest teach, in winter enjoy. / Drive your cart and your plow over the bones of the dead. / The road of excess leads to the palace of wisdom. / Prudence is a rich, ugly old maid courted by Incapacity. / He who desires but acts not, breeds pestilence..."* From: The Portable Blake, Edited by Alfred Kazin, Viking Portable Library, p. 252.

ISBN 141208398-2